AF515654

TOWARDS A FOOD SECURE INDIA

Issues and Policies

INSTITUTE FOR HUMAN DEVELOPMENT
NEW DELHI

The Institute for Human Development, set up by the Indian Society of Labour Economics in 1998, is a non-profit autonomous institution for study and action in the areas of labour, employment, poverty, health, education and other aspects of human development in developing countries, particularly India. During the short span of its existence, the Institute has completed a number of research projects, organised several seminars/workshops and brought out several books and working papers. The publications of the Institute have been favourably reviewed both in India and abroad. Significantly, the Institute has emerged as an important think-tank on the study of issues related to labour, employment and human development. The areas in which the Institute's current activities are concentrated include: impact of globalisation on poverty, employment and social development, and desired policy interventions; informal sector, poverty and employment; labour migration; empowerment of rural labour; efficacy of poverty alleviation programmes; labour markets, employment relations and human development. Special focus is on gender disparity, backward regions and vulnerable groups.

CENTRE FOR ECONOMIC AND SOCIAL STUDIES
HYDERABAD

The Centre for Economic and Social Studies, Hyderabad was set up in 1980 by the Government of Andhra Pradesh as an autonomous research institution (registered under the Societies Act) with the objective of undertaking mutually supportive and interrelated research, training and documentation activities in the field of economic and social development in general and the state of Andhra Pradesh in particular. The Centre was accorded the status of a national institute in 1986 by the Indian Council of Social Science Research (ICSSR), New Delhi and was included in its network of institutions for giving grants. The specific areas in which the Centre's current research is concentrated include: rural development and poverty; agriculture and food security; irrigation and water management; public finance; demography and health; environment and other studies. The Centre also has the M.Phil/Ph.D programme affiliated to Dr. B.R. Ambedkar Open University, Hyderabad.

TOWARDS A FOOD SECURE INDIA

Issues and Policies

Edited by

S. Mahendra Dev, K.P. Kannan and Nira Ramachandran

2003

INSTITUTE FOR HUMAN DEVELOPMENT, NEW DELHI

and

CENTRE FOR ECONOMIC AND SOCIAL STUDIES, HYDERABAD

Published by

INSTITUTE FOR HUMAN DEVELOPMENT
Old IAMR Building, 3rd Floor, I.P. Estate
Mahatma Gandhi Marg, New Delhi-110002
Phones: 23358166, 23321610; Fax: 23765410
e-mail: ihd@vsnl.com; website: www.ihdindia.org

Distributed by

MANOHAR PUBLISHERS AND DISTRIBUTORS
4753/23, Ansari Road, Daryaganj, New Delhi
Phones: 23262796, 23289100 Fax: (011) 23265126
e-mail: manbooks@vsnl.com
website: manbooks.com

Copyright © Institute for Human Development, 2003

First Published, 2003

ISBN 81-900948-7-4

All rights reserved. No part of this publications may be reproduced in any form without the prior written permission of the publishers.

Laser Typesetting & Printed at :

PRINT-WAYS, G-19, Vijaya Chowk, Laxmi Nagar, Delhi-110092
Phone: 22514076

Contents

Preface

Improving food security is an issue of considerable importance for a developing country like India where millions of people suffer from hunger and malnutrition. It is now widely recognised that food security is not confined only to production, availability and demand for food—ultimately, the key question is that of the ability of the people to access food and utilise it effectively at all times, to lead a healthy life. Nutrition security is an important dimension of food security.

In the post-independence period India has several achievements on the food front. Successive Five-Years Plans have laid considerable emphasis on policies and strategies aimed at raising the level of nutrition and standard of living of the people. The production of foodgrains has increased more than four fold since independence—from 50 million tonnes in 1950-51, it has increased to about 210 million tonnes in 1999-00. As a result, India has moved from a stage of chronic food shortages to self-sufficiency in food production, and has built up substantial buffer stocks. The level of procurement and the reach of PDS has also increased considerably, overtime. Additionally, the government has introduced several nutrition programmes such as the Integrated Child Development Services (ICDS) providing supplementary nutrition for pre-school children and expectant or nursing mothers, and the noon-meal scheme (which has been a success in Tamil Nadu and Kerala). All these have contributed greatly towards improving the availability of food and level of nutrition in the country.

However, all is not well with the food security policy, particularly with reference to procurement, PDS and nutrition programmes. With the advent of economic liberalisation and globalisation, some new challenges have also emerged. Despite the implementation of several programmes, there are concerns regarding calorie intake and malnutrition. Poverty levels remain high, despite a significant reduction in poverty in recent years. The calorie intake of the bottom 30 per cent is low. The problem of malnutrition is acute and widespread and is extremely serious among women and children. The percentage of malnutrition is much higher in the relatively poorer states like Bihar, Uttar Pradesh and Madhya Pradesh. Inequitable distribution of food among different segments of the population is one of the major factors responsible for under-nutritution.

In order to improve the food and nutrition security in the country, the present programmes such as PDS, *Antyodaya Anna Yojana*, nutrition programmes, and public works programmes have to be strengthened. It may be noted that employment security is crucial for achieving food security. As Amartya Sen and others have argued, food availability is not a major problem at the national or local level. It is the economic access at the household level which is responsible for the low accessibility of food. In this context, creating purchasing power through employment is crucial. The government can facilitate labour-intensive growth and provide direct programmes to generate productive employment which, in turn, can ensure food security. Appropriate policies have to be framed at both the national and local levels. Different regional and grass root level experiences would also be useful in framing appropriate policies at different levels. Efforts will have to be made to identify vulnerable grups/families and improve their household nutrition security. For this, we need to test and evaluate various modalities of improving the efficiency of the programmes currently in operation.

These and related issues were discussed at a national seminar organised by the Institute for Human Development (IHD), New Delhi and Centre for Economic and Social Studies (CESS), Hyderabad. Sponsored by the Ministry of Consumer Affairs and Public Distribution of the Government of India, the seminar was held at Hyderabad during March 15-17, 2000, and attended by about 75 academicians, policy makers and social activists. This volume is largely based on the selected and revised papers presented at the seminar. However, a few other papers have also been included to fill the critical gaps. All these make the present volume not only a comprehensive one, but also one which addresses critical issues and emerging concerns on food security such as the demand for and supply of foodgrains in future; policy response to domestic reforms and globalisation; regional scenario and micro-level experiences; and ongoing perspectives on issues such as the working of the PDS, nutrition and right to food.

It is hoped that this volume would be useful in placing the issue of food security at the centrestage as well as in formulating appropriate strategies and policies in moving towards a more food secure India.

S. Mahendra Dev
Director
Centre for Economic and Social Studies
Hyderabad

Alakh N. Sharma
Director
Institute for Human Development
New Delhi

Acknowledgements

The publication of this volume has been possible because of support and help from several individuals. Most of the papers in this volume were presented at a seminar organised by the Institute for Human Development (IHD) and Centre for Economic and Social Studies (CESS) during March 25-27, 2000. We are grateful to the paper writers for meeting our request for revising and updating their papers. We are also thankful to Mr. M.D. Asthana, the former Secretary of the Ministry of Consumer Affairs and Public Distribution, Government of India for sponsoring the seminar and providing it all support. Thanks are also due to Dr. Padmanabha Rao and the administrative staff of CESS, Mr. Premchandra and the administrative staff of IHD and Mr. R.P. Mamgain, Managing Editor of the *Indian Journal of Labour Economics* (IJLE) for their help in organising this seminar.

We owe immense gratitude to Professor Alakh N. Sharma, Director of the Institute for Human Development, who spent a lot of time and energy right from organising the seminar as the seminar co-ordinator to the publication of this volume. His academic as well as editorial advice have been extremely helpful to us. Without his unstinted support, the publication of this volume would not have been possible. We are also grateful to Professor C.H. Hanumantha Rao, Chairman, CESS, and Professor Yoginder K. Alagh, Chairman, IHD, for their invaluable guidance and support at every stage of the seminar and publication of the book.

The tedious job of copy-editing and proof-reading has been very ably done by Mr. Rajesh Shankar and Mrs. Dipika Sen at IHD. Ms. V. Kalpana and Ms. Uma Sarmistha—the two M.A. Trainees from Gokhale Institute of Politics and Economics at IHD—provided very helpful editorial support. Mr. Dhiraj Kumar and Mrs. Madhavi Chauhan very patiently incorporated the changes made in a series of drafts. We are thankful to all of them.

New Delhi *Editors*
July 20, 2003

Acknowledgements

1

Introduction

S. Mahendra Dev, K.P. Kannan and Nira Ramachandran

I. THE CONTEXT

Ensuring food security ought to be an issue of great importance for a country like India where more than one-fourth of the population is estimated to be absolutely poor, and one-half of all children, malnourished in one way or another. There have been many emerging issues in the context of food security particularly during the 1990s. These are: (a) economic liberalisation in the 1990s and its impact on agriculture and food security; (b) establishment of WTO and particularly the Agreement on Agriculture (AOA) under it; (c) the phenomenon of hunger amidst plenty, i.e. the accumulation of more than 60 million tonnes of food stocks while 260 million or so people still live below the poverty line; (d) the introduction of targeting in the public distribution system (PDS) for the first time in the 1990s; (e) the 'right to food campaign' for improving food security in the country and the orders of the highest judicial body – the Supreme Court of India—on mid-day meal schemes; (f) monitorable targets under the Tenth Five Year Plan similar to Millennium Development Goals (MDGs) on poverty, and women and child nutrition. These developments in the 1990s have provided opportunities and challenges for the food and nutrition security of the country.

It is by now well-known that the question of food security has a number of dimensions that go beyond the production, availability and demand for food. There has been a paradigmatic shift in the concept of food security from food availability and stability to household food insecurity, and from the assessment of input measures like energy intake to output indicators such as anthropometrical measures and clinical signs of malnutrition.

From the policy point of view, it is useful to distinguish between growth-mediated food security and support-led food security.[1] Growth-mediated security has to do with, mainly, economic growth and improving human capabilities for meeting food and other basic needs. Support-led food security recognises the importance of government provision of public support systems for food security (e.g. in the state of Kerala and in Sri Lanka). Food subsidies, food for work programmes, and nutrition schemes fall in the latter category. There can, however, be a trade-off between these two approaches. In the literature on the subject, a distinction is also made between short-term and long-term measures for food security. Policies for sustainable agriculture, for example, can come under long-term measures, while relief type programmes like public works can be included under short-term measures. However, most programmes aimed at reducing food insecurity at the household level have both short-term and long-term dimensions. For example, 'food-for-work' programmes not only provide food for the workers in the short run, but also create assets, which impart long-term food security.

India has been following both growth-led and support-led policies and has been using short and long-term measures for improving food security. A large public distribution system, supplemented by arrangements for moderating prices in the open market and concerted efforts for achieving self-sufficiency in foodgrains coupled with measures for maximising procurement from surplus areas, have been the twin objectives of the food policy in modern India, ever since the Bengal famine of 1943. These objectives have held sway over the last 55 years, though with changes in emphasis and varying degrees of rigidity, from total control to total decontrol, depending upon the prevailing situation and assessment at each point of time (GOI, 2000). Currently the food security system basically consists of three instruments: procurement prices/ minimum support prices, buffer stocks and the public distribution system (PDS).[2] In order to ensure remunerative prices to farmers, the Government of India has been intervening in the foodgrain market mainly for wheat, paddy and coarse cereals through its minimum support price (MSP)/procurement policy. The importance of building up a buffer stock of foodgrains, normally rice and wheat, is to provide food security to the country. The argument in favour of buffer stocking is that where the variability of the foodgrain output is large, either due to weather conditions or due to man-made factors, it would be essential for the state to ensure that food security is maintained for the large mass of the people by building adequate buffer stocks from the surpluses during the good production years and/or by arranging to import the requisite foodgrain in times of need.

Various committees have suggested the optimal size of the buffer stock, which varies from 15 to 25 million tonnes, depending on the season. The Expenditure Reforms Commission recommended 17 million tonnes as the total average stock to be maintained for distribution and as a buffer (GOI, 2000). The current levels are much higher than the recommended levels. The network of the public distribution system (PDS) has expanded over the years, since its inception during World War II. Currently, foodgrains from government stocks are being made available through the PDS to households through a countrywide network of about 4.6 lakh fair-price shops. Various modifications have been made to the PDS over the years in order to improve its performance, including expansion in backward areas, special subsidised rates for target groups, etc. The *Annapoorna* Scheme was introduced in 2000 to provide food security to those senior citizens, who, though eligible for pension under the National Old Age Pension Scheme, are not getting the same. The *Antyodaya Anna Yojana* was introduced in 2001 to take care of the destitute in the country. In the Budget, 2003-04, this scheme was expanded to cover 25 per cent of the poor.

The purchasing power of the poor, for meeting their food requirements, can be ensured in two ways: one, by supplying foodgrains at subsidised prices similar to the PDS; and the other, by raising the incomes of the poor through employment. The employment, in turn, can be raised through growth in different sectors and directly targeted employment programmes. By now, it is well-recognised that the instrument of the rural public works programme has become an important component of various strategies devised to alleviate poverty and hunger in India. The public works programmes have both direct and indirect benefits. They are particularly useful during droughts and other natural calamities.

In addition, India also has nutrition programmes for women and children. Programmes such as the Integrated Child Development Services (ICDS) provide supplementary nutrition for pre-school children and expectant or nursing mothers. In the case of school children, the noon-meal scheme (particularly successful in Tamil Nadu and Kerala), which provides cooked food to children, has come to assume a crucial role in the larger scheme of food security.

The food security policy pursued since Independence may be considered as a success story in some aspects. Famines have been eliminated since Independence. The overall foodgrain production has increased from 50 million tonnes in 1950-51 to 209 million tonnes in 1999-2000. The level of procurement and the reach of the PDS have increased considerably, over time. Food/cash for work programmes have also helped the poor by raising their purchasing power. Nutrition programmes have contributed to the welfare of pregnant mothers, pre-school children, and school-going children. However, as shown below, all is not well with the food security policy, particularly with reference to procurement, the PDS and nutrition programmes. With the advent of economic liberalisation and globalisation, some new challenges have also emerged.

Despite the implementation of these programmes, there are concerns regarding calorie intake and malnutrition. Poverty levels remain high, despite a significant reduction in poverty in recent years. The calorie intake of the bottom 30 per cent is low. The problem of malnutrition is acute and widespread and is extremely serious among women and children. The proportion of pregnant women with anaemia is as high as 88 per cent. At the all-India level, more than 50 per cent of the children under the age of five were under-weight in 1998-99. The percentage of malnutrition is much higher in poorer states like Bihar, Uttar Pradesh and Madhya Pradesh. Currently, the major nutrition-related public health problems are: (a) chronic energy deficiency and under-nutrition; and (b) micro-nutrient deficiencies such as anaemia due to iron and folic acid deficiency, Vitamin A deficiency and iodine deficiency disorders (GOI, 2000a).

In order to meet all the food and nutrition requirements of its growing population, the country will have to increase its current levels of foodgrain production and increase the production of fruits, vegetables, livestock and fish. This has to be achieved in the face of obstacles like shrinking arable land and farm size, low production, growing regional disparities in production and depletion of the natural resource base.

The need for a comprehensive analysis of food security in the context of emerging issues and policies forms the immediate context of this volume. It is hoped that the analyses in the book would help formulate appropriate strategies and move towards a food secure India. The volume is organised into five sections: (a) Demand for and supply of foodgrains; (b) Policy response to domestic reforms and globalisation; (c) Regional scenario; (d) Grass roots experiences; (e) Emerging perspective. Given below is an overview of the findings of the chapters and related issues in the literature.

II. DEMAND FOR AND SUPPLY OF FOODGRAINS

India is, more or less, self-sufficient in foodgrains at the national level. The immediate question, however, is whether the country will continue to be self-sufficient in foodgrain production in the years ahead. Over the next 20 years, will total cereal demand increase significantly? Or will there be a significant departure from past trends that may increase or slow down the growth in demand? Will the supply of cereals continue to keep pace with demand, or will increasing resource scarcity and degradation limit future growth opportunities?

There have been considerable differences regarding the projections on foodgrains. The cereal demand in 2020 varies on each of the following essential elements: population, per capita direct consumption, and the requirement for animal feed. The papers on this theme (chapters 2 to 4) discuss these issues on the demand for and supply of foodgrains. The projections on supply and demand show that by 2020 the supply of foodgrains would be sufficient to meet the growing food demand.

The paper on supply by Kumar and Mittal (chapter 2) examines changes in the productivity performance of cereals and provides supply projections for foodgrains under different scenarios. The supply projections range from 248 million tonnes to 289 million tonnes depending on the assumption on total factor productivity, area, etc. The demand for foodgrains in 2020 is projected to be around 269 million. The demand for cereals will be met in future with a marginal surplus of wheat. However, this balance between domestic production and the demand for cereals can be sustained only if we maintain total factor productivity growth.

There are considerable differences regarding magnitudes of demand for foodgrains.[3] According to Bansil (chapter 3), the gross requirement of foodgrains will not exceed 241 million tonnes. This includes demand for per capita consumption and animal feed. This would mean that production would have to increase by 40 million tonnes during the next 20 years or say, 2 million tonnes annually. The paper argues that if a much higher target is fixed, as proposed by many others, there is an obvious danger of giving wrong signals to the development strategy which may lead to distortions and ill-advised wasted efforts.

The changing consumption patterns have implications on food demand projections as well as on non-cereal food crops and allied agricultural activities. Rao (chapter 4) examines changes in consumption patterns and the factors contributing to the decline in demand for foodgrains. This would have important implications not only for demand projections for foodgrains but also for development policies in general. The food basket is more diversified in the 1990s as compared to the 1970s. The per capita cereal consumption between 1972-73 and 1993-94 declined for all classes except for the bottom 30 per cent in both rural and urban areas. In future, the per capita consumption may decline even for the bottom 30 per cent of the population. An increase in rural infrastructure like roads and the mechanisation of agricultural operations could be responsible for the decline in the demand for foodgrains. The decline in per capita consumption of foodgrains on account of these factors would be associated with an improvement in the welfare of the rural consumers in general. It would also have implications for the future demand estimates for foodgrains.

The consensus seems to be that India would be able to produce enough cereals to meet the food and feed demand of around 260 million tonnes by 2020 provided that there is an increase in total factor productivity.[4] As mentioned above, there are challenges for increasing the productivity of foodgrains and also for maintaining growth in foodgrain production in the wake of the shift in area to non-foodgrains.

III. RESPONSE TO MACRO AND GLOBAL POLICIES

There are several emerging issues at the national and global levels in the context of food security in the country. The papers (chapters 5 to 7) on this theme discuss macro and international trade policies for ensuring food security at the national and household levels.

What kind of economic policies are needed to ensure food security? Vyas (chapter 5) discusses the economic policies needed for improving availability of food, household entitlement to food and stability in the supply of food. The national level food supply scenario has changed from one of deficit to one of surplus. However, in the 1990s, the growth of foodgrain production and productivity declined and there has been stagnation in the per capita availability of foodgrains. A large and poor country such as India cannot afford to take the issue of imports of sizeable quantities of foodgrains lightly. As our past experience suggests, the key factors in raising productivity are the level of public investment in agriculture, strengthening of supportive institutions of credit and marketing, and above all, a steady stream of productivity-enhancing technology. The incentive prices do play their part but that should not be exaggerated. A disturbing feature of the agriculture policy in India is the large and growing amount of input subsidies. These should be gradually reduced. Even if enough foodgrains are available, access is important. The relative price of foodgrains and the public distribution system (PDS) are important here. It is important to contain the minimum support prices (MSP). In the race between population growth and foodgrain productions, even when the income-induced demand for foodgrains is slackening, the state has a big role to play in ensuring adequate availability, minimising instability and uncertainty, and facilitating access to food, especially for the poorer sections.

The policies are generally broad-based and complex. In his paper on the new paradigms of food security, Alagh (chapter 6) attempts to develop an integrated information and decision support system to achieve the objectives of food security and hunger removal, as part of a diversification, strategy consistent with the new trade regime. Such a system is posited as part of a framework of decentralisation. The sub-regional and socio-economic correlates of food security are not known. There is a need for indicators and information systems. The requirement of work to develop information systems in the light of the above description will be three-fold: the first exercise to be carried out will be of a policy kind. These will outline the relationship among economic reform policies, the strategy of agricultural policies being developed, and food security policies. The second set of work requirements will relate to data requirements of the decision needs. The third set of work requirements will relate to models and information system formats. Quantitative models of different kinds will be needed to 'forecast' base level indicators in a consistent manner. Three alternatives for food policy are also suggested in this paper.

At the international level, the inclusion of the Agreement on Agriculture (AOA) under the World Trade Organisation (WTO) agreement was a watershed in the history of world trade reforms. Dev (chapter 7) examines the impact of WTO on food security in India. The implementation of the Agreement on Agriculture (AOA) under WTO has raised concerns in India about the possibility of it destroying food security. These are justified because the agriculture sector provides employment to many and food accounts for a major share of the expenditure of the poor. The analysis in this paper shows that India does not have to change her food policies relating to minimum support price, buffer stock and the PDS. The actual tariffs for most of the commodities in

India are much lower than the Uruguay Round bound rates. As such it can easily check edible oil imports by raising its tariff. There is, however, a need for extreme vigilance in taking timely measures within the existing tariff bindings to restrict imports, which affect our producers livelihoods. Regarding domestic support, the product-specific support in India was negative at –38.5 per cent in 1995-96 (it is positive only for sugarcane and oilseeds), while the non-product specific support (input subsidies) was positive at 7.5 per cent. Thus India is under no obligation to reduce domestic support or subsidies currently extended to agriculture as the support being given is well below the permissible level of 10 per cent of the value of its agricultural output. In respect of export competitiveness also, India's policies are not in conflict with the provisions of the WTO agreement. However, the experience of the last six years shows that there has been no significant reduction in domestic as well as export subsidies given by the developed countries to their agriculture sector. The anticipated increase in the exports of agricultural products from developing countries, therefore, has not materialised.

The WTO is not responsible for the glut of foodgrains in the country. In some quarters, the WTO is blamed for the glut in the market. The fear of the import of foodgrains under the new liberalised trade regime, which is having a dampening effect on the foodgrain prices in the country, is misplaced.[5] We need to understand why there is a glut in the foodgrain market and mounting stocks with the Food Corporation of India (FCI), despite the deceleration in the growth of foodgrain output during the last decade. We have also had net exports of foodgrains, consecutively for the last six years. As mentioned above, factors such as an increase in procurement prices and issue prices and long-term factors like changes in consumption trends towards non-foodgrains may also be responsible for the surplus. The evidence in the 1990s points to this phenomenon. This also does not lend credence to the view that trade liberalisation per se would endanger India's food security.

India submitted its proposals for the current negotiations on the Agreement on Agriculture in the areas of market access, domestic support, export competition and food security to the WTO in January 2001. The guiding principles on which these are based are: food and livelihood security of our people, protection of the interest of domestic farmers and maximising export opportunities for Indian agricultural products.

The implementation of the WTO Agreement on Agriculture (AOA) since 1995 has brought out the inadequacies inherent in the agreement. The ongoing negotiations in the WTO on the AOA provide an opportunity for India to rectify these inadequacies and inequalities. India would therefore do well to use this occasion to lay stress on the implementation of the Uruguay round agreements to reduce subsidies and other distortions by developed countries. Also, it should join the Cairns group for strengthening its bargaining capacity. As the international trade in agricultural commodities is likely to be liberalised further, a greater preparedness is required to face and prepare for competition in the international market. Standards are fast becoming an important factor in global trade, particularly regarding sanitary and phyto-sanitary (SPS) measures. The challenges that the developing countries face are that the standards may sometimes not be set in a transparent manner or that they may not provide sufficient time to meet these standards.

Furthermore, appropriate domestic policies are needed to augment agricultural production and to improve food security provided to the poor. This is because the viability of agriculture depends on cost reduction in Indian agriculture and not on the higher prices of farm products. These policies would also be useful for enabling India to complete with other countries in international trade. The focus of our efforts to improve the viability of Indian agriculture has to be on raising productivity by stepping up public investment, accelerating the development and adoption of cost-reducing technologies and removing restrictions on trade, marketing and processing within the country. Investible resources have to be raised through a better tax-GDP ratio as well as better cost recovery for the input services. In order to achieve food security, the economic access of the household to food is an important requirement. A crucial need for realising this objective is employment creation. This would necessitate the introduction of policy initiatives aimed at boosting agricultural growth.

IV. REGIONAL SCENARIO

In a vast country like India, food security issues differ across states. For example, Punjab is a food surplus state while Kerala is a chronic food deficit state. The problems in the north-eastern states are different from other states. Six papers in this volume (chapters 8 to 13) discuss various issues relating to food security in different states.

Most of the existing literature on poverty and food security in India considers only the major states. The paper by Dubey and Kharpuri (chapter 8), on the other hand, delves into the problem of food security among the states in the north-eastern (NE) region of India. Unlike at the all-India level, poverty increased in the rural north-eastern region between 1987-88 and 1993-94. Out of the eight constituent states, Meghalaya and Sikkim are the only two states where poverty ratios have declined during this period. In the absence of a well-knit market mechanism in the region, the adequate supply of food needs to be ensured through PDS. It seems that the PDS is accessible to most of the households in the region and that it is the lack of purchasing power which comes in the way of ensuring food security in the region. This is quite consistent with the economic structure of the most of the states in the north-eastern region where the most important sector is services, and job opportunities are available only in government services, which are concentrated in the urban areas. Therefore, for ensuring food security in the region, more income generating opportunities need to be created and made accessible to poor households in the rural areas in the short-run. These efforts are, however, hampered by the political instability and ethnic violence in many states in the region. In the context of the overall development of the region, food security will crucially depend on the general security situation in the region.

Turning to the southern states, food security issues in Andhra Pradesh and Kerala are different from those in the north-eastern region and some of the northern states. Indrakant and Harikishan (chapter 9) examine the food security situation in Andhra Pradesh. The state is considered as foodgrain surplus one and food-secure at the macro-level. However, there is food insecurity at the household level. Around one-fourth of the state's population still suffers from chronic food insecurity and around 40 per cent of the children suffer from malnutrition. The consumption data indicate a declining per capita monthly consumption of cereals across all the income groups in the rural and urban areas of Andhra Pradesh. Within cereals, rice, which is a staple food in AP, shows mixed trends. In the case of the poorest 30 per cent in rural areas, rice consumption increased at 2 per cent per annum, while for their counterparts in the urban areas, it fluctuated without any significant trend. For the top group, both rural and urban, the rice consumption declined considerably. A high rate of decline in coarse cereal consumption is visible across all the three income groups. While the PDS covers a large section of the population, its benefits do not always reach the targeted groups. The extent of benefits realised from the PDS in terms of the quantity of cereals obtained through the system as a proportion of the total cereal consumption, income gain to the beneficiary households and the consequent decline in the level of poverty, is modest when compared to the huge amount of subsidy incurred on the subsidised rice scheme. Covering about 70 per cent of the households, the rice scheme in Andhra Pradesh is highly cost-ineffective. The rice scheme in Andhra Pradesh can be modified to make it cost-effective so that the poor can be protected without straining investments in other sectors of human development. The demand for cereals is declining because of changes in tastes and insufficient growth of the income of the poor households. In order to improve the level of food security available to the people in general, and the poor in particular, it is essential to ensure that: (a) the farmers get a remunerative price; and (b) the income of the poor is increased. Therefore, the prospect of providing the benefit of food security to the poor in the future, depends in large measure, upon the success of government policies in increasing the income of the poor, the extent to which the adverse shift in taste pattern is prevented and the provision of the necessary infrastructure facilities to the domestic farmers in the face of globalisation of trade.

It is interesting to observe the experience of Kerala, which is a food-deficit state. Kannan (chapter 10), in his assessment of the state-assisted food security system in Kerala, shows that it has contributed to the improvement of a wide-range of human development indicators that are closely related to access to food and the alleviation of poverty. As in the case of several developmental indicators in India, the state of Kerala presents itself as an interesting case in the matter of food security also. While Kerala finds itself at a lower level in terms of the average intake of food among various states in India, it is in the forefront in terms of such food security indicators as the incidence of under-nutrition, poverty, infant mortality and life expectancy. An important component of the social security programme in Kerala is that of food security. There are three major components of the food security system in Kerala: PDS, supplementary nutrition programmes for school-going and pre-school children, and old age and other disability pensions for the poor. The problem of availability may have compelled Kerala to concentrate on the distribution of food. The Kerala experience highlights the advantages of a universal PDS. Over the last 38 years, the PDS in Kerala has been institutionalised and has become an integral part of public policy. It has ensured both physical and economic access and has sought to provide an entitlement of foodgrain, which is close to 90 per cent of the requirement. Given the increasing specialisation of Kerala's agriculture in favour of high value commercial crops, the large gap (currently 80 per cent) between foodgrain production and consumption has been largely taken care of by the PDS. The shift-over to a targeted PDS has pushed states like Kerala into a fiscally difficult situation. Sustaining the present system will entail large subsidies. Reducing the present system to a targeted one would exclude a large section of the non-poor but non-rich, and would threaten the rationale as well as the survival of the PDS (chapter 10). The long-term solution is to ensure that the extent of dependency is reduced. In the case of Kerala, the potential output of rice is close to 21 lakh tonnes, i.e. a little more than half its requirement. Given that the farmers in Kerala are price takers in both the product market and the input market, the solution lies in increasing productivity. This calls for improving the water control measures, an area in which the performance of successive governments has been highly disappointing.

We move to the food security issues in Rajasthan where there is large agricultural instability (Vidya Sagar, Chapter 11). The state has been declared drought-affected for the last five consecutive years. The population affected by drought was estimated to fluctuate between 21.5 to 33 million during 1998-99 and 2000-01. An important feature of the state is its wide annual variation in agricultural production. By major indicators, food security in the state appears to have improved in spite of it registering the highest population growth in India in recent years. That agricultural development and the rural economy could keep pace with the rapidly growing population may be a matter of satisfaction. However, this is achieved at the cost of resource degradation in large parts of the state. The continuation of such pressure on natural resources may not ensure sustainable food security. Equally important is the rate of population growth. Rajasthan observes one of the highest decadal increases in population during 1991-2001. A third issue relates to the central government policies to restrict income transfers through food assistance and targeted public distribution system (TPDS). The liberalisation of edible oil imports seems to have affected the edible oil farmers and industry. It resulted in loss of income and employment in the farm sector. According to a memorandum submitted by the Rajasthan Mustard Oil Industries Association, 90 per cent of the small industrial units have suffered. There is no denying that the poor in Rajasthan, as elsewhere, were benefited by the fall in edible oil prices. However, if the total employment and income effect of such a policy are taken into account, the gains in welfare get substantially reduced. If a longer-term perspective where in the cost of providing alternative employment and/or reviving a sick industrial sector are considered, such policy may have resulted in net welfare loss.

The remaining two papers are on the states of Bihar (and the newly created state of Jharkhand) and Uttar Pradesh, which are characterised by poverty, vulnerability to food shortages and an ill-functioning PDS. The experience of PDS in Bihar and Jharkhand is interesting. Mooij (chapter 12) examines the PDS experience and the political economy of PDS in Bihar and Jharkhand. In these two states the policy works poorly. It is important to understand why this is the case. This paper describes the PDS in Bihar and Jharkhand, not only in terms of how it fails and what it does not accomplish, but also in terms of what it is and what it does. The activities and interests of the various actors involved in the PDS are described, and it is shown that many people do benefit from the present setup, but that there are also people within almost all categories of stakeholders who are dissatisfied with the large-scale misappropriation of foodgrains. There is large-scale misappropriation of foodgrains at all levels; the distribution of cards to below poverty line (BPL) families is unsatisfactory; the Bihar State Food and Civil Supplies Corporation is financially unable to perform its task. Many people benefit from the way the PDS functions at present in the state. Some PDS dealers get a reasonable income, as do many civil servants and others who are involved in monitoring the system. The Food Minister as well as some other politicians also have vested interests in the way the system works. The problems with the PDS are not exceptional; in fact, they are part of a larger pattern of governmental ineffectiveness. The reasons behind this failure on the part of the government are economic stagnation and under-development, and the changing political landscape. Given this political economic context in which the PDS is implemented, the problems observed are not surprising. There is almost no growth, so whatever scarce resources are available, they are appropriated through legal or illegal means. It is argued that there is scope for change, but change requires strategic political manoeuvring and initially a low-key approach so as not to awaken and antagonise the strong vested interests.

The paper on Uttar Pradesh (Srivastava, chapter 13) looks at food availability and food access in the state. Uttar Pradesh is a food surplus state where the cereal and calorie intake are higher than the national averages, and the spread and depth of hunger is lower than in the country as a whole. Yet, large numbers of people in the state are food-insecure. While it scores highly on food availability, it is poor in food access. The poor in the state lack adequate food and a balanced diet, leading to nutritional and health problems and growth disorders. The health indicators show that the backward regions of the state, and women, children and SC/STs are especially disadvantaged. The performance of the government's direct interventions on the food front is poor. The PDS, despite attempts to revitalise it, has largely failed to deliver and the ICDS has not drawn young mothers and children to the *anganwadis* or improved their nutritional status. There are more positive reports on the mid-day meal scheme but even here the achievement lies in its success in enhancing school enrolments rather than in providing food or nutrition to children. It remains to be seen whether the state government can ensure better implementation of the recently introduced *Sampoorna Gramin Rozgar Yojana,* a universal food-for-work programme, aimed at utilising the large stocks of foodgrains to provide food and rural employment, while at the same time building rural infrastructure.

V. GRASS ROOTS EXPERIENCES

In a vast and diverse country like India, the question of food security has diverse connotations in different regions. We need to understand the scenario of food security at the micro-level and to devise appropriate strategies to deliver effective results. The section contains four papers focused on diverse environments ranging from drought-prone areas in the southern plateau (Karnataka), a tribal village in West Bengal, to a study of remote mountain villages in Uttaranchal and the hunger hotspots of Kalahandi (chapters 14 to 17).

The paper by Rao and Deshpande (chapter 14) examines food security in a drought-prone area of Karnataka. The purpose of this paper is to suggest an approach to food security, which would be consistent with both the development of rain-fed farming and the implementation of reforms regime for agriculture. Any discussion on the present food security system often revolves around the contention as to how it can be improved by: (a) focusing the PDS on the poor; (b) excluding the better-off; and (c) reducing leakages and corruption. While improvements in the system are welcome, our plea is that the present food security system needs to be assessed in relation to the broader context of the changing agricultural and poverty scenario in India. This seems to suggest that what is urgently required is a thorough restructuring of the system rather than piecemeal improvements in it. The present food security system reflects two basic flaws in our policy-making for promoting agricultural and rural development. Firstly, the problems of the relatively better-off sections of the farmers receive far more attention in policy-making than the deprivations suffered by the poor. Secondly, while the areas lagging in development like drought-prone areas, urgently need investment and an infrastructure to support and sustain the development process, the emphasis in policies remains on temporary and ad hoc relief measures. It is important to realise that this is not a congenial setting for progress towards decentralisation, de-bureaucratisation and de-politicisation referred to above. In fact, the Panchayati Raj Institutions (PRIs) as visualised in the recent constitutional amendments, would need a long time to become operational even in the few states like Karnataka that are regarded as being in the forefront in promoting the PRIs.

There are very few studies on the food security of rural women in tribal villages. Mukherjee (chapter 15) tries to fill in this gap by looking at a case study in West Bengal. Some of the questions addressed in the study are: What kind of food do the poor women, men and children consume to fill their stomachs? What type of food relieves them from the pangs of hunger in times of stress, caused by a natural or man-made calamity? In a patriarchal society, where gender discrimination is a matter of public history, who decides on the intra-household allocation of food everyday? Do the poor people find out every day the extent of food shortfall they face? And if so, how? What coping mechanisms do they adopt to make good the shortfall or to be able to survive with the food shortages? The findings show that the nature and intensity of hunger varies from month to month, the situation being at its worst during the summer and monsoon months. Villagers face long periods of hunger from *Chaitra* to *Kartik*, and the consumption of food is lowest during the months when the need is highest due to workload on account of employment and a harsh climate. The women face an additional workload of maintaining the supply of fuel during the period under reference when (particularly the latter part of the hunger period) fuel availability from 'conventional sources' gets reduced. It is argued that the role of the secondary food system (common property resources, micro-environments, forests, etc.) is critical in reducing hunger of the poor all through the year but more so during the hunger the period. Several policy initiatives are suggested to reduce hunger and food insecurity in the tribal areas.

Similar problems can be seen in the remote hilly areas too. Ramachandran (chapter 16) assesses the food security and nutritional status of the population in the remote mountain villages of the district of Garhwal, Uttaranchal. The district, in general, and particularly, the selected block, Pauri, is largely dependent on subsistence agriculture. Traditional methods of cultivation, small and scattered land holdings and the total dependence on already overburdened women farmers, results in low productivity levels with the agricultural output being barely sufficient to supply the average household with foodgrains for a period of three to four months. The region is thus heavily dependent on the PDS, which provides a steady supply of rice, wheat and sugar. Both officials and villagers attested to the effective functioning of the PDS in the region. However, as in other regions, the amount available per family is limited and can thus only augment, but not entirely substitute other sources of foodgrain supply. Thus, seasonal food distress is common among the BPL families, who at times, have to reduce food consumption to a single meal a day. While out-migration of young able-bodied males is common, there is no significant family migration trend among the people. The paper argues for a restructured food policy. The food policy with its focus on foodgrain production and subsidised distribution, and the nutrition supplementation programmes of other departments with their emphasis on eliminating child malnutrition and micro-nutrient deficiencies, need to be synergised.

Food security in some villages of the Kalahandi district of Orissa is examined by Sarap and Mahamallik (chapter 17). More specifically, this chapter discusses the access of the rural households to the provision of foodgrains as supplied by the revamped public distribution system (RPDS) operating in the area. An analysis of the food delivery system, as it is currently functioning in the state, shows that its coverage is limited in terms of the percentage of households as well as in terms of the amount of foodgrains supplied through this system. Several factors including an inadequate and inefficient food delivery system, poor infrastructure, the quality of grain supplied and lack of income especially in the poor households, have contributed to the poor performance of the local delivery system. Even the limited amount of foodgrains supplied to the state has not been lifted fully by the fair-price shops. Given the existence of such an inefficient food delivery system, even if more and cheaper foodgrain is allotted to the poor it would be difficult to deliver it to them. Given that half the population of the state lives below the poverty line, there is no serious effort on the part of the state to raise their effective access to food. The success in delivering food to the poor depends critically on the thrust of the rural development policies, including the employment assurance programme. In the ultimate analysis, there is a need for rapid rural development through the provision of irrigation and other rural infrastructure and large-scale employment generation programmes in order to provide effective food security to the poor in the area under study.

The broad consensus that emerges from the micro-findings on PDS is that the functioning of the PDS in its present form is unwieldy, as its organisational setup is far too centralised. Further, it involves huge costs and leakages, which can partly be attributed to the centralised structure of governance, and thereby, results in inefficiency. Although economic efficiency alone cannot be an appropriate tool to assess the overall performance of the PDS and its impact on food security, the inability of the system, in its present form, to ensure the delivery of food to the vulnerable, is indisputable. This has been emphasised by studies looking into the question of food security in the tribal and dry land regions. These regions are marked by persistent hunger and extreme scarcity of food during certain months. Hunger in these regions is, to some extent, seasonal in nature. Therefore, common property resources have become the basic life-sustaining sources for poor households. These facts call for a mechanism or an organisational structure that ensures undifferentiated access to adequate food for the vulnerable households in such areas. A widely accepted modification is that of a decentralised framework for the functioning of the PDS at the village level. This could be operationalised by bringing the PDS under the purview of PRIs.

VI. PDS, NUTRITION AND RIGHT TO FOOD

The last section brings to the reader emerging perspectives on the issues pertaining to food security in the country today. The emerging concern for improved nutrition rather than food security alone, the continuing importance of the PDS as a measure to ensure food security to the vulnerable, albeit with modifications aimed at improving the efficiency of the delivery system and lastly, the growing awareness of the need for a people's movement, if food security is to be ensured to the masses, constitute the contributions in this section.

The major focus in food security provisioning in the country is on the objectives, design, functioning and impact of the PDS in India. It was contended that the original objective of the PDS in India was stabilisation of foodgrain prices and management of supply. Over time, it came to be seen as an instrument for poverty alleviation. The primary responsibility of the central government was to intervene in the market for foodgrains by announcing minimum support prices as well as procuring surplus foodgrain. The latter was offered to the states for distribution through the PDS at a subsidised price. The Government of India, however, changed this policy as part of its economic reform programme and introduced in 1997, a targeted PDS (TPDS) under which foodgrains are being allocated to states on the basis of the estimates of population 'below the poverty line'. The separate issue price is fixed for the population above poverty line (APL). Under this scheme, each poor family was originally entitled to 10 kg of foodgrains per month at a specially subsidised price. In order to improve the allocations for poor families, the government increased the allocation to BPL families from 10 kg to 20 kg of foodgrains per family per month at 50 per cent of the economic cost from April 2000 onwards. The allocation for APL was retained at the same level at the time of introduction of TPDS but the central issue price (CIP) for APL was fixed at 100 per cent of the economic cost from the date so that the entire consumer subsidy could be directed for the benefit of BPL population. In order to reduce excess stocks lying with the FCI, the government has further initiated the following measures under TPDS from July 2001: (a) The BPL allocation of foodgrains has been increased from 20 kg to 25 kg per family per month with effect from July 2001, the CIP for BPL families at Rs. 4.15 per kg for wheat and Rs. 5.65 per kg for rice is 48 per cent of the economic cost; and (b) the government has decided to allocate foodgrains to APL families at the discounted rate of 70 per cent of the economic cost. The CIP of APL wheat, which was Rs. 830 per quintal has been reduced to Rs. 610 per quintal and the CIP of APL rice, which was Rs. 1130 per quintal, has been reduced to Rs. 830 per quintal.

Two papers (chapters 18 and 19) discuss issues relating to the targeted PDS (TPDS). Jha and Srinivasan (chapter 18) discuss the rationale for and the problems faced by the recent initiatives taken by the government in reforming the PDS for foodgrains in India. The chapter examines the costs and benefits associated with the operation of the PDS and illustrates through counter-factual simulations how the benefit-cost ratio would increase when subsidies are targeted at the poor and indirect benefits are accounted for. However, the administration of directly targeted PDS (TPDS) is difficult and a large number of the poor tend to get excluded from the programme. Therefore, the paper examines alternative ways of reducing inefficiencies in the system. It compares the costs of public storage and distribution operations with those of private agents, and discusses how the rising government costs can be curtailed by making the administration more efficient and by relying on market forces for the spatial distribution of grain. The findings show that the new system is faced with several problems and does not appear to address the real issues. One of the suggestions is to limit the role of FCI to price stabilisation and the maintenance of buffer stocks. Also, geographical targeting involving the universal coverage of only those areas that have a high concentration of poverty, can be an effective way of reaching out to more and more of the poor with a given amount of resources.

Opinions are sharply divided on the question of the design of the PDS. Swaminathan (chapter 19) examines the dangers of narrow targeting. Targeting is very costly in a country with a large population that is under-nourished and vulnerable to under-nourishment. At the very least, we need to include around 70 to 80 per cent of the population (and a much higher proportion of the rural population) in a scheme of providing minimum nutritional and income support such as the PDS. So the first step of the reform process must be to redefine the population that is to be included in the PDS. Once the size of the population whose nutritional needs are to be covered by the PDS, which includes all vulnerable sections of the population, is determined, then the administrative, fiscal and welfare concerns would all indicate that near-universal coverage is a better way to reach the target group than a complicated process which involves the exclusion of those in the highest consumption quintile. A belated recognition of this problem has led to the announcement (in July 2001) that prices for APL consumers in the PDS will be lowered to 70 per cent of the economic cost of grain. This announcement, it is hoped, will bring the consumers back to the fair-price shops and result in a higher off-take from the PDS. The paper argues for a genuine reform of the PDS, which calls for a reversal of the current policies, and specifically, the policy of narrow targeting to families living below the poverty line.

One paper in the volume examines the larger issue of nutrition security. Suryanarayana (chapter 20) takes up the question of food security and examines how imperative are the policies for nutrition. The findings on declining poverty levels during the 1980s, have led to a belief that the government should no longer concern itself with any major redistributive exercise. This is all the more so with respect to policies for alleviating nutritional deficiency, because of the apparent finding that the poor, with an improvement in their economic status, have opted for a diversified consumption basket to the neglect of nutritional considerations. This paper examines the empirical basis for such conclusions. It observes that the poor have not diversified their consumption basket to the extent reflected in the estimates at current prices. At the all-India level, the poorest 40 per cent have only diversified to the extent required by the principle of complementarity among food items. As a result, their calorie intake has increased consistently, and yet the calorie levels fall short of the normative minimum. This emphasises the need for formulating policies with reference to both poverty and nutritional deficiency considerations. This point is further corroborated with reference to the contrasting growth and redistributive experiences of Kerala and Tamil Nadu. By initiating a set of policies for promoting economic as well as physical access to foodgrains, the Government of Kerala could succeed in promoting the well-being of its population with respect to both the economic and nutritional criteria. Thus the nutritional status of the state's population has increased consistently over the years unlike in the case of Maharashtra. When it comes to the nation as a whole, the question that needs to be addressed does not seem to be one of pursuing targeted policies for promoting the nutritional status of a particular section of the population. The average level of calorie intake is so low and the incidence of calorie deficiency is so high across states that there is little scope for eradicating the incidence of calorie deficiency by pursuing a targeted policy uniformly across regions. It is, therefore, imperative that the government initiates policies aimed at improving the nutritional status of the population as a whole by introducing programmes designed to ensure the economic and physical access of all sections of its population to foodgrains and also for guiding consumer choice.

In recent years, food security has been examined with a human rights perspective. Dreze (chapter 21) provides three essays on food security and the right to food. There is no greater scam in India at this time than the so-called food subsidy. Under the cover of 'food security', the government is keeping millions of tonnes of food out of the reach of poor people. The paradox of mounting food stocks amidst widespread hunger provides a natural rallying point for further popular mobilisation across the country. The second essay on the political economy of hunger in Orissa provides many lessons. One of them is that in areas like KBK (Kalahandi-Bolangir-Koraput) there is an urgent need for social security arrangements of a permanent nature. The last essay deals with the right to food and public accountability. The growing awareness of the need for a people's movement, if the goal of food security is to be achieved, has evolved into a full-fledged campaign on the 'Right to Food'. In the light of the Directives of the Supreme Court of India on various issues relating to food security in drought affected states or for school-going children, the movement has assumed added significance in the context of ensuring food security to the vulnerable. The right to food calls for greater attention from popular organisations and social movements.

VII. CONCLUSION

The papers in this volume show that we need to adopt a multi-faceted approach for improving food and nutrition security in the country. Apart from proper national level policies, there is need for state level or location-specific policies as the problem of hunger and food security may differ from region to region. As mentioned above, food security can be increased through direct food assistance or through an increase in purchasing power by creating employment or a judicious combination of the two. Despite the initiation of many a programme, the problem of food insecurity continues to pose a major challenge to policy makers in the country. Some of the worst violations of the right to food can be seen in India today. On the one hand, under-nutrition levels are among the highest in the world. The problem of malnutrition is acute and widespread. It is extremely serious among women and children. The proportion of pregnant women with anemia is as high as 88 per cent and more than half of the children under five are underweight. These proportion are particularly acute in relatively poorer states.

It is ironical that India witnesses such acute forms of food insecurity as it accumulates stocks of foodgrains in public warehouses to unprecedented levels—more than 60 million tonnes! Democracy may have averted famines but it cannot claim to have averted food insecurity. Achieving freedom from hunger still remains one of the biggest challenges of a democratically free India.

The papers in this volume show that the issue of food security needs to be seen in a holistic perspective taking into account both the macro and micro aspects and hunger and nutrition. In such a comprehensive food security system, the state is responsible for ensuring that every needy person has economic access to nutrition and food. The volume strongly advocates the strengthening and effective implementation of various schemes and programmes, food and nutrition such as PDS, *Annapurna*, mid-day meal schemes and ICDs, and extending *Antyodaya Anna Yojana* to all the destitute in the country. In a holistic scheme of food security, gender aspects of food security should be given due importance in realising every person's right to food. Women's economic and social empowerment not only improves intra-household food distribution and health-related matters but also the implementation of food and nutrition programmes.

The access of the poor to employment will help to greatly promote food security though increased purchasing power. As such, the programmes of food and nutrition and employment security should be given utmost priority in the development policy.

Notes

1. Dreze and Sen (1989) distinguish between growth-mediated security and support-led security in the context of, not only food security but also other basic needs.
2. The Food Corporation of India (FCI) and Commission on Agricultural Costs and Prices (CACP) were established in 1964-65 to oversee the countrywide procurement, distribution and stocking of foodgrains and to recommend the minimum support prices of agricultural crops to the government, respectively. These food policy operations are aimed at stabilising prices, protecting the interests of the producers, consumers and the economy, as a whole, and reducing inter-regional disparities in the production and consumption of foodgrains.
3. Bhalla et al. (1999) provide the highest estimates on the food and feed demand for cereals in 2020 at 246 and 50 million tonnes respectively assuming the population to be 1329 million. The lowest food estimate is from Dyson and Hanchate (2000), who put their food and feed demand at 194 and 30 million tonnes, projecting 2020 the population in 2020 to be 1315 million.
4. Former on this see, GOI (2002).
5. On this, see Rao (2001).

References

Bhalla, G.S.; Hazell, P. and Kerr, J. (1999), *Prospects for India's Cereal Supply and Demand to 2020*, Food, Agriculture and the Environment Discussion Paper 29, International Food Policy Research Institute (IFPRI), Washington, D.C.

Dreze, J. and Sen, A. (1989), *Hunger and Public Action*, Oxford University Press, New York.

Dyson, Tim and Hanchate, A. (2000), "India's Demographic and Food Prospects: State Level Analysis", *Economic and Political Weekly*, November 11.

GOI (2002), *Report of the High Level Committee on Long-term Grain Policy*, Department of Food and Public Distribution System, Government of India, Ministry of Consumer Affairs, Food and Public Distribution, New Delhi.

——(2000), *Report on Food Security*, Expenditure Reforms Commission, New Delhi.

——(2000a), *Mid-Term Appraisal of Ninth Five Year Plan*: 1997-2002, Planning Commission, New Delhi.

Rao, C.H. Hanumantha (2001), "WTO and Viability of Indian Agriculture", *Economic and Political Weekly*, Vol. 36, No. 36, September 8-14.

PART I

Estimates of Demand for and Supply of Foodgrains in India

2

Productivity and Supply of Foodgrains in India

Praduman Kumar* and *Surabhi Mittal

I. INTRODUCTION

Achieving food security has been the overriding goal of agricultural policy in India. The introduction and rapid spread of high-yielding rice and wheat varieties in the late 1960s and early 1970s resulted in steady output growth for foodgrains. Public investment in irrigation, other rural infrastructure and research and extension, together with improved crop production practices, has significantly helped expand production and stocks of foodgrains. Foodgrain production, which was 72 million tonnes in 1965-66, rose to about 203 million tonnes in 2000. Imports, which averaged 6 million tonnes per year from the mid-1960s to the mid-1970s, have been surplus in recent years, and grain stocks, which were just 2.2 million tonnes in 1965–66, rose to more than 55 million tonnes.

The Green Revolution phase is characterised by widespread variety, turnover and adoption of improved varieties made possible by agricultural research and policy support. It exhibits enhanced productivity growth per unit of land that resulted in steady output growth for cereals. A first 'Post-Green Revolution' phase sees continued growth in returns to land through intensification of chemical input use and labour input per hectare. A second 'Post-Green Revolution' phase begins when input use is high, and further gains in productivity are largely dependent on increased efficiency of input use. The process of intensification of agriculture is central to achieving sustained growth in output. A marked increase in agricultural output has been instrumental in the transformation of traditional to modern, commercial agriculture. Economic, technological, and institutional factors have led to changes in cropping pattern. Farmers allocate the land among alternative crops so as to maximise their expected return. India experienced considerable changes in area, production and yield of various crops since the inception of the Green Revolution. A regional pattern in crop specialisation has emerged and those in deceleration in the growth of agriculture.

Achieving and maintaining the targets of food security appear to be a daunting task, especially when growth in production has to come exclusively from growth in productivity. These evolving scenarios will change the supply and demand prospects for food in this century. The present article examines changes in productivity performance of cereals and provides the supply projections for foodgrains under different scenarios.

II. PRODUCTIVITY

1. Changes in Cropping Pattern

The cropping pattern is changing in favour of crops, which have higher yields than their competitive crops at different point of time. The relative shares of crops whose yeilds are stagnating in the total gross cropped area are either declining or increasing at a slow rate. The extension of irrigation facilities for crops like rice, maize, wheat, gram, cotton, rapeseed, mustard and sugarcane has largely been instrumental in bringing drastic changes in the yields of these crops, which explains the changing cropping pattern. Irrigation facilities have made it possible for farmers to substitute high yielding and high value crops like wheat and rice in place of coarse cereals, pulses and oilseeds, etc. The area under high yielding varieties is increasing tremendously for rice, wheat, maize and sorghum, which has resulted in high yields for these crops. These are some of the factors, which support the changes in cropping pattern towards crops with high yields. Thus, the cropping pattern has been changing in favour of rapeseed, mustard, wheat, rice and sugarcane in India. These crops have shown an impressive performance in productivity growth.

The introduction of Green Revolution varieties after 1966-67 certainly promoted the production and distribution of high quality seed. More than 90 per cent of wheat acreage in India is already under HYVs whereas in rice about 70 per cent of rice area is under high-yielding varieties (HYVs) and the coverage is increasing. About 54 per cent acreage is under modern varieties for sorghum and maize. The area has steadily increased from 35 million hectares to 43 million hectares for rice and from 13 million hectares to 26 million hectares for wheat during the last 30 years. A marginal increase in the area under maize and pulses is observed. However, the area under sorghum and pearl millet declined due to substitution.

2. Trends in Production

In the last three decades, the country's wheat production went up 4.5 times with an annual growth rate of 4.6 per cent and it stood at 71 million tonnes during 1997-2000. The boost in production is a cumulative effect of research efforts, extension of area, development of irrigation infra-structure, enhanced use of fertilisers and plant protection measures, etc. As in the case of wheat, the HYV programme was initiated in rice in 1965-66 with the introduction of dwarf rice 'Taichung Native' and the release of

'IR8' in 1966. Rice production rose from 30 million tonnes in 1966-67 to 64 million tonnes in 1985-86 and 86 million tonnes during 1997-99 mainly on account of dwarf rice varieties covering presently 27 million hectares of a total of 44.4 million hectares area under rice in India. Despite the decline in the area under sorghum and pearl millet, the production of these crops increased due to gains in yield. The production of maize and pulses has almost doubled in last three decades in India, driven mainly by yield improvement. There was a spectacular increase in the yield for rice from 1,089 kg/ha in 1967-71 to 1,898 kg/ha in 1995-2000. During this period the per hectare yield increased from 1,242 kg to 2598 kg for wheat, 505 kg to 837 kg for sorghum and 1054 kg to 1,721 kg for maize. Growth in yield has accelerated over time, rising from 1.5 per cent in 1967-81 to 2.7 per cent in 1982-96 for rice. During this period, annual growth in yield increased from 2.6 per cent to 2.8 per cent for wheat and 0.4 per cent to 2.4 per cent for maize. The growth in sorghum yield was 3.2 per cent in the green revolution period, but decelerated in the post-green revolution period, 1982-96.

3. Cost of Production and Equity

The nominal cost[1] per unit of rice output is showing an upward trend despite the rapid growth in yield due to technical changes. However, the increase in nominal unit cost of production needs to be assessed. We need to determine whether it came about mostly due to an increase in prices of farm inputs at a rate higher than the rise in productivity or whether it was due to higher use of inputs in real terms for obtaining the same yield. This question was examined by assessing cost of production at constant prices.

The unit cost of production was deflated by an input price index series to obtain the cost of production at constant prices. The annual growth rates in *real cost of production (RCP)* are computed for major cereals and presented in Table 1. The real cost of production has shown a decline in respect of nearly all the cereal crops in all the states. The decline in cost of production for maize at constant price was not significant. While new technologies have increased the use of modern inputs, the increase in crop yields has been much higher than the increase in real input costs. Hence, the cost per unit of output has declined steadily at an annual rate of 2.2 per cent for wheat, 1.7 per cent for rice, and 1.4 per cent for sorghum. The adoption of modern varieties of maize in many parts of the country has not lowered the production cost.

The decline in unit cost of production due to technological change and input subsidies has resulted in substantial increases in the marketed surplus of wheat and rice. These contributed to food security mainly by inducing a sharp decline in real prices of rice (down 3.3 per cent annually) and wheat (down 2.2 per cent annually). Both farmers and consumers shared many of the benefits of higher efficiency in the use of inputs and lower unit costs of production that technological change has generated. The farmers gain because of higher crop yields and production while the

Table 1
Annual Growth in Real Cost of Production for Cereals in India

Crop	State	Annual growth(per cent)	Period
Paddy	Andhra Pradesh	-3.39**	1973-95
	Assam	-0.76**	1973-95
	Bihar	-0.51	1974-90
	Haryana	-0.52	1979-94
	Karnataka	-1.04	1973-91
	Madhya Pradesh	0.20	1974-94
	Orissa	-2.17**	1973-95
	Punjab	-2.32**	1976-95
	Tamil Nadu	-4.07**	1973-81
	Uttar Pradesh	-2.42**	1977-92
	West Bengal	-2.00**	1973-95
	India	-1.67**	1973-95
Wheat	Haryana	-3.25**	1972-95
	Himachal Pradesh	0.76	1972-95
	Madhya Pradesh	-1.29**	1972-95
	Punjab	-2.81**	1976-94
	Rajasthan	-3.20**	1972-95
	Uttar Pradesh	-2.17**	1972-95
	India	-2.20**	1973-95
Sorghum	Andhra Pradesh	-1.92**	1971-91
	Karnataka	-1.98*	1976-95
	Madhya Pradesh	-1.07	1971-95
	Maharashtra	-4.13**	1971-92
	Rajasthan	-2.88**	1971-95
	India	-1.38**	1971-95
Maize	Himachal Pradesh	-0.89	1976-87
	Madhya Pradesh	-2.25	1983-95
	Rajasthan	-2.63*	1974-92
	Uttar Pradesh	-4.18	1989-92
	India	0.75	1976-95

Note: Asterisks indicate significance level: ** = 1 per cent; * = 5 per cent.
Source: Computed by the author.

consumers benefit from higher purchasing power due to lower prices. The fall in prices of grains has benefited the urban and rural poor more than the upper income groups, because the former spend a much larger proportion of their income on these commodities than the latter (Kumar, 1997). The adoption of modern varieties, investment in irrigation, infrastructure and research, and favourable input pricing policies appear to have lowered the unit cost mainly of rice and wheat production and benefited both consumers and producers.

4. Total Factor Productivity (TFP)

The Divisia-Tornqvist index is used for computing the total output, total input, and TFP indices for cereal crops at the state level (Christenson, 1975). Micro farm-level data on yield, use of inputs and their prices, which were collected from the "Comprehensive Scheme for the Study of Cost of Cultivation of Principal Crops," Directorate of Economics and Statistics, Government of India, provides a very rich source of data to measure TFP changes. The annual compound growth rate of input, output and TFP indices are computed for rice, wheat and major course cereals and the results are presented in Table 2.

Table 2
Annual Rate of Growth (%) in Total Factor Productivity for Cereals in India

Crop	State	Input	Output	TFP	Period
Rice	Andhra Pradesh	2.36**	3.77**	1.41**	1973-95
	Assam	1.80**	2.08**	0.28	1973-95
	Bihar	1.58**	0.88	-0.69	1974-90
	Haryana	4.05**	3.75**	-0.30	1979-94
	Karnataka	1.03*	-0.08	-1.10**	1973-91
	Madhya Pradesh	2.71**	1.79**	-0.93	1974-94
	Orissa	1.48**	2.84**	1.35**	1973-95
	Punjab	6.79**	8.23**	1.44**	1976-95
	Tamil Nadu	0.98	4.15**	3.17**	1973-81
	Uttar Pradesh	2.13**	3.47**	1.34*	1977-92
	West Bengal	2.06**	3.30**	1.25**	1973-95
	India	2.23**	2.91**	0.68**	1973-95
Wheat	Haryana	3.43**	5.17**	1.74**	1972-95
	Madhya Pradesh	3.14**	3.06**	-0.08	1972-95
	Punjab	2.61**	3.94**	1.33**	1972-95
	Rajasthan	1.69**	3.48**	1.79**	1976-94
	Uttar Pradesh	2.38**	4.02**	1.64**	1972-95
	India	2.86**	3.78**	0.92**	1972-95
Sorghum	Andhra Pradesh	-3.06*	-2.31*	0.75	973-95
	Karnataka	3.02**	3.72**	0.69	971-91
	Madhya Pradesh	-0.86	-1.25	-0.39	1976-95
	Maharashtra	2.31**	3.80**	1.49*	1971-95
	Rajasthan	1.74	1.75	0.01	1971-92
	India	1.25*	1.43*	0.18	1971-95
Maize	Himachal Pradesh	0.26	-0.25	-0.51	1976-87
	Madhya Pradesh	0.63	2.27	1.64	1983-95
	Rajasthan	3.38**	3.18*	-0.20	1974-92
	Uttar Pradesh	-0.39	1.81	2.20	1989-92
	India	1.61**	1.20*	-0.41	1976-95

Note: Asterisks indicate significance level: ** = 1 per cent; * = 5 per cent.
Source: Computed by the authors.

Rice: The average annual growth rates of output, input and TFP indices for rice revealed that in Punjab, the input index during 1970s-1990s has risen at the rate of 6.8 per cent. This rise was 4.1 per cent in Haryana, 2 to 3 per cent in Madhya Pradesh, Andhra Pradesh, Uttar Pradesh, and West Bengal, 1 to 2 per cent in Assam, Orissa, Bihar, and Karnataka, With the increase in input and technological change, the output increased 8.2 per cent in Punjab, 3 to 4 per cent in Haryana, Uttar Pradesh, Andhra Pradesh, 2 to 3 per cent in Orissa, Assam and 1.8 per cent in Madhya Pradesh. Insignificant growth in rice output for Bihar and Karnataka was observed. Thus, TFP growth rate in rice was estimated at 1 to 2 per cent for Punjab, Uttar Pradesh, Andhra Pradesh, Orissa and West Bengal. In the other states, TFP was negative and insignificant. A national figure for India is computed by taking a weighted average of the states.

The input, output and TFP indices have annually risen by around 2.2 per cent, 2.9 per cent and 0.7 per cent, respectively, and the growth in TFP was responsible for about 24 per cent increase in output growth of rice in India. During the first period (till mid-1980s) the rise was mainly contributed by the adoption of technology in the front line states, Punjab and Haryana. After the mid-1980s, TFP has risen in states such as Andhra Pradesh, Orissa and West Bengal. Among the southern states, Karnataka lags behind. The case of Haryana in the northern region is puzzling. Its performance is in sharp contrast to that of Uttar Pradesh and adjoining Punjab. Among the eastern states, West Bengal and Orissa show some significant tendencies towards the growth in TFP. Other eastern states tend to drag the national average down. Technological change has not made much headway across substantial areas. The high past growth in Andhra Pradesh, Punjab, Orissa and West Bengal may not be sustained if future technological improvements are not supported by public resource allocation to infrastructure, research and development.

Wheat: Table 2 reveals that in Punjab, the input index during 1972-95 has risen at the rate of 2.6 per cent, whereas it was 3.4 per cent in Haryana, 3.1 per cent in Madhya Pradesh, 2.4 per cent in Uttar Pradesh, and 1.7 per cent in Rajasthan. With the increase in input use and technological change, the output increased by 3 to 5 per cent per annum. On the whole, the TFP index has risen by about 1.3 per cent in Punjab, 1.7 per cent in Haryana, 1.8 per cent in Rajasthan and 1.6 per cent in Uttar Pradesh, while the increase is negligible in Madhya Pradesh. In Madhya Pradesh, increasing trend in TFP was observed just after the adoption of HYVs and in the latter period it has shown a declining trend. These fluctuations resulted in negative and insignificant growth in TFP for wheat in Madhya Pradesh. A steady rise in TFP indices are observed in the front line wheat growing states, viz., Haryana, Punjab, and Uttar Pradesh with the introduction of modern varieties of wheat in the late 1960s and early 1970s. Fluctuations in TFP indices were observed due to high weather variation in Rajasthan, Madhya Pradesh and Himachal Pradesh. The TFP growth rates in the wheat sector in the states of Punjab, Haryana, Uttar Pradesh and Rajasthan are much above the rate of growth in TFP not only in the Indian and Pakistani crops sector (around 1 per cent) but also in US post-war agriculture (around 1.5 per cent) (Rosegrant and Evenson, 1992). The productivity growth or technical change is responsible for 34 to 51 per cent of the total output growth in the front line states.

Sorghum: The growth in TFP for sorghum was found statistically insignificant for most of the states except Maharashtra, which is the major sorghum growing state of the country. Despite stable growth in input and output indices, the TFP trend is highly unstable. In the country as a whole, the input index increased at the rate of 1.25 per cent, output index grew at the rate of 1.43 per cent and TFP at the rate of 0.18 per cent during the period 1971-95. Wide fluctuations in TFP indices were observed due to variations in production as a result of the weather.

Maize: Wide fluctuations in TFP indices were observed for all states. This may be due to the variation in production as a result of the weather. The input index during 1976-95 has risen at the rate of 1.61 per cent per annum, which was higher than the growth in output resulting in negative growth in TFP. No significant trend in TFP indices was estimated. It appears that maize production is input based and role of technology is not visible.

III. SUPPLY OF FOODGRAINS

1. Supply Model

For all foodgrains, the production increment during 1971-2001 was 100 million tonnes per annum. Rice contributed 47 per cent, and wheat 50 per cent to this total, with coarse cereals and pulses, contributing 1 per cent and 2 per cent, respectively. Rice and wheat crops are the major sources of foodgrains supply. The supply model specified in Appendix 1 was estimated for rice and wheat by using the cross-section cum time-series cost of cultivation data for the period 1973-95. The results of the estimated model are presented in App. Tables 1 and 2 for rice and wheat, respectively. Most of the coefficients in the estimated system were statistically significant at the 5 per cent confidence level (one-tail test) or better. The explanatory power of the estimated system was quite high and statistically significant. The supply model is specified in double log linear form, hence, the estimated effects can be interpreted as factor demand and yield elasticities for crops with respect to price and non-price factors in the subsequent discussion.

(i) Choice of Technique

The choice of technique (irrigation, variety) within each crop is a function of investment decisions by both the farmer and the government and it induces the use of inputs and thereby yields. The within-crop choice of technique which influences the yield response of the crop, is defined in terms of the percentage of crop area under irrigation, and percentage area under HYVs. The elasticity for crop-irrigated area with respect to net sown irrigated area was estimated to be 1.103 for wheat, followed by 0.608 for rice. The farmers' choice is in favour of wheat crop with regard to the allocation of irrigated land. Literacy rate, electrification and irrigation influence the decision on the adoption of modern varieties significantly. All of these variables have expected positive signs. The elasticity of HYVs with respect to literacy was higher for wheat (0.60) than it was for rice (0.38). Higher use of inputs is indirectly induced by rural literacy rate through adoption of HYVs.

(ii) Factor Demand Function

Human Labour: The employment of human labour for each crop is explained by normalised wages, machine labour price, adoption of high yielding varieties and area under irrigation. The wage elasticity of human labour demand has the anticipated negative sign for both crops. It was estimated at -0.25 for rice and -0.44 for wheat. A negative sign for cross-price elasticity with respect to the price of other variable inputs shows that the pair are complementary and a positive sign is an indicator of a substitutive relationship. However, a positive sign for cross elasticity with respect to choice of technology indicates that the pair is complementary and a negative sign is indicative of a substitutive relationship. The cross-price elasticity in relation to machine labour price was positive and significant. The elasticity demand for human labour with respect to crop output prices was estimated to be positive, with a mild result for rice (0.09). However, the output price elasticity for labour employment was quite high for wheat (0.33). With wage inflation, human labour will be substituted by machine labour. This is likely to induce efficiency in crop production and improve productivity and yield. Irrigation has a positive significant impact on labour employment. Adoption of modern varieties had replaced human labour with machine labour for wheat and maize crops. Mechanisation of farms is of crucial importance for timely completion of farm operations, for multiple cropping and short duration varieties. Moreover, mechanised operations are easier for wheat than they are for rice, and more readily accepted by the farmers.

Machine Labour: Machine labour use is a function of wages, bullock labour charges, machine labour charges, adoption of HYVs and area under irrigation. Cross-price elasticity of use of machine labour with respect to wages and bullock labour charges was positive and significant, indicating a substitutive relationship. Substitution of machine labour for human and bullock labour will take place as a result of an increase in wages for traditional labour input. The elasticity of machine labour employment with respect to HYVs and irrigation was positive and significant for both crops. Irrigation expansion and adoption of modern varieties had induced the demand for machine labour.

Fertiliser: The study of responsiveness of fertiliser demand to price movements and changes in fixed factors is quite important in identifying the factors influencing demand for fertiliser. Demand for fertiliser is assumed to be a function of normalised price of fertiliser, machine labour use, adoption of HYV and crop area under irrigation. The results of fertiliser demand elasticity revealed that own price elasticity of fertiliser demand had an unexpected positive sign for rice and wheat. However, it was not significant in the case of rice. The results revealed that with an increase in fertiliser price, fertiliser use in rice and wheat crop would not be affected. Other crops showed that there would be a significant decline in the use of fertiliser. Rice and wheat crops are highly remunerative and responsive to fertiliser. Even with a higher fertiliser price, farmers will continue to use higher doses of fertiliser. This finding has policy implications for the fertiliser subsidy programme. Reduction in fertiliser subsidies will not affect the use of fertiliser in the rice and wheat cropping system, which is the backbone of national food and nutritional household security (Kumar, 1998). This has strong policy implication for equity and domestic output supply of these crops. Mechanisation has a positive significant effect in inducing higher use of fertiliser. Fertiliser demand was highly responsive to irrigation and HYVs. Fertiliser demand elasticity with respect to crop-irrigated area was positive and significant. Fertiliser demand with respect to HYVs is estimated to be elastic for rice (1.13) and inelastic for wheat (0.40). A complementary relationship for fertiliser use with irrigation, HYVs and mechanisation was strongly visible.

(iii) Yield Function

The structural equation of the yield function in the model is specified as a function of inputs (human labour, machine labour, fertiliser, farm yard manure), technology and quality of inputs (TFP indices are used to take care of these factors), rainfall, dummy for the eastern (control), western, northern and southern states of the country. The yield elasticity with respect to human labour was positive and significant for wheat and insignificant for rice. Machine labour had significant and positive effects. The yield elasticity for machine labour was estimated to be 0.24 for rice and 0.49 for wheat. The fertiliser yield elasticity was estimated highest for wheat (0.096), followed by rice (0.047). The effect of TFP on yield was positive and strong. The elasticity of yield with respect to TFP was estimated at 0.58 for rice and 0.56 for wheat. The TFP seems to be the most dominating source for yield growth. Organic manure had a positive and significant effect on yield for rice, however, for wheat it was not visible.

(iv) Regional Dummy

A quick glance into the region dummy estimates for rice shows that the eastern region (control) and the southern region dummy coefficients are positive, high and statistically significant. It can be inferred that a faster rate of growth in rice yield can be achieved from the eastern and southern states of India. The northern states had achieved high growth in yield mainly due to intensive use of inputs, which may not be cost effective in the long run. These findings confirm earlier findings (Kumar and Rosegrant, 1994) that future productivity gains in rice production will have to be achieved from the eastern and southern regions of India.

2. Cumulative Effects of Price and Non-price Factors on Yield

Cumulative effects of price and non-price factors on the use of inputs and yield were derived from the estimated model by using the derivations given in the Appendix and the results are presented in Tables 3 and 4 respectively, for price and non-price factors. The illustration provides crucial information on choice of technique, factor demand and yield growth for the crops under study.

(i) Price Factor

Wage: Wage has a negative effect on the use of human labour and a positive influence on machine labour and fertiliser. This implies that with an increase in wages, human labour becomes more costly. Once human

Table 3

Cumulative Effect of Price Factors on Input Demand and Yield

Crop	Crop elasticity			
	Human labour	Machine labour	Fertiliser	Yield
Total effect of wages (w/P)				
Rice	-0.25	0.90	0.30	0.23
Wheat	-0.44	0.41	0.32	0.12
Total effect of bullock labour charges (b/P)				
Rice	-	0.39	0.13	0.10
Wheat	-	0.27	0.21	0.15
Total effect of machine labour charges (m/P)				
Rice	0.16	-0.84	-0.28	-0.23
Wheat	0.11	-0.27	-0.21	-0.12
Total effect of fertiliser price (r/P)				
Rice	-	-	0.37	0.02
Wheat	-	-	0.20	0.02

Notes: Variables are not entered in the model; w=wage rate, b=bullock labour charges, m= machine labour charges, r=fertiliser price and P = crop output price.

Table 4

Cumulative Effects of Non-price Factors on Input Demand and Yield

Crop	Crop elasticity					
	CRIRR	HYV	Human labour	Machine labour	Fertiliser	Yield
Total effect of farm yard manure						
Rice	-	-	-	-	-	0.04
Wheat	-	-	-	-	-	-.001
Total effect of net sown irrigated area						
Rice	0.61	0.11	0.12	0.23	0.62	0.08
Wheat	1.10	0.35	0.38	0.66	0.88	0.50
Total effect of literacy						
Rice	-	0.38	-0.00	0.17	0.48	0.06
Wheat	-	0.60	-0.08	0.09	0.31	0.05
Total effect of rural electrification						
Rice	-	0.48	0.00	0.22	0.62	0.08
Wheat	-	0.18	-0.02	0.03	0.09	0.02
Total factor productivity effect						
Rice	-	-	-	-	-	0.58
Wheat	-	-	-	-	-	0.56

Note: Variables are not entered in the model.

labour becomes costly, the process of substitution from human labour to machine labour takes place. Mechanisation induces fertiliser use and the trade-offs between these inputs improves production efficiency. Hence, the net effect of normalised wage on yield was positive. The gain in yield growth was estimated at a rate of 2.3 per cent for rice and 1.2 per cent for wheat for every 10 per cent growth in normalised wages.

Bullock Labour Charges: Higher bullock labour charges will induce higher use of machine labour as it results in the substitution from bullock use to machine labour use. With 10 per cent growth in bullock charges, the use of machine labour will increase at the rate of 3.9 per cent for rice and 2.7 per cent for wheat. Mechanisation has induced higher use of fertilisers. Higher use of machine labour and fertiliser then result in productivity gains. The yield improvement corresponding to 10 per cent growth in real bullock charges are estimated to have a growth rate of 1.0 per cent for rice, and 1.5 per cent for wheat.

Machine Labour Charges: Own price elasticity of demand for machine labour is highly negative and significant. With a 10 per cent growth in machine labour charges, the use of machine labour will decline at a rate of 8.4 per cent for rice, and 2.7 per cent for wheat. High cost of machine labour will result in lower use of machines and fertilisers and higher use of human and bullock labour. This will result in a net negative effect on yields. With a 10 per cent increase in growth of machine labour charges, the decline in yield growth was estimated at 2.3 per cent for rice and 1.2 per cent for wheat. These results suggest that it is necessary for policies to evolve, as this keeps the price of machine labour low and helps induce crop production efficiency in the light of food needs and nutritional household security.

Fertiliser Price: Chemical fertilisers are the major nutrients in crop production. Rice and wheat are the technological advance crop and the relative profitability of these crops are high (Kumar et al., 1998). The gradual increase in fertiliser price has not declined the use of fertilisers in both crops. Yield elasticities were highly inelastic with respect to fertiliser price. Thus, the reduction in fertiliser subsidy will not affect the supply of these major staple cereals of India. This has wide implications in the trade liberalisation regime. These two crops shared more than 70 per cent of total foodgrains and are the backbone of India's food and household nutritional security.

(ii) Non-price Factor

Irrigation: Impact of net sown irrigated area induces the allocation of irrigated land under specific crops. Crop-irrigated area, consequently, induces the adoption of modern varieties. Both yield-enhancing non-price technologies induce the use of inputs and hence yield. With the expansion of irrigated land, wheat crop will share maximum irrigated land. Crop irrigation induces the adoption of HYVs with an elasticity coefficient of 0.11 for rice, and 0.35 for wheat. Crop-irrigated area and adoption of HYVs induced higher use of human labour, machine labour and fertilisers. The effect of irrigation on the use of farm inputs was highest for wheat, followed by rice. Among inputs, irrigation has the highest effect on fertiliser use, followed by machine labour and human labour employment. The total impact of irrigated land expansion on yield was higher for wheat (0.50) than for rice (0.16). If government investment in irrigation increased the growth of irrigated areas at an annual rate of 10 per cent, then yield growth would gain at a rate of 5.0 per cent for wheat, and 0.8 per cent for rice. Wheat crop growers will derive maximum benefits from investment in irrigation.

Literacy: Rural literacy has significant effects on the adoption of modern varieties. The elasticity of HYVs with respect to literacy was highest for wheat (0.60), followed by rice (0.38). Higher use of inputs is induced through HYVs as a result of a higher rural literacy rate. Impact of literacy has a negative and mild effect on the use of human labour. A 10 per cent improvement in literacy rate will induce the growth rate in yield by 0.6 per cent for rice and 0.5 per cent for wheat. An increase in yield, resulting from an improvement in literacy rate was on an average small but still has substantial implications for supply of cereals.

Electrification: Rural electrification has induced the adoption of modern inputs in rice crops (0.48) more than it has in wheat crops (0.18). The government has already invested heavily in rural electrification in the wheat growing frontier states. Capital investment in rural electrification in the eastern states will increase the use of fertilisers and machine labour and induce rice supply. Electrification has a mild negative effect on human labour employment. The higher use of modern inputs as a result of rural electrification will be responsible for increasing yield growth from its existing average level. A 10 per cent growth in rural electrification will correspond to an increase of 0.8 per cent for rice crops and 0.2 per cent for wheat crops.

Total Factor Productivity: The TFP is found to be a significant determinant for growth of yield. The elasticity of yield with respect to TFP is estimated to be 0.58 for rice and 0.56 for wheat. Literacy accounts for a 13 per cent growth in TFP for rice in India (Mittal and Kumar, 2000). Literacy, through TFP, will contribute a quite substantial 7.5 per cent improvement in yield growth for rice crops.

3. Supply Growth

TFP, price environment, infrastructure, literacy, and organic manure are the major sources of yield growth. The elasticities given in Tables 3 and 4 are used to express the yield growth equation in terms of relative changes of exogenous variables for rice and wheat crops and are presented as follows.

Rice

$$\dot{Y} = 0.23\ (\dot{w/P}) + 0.10\ (\dot{b/P}) - 0.23\ (\dot{m/P}) + 0.02\ (\dot{r/P}) + 0.04\ \dot{FYM} + 0.08\ \dot{NSIRR}$$

$$+0.06\ \dot{LIT} + 0.08\ \dot{PVELECT} + 0.58\ \dot{TFP}$$

Wheat

$$\dot{Y} = 0.12\,(\dot{w/P}) + 0.15\,(\dot{b/P}) - 0.12\,(\dot{m/P}) + 0.02\,(\dot{r/P}) - 0.001\,\dot{FYM} + 0.50\,\dot{NSIRR}$$

$$+0.05\,\dot{LIT} + 0.02\,\dot{PVELECT} + 0.56\,\dot{TFP}$$

Yield and acreage are the sources of output growth. The production growth equation would be

$$\dot{S} = \dot{Y} + \dot{CRAREA}$$

where Y is yield per unit of land, w, b, m, r, and P are wage rates, bullock labour charges, machine labour charges, fertiliser price, and crop output price, respectively. NSIRR is the percentage of net sown area under irrigation, LIT is the rural literacy, PVELECT is the percentage of total villages electrified, TFP is total factor productivity, CRAREA is crop sown area, and the dot (.) represents growth in the corresponding variable. This formulation has the advantage of separating the effect of price and non-price factors. The first four terms measure the price effects and the other terms measure the contribution of irrigation, literacy, electrification, and TFP to yield growth.

4. Supply Projections

The yield and production (supply) growth equations given above were used to predict the supply of rice and wheat under the assumptions given in App. Table 3 for factor and product prices, infrastructure variables, TFP, organic manure, and area growth. Medium- and long-term prospects of major cereal supply were explored up to 2020 under the following scenarios:

S1 = baseline assumptions as given in App. Table 3
S2 = baseline assumptions without TFP growth
S3 = baseline assumptions without area growth
S4 = baseline assumptions without TFP and area growth

(i) Rice

The projected growth in rice supply as given in Table 5 revealed that rice supply would grow at a lower rate than that achieved in the past. The predicted annual growth of rice supply, corresponding to the baseline, would decline from 2.26 per cent in 2000 to 1.71 per cent in 2010 and further to 1.60 per cent in 2020. In the absence of TFP growth, supply would grow by 1.51 per cent in 2005, 1.41 per cent in 2010, and 1.36 per cent in 2020. The possibility of area expansion is limited. Under the assumption with no growth in rice area, the supply would grow annually by 1.23 per cent in 2005, 1.08 per cent in 2010, and 0.98 per cent in 2020. Under the scenario 4 (without growth in TFP and rice area), the supply would grow at a smaller rate of about 0.87 per cent in 2005, 0.78 per cent in 2010, and 0.74 per cent in 2020 vis-à-vis the baseline. The projected growth in rice supply is lower than that achieved during 1982-90 (4.7 per cent) and

Table 5

Predicted Annual Growth (%) of Domestic Rice Production in India

Year	Scenario 1 (baseline)	Scenario 2	Scenario 3	Scenario 4
1985-97	2.51	1.98	1.95	1.42
2000	2.16	1.73	1.55	1.11
2005	1.87	1.51	1.23	0.87
2010	1.71	1.41	1.08	0.78
2015	1.66	1.39	1.03	0.76
2020	1.60	1.36	0.98	0.74

Notes: Scenario 1 = baseline assumption for price and non-price exogenous variables. Scenario 2 = baseline assumption without TFP growth. Scenario 3 = baseline assumption without area growth. Scenario 4 = baseline assumption without TFP and area growth.

1991-99 (2.1 per cent) and much less that what has been envisaged in various five year plans. In most of the areas, the investment in irrigation has remained static or has even fallen. The natural resource base is under severe pressure.

Based on the projected growth in supply given in Table 6, the domestic supply of rice is projected using TE 2000 as the base year production. The domestic supply of rice under the baseline scenario will be about 108 million tonnes in the year 2010 and grow to 127 million tonnes by the year 2020. Considering the baseline scenario without TFP growth, the domestic supply of rice will be about 103 million tonnes in 2010, and 118 million tonnes in the year 2020. In the absence of area expansion under rice crop, the rice supply is projected at the level of 100 million tonnes in the year 2010, and 111 million tonnes in the year 2020. The domestic supply in scenario 4 (without TFP and rice area growth) is projected to be 96 million tonnes in 2010 and grow to 103 million tonnes in the year 2020.

Table 6

Projected Domestic Rice Supply in India (million tonnes)

Year	Scenario 1[a] (baseline)	Scenario 2	Scenario 3	Scenario 4
TE 1999	85.7	85.7	85.7	85.7
2000	89.5	88.7	88.4	87.6
2005	98.7	96.0	94.6	91.9
2010	107.8	103.2	100.0	95.8
2015	117.1	110.6	105.4	99.5
2020	127.0	118.4	110.8	103.3

Notes: [a]Scenario 1=baseline assumption for price and non-price exogenous variables. Scenario 2=baseline assumption without TFP growth. Scenario 3=baseline assumption without area growth. Scenario 4=baseline assumption without TFP and area growth.

A comparison of scenarios 1 and 2 assesses the effect of TFP growth on rice supply. The TFP contribution to the rice supply is estimated at 4.6 million tonnes in 2010, and 8.6 million tonnes annually by the year 2020. If TFP growth is not maintained, the loss in the rice production will be substantial. The area response remained one of the most important sources of domestic supply. Several states gained in rice area as a result of substitution or expansion or both effects. The impact was substantial in the northern states, where the rice area gained 4.4 per cent annually during 1973-81 and 1.9 per cent in the recent past. All the regions have shown a positive growth in rice area expansion at about 0.6 per cent on an average nationally during 1967-99. A comparison between scenarios 1 and 3 assesses the effect of area on supply. In the absence of area expansion, the loss in rice supply will be 7.8 million tonnes in 2010, and 16.2 million tonnes in 2020, which is about 15 per cent of the total rice supply. This loss needs to be compensated for by increasing the yield levels per unit of land. A comparison between scenarios 4 and 1 assesses the effect of TFP and area response and it is estimated to be equivalent to 12 million tonnes in 2010, and 24 million tonnes in 2020.

(ii) Wheat

The projected annual growth of wheat supply is estimated to be 2.07 per cent in the year 2005, which will decline to a level of 1.43 per cent by the year 2020 corresponding to the baseline assumptions (Table 7). In the absence of TFP growth, wheat production would grow by 1.89 per cent in 2005, 1.61 per cent in 2010, and 1.37 per cent in 2020. Under the assumption with no growth in acreage, the wheat production would grow annually by 1.45 per cent in 2005, 1.19 per cent in 2010, and 1.09 per cent in 2020. Under scenario 4 (without growth in TFP and wheat area), the supply would grow at a smaller rate of about 1.28 per cent in 2005, and 1.03 per cent in 2020 vis-à-vis the baseline. The projected growth in wheat supply is higher than that predicted for rice. Based on the projected growth in wheat supply, the domestic supply of wheat is projected using TE 2000 as the base year production (Table 8). The domestic supply of wheat under the baseline scenario will be 87 million tonnes in the year 2005 and grow to 112 million tonnes by the year 2020. Considering the baseline scenario without TFP growth, the domestic supply of wheat will be about 108 million tonnes in the year 2020. In the absence of acreage response, the wheat production is projected at 87 million tonnes in the

Table 7
Predicted Annual Growth (%) of Domestic Wheat Production in India

Year	Scenario 1 (baseline)	Scenario 2	Scenario 3	Scenario 4
1985-97	2.99	2.70	1.91	1.62
2000	2.60	2.36	1.72	1.48
2005	2.07	1.89	1.45	1.28
2010	1.69	1.61	1.19	1.11
2015	1.55	1.48	1.14	1.07
2020	1.43	1.37	1.09	1.03

Notes: Scenario 1=baseline assumption for price and non-price exogenous variables. Scenario 2=baseline assumption without TFP growth. Scenario 3=baseline assumption without area growth. Scenario 4 = baseline assumption without TFP and area growth.

Table 8

Projected Domestic Wheat Supply (million tonnes) in India

Year	Scenario 1 (baseline)	Scenario 2	Scenario 3	Scenario 4
TE 1999	71.1	71.1	71.1	71.1
2000	77.2	76.6	75.0	74.4
2005	86.8	85.3	81.2	79.8
2010	95.4	93.1	86.8	84.8
2015	103.5	100.6	92.0	89.5
2020	111.5	108.1	97.3	94.3

Notes: "Scenario 1=baseline assumption for price and nonprice exogenous variables. Scenario 2=baseline assumption without TFP growth. Scenario 3=baseline assumption without area growth. Scenario 4=baseline assumption without TFP and area growth.

year 2010 and 97 million tonnes in 2020. The domestic wheat supply in scenario 4 (without TFP and rice area growth) is projected to be 85 million tonnes in 2010 and grow to only 94 million tonnes in the year 2020. Acreage and TFP growth has a substantial impact on wheat supply and it is estimated to be equivalent to 11 million tonnes in 2010, and 17 million tonnes in 2020.

(iii) Coarse Cereals

As seen in Table 9, the area under coarse cereals has declined with annual growth rate of 1.55 per cent in the last three decades. The increase in yield (2.09 per cent) has compensated the negative effect of acreage and the production of coarse cereals is noticed to be stagnating at a level of 32 million tonnes. Long-term growth in production of coarse cereals is estimated at 0.54 per cent annually. Using long-term annual growth in production, the supply of coarse cereals is projected to be 32.7 million tonnes in 2005, 33.6 million tonnes in 2010 and 35.5 million tonnes in the year 2020 (Table 10).

(iv) Pulses

The production of pulses is almost stagnating at a level of 12 to 14 million tonnes. In the long term, production of pulses has increased with

Table 9

Growth in Area, Yield and Production for Coarse Cereal and Pulses in India

Period	Area	Yield	Production
Coarse cereals			
1971-85	-0.77**	1.37**	0.60ns
1985-00	-2.02	2.66**	0.63ns
1971-00	-1.55**	2.09**	0.54*
Pulses			
1971-85	0.33ns	0.98ns	1.33ns
1985-00	-0.34ns	0.81*	0.47ns
1971-00	-0.12ns	1.03**	0.91**

Notes: Asterisks indicate significance level: **=1 per cent; *=5 per cent; hr/ha: hours per hectare.

an annual growth rate of 0.9 per cent. Using long-term growth in production of pulses, the supply of pulses is projected to be 13.3 million tonnes in the year 2005, 13.9 million tonnes in the year 2010 and 15.2 million tonnes in the year 2020 (see Table 10).

Table 10
Projected Domestic Supply of Coarse Cereals and Pulses in India (million tonnes)

Year	Coarse cereals	Pulses
Long-term annual growth in production (per cent per annum)	0.54	0.905
TE 2000	31.7	12.6
2005	32.7	13.3
2010	33.6	13.9
2015	34.5	14.6
2020	35.5	15.2

(v) Total Foodgrains

Looking at the supply scenarios given above, supply of foodgrains will be in the range of 218 to 231 million tonnes in the year 2005 and it will grow to a level of 228-251 million tonnes in the year 2010 and 248-289 million tonnes in the year 2020 (Table 11). The possibility of area expansion is minimal. Future growth in food production has to essentially come through increase in yield. It is expected that the further increase in foodgrain production will be yield-based and the scenarios 3 and 4 will be more realistic in the supply analysis. The supply of foodgrains will be about 248-259 million tonnes in the year 2020. As seen in App. Table 4, Kumar (1998) had estimated domestic demand for foodgrains at 202 million tonnes in the year 2000, 238 million tonnes in the year 2010 and 269 million tonnes in the year 2020. In the year 2020, the domestic demand will be about 110 million tonnes for rice, 91 million tonnes for wheat, 39 million tonnes for coarse cereals, and 28 million tonnes for pulses. Food demand challenges ahead are formidable considering the fast declining TFP growth and rapidly shrinking resource base. Cereal requirements will be met in future if the TFP is maintained. However, pulses will be in short supply.

Table 11
Projected Domestic Supply of Foodgrains

Year	Scenario 1 (baseline)	Scenario 2	Scenario 3	Scenario 4
2005	231.5	227.3	221.8	217.7
2010	250.7	243.8	234.3	227.6
2015	269.7	260.3	246.5	238.1
2020	289.2	277.2	258.8	248.3

Notes: [a]Scenario 1=baseline assumption for price and non-price exogenous variables. Scenario 2=baseline assumption without TFP growth. Scenario 3=baseline assumption without area growth. Scenario 4=baseline assumption without TFP and area growth.

IV. CONCLUSIONS

Demand for cereals will be met in future with a marginal surplus of wheat. Pulses will be in short supply. The policies that can help in maintaining the TFP growth in the long run can keep the balance between domestic production and demand for cereals. This emphasises the need for strengthening the efforts at increasing production by maintaining or increasing TFP through public investment in irrigation, infrastructure development, research and efficient use of water and plant nutrients. Greater research emphasis is needed for dry land agriculture. Resource productivity enhancing strategies are suggested like creation of infrastructure in less developed areas, managing infrastructure better, and introducing new technologies (Shenggen et al., 1999; Kumar, 2001).

Vast uncommon opportunities to harness agricultural potential still remain, which could be tapped to achieve future targets. There are serious gaps both in yield potential and technology transfer as the national average yields of most commodities are low, which if addressed properly could be harnessed. Improved agricultural technologies are 'size-neutral'; however, some of them are not 'resource-neutral'. Hence, in generating improved agricultural technologies, small-holder-oriented research and extension should emphasise " cost reduction without yield reduction".

Managing the rice-wheat production system, enhancing the yields of major commodities, arresting deceleration in food productivity, improving productivity in rain-fed agriculture, integrated nutrient management and post-harvest management and value addition will be the major strategies to tackle the challenges ahead. These strategies need to be blended with the farmer's wisdom to ensure the adoption of improved technologies. Thus, to ensure food security, more capital investment in agriculture, including greater support to research and development will be critical in future. The best of science and development efforts (including traditional knowledge and modern scientific approach) should be mobilised through partnerships involving national and international research institutions, non-governmental organisations and the private sector in order to tackle the present and future problems of food security and production.

Donors and governments must urgently increase funding for agricultural research targeted at the needs of the rural and urban poor, and every effort must be made to ensure the free flow of information, technology and germplasm so that a proper sustainable agriculture can be achieved. The stagnation in the research investment beyond 1990 is a matter of concern in the light of challenges ahead for attaining food security. Recent efforts to increase operational funds for research under the National Agricultural Technology Project is a welcome step and has given a jump to research intensity in the country. The investment on extension has risen sharply till the year 1990, thereafter stagnating at the level of Rs. 1218 million. The extension intensity increased from 0.09 per cent of agricultural GDP in the early 1960s to 0.14 per cent in the early

1970s, which further rose marginally to 0.15 per cent in the early 1990s after a slight fall in the early 1980s. This level of extension intensity in India is much lower than that in developing and developed countries (0.4 per cent and 0.9 per cent, respectively, Judd et al., 1986). The ratio of the amount spent on extension to research is falling. The problem of inadequate investment is much more serious in extension. It is estimated that excepting few states, there is untapped yield potential of 40-94 per cent in most important crops of the states. This coupled with complexity of second generation technologies and heterogeneity of production environment warrant much more intensive extension efforts. The slowing down emphasis on extension will further widen the gap in the adoption of technology. Extension services should be strengthened by scaling up investment levels and improving the quality of extension.

Under the liberalised economic environment, the farm situation is characterised with reduction in farm labour, higher use of fertiliser and mechanisation. This is improving efficiency and productivity in Indian agriculture. Rural literacy was found to be an important source of growth in adoption of technology, use of modern inputs and yield. In the liberalised economic environment, efficiency and growth orientation will attract maximum attention and literacy will play a far more important role than it did in the past. Policies are needed to maintain TFP growth in the long run to keep the balance of demand and supply. The declining trend in public sector agricultural investment should be reversed by increasing allocation in irrigation, power, education and so on, in order to check adverse impact on productivity and agricultural output. The increasing complexity of the production environment, demands efficient information dissemination and training in the use of modern technologies. For this, an appropriate extension service needs to be created to stimulate and encourage both top-down and bottom-up flow of information between farmers, extension workers and research scientists. The extension service should also promote generation, adoption and evaluation of location-specific farm technologies.

Appendix

Supply Model[2]

Studies on agricultural supply response at the country or regional level have mainly applied duality theory to derive systems of output supply and factor demand equations from the underlying profit function (Lau and Yotopoulos, 1972). In the application of the dual approach, the technology and levels of quasi-fixed inputs have been treated as exogenous variables that do not allow measurement of the dynamic effect of quasi-fixed inputs, technology, and investments on the supply of commodities. Mundlak (1988) has developed an alternative framework for the choice of techniques in production, which permits a separate determination of optimal input and output combinations along a given production function, and to determine the optimal combination of techniques. The approach provides a structure within which the choice of technique and quasi-fixed inputs are determined endogenously. This approach was used for food supply analysis in Indonesia (Rosegrant and Kasryno, 1992) and in India (Kumar and Rosegrant, 1997). The results have been close to reality.

Adapting this framework, a simultaneous-equation model is specified in which direct and indirect interactions are explicitly considered. It has three blocks—choice of technique, factor demand, and yield equations—and consists of endogenous variables (yield, human labour, machine labour, fertiliser, crop irrigation, and high-yielding varieties) and exogenous variables [factor product prices, irrigation, human resource development (rural literacy), infrastructure (electrification), geographical location (dummy for regions), agro-climatic factor (rainfall), and quality of inputs and technology (TFP)]. Output supply is derived indirectly through this three-block model.

Specification of Supply Model

Repetitive exercises in estimating and revising the specification of the simultaneous recursive model (in double log form) were undertaken by using seemingly unrelated regression estimates (SURE) estimation procedures. The final form of the structural equations of the model is specified as follows :

Choice of technique

CRIRR = f (NSIRR, DUMMY) (1)
HYV = f (CRIRR, LIT, PVELECT, DUMMY) (2)

Factor demand

HL = f (w/P, m/P, HYV, CRIRR) (3)
ML = f (w/P, b/P, m/P, HYV, CRIRR) (4)
FERT = f(r/P, HYV, CRIRR, ML) (5)

Yield function

Y = f (HL, ML, FERT, FYM, TFP, RAIN, DUMMY) (6)

Identity

S = Y * CRAREA

where the variables in the model are defined as follows:

Endogenous: CRIRR = percent of cropped area under irrigation (sum of both private and public irrigation); HYV = percent of rice area under high-yielding varieties; HL = human labour in hours per hectare; ML = use of machine labour (index); FERT = chemical fertilisers in terms of total plant nutrients in kilograms per hectare; Y = yield in quintals per hectare for rice; and S = domestic supply of rice.

Exogenous: NSIRR = per cent of irrigated area to net sown area; LIT = literacy rate (per cent of rural literate population, primary or above education); PVELECT = per cent of villages that are electrified; w = wage rate (Rs. h^{-1} of human labour); b = bullock labour charges (Rs h^{-1} per pair of bullock labour); m^2 = machine labour charges (index); r = fertiliser price (Rs. kg^{-1} of total plant nutrients); P = rice price; RAIN = rainfall in the critical production period; DUMMY = region dummy and defined as ERDUMMY = eastern region dummy and it takes the value one if the data pertain to the states of Bihar, Orissa, Assam, and West Bengal, and zero otherwise. WRDUMMY = western region dummy and it takes the value one if the data pertain to the states of Rajasthan, Madhya Pradesh, Maharashtra, and Gujarat, and zero otherwise. NRDUMMY = northern region dummy and it takes the value one if the data pertain to the states of Uttar Pradesh, Haryana, and Punjab, and zero otherwise. SRDUMMY = southern region dummy and it takes the value one if the data pertain to the states of Andhra Pradesh, Tamil Nadu, Karnataka, and Kerala, and zero otherwise. FYM = use of farmyard manure (q/ha); TFP = total factor productivity index (Tornqvist-Theil index). CRAREA = area under rice (predetermined endogenous variable).

Cumulative effects of price and non-price factors on rice yield :

The cumulative effects of price and non-price factors on yield were derived from the structural equations 1-6 of the supply model as specified above. The formulations are presented below. These formulations have the advantage of separating the effects of constituent forces on yield growth and help in understanding the process through which yield growth takes place.

Wage effect

$$dY/d(w/P) = \frac{\partial Y}{\partial HL} (\partial HL/\partial (w/P)) + (\partial Y/\partial ML)(\partial ML/\partial (w/P)) + (\partial Y/\partial FERT)(\partial FERT/\partial ML)(\partial ML/\partial (w/P))$$

As seen in the above equation, wages have a direct effect on the use of human labour and an indirect effect on the use of machine labour by substitution, thus inducing fertiliser use through mechanisation. Hence, there are greater yield improvement opportunities in moving from traditional to modern inputs such as machine labour and fertiliser.

Bullock labour charges

$$dY/d(b/P) = (\partial Y/\partial ML)(\partial ML/\partial (b/P)) + (\partial Y/\partial FERT)(\partial FERT/\partial ML)(\partial ML/\partial (b/P))$$

The bullock labour charges induce changes in machine labour use and also induce fertiliser demand. Bullock labour price has an indirect effect on yield through the higher use of machine labour and fertiliser.

Machine labour charges

$$dY/d(m/P) = (\partial Y/\partial HL)(\partial HL/\partial (m/P)) + (\partial Y/\partial ML)(\partial ML/\partial (m/P)) + (\partial Y/\partial FERT)(\partial FERT/\partial ML)(\partial ML/\partial (m/P))$$

Machine labour charges have both direct and indirect effects on yield. The first term measures the effect of machine price on human labour and then yield. The second term measures the direct effect of machine charges on the use of machines and then yield. The third term measures the indirect effect of machine charges on yield through fertiliser.

Fertiliser price

$$dY/d(r/P) = (\partial Y/\partial FERT)(\partial FERT/\partial (r/P))$$

The above terms measure the fertiliser price effect on yield through fertiliser.

Net sown irrigation

$$
\begin{aligned}
dY/dNSIRR = & (\partial Y/\partial HL)(\partial HL/\partial HYV)(\partial HYV/\partial CRIRR)(\partial CRIRR/\partial NSIRR) \\
& + (\partial Y/\partial ML)(\partial ML/\partial HYV)(\partial HYV/\partial CRIRR)(\partial CRIRR/\partial NSIRR) \\
& + (\partial Y/\partial FERT)(\partial FERT/\partial ML)(\partial ML/\partial HYV)(\partial HYV/\partial CRIRR) \\
& \quad (\partial CRIRR/\partial NSIRR) \\
& + (\partial Y/\partial FERT)(\partial FERT/\partial HYV)(\partial HYV/\partial CRIRR)(\partial CRIRR/\partial NSIRR) \\
& + (\partial Y/\partial HL)(\partial HL/\partial CRIRR)(\partial CRIRR/\partial NSIRR) \\
& + (\partial Y/\partial ML)(\partial ML/\partial CRIRR)(\partial CRIRR/\partial NSIRR) \\
& + (\partial Y/\partial FERT)(\partial FERT/\partial ML)(\partial ML/\partial CRIRR)(\partial CRIRR/\partial NSIRR) \\
& + (\partial Y/\partial FERT)(\partial FERT/\partial CRIRR)(\partial CRIRR/\partial NSIRR)
\end{aligned}
$$

This equation captures the effect of irrigation on yield (productivity) through yield-enhancing technologies such as the allocation of irrigated land under the crop, the adoption of improved varieties, and their effect on the use of inputs and thereby on yield.

Literacy

$$
\begin{aligned}
dY/dLIT = & (\partial Y/\partial HL)(\partial HL/\partial HYV)(\partial HYV/\partial LIT) \\
& + (\partial Y/\partial ML)(\partial ML/\partial HYV)(\partial HYV/\partial LIT) \\
& + (\partial Y/\partial FERT)(\partial FERT/\partial ML)(\partial ML/\partial HYV)(\partial HYV/\partial LIT) \\
& + (\partial Y/\partial FERT)(\partial FERT/\partial HYV)(\partial HYV/\partial LIT)
\end{aligned}
$$

This equation captures the effect of literacy on yield through improved varieties and hence changes in the use of inputs, leading to increases in yield.

Rural electrification

$$
\begin{aligned}
dY/dPVELECT = & (\partial Y/\partial HL)(\partial HL/\partial HYV)(\partial HYV/\partial PVELECT) \\
& + (\partial Y/\partial ML)(\partial ML/\partial HYV)(\partial HYV/\partial PVELECT) \\
& + (\partial Y/\partial FERT)(\partial FERT/\partial ML)(\partial ML/\partial HYV)(\partial HYV/\partial PVELECT) \\
& + (\partial Y/\partial FERT)(\partial FERT/\partial HYV)(\partial HYV/\partial PVELECT)
\end{aligned}
$$

This equation captures the effect of village electrification on yield through improved varieties and changes in the use of inputs.

TFP

dY/dTFP = coefficient of TFP in yield equation

App. Table 1
Joint Estimation of Supply Function, Factor Demand and Within-crop Choice of Technique for Rice in India (SURE estimates)

Variable	Yield function	Factor demand		Choice of technique		
		HL	ML	FERT	HYV	CRIRR
Constant	1.46059**	4.59642**	2.73718**	-1.75468	-0.35205	1.37486**
	(3.07)	(12.73)	(3.61)	(1.54)	(1.07)	(8.33)
Human Labour (hr/ha)	-0.10721	-	-	-	-	-
	(1.56)					
Machine Labour (hr/ha)	0.23875**	-	-	0.33843**	-	-
	(12.77)			(2.72)		
Fertiliser (Kg/ha)	0.04664**	-	-	-	-	-
	(3.94)					
FYM (q/ha)	0.03763**	-	-	-	-	-
	(3.40)					
TFP	0.57979**	-	-	-	-	-
	(9.88)					
Price of Inputs						
Human Labour (w/P)	-	-0.24844**	0.89776**	-	-	-
		(4.63)	(7.16)			
Bullock Labour (b/P)	-	-	0.38603**	-	-	-
			(5.31)			
Machine Labour (m/P)	-	0.15999*	-0.83797**	-	-	-
		(2.19)	(5.63)			
Fertiliser (r/P)	-	-	-	0.36646	-	-
				(1.79)		
HYV area (%)	-	0.02737	0.44705**	1.13096**	-	-
		(0.80)	(6.45)	(6.86)		
Crop irrigated area (%)	-	0.19400**	0.29036**	0.68526**	0.18813**	-
		(6.35)	(4.56)	(4.26)	(3.66)	
Net sown irrigated area(%)	-	-	-	-	-	0.60846**
						(12.25)
Literacy (%)	-	-	-	-	0.37579**	-
					(3.54)	
Villages electrified (%)	-	-	-	-	0.48095**	-
					(11.41)	
Rain (mm)	-0.03029	-	-	-	-	-
	(1.09)					
West region dummy	-0.28278**	-	-	-	0.31174**	-0.24077**
	(6.54)				(4.88)	(3.70)
North region dummy	0.08830*	-	-	-	0.37093**	0.21663**
	(2.03)				(6.12)	(3.36)
South region dummy	0.15803**	-	-	-	0.32079**	1.05061**
	(4.31)				(4.75)	(23.25)
Adjusted R-square	0.83	0.18	0.74	0.55	0.83	0.81
F-Statistics	122.24	13.44	132.60	70.47	183.47	250.29

Notes: No. of observations = 228; asterisks indicate significance level: **= 1%; *= 5%; hr/ha: hours per hectare; kg/ha: kilogramme per hectare; q/ha: quintal per hectare; w/P: real wages; b/P: real bullock labour charge; m/P: real machine labour charge; r/P: real fertiliser price; mm: millimetre; %: figures in brackets are 't' statistics.

App. Table 2

Joint Estimation of Supply Function, Factor Demand and Within-crop Choice of Technique for Wheat in India (SURE Estimates)

Variable	Yield function	Factor demand		Choice of technique		
		HL	ML	FERT	HYV	CRIRR
Constant	-1.56462**	2.88192**	0.30706	2.40013**	-0.20020	0.75801**
	(3.92)	(7.45)	(0.61)	(3.69)	(0.59)	(5.72)
Human Labour (hr/ha)	0.25813**	-	-	-	-	-
	(6.43)					
Machine Labour (hr/ha)	0.49296**	-	-	0.77456**	-	-
	(13.72)			(8.07)		
Fertiliser (Kg/ha)	0.09612**	-	-	-	-	-
	(3.22)					
FYM (q/ha)	-0.00178	-	-	-	-	-
	(0.26)					
TFP	0.55851**	-	-	-	-	-
	(7.79)					
Price of Inputs						
Human Labour (w/P)	-	-0.43694**	0.41134**	-	-	-
		(8.84)	(6.01)			
Bullock Labour (b/P)	-	-	0.26842**	-	-	-
			(3.55)			
Machine Labour (m/P)	-	0.11173*	-0.27052**	-	-	-
		(2.10)	(3.47)			
Fertiliser (r/P)	-	-	-	0.20067*	-	-
				(2.00)		
HYV area (%)	-	-0.13056**	0.14373**	0.40097**	-	-
		(2.81)	(2.52)	(4.57)		
Crop irrigated area (%)	-	0.38357**	0.54828**	0.20582*	0.31941**	-
		(10.19)	(12.84)	(2.27)	(7.64)	
Net sown irrigated area(%)	-	-	-	-	-	1.10296**
						(24.88)
Literacy (%)	-	-	-	-	0.59645**	-
					(5.25)	
Villages electrified (%)	-	-	-	-	0.17803**	-
					(3.30)	
Rain (mm)	0.00888	-	-	-	-	-
	(0.73)					
North region dummy	0.02182	-	-	-	0.27869**	-0.88717**
	(0.74)				(6.37)	(14.12)
Adjusted R-square	0.90	0.56	0.88	0.83	0.79	0.84
F-Statistics	156.80	40.03	177.70	149.80	114.55	210.69

Notes: No. of observations = 121; asterisks indicate significance level: **= 1%; *= 5%; hr/ha: hours per hectare; kg/ha: kilogram per hectare; q/ha: quantal per hectare; w/P: real wages; b/P: real bullock labour charge; m/P: real machine labour charge; r/P: real fertiliser price; mm: millimetre; %: figures in brackets are 't' statistics.

App. Table 3

Baseline Assumptions for Rice and Wheat Supply in India

Price and non-price exogenous variables	Observed annual growth (%) 1971-85	1985-97	1971-97	Predicted annual growth (%) 2005	2010	2020
Factor and product prices						
Human labour charges	8.62	12.62	10.36	10.36	10.36	10.36
Animal labour charges	7.49	10.40	8.81	8.81	8.81	8.81
Machine labour charges	10.18	6.29	8.02	8.02	8.02	8.02
Fertiliser price	4.04	5.50	4.50	4.50	4.50	4.50
Rice price	6.16	8.67	7.08	7.08	7.08	7.08
Wheat price	5.25	8.85	6.12	6.12	6.12	6.12
Infrastructure variables						
Net sown irrigated area (%)	3.20	1.09	2.26	0.51	0.23	0.11
Villages electrified (%)	6.56	2.02	5.10	0.87	0.38	0.16
Rural literacy (%)	2.95	2.08	2.46	1.62	1.26	0.98
Supply factors						
Rice TFP	0.98	0.75	0.91	0.62	0.51	0.42
Wheat TFP	1.36	0.53	1.07	0.31	0.14	0.10
Organic manure	1.66	–1.90	0.59	0.00	0.00	0.00
Rice area	0.66	0.65	0.56	0.64	0.63	0.62
Wheat area	1.90	1.08	1.17	0.61	0.50	0.34

Note:[a] It is assumed that the factor product prices would grow at the rate observed during 1971-97. The growth in the infrastructure variables, total factor productivity (TFP), and rice area will decelerate at the rate observed from 1971-85 to 1985-97. Zero growth is assumed for farmyard manure.

App. Table 4

Demand for Foodgrains in India (million tonnes)

Items	Year 2000	Year 2010	Year 2020
Rice	86.1	100.4	110.4
Wheat	69.0	81.5	91.1
Coarse cereals	29.9	34.5	39.3
Total cereals	185.0	216.4	240.8
Pulses	16.7	22.2	28.0
Foodgrains	201.7	238.5	268.8

Note: Kumar estimates are based on IARI policy paper 1998-2001 (Kumar, 1998) after using the revised population projections given by the State of World Population 1998, UNFPA.

Notes

1. Cost includes all cash and kind expenses actually incurred, rent paid, interest on owned and borrowed capital and imputed value of family labour.
2. The supply model is developed by the authors during the collaborative study on 'Equity Driven Trade and Marketing Policy Strategies for Improved Performance of Indian Agriculture: A Scooping Exercise (Project No. ANRE 1/98/91 of ACIAR)', supported by the Australian Centre for International Agricultural Research (ACIAR) and Indian Council of Agricultural Research (ICAR). The findings of the study have been published: (2001) and Kumar (2001).

References

Christenson, L.R. (1975), "Concepts and Measurement of Agricultural Productivity", *American Journal of Agricultural Economics*, Vol. 57.

Judd, M.A.; Boyce, J.K. and Evenson, R.E. (1983), "Investing in Agricultural Supply", *Economic Growth Centre*, Yale University (mimeo).

——(1994), "Productivity and Sources of Growth for Rice in India", *Economic and Political Weekly*, December 31.

Kumar, P. and Rosegrant, M.W. (1997), "Dynamic Supply Response of Rice and Other Major Foodcrops in India", *Agricultural Economic Research Review*, Vol. 10, No. 1, pp. 1-27.

Kumar (1997), "Food Security: Supply & Demand Perspective", *Indian Farming*, December.

——(1998), "Food Demand and Supply Projections for India", *Agricultural Economics Policy Paper 98-01*, Indian Agricultural Research Institute, New Delhi.

——Joshi, P.K.; Johansen, C. and Asokan, M. (1998), "Sustainability in Rice-Wheat Based Cropping Systems in India: Socio-Economic and Policy Issues", *Economic and Political Weekly*, September 26, Vol. 33, No. 39.

——(2001), "Agricultural Performance and Productivity", in Acharya, S.S. and Chaudhri, D.P. (eds.), *Indian Agricultural Policy at the Crossroads*, Rawat Publications, Jaipur and New Delhi.

Lau, L.J. and Yotopoulos, P.A. (1972), "Profit, Supply and Factor Demand Functions", *American Journal of Agricultural Economics*, Vol. 54, No. 1, pp. 11-18.

Mittal, Surabhi and Kumar, P. (2000), "Literacy, Technology Adoption, Factor Demand and Productivity: An Econometric Analysis", *Indian Journal of Agricultural Economics*, Vol. 55, No. 3, pp. 490-499.

Mundlak, Y. (1988), "Endogenous Technology and the Measurement of Productivity", in Cepalbo, S.M. and Antle, John M. (eds.) *Agricultural Productivity: Measurement and Explanation*, Resources for the Future, Washington, D.C.

Rosegrant, M.W. and Evenson, R.E. (1992), "Agricultural Productivity and Sources of Growth in South Asia", *American Journal of Agricultural Economics.*, Vol. 67.

——and Kasryno, F. (1992), *Food Crop Production Growth in Indonesia: Supply Response with Choice of Technique*, International Food Policy Research Institute, Washington, D.C.

Shenggen, Fan; Hazell, Peter; and Thorat, Sukhadeo (1999), "Linkages between Government Spending, Growth, and Poverty in Rural India", IFPRI Research Report 110, International Food Policy Research Institute, Washington, D.C.

3

Demand for Foodgrains by 2020 AD

P.C. Bansil

I. INTRODUCTION

Starting from Malthus, the question of feeding the evergrowing population has been engaging the attention of politicians and academicians alike. At the international level, the history of global carrying capacity estimates goes back a century. Nobody could make reliable global appraisals until at least two types of basic information regarding the extent of cultivated and potentially cultivable area, typical yields of dominant cereal crops, and their likely future increase were available. As with so many other developments, the time for projecting the total population that the planet could support came during the last decades of the nineteenth century. Ravenstein (1891), perhaps the first researcher to investigate the limit, came up with a maximum total of just under 6 billion people. Shortly afterwards, Pfaundler (1902), assuming that there was (a) no extension of the then existing 2,174 million hectares (mha) of cropland and good grazing land, (b) an average density of five people per hectare supported by traditional farming methods, and recycling of organic matter—ended up with a minimum of 11 billion people. Numerous other estimates followed, varying from 10 to 40 billion people. The position is more or less the same in India. Demand projections for foodgrains vary widely from 179 to 241 million tonnes even for the current year 2000 AD.

The position is even more complicated for the year 2020. Although there is no dearth of 'doomsday' crystal gazers in India, the position in the country today is that stocks of foodgrains are overflowing and the issue is one of its disposal. It is, therefore, necessary to examine the issues involved in the estimation of future requirements of foodgrains and come up with somewhat realistic estimates for 2020. While sufficiently reliable data are available on long-term series regarding human consumption, the other segment, relating to the demand for feed and seed and wastages, etc., is a completely unexplored area.

II. TRENDS IN HUMAN CONSUMPTION

As regards the demand by human beings, one of the constraints relates to human behaviour which changes not only from place to place, but also from time to time. In other words, food consumption levels are closely connected with the standard of living and the environment. Urban people with higher income, for example, consume less cereals than people in the villages. The change is not only in respect of quantity but also in quality of the grain consumed. Rice and wheat, which account for more than 80 per cent of foodgrains, constitute the staple of the majority of the people in India. Next come coarse grains and then there is a small section of the people in certain parts of Kerala, who mainly subsist on root crops like tapioca and sweet potato, commonly known as subsidiary foods. This is not in any way peculiar to India. In China, the consumption level of wheat determines the social status of a family.

Every increase in income thus has a two-way effect on food. First of all, fine grains are substituted for the coarse ones as well as tubers and then the cereals are themselves replaced to a smaller or greater extent by protective foods like milk, fruits and vegetables depending on the income, customs, habits and taste of the people. We will examine the future food consumption levels with due consideration to the changing economic scenario likely to take place in the country.

In the case of NSSO, annual data series are primarily in terms of expenditure, though for selected years quantitative information is also available. A careful study of the CSO, Directorate of E&S, NSSO and NNMB data leads us to the conclusion that there is hardly any possibility of an increase in the per capita consumption of foodgrains. Details of the data are set out below:

1. The National Accounts (CSO) data show that the share of private final consumption expenditure at constant prices on food declined by 10.5 per cent and on cereals by 23.6 per cent between 1980-81 and 1994-95.[1]
2. Likewise, the NSSO data also show that the average monthly per capita expenditure on cereals as a percentage of total MPCE, declined from 40.6 per cent in (1972-73) to 24.2 per cent in (1993-94) in rural areas and from 23.3 per cent to 14 per cent in urban areas during the same period. Although there is a decline in the share of total expenditure on food, there is a corresponding increase in expenditure on non-cereals as well as non-food items.
3. The share of household consumption expenditure for the population in the group below the poverty line came down from 80.25 per cent in 1977-78 to 75.77 per cent (rural areas) and from 75.19 per cent to 73.68 per cent (urban areas) during the same period (Planning Commission, 1993). Some economists take 20 per cent as being the irreducible proportion of income spent by the poorest in a wide range of countries on non-food essentials. Given the tendency of food requirement figures to overestimate real food needs, especially in relation to people living in warm climates, it might be more realistic to work with 80 per cent of the (FAO/WHO, 1973) weight-adjusted dietary

energy requirements. This leads to a double 80 rule, according to which people are judged to be ultra poor if 80 per cent of their income is insufficient to purchase 80 per cent of these energy requirements.

4. Per capita availability of foodgrains remained around 470 grams per day since 1961 by which time comparable data series for food production stabilised (Bansil, 1956). It did cross this figure in a few years, which could partly be explained by changes in private stocks for which no information is available. As against this, per capita availability of milk, eggs, fish, fruits, vegetables, sugar, oils, tea and coffee has increased manifold. Availability of potato increased by about 12 times, milk by seven times and meat nearly by 10 times against a population increase of two and a half times.
5. A study of the net availability of various food items at the physiological level (GOI, 1994) for the triennium ending 1993 shows that the per capita availability of food in India is 964.6 g (of all food items) providing 2400 calories and 64.9 g of protiens.
6. The comprehensive NSSO data series are available up to the year 1999-2000. A study conducted by the Techno-economic Research Institute for US AID (Bansil, 1990) converted value data into quantities and found that even in the case of lowest three deciles, per capita cereal consumption both in the urban and rural areas, declined in all the states during 1961-62 to 1983. The pattern was the same in the poorest states as well.
7. According to CSO data, expenditure on food actually declined by 1.4 per cent in 2000-2001 in nominal terms and by 2.7 per cent in inflation-adjusted terms. Since these figures refer to total consumption, this would mean that Indians, on an average, or on a per capita basis consumed less food in 2000-01 since the population increased during that year. The consumption basket of the average Indian has changed in recent years in favour of health care, transport and communication services at the cost of the basic necessities of food and clothing. But the recent CSO data show that this pattern accelerated significantly during 2000-01. Except in the case of fruits and vegetables for which expenditure rose 5 per cent (real terms), for all other major food categories expenditure has been falling. Moreover, the private final consumption expenditure (PFCE) on food products has actually declined during the year (Table 1). This is the first time since 1976-77 that the expenditure on food has actually fallen in nominal terms.
8. An FAO sponsored study by the Indian Association for the Advancement of Science on Food and Nutrition Status observes that "the poverty indicator gives large population as threatened by malnutrition or undernutrition but the ground reality is different. Most of the poor consume many local products which are not reflected in their income or even various consumer surveys. Their traditional knowledge also helps them to consume locally available foods and minor forest products, not recorded otherwise. There are, however, better-off households whose average dietary intake is low".

Table 1
Composition of PFCE (%)

Expenditure item	1993-94	1999-2000	2000-01
Food, beverages and tobacco	54.8	51.5	48.1
Food items	50.6	46.0	42.8
Clothing and footwear	11.9	10.1	11.3
Furniture and appliances	3.1	2.8	3.0
Health care	3.4	6.6	7.3
Transport and communication	11.3	12.8	13.3
Recreation and education	3.1	3.6	3.7

9. While per capita income at constant (1980-81) prices have more than doubled during the period 1951-2000, a time series data of cereal consumption under NSSO is quite revealing. Over a period of 38 years (1961-62 to 1999-2000), there has been a steady decline in the per capita consumption of cereals at the all-India level. At the same time there is a shift in the consumption pattern as between the different grains both in the rural and urban areas. While the share of rice has remained more or less constant, wheat has replaced coarse grains to a large extent (Table 1a).
10. There has been a decline in cereal consumption in the overall deciles during 1987-88 and 1999-2000, though being much sharper in the top deciles and marginal in the lower ones. This is accompanied by a corresponding increase in the consumption of non-foodgrains. While a plateau has been reached at below 11kg of cereals consumption for urban areas, the decline for cereals is sharpest for top deciles in rural India.
11. According to the *Economic Survey (2001-2002)*, the National Sample Surveys show that the proportion of household expenditure on items other than food has been increasing. Conversely, household expenditure on food as a proportion of their total expenditure has fallen from 60 per cent in 1977-78 to 48.1 per cent in 1999-2000 in urban areas, and from 64.3 per cent to 59.4 per cent in rural areas. With rising incomes, peoples' diets are becoming increasingly diversified. The share of cereals in their diet has been falling in favour of other foods. Expenditure on cereals in total household food expenditure fell from 40.8 per cent in 1977-78 to 31.8 per cent in 1999-2000 in urban areas, and from 50 per cent to 44.1 per cent in rural areas. Correspondingly, substantial increases have taken place in the expenditure on other foods such as fruits, vegetables, meat, eggs, fish and milk. Hence, though it is essential to ensure food security through adequate production of foodgrains in the country, the thrust of agricultural policy now must shift to accelerating the growth of non-cereal food products. Increasing incomes and urbanisation are also providing the demand stimulus for greater production and consumption of fruits and vegetables. As urbanisation proceeds, there will be an accelerating need for basic processed foods as well.

Table 1a
Consumption Pattern of Cereals by Period in Rural and Urban India (monthly per capita in kg)

NSS round	Year	Rice	(%)	Wheat	(%)	Coarse cereals	(%)	Total cereals	(%)
				Rural					
17	1961-62	8.77	50	2.63	15	6.15	35	17.55	100
	1970-71							15.35	100
27	1972-73	8.56	56	3.83	25	4.84	32	15.26	100
28	1973-74	6.90	46	3.52	23	4.67	31	15.09	100
32	1977-78	7.12	45	4.05	26	4.51	29	15.68	100
38	1983	6.63	45	4.46	30	3.71	25	14.80	100
42	1986-87	7.11	49	4.77	33	2.49	17	14.37	100
43	1987-88	7.04	49	4.94	34	2.49	17	14.47	100
44	1988-89	7.07	49	4.73	32	2.76	19	14.56	100
47	1991	7.10	49	4.60	32	1.70	12	13.80	100
48	1992	7.20	49	4.50	31	1.70	12	13.80	100
49	1993	7.20	49	4.50	31	1.60	11	13.60	100
50	1993-94	7.00	52	4.40	33	2.00	15	13.40	100
51	1994-95	7.10	49	4.30	30	1.40	10	13.20	100
52	1995-96	7.00	48	4.20	29	1.50	10	12.90	100
53	1997	6.70	46	4.50	31	1.40	10	12.80	100
54	1998	6.80	47	4.30	30	1.20	8	12.50	100
55	1999-2000	6.78	53	4.55	36	1.39	11	12.72	100
				Urban					
17	1961-62	6.16	50	4.10	33	2.09	17	12.35	100
	1970-71							11.36	100
27	1972-73	4.94	43	4.82	42	1.61	14	11.37	100
28	1973-74	5.38	48	4.32	38	1.62	14	11.32	100
32	1977-78	5.48	47	4.87	42	1.27	11	11.62	100
38	1983	5.32	47	4.82	43	1.16	10	11.30	100
42	1986-87	5.33	49	4.82	44	0.83	8	10.98	100
43	1987-88	5.35	48	4.98	45	0.86	8	11.19	100
44	1988-89	5.35	48	4.81	43	0.90	8	11.06	100
47	1991	5.20	47	4.90	44	0.40	4	10.70	100
48	1992	5.20	47	4.90	44	0.40	4	10.70	100
49	1993	5.30	48	4.50	41	0.60	5	10.50	100
50	1993-94	5.28	50	4.72	44	0.63	6	10.63	100
51	1994-95	5.10	46	4.90	44	0.60	5	10.70	100
52	1995-96	5.30	48	4.70	42	0.40	4	10.60	100
53	1997	5.20	47	4.60	42	0.40	4	10.30	100
54	1998	5.30	48	4.70	42	0.40	4	10.40	100
55	1999-2000	5.22	50	4.77	46	0.43	4	10.42	100

Notes: Percentage of total cereal consumption; 43rd Round, July 1987–June 1988; 47th Round, July 1991–December 1991; 48th Round , January 1992–December : 1992; 49th Round, January 1993–June 1993; 50th Round, July 1993–June 1994; 51st Round, July 1994–June 1995; 52th Round, July 1995–June 1996; 53rd Round, January 1997–December 1997; 54th Round, January1998–June 1998; and 55th Round, July 1999–June 2000.

Source: *NSSO Survey on Consumer Expenditure*, Various Rounds.

12. The average daily calorie intake went up from 1,981 kcal in the period 1961-63 to 2,090 in the period, 1979-81 and further to 2,235 kcal in 1988-90. There is no evidence of consumption inequality having increased in India. In fact, if at all it is the other way round—the nutrition level has improved and the hunger situation has eased (Alagh, 1994) indicating a narrowing of consumption inequality.
13. Even the state level study for the period shows that during the period 1970-71 to 1991-92, both in the rural and urban areas, but for a few states such as Kerala, Orissa and West Bengal, there is a clear decline in the per capita consumption of cereals. If we take into consideration the latest 50th round data, even Orissa shows a decline. A study of the consumption patterns of Kerala and Andhra Pradesh where per capita income is much below the all-India level, and which have a well developed PDS, would be of interest: If consumption of cereals stabilises of a little above 13 kg (Andhra Pradesh) and 10 kg (Kerala) in the rural areas of Andhra Pradesh and Kerala respectively and at 11 kg (Andhra Pradesh) and 9.5 kg (Kerala) in the urban areas, of these states at highly subsidised prices, the argument that consumption levels will go up with increasing incomes, will not hold good (Table 2).
14. Recent evidence (Radhakrishna, 1992; Radhakrishna and Rao, 1992) thus shows that trends in cereal consumption appear to be inconsistent with income growth. Such counter-intuitive findings cannot be explained by food expenditure elasticities, which are supposed to be generally high. Rather, a part of the explanation lies not only in changes in tastes and preferences but also development of rural infrastructure and mechanisation which again would show that during the late eighties the country was already in the second stage of Engel's law. A trend analysis suggests a distinct shift in consumption patterns away from cereals since the mid-1970s uniformly across all expenditure groups, including the poorest (Table 3).
15. The NNMB latest available Report for 1988-90 says that the average calorie consumption of rural households during sixties was around 2,070 kcal/CU/day at the aggregate level and 2,350 kcal during the seventies increase as much as 280 kcal/CU/day. However, there was no further change during the subsequent period. While the earlier surveys of NNMB showed an increase of 110 kcal between 1,975 and 1980, the repeat surveys in 1988-90 showed a decrease of 57 kcal. These changes, however, are marginal and statistically not significant as the standard deviation for the difference of means was 175 kcal after correcting for family size. In other words, it can be concluded that at the aggregate level, there has been little change in the average calorie intake of rural households during the last 15 years.
16. The NSSO data (Table 4) further show that the share of persons having two square meals a day has increased from 93.05 per cent in 1985 to 99.7 per cent in 1993 (urban) and from 81.46 per cent to 93.8 per cent (rural) during the same period. Recently according to a

Table 2
State-wise Per Capita Consumption of Cereals from 1970-71 to 1990-91 and 1999-2000

(kg/month)

State	1970-71	1983-84	1987-88	1990-91	1999-2000
			Urban		
Andhra Pradesh	13.31	11.95	11.70	11.70	10.94
Assam	11.91	12.78	12.39	12.08	12.26
Bihar	13.68	13.44	13.37	12.85	12.70
Gujarat	10.35	9.61	9.44	9.55	8.49
Haryana	11.90	11.59	10.98	10.1	1 9.36
Himachal Pradesh	11.30	11.79	13.28	N.A	10.33
Jammu & Kashmir	14.62	13.80	14.09	N.A	12.84
Karnataka	11.91	11.69	11.06	10.40	10.21
Kerala	7.55	10.12	9.60	9.60	9.25
Madhya Pradesh	12.88	12.32	11.89	11.54	11.09
Maharashtra	9.75	9.90	10.18	9.74	9.35
Orissa	13.22	14.19	13.74	13.94	14.51
Punjab	11.25	9.94	9.74	9.06	9.21
Rajasthan	13.03	12.95	12.73	12.03	11.56
Tamil Nadu	10.63	10.39	10.14	10.14	9.65
Uttar Pradesh	11.79	11.66	11.63	11.14	10.79
West Bengal	10.88	11.80	11.71	11.78	11.17
All-India	11.36	11.30	11.19	10.87	10.42
			Rural		
Andhra Pradesh	16.05	15.37	14.35	13.62	12.65
Assam	15.70	14.23	14.23	13.63	12.63
Bihar	16.39	15.77	15.39	16.45	13.75
Gujarat	15.00	12.56	12.00	11.75	10.19
Haryana	18.13	14.54	15.02	14.55	11.37
Himachal Pradesh	17.64	16.06	16.06	N.A	12.86
Jammu & Kashmir	20.14	17.59	17.26	N.A	14.68
Karnataka	15.71	15.03	13.75	11.62	11.53
Kerala	7.99	10.01	10.36	10.73	9.89
Madhya Pradesh	16.51	15.83	15.39	15.22	12.94
Maharashtra	12.83	13.79	13.03	11.48	11.32
Orissa	16.12	15.61	15.72	15.98	15.09
Punjab	15.46	13.52	12.41	11.69	10.58
Rajasthan	17.91	17.19	16.62	15.75	14.19
Tamil Nadu	13.95	13.05	12.24	12.20	10.66
Uttar Pradesh	16.32	15.17	15.32	14.79	13.62
West Bengal	13.35	14.28	15.12	15.06	13.59
All-India	15.35	14.80	14.47	14.06	12.72

Note: N.A. –Not Available.

Source: Radhakrishna (1992) and Bansil (1992).

survey conducted by the Techno-Economic Research Institute for the FAO on Food Security, more than 98 per cent of the respondents reported having two square meals, but aspired for better health facilities, skill upgradation and improved infrastructure. Their perception of 'two square meals', however, was limited to the desired/required quantities of cereals (Bansil, 1997).

17. The NNMB data for 1988-90 shows that a person with per capita monthly income of less than Rs. 30 or less than Rs. 2,000 per annum

Table 3

Percentage Distribution of MPCE over Broad Groups of Items for Different NSS Rounds in Rural and Urban Areas: All-India Average Monthly Per Capita Consumption as Percentage of Total MPCE

Item group	Rural									Urban								
	43rd round	47th round	48th round	49th round	50th round	51st round	52nd round	53rd round	54th round	43rd round	47th round	48th round	49th round	50th round	51st round	52nd round	53rd round	54th round
1	2	3	4	5	6	7	8	9	10	11	12	13	14	15	16	17	18	19
Cereals	26.3	24 4.2	3.9	4.0	3.8	3.7	3.7	3.8	3.7	3.4	3.4	3.2	3.1	3.0	3.0	3.1	2.8	2.9
Milk & milk prod.	8.6	9.0	9.4	9.4	9.5	8.9	9.4	10.0	9.6	9.5	10.0	10.4	10.7	9.8	9.7	9.4	9.7	9.5
Edible oil	5.0	5.5	5.0	4.7	4.4	4.6	4.6	4.1	4.3	5.3	5.8	5.1	4.6	4.4	4.5	4.1	3.7	3.7
Meat, egg, fish	3.3	3.4	3.4	3.6	3.3	3.2	3.2	3.0	3.3	3.6	3.6	3.6	3.7	3.4	3.4	3.2	3.0	3.2
Vegetables	5.2	6.0	5.4	5.7	6.0	5.6	5.7	5.3	6.4	5.3	5.5	5.1	5.2	5.5	4.9	5.0	4.7	5.2
Fruits and nuts	1.6	1.6	1.7	1.7	1.7	1.4	1.5	1.7	1.2	2.5	2.3	2.5	2.8	2.7	2.5	2.2	2.2	2.2
Sugar	2.9	2.6	2.6	3.1	3.1	2.9	2.6	2.7	2.7	2.4	2.1	2.1	2.5	2.4	2.2	2.0	1.9	1.9
Salt	0.2	0.2	0.2	0.2	0.2	0.2	0.2	0.2	0.2	0.1	0.1	0.1	0.1	0.1	0.1	0.2	0.2	0.2
Spices	2.7	2.7	2.8	2.7	2.5	2.4	2.3	2.2	2.2	2.2	2.0	2.2	2.1	1.9	1.9	1.6	1.6	1.6
Beverages etc.	3.9	3.8	3.8	3.9	4.2	3.8	3.7	3.7	4.0	6.8	7.0	6.6	7.3	7.2	6.6	6.1	6.3	6.1
Food total	64.0	63.1	65.0	65.2	63.2	61.0	60.3	58.7	60.8	56.4	56.0	56.0	57.6	54.7	53.4	50.1	49.6	49.6
Pan, tobacco and intox.	3.2	4.5	3.3	3.3	3.2	3.0	2.7	3.0	2.9	2.6	2.6	2.3	2.5	2.3	2.1	1.9	1.9	1.9
Fuel and light	7.5	7.0	7.0	7.6	7.4	7.0	7.1	7.2	7.9	6.8	6.4	6.3	7.0	6.6	6.7	6.4	7.1	7.3
Clothing	6.7	5.0	5.6	5.2	5.4	7.0	7.7	7.0	5.9	5.9	5.7	5.4	4.9	4.7	5.5	7.1	5.8	5.5
Footwear	1.0	0.7	0.8	0.8	0.9	1.0	1.1	1.2	1.0	1.1	0.9	0.9	0.9	0.9	1.0	1.2	1.0	1.1
Misc. goods and services	14.5	13.0	14.1	14.2	17.3	15.4	16.1	18.2	17.6	23.2	19.8	20.9	19.6	27.5	21.9	22.5	24.6	24.8
Rent	@	0.3	0.3	0.3	@	0.2	0.3	0.3	0.3	@	3.7	3.5	4.2	@	4.3	3.8	4.4	3.9
Taxes and cesses	@	0	0.0	0.1	@	0.1	0.1	0.1	0.1	@	0.3	0.3	0.3	@	0.6	0.6	0.6	0.6
Durable goods	3.1	6.3	3.8	3.3	2.7	5.2	4.5	4.4	3.5	4.1	4.6	4.3	3.0	3.3	4.5	6.5	5.0	5.2
Non-food total	36.0	36.9	35.0	34.8	36.8	39.0	39.7	41.3	39.2	43.6	44.0	44.0	42.4	45.3	46.6	49.9	50.4	50.4
Tot. cons. exp.	100.0	100.0	100.0	100.0	100.0	100.0	100.0	100.0	100.0	100.0	100.0	100.0	100.0	100.0	100.0	100.0	100.0	100.0

Note: @ Clubbed with miscellaneous goods and service; Tot. cons. exp.– total consumption expenditure.

Source: 43rd Round, July 1987–June 1988; 47th Round, July 1991–December 1991; 48th Round, January 1992–December 1992; 49th Round, Janaury 1993–June 1993; 50th Round, July 1993–June 1994; 51st Round, July 1994–June 1995; 52nd Round, July 1995–June 1996; 53rd Round, January 1997– December 1997 and 54th Round, January– 1998 June 1998.

Table 4
Proportion of Households Getting Two Square Meals a Day

(Per cent)

State	Response type						
	Throughout the year		Only some months of the year		Not even in some months of the year		Not reported
	1983	1998	1983	1998	1983	1998	1993
			Urban				
Andhra Pradesh	92.94	98.3	6.93	0.9	0.04	0.7	.1
Assam	90.77	98.1	7.23	1.2	1.79	0.6	.1
Bihar	87.60	97.0	9.14	1.1	2.89	0.9	.9
Gujarat	98.18	98.4	1.05	0.8	0.09	0.7	0
Haryana	99.47	99.4	0.53	0.6	0.00	0.0	0
Karnataka	88.65	98.6	10.37	0.1	0.58	0.3	.1
Kerala	86.05	93.9	11.67	4.8	1.85	1.1	.2
Madhya Pradesh	94.21	98.8	4.86	0.9	0.37	0.3	0
Maharashtra	94.50	98.5	5.00	1.1	0.42	0.4	0
Orissa	87.41	95.8	11.33	1.3	5.00	0.7	.2
Punjab	96.80	99.8	1.80	0.1	0.84	0.1	.1
Rajasthan	96.98	99.2	1.18	0.2	0.82	0.0	.7
Tamil Nadu	91.28	97.7	7.15	0.1	0.27	0.6	.7
Uttar Pradesh	95.17	98.5	3.86	0.8	1.05	0.2	.5
West Bengal	91.88	96.0	6.14	0.2	0.71	1.5	.5
All-India	93.25	98.1	5.56	1.1	0.77	0.5	.3
			Rural				
Andhra Pradesh	84.32	96.6	14.69	1.7	0.82	1.2	.5
Assam	83.87	90.1	12.49	6.1	3.58	0.3	.8
Bihar	62.51	92.8	31.81	5.1	5.42	1.5	.6
Gujarat	96.92	97.6	2.78	0.9	0.07	0.4	1.1
Haryana	98.61	99.2	0.73	0.8	0.12	0.0	0
Karnataka	80.91	96.0	17.81	2.7	0.93	0.8	.4
Kerala	80.80	91.0	15.29	7.4	3.68	0.4	1.2
Madhya Pradesh	84.34	97.0	13.35	2.5	1.72	0.3	.1
Maharashtra	85.80	95.4	13.42	4.1	0.68	0.4	.1
Orissa	62.79	84.4	31.80	14.9	5.02	0.5	.2
Punjab	98.26	99.9	1.35	0.1	0.24	0.0	0
Rajasthan	95.95	98.5	3.11	0.6	0.69	0.0	.8
Tamil Nadu	82.10	96.9	16.06	1.5	1.36	0.9	.7
Uttar Pradesh	88.24	96.3	10.39	2.9	0.62	0.5	.3
West Bengal	60.31	85.6	31.10	11.1	8.60	0.3	.4
All-India	81.46	94.5	16.19	4.2	2.35	0.9	.4

Source: Bansil (1990).

per family, consumed 500 grams of foodgrains per CU per day. Since the nineties have witnessed a faster growth in the availability of non-cereal foodstuff, there is very little possibility of any further increase in the consumption of foodgrains.

18. Repeat surveys of NNMB further show that an average person in the surveyed areas invariably consumed more than the RDA in terms of energy, proteins, iron, etc. However, there was severe deficiency only with regard to thiamine.

19. A study by the NCAER (Rao, 1994) shows that during 1992-93, people in the lowest income group (households having an annual income below Rs. 11,000 at 1987-88 prices) purchased 1.85 million transistor radios, 0.68 million black and white TV sets, 0.67 million pressure cookers, 4.12 million torches, 2.46 million bicycles, over 5 million wrist watches and 1.8 million electric fans. Thus, even among those in the lowest level of income, there are a sufficient number of those who aspire and are able to purchase products which offer convenience and comfort. Low-income households, owned 37 per cent of group I durable goods, (costing less than Rs. 1,000), 24 per cent of group II goods (costing Rs. 1,000 to Rs. 6,000) and 10.5 per cent of group III goods (value Rs. 6,000 and above). This shows that durable goods are owned at all income levels in significant numbers. Even at the lowest income levels, on the basis of national average and a proportionate allocation to each income class, the data show that about 18 of the durable goods are actually owned by the poor. This indicates that those in the lowest group also, having met their minimal food requirements, are showing an inclination to spend an increasing proportion of their incomes on white goods.

III. DEMAND ELASTICITIES

Demand projections for various food items are often based on demand elasticities and available data on the income and expenditure structure. The NSSO being the only source of such data series, researchers have been calculating such demand elasticities since the First Plan. These elasticities are supposed to be nothing more than an illustration of Engel's Law of Consumption as discussed earlier. Some of the functions used for calculating these elasticities have been based on log inverse, semi·log and logarithmic, etc.

Insofar as cereal consumption is concerned, all such calculations made so far have shown that:

1. Urban elasticities are always lower than rural.
2. Elasticity at different points of time beginning with the First Plan has regularly come down for cereals. It was 1.0 in the '50s, 0.65 in the '70s and as low as 0.3 in the '80s.

1. Problems in Demand Projection

With this premise before us, it is clear that any long-term projections based on this 'scientific tool' are bound to go wrong. If the National Commission on Agriculture (1976) projected the demand for foodgrains for 2000 at 240 million tonnes according to the calculated elasticity of 0.65, it must not be considered valid even by 1987-88 when the elasticity had already come down to 0.3. Similarly, all long-term projections based on such elasticities will not be valid 20 years hence.

Normally, one should assume that when the NSSO is the only data source for calculating expenditure elasticities, the results should be the same. This is not, however, so. Elasticities calculated by different authors vary from -0.037 to 0.18 for urban and from -007 to 0.29 for rural areas (Table 5). It is then left to the judgement of any individual to choose the one which best suits him/her. If so, all these numbers lose their sanctity as a scientific tool (Bansil, 1998).

As for the future, all the researchers have been using the calculated elasticities for 1987-88 to 1993-94 as applicable even 20-25 years hence. In some cases elasticities for 2020 have now been reduced arbitrarily saying that they are the 'best guesses'. Murty (1998), who used different elasticities under different methods gives demand projections for cereals for 2020 which vary from 188.7 to 3,54.0 million tonnes. All such calculations will then be based on the so-called scientific approach.

There are three more theoretical problems with these elasticities. Firstly, while the elasticities are calculated from expenditure, for projecting the demand, income is being used as a proxy for expenditure. This is not in keeping with the facts. It has been observed that total expenditure moves within the narrow band of Rs. 3,000 to Rs. 6,000 per capita per annum, irrespective of income. The gap between income and expenditure widens once income crosses the Rs. 7,500 mark at 1993-94 prices. As seen earlier, expenditure on cereals starts declining even earlier. Secondly, while elasticities have been calculated at some constant prices, all income projections are calculated at current prices of the target year.

Thirdly, there is a limit to the total calories which an average human being can consume under given climatic conditions. There is no built-in formula in the elasticities referred to above where the elasticity coefficient becomes zero and takes negative value once the satiation point is reached. As a solution to this problem, some demand studies centred around complete demand system, taking into account mutual interdependence of a large number of commodities in the budget decisions of the consumer, were undertaken by some experts. The important models which received considerable attention are the linear expenditure system (Stone, 1954) and 'almost ideal demand system (AIDS)' (Deaton and Muellbaur, 1980). These models were generally used for estimating demand equation for a group of commodities and not for commodities at a disaggregate level. But they also do not account for increasing or decreasing income elasticities.

The 'Normalised Quadratic Demand System (NQDS)', 'Generalised Leontief Demand System (GLDS)' and 'Transcendental Logarithmic Demand System (TLDS)' suggested by Swamy and Binswanger (1983) are the models which satisfy all general conditions of demand theory and also allow for estimation of cross-price elasticities within a group of close substitutes or complements, and do not assume additivity. These models also include linear and squared income terms which allow more flexibility in the response of consumer items to changes in income. In addition to econometric models, Bouis (1992) suggested a non-econometric model based on demand characteristics known as 'Food Characteristic Demand System (FCDS)'. This model requires far less data than the usual econometric approaches and so may be implemented relatively quickly and in a cost-effective manner. Several studies have shown that demand elasticities can vary widely across income groups and by regions as production environments and tastes change. The FCDS can be used easily for these subsets of consumers.

Under the FCDS, three characteristics—energy, variety, and tastes of individual food are assumed to be additive in the utility function. Energy and variety enter the utility function in such a way that utility from consumption of one food depends on the level of consumption of all other foods. By specifying an explicit functional form for these characteristics in the utility function, it turns out that the entire matrix of price and income elasticities can be derived for a system of 'n' food and one non-food from prior knowledge of just K+4 elasticities in the (n+1) by (n+2) matrix of price and income elasticities, where 'K' is the number of broad non-staple food groups. Staple foods such as rice, wheat and coarse grains which are consumed primarily for their calorie content, are treated in a unique way in the FCDS (Kumar, 1994).

This conforms to Engel's Law of Consumption (1932), that is, though the food basket of an average person undergoes changes with changes in income, once the consumption of cereals is stabilised, income calories elasticity becomes zero. This is the situation at the all-India level, but is also true insofar as hunger and poverty are concerned.

When the ground situation, both at the all-India level and state level, shows that there is a steady decline in the per capita consumption of cereals over the last 38 years and it has reached a level of saturation, any model which goes against this ground situation, has to be rejected.

The calculated elasticities on the basis of the FCDS system discussed above for 1987-88 (Table 5) show that both for wheat and coarse grains they were negative and for rice marginally positive. Since the share of rice was 36 per cent and that of wheat and coarse cereals 38 per cent in the total calories of food consumed in rural areas and a more or less similar consumption pattern prevailed in urban India, the overall elasticity coefficient for cereals for India as a whole would be negative. This would mean that every real increase in per capita income will result in a decline in the per capita consumption of cereals. A comparison of the 50th round NSSO data (between 1993-94 and 1999-2000) shows the same trend.

To sum up our discussion in the preceding pages, in accordance with Engel's Law, the behaviour of food consumption in India has dramatically changed over the last 25 years. The composition of the consumer food basket of an average Indian has changed not only by replacing coarse cereals by fine grains to a large extent, but also by reducing the quantity of foodgrains consumed. At the same time, the share of total expenditure on food has also decreased with a corresponding increase in expenditure on non-food items. This has happened in response to increasing per capita income, urbanisation, changes in food habits and tastes, etc. With the per capita income having nearly doubled at constant prices there is a

Table 5
Expenditure and Own Price Elasticities Based on FCDS by Rural and Urban Population, India

	Expenditure elasticity		Own price elasticity	
	Rural	Urban	Rural	Urban
Rice	0.064	0.016	-0.282	- 0.288
Wheat	-0.056	-0.080	-0.242	-0.217
Cereals	-0.151	-0.165	-0.268	-0.309
Pulses	0.309	0.214	-0.524	-0.516
Milk	0.458	0.372	-0.636	-0.667
Oil	0.389	0.234	-0.567	-0.522
Vegetables	0.385	0.253	-0.601	-0.683
Fruits	0.442	0.360	-0.641	-0.683
Meat	0.848	0.633	-0.879	-0.885
Sugar	0.133	0.057	-0.405	-0.394
Others	0.945	0.695	-0.967	-0.967
Non-food	2.251	1.874	-1.241	-1.235

Source: Kumar (1994).

declining trend in cereal consumption. During this period the proportion of people below the poverty line has come down from above 50 per cent to around 19 per cent, according to the old methodology of the Planning Commission and 39 per cent as per Expert Group estimates. We will, therefore, be justified in making the most optimistic assumption that the future consumption level of cereals will remain more or less stable at the 1993-94 level or say at 14 kg per capita per month for rural India and 11 kg per capita per month for urban areas.

IV. PATTERNS OF CALORIE CONSUMPTION

The other most important factor influencing consumer behaviour is that there is a limit beyond which total calories consumed by an average person will not increase. A study of the 50th round, NSSO data show that per capita per day consumption of calories in the rural areas (2,418) of the most prosperous state (Punjab) is lower than that in Jammu & Kashmir (2,507), Haryana (2,491) and Rajasthan (2,470). As for urban areas, the corresponding figure for Punjab (2089) is lower than that in 11 other states including Bihar (2,188) and Orissa (2,261). Even with regard to the intake of proteins, Punjab is way behind some other states both in rural and urban areas, though the intake of fats (59.8 g/day) is the highest in rural Punjab. This only shows that the intake of total calories or for that matter other constituents of the food basket is also not related only to income. In Punjab (both rural and urban), for example, the average person consumes the lowest share of calories from cereals but highest from milk. Similarly, with regard to meat, fish and eggs, Kerala ranks at the top followed by Assam and West Bengal both in rural and urban areas.

This discussion would lead us to conclude that though there is a limit beyond which one's intake of total calories will not increase, neither the number nor its composition is a function of income alone. There are many other factors such as climate, food habits/tastes, nature of activities and easy availability of various consumption items in rural areas, price relationship between foodgrains, non-foodgrains and non-food items, changes in energy requirement due to reduced manual labour and climatic variations, changes in the wage payment systems, improvements in health status and the resulting efficiency in conversion of food into energy, which play their own role in determining both this number and composition of calories an average person consumes.

Despite lower income levels, people in both the rural and urban areas of Himachal Pradesh and Jammu & Kashmir consume higher calories primarily because of the colder climate in these states, where the per capita intake of both proteins and fats is also one of the highest. Another interesting feature of the inter-state consumption pattern is that while the total calorie consumption is within a range of 1,922 to 2,416 calories (urban) and 1,939 to 2,507 calories (rural), per capita incomes vary between Rs. 1,042 (Bihar) to 4,053 (Punjab).

This is further confirmed by a look at the relationship between incomes and calorie consumption at the international level, where the availability of total calories in each country is more than what is required. Although the per capita income of Papua New Guinea is more than double that of China, the availability of calories in the former is 30 per cent less than in China. The highest level of calories available is in Malaysia (2,790) followed by China (2,709), though per capita income of China is six and a half times less than that of Malaysia. This also applies to the composition of the total consumer basket among different countries.

This inter-state comparison within India and international comparison among the countries in the Asian region is more than sufficient to prove that irrespective of the income of a family, there is a limit beyond which calorie consumption will not rise. If at all, there is an inverse relation between income and calories consumed, but there is again a limit at which it will tend to stabilise. There is, however, sufficient evidence available to prove that the composition of the food basket does undergo changes with increasing incomes—the share of cereals being reduced. While it may be difficult to determine the level beyond which the absolute number of calories will not go, we would be on the safe side if the availability of calories per capita per day under Indian conditions is fixed at around 2,900-3,000 and actual intake in the range of 2,100-2,400. This is the actual position in the urban areas of comparatively better-off states, where expenditure on non-food items is in the range of 40-45 per cent, assuming that every family in India will achieve the present consumption levels of Punjab—the most affluent state in the country, though it may not be possible for every state to reach the per capita income level of Punjab.

V. AVAILABILITY OF FEED, SEED AND WASTAGE RATES

In India, the only information available is in terms of conventional assumptions about the quantity of foodgrains used as feed, seed and that being wasted. Some rough estimates were formulated during the late '50s aggregating to a broad average of 12.5 per cent of production as accounting for feed, seed and wastages. For all official calculations, this is the netting factor being adopted to calculate the availability of foodgrains for human consumption.

None of these three items is in any way related to the gross production of foodgrains. The availability of seed, for example, is primarily a function of the area under the crop and is determined by the seed rate required under different cropping systems and the type of seed used. In a situation where gross area under foodgrains has steadily declined from a peak of 131.16 million hectares in 1983-84 to 124.1 million in 1997-98 the quantity of foodgrains used as seeds had actually declined and would be reduced further. Even wastage rates will depend not only on the quantity stored, but also the types of storage available and marketable surplus. Imported stored grains are not included in any of the calculations being made at present. Similarly exported grain should be excluded from storage losses. Here also, with improvements in storage systems, the quantity lost should come down.

With regard to feed rates, these have a direct relation with animal husbandry and poultry development programmes. Again, data available has no relevance under the conditions as they exist today. While feeding of gram to animals is not very common these days, the consumption of maize has gone up appreciably because of poultry development.

At the international level, according to FAO estimates, as much as 34 per cent of cereals were used as feed during 1984-85 which increased mildly (34.6 per cent) during 1995-96. Interestingly, even the physical quantity of foodgrains in the latter year is less by 2.0 million tonnes compared to that in 1984-85. The estimated consumption of wheat, coarse grains and rice during 1994-95 was 647.0 million tonnes as estimated by the FAO when the world production of meat, milk and eggs was less than that in 1995-96. The situation is somewhat different according to the USDA sources.

Data from the two sources do not tally possibly because the methodology in each case may be different. But what is significant is that while, according to FAO the total quantity of coarse grains, wheat and rice fed to animals came down from 622 to 620 million tonnes during the 11 year-period, the corresponding figures for USDA are 608.7 and 641.9 million tonnes, showing an increase during the period. A long time data series of USDA shows that the consumption of wheat and coarse cereals as a feed increased from 60.6 million tonnes and 336.4 million tonnes respectively in 1968-69 to 97.2 million tonnes (62.3 per cent) and 56.8 million tonnes (59.2 per cent in 1995-96). There is a steady increase in the production of feed (wheat and coarse grain) up to 1987-88 when it peaked at 661.5 million tonnes. Eight years later (1995-96), the estimated production was is only 641.9 million tonnes nearly 20 million tonnes less than in the base year 1987-88.

According to USDA, rice is not being fed to animals anywhere in the world, but FAO shows that this has increased from 7.0 to 9.0 million tonnes during the same period. Our studies in Punjab, Haryana and Uttar Pradesh show that small quantities of rice are being consumed by livestock in India. But the most interesting case is that of China, where during 1993 as much as 20.0 million tonnes of rice was consumed by the animals. Again in 1980 a study by IFPRI shows that the estimated consumption of paddy as feed during 32.0 million tonnes represented 8.0 per cent of production during the year. The total consumption of cereals as feed according to the study during that year was 681.0 million tonnes, which included 17 per cent by-products of cereals, giving a net cereal consumption of 565.6 million tonnes. The IFPRI study does not make it clear whether the original figure of 681.4 million for total cereal consumption includes by-products of this very grain or is additional from outside. Normally, in India, for example, grain is fed to livestock along with additional by-products like *bran/choker,* etc. For purposes of comparison, it is assumed that whole grain equivalent of consumption during 1980 was 681.4 million tonnes including by-products, according to IFPRI, representing 43.5 per cent of total production.

A comparison of these three sources of data (FAO, USDA and IFPRI) depicts a rather confusing picture. IFPRI does not give any annual data series. But for 1980 its estimate is 681.4 million tonnes as against 559.6 million tonnes by USDA. Again, for 1984 the FAO estimate is 622 million tonnes against USDA 582.2 million tonnes. Besides these varied estimates, one striking feature is that while cereal feed consumption, according to FAO and USDA, has come down during the last 10-11 years, world production of eggs, meat and milk increased manifold during the same period. IFRPI appreciates the fact that the use of cereals as livestock feed is growing rapidly in developing countries and is reaching significant proportions, and that this has profound implications for food security of low-income people, employment, and the size of markets available to exporters of cereals. It did undertake a few studies, but no one has ventured into the field to find out the ground situation which has its own peculiarities.

VI. THE INDIAN SCENARIO

Most of the researchers engaged in projecting the demand for foodgrains for India, base their calculations on the experience abroad and come up with conclusions which have no relevance to the ground situation. China is perhaps the only country in the Asian region where the quantity of foodgrains fed to livestock is rather high. But our researchers also project such high requirements for India on this account without understanding the implications of the Chinese data. The fact remained that even there, leaving aside projections, current consumption estimates vary widely between different sources (Bhalla, 1997).

In India, there is only one study, conducted by the Techno-Economic Research Institute under the sponsorship of the Planning Commission (1993) which addressed itself to this specific question. It is based on an interview of 1800 farmers spread over 15 districts in Punjab, Haryana and Western Uttar Pradesh during 1986-87. The results of the study are revealing. They show that only 3.24 per cent of the foodgrains consumed is used as feed and a total of 9.78 per cent as feed, seed and wastages as against the conventional estimates of 5 per cent and 12.5 per cent respectively in India.

1. Peculiar Indian Conditions

Let us examine the problem of estimating the demand for feed in India. Normally the farmer either buys the concentrate from the market or prepares it himself according to his own experience and circumstances. Such decisions certainly have inter- and intra-regional/country variations. Theoretically, animal nutritionists have laid down recommended composition of concentrates containing specified quantities of digested crude proteins, total digestible nutrients, etc. They are grouped into some sort of maintenance packages for mature animals, growing calves, milk production, etc. These now consist of oilcakes, foodgrains, fish meal, pulses, root crops like cassava and various agricultural wastes. The composition of various commodities in the package will depend upon the easy availability of a particular item, traditional feeds and systems, inter-commodity price differential, economics of feeding livestock and changes in the production, pattern of livestock products.

It is true that we cannot produce milk or meat just on air and water. But it is also true that various factors referred to above play a very significant role in determining the amount of concentrates that can be given to animals. If China produces 150 million tonnes of sweet potato and potato, it is no wonder that half of this is fed to animals. In India, given the economic condition in the country, if the prices of foodgrains go up, it is uneconomical for the farmer to give concentrates to animals which give, say 1-2 kg of milk. Instead, he may keep them grazing on dry or some green fodder, if available, plus by-products of foodgrains, kitchen or other agricultural wastes, etc. Such flexibility is much more feasible with regard to dairy animals and piggery, than in the case of poultry-layers (particularly the organised sector) and broilers in whose case research findings available show that a certain percentage of maize is an essential component of the feed. This would then mean that there is nothing like a fixed relationship between the various constituents of the concentrate at a given time. This will vary from time to time, depending on the specific factors mentioned earlier. The problem is further complicated in the case of India where conditions are marked by certain peculiarities as:

1. A major part of the milk in India is produced by the animals which yield less than 2-2.5 kg/day and as a result, it is neither economical nor practical to give them any concentrates.
2. There is double counting insofar as wastage and livestock feeding is concerned and a major part of the so-called wasted grain is fed to livestock.

3. Out of a total of around 3.5 million tonnes of meat, a major part (about 3.1 million) excluding chicken, is a by-product of the livestock industry. We do not have separate beef or pig fattening programmes and a major part of the sheep or goat are also not stall fed. Even with regard to chicken meat, not more than half is broilers which have to be fed to get good results. The remaining half is from the culled layers which again is a by-product.
4. With regard to egg production, at least 12 per cent come from *desi* birds, the productivity of which is only 40 eggs per annum per bird compared with around 240 eggs of those in the organised sector. *Desi* birds just scavenge around and live on kitchen waste. They are not given any additional concentrates.
5. Obviously, all studies which convert livestock products into meat livestock units and calculate feed requirements on the basis of theoretical norms are bound to go wrong.
6. In India, draught animal power (DAP) of bullocks (72 million) and buffaloes (8 million) as well as equines (1 million of horses and donkeys) and camels (1 million) make available 50,000 million units of energy per year, worth Rs. 100,000 million. Draught animals plough 100 million hectare of farm land, constituting 60 per cent of the area cultivated and the power generated by them saves 6 million tonnes of petroleum per year, worth Rs. 40,000 million in foreign exchange. Draught animal power is an appropriate technology, that can best serve the need of 60 million small farms and small scale transportation. The asset value of draught animal power is Rs. 200,000 million, and its replacement by mechanised system would need Rs. 1,000,000 million. According to a study conducted by the Institute of Economic Growth, to replace our draught animals, we would require about 20 million tractors and the petroleum products worth $20 billion. Another study by Dr. Jugner Lansh, who lived in Indian villages for three months found that if the cattle were to be eliminated, as many as 100-200 million of people would migrate to cities. Given the trend towards increasing tractorisation, however, the importance of draught animal power will be decreasing in the future.

2. Research on Alternative Sources of DLP/TDN

While projecting the demand for feedgrains for livestock feeding in the developing world, one has also to take into consideration the likely impact of research activity which is directed at providing the required DCP/TDN from sources other than foodgrains. Steps taken and new initiatives needed in this direction are discussed below:

(i) There is an ongoing debate on how a large proportion of cereals can be saved in poultry feeding by increasing the caloric density of the diet. It has been observed that cereals as a source of poultry feeding can be replaced by other alternative sources which include fats and oils, preferably the non-conventional ones like *mahua*/mustard oil, which are very rich source of energy in poultry rations. Since vegetable oils are mostly used for human consumption, the use of rendered animal fats as a poultry feed may be a better proposition. Despite social constraints on the use of rendered animal fats, the organised feed industry can make use of this product which is being practically wasted today. Failing this, import of mutton tallow holds promise for maintaining poultry production at the desired levels (World Bank, 1996).

(ii) Present research efforts have to be intensified to sustain animal production on crop residues and industrial by-products. The present research on animal nutrition and physiology for promoting traditional feeding systems will no longer deliver high productivity levels as the basic raw materials have a low digestibility (2-3 per cent). However, a major reserve of energy is found in the untapped plant cell wall in terms of ligno-cellulose complex, which, if tapped, will yield enough energy to feed all the 400 million livestock. But this will require large investments in research on feed biotechnology, manipulating and constructing microbes which can digest thc ligin ring. Current nutrition research has to focus on this area to generate and release carbohydrates from plant cell wall. A method has to be found to remove various chemical moieties like tannin and other anti-growth factors from cakes and meals so that the abundant protein in the meal is made available to livestock.

(iii) New technologies are being developed here to improve the utilisation of crop residues. Fodder production and cut-and-carry systems offer an alternative to communal grazing. The quality of crop residue (i.e., straw) can be improved by urea treatment to improve its nutritive value. A highly successful and acceptable urea-molasses-mineral block-lick has been developed for improved utilisation of straws by growing animals. The supplement can be used during natural calamities to save the animal. Compact straw blocks supplemented with urea, mineral mixture, and molasses, cakes, bran and green fodder have been developed to make a complete feed for different categories of dairy animals. Similar low-cost feed and fodder need to be developed. Increased milk yields of 20 per cent as a result of using urea-molasses blocks have been reported.

The application of by-pass protein technology in combination with straw has been found to quadruple the efficiency of the supply of amino-acids from feed to milk production. Bypass protein technology, which refers to the use of special protein sources (e.g., brewer's grain, corn gluten meal, cotton seed cake, soybean meal) and processes (e.g., heating) to reduce the digestive losses in the rumen and improve the efficiency of protein utilisation, under experimental conditions, has reportedly allowed the reduction of concentrate requirement by 40 per cent, the increase in the conversion of protein in dry matter by over 30 per cent, and the reduction of dry matter requirement by 24 per cent (Bansil, 1985). Important constraints to the utilisation and dissemination of these technologies however, still remain and include the applicability of these technologies to high-yielding cross-bred cows only, their commercial production and utilisation potential, and weaknesses in the existing technology transfer system which could introduce such technologies to farmers.

(iv) Extensive research and feeding trials have been conducted on many agro-industrial by-products and non-conventional feeds aimed at using these as protein and energy supplements, such as apple pomace, groundnut hulls, *mesta* cake, *mahua* cake, *neem* cake, salseed meal, leaucena leaf meal, soya pulp, rice bran, brewery waste, etc. The compounded feed industry has been greatly benefited by these findings. Appropriate technologies have been developed for detoxifying toxins in certain agro-industrial feeds like mahua cake, neem cake and sal seed meals for providing cheep alternative feed to growing calves. The development of cheap good quality feed is expected to pose a great challenge for the scientists in the coming years.

(v) In Cuba, farmers add pumpkin (squash gourds) to the bird's feed. They chop and dry pumpkins and feed them to laying hens with good results. Pumpkins have as much or more protein and fat as maize and cassava flours which are used to feed chicken. Taro (*colocasia esculenta*) is another plant which is used to feed poultry. It is also a tuber known as *dasheen* or coco yam. The taro is ground into flour, 15 per cent of which is added to the diet of chicken between the age of one day to four weeks. Chicken fed on this diet can gain 10 times their weight in the first four weeks of life. Similarly an alternative feed for pigs consists of local plants as feed substitutes. These include 'cassava' *(manihot esculenta)*, which can be used to replace maize or other grains. The farmers gather cassava tubers, leaves and the juicy parts of the stem, boil them together in water, and add a little salt and a little amount of fish meal. The fish meal provides protein which is an essential part of the pigs' diet.

It is hoped that over a span of more than two decades, the dissemination of results of research underway, as set out above, would reduce substantially the use of cereals in animal food, leading to the utilisation of alternative sources of energy and protein.

3. Some Problems in Projecting Demand

The use of certain coefficients for converting milk, meat and egg, etc., into foodgrains which have neither any scientific basis behind them, nor takes into consideration peculiar Indian conditions poses a problem: the projected demand figures presented are not realistic in that they do not reflect the ground realities giving completely wrong signals to the policy makers.

It is unfortunate that over the last five decades, no serious effort has been made in India or for that matter in other developing countries to establish any empirical basis in this respect. This can be attributed to two reasons: Firstly, feed is wrongly grouped with seed and wastages for reasons explained earlier. Secondly, the projections are not based on any scientific study but on pure guess—work varying from the magical figure of 12.5 per cent (which itself has no basis) to anything like 15 per cent for say the year 2000 and more for subsequent periods. The fallacy of such an exercise is obvious. During the last 50 years milk production has increased fourfold, egg by over 15 times, chicken from 0 to 0.4 million tonnes, (of course, with about four times increase in food production). The conventional adjustment factor of 12.5 per cent has been assumed to remain constant. One would then wonder why this should be assumed to go up to 15 or 20 per cent in the coming few years, particularly when foodgrain production is also assumed to grow more or less at the prevailing rates or even a bit higher.

VII. THE INCREMENTAL DEMAND MODEL

There is presently no empirical study available which can give any idea about the consumption levels of foodgrains by the livestock (Bansil, 1997). To fill this need, a Simple Incremental Demand Model has been developed to project the demand for foodgrains by 2020 AD. The year 1993 is taken as the base. The production of foodgrains during the year was 179.5 mt, milk 58 mt, eggs 23 billion (1.15 mt) and meat 3.5 mt. The prevailing system of distribution was not geared to absorb such a large quantity of grains for meeting the human as well as livestock requirements at the then exisiting pattern of consumption, existing levels of prices and poverty (whatever its dimension and definition). It is estimated that as much as 9.6 million tonnes were added to public sector stocks. With imports of 2.4 million tonnes, total quantity of foodgrains available in the system was as high as 172.28 million tonnes (Table 6).

Starting from this base, the population of India by 2020 as projected by UNFPA will be 1280.4 million, which will be equally distributed between rural and urban regions. Human cereal consumption levels both for rural and urban India will not remain constant at the 1993-94 levels of 13.4 kg per capita per month (rural) and 10.63 kg per capita per month (urban), since past experience is a clear indicator of a further decline. Well-fed states like Punjab (10.78 kg rural and 9.01 kg urban), Haryana (11.92 kg rural and 10.46 kg urban), Gujarat (10.66 kg rural and 8.96 kg urban) and Maharashtra (11.39 kg rural and 9.37 kg urban) have registered a steep decline in their consumption pattern of cereals. It will then be reasonable to assume that per capita per month consumption of cereals for the country as a whole will not be more than 12 kg (rural) and 10 kg (urban)—somewhat above the present consumption levels of these states. This may actually be reduced further.

Recent studies throw an interesting sidelight by establishing an inverse relation between consumption of cereals and availability of labour-saving devices like an increase in the horse power of tractors and pumpsets. The decline in consumption also results from an increase in road length in rural areas. Notably, a study by Professor Hanumantha Rao (1999) based on a discussion of other indicators like nutritional efficiency, etc., arrives at an interesting though apparently paradoxical conclusion that, upto a point, a reduction in the intake of foodgrains on certain counts should in fact be associated with improvement in human welfare. Since our future projections for rural and urban consumption levels are assumed to be 12 kg (rural) and 10 kg (urban) respectively as mentioned above, there would be a reduction of only 5 per cent for urban and 10 per cent for rural areas over the 1993-94 consumption levels of cereals over a period of 27 years. This may actually stabilise at lower rates.

On the basis of the assumptions as below production targets for various livestock products are determined. Although a major part of additional production of livestock products is likely to be continuously produced under the existing systems, it is assumed that the total additional production will be under the improved system.

1. Availability of milk hovered around 40 kg per capita per annum up to 1977-78, when it started moving up steadily. It rose from 44 kg to 65.6 kg during 1992-93 an annual compound growth rate of 2.8 per cent in response to a per capita income growth rate of 2 per cent. Production of milk during this 15 year period increased at an annual compound rate of 4.9 per cent. There has, however, been a deceleration in the growth pattern during the nineties when production increased at a rate of around 3 per cent per annum. As against this, the decade witnessed an all-round increase in milk prices and the production of synthetic milk, particularly in North India, the milk bowl of the country. Special efforts will, therefore, have to be made to remove constraints in production due to various factors such as breeding, feeding, management and disease control problems. Demand, the targeted growth rate has to be atleast 3 per cent. If so, milk production target for 2020 will have to be 163 million tonnes. Although the organised sector today contributes hardly 10-15 per cent of total milk output, if the whole of the additional (163-58)=105 million tonnes, is to be produced in the organised sector, the recommended norm will have to be 1 kg of foodgrains for 14.45 kg of milk (Bansil, 1985). Hence, the additional requirement of foodgrains will be 7.27 million tonnes.

   It would be of interest to know that the compound animal feed industry in India has been growing at an average rate of 10-12 per cent annually. In order to feed the growing population with a nutritive diet containing adequate calories and protein, it was necessary to bring about a revolution in agricultural production, animal husbandry and aqua-culture. The compound animal feed industry has utilised the nutritional qualities of various conventional and non-conventional raw materials and scientifically compounded them to prepare animal feed according to the nutritional requirements of the animals. It has thus contributed in achieving the main objective directly by increasing the yield and production of animal protein and indirectly by augmenting the availability of foodgrains and edible oil bearing material useful for human consumption by reducing their use in feeding animals. Thus, from less than about 50,000 tonnes of production per annum in the early sixties, the compound animal feed industry in India has grown to produce about 8 million tonnes of compound feed annually. The Indian compound animal feed industry has also been improving the quality of compound food. The efficiency of animal feed is always expressed in terms of feed conversion ratio, i.e., output (animal production) in relation to input (feed) per unit.

To produce balanced feed for animal, poultry or aqua, the main oil meals used are soybean meal, groundnut meal, sunflower seed meal, rice bran extraction, rapeseed meal, cottonseed meal. India produces 32 million tonnes of oilseeds and oil bearing material which gives about 20-22 tonnes of oilcake-meal. The current production of oil meal is about 10 million tonnes out of which about 3 million tonnes is exported. Thus, exploiting the full potential of oil meals will go a long way to save foodgrains and improve animal nutrition.

2. In 1993, the annual per capita availability of eggs was 28. With the growth rate of 5-6 per cent in production during the past few years, and increasing incomes supported by the educational campaigns by the National Egg Coordination Committee (NECC) along with improved infrastructural facilities for rural poultry development, demand is projected to go up by over three times to say 90 eggs per capita per annum. This would mean that the production target would have to be 119.7 or say 120 billion (6.0 million tonnes) eggs. It may be noted that the present annual per capita consumption of eggs in rural India is only 10 eggs and in urban areas 80 eggs. Demand for foodgrains (at 1.2 kg of foodgrains for 1 kg (20) eggs) for an additional 92 billion eggs in the organised sector will calculate to 5.5 million tonnes (Bansil and Bhat, 1996). The present free range system at the village level under which about 12 per cent of total eggs are provided will be completely eliminated.
3. Per capita availability of poultry meat during 1993 was 517 grams per annum. As against this the demand for poultry meat is increasing fast at around 12-14 per cent. Assuming an annual growth in production of around 9 per cent, for the whole period, total availability of poultry meat is projected at 6.5 million tonnes. As a result, the per capita consumption will be 5 kg or nearly 10 times the consumption levels of 1993. Of the total poultry meat of 454 thousand tonnes available during 1993, only 254 thousand tonnes was from broilers and the remaining

200 thousand tonnes from culled layers after 18 months of their productive life. Assuming that all the additional egg production of 92 billion will come from pedigree hens which produce over 240 eggs each, the total number of hens will work out at around 400 million. At the rate of 2 kg per bird, they will produce 800 thousand tonnes of chicken meat. Additional chicken meat which will be produced by broilers will work out to 6500-(454+800) = 5246 thousand tonnes. To produce this quantity of broiler meat, foodgrain requirement (at 1.2 kg foodgrains for 1.0 kg meat), will work out at 6.3 million tonnes.

4. There is a growing view that a large proportion of cereals can be saved in poultry feeding by increasing the caloric density of the diet. Since the availability of cereals for poultry feeding would continue to be a problem, the other alternative is to use fats and oils, maybe the non-conventional ones like *mahua* oil, mustard oil, etc., which are a rich source of energy in poultry rations. But since vegetable oils are mostly used for human consumption the use of rendered animal fats as poultry feed may be a better proposition. Although social constraints exist on the use of rendered animal fats, this should not deter the organised feed industry from making use of this product which today is being practically wasted. Failing this, import of mutton tallow holds promise for maintaining poultry production at the desired levels.
5. Meat from culled birds and other animals like buffalo, etc., is a by-product of the livestock industry. Of the total meat production of about 3.5 million tonnes during 1993, the share of goat, sheep and pig was about a million tonnes. There are no well focused programmes to increase the production of these categories of meat. The most optimistic assumption can be that at best another 1 million tonnes of meat can be added from these sources. While sheep and goat will continue to be raised as before, piggery can be assumed to come within the organised sector to some extent. This would possibly need a total of around 2 million tonnes of additional foodgrains.
6. India has a special place for draught animals and breeding stock and though, with increasing mechanisation of agriculture, the demand for draught power should possibly be decreasing, a provision of 2.0 million tonnes of foodgrains had been made for these animals in 1993-94. Similarly, with the increasing application of artificial insemination, the number of breeding bulls might also decrease and allocations already made for 1993-94 should be sufficient to meet the requirement of food on this account.
7. Since a major part of the so-called wastage in foodgrains is used to feed livestock, and there is a strong possibility of new technology being introduced both in the public and private sectors, storage losses on this account will be minimal. Even then, it would be better to allow for wastages on the additional production of 69.0 million tonnes. Accordingly provision for an additional 1.5 million tonnes has been made on this account.

8. Seed requirements are related to the area under cultivation. Total area under foodgrains peaked at 131.16 million hectares during 1983-84 and steadily came down to 124.1 million hectare in 1997-98. There being hardly any possibility of any increase in the area under foodgrains, no allowance is being made for additional seed requirements.
9. With growing industrialisation, industry is likely to become a very important user of foodgrains in times to come. Industrial uses of foodgrains can be divided into two categories—indirect human consumption like biscuits, bread, etc., and non-human consumption like starch and malt. The demand for starch is expected to go up primarily with the development of textile and paper industries, though small quantities are also used in the production of glucose, cosmetics and pharmaceuticals. Estimated production of starch for the year 2000 was around 637 thousand tonnes. With an annual increase in foodgrain production being about 40 thousand tonnes the projected production for 2020 may then be placed at about 1.5 million tonnes. The production of starch today is based on tapioca and maize. In Kerala, both production and human consumption of tapioca are decreasing, while in other states like Tamil Nadu the production is increasing. The additional starch requirement works out to be (1.5–0.637) 0.863 million tonnes, part of which is being met by tapioca. The quality of maize required for maintaining the required production of starch will work out to, say 1.0 million tonnes.

   Further, industrial units manufacturing beer, nutritious food products, pharmaceutical items and even cattle feed use malt in different proportions. The total demand for malt by these units today is 2.5 lakh tonnes, for which the source is primarily barley. Since the demand for these products using malt has a very high growth rate—over 10 per cent—malt requirements are likely to go up to around 2.5 million tonnes. Total production of malt in the country is hardly 1.7 lakh tonnes while the rest is being imported. If the total demand of 2.5 million tonnes of malt is to be met out of production in India as much as 3.5 million tonnes of barely would need to be produced. The present production of barley in India is around 1.6 million tonnes which has come down from over 3.0 million tonnes 50 years back. Since it is basically rainfed crop, it is replaced by wheat or even mustard to come extent once irrigation facilities are available. The possibilities of increasing the production of quality barley to meet the total demand for malt are remote. As imported barley is superior in quality to the one produced in India for the purpose of making malt and costs less than that produced at home, the units based on imported barley can also earn a considerable quantum of foreign exchange through exports particularly when the Union and state governments have delicensed the manufacture of beer.

   In the light of the above, there will be only two options left for the malt manufacturing companies: either import barley from outside or shift to other bases like molasses and beetroot etc., at least for non-beer uses. To meet the requirement of these units a provision for a total 4.5 million tonnes of foodgrains (3.5 for malt and 1.5 for starch) has been made, All other industrial uses like biscuits, etc., are included in the calculations for human consumption of cereals.

10. Requirements for human consumption do not include pulses. The demand for this commodity has been assumed to go up by around 50 per cent per capita. Thus, efforts will have to be made to find alternative sources like soya cake, etc., as a substitute for pulses to provide for any additional demand arising because of production constraints. Against the availability of 12.8 million tonnes in 1998 and the highest ever production of 14.26 million tonnes, 20.0 million tonnes has been provided under the model.

To sum up, (Table 6), the gross requirement of foodgrains will not exceed 241 million tonnes. This would mean that production would have to increase by 40 million tonnes during the next 20 years or, say 2 million tonnes annually. This should be an attainable objective. It merits mention here that each of the assumptions made above with regard to demand, errs, if at all, on the higher side. This is because, (i) total additonal production of livestock products is assumed to be produced within the modern organised sector, resulting in an allocation of over 32 per cent of the additional production of foodgrains for livestock feeding; and (ii) new

Table 6

Demand for Foodgrains by 2020 AD

	Population (million)		
Item	Urban	Rural	Total
1993	221	663	884
2020	640	640	1280
1993-2020*	419	-23	446
Additional foodgrains requirement (million tonnes)			
Human consumption			
Cereals	48.6	-14.3	34.3
Pulses	20	-12.8	7.2**
Egg (additional 105 million tonnes)	7.27		
Eggs (additonal 92 Billion eggs)	5.5		
Chicken (additional 4.4 million tonnes)	5.3		
Other meat			2.0
Draught and other animals			0.5
Wastage			2.5
Industrial uses			1.5
Total quantity available in the system during 1993			69.07
179.48-9.6 (Public sector stock) = 169.88 + 2.4 (Imports)=			172.28
Grand Total			241.35

Notes: *Additional population during period.

** Present per capita consumption of pulses is 10-3 kg/annum for urban and 9.1 kg/annum for rural areas.

Calculated at this rate, total demand for pulses works out to 13.0 million tonnes. Our estimated demand at 20.0 million tonnes gives an increase of over 50 per cent.

researches in the pipeline aiming at substituting foodgrains for livestock feeding have not been taken into account. The former is unlikely to happen. These projections would, therefore, appear to be optimistic. The reconstituted food basket for 2020 (Table 7) gives a total per capita availability of 2849 calories. Total availability of protein is 90.5 g and the share of calories from animal sources is 14.4 per cent as against 7.8 per cent during 1993.

Table 7
Available Consumer Basket, 2020

Item	Total production (million tonnes) TE-ending 1993	2020	Per capita availability Annual kg	Daily g	Calories	Proteins g
Cereals*	123.30	169.00	132.03	361.7	1266.0	31.2
Pulses	13.0	20.0	15.62	42.8	150.9	9.0
Milk	53.90	163.2	127.50	349.3	366.5	12.7
Oils	6.2	14.96	11.69	32.0	288.0	-
Egg	1.1	5.98	4.67	12.8	23.1	5.4
Meat	3.08	12.24	9.56	26.2	29.5	4.1
Fish	3.09	10.88	8.50	23.3	23.4	1.4
Fruits	24.12	62.56	48.88	133.9	100.2	
Vegetables	43.02	140.08	109.44	299.8	185.0	7.8
Sugar**	20.36	40.8	31.88	87.3	346.2	-
Total	-	1369.1	2778.8	89.4	-	
Miscellaneous not	-	-	-	-	-	-
already covered	-	-	-	70.0	-	-
Grand total	-	-	2848.8	-	-	-

Notes : * This is the actual consumption level for humans.
** Includes Jaggery;
Per capita consumption of milk in Delhi during 1996-97 was only 282 grams.
Source: Estimated by the author.

It must be highlighted that the northern region which has so far contributed more than 50 per cent in the average incremental production of foodgrains during 1962-65 to 1990-93 (Table 8) will not be able to maintain its performance. Neither can one be very hopeful of the western, southern and central regions of being able to do so. Only the eastern region can be expected to make a major contribution to the food basket. During the 27 years (1962-66 to 1990-93), of which the previous seven years happened to have good monsoons in a row, additional foodgrain production sustained fully by the green revolutions totalled, 91.7 million tonnes. We will now have to add another 41 million tonnes during the next 20 years (2000-2020)—the period under discussion. Clearly, there is no room for complacency on the food front. While Krishi Bhavan need not lose its sleep, it certainly cannot afford to take the matter lightly.

Table 8

Average and Incremental Production of Foodgrains Regionwise 1962-65 to 1990-93

(Million tonnes)

Year	North-western region		Eastern region		Central western region		Southern region		All-India	
					Average production					
1962-65	20.9		19.7		23.5		18.7		82.8	
1970-73	32.5		23.0		26.0		21.1		102.6	
1980-83	47.0		23.4		34.4		24.5		129.3	
1990-93	67.8		33.8		43.0		28.5		173.1	
1994-97	74.8		38.0		47.8		29.4		190.0	
					Incremental average production					
2 over 1	11.6	(58.6)	3.3	(16.7)	2.5	(12.6)	2.4	(12.1)	19.8	(100)
3 over 2	14.5	(54.3)	0.4	(1.5)	8.4	(31.5)	3.4	(12.7)	26.7	(100)
4 over 3	20.8	(47.5)	10.4	(23.7)	8.6	(19.6)	4.0	(9.1)	43.8	(100)
4 over 1	46.9	(51.9)	14.1	(15.6)	19.5	(21.6)	9.8	(10.9)	90.3	(100)
5 over 4	7.0	(41.4)	4.2	(24.9)	4.8	(28.4)	0.9	(5.3)	16.9	(100)
5 over 1	53.9	(50.3)	18.3	(17.1)	24.3	(22.7)	10.7	(9.10)	107.2	(100)

Note: North-western–Uttar Pradesh, Punjab, Hayana, Himachal Pradesh and J & K; Central western–Madhya Pradesh, Maharashtra, Gujarat and Rajasthan; Southern–Andhra Pradesh, Karnataka, Kerala and Tamil Nadu, Eastern–Arunachal Pradesh, Assam, Manipur, Meghalaya, Mizoram, Nagaland, Tripura, West Bengal, Orissa and Bihar.

Source: Calculated by the author from the production data.

VIII. CONCLUSION

An effort has been made to prepare optimistic demand projections both for human consumption and other uses. Accordingly, an allocation of 23.6 million tonnes of foodgrains for annual feed alone, from the additional production of 69 million tonnes (over 32.0 per cent), would certainly be the highest. Most of the other estimates of total demand for foodgrains based on these projections, made by the national and international agencies being much higher, this exercise raises important policy issues. The realisation of a target of, say 241.0 million tonnes of foodgrains, for 2020 AD, though achievable will need special efforts. The actual requirements will certainly be much less because of the optimistic assumptions (giving higher estimates) on which these are based under the model. We will then be playing safe. But if a much higher target is fixed, as proposed by many others (Bhalla, 1997) there is an obvious danger of giving wrong signals to the development strategy which might lead to distortions and ill-advised wasted efforts.

This paper, which is of an indicative nature, aims at serving as an important input in this major issue of national significance. It underscores the importance of having realistic estimates. There is also an urgent need to undertake comprehensive studies on livestock feeding, the only major grey area in the country, the ground situation being very different as mentioned in the introductory section. At the same time, a micro-level study about the problems, constraints and potentials of production of foodgrains at the regional and sub-regional levels is another area where research is called for. In fact, it is now imperative to shed orthodoxy of regional self-sufficiency and come up with an optimal cropping pattern with due consideration to the need for optimising production potential in the country.

In the end, it may be stated that today there is a vital need to initiate special studies to obtain more detailed information about the existing food basket of people in the various strata of society. Unfortunately, the available information is not sufficient to provide a realistic estimate of the demand for foodgrain for 2000 AD. There are a number of scattered micro-level studies available which are quite revealing. Both human beings and livestock today consume a large number of locally available material which does not figure anywhere in our production estimates. Even the NSSO methodology as it exists today cannot provide any answer to these intricate issues. As matters stand, with models imported from outside and developed by various interests, the issue will remain shrouded in controversy adding to the confusion. There is otherwise no reason why the projection for foodgrains demand for 2000 projected by responsible quarters at, say 240 million tonnes as the minimum requirement just a few years back have already been proved wrong today. And, if this is so, it is very likely that their projections for the future will also be wrong.

Note

1. Various Issues of *National Accounts*, Central Statistical Organisation (CSO), Government of India.

References

Alagh, Y.K. (1994), "Export Peripheral to Farm Growth", *Economic Times*, October 31.

—— "Institution for Price Policy and Supply Management of Food in India", Paper presented at the Seminar on the *Role of Foodgrain Agencies in Food Security in Asia and the Pacific,* sponsored by FAO and FCI, April 23-25, New Delhi.

Bansil, P. C. (1998), "Inter-Country Comparisons in Feed Production and Consumption", Techno-Economic Research Institute, New Delhi (mimeo).

—— (1997), "Food Security—Perceptions and Aspirations of Villagers", Techno- Economic Research Institute, New Delhi (mimeo).

—— (1990), *Agricultural Statistical Compendium*, Vol. 1 & Supplement, Techno-Economic Research Institute, New Delhi.

—— (1985) *Feed, Seed and Wastage Rates-A Regional Study*, Techno-Economic Research Institute, New Delhi.

—— (1956), Food Statistics, *Sankhya*, December.

—— and Bhat, P.N. (1996), "Problems and Prospects of Poultry Industry in India", *Indian Journal of Animal Production*, December.

Bhalla G.S. (1997), "Demand for Foodgrains to 2020", *Economic and Political Weekly,* December.

Bouis, Howarth (1992), *A Food Demand System Based on Demand for Characteristics: If There is Curvature in the Slutsky Matrix, What Do the Curves Look Like and Why?* International Food Policy Research Institute, Washington, D.C.

Deaton, A. and Muellbauer, J. (1980), "An almost Ideal Demand System", *American Economic Review*, Vol. 3, pp. 312-25.

FAO/WHO (1973), Energy and Protein Requirements, *Report of a Joint FAO/WHO Ad Hoc Expert Committee,* March 22–April 2,1971, FAO Nutrition Meetings Report Series No. 522, Rome, Italy; Geneva, Switzerland.

Kumar, Praduman (1994), "Demand for Foodgrains", New Delhi (mimeo).

GOI (1994), "Report of the Working Group on Foodgrains Requirements by the Year 2000 A.D.", Government of India, Ministry of Agriculture, New Delhi.

Murty, K.N. (1998), "Foodgrain Demand in India to 2020", *Economic and Political Weekly,* November 14.

Pfaundler, L. (1902), "Die Weltwirtschaft im Lichte der Physik," *Deutsche Revue,* Vol. 22, No: 2, pp. 29-38; 171-182.

Planning Commission (1993), "A Report of the Expert Group on Estimation of the Proportion and Number of Poor", New Delhi.

Radhakrishna, R. (1992), "Trends in Nutrition, Emerging Challenges and Nutrition Need for Effective Intervention", *The Economic Times,* New Delhi, February 10 and 11.

——Rao, C. (1992), *Effects of Growth, Relative Price and Prefereances on Food and Nutrition,* Centre for Economic and Social Studies, Hyderabad.

Rao, C.H. Hanumantha (1999), "Declining Per Capita Demand for Foodgrains in India: Why and What Does This Imply", *Presidential Address Delivered at the 13th National Conference on Agricultural Marketing* held at N.I.R.D., Hyderabad, on 12 October,

Rao, S.L. (1994), "Consumer Goods Market", *Economic Times,* September 30.

Ravenstein, E.G. (1891), "Lands of the Globe Still Available for European Settlement", Proceedings of the Royal Geographic Society, Vol. 13, pp. 27-35, 64.

Stone J.R.N. (1954), "Linear Expenditure System and Demand Analysis: An Application to the Pattern of British Demand", *Economic Journal,* Vol. 64, pp. 511-527.

Swamy, Gurusnri and Binswangar, Hans P. (1983), "Flexible Consumer Demand System and Linear Estimation, Food in India", *American Journal of Agricultural Economics.*

World Bank (1996), *India Livestock Sector Review,* New Delhi.

4

Declining Per Capita Demand for Foodgrains in India: Why and What Does This Imply?

C.H. Hanumantha Rao

I. INTRODUCTION

While some of the projections in regard to the demand for foodgrains in India in the next 20 years have been mind-boggling (Murty, 1998), scholars like Radhakrishna, and Ravi (1992), Kumar and Mathur (1996) and Murty (1999), in recent years have come out with a sobering—though startling—finding, based on the National Sample Survey (NSS) data: that the per capita household demand for foodgrains has been declining. Since per capita income has been rising over the years, this would have led to some rise in per capita demand for foodgrains. Moreover, the prices of foodgrains relative to the index of non-foodgrains prices have declined over a greater part of the last two decades, which would also have resulted in some rise in the demand for foodgrains. If, despite these factors favouring an increased demand for foodgrains, the actual per capita demand for foodgrains has been declining, there must be powerful forces operating in our economic system which are dampening the demand for foodgrains.

Radhakrishna and Ravi (1992) and Murty (1999) in their studies mentioned earlier, have attributed this dampening demand to the changes in tastes and preferences of consumers away from foodgrains. There can, no doubt, be such changes in tastes and preferences. But the question arises as to whether we have exhausted all the identifiable economic factors in explaining the observed decline in per capita demand for foodgrains. This paper aims to probe into some such factors—other than changes in tastes and preferences. Needless to say, an understanding of the factors contributing to the decline in demand for foodgrains would have important implications not only for demand projections for foodgrains but also for development policies in general. In particular, the unearthing of some of these factors could have implications for the development of marketing infrastructure in rural areas.

II. TRENDS IN PER CAPITA CEREAL CONSUMPTION

Let us, at the outset, look at the broad trends in regard to the per capita demand for foodgrains in the rural and urban areas and the associated factors like changes in expenditure and prices, as revealed by the National Sample Survey data. For the sake of convenience, the present analysis is restricted to cereals only, as it is well known that the per capita consumption of pulses has also been declining. Over a period of two decades—that is, between 1972-73 and 1993-94—the per capita consumption of cereals has shown a sharper decline (by around 12 per cent) in rural areas than in urban areas (around 5 per cent). It is also significant to note that the per capita consumption of cereals in both the periods was higher in rural when compared to urban areas. However, this rural-urban differential has come down, even though rural per capita consumption was still higher by as much as 26 per cent in 1993-94.

There are significant regional variations in these trends. For example, while in states like Kerala and West Bengal, where per capita consumption of cereals both in rural and urban areas was way below the national average in 1972-73, a significant increase was registered in 1993-94, in other states such as Haryana and Punjab which show a sharper decline in per capita rural consumption, the per capita consumption was higher than the national average to start with (in 1972-73), accompanied by a higher rate of mechanisation of agriculture (Table 1).

Table 1
Per capita Cereal Consumption: States (Kg per month)

	Rural			Urban		
State	1972-73	1993-94	% change	1972--73	1993-94	% change
Andhra Pradesh	15.25	13.27	-12.98	12.68	11.3	-10.88
Assam	14.81	13.17	-11.07	12.55	12.05	-3.98
Bihar	15.58	14.31	-8.15	13.49	12.82	-4.97
Gujarat	13.32	10.66	-19.97	10.77	8.96	-16.81
Haryana	17.57	12.92	-26.47	11.86	10.46	-11.80
Karnataka	15.63	13.15	-15.87	11.32	10.87	-3.98
Kerala	7.97	10.11	26.85	8.17	9.46	15.79
Madhya Pradesh	17.28	14.20	-17.82	12.88	11.32	-12.11
Maharashtra	12.60	11.39	-9.60	8.95	9.37	4.69
Orissa	15.22	15.93	4.66	13.77	13.36	-2.98
Punjab	15.38	10.78	-29.91	10.71	9.01	-15.87
Rajasthan	18.17	14.85	-18.27	13.21	11.52	-12.79
Tamil Nadu	14.53	11.72	-19.34	11.12	10.05	-9.62
Uttar Pradesh	16.83	13.91	-17.35	12.24	11.08	-9.48
West Bengal	13.64	14.96	9.68	10.53	11.64	10.54
All-India	15.26	13.4	-12.19	11.24	10.63	-5.43

Another notable feature is that the poorest or the bottom 30 per cent of the population have experienced an increase in per capita consumption of cereals between these two periods, while the middle 40 per cent and the top 30 per cent of the population have shown a decline in their per capita consumption, the decline being sharper for the top 30 per cent both in rural and urban areas. The rural-urban difference in the per capita consumption of cereals for the top 30 per cent was as high as 64 per cent in 1972-73, which still remained quite high in 1993-94 at around 40 per cent (Table 2). These facts underscore the point that to identify the factors accounting for the observed decline in per capita consumption of cereals in the country, one should look closely at the consumption behaviour in rural areas and among upper expenditure groups in certain states.

Table 2
Per Capita Cereal Consumption: All-India (Kg per month)

	1972-73			1993-94		
	Rural	Urban	R/U	Rural	Urban	R/U
Bottom 30%	11.36	10.12	112.25	11.76	10.29	114.29
Middle 40%	15.32	11.78	130.05	13.61	10.94	124.41
Top 30%	19.08	11.64	163.92	14.77	10.56	139.87
All	15.26	11.24	135.77	13.40	10.63	126.06

Note: R/U indicates rural consumption as a percentage of urban consumption.

The rural-urban disparity in per capita total expenditure has widened over the last two decades. The per capita total expenditure in rural areas in 1972-73 was around 30 per cent lower than that in urban areas, but by 1993-94, this disparity had risen to 39 per cent (Table 3). The fact that despite the lower per capita total expenditure in rural areas when compared to urban areas in both the periods, the per capita consumption of cereals was significantly higher in rural areas points to the importance of factors other than income working in the opposite direction.

Table 3
Per Capita Total Expenditure: All-India (Rs. per month)

	1972-73			1993-94		
	Rural	Urban	R/U	Rural	Urban	R/U
Bottom 30%	22.04	29.26	75.32	149.70	207.03	72.31
Middle 40%	37.69	50.47	74.68	240.32	363.91	66.04
Top 30%	74.94	114.54	65.43	467.87	834.55	56.06
All	44.17	63.33	69.75	281.40	458.04	61.44

Note: R/U indicates rural expenditure as a percentage of urban expenditure.

The prices of cereals were about 11 per cent lower in rural areas when compared to urban areas in 1972-73 and the rural-urban difference in cereal prices had risen to 16 per cent in 1993-94 (Table 4). It is significant that the rural-urban difference in the per capita consumption of cereals has narrowed down somewhat despite the rising price difference. This again underscores the importance of factors other than income and prices in explaining the rural-urban difference in cereal consumption. In both the periods, the rural-urban disparity in cereal prices was smaller for the lower expenditure groups when compared to that for the top 30 per cent. This is understandable as the rural poor have to buy a good part of their cereal requirements from the market whereas the rural rich meet their requirements from their own produce. This is consistent with the fact, noted earlier, that the rural-urban difference in the per capita consumption of cereals is sharper in the case of the top expenditure group.

Table 4
Average Cereal Price: All-India(Rs./Kg)

	1972-73			1993-94		
	Rural	Urban	R/U	Rural	Urban	R/U
Bottom 30%	1.09	1.21	90.08	4.73	5.35	88.41
Middle 40%	1.17	1.32	88.64	5.15	5.97	86.26
Top 30%	1.22	1.40	87.14	5.28	6.82	77.42
All	1.17	1.31	89.31	5.08	6.05	83.97

Note: R/U indicates rural cereal price as a percentage of urban price.

III. FACTORS BEHIND HIGHER CEREAL CONSUMPTION IN RURAL AREAS

For explaining the higher per capita consumption of cereals in rural areas, one can think of at least four factors other than income and foodgrain prices. They are: (a) higher prices of non-foodgrain and non-food items; (b) higher energy requirement of the rural poor due to heavy manual labour; (c) payment of wages in kind by the large farmers in the form of cooked food; and (d) the poor state of health and environment resulting in low efficiency of conversion of food into energy. The discussion on the first two factors, which are quantifiable to some extent, is based on the ideas borrowed from a paper written in 1969 (Rao, 1969; Srinivasan and Bardhan, 1969; Rao, 1969a).

1. Higher Prices of Non-foodgrain and Non-food Items

To start with, the first factor, goods and services other than foodgrains, in rural areas, range from food items such as milk, eggs, meat and fish to a host of urban goods and services such as textiles, modern furniture, cosmetics, medicines, radio and television sets and access to cinema houses and other forms of entertainment, to mention only a few. While we do not have readily available data on rural prices of several of these urban goods of consumption, at least in the case of some of the essential urban goods of consumption which are traditionally marketed in rural areas, such as coarse cloth, edible oil, sugar, kerosene, etc., it would be reasonable to assume that their prices would be higher in rural areas when compared to their urban prices, at least to the same extent as the foodgrain prices in urban areas are over their rural prices. This is because transport costs and traders' margins are involved in both the cases.

With regard to several other urban goods of consumption, their rural marketing is not as well developed as the traditional foodgrain marketing in urban centres, though the position would have improved somewhat over the last few decades. As such, the rural-urban price differential in their case can be expected to be greater than for those having an established market in rural areas. Moreover, even the food basket effectively opened to the rural population is restricted when compared to the one opened to the urban population which largely contains protective foods, e.g., meat, eggs, milk, vegetables, fruits, etc., which are available to the urban population in a greater measure owing to the existence of a large market for these commodities. In any single village, the availability of some of these goods is limited, even excluded in quite a few cases, because of their restricted market and the resulting diseconomies of (small) scale in marketing.

The basket of the non-agricultural goods available for the urban population is far more diversified because of the existence of the large market coupled with the availability of necessary infrastructure leading to economies of scale in marketing. For individual villages, in a large number of cases, the availability of many of these urban goods and services is ruled out owing to the non-availability of adequate supporting infrastructure like electricity and roads and the resulting extreme diseconomies of (small) scale in marketing. The position has, of course, improved somewhat over a period of time with some of these urban goods and services becoming available in rural areas. However, to the extent that some such goods and services—food as well as non-food—can be obtained by the rural consumers only by visiting urban markets, they add to the cost of purchase or prices of these goods and services for rural consumers. Indeed, it is possible that certain higher expenditure groups in rural areas, whose budget consists predominantly of expenditure on urban goods and services, may be experiencing lower real incomes as compared to their urban counterparts because of higher prices and high cost for getting access to such goods and services (Rao, 1969; Srinivasan and Bardhan, 1969).

Because of the large cultural diversity and consequent differences in food histories across different regions in the country, there can be some differences in tastes and preferences of consumers across the regions (Minhas, 1991). However, within any region, the rural-urban differences in tastes and preferences of people are unlikely to be a major factor in accounting for the rural-urban difference in per capita consumption of foodgrains. Indeed, in the course of the debate on this theme in 1969, mentioned before, on the basis of the National Sample Survey data on per capita consumption of foodgrains for the year 1959-60, Srinivasan and Bardhan concluded that "the assumption that the preference structures of rural and urban consumers for same expenditure class are identical is not contradicted" (Srinivasan and Bardhan, 1969).

Therefore, in view of high prices or high cost of obtaining urban goods and services in rural areas, high per capita consumption of foodgrains in rural areas can be explained in terms of the familiar demand theory: apart from income and prices of foodgrains, the cross elasticity of demand for foodgrains in rural areas with respect to the prices or the actual cost of obtaining the basket of non-foodgrain items in rural areas would be a relevant factor (see Appendix). It should be clear from the above discussion, that the prices of foodgrains relative to the overall index of non-foodgrains prices may not fully reflect the true cost of obtaining access to urban goods and services in rural areas.

2. Higher Energy Requirement in Rural Areas

Owing to the heavy manual or physical labour involved in agriculture arising from the labour-intensity of operations as well as harder physical environment in rural areas, the requirements of foodgrains for providing the required calories can be expected to be higher than in urban areas. This part of the requirement may be lower now than a few decades ago but may persist, though at a diminishing rate, until most of the agricultural operations and rural transportation are mechanised.

3. Wage Payment in Kind

The third factor relates to the payment of wages in kind in the form of cooked meals for agricultural labour as well as for domestic services. According to Minhas, "The NSS records all 'cooked' meals in the budgets of the serving households. Meals provided to employees, guests visiting the household or invited to ceremonies, cleaning ladies, religious functionaries, etc., whether prepared in the household kitchen, in the field or at some ceremonial location, get included in the domestic consumption account of the household. Also, the food served to household pets is booked in the domestic consumption account of the household" (Minhas, 1991). With increasing monetisation of agricultural and rural wages over a period of time, the average per capita consumption of foodgrains can be expected to come down, as the quantity of foodgrains purchased by wage earners at market prices could be lower than when it is received in the form of cooked meals. However, while the relevance of this issue becomes apparent now, it would be difficult at this stage to empirically test the possible impact of monetisation of such wages on the rural per capita consumption of foodgrains. This is because of the "practical difficulty of estimating the quantities and values of individual items used in preparing the meals served to employees and others" (Minhas, op.cit.), and the non-availability of other relevant data.

4. Poor State of Health and Environment

The pioneering contributions of late Professor P.V. Sukhatme to the nutrition theory, particularly with respect to the interaction between genetic and environmental factors, are well known. He explained how efficiency of conversion of food intake into energy would depend on the access to primary health care, primary education and environmental factors bearing on health. This accounts for the higher demand for foodgrain in the rural areas. Since the position in this regard has been improving over a period of time, especially in rural areas, one should expect at best a slow— almost invisible—decline in the quantity of foodgrains consumed per head without any adverse effect on the efficiency of work. Again, one can only flag this issue without venturing into any empirical examination, as that would be intractable at the moment.

The effects of per capita income or expenditure and prices of foodgrains on per capita consumption have been studied extensively in the existing literature. The general conclusion from these studies is that both the income and price variables do influence the per capita consumption of foodgrains in the expected direction, but that their impact is more pronounced among the lower expenditure groups and their overall impact is wearing out over a period of time. This conclusion is generally borne out by the findings from the exercises undertaken for this paper.

IV. IMPACT OF RURAL INFRASTRUCTURE AND FARM MECHANISATION ON FOOD CONSUMPTION

The main concern in this paper is to explore the possible impact of rural infrastructure—bearing on the marketing of non-foodgrain items of consumption—and mechanisation of agriculture, on the rural per capita consumption of cereals. Given the dearth of data on rural infrastructure or urbanisation of rural areas, one cannot think of a better proxy than the road length (km) per '000 sq. km of geographical area. The combined units of horse power from tractors, electric motors and oil engines per '000 hectares of net sown area have been used to show the mechanisation of agriculture (Table 5). Road length, insofar as it facilitates mechanised transportation, reflects, to some extent, the declining need for physical labour.

Between states, the rural per capita consumption of cereals is negatively correlated with road length both in 1973-74 and 1993-94, implying that better availability of urban goods and services consequent to the urbanisation of rural areas may lead to a decline in per capita consumption of cereals in rural areas. Mechanisation of agriculture also bears a similar negative relationship with the per capita consumption of cereals, particularly in 1993-94 when the rate of mechanisation was quite high in certain states. The negative correlation with road length looks stronger than with mechanisation (Table 6). These correlations are in line with the argument by Kumar and Mathur (1996) that "the demand for food is not only influenced by income changes, but also by differences in the urban and rural lifestyles, the development of more advanced marketing systems, occupational changes that are closely linked with increasing per capita income".

An attempt is made to explain the inter-state variation in the rural per capita consumption of cereals in terms of road length and mechanisation

Table 5
Road Length and Horse Power from Tractors and Pump-sets

State	Road length (km/'000 sq. km)		HP from tractors and pump sets	
	1975-76*	1991-92**	1972*	1987**
Andhra Pradesh	379.0	556.0	133.4	551.4
Assam	689.0	878.0	9.5	18.4
Bihar	536.0	504.0	83.5	313.5
Gujarat	248.0	472.0	258.9	30.7
Haryana	583.0	673.0	343.1	1572.2
Karnataka	525.0	711.0	121.8	354.2
Kerala	2248.0	3534.0	87.5	519.5
Madhya Pradesh	211.0	309.0	40.0	248.8
Maharashtra	368.0	799.0	116.3	204.7
Orissa	310.0	428.0	17.0	43.1
Punjab	797.0	1116.0	763.5	1666.2
Rajasthan	164.0	358.0	51.6	400.3
Tamil Nadu	847.0	1434.0	731.0	1143.3
Uttar Pradesh	653.0	756.0	146.2	960.3
West Bengal	610.0	665.0	10.4	723.4
All-India	380.0	628.0	153.7	761.8

Notes: 1. Pump-sets include both electric and diesel pump-sets.
2. * Data used for 1972-73; ** Data used for 1993-94.
3. In case of Orissa, the total road length in 1991-92 is arrived at by assuming the growth rate of surface road length.

Sources: 1. For cols. 1 & 2, Centre for Monitoring Indian Economy (1996).
2. For cols. 3 & 4, GOI (1997).

Table 6
Correlation Ratio between Rural Cereal Consumption and Related Variables

Variable	Rural per capita cereal consumption							
	1972-73				1993-94			
	Bottom (30%)	Middle (40%)	Top (30%)	All	Bottom (30%)	Middle (40%)	Top (30%)	All
Total expenditure	0.4647 (1.8922)	0.2601 (0.9712)	0.1521 (0.5549)	0.2688 (1.0062)	-0.4492 (-1.8128)	-0.6417 (-3.0167)	-0.6114 (-2.7858)	-0.6301 (-2.9257)
Price	-0.8792 (-6.6533)	-0.8382 (-5.5416)	-0.7420 (-3.9906)	-0.8531 (-5.8954)	0.0032 (0.0115)	0.0179 (0.0645)	-0.0939 (-0.3401)	-0.0244 (-0.088)
Road length	-0.5901 (-2.6354)	-0.7983 (-4.7792)	-0.7420 (-3.9906)	-0.7449 (-4.0256)	-0.6545 (-3.1212)	-0.5918 (-2.6471)	-0.5930 (-2.6553)	-0.6142 (-2.8062)
Tractor and pump-sets (H.P.)	0.1368 (0.4979)	0.0475 (0.1715)	-0.0385 (-0.1389)	0.0481 (0.1736)	-0.3091 (-1.1719)	-0.3709 (-1.44)	-0.3684 (-1.4288)	-0.3592 (-1.3877)

Note: Figures in the parentheses are t-ratios.

of agriculture, apart from per capita total expenditure and prices of cereals. These four variables together explain nearly 80 per cent of the variation in per capita consumption of cereals in 1973-74 and 65 per cent in 1993-94. Roads show a negative relationship in 1973-74, which seems to have been blurred in 1993-94, except perhaps for the bottom 30 per cent of the population. The index of agricultural mechanisation, on the other hand, shows a negative relationship in both the periods, the relationship being significant in 1993-94 (Table 7).

Table 7
Results of Regression Analysis; Dependent Variable: Rural Per Capita Consumption: Equation: Log-log

Variable	1972-73 Bottom 30%	1972-73 Middle 40%	1972-73 Top 30%	1972-73 All	1993-94 Bottom 30%	1993-94 Middle 40%	1993-94 Top 30%	1993-94 All
Total	0.3908	0.1062	-0.0363	0.0490	-0.1332	-0.3720	-0.3210	-0.3388
expenditure	(2.704)	(0.636)	(-0.219)	(0.303)	(-0.74)	(-2.032)	(-1.72)	(-1.792)
Price	-1.3351	-1.0163	-0.6704	-0.9908	-0.0309	-0.2873	-0.3415	-0.3019
	(-6.191)	(-3.458)	(-2.814)	(-4.012)	(-0.152)	(-1.359)	(-1.727)	(-1.417)
Road length	-0.1117	-0.1013	-0.0834	-0.0817	-0.0735	0.0094	0.0152	0.0070
	(-2.379)	(-1.734)	(-1.469)	(-1.531)	(-1.164)	(0.151)	(0.238)	(0.109)
Tractor and								
pump-sets	-0.0487	-0.0358	-0.0178	-0.0315	-0.0492	-0.0609	-0.0539	-0.0571
(H.P)	(-2.005)	(-1.26)	(-0.601)	(-1.155)	(-1.775)	(-2.355)	(-2.025)	(-2.211)
Constant	2.2157	3.2675	3.8308	3.3334	3.7991	5.3015	5.3867	5.1834
	(4.65)	(5.326)	(5.133)	(5.287)	(4.327)	(5.409)	(4.947)	(5.043)
R-Square	0.8946	0.7879	0.6758	0.7933	0.5773	0.6658	0.6415	0.6551

Note: All the variables are taken in log form. Figures in the parentheses are t- ratios.

Before discussing some of the implications of this analysis, one must add a note of caution. Inter-state comparison is necessarily at a high level of aggregation. A state is generally a highly heterogenous unit, both in regard to infrastructure development like roads and the degree of mechanisation of agriculture. This is more so in the case of larger states. It would, therefore, be rewarding if a similar exercise is undertaken at the disaggregated level of NSS regions which, incidentally, would provide a much larger number of observations.

V. IMPLICATIONS

One obvious question that arises from the declining trend in per capita consumption of cereals is in regard to the nutritional status of the poor. In fact, the per capita consumption of cereals by the bottom 30 per cent of the population had increased marginally over the two decades under study. Since the expenditure and price elasticities of demand for cereals are higher for the poor, given the significant increase in their employment, income and wages, and if the cereal prices faced by them relative to those faced by their urban counterparts were lower as in the case of the top 30 per cent of population, the per capita consumption of cereals among them would have been substantially higher. To this extent the decline in the average per capita consumption of cereals in the country would have been lower.

However, it appears that the saturation point in regard to the consumption of cereals would soon be reached even among the poor. This is evident from the significant decline in per capita consumption of cereals among the middle 40 per cent of the population and the strong negative impact of roads and mechanisation on cereal consumption among the poor. Even so, cereals being a low cost source of energy, the nutritional status of the poor can be improved substantially through the subsidised sale of foodgrains from the public distribution system (PDS). However, the quantity of foodgrain per head that the non-poor are found to be purchasing from the PDS is almost as much as that purchased by the poor (Radhakrishna et al., 1997). Therefore, if the PDS is effectively targeted to the poor, it has the potential of trebling their access to foodgrains without increasing its total commitment.

Another major implication of this analysis is that the demand projections for foodgrains need to take into account the possibility of a further fall in per capita demand on account of the development of rural infrastructure and mechanisation as indicated earlier. The average road length per square kilometer of geographical area in the country in 1991-92 was only about half of that in states like Punjab and Tamil Nadu—not to speak of Kerala, where one can see a rural-urban continuum. Similarly, the average rate of agricultural mechanisation in the country in 1987 was less than half of that in Punjab and Haryana (See Table 5). There is thus a considerable potential for modernisation of rural areas on these counts.

Further, since the rural-urban differential in per capita consumption of foodgrains is quite high even now, one should expect a significant decline in the average per capita consumption of foodgrains in the country with increasing urbanisation. On account of all these factors, it would not be unreasonable to expect a further decline in per capita consumption of foodgrains, say, by 2020 AD, at the same rate as witnessed over the two decades covered by our analysis, i.e., by about 10 per cent. Given the expected population growth by 2020, this declining trend in per capita consumption on account of the development of rural infrastructure, mechanisation, urbanisation, and other factors including changes in tastes and preferences, is likely to result in a decline in the household demand for foodgrains by about 20 million tonnes in 2020. However, this may be neutralised by the increasing demand for cereals as animal feed to the extent of about 10 million tonnes (Radhakrishna and Ravi, 1992). Despite this fall in per capita demand, the total demand for foodgrains will increase on account of population growth.

The actual outcome would, of course, depend upon the pace of development of rural areas, particularly the development of market infrastructure in rural areas for the sale of non-foodgrain items of food and other urban goods and services. In particular, innovative marketing methods and strategies for minimising the diseconomies of small scale in marketing of such goods and services in rural areas have a great potential for reducing their cost to the consumers, and thus inducing them to exchange part of the foodgrains for non-foodgrain items of food and other urban goods and services. This will reflect on the consumption of foodgrains in these areas.

Finally, it is clear that the decline in per capita consumption of foodgrains on account of the factors enumerated above would be associated with an improvement in the welfare of the rural consumers in general: the decline in the cost of accessing non-foodgrain items would raise the real income of large sections of rural consumers; while the decline in consumption on account of reduced physical labour would be associated with freedom from drudgery and higher nutritional efficiency with improved health and environment. Further, even the reduced dependence of rural workers on cooked meals from the rural rich should be welcome, as it would enhance human dignity. Paradoxical as it may seem, it is interesting to note that, up to a point, a reduction in the intake of foodgrains on certain counts should in fact be associated with an improvement in human welfare.

Appendix

I. Objective and Findings

The purpose of this note is to illustrate (a) the higher per capita consumption of cereals in rural areas on account of greater manual labour requirements; (b) the higher cost of obtaining urban goods of consumption in rural areas; and consequently the higher per capita consumption of cereals in rural areas attributable to the cross elasticity of demand with respect to the prices of urban goods of consumption.

The main findings are: (a) the higher cereal intake in rural areas, on account of higher manual labour put in, is the single largest factor behind the rural-urban difference in per capita consumption of cereals. Although this component has been declining over time, it still accounts for nearly 50 per cent of the rural-urban difference in per capita consumption of cereals in the early 1990s (App. Table 1); (b) though the cost of obtaining urban goods of consumption in rural areas, when compared to their urban prices, has declined over a period of time, it was still quite high in the early 1990s —over 50 per cent higher when compared to their urban prices; and consequently, nearly 25 per cent of the higher per capita consumption of cereals in rural areas can be attributed to this cross elasticity of demand (App. Table 1).

App. Table 1

Components of Rural-Urban Difference in Per Capita Consumption of Cereals

(Percentage rural over urban)

	Bottom (30%)		Middle (30%)		All expenditure groups	
	1972-73	1993-94	1972-73	1993-94	1972-73	1993-94
1. Expenditure	-8.14	-9.14	-8.36	-11.21	-9.98	-12.72
2. Own price	4.96	5.80	5.68	6.87	5.35	8.02
3. Cross price	1.69	1.97	1.93	2.34	18.13	9.72
4. Manual labour	13.74	15.66	30.80	26.41	22.27	21.04

II. Methodology

It is difficult to arrive at an estimate of the rural-urban difference in per capita consumption of cereals due to manual labour independently on the basis of any extraneous information. We have, therefore, assumed that the rural-urban difference in the consumption of cereals pertaining to the bottom three as well as the middle four expenditure groups is attributed to this factor apart from that arising from the difference in price and per capita expenditure. We also assume that the urban goods of consumption demanded by these lower expenditure groups are available in rural areas and that the rural-urban difference in the prices of such goods is the same as that for cereals, albeit, in the opposite direction. This assumption may not be unreasonable because the urban goods entering into the consumption basket of such groups are basic necessities having a long-standing market in rural areas.

On the basis of the findings from the existing studies on the demand for foodgrains, we have assumed an expenditure elasticity of 0.33 and price elasticity of -0.50. We do not have widely accepted empirical estimates of the cross elasticity of demand for foodgrains with respect to the prices of urban goods of consumption. However, we know from the Slutsky-Schultz' relation that the algebraic sum of income, price and cross elasticities of demand for any commodity equals zero (Srinivasan and Bardhan, 1969), which gives us the cross elasticity of 0.17.

The component of cereals, demand due to manual labour in rural areas has been estimated as the residual after accounting for expenditure, price and cross elasticities of demand for the lower seven expenditure groups. This relation implies that the cross elasticity of demand for cereals with respect to the prices of other rural goods and services is zero. However, this cross elasticity is likely to be positive. Owing to this omission, the cross elasticity we are using may be on the high side. Since the prices of rural goods and services (other than cereals) can be expected to be lower than those of similar items in urban areas, this omission may have overestimated the component due to cross elasticity and hence underestimated this due to manual labour. Since, for lower expenditure groups, basic necessities like foodgrains and clothing, etc., account for the bulk of the budget—the expenditure on other rural goods and services claiming a very small proportion—the error on account of their exclusion may not turn out to be serious.

We have arrived at the components of average (all classes) difference in per capita consumption of cereals in rural areas due to per capita expenditure

App. Table 2

Percentage Shares of Different Components (All expenditure groups)

	1972-73	1993-94
Per cent difference in rural per capita consumption of cereals over urban consumption:		
Observed	35.77	26.06
After accounting for expenditure differences	45.75	38.78
Per cent share:		
1. Own price	11.7	20.7
2. Cross price	39.6	25.1
3. Manual labour	48.7	54.2

differences, manual labour and difference in price. The residual is attributable to the cross elasticity of demand with respect to the price or cost of obtaining the urban goods of consumption (App. Table 2). By using the coefficient of cross elasticity, we can obtain the rural-urban price difference in regard to urban goods of consumption. This gives a measure of the cost to the rural consumers of obtaining urban goods of consumption in rural areas, if available, or of obtaining them from urban areas.

Since, as mentioned, we may have overestimated the cross elasticity with respect to the prices of urban goods, we would only be underestimating and not exaggerating the cost of obtaining urban goods of consumption in rural areas. These costs seem to be much higher (57%) than the rural-urban differences in the prices of cereals (-16%) even in 1993-94. The corresponding differences in rural-urban prices in 1972-73 were 106.6 per cent and -10.7 per cent respectively.

Finally, we would like to state that this exercise should be regarded as merely illustrative, as it is based on certain restrictive assumptions. One such obvious limitation is that the expenditure and price elasticities assumed are invariant over time as well as with respect to different expenditure groups.

(This paper is based on the presidential address delivered at the 13th National Conference on Agricultural Marketing, Indian Society of Agricultural Marketing, held at the National Institute of Rural Development, Hyderabad, October, 12, 1999. The author is highly indebted to C. Ravi for his help with the statistical analysis).

References

Centre for Monitoring Economy (1996), *Infrastructure in India*, Mumbai, November.

GOI (1997), *Statistical Abstract of India*, Vol. I, Government of India, Central Statistical Organisation, New Delhi.

Kumar, Praduman and Mathur, V.C. (1996), "Structural Changes in the Demand for Foodgrains in India", *Indian Journal of Agricultural Economics*, Vol. 51, No. 4, October-December, pp. 664-673.

Minhas, B.S. (1991), "On Estimating the Inadequacy of Energy Intakes: Revealed Food Consumption Behaviour *versus* Nutritional Norms (Nutritional Status of Indian People in 1983)", *The Journal of Development Studies*, Vol. 28, No. 1, October, pp. 1-38.

Murty, K.N. (1998), "Foodgrain Demand in India to 2020—A Comment", *Economic and Political Weekly*, November 14, pp. 2943-2944.

—— (1999), "Decomposition of Changes in Cereals Demand into Its Components in Semi-Arid Tropical Area", Paper presented at the *35th Indian Econometric Society Meeting* held at the Department of Economics, University of Rajasthan, Jaipur, March 11-13.

Radhakrishna, R. and Ravi, C. (1992), "Effects of Growth, Relative Price and Preferences of Food and Nutrition", *The Indian Economic Review*, Special Number in Memory of Sukhamoy Chakravarty, Vol. 27, pp. 303-323.

Radhakrishna, R.; Subbarao, K. with Indrakant, S. and Ravi, C. (1997), *India's Public Distribution System—A National and International Perspective*, World Bank Discussion Paper No. 380, World Bank, Washington, D.C.

Rao, C.H. Hanumantha (1969), "Resource Prospects from the Rural Sector—The Case of Indirect Taxes", *Economic and Political Weekly*, Review of Agriculture, March, pp. A-53-58.

—— (1969a), "Reply", *Economic and Political Weekly*, Vol. 4, No. 26, Review of Agriculture, June.

Srinivasan, T.N. and Bardhan, P.K. (1969), "Resource Prospects from the Rural Sector: A Comment", *Economic and Political Weekly*, Review of Agriculture, Vol. 4, No. 26, June, pp. 1-4.

PART II

Response to Macro Policy and Globalisation

5

Economic Policies for Ensuring Food Security

Vijay S. Vyas

I. INTRODUCTION

There is a general consensus among the nations of the world that food security is a primary responsibility of the state towards its citizens. This has been articulated in the successive World Food Congresses, and has been reiterated on several international and regional fora. A broadly accepted definition of food security is: access to food at the household level at all times to ensure a healthy and active life.

Apart from consensus on the responsibility for, and definition of, food security, there are two other aspects on which there is a general agreement. In the first place, it is recognised that food availability at the macro level cannot be equated with the food security at the household level. To ensure food security the household should have 'entitlement' to access adequate food. Second, it is now recognised that the concept of food security should go beyond the availability of a given quantity of calories for the individuals in a household; it should also meet their nutritional requirements. While there is a general agreement on these extensions to the original concept of food security (which earlier was narrowly interpreted as the availability of foodgrains at the national level), in practice much remains to be done in most of the countries, including our own.

The concept of food security in its wider connotation comprises of four elements: (i) availability of food; (ii) household's entitlement to food; (iii) stability in the supply of food throughout the year; and (iv) protection against malnutrition. In meeting all these requirements economic policies play an important role. In this presentation we will be concentrating on the first three elements. It should be recognised at the outset that in terms of avoiding malnutrition, our performance is not at all satisfactory. Impartial agencies, such as UNICEF, have stated that in the area of nutrition our record is worse than that of some of the countries of Africa. However, due to the paucity of time, I will not be able to comment on this aspect of food security.

II. FOOD AVAILABILITY

Let us first look at the aspect of *availability*. Thanks to the efforts of the scientists supported by appropriate economic policies and institutions, India could boast of producing adequate quantities of foodgrains to meet its domestic requirements. As is now well known, and often stated, within a span of just two decades the increase in foodgrains production has converted this country from a critically food deficit country to a marginally surplus one.

In recent years, however, there has been stagnation in the per capita availability of foodgrains from domestic production. In other words, foodgrains production has not been able to keep pace with increasing population. As is well known, two principal factors affecting the demand for food in the short run are, increase in population and increase in income, while in the long run the changes in taste also effect demand, especially the composition of food basket. With the rising income Engel's law starts operating, i.e., expenditure on food as a proportion of total income declines, and expenditure on foodgrains declines even faster. Normally, the demand for foodgrains will not fall so long as population continues to rise. Population growth will continue to propel the demand for food. Also, so long as a vast number of people are below the poverty line the increase in their income up to certain threshold would fuel demand for foodgrains. Based on these considerations various estimates of demand for foodgrains have been attempted. An exercise by Paroda and Kumar suggests that the demand for foodgrains by the year 2030 will range between 260 million tonnes to 264 million tonnes depending on the growth in per capita income (Paroda and Kumar, 2000). The other estimates of foodgrains demand are more or less in a similar range. The rate of growth in foodgrains production has to be substantially accelerated to meet the projected demand if we wish to adhere to the goal of food self-sufficiency.

With the emphasis on globalisation and market orientation, it is suggested in some quarters that a time has come to abandon the objective of food self-sufficiency and rely on international trade to obtain foodgrains, more so if we do not have a comparative advantage in producing additional food.

However, a large and poor country, such as India cannot afford to take the issue of sizeable quantities of imports of foodgrains lightly. The policy of food self-sufficiency, which has remained the cornerstone of our agricultural policy, paid us rich dividends. It encouraged our scientists to strive for higher productivity with better utilisation of resources and application of science and technology to make adequate quantities of food available for the growing masses. It is true, that with progressive integration of Indian economy (and Indian agriculture) with global economy we will not be able to totally ignore the principle of comparative advantage. Nevertheless, at the present stage of our development we cannot afford to take a doctrinaire approach in such vital a matter as foodgrains production. Apart from the fact that 'comparative advantage' is a rather nebulous concept, (more so its indicator, i.e., the border prices), there is ample evidence to show that international prices are more volatile. (Chand and Jha, 2000). An important issue that needs to be addressed is: should a large mass of poor consumers and poor producers be exposed to the uncertainty and instability in as vital a sector as the food sector?

Food self-sufficiency is not a matter of faith. We can review this policy once the internal and external circumstances change. In other words, this can be done when (a) a large portion of the workforce—at present estimated to be more than 50 per cent—is not dependent for their livelihood on foodgrains production; (b) a large number of households will not be spending a sizeable amount of their incomes on procuring their daily requirements of food; (c) the economy will not have the constraint of foreign exchange needed to import food; and (d) international trade regime ensures that our trading partners, who in most of the cases will be multinational companies from the developed countries, adhere to the 'rules of the game' (Vyas, 1998). We will have to wait atleast for five to 10 years before we can fully expose our food economy to the vagaries of international trade.

As is well known, India is now producing enough food, which if equitably distributed, can meet the calorie requirements of the citizens. However, the fact of the matter is that the available food is not equitably distributed and as a result the lower 30 per cent of the households do not have adequate intake of calories. Besides, as mentioned earlier, given the inadequate growth in foodgrains production, which in per capita terms, seems to have reached a plateau, and the continuing growth in population and incomes there is a clear danger of India becoming a foodgrains importing country. This is a risk which we cannot afford to take at least for the coming few years.

As our past experience suggests, the key requirements for raising the productivity level are enhancing public investments in agriculture, strengthening of supportive institutions of credit, marketing, etc., and above all a steady stream of productivity enchancing technology. The incentive prices do play their parts but their role should not be exaggerated. It should be remembered that farmers, like any one else, are interested in higher incomes not in higher prices *per se*. As long as the farmers are able to raise their income by increasing productivity, i.e., so long as income terms of trade are in favour of agriculture, merely raising prices has very little positive effect. In fact, such a policy can be detrimental to food security.

1. Input Subsidies

A disturbing feature of agricultural policy in our country is the large and growing amount of input subsidies. These subsidies are progressively losing their relevance and are becoming an unbearable fiscal burden. Input subsidies were justified on the ground that the agricultural producers, as well as consumers of the agricultural products are poor, and it is the state's obligation to subsidise the poor producers as well as poor consumers. This has come to be known as 'cheap-input cheap-output policy'. The case for subsidies was further strengthened by the argument that these lead to an increase in the use of inputs resulting in improved productivity. These, then, were the main arguments for the introduction and continuation of subsidies in agriculture.

Specifically a policy of subsidising inputs can be justified if:

(i) Introduction of a new input warrants sharing of risks by the state;

(ii) Use of subsidised inputs ensures continuous increase in productivity which is shared both by the producers and consumers;

(iii) Subsidising inputs is the only way to transfer income to the poor producers;

(iv) In the case of heavily traded products, the trading partners are resorting to overt or covert subsidisation, and there is no other way for redressal.

A close scrutiny of the functioning of the subsidy regime in agriculture suggests that none of the arguments for input subsidisation apply in the present circumstances. Neither fertilisers, nor irrigation, nor for that matter, power, is an unfamiliar input. The increasing use of the subsidised inputs is not contributing to productivity at the margin. In fact the reverse seems to be true. The marginal productivity of fertilisers and water applications is declining, largely because of weaknesses in the organisation and functioning of the extension system. There are better ways of transferring incomes to the producers such as by improving the income terms of trade. The provision for subsidies—and that too in the case of heavily-traded agricultural produce—can be justified only when our trading partners are not playing according to the rules of the game. Even in that case, we have to take recourse first to WTO provisions since we and practically all our trading partners are members of the same.

2. Role of State

A determined move, therefore, needs to be made to dismantle the subsidy regime in agriculture. It should be recognised, however, that our system has been addicted to subsidies. Also, in the case of some major subsidies—irrigation and power in particular—while the centre has a limited role, the states have to take the initiative. We need to take action in the following directions to enable us to ' retreat without disarray':

(i) Capping the subsidies in the current year's budget.

(ii) Announcing the progressive withdrawal of subsidies according to a phased programme.

(iii) Earmarking the amount thus saved from input subsidies as addition to the funds for strengthening rural infrastructure, research and extension.

(iv) Initiating well-defined measures to improve efficiency and plugging leakages in input supplies.

(v) Impressing upon the states the need for cost recovery, particularly in irrigation and power.

None of these are likely to prove to be easy options. But continuing the same regime will make future tasks all the more difficult. This places a major responsibility on the scientists for developing yield-enchancing technologies, and on administrators and policy makers for allocating adequate resources for promoting scientific efforts and for infrastructure building. Besides, it requires the leadership of the supportive institutions of credit, input supply and marketing to measure up to the challenge. These are difficult tasks. Raising administered prices by state fiat, on the other hand, is relatively easy.

However, the farming community will benefit, and our agriculture will become more sustainable if the productivity levels rise continuously. It is not the higher prices for agricultural produce but higher investment in scientific research and infrastructure and the strengthening of the supportive institutions, which are the keys to sustainable agricultural growth. The state has to take up the primary task of investing in these activities; the private investment can only complement public investment.

Another area where state policies have an important role to play in ensuring food security is that of maintaining relative *stability* of prices, and adequate availability of food in all regions while accounting, of course, for reasonable price differences due to transport and storage costs, and returns to labour and capital involved. This aspect is directly related to the functioning of the markets. There may be adequate supplies at the national level but its access over time and over space may be skewed. This is where the role of markets assumes crucial importance. The efficient markets should be able to move agricultural produce from producing regions to the consuming regions, from the flush harvest season to the lean post-harvest season, without increasing the costs beyond a justifiable limit. It is now well established that the food markets in India do perform these tasks, of adding place and time utilities, at reasonable costs. But this is true only in organised markets and that too for the crops which are widely traded. This, however, is not the case with respect to remote, inaccessible places, or for some of the so called 'minor' crops which the poor consume in larger quantities. In respect of these crops, both the seasonal price differences as well as the price differences between the producing and the consuming regions are unconscionably large. Here, the state can make its contribution in improving marketing efficiency by investing in infrastructure and the development of market places, and also by introducing regulatory measures to ensure that (a) there is free and fair competition, (b) the necessary information is available to the buyer and the sellers, and (c) there are no barriers to entry and exit.

The stability aspect of food security has another dimension where the role of state policies becomes important, and that relates to the element of risk and uncertainty. The poor producers as well as poor consumers are the worst hit by the instability in the production and/or prices of agricultural commodities. To some measure state instability in their production and prices is unavoidable. As in the area of overall production, in ensuring stability in production also, scientific research initiated by the state has played an important part, mainly by developing stress resisting varieties.

Furthermore, the state can mitigate to a great extent uncertainty about the availability and prices of agricultural commodities by initiating policies aimed at insuring crops, establishing forward markets creating and or strengthening storage and warehousing facilities, ensuring the orderly release of buffer stocks, etc. In India, the state policies have largely succeeded in meeting this objective. Yet much remains to be done, especially in the area of crop insurance.

III. ENTITLEMENT OF HOUSEHOLDS TO FOOD

Even if we can produce enough food and make it available in all seasons and in all regions, the problem of *entitlement* will have to be resolved. The major source of entitlement in our society is the stream of income which a household can claim. To the extent a household's income falls short of the cost of procuring nutritional food, food security looses its meaning. If we take poverty as an indicator of food insecurity (which, admittedly, is a rather rough approximation) we have in this country nearly one-third of the households who do not have adequate entitlement. The economic policies directed towards poverty alleviation have only been partially successful. Although these policies have been in place for the last 25 years or more, enough resources have been expended on poverty alleviation programmes (PAP) and, more importantly, there is a national consensus on pursuing these policies, our success has at best been partial. There are several reasons why we have not been able to reach the poor, and empower them to cross the poverty line. I have dealt with the reasons for the inadequate success of PAP on a different occasion (Vyas, 1999). Briefly, the success of these programmes depend on: the rate and composition of economic growth, access of the poor to assets, economic returns to their enterprises, congruence of the delivery systems to the needs of the poor, role played by the civil society institutions, nature of deprivations and the like.

There are two other aspects, which impinge on the entitlement for food in our country. One is the relative price of foodgrains in the market place, and other is their public distribution.

In India, till recently 'real' prices of foodgrains (i.e., prices of foodgrains after taking into account inflation in the general level of prices) have remained stable—in fact, they have marginally declined, mainly because of a rise in productivity in the foodgrains sector, coupled with the implementation of an integrated food policy. This policy comprises of minimum support price, procurement arrangements at the support price and public distribution of foodgrains through the PDS. It was possible to contain a rise in the 'real' prices of foodgrains by maintaining the right balance between the minimum support prices for producers and issue prices for the consumers. Once this balance is disturbed by an unjustifiable increase in the minimum support prices, or inordinate rise in the issue prices the real losers are the poor and food insecure, both in urban and rural areas. Policies which do not recognise the need for maintaining stability in the 'real' prices of foodgrains, adversely affect the food security of the poor. Indeed, this is one of the important indicators to judge whether the state is serious about ensuring food security for its people, especially the poor population.

IV. MAINTAINING STABILITY IN FOOD SUPPLY

My last point pertains to the entitlement of foodgrains to needy persons through the Public Distribution System. In India, we have developed a large network of fair-price shops where the grains are supplied out of the stocks procured by the state at prices which are generally below the ruling market prices, i.e., at the minimum support prices. It is argued that though the system is meant to meet the requirements of the poor, in effect it is taken advantage of by the 'not-so-poor'. It is also contended that the cost incurred on the PDS is unjustifiably high. There is force in both these comments. However, the alternative is not to abandon the system, but to ensure that proper targeting is done, and the distribution costs are controlled. For realising these objectives the involvement of the local level institutions can be extremely helpful. In our country such involvement could now be facilitated with the establishment of the Panchyat Raj System.

In the race between population growth and foodgrains productions, even when the income-induced demand for foodgrains is slackening, the state has a big role to play in ensuring the adequate availability of the same minimising instability and uncertainty, and initating appropriate measures to ensure access, especially of the poorer sections, to food. In this regard the economic agenda is clear. It would require encouraging production by investment in infrastructure and promoting scientific research and extension, by (i) strengthening supportive institutions of credit and marketing; (ii) providing appropriate subsidies and fixing fair procurement prices; (iii) regulating the markets to foster competition and discourage exploitation; and (iv) mitigating or at least minimising uncertainty by introducing measures such as crop insurance, establishing forward markets and fixing minimum support prices.

These are clearly the goals to which the state policies have to be directed. At the same time it should be recognised that food security is too complex an issue to be left only to the state to resolve. The markets and civil society institutions also have a role to perform towards achieving these objectives. In some situations they play a supplementary role; in others a watch-dog role, and on many more occasions a proactive role. (Vyas, 2000). It is only when the civil society institutions, markets and state policies converge that we will come closer to the ideal of food security for all.

(*This paper is based on the presentation made at 88th Conference of the Indian Congress, New Delhi*).

References

Chand, Ramesh and Jha, Dayanath (2000), *Trade Liberalisation, Agricultural Prices and Net Social Welfare* (mimeo).

Paroda, R.S. and Kumar, Praduman (2000), "Food Production and Demand in South Asia", *Agricultural Economics Research Review*, Vol. 13., No. 1

Vyas, V.S. (2000), "Ensuring Food Security—Role of the State, Market and Civil Society", *Presidential Address to 3rd Asian Conference of Agricultural Economists*, Jaipur.

——(1999), "Seven Lessons of Poverty Alleviation", (mimeo).

——(1998), "Agricultural Trade Policy and Export Strategy", *Presidential Address to 12th Annual Conference on Agricultural Marketing*, Jaipur.

6

Towards Newer Paradigms of Food Security

Yoginder K. Alagh

I. THE CONTEXT

It is time that the priorities of action and research changed from measurement of poverty and broad-based anti-poverty and employment programmes to a more focused attention on solving the problems of hunger and extreme deprivation. It is unlikely that this focused problem will be solved by a free market by itself. However, commodity and factor markets will have to be a large part of the solution. The poverty line currently used was developed by a Task Force the present author chaired, in the period 1977-79 and the poverty line has endured. We begin by discussing it and show that some of the rich behavioural characteristics of the earlier studies have given way to a very sterile posturing with little fresh analytical insights. The problem of hunger is more amenable to structural analysis and policy action. Indian data on hunger and deprivation are a part of a global discourse on the problem.

The measurement and correlation of hunger are broadly known in India, but the analysis is poor in comparison to the discussion in other countries, including some developing societies. The structure of organisations, management systems, information and decision support systems does not exist in India, to frontally attack the hunger problem. The global discussion of the systems to attack the problem of hunger is much better focused and a lot of action has been taken in this regard outside India. The problem of hunger will have to get into the issues of entitlements and, therefore, class and spatial correlates of consumption have to be identified, and more importantly, used in a management information system, which aims at solving the problem. Availability of foodgrains has to be accompanied with the employment and income generation programmes of a targeted kind.

It is well known that the widespread agricultural growth based on foodgrains and sustainable land and water development and management programmes, has a dual effect—food commodities become available at cheaper prices and employment is generated. Food producers are a large part of the poor and hungry segments of the workforce. This is another reason for precise demarcation of hunger zones—to identify targeted programmes.

Recent work with participative rural appraisal analysis suggests that the earning power of hungry households is related in a significant manner with the demographic status of the household (hungry households more often tend to be women headed or consist of disabled workers) and health status of the members of the household (morbidity significantly reduces economic status). On the positive side, hungry households in rural areas showed considerable dignity and desire to improve their status. The democratic polity was seen as a factor empowering them and in fact there was considerable resistance in classifying themselves as destitute or hungry. A hunger removal programme, embedded in a food security strategy will have to be a part of the wider process of diversification of Indian agriculture and larger exposure to trade sustainability considerations will also require release of land from low productivity cereals to more appropriate cropping sequences in different agro-climatic regimes.

The requirements of the policy regime are both broad-based and complex. Instead of an abstract discussion of past principles, we attempt in this paper to develop an integrated information and decision support system to achieve the objectives of a food security and hunger removal strategy as part of a diversifying trade consistent strategy. We posit such a system as part of a framework of decentralisation.

II. FOOD PRICES, POVERTY, HUNGER AND FOOD SECURITY

An increase in food prices makes the poor relatively worse off, as the classic study by Radhakrishna and Sarma (1975) has shown. A faster increase in food prices would make the poor justifiably feel relatively more deprived. With high food stocks and large foreign exchange reserves, these trends can be avoided; we must monitor these trends more closely and put into force remedial policies. Our concern is with the identification of the poor in a manner such that in a period of structural reform, targeted groups can be quickly isolated and remedial policies adopted.

The Expert Group on Estimation of Proportion and Number of Poor of the Planning Commission (for brevity Expert Group) has missed a good opportunity to provide an analytical framework and database for the next round of food security and employment policies (GOI, 1993). The world over 'expert groups' are identifying the hard-core poor and their empirical correlates and developing policies of direct intervention and institutional reform to help them. Recent international conferences show the richness of the material (WFP and FAO, 1993). The Indian report however stays aseptically away from relevance and has as a consequence also created no 'expert' waves.

Beginning with a literature review, the Expert Group states that the "early 1970s generated a rich and extensive literature on poverty", and that the "Task Force on Projections of Minimum Needs and Effective

Consumption Demand, January 1979, was able to bring together at one place the results of some of these studies and redefine the poverty line". (Since the present author was the chairman of this group for brevity we shall call it the Alagh Task Force) (GOI, 1979).

The Alagh Task Force made four important recommendations, two of which have been accepted by the expert group. First, the poverty norm at 2,400 kcal per person for rural areas and 2,100 kcal for urban areas, or the poverty line is 'anchored in a given calorie norm and the corresponding all-India consumption basket for 1973-74'. Second, it developed a procedure for updating the poverty norm for years for which household consumption surveys were not available. The expert group was 'in favour of using the same', as far as these practices are concerned.

A third recommendation of the Alagh Task Force was based on one of the most detailed demand and income distribution studies done anywhere in the world. Taking account of household budgetary survey data, price information and aggregate consumption patterns, it developed the income and price response of both poor and rich households separately, in rural and urban areas. This meant that income supplementation and public distribution policies working through pricing and dual markets (an open market and a rationing system) could be integrated quantitatively into commodity market and parastatal policies specifically aimed at households below the poverty line. The late D.T. Lakadawala (1977) and the present author (1994) have written about this extensively. The price elasticities of rich and poor Indians in rural and urban areas attracted Lakadawala immensely for, price theory, common sense and a concern for the poor were his forte up to the last day of his life. For example, if price elasticities of the kind contained in Table 1 estimated from the NSS consumer expenditure data of 1998 are known and the target of public distribution is given, it is possible to derive the open market share which would give the producer a price required to ensure long-run supply for an efficient firm (ibid., p. 262).

Table 1
Price Elasticities, 1998

	Rural		Urban	
Commodity	Persons below poverty line	Persons above poverty line	Persons below poverty line	Persons above poverty line
Cereals	-0.530	-0.161	-0.430	-0.099
Edible oils	-0.794	-0.589	-0.799	-0.417
Sugar	-0.941	-0.800	-0.740	-0.294

Source: Ravi (2001).

The Draft Sixth-Plan stated: It would be desirable to adopt a system of dual pricing in respect of selected goods of mass consumption. The rationale of such a policy is derived from the fact that price elasticity in respect of essential commodities—cereals, pulses, edible oils—is relatively higher for persons below the poverty line both in urban and rural areas (GOI, 1979).

The Fourth recommendation of the Alagh Group was to define a modified poverty line of hunger; this was the contribution of Sukhatme. The Expert Group strangely gives data in an annexure to show that the population proportions of hunger are less than 20 per cent, but does not say anything substantive about this in the main report. They also have nothing to say on the behavioural aspects of consumption of poor households. This is important since 'well behaved' results validate results and if the expert group had worked on these same numbers the problem could have been avoided. For example, the elasticities reported in Table 1 conform in the well-known requirements of demand theory, which enhances 'confidence' in the numbers.

The empirical results of the Expert Group need considerable discussion. They came out with the somewhat strange result that rural poverty in India is less than urban poverty in 1987-88—a drought year. Table 2 shows that according to them, urban poverty in that year was 40.12 per cent and rural poverty 39.06 per cent of the population. This is particularly so in some of the most advanced industrial states of India. As the table shows, according to the Group in 1987-88, in some of the worst hit states in the drought year, rural poverty was much lower than urban poverty. Thus, in Andhra Pradesh, rural poverty was 20.92 per cent but urban poverty was 44.63 per cent. In Gujarat, rural poverty was 28.67 per cent and urban poverty 39.63 per cent. In Karnataka, another badly hit state, rural poverty was 32.82 per cent but urban poverty 49.06 per cent. In Kerala, the corresponding numbers were 29.10 and 43.36 per cent. The same relative structure, according to the Group, was obtained in some of the poorest states. In Bihar, the numbers were 52.63 and 57.71 per cent, in Madhya Pradesh 41.92 and 48.17 per cent. States, which have high industrial growth rates and where the structure of the labour force has been transformed, urban poverty rates are also higher than rural poverty rates, according to the Group. This is a 'surprising' result in itself and should have raised many questions when estimated for states such as Gujarat, Maharashtra, Karnataka and Haryana.

The industrialised states with high urban poverty, according to the Group, have high proportions of urban male labour force in the manufacturing sector (25 to 30 per cent) and low and declining shares of agriculture in labour force. Bhalla (1983) and the present author (1986) had made the point in the mid-1980s that a structural transformation of the labour force has begun. Later work, including by a member of the Expert Group, confirmed that this transformation is on account of labour demand pull factors (Vaidyanathan, 1994). Hence the Expert Group's numbers on high urban poverty in these states need close scrutiny. They also have estimated 'facts', such as that urban poverty in Gujarat in some years is more than in Assam, or that poverty in Tamil Nadu is more than in Uttar Pradesh, and in West Bengal more than Bihar.

Table 2
Number and Percentage of Poor Based on Poverty Lines, 1987-88

State/UTs	Rural		Urban		Combined	
	No. of persons (lakhs)	Per cent of persons	No. of persons (lakhs)	Per cent of persons	No. of persons (lakhs)	Per cent of persons
Andhra Pradesh	94.89	20.92	72.88	44.63	167.77	27.20
Arunachal Pradesh	2.73	39.35	0.11	17.34	2.84	37.47
Assam	80.86	39.35	4.58	17.34	85.44	36.84
Bihar	370.36	52.63	69.48	57.71	439.84	53.37
Goa	1.32	17.64	1.42	33.71	2.74	23.42
Gujarat	75.95	28.67	52.63	39.63	128.58	32.33
Haryana	18.75	16.22	7.15	17.79	25.90	16.63
Himachal Pradesh	7.37	16.28	0.25	6.18	7.62	15.46
Jammu & Kashmir	13.96	25.70	2.40	14.82	16.36	23.20
Karnataka	93.96	32.82	68.39	49.06	162.35	38.14
Kerala	66.20	29.10	26.02	43.36	92.22	32.08
Madhya Pradesh	195.85	41.92	70.04	48.17	265.89	43.40
Maharashtra	185.59	40.78	108.59	38.99	294.18	40.10
Manipur	4.68	39.35	0.85	17.34	5.53	32.93
Meghalaya	4.89	39.35	0.59	17.34	5.48	34.60
Mizoram	1.68	39.35	0.33	17.34	2.01	32.52
Nagaland	3.05	39.35	0.35	17.34	3.40	34.85
Orissa	148.02	57.64	19.94	44.11	167.96	55.61
Punjab	16.78	12.60	7.77	12.91	24.56	12.70
Rajasthan	103.02	33.21	38.17	38.99	141.19	34.60
Sikkim	1.25	39.35	0.15	17.34	1.40	34.67
Tamil Nadu	160.67	45.80	82.54	43.88	243.20	45.13
Tripura	8.49	39.35	0.48	17.34	8.97	36.84
Uttar Pradesh	412.03	41.10	125.02	45.22	537.05	41.99
West Bengal	219.09	48.30	57.63	32.84	276.72	43.99
Delhi	0.06	1.29	12.74	16.91	12.80	16.04
A & N Island	0.80	45.80	0.32	43.88	1.12	45.24
Chandigarh	0.40	12.91	0.76	12.91	0.80	12.91
D and N Haveli	0.21	17.64	0.03	33.71	0.24	18.71
Lakshadweep	0.06	29.10	0.12	43.36	0.18	37.26
Pondicherry	1.35	45.80	1.80	43.88	3.15	44.68
All-India	2293.96	39.06	833.52	40.12	3127.48	39.34

Source: GOI (1993).

The Expert Group does not make any serious comment on the discrepancy between National Accounts (NAS) and National Sample Survey (NSS) estimates of per capita consumption expenditure, apart from relying only on the latter. This is a serious matter. One of the most careful analyses of such differences by Mukherjee in 1972 concluded that "without an intensive study of the discrepancy between the two sources of consumption data, it is not possible to conclude in favour of either". The arguments of their classic study are still valid but have not been discussed at all. This is particularly so when the Expert Group recognises that "NAS based estimates are higher by a very large factor for commodity groups like sugar, edible oils, clothing and footwear, durable consumer goods and rent, fuel and power" and that "NSS based estimates of cereals are higher than NAS based estimates". In the 1980s cereal consumption has not been rising but the consumption of sugar, etc., has been rising very fast along with aggregate calorie consumption per capita.

The poverty ratios for the year 1999-2000 released by the Planning Commission (Table 3) also show that urban poverty is higher in nine states (Andhra Pradesh, Gujarat, Haryana, Karnataka, Kerala, Madhya Pradesh, Maharashtra, Rajasthan and Tamil Nadu). These estimates also prove that there is a need for examining the methodology of the expert group.

Table 3

Number and Percentage of Population Below Poverty Line by States, 1999-2000 (30-day Recall Period)

		Rural		Urban		Combined	
Sl. no.	State	No. of persons (lakhs)	Per cent of persons	No. of persons (lakhs)	Per cent of persons	No. of persons (lakhs)	Per cent of persons
1	Andhra Pradesh	58.13	11.05	60.88	26.63	119.01	15.77
2	Assam	92.17	40.04	0.18	7.47	3.98	33.47
3	Bihar	376.51	44.30	49.13	32.91	425.64	42.60
4	Gujarat	39.80	13.17	28.09	15.59	67.89	14.07
5	Haryana	11.94	8.27	5.39	9.99	17.34	8.74
6	Jammu & Kashmir	2.97	3.97	0.49	1.98	3.46	3.48
7	Karnataka	59.91	17.38	44.49	25.25	104.40	20.04
8	Kerala	20.97	9.38	20.07	20.27	41.04	12.72
9	Madhya Pradesh	217.32	37.06	81.22	38.44	298.54	37.43
10	Maharashtra	125.12	23.72	102.87	26.81	227.99	25.02
11	Orissa	143.69	48.01	25.40	42.83	169.09	47.15
12	Punjab	10.20	6.35	4.29	5.75	14.49	6.16
13	Rajasthan	55.06	13.74	26.78	19.85	81.83	15.28
14	Tamil Nadu	80.51	20.55	49.97	22.11	130.48	21.12
15	Uttar Pradesh	412.01	31.22	117.88	30.89	529.89	31.15
16	West Bengal	180.11	31.85	33.38	14.86	213.49	27.02
	All-India	1932.43	27.09	670.07	23.62	2602.50	26.10

Source: GOI (2001).

The 1980s and 1990s record a much faster growth of agro-based consumption in the Indian demand basket. For example, per capita consumption of sugar goes up from 6.2 kg/year in 1975-76 to 14.9 kg/year (Table 4) and that level is not only much higher than in comparable countries, but also than in countries which have much higher levels of per capita income. Also, there has been a very rapid increase in consumption of non-crop based commodities like eggs and milk. Egg consumption per capita goes up from 15 to 30 per year in the period of 1975-98. Thus, as discussed in the author's Lal Bahadur Shastri Lecture, expansion and diversification of the consumption basket is basically driven by a higher growth performance in the 1980s (Alagh, 1994a and also see Radhakrishna and Ravi, 1990). This in turn leads to another problem.

Demand driven growth and diversification would be in serious jeopardy if the 1990s persist in low rates of aggregate growth. It needs to be noted that the agro-based items of consumption are important in the demand baskets of different income groups (ibid.). These consumer items are not for elite consumption alone (Table 4).

Table 4
Per Capita Consumption of Agricultural Processed Commodities in India

Sl.no.	Commodity	1955-56	1975-76	1990-91	1998-99
1	Foodgrains (per capita net production: two year average of kg ending with year)	155.6	158.5	180.6	176.7
2	Edible oil and vanaspati (kg/yr.)	3.2	4.2	6.5	11.7
3	Sugar (kg/yr.)	5.0	6.2	12.5	14.9
4	Textiles (cotton equivalents) (meter/yr.)	14.4	17.6	24.8	28.2
5	Tea (kg/yr.)	0.36	0.45	0.61	0.68
6	Milk (ltr/yr.)	4.7	4.6	6.3	7.5
7	Eggs (no/yr.)	5.3	15.5	26.0	30.4

Source: Rows 1 to 7, Government of India, *Economic Survey, 2000-01*, Vol. 2, pp. S-24, S-26.

The increase in average calorie consumption in India is from about 1,981 kcal in the early 1960s to around 2,235 kcal in the late 1980s (Table 5). With this record it would be difficult to justify poverty rates as high as 38 per cent, particularly when it is being argued that income distribution is more or less invariant through time. The average intake of the Indian has gone up by over 10 per cent in the last three decades. The highest improvement as we see in Table 4 is in the 1980s. (For the purpose of this calculation Akroyd conversion factors have been used. Foodgrain, edible oil, sugar, milk, eggs, meat, fruits and vegetables consumption have accounted for 50 cal/person/day: 50 cal have been added for other consumption.) There is no evidence to suggest that consumption inequality has increased in India. In fact, if at all, the evidence is the other way around. The nutrition and hunger situation has definitely improved. The procedure of state level price adjustment basically using state level consumption weights and all-India prices may have led to the problem in their estimates, in addition to the question of 'missing calories.'

Table 5
Average Daily Calorie Intake Per Indian

Year	Daily kcal/person
1961-63	1981
1969-71	2020
1979-81	2090
1988-90	2235

Source: Alagh (1994a).

The real issue of behavioural and spatial correlates to poverty at a level of disaggregation still needs examination, and it is no wonder that the policy approximations of a *Yugandhar* or a *Venugopal* have been more illuminating than some 'expert estimates'. The world over, poverty research is reaching a level where empirical work and modeling helps in developing food security and targeted employment augmentation programmes. Indian academic has to catch up. It has been decided that the PDS should be concentrated in areas (*taluka*) with concentrations of nutritionally-at-risk persons (mainly landless labourers). While the new definition of persons below the poverty line are not very helpful, the country can mount a decisive attack on the hunger problem. In the selected blocks, management information system should now be operationalised to monitor food prices, availability, and the nutritionally-at-risk population. ICAR and agricultural universities should also join a national effort to eradicate hunger in these areas with realistic technological and institutional answers. In the medium term, local agricultural plans must also be integrated with food security objectives.

III. HUNGER AND HUMAN SECURITY

Special programmes need to be formulated to remove hunger since trade and market dominated policy strategies can lead to rising food prices and affect poor farmers and landless labourers adversely. This has been shown by a number of Indian studies as documented by D.S. Tyagi (1990). The literature on the issue has been extensively dealt with by Tyagi and is not being repeated here.

The need for a well-focused scheme on hunger removal is being made globally and the Indian discussion will benefit from a summary of them.

1. Aspects of Social and Environmental Degradation: Hunger and Poverty

Human security implies safety from chronic threats such as hunger, disease and oppression, linking it to the broader concept of human development. One-third of the people in the world live on less than 2 US $ per day. Table 6 provides the number of people suffering from hunger and poverty in developing countries. More than one billion people in developing countries live without adequate housing, and an estimated 100 million are homeless (UNDP, 2000). What is it that makes individual households as well as national and regional societies vulnerable to hunger and famine? How does the affected population cope with vulnerability and risks? And how far can interdisciplinary research contribute to a reduction of these risks and strengthen the coping capabilities of these communities? Does environmental stress leading to famine situation has a different impact on women, children or the aged?

The questions about the linkages between hunger, poverty, land degradation, destruction of resources and demographic changes have been discussed for decades. The Brundtland Commission on Environment

Table 6
Hunger and Poverty in Developing Countries: 1994-96

Region	Hunger (1995)* (Million people)	Region	Poverty (1993) (Million people)
Africa	241	Sub-Saharan Africa	218.6
China	210	China	372.3
Eastern Europe and Central Asia	6.3	Eastern Europe and Central Asia	14.5
Latin America and the Caribbean	65	Latin America and the Caribbean	109.6
Middle East	29	Middle East and North Africa	10.7
South and South-east Asia	337	South Asia	514.7
North America	7	North America	0#
Pacific OECD	1	Pacific OECD	0#
Western Europe	3	Western Europe	0#
World	889	World	1313.9

Notes : For data on hunger, see Raskin et al., 1998; for data on poverty, see World Bank, 1999.
* Data for hunger are taken from the Reference Scenario in Raskin et al., 1998. See also Chapter 3.
\# A different measure of poverty is used for OECD countries.
Source: World Bank (1999), Stastical Annexe for data on poverty and FAO (1997) for data on hunger.

and Development stated: "Poverty is a major cause and effect of global environmental problems. It is theoretically futile to attempt to deal with environmental problems without a broader perspective that encompasses the factors underlying world poverty and international equality (WCED, 1987).

It is mainly the poor that suffer from famine, hunger and malnutrition. But not all poor people are equally vulnerable to hunger, and it is not always the poorest who are exposed to the greatest risks. There are many other factors that determine the vulnerability to hunger. These include the risk of exposure to crises, stress and shocks.

As vulnerability is not coincident with poverty, malnutrition or other indices of human deprivation, more research should be based on a better understanding of such environmental crises. Also public responses to improve the coping facilities of social groups should be assisted by targeted research and development projects, and not just by relief. A number of approaches have been chosen to address these problems (e.g., entitlement, empowerment, enfranchisement). Food security should be closely tied to human security. While food supply to the rural poor is still a major problem, more emphasis on urban food security is needed.

The general tendency to combat environmental and social forms of degradation as expressed in famine and poverty should not only be 'reactive' but should stress on preventive measures. The term 'preparedness' should move into the centre of attention. This leads to the increased necessity of early warning systems. Policy makers have already reacted by establishing short and medium term early warning systems for the most vulnerable regions. The Famine Early Warning System being developed by the United Nations is an example of such a reaction. However, without accurate socio-economic and political information from the field, such computer assisted warning systems based mainly on biophysical parameters, will not be able to accurately predict famines in a given region.

The Indian discussion is not particularly illuminating as shown earlier. We only know that according to the NSS people who claimed that those who do not have two square meals a day went down to less than a twelfth of the population in 1993 from around a fifth in 1983 (Table 7). But the sub-regional and socio-economic correlates of this are not known.[1] Hence the need for indicators and information systems.

Table 7
Incidence of Hunger in Rural India, 1983-1993

Sl. no.	Year	Incidence of hunger (%)
1.	1983	19.0
2.	1993	7.0

Source: National Sample Survey Organisation.

2. Information System Requirement

The requirement of work to develop information systems in the light of the above description will be three-fold—the first exercise to be done will be of a policy kind. These will outline the relationship among economic reform policies, the strategy of agricultural policies being developed, and food security policies. The emphasis here will be on the pursuit of market policies to improve availabilities and distribution channels, particularly in areas with less developed infrastructure. The minimum degree of government intervention of a physical kind—distribution of food and subsidies in kind, given equity objective—will have to be determined. The study will have to begin with a reasonable description of the existing institutions involved in decision-making roles regarding food security like ministries, parastatals, etc., and changes taking place in these roles. Also, the set of economic policies towards agriculture to ensure steady improvement in food availability will need to be worked out as part of increasing reliance on market policies in the sector. This part of the work will require policy analysis, synthesis of existing studies and development of operational food security policies. It will include high level policy judgments to develop indicators for decision making as outlined above, also the nature of demand for food security analysis required in the next phase, for example, commodity coverage of policies and nature of interventions expected.

The second set of work requirements will relate to data requirements of the decision needs spelt out above. Again this work will need to be spelt out in detail. The third set of work requirements will relate to models and information system formats. Quantitative models of different kinds will be needed to 'forecast' base level indicators in a consistent manner.

Generally, information on prices and quantities for recent periods will not be known. Three additional formal models may be required. The first will be optimal stocking models under uncertainty. The second will be policy models with government policies working through food demand and supply which may be called market determined models. The third kind will be questions of development of information systems both for numeric and file based systems in an efficient manner.

IV. DECISION MAKING SYSTEM FOR FOOD SECURITY

Assuming that a careful analysis of food availabilities and vulnerable sectors of the population is completed, we now turn our attention to the requirements of decision making for a food security system.

1. National Level Decision Making

The national decision making level will be pivotal for food security. Major critical decisions will have to be made at this level. Illustrative kinds of decisions will be as follows:

(i) Purchase of food items in international markets, or establishing access, for example, through 'future' markets, or recourse to bilateral or multilateral agencies, for example, 'food aid' or 'cereal facilities';

(ii) Decisions on adjustment of domestic stocks through national policies. These may include purchase or sale of public stocks and attempts to influence private inventories, as also the related questions of desired levels of domestic prices of food items;

(iii) Use of support prices, tariff mechanisms and domestic taxes, restrictions and subsidies;

(iv) Optimal internal stock movements and the related question of domestic availabilities and price spreads in regional markets;

(v) Access and vulnerability question of classes of consumers, for example in mofussil areas, or categories like women, children, the unemployed and the destitute or disabled;

(vi) Short-run decisions relating to financing, credit and foreign exchange requirements of operational food policies;

(vii) Decisions with a medium-term horizon like assessment of food demand, incentives and support policies for domestic producers, development of improved processing and marketing infrastructure, standardisation, nutritional and quality aspects, and employment and income supplements for marginal populations and areas.

It is quite obvious that national decision systems support will be required at core economic policy-making centres relating to food security, for example, the Cabinet, Finance Ministry, Planning Ministry and in this case the Civil Supplies, Rural Development and Agriculture Ministries. Second, the same will be required for sectoral levels, for example, Health

Ministry and Local Government Ministry. Finally, the national level parastatals and institutes may require such information, such as the Central Bank, Agricultural Bank and nutrition and agricultural technology related institutions. It needs to be noted that while the decisions and agencies taking them have been listed separately, the information system itself will play a coordinating and integrating role. A decision to import, for example, has to be based on simultaneous considerations of expected international and domestic prices and availabilities, both with government and likely behaviour of private trade. While the output for the decision makers of the decision support system will be a select list of indicators required by him, in these will have to be integrated, processes of reasoning and analysis. These will be in the nature, to the extent possible, of a comprehensive set of models, but will most certainly consist of a set of sub-models operationalised at the level of international markets, the national market, regional markets and different segments of the population. Core scarcities will have to be incorporated; for example, in the short run domestic and foreign exchange resources, transport and marketing infrastructure, and in the medium term sustainable land water resources availabilities, estimated demands and policy generated parameters emerging from the structural adjustment programme and, in particular, the nation's projected agricultural strategy for the 1990s.

2. State Level Decision Making

At the state level the requirements of information for decisions will be more direct and pressing. These will include data of a continuous kind on prices and quantities marketed in agricultural markets and retail prices by location. If base level models show, as is likely, a relationship between local food production and local prices, then estimates for area, production and yield and forecasts for the current agricultural season will be required. Data on government stocks and improvements will be needed. If possible, effort should be made to develop indicators of private stocks. Direct data from trade channels is a possibility. Alternately, stock movements or market arrival or turnover data may be used. If none of these are available, estimates may have to be inferred from price data and movements in it, for which a back up relational model may be required. At the market level, it will be important to standardise in terms of quality, weight and related considerations. Quality noise can distort price data in a significant manner.

On the demand side, population and workforce data will be required by location, sex and age distribution. Forecasts for post census years will be necessary. The Benchmark analysis of household budgetary surveys of the kind conducted by statistical survey agencies or the nutrition survey of the kind undertaken by the National Nutrition Institute will be used to prepare indications of 'vulnerable' or 'at risk' segments of the population. Their magnitude and location will have to be constantly updated.

Again modelling effort will be required. Three kinds of efforts can be anticipated. The first will be the attempts at updating data bases with historical information being continuously updated in a reasonably accurate manner, ensuring consistencies with currently available information of a limited kind. The second will be behavioural modelling, for example, of demand-supply markets and price impacts. The third requirement will be aggregating of market information to regional and national aggregates. This is a complex problem since the regions are open economies.

Information requirements for medium term decisions at the state level will be of very high priority, as they would relate to higher levels of efficiency and capabilities of the system to meet food security needs through time. Three kinds of broad requirements can be indicated to outline the nature of work requirements for the information system for decision support. Each would need considerable operational detailing. The first would relate to expansion of supply potentials, the second to marketing, trading, distribution and information infrastructure and the third to improvements in access to food by different segments of the population.

Information on expansion of agricultural supply potential at the state level would be available in the five year plan. In our context, this would relate to expansion of land and water availabilities either through investment plans or improved efficiency of water use.

For food security the important question will be the medium term economic price incentives, access to improved and cheaper inputs, and credit policies such that the economic environment is to encourage expansion of agricultural potential or improved use of existing resources for food crops. Such policies would vary depending on the agro-climatic regime, for example, in the different soil and water regimes; they would also vary between the old lands and those recently reclaimed—as also those areas, which primarily depend on canal irrigation and those on groundwater use or both.

As the reform process strengthens itself, the effort will have to be taken to work out operationally the concept detailed in economics for agricultural strategy in the 1990s, namely, the long-range marginal cost of agricultural supply potential in each region, and to encourage policies towards output prices and input availabilities and key in approximately this supply price objective. This would encourage peasant households to meet the desired output objectives, expand food supply possibilities as part of this effort and more importantly, generate additional income and employment, which can come on the medium term only through widespread agricultural development.

The attempt will have to be to cost and economically evaluate water and land development schemes, since this would provide the information back up for implementing concrete policies for food supply and income/ employment generation outcomes of an operational kind. Examples are given in the World Development Report 1992 and in the investment proposals of the Agricultural Bank's national agricultural policy paper.

Marketing information and distribution infrastructures relate with food security by ensuring access to available supplies in an efficient manner. Regional spreads in food prices emerge from market imperfections. Generally, regions of food deprivation or access difficulties, i.e., upper hills and rural areas outside the valleys and deltas, are also areas of poor communications and agriculture marketing infrastructure. Improved information on food prices is the first step, but wider and more efficient markets are very important. Modern communication and data networking facilities should be used not only to collate, analyse and transmit data from rural markets, but for interactive communication.

As the rural economy diversifies, there is every reason for the peasant in upper hills or other backward areas, for example, to have available to him data on prices of crops to be considered by him for sowing, in other regions and in other countries, with which his output will compete at harvest time. Thus, extra superior long cotton prices in the Philippines or Pakistan may also be important for his decision.

Information systems will, of course, have to be built up on storage facilities, stock and movements of public stocks of food items. Efficient deployment of such stock through regions and time is important from the cost saving angle of public interventions. Inventory management under uncertainty and optimal transportation models become important here – as also improved storage processes. Seasonal aspects of the crop season and post-harvest assessments of stocks and prices are generally necessary for sound policy decisions.

Problems like iron deficiency in women, female rural illiteracy, low nutritional levels in some areas, and emerging trends of decline in protein/ energy intake in some population segments hit by adjustment, may need to be isolated and reversed targeting of deliveries and social adjustment programmes of short run employment and income generation may need to be developed. Data bases which will provide labour market trends, information on successful community intervention strategies and filtering data mechanisms for isolating the truly needy populations at the household level will also be required. Information will also have to be planned for taste patterns, food storage, cooking and consumption habits and local technologies, either traditional or new, with application possibilities for resolving food gaps in an efficient manner. Delivery systems, which work particularly in market channels integrated with community efforts or public objectives, will need to be actively searched for.

V. GENERAL CONSIDERATIONS

While decision making requirements at each level will be specific, the data bases will need to be in a common format and with uniform concepts. This will introduce system complexities. Aggregation will have to be conceptually possible both through space (village market—household—governorate—national—global) and real time (week—season—year—farmers' investment horizon of medium term). Coding and conceptual problems of a fairly complex kind will need to be planned for and resolved. Numerical data systems will have to be compatible with modelling as well as indicator requirements. In addition, life-based systems of a non-numeric kind will also be required.

1. Preliminary List of Indicators

In view of the above discussion, a very preliminary illustrative list of indicators to be developed by a food security information system is discussed below. This list is prepared by way of examples. In the first phase, the emphasis will be on collecting information at the national level and developing information systems at this level. Such information, of course, has also a regional (rural/urban: state, market centre) component, but the purpose of the exercise will be a national food security decision system.

2. National Level Indicators for Short-run Decisions

Some of the required indicators for short-run decisions will be:

(i) Estimates of public stocks of food items; beginning/middle/end of each crop season; comparisons through years; deviation from desired level of stocks, at different times of the year; location of stocks.

(ii) Price trends of food items and comparisons with earlier years; seasonally adjusted trends; variation and spread between markets through space; wholesale-retail spread.

(iii) Estimates of private trader stocks of food items at agricultural/ wholesale market levels or inferences on them from price trends.

(iv) Crop output expectations.

(v) International price trends. For example, wheat in Chicago/ Winnipeg/Argentina/Australia, etc.; international stock change, future markets' trends.

(vi) Short-run domestic demand trends; fluctuations in income and impact.

(vii) Weather fluctuations, disasters, food import indicators.

(viii) Estimates of infrastructure relating to food performance; storage capacities; performance of milling industry/cold storage; transport; port capacities.

(ix) Agricultural credit for trade/farm operations.

(x) Government decisions on support prices, relation to market trends/costs of production.

(xi) Trends in food risk and nutritionally-at-risk segments of the population.

(xii) Taxes/tariffs/quantitative restrictions on food movements; domestic and abroad.

(xiii) Major technological achievements relating to food availability, transport, processing.

(xiv) Food aid indicators.

3. Medium-term Indicators at National Level

(i) Expected increase in agricultural potential in the next three to five years; realistic assessments of plans.

(ii) Expected trends in food crop acreages.

(iii) Expected increases in demand for food items.

(iv) Expected changes in price environment for agricultural sector; outputs/inputs.

(v) Policy adjustment expected in economic incentives to agriculture and their impacts particularly on food items.

(vi) Expected developments in agricultural markets/storage/cold chains.

(vii) Impact of economic policies on food demand.

(viii) Likely trends in nutritionally-at-risk populations and their regional spread.

(ix) Food aid trends.

(x) International price trends in view of policy changes expected, i.e., GATT agreements.

(xi) Major changes in regional demand/supply configuration in three to five years such as new cities, new agricultural lands, development and impact on food availability.

VI. CONCLUSION

We sum up the alternatives available in the schematic framework in the Panel below. Our own preference is for alternative I, but both are listed to clarify the issues for debate.

Alternatives for Food Policy

A. Availability

Medium Term (three year)

Alternative I

1. Maintain, as stated by the World Bank a long range marginal cost based agricultural price policy to achieve high agricultural growth such that the farmer gets an adequate rate of return on fresh investment and utilisation of existing capacity based on development of soil and water. Align agricultural prices and input prices with global prices as in (1) and (2) in alternative II. Intervene on either side if rates of return fall below required levels of World Bank recommended LRMC (long range marginal cost); work generally with tariff and tax policies; if absolutely necessary, agricultural support prices and consequent purchases by parastatals to maintain such prices. The objective would be to maintain economic environment in which agricultural supply potential expands by about 4 per cent annually.

2. Align relative crop prices to international prices, but at the margin build in an edge for important food crops like wheat, oil and sugar (possibly, milk?). Operate the system within the constraints of the GATT framework.
3. Policies to be designed to improve the economic incentive structure for farmers; special care to be taken for new lands and areas of low capacity use. Emphasis on market based solutions. In well identified problem areas development of cooperatives and public investment packages, for example, completion and modernisation of canal systems, drainage policies, agricultural research and extension strategies. Development of agricultural markets, private channels for inputs, agricultural credit markets, etc. State may need to play demonstration role.
4. Phase out widespread public distribution systems, but maintain a minimum system for limited supplies of a small basket of commodities (bread, oil and sugar) to specified vulnerable sections of society, i.e., poor.
5. Households particularly in areas where hunger and anaemia incidence is higher, school children, pregnant and lactating mothers in well defined areas.

Alternative II

1. Adjust agricultural output and input prices in global prices and ensure availabilities at that level. Abolish quantitative interventions in domestic markets and import restrictions and export quota. Phase out commodity and input trade by parastatals. Agricultural investment would depend on the impact of the emerging international economic environment for the agricultural sector in the developing world. At the present phase it is reasonable to expect that increased market orientation will improve resource use efficiency in agriculture.
2. Improve marketing channels such that import and export of specific commodities can be eased out and made more efficient. Let international trade even out the impact of fluctuations in domestic output.
3. Development of markets for agricultural produce and agricultural inputs. Reduction of tariff and tax barriers. Phasing out of state and parastatal activity. Research and demonstration role of state to continue.
4. A minimum degree of regulation to continue in view of environmental and other concern.
5. Abolish all distribution interventions in a phased manner.

Alternative I	Alternative II
B. Access	
1. The widespread agricultural growth programme would generate employment/income. To be supplemented with special employment programmes integrated with rural/urban infrastructure—economic development programmes. Emphasis on voluntary organisations, community participation programmes. Selectivity to be ensured. 2. Improvements in markets to ensure access to supplies at favourable prices. 3. Nutrition education and technology programmes to improve access to nutrition with limited budgets. Emphasis on literacy, drinking water, women's programmes. 4. Public distribution systems or intervention mechanisms like food stamps as a method of last resort. Phasing policies will have to be worked out in each alternative.	1, 2 and 3 as in Alternative I
C. Stability	
1. Improve market channels so that inter-regional inter-seasonal and inter-year price spreads are minimised. 2. Introduce future markets to stabilise prices. 3. Government inventory policies with domestic purchases and imports to work on the margin with well developed inventory management rules, to operate food prices in a specified band. 4. Minimum supplies to be ensured on a regular basis in specified regions/for limited supplies to specified households/classes.	1 and 2 as in Alternative I
D. Short run	
1. Use imports to even out fluctuations in domestic production of a selected basket of food commodities in particular those in which limited public distribution for vulnerable sections is required. Such imports will supplement the domestic stocks which may emerge from the pursuit of an LRMC policy as outlined above. 2. Develop optimal inventory and stocking policies with the aim of influencing food prices, particularly in backward areas. Work through markets. 3. Design and work out optional distribution policies with the objectives of minimising cost of public intervention mechanisms.	Let trade flows bring prices close to international levels, taking transport and distribution margins into account. At such prices supplies should be perfectly elastic.

Notes

1. A significant exception is Rao, Sharma and Shrivastava (1999).
2. Desired level of stocks will be developed by inventory; risk adjustment on international markets/futures.

References

Alagh, Y.K. (1994), *Indian Development Planning and Policy*, Second Edition, Vikas, Delhi, Chapters 2 and 4.

——(1994a), "Planning and Policies for Indian Agricultural Research", *XXV Lal Bahadur Shastri Memorial Lecture*, February, Indian Council of Agricultural Research, New Delhi.

——(1986), *Some Aspects of Planning Policies in India*, Vora, Allahabad.

Bhalla, Sheila (1983), *Growth Employment and Wages in Indian Agriculture*, Jawaharlal Nehru University, Delhi.

FAO (1997), *World Food Conference 1997*, Food and Agricultural Organisation, Rome.

GOI (2001), *Mid-term Review of the Ninth Five Year Plan*, Planning Commission, Government of India, New Delhi.

——(1993), *Report of the Expert Group on Estimation of Proportion and Number of Poor*, Perspective Planning Division, Planning Commission, Government of India, Delhi.

——(1979), *Report of the Task Force on Projections of Minimum Needs and Effective Consumption Demand*, Planning Commission, (PPD), Government of India, Delhi.

Lakadawala, D.T. (1977), "Growth, Unemployment and Poverty", *Presidential Address to the Indian Society of Labour Economics*, Tirupati.

Mukherjee, M. and Chaterji, G.C. (1990), "Trends in Distribution of National Income, 1950-51 to 1965-66", in Krishnaswamy, K.S. (ed.), *Poverty and Income Distribution*, Oxford University Press, Delhi.

Rao, V.M.; Sharma, Alakh N. and Srivastava, Ravi (1999), *Voices of the Poor*, Institute for Human Development, New Delhi (mimeo).

Ravi, C. (2001), *Complete Demand System, Welfare and Nutrition: An Analysis of Indian Consumption Data*, Ph.D. Dissertation, Centre for Economic and Social Studies, Hyderabad.

Radhakrishna, R., and Sarma, Atul (1975), *Price Indices by Income Class in Rural and Urban Areas*, Sardar Patel Institute of Economics and Social Research, Ahmedabad.

—— and Ravi, C. (1990), *Food Demand Projections for India*, Centre for Economic and Social Studies, Hyderabad.

Tyagi, D.S. (1990), *Managing India's Food Economy Publications*, Sage, New Delhi.

UNDP (2000), *Human Development Report*, Oxford University Press, New York.

Vaidyanathan, A. (1994), "Employment Situation: Some Emerging Perspectives", *Economic and Political Weekly*, Vol. 29, No. 50, December 10.

WCED (1987), *Report of the World Commission on Environment and Development* (Brandtland Commission), Geneva.

WFP and FAO (1993), *World Food Conference*, World Food Programme and FAO, Rome.

World Bank (1999), *World Development Report*, Washington, D.C.

7

World Trade Organisation and Food Security

S. Mahendra Dev

I. INTRODUCTION

The inclusion of Agreement on Agriculture (AOA) under World Trade Organisation (WTO) agreement was a watershed in the history of world trade reforms. The AOA and other agreements like trade-related intellectual property rights (TRIPS), sanitary and phytosanitary measures (SPS) are expected to have considerable impact on Indian agriculture the performance of which has significant implications for the employment and incomes of a majority of the population. There have been concerns on food security in India with the implementation of the WTO Agreement on Agriculture in 1995. The broad objective of this paper is to examine (a) the implications of AOA for Indian agriculture and food security; and (b) suggest measures for improving food security in India. Specifically, it addresses the following questions:

(a) What are the characteristics of Indian agriculture and how has it performed?

(b) What are the conditions or rules provided under Agreement on Agriculture (AOA)?

(c) How does AOA impact or influence on food security and agriculture in India?

(e) What measures are needed to improve the viability of agriculture and food security in India?

These issues are discussed in sections 2, 3, 4 and 5, respectively. The concluding section presents a summary of the issues discussed in the paper.

II. CHARACTERISTICS AND PERFORMANCE OF INDIAN AGRICULTURE

As a background to our analysis on WTO and food security, it is important to know the characteristics of Indian agriculture and how it has performed over the years. It is well known that the Indian economy is predominantly agrarian as far as the disposition of the workforce is concerned. Apart from the direct effect of agriculture growth on the workers dependent on agriculture, its indirect benefits and linkages with the rest of the economy are also important. This is because, agricultural growth has an economy wide impact and can also achieve equity if it spreads across poor regions.

One of the paradoxes of Indian agriculture is that there has been a significant decline in its share in GDP, while its share in employment is still 60 per cent. Therefore, demographic pressures on land have increased over the years. As a result, disparities between labour productivity in agriculture and non-agriculture also increased. The fact that small and marginal farmers dominate Indian agriculture assumes importance in the context of trade in farm products because in international trade, the small farmer in India has to compete with large farmers in the US, Europe and many other countries.

Growth of Indian Agriculture in the Post-independence Period

In terms of growth, the performance of Indian agricultures has been quite impressive in the post-independence period. As against the all crop output growth of around 2.7 per cent per annum during this period, that in the first half of 20th century was around 0.3 per cent, indicating a significant increase in the output after the country's independence. The growth of agriculture in GDP in the 1980s and 1990s was 3.03 per cent and 3.05 per cent per annum respectively. The steady growth of aggregate output at the national level hides a great deal of variation in the performance of different crops and regions. While wheat and rice have benefited from the green revolution, others like coarse cereals and pulses have not improved their performance. In the 1990s, there has been a shift towards non-cereal crops like oilseeds, fruits and vegetables. The share of allied activities like milk production, poultry, and fisheries has increased during the period. And yet India's share in world trade is negligible though the share of agriculture in world agriculture production is not insignificant. The WTO is expected to provide, at least theoretically, opportunities for exports of several agricultural commodities from India.

The economic reforms in India since 1991 have improved the incentive framework and agriculture has benefited from reduced protection to industry. Further, the terms of trade for agriculture improved and private investment in it increased. Export of commodities, particularly cereals, improved, and market reforms have resulted in the removal of domestic and external controls. However, the 1990s saw the emergence of concerns on agriculture and food security in particular. The general concern is that reforms have neglected agriculture in the 1990s as is reflected in agriculture growth during the 9th plan period (1997-2002) which is only 2.1 per cent per annum. There is also a concern over the decline in the growth rate of productivity and the unsatisfactory food management—we have an accumulation of 60 million tonnes of foodgrains in buffer stock with 260 million people living below the poverty line. Moreover, there had been no increase in public investment in agriculture during the nineties while diversification led to risk and uncertainty in the period.

As regards trade policies in India, during the last five decades, these have been of a highly interventionist nature and discriminated against agriculture. In particular, basic foods like cereals were highly regulated and private trade was practically banned during the period 1950-1995. Whatever little trade existed was restricted to basmati or maize imports for poultry. On the external trade front, the year 1995 marked the onset of a new era for agriculture. It saw the inclusion of agriculture in the Uruguay Round for the first time. Notably, the rules of trade in agriculture were rewritten under AOA.

III. WTO AND AGREEMENT ON AGRICULTURE

The developed countries have been subsidising their agriculture and selling their produce at artificially lower prices. This shows that the playing field is highly uneven as the principle of comparative advantage in international trade is not followed. Similarly, developing countries have been taxing or discriminating against agriculture by heavily protecting their industry and through overvalued exchange rates. Here also, the principle of comparative advantage is not adhered to. However, some poor countries need some protection because of their inherent disadvantages in infrastructure, technology and skills. Institutional arrangements such as the WTO are, therefore, important for ensuring that level playing field is observed by trading nations so that the principle of comparative advantage can have a free and fair play (Rao, 2001). As a founder member and signatory to the General Agreement on Tariffs and Trade (GATT), and a member of the WTO as the former has been revamped after its reorgnisation, India committed itself to dismantling of trade barriers.

While the subject of agriculture was discussed even in some earlier GATT rounds, the issue of agricultural subsidies and the consequent distortions in trade was not because of pressures from the US and Europe. In recent times, the protection given to agriculture by European Union was much higher than that to agriculture in the US. Partly due to pressures from the US, the subject of agriculture and subsidies was brought into the agenda of the Uruguay Round. The WTO Agreement on Agriculture (AOA) came into force with effect from January 1, 1995. It has stipulated a six-year implementation period for developed countries and 10 years for developing countries. The three pillars of AOA are: Market Access, Domestic Support and Export Competition. These are discussed below.

1. Market Access

Market access implies access to or penetration of markets protected by restrictions imposed over the years. It aims to replace quantitative restrictions on imports by appropriate tariffs, which would be brought down gradually. According to AOA, the developed countries should reduce their tariffs by 36 per cent over six years (2000 AD), while developing countries should do so by 24 per cent over 10 years (2004 AD). As per the agreement the member countries are committed to reduce duty levels to those as on 1986-88 and the least developed countries are exempted from any reduction in tariffs. Special and Differential Treatment (SDT) is given in some respects and exemption from liberalising was given to any agricultural product that is predominantly staple in the traditional diet. Further, AOA permits quantitative restrictions (QRs) for a limited period as per the balance of payments clause (BOP). Accordingly, India was initially allowed to retain the restrictions for the stipulated period but was required to remove them from April, 2000. The agreement further provides for permitting countries to increase their access to markets from a minimum of 3 per cent of the base period (1986-88) to 5 per cent in 2000.

2. Domestic Support

The Domestic Support permitted under AOA is specified through a ceiling on the aggregate measure of support (AMS). The AMS is defined as an annual aggregate of market support, direct payments and other subsidies (some are exempted). The calculation of AMS covers product specific support and non-product specific support. The former is done through (a) market price support; (b) non-exempt direct payments; and (c) other non-exempt subsidies. Total non-product specific support (e.g., subsidies on electricity, credit, fertiliser, transport, irrigation, livestock feed, crop insurance etc.) is available to several crops taken together. Minimum trade distorting measures like provision of government assistance for general services like (a) research, pest and disease control, training, extension and advisory services; (b) domestic food aid; and (c) direct payment to producers through government participation in income insurance and safety nets, relief from natural disasters, and environmental assistance programmes referred to as 'Green Box' measures are exempted from AMS calculations. 'Blue box' measures representing direct payments to farmers under production limiting programmes are also exempted. Measures like investment subsidies and agricultural input services to low income and resource-poor producers are exempted under SDT. The product specific AMS is calculated as the gap between fixed external reference price and the administered price in the domestic economy. The external reference price is 1986-88. The non-product specific support applies to all commodities. AOA fixes AMS ceiling for both product specific and non-product specific subsidies. The ceiling is fixed at 10 per cent of the total value of agricultural production for developing countries and 5 per cent of that for developed countries. This level is called *di minimus* level. If the AMS exceeds this level, developing countries have to reduce theirs by 13.3 per cent over 10 years and developed countries, by 20 per cent in six years.

3. Export Competitiveness

AOA requires member countries to effect reductions in export subsidies over a time period. The commitment on export subsidy pertains to reduction in (a) the total budgetary outlays on export subsidies, and (b) the total quantity of exports covered by the subsidy. These reductions are to be brought about on a product specific basis. The developed countries should reduce the value of their expenditure on export subsidies by 36 per cent and that on the quantity covered under export subsidies by 21 per cent over six years.

The targets for reduction in agricultural subsidies and protection under three pillars of AOA are summarised in Table 1.

Table 1
Reduction in Agricultural Subsidies and Protection Agreed in the Uruguay Round

	Developed countries 6 years: 1995-2000	Developing countries 10 years: 1995-2004
Tariffs		
Average cut for all agricultural products	-36%	-24%
Minimum cut per product	-15%	-10%
Domestic support		
Cuts in total (AMS) support for the sector	-20%	-13%
Export subsidies		
Value of subsidies (outlays)	-36%	-24%
Subsidised quantities	-21%	-14%

Notes: 1. Least developed countries do not have to reduce tariffs or subsidies. The base level for tariff cuts was the bound rate before January 1, 1995; or, for unbound tariffs, the actual rate charged in September 1986 when the Uruguay Round began.
2. Only the figures for cutting export subsidies appear in the agreement. The other figures were targets used to calculate countries' legally binding 'schedules' of commitments. Each country's specific commitments vary according to the outcome of negotiations. As a result of those negotiations, several developing countries chose to set fixed bound tariff ceilings that do not decline over the years.

Source: WTO (2002).

4. Sanitary and Phytosanitary Measures (SPS), Trade-related Intellectual Property Rights (TRIPS) and Non-trade Concerns

The SPS agreement basically aims at ensuring the provision of safe food for human consumption. With a view to providing a system for food safety and for regulating animal and plant health, the agreement recognises that governments have the right to take sanitary and phytosanitary measures but that they should not arbitrarily or unjustifiably discriminate between members. In order to harmonise sanitary and phytosanitary measures as widely as possible, member countries are encouraged to base their measures on international standards, guidelines and recommendations where they exist. This should ensure that the commodities consumed by the people of the importing country are safe and enable them to lead to a healthy and active life. In order to ensure that the adoption of a new SPS regulation does not create any trade barriers, the agreement provides for a reasonable interval between its publication and its enforcement and further for "longer time-frames for compliance" for developing countries. The basic purpose of these provisions is to provide sufficient time to the producers in developing countries to adapt their products to the requirements of the new regulations.

The agreement on Trade-Related Intellectual Property Rights (TRIPS) provides for the patenting of all life forms including plants and micro-organisms and requires a switch over from the process patenting to product patenting. Patent protection will be available for a period of 20 years for all inventions, whether of products or processes, in almost all fields of technology. Plant varieties, however, must be protected either by patents or by a *sui generis* system (such as the breeder's rights provided in a UPOV Convention).

The AOA provides significant scope for governments to pursue important 'non-trade' concerns such as food security, environmental protection, structural adjustment, rural development, poverty alleviation, and so on. Article 20 says that the negotiations have to take non-trade concerns into account suggesting that, most countries accept the fact that agriculture is not only about producing food and fibre but also has other functions, including those of meeting non-trade objectives. The question debated in the WTO is whether 'trade distorting' subsidies or subsidies outside the 'green box' are needed in order to help agriculture perform its many roles.

IV. IMPACT OF AOA ON INDIAN AGRICULTURE AND FOOD SECURITY

The implementation of Agreement on Agriculture (AOA) under WTO has raised concerns in India about the possibility of its destroying food security. These are justified because agriculture provides a lot of employment and food accounts for a major share of the expenditure of the poor. Some of these concerns are:

(i) Trade liberalisation under AOA and integration of Indian agriculture with world markets through elimination of quantitative restrictions and reduction in tariffs would lead to huge imports from other countries. This would have an adverse impact on domestic agriculture, leading to unemployment and poverty. In this context, the cases of edible oils, coconut etc., are cited in support of this argument. It may be added here that for political reasons also, India does not want to depend on other countries for preserving food security.

(ii) Integration of Indian agriculture with world markets would lead to price volatility. The resulting fluctuations would have an adverse impact on both producers and consumers and threaten food security. Safety nets are mentioned, but they are not effective.

(iii) Reduction in input and food subsidies would impair food security of the country.

(iv) The absence of any level playing field in WTO agreements is indicative of a western bias in the agreement. While the agreement provides Indian agriculture with an opportunity for larger exports, there are also fears that the agreements will make Indian markets vulnerable to competition from imports and may not lead to reduced tariffs/subsidies for those commodities of interest to India.

1. AOA and Food Security in India

Does the minimum access commitment hurt India? India offered tariff bindings at three levels: 100 per cent for raw commodities, 150 per cent for processed agro-commodities and 300 per cent for most of edible oils (Soya oil at 45 per cent). Out of 686 tariff lines, for 587 lines the basic customs duty was at least 50 per cent points below the Uruguay Round (UR) bound rates. Only in 10 tariff lines did it exceed UR bound rates. But they belong to the liquor group, which shows that India has enough leverage in the bound rates. Thus, India can check edible oil imports easily and so there is no risk of either agriculture or food security in this country facing any threat on the basis of market access.

Regarding India's stand on domestic support one needs to first look at the position in this respect in different countries. OECD countries had the highest domestic support ($361 billion) in 1999 with roughly 40 per cent of it being in amber box, and therefore subject to reduction commitments, while 60 per cent fall under green and blue boxes, which are exempted from these commitments. Based on producer support estimates (PSEs), the countries can be divided into five blocks (Gulati, 2001): First, Japan, Korea, Iceland, Norway, Switzerland etc., which have domestic support to the extent of over 60 per cent; second, countries within Europe which have 44 per cent, third, USA, which has 20 per cent, the Cairns group (Australia, New Zealand) which falls in the fourth category with less than 10 per cent. In the last group, South Asian countries have negative support for most of the commodities.

In the case of India the product specific support was negative (at -38.5 per cent) in 1995-96 (except for sugarcane and oilseeds for which it was positive), while the non-product specific support (input subsidies) is positive at 7.5 per cent. Thus, India is under no obligation to reduce domestic support or subsidies currently extended to agriculture as the support being given is well below the permissible level of 10 per cent of the value of its agricultural output.

In respect of export competitiveness, the direct export subsidies were being progressively eliminated in India since 1991. But, it provides income tax exemption benefits on export earnings and interest subsidy. These will be phased out over time.

To conclude, the crash in international prices of commodities without any improved access for Indian exports and low rate of tariff applied on imports of commodities like edible oils, sugar etc., have caused problems for farmers in the country. However, in general, there is no threat of imports on a large scale flowing into India (Blarel et al., 1999; and Sharma, 1999). Do we have to change our food policies due to AOA? The major food and agricultural policies initiated in India are those of: procurement policy, buffer stocking, public distribution system, public investment, input subsidies, and government support to research, clearly. Although India does not have to change any of these policies because of AOA (Hoda and Gulati, 2002), the country has to be vigilant regarding international markets.

2. Concerns Regarding Continuation of High Subsidies and Protection by Developed Countries

It is true that there are no fears of large scale imports into India due to AOA. However, there are concerns about the level playing field for India, which is required to enable it to benefit from the liberalisation of agricultural trade (CMA, 2001; Panchamukhi, 2001; Dhar and Ray, 2001; and Reddy, 2001). The Uruguay Round of Trade Negotiations did not bring about trade liberalisation in agriculture, as expected. There has been no significant reduction in domestic as well as export subsidies given by the developed countries to their agriculture and thus the anticipated increase in exports of agricultural products from developing countries like India has not materialised. Therefore, a major issue is the continuation of high domestic support being provided to agriculture in the developed countries, especially the European Union (EU) in the West and Japan in the East.

As measured by world price effects, a small number of countries cause most of the agricultural market distortions—the EU accounts for 38 per cent of world price distortions, compared to Japan plus Korea (12 per cent), the United States (16 per cent), and Canada (2 per cent) (Table 2). The complete elimination of agricultural tariffs, domestic subsidies and export subsidies would increase world agricultural prices to 12 per cent above their expected level (see Table 2). Eliminating tariffs, which distort both consumer's choice and producer's decisions, would account for more (52 per cent) of the potential price increase (Burfisher, 2001). In developed countries, the tariffs are high for some commodities. In EU, for instance, the out-of-quota tariff for bananas is 180 per cent; in Japan these tariffs range between 460 to 600 per cent for dried beans, peas and lentils and in the US., groundnuts in shell attract a tariff of 164 per cent. Recently, Japan has levied a tariff of about 1000 per cent on rice. Domestic subsidies account for 31 per cent of the total agricultural price impacts. The EU has a relatively high level of distorting domestic agricultural subsidies with export subsidies accounting for a relatively small share (13 per cent) of the total price distortions. The three policies add up to less than 100 per cent in distorting prices as interaction effects account for rest of the distortions.

Some attempts have been made to show the aggregate agricultural price impact broken down by commodity and type of protectionist policy

Table 2
Effects on World Agricultural Prices of Eliminating Agricultural Policy Distortions

	Percentage change from base price				
Elimination of	World	US	EU	Japan/Korea	LDCs
All policies	11.6	1.8	4.4	1.5	2.3
Tariffs	6.0	0.7	1.5	1.4	2.3
Domestic support	3.6	0.9	2.0	0.2	n.a.
Export subsidies	1.5	0.1	0.9	n.a.	0.0

Source: Diao et al. (2001).

Table 3
Effects on World Agricultural Prices of Eliminating All Agricultural Policy Distortions by Commodity and Policy

	Percentage change from base price			
Commodity	Full policy elimination	Global removal	OECD domestic subsidy removal	Global export subsidy removal
Wheat	18.1	3.4	12.0	2.0
Rice	10.1	5.9	2.4	1.5
Other grains	15.2	1.4	12.2	0.6
Vegetables and fruits	8.2	4.9	-0.1	3.0
Oil and oilseeds	11.2	3.1	7.8	0.1
Sugar	16.4	10.9	1.6	3.3
Other crops	5.6	4.2	1.2	0.1
Livestock and products	22.3	12.2	5.5	3.1
Processed foods	7.6	4.8	1.8	1.0

Source: Diao et al. (2001).

initiated with respect to different commodities. The largest distortions have been found to be due to protection given to livestock (including dairy) products, wheat, sugar and other grains (see Table 3). Tariff elimination alone will have a significant effect on livestock and sugar prices, while the elimination of domestic subsidies will affect mainly wheat and other grains (Burfisher, 2001). The distortions due to export subsidies mainly pertain to sugar, livestock products, fruits and vegetables, and wheat.

Apart from imposition of restrictions on the imports of farm products through various tariff and non-tariff barriers, this support consisted of measures such as fixing high support prices for farm produce and the provision of export subsidies, which have now been changed to direct measures for income support under the so-called 'blue box', such as provision of deficiency payments in the USA, and compensations to farmers in the European Union *via* acreage and headage premiums which are exempted from reduction commitments (Rao, 2001). The developed countries have agreed to a modest reduction in the domestic support, but the experience in the last six years indicates that the implementation of such reduction commitments has been tardy, as evidenced by a significant rise in the share of advanced countries in global exports (Rakshit, 2000; WTO, 2001). In fact, the support to agriculture increased marginally for OECD countries since 1995. According to the latest monitoring and evaluation report, the level of support to farmers in the OECD is very high and increased in 2002 as compared to 2001. Total support to agriculture remained really high at $ 318 billion in 2002, up from $ 311 billion in 2001.

There is however a marked shift away from subsidies, which are considered highly trade distorting, towards direct payments in the form of deficiency payments and compensations related to acreage and livestock numbers, which are considered 'minimally trade distorting' and hence placed under the 'blue' and 'green' boxes which are exempted from reduction commitments. However, it would be a misnomer to call these payments as 'minimally trade distorting' (Rao, 2001). This is because such payments insofar as they are not fully delinked or decoupled from the use of inputs, do influence the allocation of resources, in the sense that in the absence of such payments, fewer resources would be committed to agriculture, leading to lower output, higher prices, and smaller export surpluses (WTO, 2001).

India and other developing countries would benefit in terms of higher agriculture commodity prices if developed countries reduce their farm subsidies. There are, however, indications that in EU agriculture, where the distortion in the allocation of resources appears to be highest, there is a significant scope for reducing unit costs through the wider application of known technologies (Rao, 2001). Developing countries like India need therefore to prepare themselves for competing with low-cost farm products rather than expecting a significant rise in their prices *via* reform-induced reduction in the export surpluses from the developed countries. If the low-cost scenario is going to materialise, the countries, which are net importers, should not worry because prices may not increase even if developed countries reduce subsidies.

While the developed countries have been protecting agriculture, leading to over-production and rise in costs and distortion in world trade, several developing countries have been disprotecting agriculture in terms of protecting domestic industry and overvaluing exchange rates. In recent years, however, there have been market reforms aimed at disprotecting industry and liberalising agriculture in several countries. The reforms in agriculture in developing countries like China and Vietnam have led to high agricultural growth and a rise in their trade in agricultural commodities. The total factor productivity in agriculture in many developing countries may increase and consequently the world prices may not increase even if the developed countries reduce their subsidies.

SPS and TRIPS

The second implication concerns WTO rules on sanitary and phytosanitary measures (SPS), which makes it difficult exporting our agricultural produce to developed country markets. Standards are fast becoming an important factor in global trade. The challenges that the developing countries face is that the standards may sometimes not be set in a transparent manner or they do not provide sufficient time to meet these standards. The third concern relates to the impact of TRIPS provisions calling for introduction of *Sui generis* protection to seeds, the interpretation of rules on biodiversity and provisions on geographical indications. The increasing role of the private sector in seed supply may result in seeds becoming more expensive thus preventing farmers from using their own seeds. However, the latter problem can be tackled with *sui generis* system.

3. Measures Undertaken by India to Meet Challenges of WTO

In order to safeguard India's interests, the government had taken several remedial measures. At the outset it has consulted all stakeholders in preparing proposals for the WTO negotiations on agriculture. These included state governments, farmers' organisations, political parties, NGOs, agricultural universities, etc. Import duties on a number of commodities have been increased—the duties on (a) arecanut and poultry have been increased from 35 per cent to 100 per cent; (b) wheat from 0 to 50 per cent; (c) skimmed milk from 0 to 60 per cent; and (d) rice from 0 to 70 per cent. In the budget 2000-2001, customs duty on tea, coffee, copra and coconut has been increased from 35 per cent to 70 per cent. In the budget 2002-03, customs duty on tea and coffee has been increased to 100 per cent and on natural rubber, poppy seeds, pepper, cloves and cardamom to 70 per cent. Duty on pulses has been increased from 5 per cent to 10 per cent. Further, the import of 131 products have been allowed, subject to compliance with Indian quality standards as applicable to domestic goods. Although maintenance of QRs on imports are not permitted, the government can, if the situation so warrants, raise the applied tariffs within the bound levels and also take measures such as introduction of anti-dumping regulations, initiation of safeguard action, levy of countervailing duties under certain circumstances as specified under the WTO Agreement. However, India has been using anti-dumping instrument frequently in recent years. This should be avoided because other countries would also resort to this practice to Indian exports.

India had submitted its proposals in January 2001 to the WTO for the current negotiations on the Agreement on Agriculture (AOA) in the areas of market access, domestic support, export competition and food security. These are based on certain guiding principles, namely, food and livelihood security of our people, protection of the interest of domestic farmers and maximising export opportunities for Indian agricultural products.

Agriculture is a way of life in most developing agrarian economies. Rapid agricultural growth is therefore essential for ensuring food security and alleviation of poverty. And for large agrarian developing countries like India, food security is an important and integral element of national security. To maintain the income entitlement of people engaged in agriculture it is imperative that the developing countries are allowed to maintain tariffs commensurate with their development and trade needs while at the same time undertake relevant measures to enhance productivity and improve the quality of output. In this context, India's proposal says that the 'food security and livelihood concerns' of developing countries are on a totally different plane and should not be confused or equated with the non-trade concerns advocated under 'Multifunctionality of Agriculture' by a few developed countries with a view to providing legitimacy to and thereby perpetuate their trade distorting subsidies. Understandably, India has proposed a 'food security box' for developing countries to protect the livelihoods of the population.

4. What Should be India's Stand in the Negotiations?

Implementation of the WTO Agreement on Agriculture since 1995 has brought out the inadequacies inherent in the agreement. The ongoing negotiations in the WTO on the AOA provide an opportunity for India to rectify these inadequacies and inequalities. India should stress on the implementation of Uruguay Round agreements to reduce subsidies and other distortions caused by policies pursued by developed countries. There were some positive developments at the Fourth WTO Ministerial Conference at Doha in November, 2001. Its Declaration commits member countries to enter into comprehensive negotiations aimed at: substantial improvements in market access for developing countries; reductions of, with a view to phasing out, all forms of export subsidies; and substantial reductions in trade distorting domestic support being given by the developed countries. It also takes note of non-trade concerns of developing countries and their development needs including food security and rural development. Special and differential treatment for developing countries would be an integral part of the negotiations. It remains to be seen how soon these declarations will be implemented. It would be in the interest of India to aggressively push for the removal of all non-tariff barriers. It is also suggested that India should join Cairns group in order get support for the campaign against the provision of subsidies and protection to agriculture by developed countries like US and EU.

In respect of market access, India should propose a maximum tariff of 100 per cent initially and later advocate for a maximum tariff bound of 40-50 per cent on all agricultural commodities by any country. Special and differential treatment (SDT) should not be used in this case. However, India should invoke the provision of Special Safeguards (SSG) if there is a deluge of imports. As rightly mentioned in the proposals made to WTO, India should argue for the abolition of tariff quotas.

On domestic support, there is no need for introducing measures under 'blue box' and they should be brought to 'amber box' because the former is also trade distorting. Also, total AMS for any country should be brought down to the level of 10 to 15 per cent of agricultural production.

There is also a need for product specific ceiling on AMS. Among the green box measures, the expenditure on 'decoupled income support' and direct income payments has increased substantially during the implementation period. The share of the total direct payments has also increased significantly during this period—their share under the green box measures is estimated to have increased from 23 per cent in 1995 to 43 per cent in 1998. Direct payments along with decoupled income support as well as under production limiting programmes should be included in the non-product specific AMS. In the case of India, input subsidies for resource-poor farmers and areas can be deducted from the non-product specific support.

On export competition, India should make the following proposals: (i) export subsidies on all agricultural products should be eliminated in the first two years of implementation, both in terms of export subsidy outlays and subsidised volumes; (ii) during the transition period also, no 'rolling over' of unused export subsidies should be allowed; and (iii) all forms of export subsidisation including export credit, guarantees, price discounts and insurance programmes, etc., in developed countries should be added to the export subsidies and subjected to the overall regulations applicable to export subsidies.

Developed countries may resort to arbitrary as well as restrictive sanitary and phytosanitary (SPS) measures, which continue to represent a major obstacle to international trade in agricultural products. This usually affects exports of developing countries because the SPS measures are often developed in a non-transparent manner. A number of international standards are thus being developed without the participation of developing countries, which emphasises the need for providing special help to India on technical matters relating to sanitary and phytosanitary (SPS) measures.

More transparent and participatory preparation of standards should be insisted. For developing countries like India, a very high standard, set by importing countries, will act as a trade barrier. As such, standards should be reasonably set, so that they can be achieved. India should join other developing countries to raise the voice against undue privileges enjoyed by the developed countries on SPS and TRIPS. It is not clear how they would coordinate so many small farmers regarding SPS.

As mentioned above, India proposes to introduce a 'food security box' for protecting the livelihoods of people in developing countries. This is a debatable point because if India argues for this box, the developed countries may ask for many exemptions under 'multifunctionality of agriculture' (Hoda and Gulati, 2002).

V. REFORM BEHIND THE BORDER POLICIES TO IMPROVE FOOD SECURITY

Food security consists of three elements: food availability, economic access and food absorption. It is mainly a question of economic access to households as food availability at the national level is not a problem and food absorption depends mainly on factors such as health of the people, sanitation, etc. Clearly, better food and agriculture policies are needed to improve the accessibility of food to the poor. Even if developed countries reduce subsidies on agriculture, it is possible that India may not benefit much as the rich countries may go for cost-reducing technologies and as a result international prices for agricultural commodities may not increase. Therefore, viability depends on cost reduction in Indian agriculture and not on higher prices. These policies would also be useful in enabling India to compete with other countries in international trade. There is a need to reform the behind-the-border (domestic) policies to improve food and nutrition security. The basic focus of the policy mix must be on employment generation. However, better food management and increase in the growth of agriculture and rural non-farm sector would lead to improvements in food security.

1. Poor Food Management

The government's food management has not been satisfactory. This is clearly evident from the paradox whereby we have 60 million food stocks even as 260 million people are living below the poverty line. Food subsidy for the fiscal year, 2003-04 is budgeted around Rs. 27,000 crore.

Despite the slow growth in foodgrain production, the stocks have increased. The three main pillars of our food policy are: procurement policy, available buffer stock and the public distribution system.

The increase in the procurement and issue prices of foodgrains and the obligation of the public distribution agencies to purchase all grains offered by the farmers, changes in consumption patterns marked by a shift away from foodgrains, low purchasing power of the poor, etc., are factors that could be responsible for high food surpluses. The food surpluses are a direct consequence of a steep rise in the procurement prices in the recent period which, apart from rendering exports competitive and discouraging the holding of stocks by the private sector, reduced the domestic consumption of foodgrains, particularly by the poor (Rao, 2002).

Food subsidy as a percentage of GDP and total expenditure increased significantly in the last two years (Fig. 1 and Table 4). Subsidy on buffer stock has been increasing while consumer subsidy has declined (Table 5).

With regard to the PDS, there has been significant diversion of the PDS commodities. While poor states have not benefited, the Targeted PDS is faced with many problems. With the decline in APL prices, the off-take seems to have increased recently.

2. What are the Needed Reforms?

The policies in regard to the procurement and distribution of food have adversely affected private trade. The present food management has become expensive and unsustainable, bringing to fore the question: how can the existing system be made economically efficient, more targeted and

Fig. 1
Food Subsidy as a Percentage of Total Government Expenditure

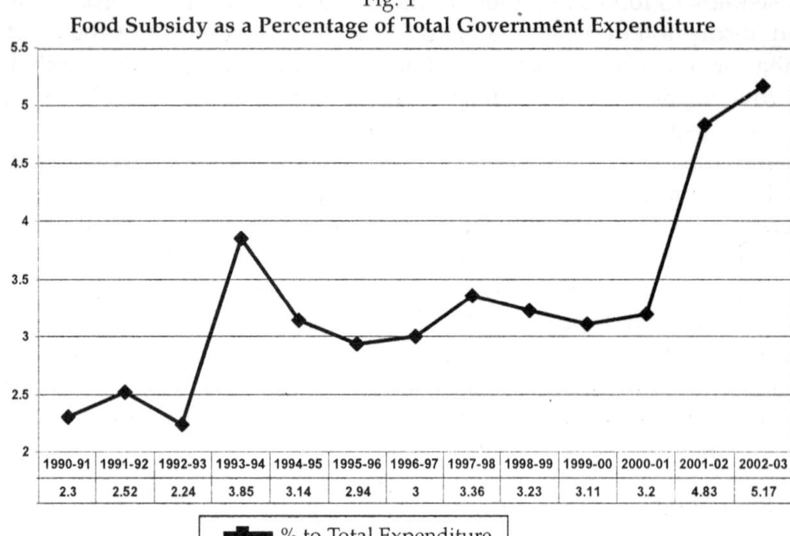

Table 4
Food Subsidy of the Central Government

Year	Food subsidy (in Rs. crore)	Food subsidy as % of GDP	Food subsidy as % of govt. total expenditure
1990-91	2450	0.43	2.30
1991-92	2850	0.44	2.52
1992-93	2800	0.37	2.24
1993-94	5537	0.61	3.85
1994-95	5100	0.50	3.14
1995-96	5377	0.47	2.94
1996-97	6066	0.45	3.00
1997-98	7500	0.52	3.36
1998-99	8700	0.51	3.23
1999-00	9200	0.48	3.11
2000-01	12010	0.58	3.20
2001-02	17612	0.76	4.83
2002-03	21200	0.83	5.17

Source: Budget documents of the Government of India.

Table 5
Buffer Component of Food Subsidy

Year	Food subsidy (in Rs. crore)	Buffer component (Rs. crore)	Buffer subsidy as % of food subsidy
1997-98	7500	937	12.5
1998-99	8700	1552	17.8
1999-00	9200	1754	19.1
2000-01	12010	4233	35.2
2001-02 (BE)	13670	5680	41.6

Source: Economic Survey, 2001-02, Government of India.

financially sustainable? There is a need to reduce the role of the Food Corporation of India (FCI) and increase that of private trade in handling foodgrains. Freezing procurement prices for a few years is one option. It merits mention in this context that the farmers' income depends on yield and prices, but the government has been concentrating only on the price factor. Another suggestion is to decentralise the procurement system. The minimum support price (MSP) scheme has to be modified in order to encourage diversification. The Department of Agriculture has been thinking of directly compensating the farmers to the extent of the difference between the market price and the MSP. This income policy is not viable in a country like India where there are more than 100 million farm holdings. The role of the FCI has to be restricted to price stabilisation and the management of buffer stock and the PDS can be left to states. The Expenditure Reforms Commission suggested that the buffer stock should be around 17 million tonnes and the private sector had to be involved in the storage and handling of grains. In spite of the high subsidy, (Rs. 27000 crores) the PDS does not reach the poor. Therefore, methods have to be formulated to reduce costs of distribution. Measures such as geographic targeting, food coupons, linking the PDS to food-for-work and nutrition programmes have to be tried. Rao (2002) has suggested a six-fold policy framework for the foodgrain sector. They are: "(1) to consolidate the food security achieved so far in the country and strengthen it further; (2) to encourage diversification of cropping pattern so as to ensure efficiency of resource use in agriculture; (3) to enhance our competitiveness in the export market; (4) to allow a rise in the domestic consumption of foodgrains among the poor; (5) to reduce the subsidy bill for the exchequer; and (6) to reduce the cost of distribution" (p. 11). These measures, if undertaken, will hopefully lead to better management of our food economy.

3. Policies for Accelerating Agricultural Growth

In order to revive agricultural growth, measures such as increasing public and private investment, and the availability of rural credit, strengthening the infrastructure such as irrigation, improving the marketing system, promoting agricultural research and technology and liberalising domestic and trade policies are needed. Also, as mentioned above, we need to induct cost-reducing technology in order to develop a viable agriculture and thus be able to compete with other countries within the WTO framework. Policy issues in respect of these are discussed below:

(i) Credit

The institutional credit is expected to increase from Rs. 64,000 crore in 2001-02 to Rs. 82,073 crore in 2002-03—an increase of 28 per cent. For the 10th Plan period, the credit flow into agriculture and allied activities is projected to be more than three times the credit flow during the Ninth

Plan (GOI, 2003). These are welcome and expected to raise agricultural growth. However, the share of agriculture in the non-food bank credit has been between 11 to 12 per cent in recent years. About 60 per cent of credit requirements of farmers are now met by institutional sources and the remaining 40 per cent by informal sources like money-lenders. Despite the existence of a wide network of rural bank branches and many schemes and programmes for providing credit for promoting agricultural and rural development, a large number of very poor people still continue to remain outside the fold of the formal banking system. The credit system should reach marginal and small farmers. In fact, the growth rate of agricultural credit for small and marginal farmers declined in the 1990s as compared with the 1980s (RBI, 2002). Significantly, during the same period, there was no decline in the growth in credit for large farmers. Some of the suicides committed by farmers in recent years have been mainly due to their being caught in a debt trap, which in turn could be attributed to the non-availability of institutional credit, thus forcing farmers to take loans from moneylenders at high interest rates. With rising income, there will be diversification of crops. Investment needs for the production of high income-elastic agricultural products, such as dairying and livestock, horticulture, agro-forests would rise much faster now. Due to these factors, rural credit has to expand at a rate faster than in the recent past.

(ii) Public Investment

The decline in public investment in agriculture has been a cause for concern because of its crucial role in the development of infrastructure such as irrigation, agricultural research, electricity, roads, markets and communications. In 2000-01, public investment in agriculture was Rs. 4007 crore, which was less than that of 1999-00 (GOI, 2002). As a percentage of agricultural GDP, public investment in agriculture, which was between 7 and 8 per cent in the 1980s, was less than that in the 1980s. It is true that private investment in agriculture has been increasing, but, it is well known that there has been complementarity between public and private investment. For example, in West Bengal, private investment in irrigation increased only after rural electrification. Public investment needs to be stepped up in rain-fed and marginal areas where poverty is concentrated.

Regarding the Rural Infrastructure Development Fund (RIDF), recent budgets have increased the allocation of funds for this scheme. A look at the RIDF, however, shows that the utilisation rate is low (around 40 per cent), except in a few states like Andhra Pradesh and Maharashtra, which utilise more funds than others. The low utilisation of the RIDF is attributed to a number of factors ranging from bureaucratic delays in submitting proposals, evaluating and sanctioning them and finally releasing the amount in instalments. In this year's budget, the release of funds to states is linked to reforms in agriculture and rural development.

The criteria regarding this linkage are not clear.

(iii) Technology, Trade and Institutions

The 1990s witnessed a decline in the yield growth for many crops. Technology plays an important role in improving the yields. A fresh look at the priorities of Indian agricultural research system is necessary in the light of the emerging prospects. There is only a marginal increase in the funds for research in the recent budget. The states, of course, must take a lead in research and extension. It is known that India spends only 0.5 per cent of GDP on agricultural research as compared to more than 1 per cent by other developing countries. Regarding institutional reforms, land reforms still have relevance. Apart from some redistribution measures, the focus has to be on tenancy reforms and consolidation of holdings. On areas under canal irrigation and rain-fed areas, water user's associations and watershed programmes have to be strengthened.

(iv) Diversification Activities

There seems to be an increasing interest in 'diversification' into fruits, vegetables, animal husbandry and fisheries. Given the changes in consumption patterns away from cereals, there is a need to increase the supply of non-cereal commodities. This will also have the benefit of increasing employment. Diversification, of course, is easier said than done. First, the risks and volatility are higher for non-food crops. The farmer has to be convinced of the need to market his produce, which cannot be done without providing her/him infrastructure support—roads, cold chain, etc. Apart from supply side, demand side aspects like market for the product has to be taken care of for the diversification of crops. Crop insurance appears to be more important for these crops than for rice and wheat. Notably, private investment may not be forthcoming till some of these problems are solved.

4. Augmenting Rural Employment for Food Security

The decline in the growth of rural employment and increase in unemployment rate in the 1990s in spite of higher GDP growth rate during the period are the matters of concern. It is known that food security of the poor people can be increased by enhancing their purchasing power (economic access) through the generation of more employment and higher wages. As mentioned above, one of the reasons for surplus foodgrains in the country is low purchasing power of the poor.

How can employment opportunities be increased and the quality of employment improved? There are mainly two approaches to this problem: One is through sectoral programmes and the other through direct employment programmes. The elasticity of employment to GDP for the entire economy was 0.53 during 1977-83 and declined to 0.41 in the period 1983-94. The elasticity declined sharply to 0.15 during 1993-2000. Employment elasticities in agriculture and community social and personal services were nil during the same period. In the case of manufacturing it was 0.26, while in that of services it was more than 0.50 during this period.

Sector-wise, the experience of developing countries shows that the greatest stimulant for pro-poor growth is a dynamic agriculture. Agriculture still contributes 60 per cent of the total employment in the country. In the decade, 1983-94, agriculture accounted for 50 per cent of the additional employment, while the period between 1993 and 1999-00 saw an absolute decline in agricultural employment. In the process of economic development, the workers engaged in agriculture shift to non-agriculture sectors. However, underemployment can be removed with a higher agricultural growth. Also, agriculture still has the potential of absorbing workers in regions with higher incidence of rural poverty such as Orissa, Bihar, Assam, Madhya Pradesh, West Bengal and Uttar Pradesh.

Within agriculture and allied activities, there seems to be some diversification towards non-cereal crops such as fruits and vegetables, fisheries and animal husbandry, which is expected to promote employment. For example, in Maharashtra, the requirement of person days per hectare per crop season for wheat is 143, while for vegetables it is 200. The corresponding numbers for fruits and grapes are 855 and 2,510 respectively. Thus, fruits in general require nearly six times, and grapes in particular, over 17 times the person days required per hectare as compared to wheat. However, as mentioned above, an element of risk and uncertainty is associated with diversification.

Development of wastelands will also contribute towards increasing employment opportunities to a substantial extent. Currently, there are about 24 million hectares of land that are categorised as culturable wasteland and permanent fallows, which can be developed and brought into cultivation. The wastelands can be given to either farmers or the corporate sector and panchayats while ensuring against the possibility of the corporate sector occupying the fertile land in the name of wastelands.

Turning to the rural non-farm sector, it is recognised that this sector is important both in generating productive employment and alleviating poverty in rural areas. Clearly, there cannot be one policy package for the entire rural non-farm sector (RNFS). There is a need for formulating sub-sectoral policies for different regions. Essentially, a combination of inputs and services including technology and skill development, infrastructure, development of markets and institutions, and credit availability is needed in order to give a boost to the rural non-farm sector.

As regards direct programmes, self-employment and wage employment schemes assume importance. Appropriately, the group approach in the form of self-help groups is being adopted for self employment. However, the problem with women's self-help groups is that most of the schemes undertaken by them are subsistence type and not high income-generating activities. In regard to wage employment, it needs to be recognised that public works programmes are the most important wage employment programmes. Presently, the government has huge surplus stocks. This provides the government with the opportunity to undertake a massive food-for-work programme, which would help in creating employment and partly solve the problem of food stocks.

VI. CONCLUSION

Our analysis in this paper shows that there are some concerns regarding the impact of WTO on food security in the country. India does not have to change her food policies relating to minimum support price, buffer stock and the public distribution system. The actual tariffs for most of the commodities in India are much lower than the Uruguay Round bound rates. As such it can easily check edible oil imports by raising its tariff. There is, however, a need for extreme vigilance in taking timely measures within the existing tariff bindings to restrict imports which affect our producers' livelihoods. Regarding domestic support, the product specific support in India was negative at -38.5 per cent in 1995-96 (only for sugarcane and oilseeds it is positive), while the non-product specific support (input subsidies) was positive at 7.5 per cent. Thus, India is under no obligation to reduce domestic support or subsidies currently extended to agriculture as the support being given is well below the permissible level of 10 per cent of the value of its agricultural output. In respect of export competitiveness also, India's policies do not conflict with the provisions of the WTO agreement.

However, the experience of the last six years shows that there has been no significant reduction in domestic as well as export subsidies given by the developed countries to their agriculture. The anticipated increase in exports of agricultural products from developing countries, therefore, has not materialised. The total support to agriculture by the OECD countries remains really high at $ 318 billion in 2002.

Developing countries like India also need to prepare themselves for competing with low-cost farm products from developed countries in case world prices do not improve due to increase in low-cost technologies in developed countries. If the low-cost scenario is going to materialise, the countries that are net importers should not have any reason to worry because prices may not increase even if developed countries reduce subsidies.

India has submitted its proposals for the current negotiations on the Agreement on Agriculture in the areas of market access, domestic support, export competition and food security to the WTO in January 2001. The guiding principles on which these are based are: Food and livelihood security of our people, protection of the interest of domestic farmers and maximising export opportunities for Indian agricultural products.

Implementation of the WTO agreement on agriculture (AOA) since 1995 has brought out the inadequacies inherent in the agreement. The ongoing negotiations in the WTO on the AOA provide an opportunity for India to rectify these inadequacies and inequalities. India would therefore do well to use this occasion to lay stress on the implementation of Uruguay Round agreements to reduce subsidies and other distortions by developed countries. Also, it should join Cairns group for strengthening its bargaining capacity.

As the international trade in agricultural commodities is likely to be liberalised further, a greater preparedness is required to face the competition in the international market. Standards are fast becoming an important factor in global trade particularly regarding sanitary and phytosanitary (SPS) measures. The challenges that the developing countries face is that they may sometimes not be set in transparent manner or that they do not provide with sufficient time to meet these standards.

Food security is mainly a question of ensuring economic access to households as food availability at the national level is not a problem and food absorption depends mainly on people's health, state of sanitation etc. Furthermore, appropriate domestic policies are needed to augment agricultural production and improve food security provided to the poor. This is because the viability of agriculture depends on cost reduction in Indian agriculture and not on higher prices of farm products. These policies would also be useful for enabling India to compete with other countries in international trade.

The focus of our efforts to improve the viability of Indian agriculture has to be on raising productivity by stepping up public investment, accelerating the development and adoption of cost-reducing technologies and removing restrictions on trade, marketing and processing within the country. Investible resources have to be raised through better tax-GDP ratio as well as better cost recovery for the input services. In order to achieve food security economic access of household to food is an important requirement. This can be realised by creating productive employment. This would necessitate the introduction of policy initiatives aimed at boosting agriculture growth.

To sum up, increase in employment opportunities and their quality would enhance economic access of poor households to food and other items. This in turn, would increase food security and reduce poverty. Apart from increasing public investment, the government should act as a facilitator to improve private investment in agriculture and non-agricultural activities. In the 1990s, inter-state disparities in economic growth and employment had increased, which underscores the need to look at employment elasticities and opportunities in different regions and sub-sectors to undertake policy actions.

References

Blarel, B.; Pursell, Garry and Valdes, A. (1999) (eds.), *Implications of the Uruguay Round Agreement for South Asia: The Case of Agriculture* World Bank, Washington, D.C.

Burfisher, M.E. (ed.), (2001), *Agricultural Policy Reform in the WTO–The Road Ahead*, Market and Trade Economics Division, Economic Research Service, US Department of Agriculture, Agricultural Economic Report No. 802.

CMA (2001), *Implications of WTO Agreements for Indian Agriculture*, Centre for Management in Agriculture, IIM, Ahmedabad, and Oxford & IBH Publishing Co. Pvt. Ltd, New Delhi.

Dhar, B. and Ray, S. (2001), "Review of the WTO Agreement on Agriculture: The Current State of Negotiations", *RIS digest.*

Diao, X; Somwaru, A. and Roe, T. (2001), "Global Analysis of Agricultural Reform in WTO Member Countries", in Burfisher (ed.).

Hoda, A. and Gulati, A. (2002), "Indian Agriculture, Food Security and the WTO-AOA", Paper presented at the ICRIER-ICAR- IFPRI *Conference on Economic Reforms and Food Security–The Role of Trade and Technology,* New Delhi, April 24-25.

GOI (2003), *Economic Survey 2002-03,* Government of India.

—— (2002), *Economic Survey 2001-02,* Government of India.

Gulati, Ashok (2001), *Trade Liberalisation and Food Security: Challenges to Indian Policy Makers,* International Food Policy Research Institute (IFPRI), Washington, D.C., January, (mimeo).

Panchamukhi, V.R. (2001), "World Trade Organization and Developing Countries: Challenges and Perspectives", *RIS Digest*, September.

Rakshit, Mihir (2000), "Post-Uruguay Round Negotiations: A Developing Country Perspective", *Artha Vijnana,* March.

Rao, C.H. Hanumantha (2002), "Food Grain Surpluses: Causes and Policy Implications", *Fifth Dr. C.D. Deshmukh Memorial Lecture,* Hyderabad, March 16.

—— (2001), "WTO and Viability of Indian Agriculture", *Economic and Political Weekly*, Vol. 36, No. 36, September 8-14.

RBI (2002), *Report on Currency and Finance 2000-01*, Reserve Bank of India, Mumbai.

Reddy, D.N. (2001), "WTO and Food Security: Issues in the Context of Small Farmer Economies Like India", Proceedings of *National Consultation on Towards Hunger Free India,* Institute for Human Development, New Delhi, April, 24-26.

Sharma, R.; Konandreas, P.; and Greenfield, Jim (1999), "A Synthesis of Assessments of the Impact of the Uruguay Round on Global and South Asian Agriculture", in Blarel, Pursell and Valdes (eds.).

WTO (2002), *WTO* Agricultural Negotiations: The Issues and Where We are Now, *http://www.wto.org.*

—— (2001), *Negotiations on WTO Agreement on Agriculture: Proposals by India in the Area of : (i) Food Security, (ii) Market Access, (iii) Domestic Support, and (iv) Export Competition,* Ministry of Commerce, Government of India, January 15.

PART III

Regional Scenario

8

Hunger and Poverty in North-eastern States: Implications for Food Security

Amaresh Dubey and *Orester Kharpuri*

I. INTRODUCTION

This paper delves into the problem of food security among the states in the North-eastern (NE) region of India. Basically food security implies that the entire population in a community has access to enough food at all times for leading an active and healthy life (World Bank, 1986; Parikh, 1998). India has achieved food security at the national level, which means that there is an adequate supply of food for the entire population.[1] But food security at the individual or household level is yet to be achieved as a considerably large proportion of households do not have access to enough food. Poverty is regarded as the principal cause of hunger, and hence, food insecurity. In India, about 35 per cent of population lives below the poverty line (GOI, 1997) which means that they do not have the means to buy enough food that is considered biologically sufficient. There is wide variation in the incidence of poverty across the states in the country. Since poverty is related to the inability to have enough food, there will be wide variation in food security at the individual level. Thus, the study of regional variations in individual food security is closely associated with variation in poverty levels. The state and region level poverty incidence is usually calculated for 15 or 16 bigger states (GOI, 1993; Jain and Tendulkar, 1995). Thus, very little is known about the poverty incidence among the smaller states in general and the smaller states in the north-eastern region, in particular.

Our motivation behind writing this paper is that most of the existing literature on poverty (and food security) in India considers only the major states that account for more than 96 per cent of the population in India. Most of the states in the NE region, excepting Assam, are very small in size—both in terms of population and geographical area—and do not figure in this vast literature separately. For the purpose of policy-making, most of the socio-economic characteristics of Assam (comparatively bigger state which is included in most of the studies including poverty ratios) have been assigned to the remaining states in the NE region (GOI, 1993).

Since poverty emerges as the singlemost important cause of individual level food insecurity, poverty incidence is separately calculated for all the states in the NE region and its implication for food security is examined by taking a close look at the various aspects of accessing food through the public distribution system.

The NE region comprises of six states besides Assam, namely, Arunachal Pradesh, Manipur, Meghalaya, Mizoram, Nagaland and Tripura. One more state, Sikkim, is also included in this region as this state is considered to be very similar to other NE states in respect of agro-climatic and demographic characteristics.[2]

These states cover an area of 2,60,000 square km and have a small population—about 40 million. They have a small cultivable area, and their agricultural yields, being based on traditional methods of farming, are low (compared to other parts of the country). All the states are special category states and depend upon the centre for most of their developmental expenditure. Most of the development indices are considered to be well below the national average (GOI, 1997). There is a general lack of reliable statistical data base that can be used for evaluating the development in the region. In this paper, the consumer expenditure data from two most recent quinquennial rounds of survey, 1987-88 and 1993-94, are used to study the incidence of poverty and food security among these states.

The paper is structured as follows: in the next section we shall discuss the issues related to the measurement of poverty and food security in the light of the special features of the states in the NE region. This is followed by a discussion in poverty incidence on the eight constituent states comprising the NE region in section III. The estimates of food insufficiency and hunger in the NE region is examined in section IV. In section V, we analyse the role of government in ensuring food security and section VI presents the concluding observations of the study.

II. MEASUREMENT OF POVERTY AND FOOD SECURITY

As stated earlier, separate poverty estimates for the states in the north-eastern region are not reported in the official circles. In this section, we examine these data related issues and argue that there is scope for obtaining reliable estimates for individual states in the NE region.

1. Data-related Issues

The household level consumer expenditure data collected by the National Sample Survey Organisation (NSSO) are used to study poverty incidence and access to food in the region. The data were collected during the periods, July 1987 to June 1988 (the 43rd round) and July 1993 to June 1994 (the 50th round). The area covered by the NSSO for the urban sector in the NE region is that of the entire territory of all the eight states in both the

43rd (1987-88) and the 50th (1993-94) rounds (GOI, 1988; 1994a). The rural areas of all the states except Nagaland were surveyed in 1987-88. However, a limited survey was conducted in the villages in Nagaland falling within 5 km of a bus route in 1993-94.[3]

For purposes of surveying the households, Assam was divided into three NSS regions in both the rural and urban sectors (Dubey and Gangopadhyay, 1998; Gangopadhyay, Jain and Dubey, 1997), and Manipur into two NSS regions in each sector. All other states have only one rural and one urban region. Thus, in the entire NE region we have 11 urban regions in the two rounds of NSSO. In rural sector there were 10 regions in 1987-88 and 11 regions in 1993-94.

Before going into the discussion of poverty measures, we look at the sample size (the number of households surveyed) in each state. It may be recalled that the Expert Group (GOI, 1993) did not calculate the poverty ratios for the states in the NE region except for Assam, citing small sample size as the reason. The number of the rural villages and urban blocks and that of households in the rural and urban sectors of each state suggest that there is no reason to suspect the data on the basis of sample size (Dubey and Kharpuri, 2000). The eight states in NE region have only 3.81 per cent share in the total population of India, while their share in the sampled FSUs and households is over 10 per cent. Thus, the states in the NE region are in fact over-represented in the NSS sample. There is no reason, then, why we should have doubts about the accuracy of the estimates of poverty and the consumer expenditure among the states in the NE region.

2. Poverty Lines

The extent of poverty is calculated by using a predefined poverty norm. In this paper, we have used the poverty norm, defined as the minimum consumption expenditure of Rs. 20 per capita per month at 1960-61 prices above which a person is considered non-poor. The poverty line at 1973-74 prices is available from the Report of the Task Force (GOI, 1979). For the year 1987-88 and 1993-94 these were to be updated at current prices, since household expenditure is given in current rupees..

There are two methodologies one can follow for updating the poverty line at 1987-88 and 1993-94 prices. One was suggested by the Expert Group (1993) and the other by Minhas et al. (1988). The latter adjustment is more detailed than that of the Expert Group. It takes the prices across different regions for the entire basket of commodities (Dubey and Gangopadhyay, 1998), while the former takes only five major commodity groups.

Given the two benchmark poverty norms and two methodologies to update these norms to current prices, we get at least four poverty lines. One possibility is to use all the available poverty lines and check for the sensitivity of the poverty measures. This exercise was carried out by Dubey and Gangopadhyay (1998). Using six poverty lines, they showed that the direction of change in the poverty measures and ranking of the states and regions was not affected by the poverty lines used. This led them to conclude that the incidence of poverty reported in this paper was based on the Official Poverty Line, updated at current prices on the methodology suggested by Minhas et al., (1988; Minhas and Jain, 1989; Minhas and Tendulkar, 1991).

Since we are interested in spatial disparities also, we have to allow for different price vectors in different regions. For the states in the NE region, we have price data for five regions only[4] namely, Assam rural, Assam urban, Manipur rural, Meghalaya urban and Tripura rural (Table 5). For purposes of computing poverty incidence, we have assigned the Assam urban poverty line to the urban sector of Tripura. Meghalaya urban poverty line has been used for Arunachal Pradesh, Manipur, Mizoram, Nagaland and Sikkim. Similarly, Manipur rural poverty line has been used for rural areas of Arunachal Pradesh, Meghalaya, Mizoram, Nagaland and Sikkim. Notably, unlike the major states, for the states in the NE region, the rural poverty lines are higher than that in the urban sector.

3. Poverty Measures

As a first step, the incidence of poverty is usually measured by the proportion of the poor in the total population, popularly known as the head count ratio (HCR). If the total population is n and the number of poor out of n are q, then

$$HCR = \frac{q}{n} * 100 \tag{1}$$

The limitation of this measure is that it does not take into account the *depth* of poverty.

The poverty measures suggested by Foster, Greer and Thorbecke (1984), on the other hand, in addition to providing the HCR, gives both depth and the severity of the poverty also.[5] It has a number of useful properties. We look at three particular forms of the generalised FGT measure, given the OPL. The generalised FGT measure is given as

$$P_\alpha = \frac{1}{n}\sum_{i=1}^{q}\left(1-\frac{x_i}{z}\right)^\alpha \tag{2}$$

where P_a is the index, n and q have been defined before, x_i is the PCTE of the ith individual and z is the poverty line. When a=0, we get the HCR. At a=1, we get the second measure of poverty, called the Poverty Gap Index (PGI), which captures the 'depth' of poverty. When a=2, we get a special case of the generalised FGT measures. For all values of a >1, the FGT reflects the 'severity' of the poverty.

III. POVERTY INCIDENCE AMONG THE STATES IN THE NE REGION

As pointed out in the last section, there is a huge literature on poverty in India that looks into state-level poverty ratios for 15 or 16 so-called bigger states (Jain and Tendulkar, 1995). It may be recalled that seven states out of eight, which now constitute NE region, are small states and do not figure in most studies. The official poverty calculations use poverty ratios of Assam for these states (GOI, 1995; 1997).[6]

Now, if the GOI (1993) recommendations are accepted, more than 50 per cent (i.e., over 20 million) of the population in this region should be below the poverty line. This would imply that over 50 per cent of the population is malnourished in the region and has a severe food security problem. Dubey and Kharpuri (1999), who have examined the incidence of poverty in these states separately, argue that since the socio-economic characteristics of the states in this region are different, poverty ratios of Assam appear to overestimate the incidence of poverty in these states.

A look at the state-wise (i.e., combining rural and urban sectors together) poverty measures, the HCR, PGI, FGT and APCTEP) shows that the HCR in the NE region was 39.98, which is lower than the all-India HCR (47.09 per cent) in 1987-88, (Table 1). There are large variations among the state level poverty indices within the NE region.

Table 1
State-wise Poverty Measures in 1987-88 and 1993-94

State	43rd round (1987-88)				50th round (1993-94)			
	HCR per cent	PGI	FGT	APCTEP	HCR	PGI	FGT	APCTEP
Arunachal Pradesh	29.76	0.0653	0.0233	105.26	47.70	0.1145	0.0406	192.34
Assam	45.50	0.0947	0.0280	108.62	52.26	0.1127	0.0336	200.77
Manipur	18.33	0.0243	0.0050	117.67	31.33	0.0384	0.0081	222.00
Meghalaya	35.27	0.0935	0.0350	99.12	30.12	0.0484	0.0115	212.42
Mizoram	3.85	0.0067	0.0025	111.39	7.01	0.0099	0.0023	217.17
Nagaland*	0.00	0.0000	0.0000	0.00	3.86	0.0041	0.0006	226.45
Sikkim	42.99	0.0795	0.0222	110.08	37.31	0.0734	0.0205	203.26
Tripura	27.01	0.0592	0.0197	105.61	28.75	0.0652	0.0221	195.90
NE region**	26.37	0.0571	0.0193	105.85	34.33	0.0706	0.0227	201.12
NE region	39.98	0.0838	0.0254	108.11	45.87	0.0978	0.0296	200.89
All -India	47.09	0.1241	0.0461	100.28	40.26	0.0978	0.0341	177.54

Notes: 1. PGI and FGT are ratios and average per capita total expenditure of the poor (APCTEP) is in Rupees/month.
2. *indicates that the state is not strictly comparable. The survey was not conducted in the rural areas of Nagaland in 1987-88.
3. **denotes that results are reported excluding Assam and Nagaland.

Source: Poverty indices for combined NE region are calculated by the author as weighted average of all the states in the NE region. The source for the all-India poverty incidence, and also for sates in the region, is Dubey and Gangopadhyay (1998) and Dubey and Kharpuri (1999).

For the NE region as a whole, all the poverty indices had increased in 1993-94 over that in 1987-88. In 1993-94, the HCR at 45.87 per cent was much higher than the all-India HCR (40.26 per cent). Out of eight constituent states, Arunachal Pradesh and Assam had a higher proportion of poor than the all-India average. As posited earlier, the poverty ratios are different for different states with large variations. In fact, in 1987-88 and also in 1993-94, Assam had the highest poverty incidence among the NE region states. At the other end of the spectrum is Mizoram with HCR at 3.85. Manipur, for which the Expert Group (1993) stated that poverty ratios are not in line with the rest of the NE region states, has the second lowest (18.33 per cent) HCR in 1987-88. Out of seven comparable states, only two states, Meghalaya and Sikkim, showed a decline in the poverty indices.

Disparities in Development

As stated earlier, there are variations in the socio-economic development among these states (Table 2). Some of these characteristics are reported in Table 2. The table very clearly brings out the disparities among the states in the NE region. For example, household density per square kilometre varies from two in Arunachal Pradesh to 50 in Tripura. The urbanisation level is the lowest in Sikkim (9.10 per cent) and highest in Mizoram (46.10 per cent). Hence, the differential poverty incidence is compatible with their disparate socio-economic development.

Table 2
Socio-economic Indicators of the States in NE Region

State	Literacy rate (%)			FWFP	HH per sq.km	Prop. of workers		U. level	Average growth
	Total	Male	Female			Primary	Tertiary		
Arunachal Pradesh	41.59	51.45	29.69	37.49	02	67.44	23.90	12.80	5.63
Assam	52.89	61.87	43.03	NA	49	73.99	20.45	11.10	2.72
Manipur	59.89	71.63	47.60	38.96	13	70.00	20.34	27.52	1.48
Meghalaya	49.10	53.12	44.85	34.93	15	74.81	21.46	18,60	5.49
Mizoram	82.27	85.61	78.60	43.25	06	65.99	28.94	46.10	3.77
Nagaland*	61.65	67.62	54.75	37.96	13	75.26	21.26	17.21	7.02
Sikkim	56.94	65.74	46.69	30.41	11	68.40	20.48	9.10	-1.70
Tripura	60.44	70.58	49.65	13.16	50	64.08	29.51	15.30	2.90
All-India	52.21	64.13	39.29	22 27	50	67.53	20.50	25.71	5.50

Notes: 1. FWFP is Female Work Force Participation Rate (in per cent), HH per sq. km is household density per square kilometre; prop. of workers refers to the proportion of workers in the primary and tertiary sectors (in per cent), U. Level is urbanisation level, in per cent and Average Growth refer to the average growth of SDP during 1987-88 and 1993-94 (in per cent). For all-India, the average growth rate is for GDP.

Sources: GOI (1994b; 1996a; 1996b).

Table 3 shows that while the poverty incidence in the rural areas of the states is almost similar to that at the aggregate level in the states in 1987-88, the socio-economic conditions in the rural areas of the NE region with 43.52 per cent poor were better than in other areas of India (49.38 per cent). There is also a lot of spatial variation within the NE states. Mizoram, with only 5.5 per cent HCR, is the best performing state whereas the HCR in Sikkim was 49.30 per cent, which showed that it had the highest

Table 3
Poverty Measures in Rural Areas for 1987-88 and 1993-94

	43rd round (1987-88)				50th round (1993-94)			
State	APCTEP	HCR	PGI	FGT	APCTEP@	HCR	PGI	FGT
Arunachal Pradesh	105.12	30.14	0.0663	0.0238	102.38	48.75	0.1171	0.0415
Assam	108.58	48.42	0.1014	0.0300	107.48	57.05	0.1241	0.0371
Manipur	116.31	21.11	0.0289	0.0062	117.30	33.08	0.0428	0.0091
Meghalaya	98.72	40.39	0.1080	0.0406	113.10	34.36	0.0552	0.0132
Mizoram	114.34	5.50	0.0083	0.0022	115.41	10.10	0.0145	0.0034
Nagaland*	NA	NA	NA	NA	119.55	4.24	0.0048	0.0007
Sikkim	109.45	49.30	0.0926	0.0260	108.12	40.24	0.0795	0.0222
Tripura	105.86	28.91	0.0633	0.0212	104.62	32.04	0.0731	0.0249
NE Region**	105.29	29.74	0.0655	0.0223	117.46	37.67	0.0790	0.0256
NE Region	107.99	43.52	0.0920	0.0280	117.76	50.42	0.1087	0.0331
All-India	95.46	49.38	0.1298	0.0480	98.39	42.70	0.1030	0.0356

Notes: 1. * and ** as mentioned in Table 1.
2. @ APCTEP is reported at constant (1987-88) prices.
3. NA denotes : Not Available.

Source: As in Table 1.

proportion of poor. Assam had the second highest HCR in the region (48.42 per cent), while all other states were placed between these two extremes. It needs to be noted that all the states had poverty ratios which were less than the average (all-India) HCR.

During 1993-94 we had a completely different scenario. First, the HCR in the NE region increased by about 7 per cent points whereas the all-India HCR in the rural sector went down by almost the same amount (Dubey and Gangopadhyay, 1998). In 1987-88, the rural poverty indices in all the states in the region were lower than the average for all-India. In 1993-94, these were higher in two states (Arunachal Pradesh and Assam) than the average (all-India). The lowest HCR was recorded in Nagaland and Mizoram was pushed to the second place during the year. Meghalaya and Sikkim are the only two states in which rural poverty indices declined as in the states as a whole. The remaining comparable states saw an increase in their rural poverty levels. When we leave out Assam and Nagaland, the revised NE region indices were below the national average but there is perceptible deterioration in 1993-94 over that in 1987-88.

Turning to urban sector, we find that NE region had performed much better than the rural sector (Table 4). There was a nominal decline in the HCR in the corresponding years from 10.72 per cent in 1987-88 to 10.64 per cent in 1993-94. It was far below the average (all-India) HCRs (39.20 per cent in 1987-88 and 32.87 per cent in 1993-94). In both the rounds, all the states have lower HCRs than that in India as a whole.

The measure of the depth and severity of poverty reported in the tables exhibit similar inter-state variations, and temporal change like the HCR discussed above.

IV. ACCESS TO FOOD IN THE NE REGION

The poverty incidence in different states reported in the last section suggests that the states in the NE region also face the problem of food security in varying degrees. Since a majority of the poor live in the rural sector, the problem is relatively more acute in the rural areas of the region.

The rural areas of these states are inhabited by indigenous tribals, who have their own traditional institutions and much of whose land is community-owned (GOI, 1997). The measurement of poverty by using the food energy intake as the yardstick poses conceptual problems. Our effort in calculating the cost of the minimum food basket at 1987-88 and 1993-94 prices based on official poverty norms suggests that the rural poverty norm turns out be higher than that of urban poverty. As reported (Table 5), these poverty norms could be calculated for two states only if they were adopted for other states.

Table 4

Urban State-wise Poverty Measures for 1987-88 and 1993-94

	43rd round (1987-88)				50th round (1993-94)			
State	APCTEP	HCR	PGI	FGT	APCTEP@	HCR	PGI	FGT
Arunachal Pradesh	110.55	20.10	0.0418	0.0105	109.85	12.12	0.0258	0.0089
Assam	110.36	12.60	0.0183	0.0048	112.81	10.03	0.0127	0.0030
Manipur	123.73	11.52	0.0131	0.0022	125.73	26.67	0.0264	0.0052
Meghalaya	123.75	4.02	0.0046	0.0009	117.23	3.48	0.0056	0.0012
Mizoram	60.43	0.62	0.0035	0.0031	135.32	0.33	0.0001	0.0000
Nagaland*	0.0000	0.00	0.0000	0.0000	129.51	2.82	0.0020	0.0002
Sikkim	119.59	14.68	0.0210	0.0053	127.48	3.39	0.0029	0.0005
Tripura	100.99	12.22	0.0266	0.0081	104.11	7.31	0.0142	0.0043
NE region**	115.03	8.49	0.0135	0.0036	126.01	11.56	0.0142	0.0034
NE region	112.06	10.72	0.0161	0.0042	118.23	10.64	0.0133	0.0032
All-India	121.22	39.201	0.1044	0.0393	125.11	32.87	0.0820	0.0298

Note: As in Table 3.
Source: As in Table 1.

Table 5

Poverty Lines for the States in the NE Region

	1987-88		1993-94	
State	Rural PL	Urban PL	Rural PL	Urban PL
Assam	137.35	129.11	256.73	221.94
Manipur	134.75	NA	253.08	NA
Meghalaya	NA	139.57	NA	252.65
Tripura	135.55	NA	254.58	NA
All-India	125.68	161.31	214.31	278.68

Source: Dubey and Gangopadhyay (1998).

Table 6
Perception of Households Regarding Food Sufficiency, 1993-94

	Rural		Urban	
State	Insufficient in some months	Insufficient throughout the year	Insufficient in some months	Insufficient throughout the year
Arunachal Pradesh	16.32	0.00	0.00	0.00
Assam	6.19	0.03	1.18	0.65
Manipur	1.29	7.89	0.95	9.67
Meghalaya	0.54	0.04	0.07	0.00
Mizoram	0.00	0.00	1.08	0.03
Nagaland	0.00	0.00	0.00	0.00
Sikkim	0.00	0.00	0.00	0.00
Tripura	3.09	2.85	0.75	1.11
NE region	5.34	0.65	0.95	1.52
All-India	5.15	0.75	1.13	0.55

Source: Special tabulation by the author using 1993-94 NSS consumer expenditure data.

In these circumstances, it would be instructive to look at the perception of the households about food sufficiency in different states. Table 6 shows that, in general, the proportion of households in the region as a whole having insufficient food in some months is marginally higher than the national average in the rural sector. The wide variation shows that some of the inaccessible areas have a greater incidence of hunger.

Another specific feature of poverty incidence, and hence food security, is the increase in rural poverty in six out of eight states in the region between 1987-88 and 1993-94. The two states that have recorded a decline in poverty are Meghalaya and Sikkim. This can be attributed to the fact that these two states have been relatively peaceful during this period.

V. ENSURING FOOD SECURITY IN THE NE REGION: ROLE OF PDS AND IRDP

In view of the increasing poverty and higher incidence of hunger as perceived by the households in the region, ensuring food security becomes a challenging task. There are two aspects of achieving this objective: One, to ensure adequate supply of food and two, to help households to have enough income to buy adequate food.

In the absence of a well-knit market mechanism in the region, adequate supply of food is to be ensured through the PDS. Table 7a shows the proportion of households that have access to the PDS in the rural sector in each state for these two years. In 1987-88, except for Manipur and Meghalaya, most of the households had access to the PDS, which increased significantly in 1993-94. Table 7b provides the same information for the urban areas.

Surprisingly, despite the accessibility of the PDS to most of the households, both poor and non-poor, a very high proportion of the households are still poor. This finding points to the lack of adequate income

Table 7a

Access to PDS in the Rural Sector in the NE Region, 1987-88 and 1993-94

	1987-88			1993-94		
State	Poor HHDs	Access to PDS (Total)	Access to PDS (Poor)	Poor HHDs	Access to PDS (Total)	Access to PDS (Poor)
Arunachal Pradesh	25.23	84.05	92.74	44.74	90.42	92.16
Assam	42.86	74.32	76.94	52.86	86.35	86.00
Manipur	18.50	11.03	10.75	30.49	35.73	36.69
Meghalaya	38.05	47.18	35.41	29.05	81.85	81.21
Mizoram	4.78	84.25	73.70	8.92	91.59	97.49
Nagaland	NA	NA	NA	3.29	42.67	8.74
Sikkim	40.67	67.13	73.74	31.56	60.33	61.61
Tripura	25.63	91.22	95.63	28.65	88.44	89.57
NE region	38.23	72.29	74.91	46.15	83.31	84 54
All-India	44.86	62.85	59.42	38.46	77.23	76.57

Source: As in Table 6.

Table 7b

Access to PDS in the Urban Sector in the NE Region, 1987-88 and 1993-94

	1987-88			1993-94		
State	Poor HHDs	Access to PDS (total)	Access to PDS (poor)	Poor HHDs	Access to PDS (total)	Access to PDS (poor)
Arunachal Pradesh	13.56	68.95	61.55	8.82	88.02	90.82
Assam	8.67	50.61	59.80	7.61	57.91	63.66
Manipur	8.95	15.89	7.05	21.74	44.52	58.25
Meghalaya	3.12	47.07	47.79	2.37	71.19	62.01
Mizoram	0.47	94.09	100.00	0.29	96.78	100.00
Nagaland	0.00	10.02	0.00	1.86	34.21	0.00
Sikkim	9.45	64.34	89.88	2.53	53.32	53.41
Tripura	10.13	82.92	98.11	6.02	75.56	96.01
NE Region	7.57	50.48	58.27	8.05	60.86	64.89
All India	31.62	63.86	67.57	26.89	68.97	72.40

Source: As in Table 6.

among the households that could account for the higher incidence of poverty and food insecurity among them. To examine this aspect, one must look at the income-earning opportunities in the region. As mentioned earlier, the NE region is the most underdeveloped region in the country. Most of the population is engaged in subsistence farming (GOI, 1997) though there have been attempts to generate income through various employment schemes, the IRDP, etc. Table 8a shows the distribution of households receiving IRDP help in the rural areas of the states in the region.

The proportion of households covered under the IRDP scheme in the region appeared to be lower than the national average in 1987-88 (Table 8a) and declined further in 1993-94. This probably explains the increase in poverty in 1993-94 over 1987-88. This observation is confirmed if we took at the access to the IRDP in the urban areas (Table 8b). In 1987-88, it was much above the national average and increased in 1993-94.

Table 8a

IRDP Help to the Households in the Rural Sector

	1987-88			1993-94		
State	Poor HHDs	IRDP help (total)	IRDP help (poor)	Poor HHDs	RDP help (total)	RDP help (poor)
Arunachal Pradesh	25.23	17.15	19.94	44.74	18.43	22.78
Assam	42.86	3.17	3.61	52.86	2.69	3.24
Manipur	18.50	9.61	10.91	30.49	6.10	5.76
Meghalaya	38.05	7.40	2.29	29.05	2.01	2.15
Mizoram	4.78	13.77	4.41	8.92	9.66	36.13
Nagaland	NA	·NA	NA	3.29	3.41	0.00
Sikkim	40.67	35.73	36.98	31.56	4.21	4.43
Tripura	25.63	12.14	11.15	28.65	18.27	15.42
NE region	38.23	5.91	5.21	46.15	4.95	4.66
All-India	44.86	6.83	7.05	38.46	7.51	8.51

Source: As in Table 6.

Table 8b

IRDP Help to the Households in the Urban Sector

	1987-88			1993-94		
State	Poor HHDs	IRDP help (total)	IRDP help (poor)	Poor HHDs	RDP Help (total)	RDP Help (poor)
Arunachal Pradesh	13.56	17.15	38.80	8.82	0.69	0.00
Assam	8.67	3.17	2.41	7.61	1.74	1.38
Manipur	8.95	9.61	10.08	21.74	2.34	3.26
Meghalaya	3.12	7.40	0.00	2.37	1.01	24.44
Mizoram	0.47	13.77	0.00	0.29	4.18	77.45
Nagaland	0.00	0.00	0.00	1.86	0.55	0.00
Sikkim	9.45	35.73	9.10	2.53	0.07	0.00
Tripura	10.13	12.14	1.89	6.02	12.66	11.46
NE region	7.57	5.91	4.45	8.05	2.88	3.18
All-India	31.62	2.26	2.18	26.89	1.29	1.75

Source: As in Table 6.

VI. CONCLUSION AND POLICY IMPLICATIONS

This paper examines the problem of food security in the NE region. Since food security at the individual and household level is closely associated with the incidence of poverty, we calculated the latter in eight states in the region. This appears to be the first exercise of its kind in which NSS consumer expenditure survey data is used for counting the poor in the NE region which includes Sikkim also.

The main finding of this paper is that in 1993-94 the NE region had become poorer (than the national average in 1993-99) as compared to 1987-88. The change over the two rounds happened to be exactly the opposite of what had happened at the all-India level. It can be said that this is not due to a particular poverty norm used in our calculations. Out of the eight constituent states, Meghalaya and Sikhim are the only two states where poverty ratios have declined over the two years. The urban sector has a much lower incidence of poverty than the rural areas of the region.

This finding has important implications for food security in the region as a whole as well as within the states the region. It appears that the PDS is accessible to most of the households in the region and that it is the lack of purchasing power that comes in the way of ensuring food security to them. This is quite consistent with the economic structure of most of the states in the NE region where the most important sector is services, and job opportunities are available only in the government services which are concentrated in the urban areas. Therefore, for ensuring food security in this region, more income generating opportunities need to be created and made accessible to the poor households in the rural areas in the short run. These efforts are, however, hampered by the political instability and ethnic violence prevalent in many states in the region. It needs to be recognised that both the overall development of the NE region and the level of food security in it will crucially depend on the general security situation in the region.

Notes

1. From a net importer of foodgrains, India has not only achieved self-sufficiency in food, but has now become a net exporter.
2. Hereafter, any reference to the NE region would include Sikkim also, unless otherwise specified. In 1996, a high-powered commission (Shukla Commission) was set up by the Government of India. The Commission has also recommended the inclusion of Sikkim as part of the NE region. See Government of India (1997) for details.
3. For details of sampling design and coverage, please refer to NSSO (1996) for the 50th round and *Sarvekshana*, Vol. 28, (1993) for the 43rd round. It is to be noted here that NSSO conducts mini consumer expenditure surveys every year. It has been pointed out that the results obtained from these mini-surveys are subject to large sampling errors and hence, not reliable.
4. For state specific and all-India urban poverty lines in 1987-88 and 1993-94, refer to Dubey and Gangopadhyay (1998).
5. There are several other measures suggested and used in the literature.
6. See GOI (1993; 1997). While reporting the 1987-88 poverty incidence among the states, the Expert Group (GOI, 1993) has recommended that the since the sample size in the National Sample Survey (NSS) data for NE region states is small, these states should be assigned same poverty level as that in Assam. See GOI (1993), page 34, para 4.7 (7) (i).
7. Despite several criticisms of the food energy-based poverty norm used in this paper, it does indicate the varying degree of food insecurity among the states in the NE region.
8. The access to PDS is based on the purchase of any item from the ration/fair-price shop by the household.
9. Dubey and Gangopadhyay (1998) have shown that poverty ratios have declined by 6 to 7 percentage points at the all-India level. What is important in their calculations is that this reduction is independent of the poverty norm used.

References

Dubey, A. and Gangopadhyay, S. (1998), "Counting the Poor: Where are the Poor in India?", *Sarvekshana: Analytical Report*, No. 1, February.

——and Kharpuri, O.J. (2000), "Poverty Incidence in North-eastern States", *Labour and Development*, Vol 4, Nos 1 and 2, pp. 32-51.

Gangopadhyay, S.; Jain, L.R.; and Dubey, A. (1997), *Poverty Measures and Socio-economic Characteristics: 1987-88 and 1993-94*, Report submitted to the CSO, Department of Statistics, Government of India.

GOI (1997), *Transforming the North East: High Level Commission Report to the Prime Minister*, Planning Commission, March.

——(1996a), *Basic Statistics of the North-eastern Region*, North-East Council, Shillong.

——(1996b), *Economic Survey 1996-97*, Ministry of Finance, New Delhi.

——(1994a), *NSSO, 50th Round: Note on Sample Design and Estimation Procedure*, SDRD, March.

——(1994b), *Census of India 1991*: Series I, Primary Census Abstract, Part II-B(i), Ministry of Home Affairs, August.

——(1993), *Report of the Expert Group on Estimation of Proportion and Number of Poor*, Planning Commission, Perspective Planning Division, July.

——(1988), *NSSO, 43rd Round: Note on Sample Design and Estimation Procedure*, SDRD, Government of India, October.

——(1979), *Report of the Task Force on Projections of Minimum Needs and Effective Consemption Demand*, Perspective Planning Division, Planning Commission, Government of India, New Delhi.

Jain, L.R. and Tendulkar, S.D. (1995), "Economic Reforms and Poverty," *Economic and Political Weekly* , June 10, pp. 1373-1377.

Minhas, B.S. and Jain, L.R. (1989), "Incidence of Rural Poverty in Different States and All-India: 1970-71 to 1983", *Agricutural Development Policy, Adjustment and Reorientation* (Golden Jubilee Volume of *Journal of Indian Society of Agricultural Economics*), Oxford and IBH, New Delhi, pp. 342-81.

——Kansal, S.M. and Saluja, M.R. (1988), "Measurement of General Cost of Living for Urban India, All-India and Different States", *Sarvekshana*, Vol. 12, pp. 1-23.

Minhas, B.S. and Tendulkar, S.D. (1991), "Rural and Urban Cost of Living: 1983 to 1987-88, State-wise and All-India", *Journal of Indian School of Political Economy*, No. 3, pp. 420-442.

Parikh, K. (1998), "Food Security: Individual and National", in Ahluwalia, I.J. and Little, I.M.D. (eds.), *India's Economic Reforms and Development: Essays for Manmohan Singh*, Oxford University Press, Delhi.

World Bank (1986), *Poverty and Hunger: Issues and Options for Food Security in Developing Countries*, World Bank Policy Study, Washington.

9

Food Security in Andhra Pradesh in Retrospect and Prospect

S. Indrakant and S. Harikishan

Our experience with poverty reduction programmes and policies is remarkably diverse. There are cases of spectacular successes as well as total failures. This only points to the fact that it is hard to make generalisations and therefore there is a need for an emphasis on regional studies.

Andhra Pradesh ranks fifth in both area and population of the country. Thanks to the calorie-based poverty line, the state is credited with remarkable success in effecting poverty reduction. In addition, consumer price indices are lower in Andhra Pradesh than the all-India average, indicating that the rate of increase in prices is relatively lower in the state. According to the Modified Expert Group, the percentage of persons living below the poverty line in the state is only 22 per cent with the state ranking second, next only to Punjab, in this respect. It is also true that the Andhra Pradesh government is pursuing a vigorous PDS policy, which in fact, has become an important issue in the election battles in the state. In this background, it is appropriate to begin this paper with an analysis of macrovariables concerning food security.

I. ANALYSIS OF MACRO VARIABLES

1. Trends in Production of Rice and Cereals

During the last four decades, Andhra Pradesh has achieved a significant growth in cereal production in general and rice production in particular. The average annual production of cereals increased from 6.8 million tonnes during 1961-65 to nearly 12 million tonnes during 1996-99 (Table 1). The same periods saw an increase in the average annual production of rice from 4.4 million tonnes to 10 million tonnes. In other words, the output more than doubled during the period under study. On account of the improvements in irrigation facilities, the share of rice in cereal production increased from 64 per cent to 86 per cent. It is observed that 70-75 per cent of rice production comes from the *kharif* harvest. However, the achievements in per capita terms are not as impressive as in aggregate terms. The per capita cereal production has ranged between 162 kg and 185 kg. It reached a peak level of 188 kg in the sub-period, 1981-85, while the subsequent two sub-periods witnessed a drastic reduction. It declined to 162 kg during the sub-period 1991-95. The last sub-period, i.e., 1996-99—thanks to good monsoons—saw a substantial improvement (173 kg), though this is much lower than the peak level registered during 1981-88. This implies that the production of cereals has not kept pace with the growth of population. In respect of rice, it is observed that the per capita production has moderately increased with some fluctuations from 118 kg during 1961-65 to 140 kg in 1996-99.

Table 1
Trends in Production of Rice and Cereals in Andhra Pradesh

	Average production (in '000 tonnes)				Per capita production (in kg)	
		Rice				
Period	Cereals	*Kharif**	*Rabi***	Total***	Cereals	Rice
1961-65	6875	NA	NA	4412.6 (64.3)	183.28	117.78
1966-70	6862	3116.8 (74.6)	1057.5 (25.4)	4174.3 (60.8)	166.26	101.12
1971-75	7849.6	3830.4 (71.7)	1746.2 (28.3)	5341.4 (68.0)	171.96	116.96
1976-80	8962.2	4509.6 (72.11)	1746.6 (27.9)	6254.4 (69.7)	177	123.42
1981-85	10341	5607.2 (70.0)	2162.2 (30.0)	7770 (75.1)	184.68	138.6
1986-90	10743.6	6160 (70.0)	2622.6 (30.0)	8782.4 (81.7)	171.08	139.72
1991-95	11240.06	6570.61 (70.5)	2749.4 (29.5)	9320.01 (82.91)	162.38	134.3
1996-99	11789.99	7331.5 (72.43)	2791 (27.57)	10122.5 (85.86)	172.79	139.63

Note :* Figures in parentheses indicate the percentage of kharif production in the total production of rice.

** Figures in parentheses indicate the percentage of rabi production in the total production of rice..

*** Figures in parentheses indicate the percentage of rice in total cereal production.

Sources: *Statistical Abstract*, Government of Andhra Pradesh; *Season and Crop Report*, Government of Andhra Pradesh, Various Issues.

2. Classification of Districts

Andhra Pradesh is a surplus state in respect of rice production. However, this is not true for all the districts of the state. Therefore, the government has to regulate the movement of rice from surplus districts to the deficit districts. The form of intervention may be either direct, i.e., through the public distribution system or indirect, i.e., by imposing restrictions on the movement of paddy and rice. Further, the status of a district may change from year to year. It is observed that seven districts in the state, which account for 30 per cent of the state population and 44 per cent of the rural poor in the state were always in deficit (Table 2). The severity of the food insecurity problem is likely to be greater in districts coming under the

Table 2
Classification of Districts in Andhra Pradesh by Surplus/Deficit Status

Type	Districts	Percentage of state population (1991)	Percentage of rural poor in state
Always surplus	East Godavari, West Godavari, Krishna and Guntur	25%	14.29
Mostly surplus	Nizamabad, Nalgonda, Srikakulam, Nellore	15%	14.92
Mostly deficit	Vizianagaram, Prakasam, Chitoor, Medak, Warangal, Mahaboobnagar, Khamam and Karimnagar	30%	44.16
Always deficit	Visakhapatnam, Kurnool, Ananthapur, Cuddapah, Ranga Reddy, Hyderabad and Adilabad	30%	26.63

Source: Same as for Table 1 and Reddy (1991).

third and the fourth classes, which emphasises the need to have special area programmes.

3. Trends in Consumer Expenditure

It is logical that a discussion of trends in production should be followed by one of consumption trends. The National Sample Survey (NSS) data of five rounds viz., 27th round (1973-74), 32nd round (1977-78), 38th round (1983), 43rd round (1987-88) and 50th round (1993-94), have been used to study the trends in the pattern of consumer expenditure in the rural and urban districts in Andhra Pradesh. The nominal expenditure on various items of consumption has been converted into real terms by using the price indices derived from retail prices of different items and the weights based on 50th round expenditure data.

The per capita consumer expenditure in rural Andhra Pradesh at 1993-94 prices increased from Rs. 247 in 1973-74 to Rs. 288 in 1993-94 registering an annual growth rate of 0.8 per cent (Table 3). This increase occurred only in non-food expenditure, which grew at a rate of 2.4 per cent. Consequently, the share of food in total expenditure declined from 71 per cent to 60 per cent.

Although the expenditure on food remained constant, there are significant changes in the composition of the food basket. For example, expenditure on cereals and meat group declined sharply at an annual rate of 1.5 per cent and 0.5 per cent, respectively.

The decline in the consumption of cereals and meat products is compensated by an increase in that of all other components of food. Expenditure on edible oil, sugar and vegetables increased at a high rate ranging from 2.8 to 4.5 per cent per annum, while that on pulses and milk products increased at a moderate rate of about 1.5 per cent per annum. As

Table 3
Consumer Expenditure Pattern in Rural Areas in Andhra Pradesh
(in percentage terms)

Commodity	1973-74	1977-78	1983	1987-88	1993-94	Annual compound growth rate
Cereals	43.7	35.6	30.1	24.8	24.6	-1.5
Pulses	2.8	3.1	3.4	4	3.8	1.3
Milk group	4.2	6	4.5	5	5.3	1.5
Edible oil	3.9	3.3	4.1	5	4.9	2.8
Meat group	3.6	4	4.6	4.3	4.5	-0.5
Sugar	1.5	1.5	1.5	1.7	1.9	4.5
Fruit & veg.	4.2	4.6	5.1	6.7	7.5	3.7
Food	70.7	65.1	60.3	59.4	59.7	0
Clothing	8.3	10	10.7	9.4	7.5	2
Non-food	29.3	34.9	39.7	40.6	40.3	2.4
Total expenditure	100 (246.7)	100 (277.6)	100 (291.2)	100 (268.2)	100 (288.0)	100

Note: Figures in parentheses represent per capita real consumer expenditure per month in Rupees.
Source: Rearranged from Subrahmanyam et al. (2000).

a result of these differential growth rates, the share of cereals declined from 44 per cent to 25 per cent and that of other food items increased marginally. In the urban areas, the monthly per capita real consumer expenditure during the two decades under study increased from Rs. 338 to Rs. 408 registering an annual growth rate of 0.9 per cent, which happens to be marginally higher than that of rural areas, i.e., 0.8 per cent (Table 4). The expenditure on food, as in the rural areas remained constant while that on non-food items increased at 2.7 per cent per annum. The changes in composition are also similar to those observed in the rural areas. However, the extent of decline in cereal expenditure is lower in urban areas (1.1 per cent per annum). The growth in expenditure is relatively high for sugar (3.2 per cent), vegetables (2.9 per cent) and edible oil (1.9 per cent), while pulses (0.6 per cent) and milk products (1.0 per cent) experienced moderate growth. Thus, the pattern of growth of consumer expenditure is similar in both rural and urban areas. In terms of the share in total expenditure, the share of food declined from 70 per cent to 54 per cent and that of cereals from 34 per cent to 18 per cent.

It is more appropriate to examine the changes in cereal consumption in quantitative terms: the per capita monthly consumption of cereals declined from 15.25 kg in 1972-73 to 13.27 kg in 1993-94, indicating an annual decline of 0.7 per cent per annum. This decline is only due to a fall in the consumption of coarse cereals. But the consumption of rice increased from 9.0 kg to 11.6 kg per month by 2.5 kg per capita per month. Despite this increase in the demand for rice, the demand for total cereals declined by 2 kg, indicating that the consumption of other cereals declined by 4.5 kg per month. The changes in cereal consumption differ between rural and urban areas in three ways: Firstly, the intake level of cereals is

Table 4
Consumer Expenditure Pattern in Urban Areas in Andhra Pradesh (Percentages)

Commodity	1973-74	1977-78	1983	1987-88	1993-94	Annual compound growth rate
Cereals	33.6	25.3	20.7	16.7	18.0	-1.1
Pulses	3.3	3.4	3.3	3.4	3.4	0.6
Milk group	6.8	6.6	6.9	6.5	6.9	1.0
Edible oil	4.8	3.8	4.5	4.7	4.5	1.9
Meat group	4.1	4.1	4.6	4.0	3.9	-1.1
Sugar	2.2	1.6	1.7	1.6	1.7	3.2
Fruit & veg.	5.2	5.0	6.4	6.6	6.9	2.9
Food	70.2	59.2	56.4	52.7	53.9	0.0
Clothing	5.8	8.5	9.3	7.2	5.5	3.3
Non-food	29.8	40.8	43.6	47.3	46.1	2.7
Total expenditure	100 (338.0)	100 (392.5)	100 (411.2)	100 (380.3)	100 (408.0)	0.9

Note: Figures in parenthesis represent per capita real consumer expenditure per month in Rupees.
Source: Rearranged from Subrahmanyam et al. (2000).

lower in the urban areas than in the rural areas (11.3 kg against 13.3 kg per capita per month). Secondly, the decline during the two decades is less in the urban areas than in the rural areas (1.4 kg against 2.0 kg per month), and thirdly, while consumption of rice increased in the rural areas, it has marginally declined in the urban areas.

Table 5
Per Capita Monthly Consumption of Rice and Total Cereals (kg)

Year	Rural		Urban	
	Rice	Total cereals	Rice	Total cereals
1972-73	8.96	15.25	10.33	12.68
1977-78	10.86	15.85	10.69	12.83
1987-88	11.39	14.35	10.28	11.70
1993-94	11.57	13.27	10.13	11.30

Source: Subramanyam et al. (2000, p. 4).

II. TRENDS IN PROCUREMENT AND DISTRIBUTION OF RICE IN ANDHRA PRADESH

1. Recent Trends

Right up to 1980-81, the procurement of rice in the state was generally low (Table 6). In 1981-82, the level of procurement crossed the one million tonne-mark. In the following year, i.e., 1982-83, on account of the introduction of subsidised rice scheme and procurement by the Andhra Pradesh State Civil Supplies Corporation (APSCSC) the procurement of rice crossed the 2 million tonne-mark. From 1982-83 to 1989-90, the Corporation purchased about one million tonnes of rice from rice mill owners at a negotiated price, which happens to be higher than the procurement price of the Food Corporation of India as the quantity received from the FCI (about one million tonnes) for distribution was insufficient to implement the subsidised rice scheme. However, this practice was given up in 1989-90 as the FCI started releasing sufficient quantities of rice. There has been an upward trend in rice procurement during the late 1990s—in 1998-99, the procurement of rice had crossed 5 million tonnes and in 1999-2000 it touched a record level of 5.52 million tonnes. Procurement as a percentage of production has increased from a low level of 14 per cent in 1981-82 to nearly 52 per cent in 1999-2000.

The quantity of rice distributed through the PDS generally varied within a range of 2 to 2.5 million tonnes. Generally, 50-60 per cent of rice procured in the state is distributed within the state. The annual per capita quantity distributed through the PDS generally varied between 30 and 37 kg. During the last five years there has not been much change in the

Table 6

Trends in Procurement and Distributions of Rice in Andhra Pradesh

Years	Procurement (in million tonnes)	Production	Procurement as a per cent	Distribution (million)	Distribution as a per cent	Per capita quantity
1970-71	0.47	4.78	9.83	-	-	-
1971-72	0.27	4.72	5.72	-	-	-
1972-73	0.33	4.25	7.76	-	-	-
1973-74	0.70	5.58	12.54	-	-	-
1974-75	0.89	5.07	15.61	-	-	-
1975-76	1.38	6.45	21.39	-	-	-
1976-77	0.48	4.93	9.74	-	-	-
1977-78	0.61	5.59	10.91	-	-	-
1978-79	1.04	7.43	13.99	-	-	-
1979-80	0.47	6.31	7.45	-	-	-
1980-81	0.70	7.01	9.98	-	-	-
1981-82	1.10	7.87	13.97	-	-	-
1982-83	1.64	7.67	26.07	1.37	68.50	24.98
1983-84	1.48	8.79	27.53	1.83	75.62	32.59
1984-85	1.77	6.91	39.65	1.89	68.98	32.91
1985-86	1.57	7.61	32.58	2.15	86.69	36.61
1986-87	1.47	6.59	34.90	2.21	96.08	36.82
1987-88	1.51	7.08	34.04	1.87	77.59	30.49
1988-89	1.48	10.62	26.18	2.00	71.94	31.94
1989-90	2.32	9.96	36.04	2.12	59.05	33.17
1990-91	3.32	9.65	34.04	2.42	72.89	37.11
1991-92	2.26	9.25	24.43	2.24	99.10	33.67
1992-93	3.30	8.79	37.54	1.82	55.15	26.99
1993-94	3.97	9.56	41.52	2.15	54.15	31.45
1994-95	4.02	9.27	43.36	2.26	56.22	32.63
1995-96	3.67	9.01	40.70	2.52	68.66	35.90
1996-97	4.50	10.68	42.13	2.36	52.44	33.18
1997-98	3.85	8.51	45.24	2.28	59.22	31.65
1998-99	5.07	10.66	47.56	2.28	49.97	31.25
1999-00	5.52	10.64	51.88	2.21	41.30	29.92

Note: - Data not available.

Source: *Bulletin of Food Statistics*, Government of India; and Civil Supplies Demand (1994-95) and (2001-2002), Government of Andhra Pradesh.

quantity of rice distributed through the PDS, though the population of the state has been steadily increasing. Therefore, the per capita quantity distributed has been declining, indicating a decline in the extent of food security provided by the PDS in the state.

2. Rice Subsidy Scheme

The Government of Andhra Pradesh introduced the subsidised rice scheme in the early 1980s to improve the consumption levels of the weaker sections of society. Under the scheme, households with an annual income of less than Rs. 6,000 were regarded as 'poor' and were issued green cards, while other households were issued yellow cards. A few years ago, the ceiling on annual income of households was raised to Rs. 11,000. A household with a green card was entitled to 5 kg of rice per person per month subject to a ceiling of 25 kg at Rs. 2 per kg. In 1991, the green cards were replaced by white cards and yellow cards by pink cards. The ration price was increased to Rs. 3.50. per kg and the ceiling was reduced to 20 kg per card. On political and economic grounds, the ration price and the scale of ration have been altered several times. Presently, the ration price of rice is Rs. 5.25 per kg and the quantity distributed per head is 4 kg per month subject to a ceiling of 20 kg per card.

Presently, there are 113 lakh white card holders and 52 lakh pink card holders in the state. The subsidised rice scheme covers nearly 70 per cent of the population, while only about 20 per cent of the population are estimated to be poor. Thus, non-poor households benefit from the scheme also. At the same time micro-level studies reveal that a large number of poor households do not have ration cards.

The subsidised rice scheme involves the provision of subsidy by both the state and central governments. The central subsidy per tonne increased from Rs. 534 in 1982-83 to Rs. 4748 in 1998-99 (Table 7). This increase was due partly to regular enhancement in procurement price and partly to a rise in the administrative cost of the FCI. The mounting buffer stock is responsible for an increase in the storage cost. During the same period, the state subsidy per tonne increased from Rs. 29 to Rs. 3416. It may be noted that in 1983-84, the state subsidy per tonne jumped by about Rs. 500, i.e., from a low level of Rs. 29 to Rs. 523, due to the introduction of the subsidised rice scheme. In spite of hikes in the central issue price, the Government of Andhra Pradesh kept the retail issue price pegged at Rs. 2 per kg. In 1991 it was raised to Rs. 3.50 per kg but in January 1995 it was again reduced to Rs. 2 per kg. As a result, in 1995-96, the subsidy per tonne registered a high level of Rs. 4463. It declined during the latter half of the 1990s as the retail issue price was raised to Rs. 3.50 per kg in August 1996. Due to the scheme, the government expenditure on subsidy increased substantially during the period under study touching a new high of Rs. 1,124 crore in the year, 1995-96. However, in 1998-99 it declined to Rs. 781 crore. The introduction of the Targeted Public Distribution System (TPDS) in 1997 provided some relief to the state government. Under the scheme, a

Table 7
Central and State Rice Subsidy in Andhra Pradesh

(in Rs./tonne)

Year	Central	State	Total
1980-81	340	-	340
1981-82	429	-	429
1982-83	534	29	563
1983-84	667	524	1191
1984-85	749	725	1474
1985-86	773	613	1386
1986-87	804	818	1622
1987-88	809	994	1803
1988-89	817	809	1626
1989-90	1242	1390	2632
1990-91	1280	1512	2792
1991-92	805	1568	2373
1992-93	869	1894	2763
1993-94	967	1900	2867
1994-95	1379	3415	4794
1995-96	1495	4463	5958
1996-97	2371	3351	5722
1997-98	3296	2885	6181
1998-99	4748	3416	8164

Note : - Date not available.

*Sources:*1. *Economic Survey,* Ministry of Finance, Government of India.
2. Budget papers of the Food Corporation of India.
3. Memorandum of Andhra Pradesh submitted to the 10th Finance Commission and Explanatory Memorandum of Andhra Pradesh, Volume IV, No. 2, pp. 240-241.

quantity of 10 kg of rice per month per family living below the poverty line was released by the central government at half the central issue price (CIP). Consequently, the state government was able to obtain 30 per cent of its requirement of rice at a reduced rate. In other words, the introduction of the TPDS has merely amounted to a partial transfer of the state burden to the centre. The state subsidy was again increased to Rs. 1,063 crore in 1999-2000 as the central issue price was enhanced from Rs. 7.50 per kg. to Rs. 9.05 per kg. with effect from 01-02-1999. However, in April 2000, the CIP of BPL rice was hiked from Rs. 3.50 to Rs. 5.90 per kg and of APL rice from Rs. 9.05 to Rs. 11.30 per kg which was expected to increase the state subsidy from Rs. 1,100 crore to Rs. 1,500 crore per annum. But to clear the accumulated stock, the CIP for BPL rice was reduced by 25 paise per kg and that of APL rice by 50 paise per kg in August 2000.

Some critical studies have been initiated on the extent and usefulness of the subsidy provided by the state government. For instance, Olsen (1989), who examined the cost involved in operating the subsidised rice scheme, pointed out that in 1987-88, the subsidy was more than the entire state expenditure on public health. It matched the entire cost of elementary education in the state. Subba Rao (1987) found that in 1985-86, the cost to the state for providing subsidy worth Re. 1.00 was Re. 1.00.

3. Key Aspects of the PDS

(i) Utilisation of the System

The National Sample Survey Organisation (NSSO) in its 42nd round, i.e., 1986-87, collected information on the utilisation of the PDS (Public Distribution System). The results of the survey revealed that in the case of rice and sugar, nearly 60 per cent of the rural households depended partially or wholly on the PDS, while in the case of kerosene, the percentage was slightly higher (65 per cent) (Table 8). In urban areas, half of the households purchased rice and kerosene from fair-price shops (FPS's) and around 70 per cent of urban households visited FPS's to purchase sugar. A rural household with a ration card, on an average, bought slightly over 4 kg of rice and about ½ kg of sugar per person per month. If the total population is considered, then the per capita quantity of rice distributed through the PDS would be only 2.5 kg. This is mainly because only white card holders are entitled to get rice. The per capita quantity of sugar distributed through the PDS was only 0.33 kg. The difference in per capita quantity distributed through the PDS and quantity purchased per user arose because of incomplete coverage of the PDS—rice distributed through the PDS forms about 18 per cent of cereal consumption per household in Andhra Pradesh. About one quarter of the households in rural areas could not buy rice because they had either no entitlement or no ration card (Table 9). For similar reasons, about 17 per cent of the households could not buy sugar. The corresponding figure for kerosene is much higher (over 40 per cent). In urban areas, one half of the households could not buy from ration shops because they had either no entitlement or no ration card.

Table 8
Purchases from PDS in Andhra Pradesh

Item	Rural		Urban	
	Per capita quantity kg/month	Per user quantity kg/month	Per capita quantity kg/month	Per user quantity kg/month
Rice	2.52	4.24	1.98	4.23
Wheat	0.01	0.76	0.23	1.60
Sugar	0.33	0.56	0.56	0.65
Kerosene	0.38	0.53	0.65	1.26
Edible oil	0.09	0.19	0.14	0.27

Source: *NSSO Report* No. 362.

Table 9
Percentage of Persons with No Entitlement/Ration Card in Andhra Pradesh

Item	Rural	Urban
Rice	24.14	44.83
Sugar	17.53	53.82
Kerosene	41.60	53.42

Source: *NSSO Report*, Nos. 362 and 355.

(ii) Leakages at Various Levels

Due to the policy of ensuring delivery of foodgrains at the doorstep of the fair-price shop (FPS), the leakages at the first level, i.e., at the FCI godown level with existing PDS network are minimal. This system of delivering foodgrains appears to be working reasonably well in most parts of the state. In states like Uttar Pradesh and Bihar, the FPS dealers have to lift their allotment from the FCI godowns and transport it to their shops at their own expense and consequently, leakages at first level are high and many times the foodgrains do not reach the villages.

The leakages at the second stage, i.e., village or town level in Andhra Pradesh are likely to be substantial. As the income of FPS dealers is very low, with the gross margin per month varying in the range of Rs. 700-1165 (Indrakant, 1996), they tend to increase their income through issuing of bogus cards, the diversion of quantities not taken by the card holders, etc. Venugopal (1992) found that in 1986 the number of ration cards in circulation (139 lakh) exceeded the estimated number of households (121 lakh) by about 15 per cent or by as much as 8 lakh.

The leakages at the third level, i.e., the household level are not likely to be significant because the price of rice in the fair-price shop is much lower than the open market price of coarse cereals.

(iii) Targeting the Poor

A field study by Indrakant (1996), which covered two backward villages, viz., Nettampadu and Singtham, two developed villages, viz., Narsayapalem and Machavaram, and a moderately developed village, i.e., Jaggasagar spread across the districts of Mahaboobnagar, Medak, Karimnagar and Guntur, indicates the extent to which poor persons are excluded and non-poor persons are included in the PDS.

In the backward villages nearly half of the poor (i.e., those whose monthly per capita expenditure is below Rs. 182) did not possess a white card (Table 10). On the other hand, in the two developed villages almost all the poor households had the white card. It is interesting to note that a large percentage of non-poor households in these villages manage to obtain a white card.

Cornia and Stewart (1993) have classified the errors of targeting into two types, viz., 'E' error, i.e., inclusion of non-poor in the scheme and 'F' error, i.e., exclusion of poor from the scheme. Table 11 shows the extent to which these two types of errors occur in targeting in the five selected villages. In the two developed villages, almost all the poor households are covered by the scheme. However, a large percentage (70-80 per cent) of the beneficiaries of the scheme belong to the non-poor category. In the irrigated area, households having less than 2 acres have been issued white cards. There are many non-poor households which have less than 2 acres of land. Venugopal (1992) has estimated that in 1983, there were about 30-45 lakh ineligible white card-holders in the state. In backward villages, both types of errors in targeting are found in large measure. A large

Table 10

Percentage Distribution of Households in Selected Villages in Andhra Pradesh

Class	Nettampadu		Singtham		Jaggasagar		Narsayapalem		Machavaram	
	Coverage	% of HH	Coverage	% of HH	Coverage	% of HH	Coverage	% of HH	Coverage	% of HH
VP										
Rs. (-137)	100.00	17.19	27.38	19.61	73.14	15.97	–	–	100.00	3.16
MP										
Rs. (137-182)	55.65	42.46	40.94	32.80	77.75	18.49	97.85	19.09	100.00	15.07
MC										
Rs. (182-228)	56.67	28.09	73.27	25.85	44.01	32.31	63.58	27.6	94.99	38.73
R										
Rs. (228-273)	38.95	7.24	21.47	10.62	39.68	16.23	92.54	23.86	77.71	15.48
VR										
Rs. (above 273)	–	5.02	–	11.12	–	17.06	24.82	29.45	38.24	27.56
Total	59.56	100.00	40.02	100.00	46.67	100.00	65.62	100.00	77.59	100.00

Note: VP = Very Poor, MP = Moderately Poor, MC = Middle Class, R = Rich, VR = Very Rich; HH = Household.
Source: Indrakant (1996).

percentage of poor households are excluded from the scheme, while a sizeable percentage of its beneficiaries belong to the non-poor category. In developed villages, the scheme has enabled most of the poor to have access to food. However, a large percentage of beneficiaries are non-poor households.

Table 11

Errors in Targeting in Selected Villages in Andhra Pradesh

Village (in %)	'E' Error (in %)	'F' Error
Nettampadu	39.36	30.48
Singtham	63.08	59.85
Jaggasagar	59.32	20.66
Narsayapalem	71.94	3.41
Machavaram	80.24	0.00

Notes: 1. Type 'E' means percentage of non-poor households among the white card-holders.
2. Type 'F' means percentage of poor households without a white card.
3. Households having a monthly per capita expenditure or less than Rs. 182 are considered as poor households.

Source: Indrakant (1996).

(iv) Impact on Incomes

The subsidised rice scheme has improved income levels and the calorie intake of the people. The magnitude of monthly income gain per person in the selected villages ranged between Rs. 5 to Rs. 14 during the first round (when the ration price of rice was Rs. 3.50 per kg) and between Rs. 8 to Rs. 20 during the second round (when the ration price of rice was Rs. 2 per kg). It formed about 3 to 6 per cent of per capita expenditure during the first round and 4 to 7 per cent of per capita expenditure during the second round. The extent of benefit reaped by the poor is relatively higher in the developed villages. Consequent to these income gains, poverty declined by 4 to 13 percentage points in the five selected villages during the first round and by a higher number of points during the second round. In three villages, the benefits match the cost of implementation of the scheme, while in the remaining two villages, the cost of implementation exceeds the benefits derived from the scheme. In short, the impact of the scheme is not uniform across the five selected villages and the developed villages have benefitted more than the backward villages.

Attempts have been made to provide macro-level estimates on gains of the poor from the scheme (Table 12). The first estimate shows the net gain after allowing for changes in the open market prices brought about by a reduction in supplies due to procurement as well as the farm income feedback effects on demand. The other estimates do not account for these secondary effects. The effects of the open market prices become important since out of the bottom 20 per cent, less than 14 per cent buy all their rice from the PDS, 56 per cent buy only a part of their requirements from the PDS and the other 30 per cent rely entirely on the open market (Parikh, 1994).

Table 12
Estimated Income Gain from Rice Subsidy for Poor in Andhra Pradesh

Source	Rural population segment	Per capita gain /annum
Radhakrishna and Indrakant (1988)	Bottom 40 per cent	23
Parikh (1994)	Bottom 20 per cent	31(1)
Howes and Jha (1992)	Bottom 20 per cent	35(2)
Hanumantha Rao and Jayashree (1994)	Below poverty line	15(3)

Notes: 1. Estimate of subsidy for those buying wholly and partly from the PDS is averaged out for all (including those not availing the PDS) in bottom two deciles.
2. Estimate for separate two bottom deciles is averaged.
3. Estimated benefit per household is reduced to per capita terms assuming the average household size of 5.

In a more recent study, Radhakrishna et al. (1997) have estimated that the per capita monthly gain in income due to the PDS in 1986-87 was nearly Rs. 6 in rural areas and nearly Rs. 8 in urban areas. Consequently, poverty in rural and urban areas of the state declined by 5 and 3 percentage points, respectively. Clearly, with better targeting much better results could have been achieved. A more rational policy aimed at providing food security would be to issue larger quantities of foodgrains through the PDS at a price higher than the existing ones instead of issuing a small quantity of foodgrains at a highly subsidised price.

III. RECENT GOVERNMENT MEASURES

1. Price Control

All the essential commodities are not supplied through the PDS, and even those which are supplied are inadequate to meet the requirement of the households. Hence, the poor are compelled to depend on the open market. Therefore, measures to control open market prices of essential commodities will go a long way providing food security to the poor. Towards this end, the Government of Andhra Pradesh in November 1998, established the Research and Monitoring Wing for Essential Commodities in Andhra Pradesh. The main objectives of the Research Wing are:

1. To anticipate, identify, monitor and analyse sudden escalation in the prices of essential commodities,
2. To suggest to the government an effective, responsive mechanism to redress the situation, and
3. To develop a comprehensive database to facilitate easy and fast decision making by the state government.

Due to the policy of procurement of essential commodities and market interventions which are based on the recommendations of the research wing, the prices of essential commodities were brought down in December 1998 from their earlier level in September 1998. In 1999, during the same period, prices were stabilised (Table 13).

Table 13
Prices of Essential Commodities in Andhra Pradesh

	Average retail price (in Rs. per kg.)			
Item	September 98	December 98	September 99	December 99
Onion	20.54	15.16	5.71	4.60
Chillies	50.85	44.54	32.85	33.99
Red gram	33.18	31.88	28.69	25.24
Ground nut oil	57.34	43.69	40.70	38.58
Tamarind	26.35	20.11	36.07	32.89

Source: Records of Research and Monitoring wing for Essential Commodities in Andhra Pradesh, Andhra Pradesh State Civil Supplies Corporation.

2. Introduction of the Raithu Bazaar Scheme

A novel scheme called Raithu Bazaar (Farmers, Market) has been launched in the state to (a) ensure remunerative prices to the farmers; (b) make essential commodities available to the consumers at reasonable prices; and (c) eliminate middlemen by bringing farmers in direct contact with the consumers. To start with, Raithu Bazaars were established in major municipalities like Hyderabad, Vijayawada, Tirupathi, etc. By January 1999, there were 49 Raithu Bazaars. The scheme will be extended to all the municipalities. To help the farmers bring their produce from different villages to the concerned Raithu Bazaar as quickly as possible, the government has provided the facility of specially designed buses. To prevent the middlemen from entering the bazaar, the government issues photo identity cards to the farmers. Alongside, it is making efforts to provide requisite infrastructure facilities to the farmers. Generally, items like vegetables, fruits, eggs, rice, pulses, oil, etc., are traded in the Raithu Bazaar. It is claimed that due to the establishment of Raithu Bazaar, the prices in the retail market are declining. However, it is alleged that retailers still manage to enter the Raithu Bazaar. Further, doubts have been expressed about the ability of the farmers to stay for the whole day in the Raithu Bazaar leaving their farm work untended. Some people express the fear that such a scheme could seriously affect the small hawkers and vegetable vendors. Hence, there is a need to conduct an independent study covering all aspects of the scheme and its implications.

3. Launching of the Deepam Scheme

The Government of Andhra Pradesh has launched a welfare scheme called Deepam Scheme to provide LPG connections to women of BPL families with a view to help them in improving their health and to remove the drudgery related to conventional cooking. This will also reduce the pressure on the forests for firewood and thus improve the environment. Under the scheme, the state government will meet the initial deposit expense of Rs. 1,000 per connection. The beneficiary has to bear the expenses for stove, pipe and other items. The scheme is likely to benefit 10 lakh women in rural areas and 5 lakh women in urban areas. The beneficiaries are selected from the members of Thrift and Credit Groups, Self-Help Groups, DWCRA/DWCUA Groups who belong to BPL families. Doubts have been expressed about the feasibility of supplying refilled cylinders in rural areas, availability of the refilled cylinders when required and the ability of the beneficiaries to pay the charges for refilled cylinders in one instalment. There is also the possibility of transferring the connection to the others by the selected beneficiaries. It is too early to say how far the programme has been successful.

4. Introduction of the Coupon System

To check the diversion of the PDS supplies to the open market by the FPS dealer and to improve the targeting of the public distribution system, the state government in recent years has introduced the coupon system. Under this scheme, coupons are distributed to the card holders by the officials of the civil supplies department. The card holder is supplied with rations at fair-price shops against these coupons. The FPS dealer has to hand over these coupons to the civil supplies department to get fresh supplies. This procedure enables the civil supplies authorities to know the actual off-take by the card holders. On this basis, the quota for the next month to the FPS dealer is released. This system, it is hoped, is likely to weed out some of the bogus cards.

The coupon system was first introduced on an experimental basis in selected areas for the distribution of kerosene. The initial results, which show that about 15-20 per cent savings are effected in the quantity of kerosene released, are encouraging. It is not clear whether these savings are on account of weeding out of bogus cards or the inability of card holders to obtain coupons. Unless the distribution of coupons is streamlined, the card holders will face difficulties in collecting the coupons. Above all, a collusion between the staff entrusted with the task of distribution of coupons and the FPS dealers would lead to the scheme's failure.

Based on the initial success of the coupon scheme for kerosene distribution the government has extended it for the distribution of rice throughout the state. The officers of the Civil Supplies Department have distributed books containing coupons to the card holder, who uses each book for a period of two years. The card holder has to come in person to obtain the book containing coupons and has to carefully preserve both the ration card and the coupons. This may be difficult for poor and illiterate persons. There are reports that many FPS dealers had expressed their reluctance to continue in the job on account of the coupon system. Clearly, a detailed study on the working of the scheme is called for.

IV. CONCLUSION

During the last four decades the production of both rice and cereals in the state has increased substantially. However, in per capita terms, the improvement is not substantial. The trends in consumption pattern indicate a shift from cereals to non-cereal food items and to non-food items.

While the PDS covers a large section of the population, its benefits do not always reach the targeted groups. The extent of benefits realised from the PDS in terms of the quantity of cereals obtained through the system as a proportion of the total cereal consumption, income gain to the beneficiary households and the consequent decline in the level of poverty is modest when compared to the huge amount of subsidy incurred on the subsidised rice scheme. A more rational policy aimed at providing food security would be to issue larger quantities of foodgrains through the PDS at a price higher than the existing one, instead of issuing a small quantity of foodgrains at a highly subsidised price.

Both supply and demand factors appear to be responsible for the recent glut in production. The demand for cereals is declining because of changes in tastes and insufficient growth of the income of the poor households. To improve the level of food security available to the people in general and the poor in particular, it is essential to ensure that (a) the farmers get a remunerative price, and (b) the income of the poor is increased. Therefore, the prospect of providing food security to the poor in the future, to a large extent, depends upon the success of government policies in increasing the income of the poor, the extent to which the adverse shift in taste patterns is prevented, and the provision of the necessary infrastructural facilities to domestic farmers in the face of globalisation of trade.

References

Cornia, G.A. and Frances, Stewart (1993), "Two Errors of Targeting", *Journal of International Development*, Vol. 5, No. 5 pp. 459-490.

Howes, Stephen and Jha, Shikha (1992), "Urban Bias in the Public Distribution System", *Economic and Political Weekly*, Vol. 27, pp. 1022-1030.

Hanumantha Rao, K. and Jayashree (1994), "Food Insecurity and Impact of Programmes to Reduce It: Case of Andhra Pradesh", Paper presented at *Seminar on Food Security*, organised by Padmavathi Mahila University, Thirupathi.

Indrakant, S. (1996), *Centre for Economic & Social Studies*, "Food Security and Public Distribution System in Andhra Pradesh: A Case Study", Hyderabad (mimeo).

Parikh, K.S. (1994), "Who Gets How Much from PDS: How Effectively Does It Reach the Poor," *Sarvekshana*, Vol. 17, No. 3

Olsen, Wendy K. (1989), "Eat Now Pay Later: Impact of Rice Subsidy Scheme", *Economic and Political Weekly*, Vol. 24, No. 28, pp. 1597-1611.

Radhakrishna, R. and Indrakant, S. (1988), "Effects of Rice Market Intervention Policies in India: The Case of Andhra Pradesh," in Johnson, J.K. (ed.), *Evaluating Rice Market Intervention Policies: Some Asian Examples*, Asian Development Bank, Movila.

—— Subba Rao, K.; Indrakant, S. and Ravi, C. (1997), "India's Public Distribution System: A National and International Perspectives", World Bank Discussion Paper No. 380.

Reddy, Sudhakar S. (1991), "Poverty and Agriculture Growth in Rural Inter District Analysis", Centre for Economic and Social Studies, Hyderabad (mimeo).

Subba Rao, K. (1987), "Interventions to Fill Nutrition Gaps at the Household Level: A Review of India's Experience", Institute of Economic Growth, New Delhi (mimeo).

Subrahmanyam, S., Indrakant and Ravi, C. (2000), "Consumption Patterns and Demand in Andhra Pradesh" Research and Monitoring Wing for Essential Commodities in Andhra Pradesh, Andhra Pradesh Civil Supplies Corporation (mimeo).

Venugopal, K.R. (1992), *Deliverance from Hunger: The Public,* Distribution System in India, Sage Publications, New Delhi.

10

Food Security in a Regional Perspective: A View from Food Deficit Kerala

K.P. Kannan

The recent shift in policy in the allocation and pricing of foodgrains, announced by the Government of India through its budget proposals for 2000-01, constitutes a major departure with regard to the food security policy in the country. On one hand, it has sought to restrict the coverage of the subsidised Public Distribution System to what it considers to be the poor. On the other, it has unilaterally increased the price of the foodgrains and other essential commodities for both the poor and the non-poor. One of the hard-hit states of this policy shift is the foodgrain deficit state of Kerala. In the process, its Public Distribution System, assiduously built up over a long period of time and hailed as a model one, is now facing several problems. What should have been a model for other states in the matter of food security, given the acute inequalities in accessing food in this country, is now left to fight for its very survival. This paper is an attempt to assess the state-assisted food security system in Kerala to show that it has contributed to improve a wide-range of human development indicators that are closely related to access to food and the alleviation of poverty. At a time when the food security system in Kerala is poised for a quantitative as well as qualitative improvement, the changes in national policy that are patently anti-poor have come as a devastating blow.

I. FOOD PRODUCTION AND AVAILABILITY

As in the case of several developmental indicators in India, the state of Kerala presents itself as an interesting case in the matter of food security, too. While Kerala finds itself at a lower level in terms of the average intake of food among various states in India, it is in the forefront in such food security indicators as the incidence of undernutrition, poverty, infant mortality and life expectancy. The problem of availability may have compelled Kerala, in a manner of speaking, to concentrate on the distribution of food. But an important aspect of availability is the question of internal production of food. What is Kerala's record in this aspect? Kerala is known as a 'food deficit' state in India because of the wide gap in the consumption and production of foodgrains especially rice which is the staple diet of the population. However, if food is viewed from a broader angle in terms of a food basket consisting of a number of items of daily consumption, a different picture emerges. Of the 15 items for which actual consumption data were calculated, it is found that Kerala produces more than its requirement for two-thirds, i.e., 10 items (Table 1).

The food consumption data shown in Table 1 was calculated on the basis of household consumption in selected localities in both urban and rural Kerala in 1990-91. The pooled results of these were found to correspond to the consumer expenditure data as per the 45th round of the NSS.[1]

Table 1

Major Food Items in Kerala: Requirement and Production '000 tonnes

Item	Consumption (g.) @	1991		1992	
		Requirement	Production	Requirement	Production
Rice	2249	3403	1087	3637	953
Other cereals	228	345	4	369	6
Pulses	108	163	16	175	15
Tapioca	245	371	3803	396	2602
Vegetables	499	755	#143	807	#154
Milk	521	788	1690	843	2246
Sugar	192	291	0	311	0
Tea	20	30	61	32	65
Coffee	8	12	21	13	22
Gur	19	29	52	31	51
Fish	308	466	607	498	851
Meat	60	91	117	97	138
Cooking oil	59	89	**	95	**
Eggs (million)	*0.56	847	1550	905	1991
Coconut (million)	*0.93	1407	4232	1504	5906

Notes: # Vegetable, pineapple, sweet potato, papaya and drumstick.

@ Quantity consumed per person per week.

* Egg and coconut in numbers.

** Data not available. It can be safely assumed that the production of coconut oil is more than the requirement because coconut production exceeds the consumption by a factor of 3 to 4 as revealed by the last row.

Source: Government of Kerala (1999), p. 25.

Kerala experiences a deficit of foodgrains, mainly rice. The production of other items, except vegetables, are limited by agro-climatic conditions. The deficit in foodgrain production assumes a greater importance than any other food because cereals (including substitutes) account for more than half of the intake of calories (64 per cent for rural and 57 per cent urban) and around half of the intake of proteins (52 and 48 for rural and urban areas respectively) in Kerala (ORF, 1999, pp. 51-52). Hence, the foodgrain deficit is almost tantamount to food deficit in Kerala.

This state of affairs is reflected in the position of Kerala compared to the country as a whole in respect of the availability and actual average consumption of food. In the country as a whole the area under foodgrains has declined marginally (around 2 per cent) during the nineties, but the output increased by around 15 per cent. At the beginning of the nineties, when the process of economic reform was started, foodgrain production stood at 176 million tonnes and increased to 203 million tonnes in 1998-99. Kerala experienced a different trend: area under foodgrains declined by 37 per cent and the output by 33 per cent. Per capita monthly cereal consumption in rural India declined from 15.35 kg in 1971-72 to 13.50 kg in 1991-92. This decline was spread over in most states but in Kerala it increased from 7.99 kg to 10.0 kg (ORF, 1999, pp. 45-46). The average is however still below the national average. Substitution of coarse grains with fine grains along with a diversification in food consumption is presumed to be the reason for this decline. The increase in Kerala could be the result of an increased availability of rice through the PDS; however, this calls for a detailed investigation.

Although Kerala is one of the five states with the least incidence of poverty (as per the 45th round of NSS 1993-94 figures), the problem of hunger seems to persist. The share of households having two square meals a day was the lowest in Kerala among the 17 states both in 1983 and 1993. The figures for urban Kerala were 86.05 and 92.5 per cent whereas for the country as a whole they were 93.25 and 97.7 per cent respectively. For rural Kerala the rank is fifth lowest in 1993 with 91.2 per cent but higher than West Bengal (81.4), Orissa (83.5), Assam (90.4) and Bihar (91.0). To this we should also note the relatively low level of calorie intake in Kerala at 1,965 kilocalories as against 2,400 in India for 1993-94. Kerala's position is the third lowest after Tamil Nadu (1,884) and Maharashtra (1,939). However, NNMB data for 1988-90 show that the energy intake in Kerala was 2,140 kilocalories, also higher than Tamil Nadu (1,871) and Maharashtra (2,221). It is quite possible that the diversified nature of food availability in Kerala (such as coconut, tapioca, banana, etc.) as well as the habit of eating out (also in rural areas) may account for the disparity in figures for Kerala.

All these point to a picture wherein Kerala's position with regard to the availability of food is below the national average leading to the characterisation of the state as a 'food deficit' one. The extent of this deficit has increased over time in Kerala, increasing its vulnerability to food security in the event of a shortage or crisis at the national level. In other words, Kerala is perhaps the most vulnerable to any short-term or long-term foodgrain deficit at the national level. This is borne out by the experience of Kerala since its formation in 1956 to the mid-seventies when the country experienced shortfalls in foodgrain production and consequent introduction of restrictions on the movement of foodgrains. The 'food problem' then assumed a critical place in the politics of the state as well as its relations with the central government.

What is the extent of the foodgrain deficit in Kerala? As Table 2 shows Kerala's deficit in rice was 50 to 55 per cent from the early fifties to the mid-seventies. Since then the deficit has increased steadily and now stands at more than 75 per cent of its requirement. From the national view, Kerala accounted for only 1.3 per cent of the production in India till the mid-seventies; this has now come down to 0.5 per cent. Till the mid-seventies, Kerala accounted for only 4 per cent of India's population which had declined to 3.3 per cent by the end of the century. Given the continuing trend in the decline of the area under rice, and the continuing increase in the requirement as a result of population increase, although at a slower rate, the deficit is likely to go up to 80-85 per cent of the requirement within the next few years. Latest figures (for 1998-99) show that the rice production in the state has declined to 7.3 lakh tonnes, i.e., only around 20 per cent of the requirement. In sum, Kerala has ceased to be a foodgrain producing state of any significance.

Table 2
Requirement and Availability of Rice (lakh tonnes)

Year	Population (lakhs)	Requirement	Own production		External supply		Deficit %
			Total	Available	PDS	Private	(5 as % of 3)
1951	135.49	14.22	7.12	6.41	-	7.81	55
1961	169.04	19.77	10.68	9.61	-	10.16	51
1971	213.47	24.96	120.98	11.68	7.37	5.91	53
1981	254.54	29.77	12.72	11.45	10.63	7.69	61
1991	290.99	34.03	10.87	9.78	17.50	6.75	71
1996	311.01	36.37	9.53	8.58	13.50	14.29	76

Note: Ten per cent of the production of rice is treated as seed requirement to arrive at availability.
Source: Government of Kerala (1999), p. 26.

It is not the main aim of this paper to go into the causes of such a rapid decline in foodgrain production in Kerala. The nature and extent of the decline has been studied by several scholars (e.g., George and Mukherjee, 1986; Kannan and Pushpangadan, 1988 and 1990). The political economy of the decline in rice cultivation is closely related to the larger political economy of development in Kerala (Kannan, 1999a) in which farmers have opted for shifting land out of rice into more remunerative and less labour-absorbing cash crops such as coconut, rubber, banana and others. On one hand, farmers face a high cost regime in cultivation mainly due to high wages (the prices of other inputs being comparable to other states) without a corresponding increase in labour productivity. Since prices are not determined by the Kerala market, farmers do not enjoy any significant price advantage as well. This has resulted in a change in the cropping pattern in Kerala, dominated by cash crops, both food and non-food ones. In fact, the area under rice which was 30 per cent of the gross cropped area in the sixties has declined to around 15 per cent in the nineties (see Table 3).

Table 3
Percentage Share of Area under Major Crops in Kerala

Crop	Trennium ending 1965-66	1985-86	1995-96
Rice	32.1(1)	25.5(1)	16.4(2)
Coconut	22.5(2)	24.7(2)	30.3(1)
Tapioca	8.6(3)	7.8(4)	4.1(5)
Rubber	5.9(4)	10.8(3)	14.5(3)
Pepper	4.0(5)	4.0(6)	6.1(4)
Cashew	3.4(6)	5.0(5)	3.6(6)
Arecanut	2.4(7)	2.1(8)	23.(8)
Banana	1.8(8)	1.8(10)	2.3(8)
Tea	1.6(9)	1.2(11)	1.1(10)
Cardamom	1.2(10)	2.0(9)	1.4(9)
Coffee	0.9(11)	2.3(7)	2.7(7)
Other crops	15.6	12.8	15.2
All crops	100.0	100.0	100.0
(In 000 hectares)	2501	2807	3052

Note: Figures in brackets show ranking.
Source: Computed from data given in Government of Kerala, *Statistics for Planning,* and *Economic Review,* Various Issues.

An important question before Kerala is whether it can hope to reduce its gap between foodgrains production and consumption. An expert committee (Government of Kerala, 1999) which examined this issue recently, arrived at the following conclusion:

> "Food self-sufficiency for Kerala, in the sense of the state's ability to produce all the food items to meet its requirements, is not an economically feasible one. This is especially true for its requirement of rice. Therefore, the policy of the state should be redefined in terms of *achieving food security rather than food self-sufficiency* (emphasis in original)".
>
> "Food security on the other hand refers to the ability of a society to ensure access to food to its population through a variety of means that include both enhancing production and its equitable and fair distribution. The Public Distribution System in Kerala is part of such a food security system. The aim of the government should be to reduce the vulnerability of the state in food security arising out of external shocks such as a decline in the national level production and movement restrictions. The government should try to reduce the gap between internal production and the requirements of its population. The Committee recommends that the aim should be to reduce this gap to 50 per cent from the current level of more than 75 per cent within a period of 10 years. Population projections for Kerala suggest that its total population in the year 2010 will be around 360 lakh. Thus, the total requirement of rice would be around 42 lakh tonnes per annum, estimated at an average daily requirement of 320 g. per person per day as evidenced by some recent consumption pattern studies. This means that the objective should be to increase the production of rice from the current level of 9 lakh tonnes [1998 figures] to 21 lakh tonnes by 2010."
>
> "The broad strategy to achieve this objective should be to increase (i) the total productivity, and (ii) the cropping intensity on paddy lands.

Productivity per hectare of land should be increased from the present state average of 2000 to 3500 kg of rice. Cropping intensity, defined as the ratio of gross cropped area to net area, should be increased from the current level of 1.5 to 2.0. If a net area of 3.00 lakh hectares (which is less than the original wetland area of 5.74 lakh hectares as per the Basic Tax Register and 3.33 lakh hectares utilised for paddy cultivation during 1992-93) can be retained for rice cultivation with a cropping intensity of 2.0, it will have the potential for a gross cropped area of 6 lakh hectares. With a yield rate of around 3,500 kg of rice (5,250 kg of paddy) per hectare, this will ensure a total production of 21 lakh tonnes of rice, i.e., 50 per cent of the projected requirement in 2010 (emphasis in original). This warrants a compound annual rate of growth (CARG) of a little more than 7 per cent in rice production in the state, which is achievable provided all the actors involved, the government, the farmers, the farm workers and the scientists, commit themselves to the proposed total package" (p. 114-15).

II. FOOD SECURITY AND ACCESS TO FOOD

Two important factors seemed to have weighed in accordance with a higher priority for food security by the Government in Kerala. One is the generalised nature of food shortage, especially that of foodgrains, and the consequent political implications and the other is the people's priority in social development including social security, so that successive governments are compelled to accord a high priority for food security as part of a wider system of social security for the people. In an otherwise highly contested political terrain in Kerala, the question of food security has enjoyed, for the above reasons, a remarkable degree of political consensus cutting across the ideological spectrum.

Perhaps the most important protective social security in Kerala is the food security system (Kannan, 1999b). This has three important components: (1) the PDS for all households; (2) the supplementary nutrition programme for children in the age groups of 0-4 and 5-12; and (3) old age pension for the poorer sections.

1. Public Distribution System

Although the PDS in Kerala does not have the advantage of such a long period of positive public policy, as in the case of health care, its origins also go back to the pre-independent days when food rationing was introduced in India at the outbreak of the second World War. It took almost a quarter of a century to establish a Public Distribution System in India as part of the public policy on food security (e.g., see Mooij 1996, pp. 69-76). In Kerala the system was expanded during 1965 at a time when the state was undergoing an acute food shortage. This shortage, as we saw earlier, is structural to the Kerala economy in that a major share of value added in the agricultural sector is through the production of cash crops such as coconut, rubber, tea, coffee, spices, etc., earning or saving considerable foreign exchange to the national economy. Even at the best of times, Kerala could not produce more than 50 per cent of its foodgrain requirements. This has been recognised by the central government which agreed to supply foodgrains (mainly rice and wheat) to meet the requirements of the PDS. Therefore, the introduction of the PDS in Kerala is part of the overall concern of the state to take care of its food security. As such almost all the households have been brought under the PDS. This resulted in the establishment of a large network of ration shops throughout the state. The relevant details are given in Table 4.

Table 4
Public Distribution System in Kerala

Year	Household ration cards (lakhs)	Ration permits to institutions (nos.)	Distribution of			
			Rice ('000	Wheat ('000 m.ts)	Sugar* ('000 m.ts)	Kerosene* ('000 kl)
1975	36.16	7634	531	490	97	107
1985	43.73	7922	1412	110	142	235
1995	56.54	13173	1130	423	150	360
1997	59.52	-	1608	353	154	372

Note: *allotment only.
Source: Government of Kerala, *Economic Review*, Various Issues.

Several studies have underlined that the Kerala PDS is by far the most efficient and egalitarian under Indian conditions where access of the poor to food remains the single most factor in their poverty status. The salient features of the Kerala PDS, which has been showing signs of strain since the policy shift at the centre from the early nineties, may be summarised as follows since they assume much importance in the all-India context of the need for an effective PDS.

(i) *Universal Coverage*: The coverage is universal in that 97 per cent of the households have ration cards. In addition, a number of institutions have also been issued ration cards. This has been the case for the last three-and-a-half decades. As of 1998 there were 61 lakh family ration cards and more than 17 thousand ration permits to institutions.

(ii) *Physical Access:* This is an important consideration in the Indian context. If the time and energy required to purchase the ration is significantly higher than what it would have otherwise taken, it involves an opportunity cost to the families. The widespread network of ration shops in Kerala amounting to more than 14 thousand has ensured physical access in both rural and urban areas. The first Economic Census of India, carried out in 1977, reported that 99 per cent of the villages in Kerala have a fair-price shop within two km distance; Maharashtra came second with 67 per cent. The all-India average was just 35 per cent.

(iii) *Urban Bias:* One of the major drawbacks of the Indian PDS is its urban bias, something which is absent in Kerala. As Suryanarayana (1996) pointed out, if anything, it is somewhat rural biased—the share of the rural segment in the total purchase of rice, wheat, sugar and kerosene is higher than its population. In the case of edible oil (70 per cent), it is only somewhat lower than its population share (74 per cent).

(iv) *Economic Access:* One of the most powerful arguments for a PDS is the question of economic access. This is because of the unequal distribution of income and purchasing power rendering the poorer sections vulnerable to food security. Given the fundamental constraints (such as distribution of assets and income), the Kerala PDS seems to have addressed this issue effectively in a relative sense. Studies (e.g., UN/CDS, 1975; George, 1979; Suryanarayana, 1996) have revealed that nearly two-thirds of the total purchase of rice of the poor in Kerala come from the PDS. For the whole population this is around half (51 per cent for rural and 46 per cent for urban in 1986-87). The picture is similar for sugar but more than 90 per cent for wheat for all the population. Consumption of wheat is low but is slowly picking up. It would appear that while the per capita consumption of cereal has increased in Kerala for all the population—unlike all India—the increase among the poor is considerably higher than that of the population as a whole. Between 1961-94, the lowest three deciles increased their consumption between 32 and 49 per cent in rural areas and 27 to 59 per cent in urban areas whereas it was only a 2 per cent increase in rural areas and a 6 per cent decrease in urban areas for the population as a whole (Suryanarayana, 1996, pp. 23-24). While the average monthly per capita consumption of cereals of the lowest decile was only 52 per cent of the average consumption of the population in 1961-62, it was 71 per cent in 1993-94 in rural areas and 45 and 76 per cent for urban areas. One of the facilitating features of the Kerala PDS in terms of economic access is its flexibility in permitting the card holders to purchase their ration in instalments rather than in one lot for a given period.

All these features should have led to a serious consideration of the Kerala PDS for replication in other parts of India where economic and physical access of the poor to food remains a major problem in ensuring their food security and, consequently, on alleviating poverty. Instead, the recent policy changes of the central government seem to threaten not only the well-established and institutionalised PDS in the food deficit Kerala but even the fragile system in the rest of the country (Suryanaraya, 2000). The consequences of the change in the PDS policy of the central government to the Kerala PDS has been dealt with elsewhere in this paper.

2. State Intervention in the Food Market

In addition to the PDS, the state government intervenes in the market through procurement and distribution of essential commodities with a view to controlling market prices. This is done through the Kerala State Civil Supplies Corporation which has a network of 61 Taluk Depots, 665 retail outlets, 18 super markets and 29 mobile stores. The prices in these shops are lower than the open market prices by a reasonable margin. In addition, by their strong market intervention to sell essential items during festival seasons such as Onam, Christmas and Ramzan, the state is able to provide a measure of stability to the prices of essential commodities. The total sales of the Corporation rose from Rs. 231 crore in 1993-94 to Rs. 473 crore in 1997-98. Although there is a considerable scope for improving the organisational efficiency of the Corporation (e.g., overstaffing), intervention in the food market has helped check the prices in the private trading sector.

3. Free Noon Meal Scheme for School Children

While the PDS in Kerala is the most important component of food security for the people in general and poorer sections in particular, provision of cooked food to the vulnerable among the poor (by self-selection) has come to assume a crucial role in the larger scheme of social security.

The notable feature of this scheme is that food is distributed free to the targeted groups as against distribution of foodgrains at subsidised prices under the PDS. This scheme is also characterised by its relatively earlier vintage (introduced in 1961) as well as its spread throughout the state. The scheme provides approximately 410 calories and 15 grams of protein to the school going children. Till the mid-eighties it was confined to children in the primary classes (I to IV) and in class V wherever these are attached to the primary schools. Since then the scheme has been extended to children up to Class VII. This roughly corresponds to children in the age group of six to 12 years. The food (usually cooked rice and a curry) is usually prepared in the schools for which the services of an assistant are provided. The Head Teacher is responsible for organising the scheme and the teachers help in seating the children and serving the food. The budget provides for noon meals during 180 school days in a year.

As mentioned earlier the scheme also has a pre-independence history. The CDS study on poverty and public policy, traced its origins to the mid-1940s when "the princely states of Travancore and Cochin had established a system of free mid-day meals for poor children in the lower primary schools' (UN/CDS, 1975, p. 35). However, the scheme in its present form was introduced in 1961, much earlier than the currently well-known scheme introduced in the State of Tamil Nadu in 1982, covering the entire state. Until the mid-seventies commodity aid for the programme was received from a consortium of American voluntary organisations known as Co-operative for American Relief Everywhere (CARE); since then the state government has been providing the commodities required from its stock.

Table 5 gives an idea of the coverage of this programme. During the sixties and until the en d of the seventies the coverage of more than 70 per cent of the children in the primary school age group (since Kerala had already achieved high enrolment at the primary stage). The declining coverage ratio during the eighties may be interpreted as a sign of the declining incidence of poverty as families pull out their children from the

Table 5
Free Noon Meal for School Children (in lakh)

Year	No. of students in primary level	No. of students in upper primary level	Total eligible students	Students enrolled in the scheme	(5) as % of (4)
1979-80	25.76	–	–	18.12	70
1984-85	25.01	–	–	14.81	59
1987-88	25.86	17.90	43.76*	32.00	73
1990-91	25.27	19.00	44.27	20.57	46
1991-92	24.72	19.30	44.02	24.10	55
1992-93	24.21	19.33	43.54	23.42	54
1993-94	23.72	19.08	42.80	24.00	56
1994-95	23.25	18.67	41.92	21.21	51
1995-96	22.51	18.39	40.90	20.86	51
1996-97	21.98	18.13	40.11	23.75	59

Note: *Year in which the scheme was extended upto Class VII.
Source: GOK, *Economic Review*, Various Issues.

scheme when they no longer consider it as a much-needed relief. When the scheme was extended to children in the upper primary stage, the coverage ratio increased but the nineties have been registering a declining ratio, again a sign of the continuing decline in the incidence of poverty. At the same time, one should note that the coverage ratio is well above 50 per cent, almost double the incidence of head-count poverty estimate for Kerala in 1993-94. While the latter provides a clear cut-off mark for poverty, the coverage ratio may be interpreted as a sign of families at the margin of the poverty line, even if somewhat above it, and consider the free noon meal for their children as a welcome relief.

4. Supplementary Nutrition for Pre-school Children and Nursing Mothers

A third and equally important component in food security is the various schemes for providing supplementary, but free nutrition to pre-school children and expectant or nursing mothers. This scheme is relatively recent (compared to the above two) in terms of its coverage. The CDS study, while noting the existence of such a programme, stated that "in terms of the quantity involved, this programme is not significant" (UN/CDS, 1975, p. 41). However, by the late seventies, the programme assumed such a dimension as to cover more than a million pre-school children, i.e., close to 40 per cent of the total number of children up to five years of age. This programme in fact was a combination of a number of schemes such as Special Nutrition Programme (SNP), Applied Nutrition Programme (ANP), Composite Programme for Women and Children (CPWP), World Food Programme Supported Feeding Scheme, One-Meal-a-Day Scheme, Health and Nutrition Programme and the by now well-known national programme called Integrated Child Development Scheme (ICDS). Through a series of reorganisations, the ICDS has now emerged as the most important scheme followed by the ANP/CPWP and SNP.

The ICDS was started in the mid-seventies and is intended to provide 300 calories and 8.15 grams of protein per child. For women the provision is 500 calories and 15 grams of protein per day per person. These rates are roughly equivalent to one-fourth of the requirements of the beneficiary groups. This has to be provided for 300 days in a year. In Kerala approximately 84 per cent of the beneficiaries are children and the rest expectant/nursing mothers. Table 6 shows that close to a million beneficiaries are now covered by the scheme. The scheme is 80 per cent supported by financial assistance from the central government. The Applied Nutrition and Composite Programme for Women and Children are slightly different in orientation and are also sponsored by the central government. The Special Nutrition Programme, started by the state through commodity aid from various agencies, has progressively been integrated into the ICDS. Its aims are the same as that of the ICDS. Currently, the SNP is in existence in areas which are not covered by the ICDS.

Table 6
Number of Beneficiaries in Nutritional Programme for Children and Women ('000s)

Year	ICDS	SNP	ANP/ CPWP	WFP	OMD**	HNP	Total
1977-78	57	200		200	–	–	457
1980-81	117	319	610	230	462	165	1903
1991-92	855	47	200	–	–	99*	1201
1995-96	960	–	123	–	–	–	1083

Notes: *refers to beneficiaries under the Feeding Centre Programme.
**OMD was closed in April 1985 as part of streamlining the nutrition programmes.
Source: Government of Kerala, *Economic Review,* Various Issues.

The supplementary nutrition programmes are implemented with the help of a large number of women's welfare organisations called *Mahila Samajams* and other organisations in the state. *Anganwadis* and *Balwadis* have been set up with the help of these organisations. Young educated women in rural areas who face the highest incidence of unemployment in Kerala are recruited as volunteers and receive only a monthly honorarium. The 1999 rate of honorarium was around Rs. 600 per month, which is equivalent to nine days of the wages of female agricultural labourers. But there is a high social premium attached to a regular job outside the farm and hence this abundant supply at a very low wage. For all these programmes there are about 18,500 centres including 11,268 centres under the ICDS.

5. Old-age Pensions to Destitutes and Rural Labourers

Unlike the primary health care system and the PDS, this one is targeted only on the poor based on their social or physical vulnerability or their status as labourers in the unorganised sector. The system of giving old age pension has come to occupy an important place in the social security provisioning in Kerala because of its coverage, progressively being extended to most rural labourers, covering around 60 per cent of the old aged poor in Kerala in 1991 under the two major pension programmes viz., destitutes and agricultural labourers (Table 7). The four most prominent schemes for old age pension for the poor are (1) Pension to the destitute and widows, (2) Pension for the handicapped, (3) Pension for old aged agricultural labourers, and (4) Pension for the old aged fish workers. All these have been in existence for more than 10 years now with the first one for 40 years. The number of pension schemes now in vogue in Kerala is around 17.

The pension schemes can be divided into those that are directly borne by the state out of its budgetary resources and those that are introduced through the creation of social insurance mechanisms such as the setting of welfare funds. The four prominent ones mentioned above are directly met by the state. The schemes introduced through the welfare funds are yet to find a firm footing. There are problems of collection of contributions from the employers and employees. Although these schemes such as the ones for old aged coir, cashew and handloom workers are in existence for the last 10 years or so, there is no evidence to show that pensions are disbursed on a regular basis.

III. A PRELIMINARY ASSESSMENT

It is well known that social security programmes in Kerala are part of its public policy on economic development in general, and poverty alleviation in particular. The emphasis on the latter has led not only to protective measures but also promotional measures thus implicitly recognising the importance of what is now called advancing 'entitlement' and 'capabilities'. Such divisions are more conceptual than practical, in that those programmes intended as protective measures often have strong promotional implications. Programmes such as health care, supplementary nutrition are cases in point.

An important component of the social security programme in Kerala is that of food security. There are three major components to the food security system in Kerala. One is the PDS which covers 97 per cent of the population. The needs of the poor are taken into account in this universal system by giving a higher level of subsidy. Apart from food, the system also meets almost the entire requirement of kerosene which is a basic need for cooking and/or lighting in poorer households. The second is the supplementary nutrition programme targeted on children; one on pre-school children with some health care elements and the other, noon-meal for school-going children up to 12 years of age. The third is the old age and the other disability pension for the poor. This started with destitutes and subsequently extended to physically handicapped, widows and rural labourers. This could be treated as food security as they are targeted only on the poor. We have attempted an estimation of the coverage of these food security schemes for 1991 which is presented in Table 7. It is interesting to note that the major programmes such as the PDS,

Table 7

Selected Food Security Cover for the Poor in Kerala: Some Estimates for 1991 (Nos. in 000s)

Total population			Estimated poor	Beneficiaries	(5) as % of (4)	(5) as % of (3)
1	2	3	4	5	6	7
				Public Distribution		
Male	Female	Total				
14289	14810	29099	9602	26696	278	92
	Children (0-4)			Supplementary Nutrition		
Boys	Girls	Total				
1410	1349	2759	911	1201	132	44
	Children (5-12)			Free Noon Meals		
Boys	Girls	Total				
1760	1701	3461	1142	2410	211	70
	Old aged (60+)			Old age Pensions		
Male	Female	Total				
1689	1371	2560	845	505.3	60	20
	Widows			Widows Pension		
Male	Female	Total				
137	1298	1435	474	129.3	27	9
Total Agricultural labourers(60+) Main Workers (Total cultivators + AL 60+ Main Workers)			Pension for Agricultural Labourers			
Male	Female	Total				
108 (298)	40 (55)	148 (353)	87 (151)	344.3	396 (228)	233 (96)
	Divorced/ Deserted/Widowed			Pension		
Male	Female	Total				
167	1461	1628	537	51.76	10	3
	Physically Disabled			Pension		
Male	Female	Total				
–	–	145	48	8.35	17	6

Notes: 1. Except for 'physically disabled', columns 1, 2 and 3 are from the 1991 Population Census Reports for physically disabled, the source is the Report of the National Family and Health Survey: Kerala for 1992-93. The information pertain to, on a per 1000 population basis, 11.0 for partial blindness, 3.0 for complete blindness and 6.6 for physical impairment. The number of estimated poor is based on an incidence of 33.3 per cent as the Head Count Ratio for 1991.

2. The number of estimated poor for 1991 is based on the highest estimate of the available figures. The Planning Commission's Expert Committee estimated the percentage of population below the poverty line in Kerala as 25.43 for 1993-94 while the World Bank estimated it at 33.8 for 1990-91 and 31.07 for 1993-94. We have taken the 1990-91 estimate and estimated the number of poor by taking the HCR at one-third of the population (33.33%). For agricultural labourers, it is well known that the HCR is much higher than for the general population for 1993-94 this has been estimated as 58.8 per cent for India. We have applied this for Kerala. The HCR for self-employed in agriculture was 31.1 per cent in 1993-94.

3. The estimate of the number of physically disabled is from the National Family Health Survey for Kerala in 1992-93.

4. The beneficiaries under children of 0-4 years refer to the various nutritional care programmes such as the Integrated Child Development Service, Special Nutrition Programme, etc. The number of beneficiaries may include women (as mothers) but is likely to form only a small proportion of the total.

5. The beneficiaries under children of 5-12 years refer to the number of children availing of the free noon meal in Schools.

6. The old aged (60+) beneficiaries refer to those receiving old age pension from the state. The categories included here are destitute and agricultural labourers.

7. All other beneficiaries refer to those receiving old age or special (as in the case of widows) pension.

supplementary nutrition and pension for agricultural workers cover more than the estimated poor below the poverty line. In fact, 92 per cent of the population are covered under the PDS, 44 per cent of pre-school children are covered under the supplementary nutrition programme, 70 per cent of the children between five and 12 years are covered by the free noon-meal scheme and 100 per cent of the 'main agricultural labourers' above 60 years are covered by the old age pension scheme. In the case of agricultural labourers, the much higher coverage is perhaps due to the fact that many of them are only marginal agricultural labourers and have to do a variety of jobs in the casual labour market because of the declining employment in agriculture. However, they identify themselves as agricultural labourers during enumeration.

A valid question that could be raised here is: why should there be people below the poverty line in Kerala (the head-count varied from 25 per cent to 33 per cent in 1991) when more than the estimated poor are covered by one or more of the social security schemes? The answer lies in the fact that the benefits are still so meagre as to pull them out of even the officially determined low poverty line. For instance, the PDS is able to cover only two-thirds of the requirements of rice of the poorer households, the calories provided for children cover only one-fourth of their daily requirements and the real value of old age and other pensions has steadily declined over the years as to hardly cover one meal a day. In 1980, the agricultural labourers' pension was Rs. 45 per month; in 1991 the real (deflating it with the CPI-AL) value was only Rs. 25.

There are few income/employment generating programmes in Kerala that could come under food security. Those that are implemented are centrally sponsored poverty alleviation programmes such as the IRDP, JRY, etc. The per capita benefit of these programme is so meagre as to make any perceptible dent on poverty (see, e.g., Kannan 1995). In terms of employment generation, they hardly give employment for more than a few days per labourer. Here again, funds have been spread too thinly without being able to make significant reductions in poverty on their own.

IV. PERFORMANCE INDICATORS OF FOOD SECURITY

The various state interventions in ensuring food security can only give us an idea of the effort but not their outcome. The latter will have to be examined in the light of the human development indicators that are related to food security. Nutritional status of a population, especially its vulnerable sections, is perhaps the closest to find out the impact of food security measures. However, this will have a bearing on more broader and perhaps robust indicators such as life expectancy, infant mortality and, to some extent, on the incidence of absolute poverty. When we examine Kerala's food security in terms of these indicators, its performance is the best (or one among the best achievers). This relatively better record of Kerala is well known in informed circles but what makes it exceptional is the fact that it scores over states which are economically much more advanced in terms of per capita income, food consumption, urbanisation and industrialisation.

According to a study by the National Nutritional Monitoring Bureau, Kerala ranked first in terms of lowest percentage of undernutrition among children (below four years) among the eight states studied in two time periods, viz., 1974-79 and 1988-90. At the same time, it improved its position by reducing the incidence of severe undernutrition among children by 59 per cent and overall undernutrition by 31 per cent. In 1988-90 Kerala was followed by Tamil Nadu, Maharashtra and the three other southern states. This performance sharply contrasts with Kerala's position in average consumption of nutrients at the household level as the second lowest both in terms of energy and protein. Tamil Nadu, equally interestingly, has the lowest position (Table 8).

Nearly half the children (51 per cent) suffered from malnutrition in India in 1994 and the picture was reportedly the same for adult rural population at 46 per cent. The regional pattern was similar to those among children with Kerala recording the lowest (33 per cent) followed by Tamil Nadu (37 per cent) and higher in Gujarat, Maharashtra and Madhya Pradesh—all above 50 per cent (Radhakrishna, 1999, p. 96). Commenting on the interstate variations in the malnutrition levels of children under five years, Radhakrishna writes that, in 1994, the percentage of moderately and severely malnourished children varied between 34 per cent in Kerala and 57 per cent in Gujarat. Middle-income states such as Kerala, Tamil Nadu and Andhra Pradesh performed better than high-income states like Gujarat and Maharashtra in terms of the nutritional status of children. Not surprisingly, poorer states such as Madhya Pradesh and Orissa performed the worst. Tamil Nadu could perform better. The National Family Health Survey data also reveal more or less similar patterns as the NNMB data' (ibid., p. 96).

Table 8
Ranking of States according to Nutritional Status and Energy Consumption (NNMB data 1988-90 and 1974-79)

State	Ranking* according to nutritional status	Nutritional status of children below four years		Ranking according to energy consumption**	Average consumption of nutrients (cu/day) (at household level)	
		<-2SD	<-3SD		Energy (kcal)	Protein (g)
Kerala	1(1)	42.5(61.2)	11.8(28.9)	6(7)	2,140(1,978)	52.9(46.4)
Tamil Nadu	2(3)	56.6(66.3)	22.6(34.7)	7(5)	1,871(2,275)	45.6(54.8)
Maharashtra	3(7)	60.1(72.8)	24.0(40.6)	5(3)	2,211(2,300)	61.7(64.5)
Andhra Pradesh	4(4)	60.7(66.9)	28.4(35.6)	4(2)	2,340(2,447)	55.7(59.8)
Karnataka	5(6)	65.9(71.6)	31.1(36.4)	2(1)	2,431(2,932)	65.4(79.3)
Gujarat	6(8)	67.2(74.4)	36.9(43.4)	3(6)	2,375(2,162)	69.3(64.2)
Madhya Pradesh	7(5)	68.9(70.8)	41.8(41.3)	1(4)	2,614(2,283)	82.5(71.5)
Orissa	8(2)	69.5(62.8)	35.7(33.2)	NA	U	U

Notes: Figures in parentheses correspond to 1974-79 values. *Rank of state with lowest per cent of undernutrition=1. ** Rank of the state with highest level of energy consumption=1. U=Not Available; NA=Not Applicable. <-3SD indicates severe under-nutrition. <-2SD indicates overall (mild, moderate and severe) undernutrition.

Table 9

State-wise Comparison of Nutritional Status and Mortality Rates of Children Under Four Years (NFHS, 1992-93)

		Nutritional status (weight –for-age) per cent		Mortality rates*			Death rate**
State	Sex of child	<-3SD	<-2SD	Neonatal	Infant	under five	(0-4) years
India	M	20.2	20.2	57.0	88.6	115.4	23.0
	F	20.2	48.1	48.1	83.9	122.4	23.6
	T	20.6	52.7	52.7	86.3	118.8	23.3
Kerala	T	6.1	28.5	15.5	23.8	32.0	3.8
Tamil Nadu	T	13.3	48.2	46.2	67.7	86.5	17.7
Karnataka	T	19.4	54.3	45.3	65.4	87.3	13.7
Andhra Pradesh	T	15.6	49.1	45.3	70.4	91.2	18.5
Haryana	T	9.0	37.9	38.4	73.3	98.7	22.1
Delhi	T	12.0	41.6	34.9	65.4	83.1	18.6
Punjab	T	14.2	45.9	31.2	53.7	68.0	14.9
Rajasthan	T	19.2	41.6	37.2	72.6	102.6	26.3
Gujarat	T	17.6	50.1	42.3	68.7	104.0	20.6
Maharashtra	T	21.3	54.2	36.4	50.5	70.3	12.1
Goa	T	8.9	35.0	20.6	31.9	38.9	4.9
Madhya Pradesh	T	22.3	57.4	53.2	85.2	130.3	27.3
Bihar	T	31.1	62.6	54.8	89.2	127.5	28.0
Uttar Pradesh	T	24.6	59.0	59.9	99.9	141.3	31.6
Himachal Pradesh	T	12.9	47.0	34.2	55.8	69.1	15.5
Jammu & Kashmir	T	13.8	44.5	31.9	45.4	59.1	15.6
Orissa	T	22.7	53.3	64.7	112.1	131.0	27.3
West Bengal	T	18.6	48.8	51.8	75.3	99.3	18.7
Assam	T	18.7	50.4	50.9	88.7	142.2	32.1
Arunachal Pradesh	T	14.5	39.7	17.5	40.0	72.0	U
Manipur	T	7.2	30.1	25.1	42.4	61.7	U
Meghalaya	T	17.2	45.5	37.8	64.2	86.9	U
Mizoram	T	5.3	28.1	8.3	14.6	29.3	U
Nagaland	T	7.6	28.7	10.0	17.2	20.7	U
Tripura	T	18.6	48.8	43.6	75.8	104.6	U

Notes: U=Not Available, M=Male, F=Female, T=Total (M+F). *Mortality rates for India are calculated for the 10 year period preceding the survey while mortality rates for the states are for a five-year period preceding the survey in 1992-93. **The age-specific death rate is based on the annual number of deaths reported during the two-year period prior to the NFHS, 1992-93.

However, when all states are compared for another measure of nutritional status, viz., weight-for-age available from the National Family and Health Survey (1992-93), the 'southern advantage', suggested by Radhakrishna, disappears. Kerala retains its first place along with such north-eastern states as Mizoram and Nagaland (at 28 per cent), almost half of the national average of 53 per cent. Andhra Pradesh (49 per cent), Karnataka (54 per cent) and Tamil Nadu (47 per cent) are behind the north-eastern states (except Tripura) as well as the north-western states of Punjab, Haryana Rajasthan and Gujarat and Jammu & Kashmir (Table 9).

In terms of life expectancy at birth, Kerala (more than 70 years in 1991) is at least 10 years higher than the all-India estimate (close to 60 years). As Amartya Sen has argued, this measure has to be reckoned as a robust one, for, all efforts at human improvement are intended to achieve a longer and healthy life. Under-five and infant mortality rates are also one of the lowest in Kerala outperformed by only two states, viz., Mizoram and Nagaland (Table 9).

The comparatively better performance of some of the north-eastern states in a number of human development indicators and the similarity to Kerala's achievement in many others warrants a closer study of these societies in terms of their traditional socio-economic organisation and the current dynamics of state and society. While Kerala has received considerable attention and subjected to close examinations through several studies, a similar focus on the north-east is lacking. It is my view that the social science community needs to be alerted to what may promise to be another interesting development within the otherwise depressing Indian scenario in human development.

V. CONCERNS OVER SUSTAINING FOOD SECURITY: THE IMPACT OF ECONOMIC REFORMS

One of the consequences of the change in the policy of the central government, arising out of the process of economic reform, has been on the PDS. The decision to limit the PDS subsidy to those 'below the poverty line' from 1997 has meant a decline in the availability of foodgrains at a subsidised price to the states for their Public Distribution Systems. Secondly, the differing interpretations of those 'below the poverty line' by the central and state governments have led to an additional burden on the states. In Kerala, the state government continued its universal coverage of the PDS but introduced a dual pricing system. Under this system, 42 per cent of the family ration card holders were treated as 'below poverty line'. This 42 per cent was identified as part of the exercise for implementation of the Integrated Rural Development Programme (IRDP). This has meant that 17 per cent of the card holders were supplied with foodgrains at a subsidised price over and above the 25 per cent recognised by the central government. In 1998, these card holders were given 10 kg of rice per family (as per the central government norm) at a subsidised price of Rs. 3.90 per kg (revised to Rs. 4 from January 1999). Any additional requirement of rice for these families was met at a price of Rs. 8.60 inclusive of a one rupee subsidy by the state government. All the non-poor card holders were also given rice at this subsidised price of Rs. 8.60 per kg. The estimated subsidy for rice alone works out to nearly Rs. 188 crore per annum.

The recent hike in issue prices for the PDS announced by the Union Finance Minister in his Budget Speech (February 29, 2000) has been a severe blow to the PDS in Kerala, threatening its very survival. If that happens, it will be the end of a PDS hailed as a model for other states. The contours of the emerging economics of Kerala's PDS are only beginning to be realised. Take the case of rice which is the single most important item in the PDS. Kerala's PDS distributed, on an average, around 15 lakh tonnes of rice per annum in the nineties. The poor (taking 42 per cent of the 61 lakh family card holders) consume around 8.7 kg of rice per capita per month of which only 5 kg was purchased from the PDS. The state government has announced that it will continue the existing prices (i.e., Rs. 4 per kg for the poor and Rs. 8.60 for the non-poor) and will continue the universal coverage of the PDS. The issue price of the central government is pegged at 50 per cent of the economic cost for those 'below the poverty line' (BPL) and full cost for those 'above the poverty line' (APL). This works out, including handling charges around Rs. 6 per kg for the BPL and Rs. 12 per kg for the APL. The subsidy involved will then range from Rs. 450 crore per annum assuming 20 kg of rice per poor family per month to Rs. 645 crore assuming 25 kg per poor family per month actually purchased by them.

There are a number of issues involved in the changed context of the role of the PDS. First, the strict application of official 'poverty line' will exclude a number of households who are just above but around the poverty line. This calls for a broad band in determining the eligible poor households rather than a strict line. Such an approach is already in existence in the case of the implementation of IRDP. Second, pegging the PDS price to the 'economic cost' will have no incentive for enhancing the efficiency of the Food Corporation of India in storage and handling. In fact, there are already complaints on the inefficiency of the FCI. The question therefore is one of adopting 'cost effective' approaches in handling and storage. Third, and linked to the above point, is the increasing bufferstock and the consequent cost increase to the government.[2] This calls for determining the basic minimum for buffer and the speedy disposal of the surplus stocks. Fourth, can the PDS sustain itself by excluding the non-poor, a majority of whom are not really rich? If such an exclusion is implemented, what will be the impact on the open market prices and the possibility of speculative price increases of an unexpected nature. Last, but not the least, is the question of priorities in reducing government subsidies. Should the PDS be targeted first or should it come last, if at all. The procurement prices, benefiting the rich farmers, have by now become a sort of subsidy. As soon as the cut in PDS subsidies were announced, the central government has enhanced the procurement prices. Is this administered price mechanism the best way to encourage foodgrains production or should the government concentrate on long-term technological and institutional solutions? There are also other implicit and explicit subsidies to the non-poor. Take the case of zero income tax of agricultural income, subsidies to the public sector, etc. Given such a scenario the anti-poor bias in the policy of the central government has come in for sharp criticism.

VI. LONG TERM SOLUTIONS FOR FOOD SECURITY IN KERALA

The regional perspective on food security, from the point of view of a 'food deficit' state like Kerala, is that a region may remain vulnerable even when national self-reliance is achieved in terms of availability. In Kerala's case, the increasing specialisation of its agriculture towards non-foodgrain crops has meant a sharp decline in the regional availability of foodgrains. While the better-off sections in the state are able to take care of their foodgrain requirements through the open market, a large section of the population, both absolutely poor and nearly-poor, have come to depend on the PDS for a major part of their foodgrain requirements. Since the state has to depend on the centre for allocation of foodgrains for the PDS, the system is also vulnerable to changes in national policy. The long-term solution is to ensure that the extent of dependency is reduced. In the case of Kerala, the potential output of rice is close to 21 lakh tonnes, i.e., a little more than half its requirement. Given that the farmers in Kerala are price takers in both the product market and the input market, the solution lies in increasing productivity. This calls for improving the water control measures. It is in this sphere that the state has failed miserably. Scarce public resources invested in medium and major irrigation projects have become sunk costs with project time and cost overruns. A majority of the projects are still in a state of incompleteness for periods ranging from 20 to 35 years! Very little work has been done beyond irrigation. Watershed management is yet to make any headway. This has resulted in a very slow diffusion of innovation in agriculture. In fact, the area under high-yielding varieties is on the decline for quite some time. Farmers' attempts at introducing mechanical technology in the context of increasing labour costs have also met with a resistance from organised labour. This is ultimately a reflection of the state of underemployment in the rural economy of Kerala.

The establishment of the new Panchayati Raj since 1995, following the constitutional amendments, has opened up possibilities for strengthening the basic developmental works for agricultural development. Nearly 40 per cent of the plan funds are now being earmarked for the panchayats. Land and water management at the level of the village, block and district panchayats should have been taken up as a first priority for strengthening the agricultural sector. In the first few years of the working of the new panchayats, the priorities continue to be dominated by welfare programmes for individuals and households (with some honourable exceptions where voluntary organisations worked hard to change priorities in favour of public goods). Distributional programmes with considerable scope for decentralised rent-seeking within a culture of patently partisan politics is what characterises the so-called 'People's Planning' in 'progressive' Kerala. A concerted effort is needed to focus on the problem of developing public and collective goods at the local level especially for the agricultural sector.

VII. CONCLUDING REMARKS

There are important lessons to be learnt from the Kerala experience of ensuring food security in the context of food deficit in internal supply as well as the existence of a sizeable section of the population below the poverty line. The policy change at the national level with a view to cut subsidy to the Public Distribution System has however raised questions about the sustainability of Kerala's PDS. The state government has been forced to choose between continuation of the existing PDS with universal coverage involving unsustainable subsidies and restricting the PDS only to the poor with the implications for enhancing the state's vulnerability to food security. Either way, it will be a hard choice.

Notes

1. The food consumption data presented here is based on a survey of 2000 households (30 per cent in urban areas and 70 per cent in rural areas) as part of a study on "Socio-Economic Changes in Kerala" conducted during 1990-91 by the Kerala Statistical Institute, Thiruvananthapuram. The results of this survey (for consumption data) were found to be compared to the results obtained in the 45th round (1998-90) of National Sample Survey. This means that the results of the study carried out in different localities, when pooled together, could give reasonably satisfactory state level estimates; for details, see KSI (1992).
2. The problem has already surfaced within a few months of the announcement of the new policy on Public Distribution System. The Government of India is now saddled with a huge stock of foodgrains (around 41 million tonnes as against the 25 million it wants to handle) leading to damage due to paucity of storage facilities and an increase in cost of stocking.

References

George, P.S. (1979), *Public Distribution of Foodgrains in Kerala—Income Distribution Implications and Effectiveness*, Research Report 7, International Food Policy Research Institute, Washington.

—— and Mukherjee, C. (1986), "Rice Economy of Kerala: A Disaggregated Analysis of Performance", *Indian Journal of Agricultural Economics*, Vol. 41, No. 1.

Government of Kerala (1999), *Report of the Expert Committee on Paddy Cultivation in Kerala*, July.

Kannan, K.P. (1999a), "Rural Labour Relations and Development Dilemmas in Kerala: Reflections on the Dilemmas of a Socially Transforming Labour Force in a Slowly Growing Economy", *Journal of Peasant Studies*, January-March.

—— (1999b), "State Assisted Social Security in Kerala", Paper presented at the *National Seminar on Social Security in India*, India International Centre, New Delhi during 15-17 April 1999 and organised by the Institute of Human Development, New Delhi.

—— (1995), "Public Intervention and Poverty Alleviation: A Study of the Declining Incidence of Rural Poverty in Kerala, India", *Development and Change*, Vol. 26, No. 4, October.

—— (1990), "Dissecting Agricultural Stagnation in Kerala: An Analysis across Crops, Seasons and Regions", *Economic and Political Weekly*, September 1-9.

—— and Pushpangadan, K. (1988), "Agricultural Stagnation in Kerala: An Exploratory Analysis", *Economic and Political Weekly*, Review of Agriculture, September 24.

KSI (1992), *Socio-economic Changes in Kerala: A Study Based on Selected Localities*, Kerala Statistical Institute, Thiruvananthapuram.

Mooij, Jos (1996), *Food Policy and the Indian State: The Public Distribution System in South India*, Oxford University Press, New Delhi.

Observer Research Foundation (1999), *Demand for Foodgrains by 2020*, New Delhi.

Radhakrishna, R. (1999), "Food Security and the Poor", in Chelliah, R.J. and Sudarshan, R. (eds.), *Income Poverty and Beyond: Human Development in India*, Social Science Press, New Delhi.

Suryanarayana, M.H. (1996), "Food Security and PDS in Kerala: Form and Scope for Reform", Paper presented at the *International Conference on Kerala's Development Experience: National and Global Dimensions*, December 9-11, New Delhi.

—— (2000), "Backdoor Closure of PDS?", *The Hindu*, March.

United Nations (UN/CDS) (1975), *Poverty, Unemployment and Development Policy: A Case Study of Selected Issues with Special Reference to Kerala*, New York.

11

Food Security Issues in a State of Large Agricultural Instability: The Case of Rajasthan

Vidya Sagar

I. INTRODUCTION

Rajasthan is passing through yet another crisis. The drought this year (2002-03) appears to be more severe than the one in 1987-88. By one estimate the state spent as much as Rs 9.5 billion on mitigating its effects. The severity of the drought this year is due to the fact that the state itself is hit by a financial crunch. The problem is compounded by the directives of the Government of India for identifying families below poverty line (BPL) as a result of which their number has halved—having declined from 2.6 million households in 1997 to 1.3 million households in 2002. The figures are drawn from the latest quinquinnial round of NSSO's survey on consumption which shows the extent of rural poverty in Rajasthan in the year 1999-2000 at 13.4 per cent. In this paper we shall examine the present and the future status of food security scenario in the state in the light of these developments and their implications for food security in the long term.

Food security has been variously defined in the literature, but the generally accepted definition is that of the World Bank (1986): "access by all people at all times to enough food for an active healthy life". In a large number of alternative definitions of this term, the emphasis, however, remains on just *sort* of 'access to enough food for all, ensured through a right to secured livelihood during' normal time and (a right) to get compensated for the loss (decline or deterioration) in it during emergency. At the macro-level food security is achieved by the state when (a) it has sufficient access to food for all its citizens—through own production, stocks or trade, and (b) it can guarantee everyone (right to) such access. It represents "a condition in which the probability of a country's citizens falling below a minimum level of food consumption—a function of international and domestic variables—is very low". The focus of most of the definitions of household food security is its transitory component. It aims at saving the vulnerable groups from the adverse impact of wide fluctuations in agricultural production by (a) making foodgrains accessible to nearby regions; and (b) protecting them from the sharp increases in foodgrain prices.

The operational part of this definition may be described as the interplay of two components of food security, viz., availability of and access to adequate food. 'Availability' is defined as stable aggregate supply, ensured either through sustainable growth in production or through imports, or both. It encompasses both the inter-temporal and spatial stability of supplies for every section of the population. 'Accessibility' is largely defined in terms of entitlement to access adequate food. In the regional context adequate food production within the region may not have much relevance if alternative farming systems provide adequate income/ employment to absorb food surplus generated elsewhere in the country. This is more so in the present-day context of large food surpluses and when economic liberalisation and comparative advantage tend to define farm production trends. A dependable network of the PDS across the country does ensure food security if access to food, whether through production, labour, trade or transfer-based entitlements, is ensured. We begin our discussion with the issues relating to the production and availability of foodgrains in section II. This includes instability in production besides growth in crop production. Section III analyses distribution of consumption expenditure and poverty in the state. Factors contributing to food security, which include livestock economy besides various public interventions aimed at alleviating transitory and chronic food security are described in section IV. Challenges to food and nutrition security are discussed in section V. The final section presents the concluding observations.

II. PRODUCTION, AVAILABILITY AND INSTABILITY IN FOODGRAINS

1. Availability of Foodgrains from Domestic Production

Agriculture continues to be the major economic activity in rural Rajasthan. The cropping pattern was heavily biased towards foodgrains until the seventies. A major shift in the cropping pattern had taken place during the eighties. During the last four decades agricultural performance of the state has kept pace with population growth (Table 1). Index number of agricultural production, with the base period 1979-82 as 100, has increased to 249 during the triennium ending 1999-2000. Population growth during the same period has been 65 per cent, which is somewhat lower than the growth in production of foodgrains. As a result, the per capita production of foodgrain has improved. As against the ICMR norm of per capita foodgrains consumption of 195 kg, production in the state has been significantly below this norm only once (1993-94) since the severe drought of 1987-88 (Fig 1). Even during that year (1993-94) the loss was partly compensated by per capita production in oilseed. The surplus exceeding 50 kg per capita is estimated in seven crop years since 1987-88.

A marginal deficit of 14 kg and 6 kg is reported during 1991 and 2000-01, respectively (Table 2). The state is thus surplus in foodgrain production on a triennium basis. This is in spite of a shift in cropping pattern and diversion of irrigation, (mostly additional capacity), to non-food crops. As a result of this and other supporting factors, the index of production of non-food crops increased to 472 during the triennium ending, 1999-2000.

At the disaggregated level, three western arid districts of Barmer, Jodhpur and Jaisalmer produce below 100 kg of foodgrain per capita. For another 10 districts the per capita production figures are below 160 kg. These include districts with a high proportion of urban population such as Jaipur, Ajmer, Bikaner and Udaipur. The remaining 19 districts are self-sufficient in providing adequate foodgrain for their own populations. Surpluses from these districts are sufficient to take care of the deficit districts on the triennium basis (Table 3).

2. Instability in Agricultural Production

An important feature of the agricultural scenerio in the state is the wide annual variation in agricultural production—coefficient of variation in foodgrain production at the aggregate level in Rajasthan increased marginally to 20.5 per cent during the eighties and the nineties, as compared to 18.2 and 18.3 per cent during the sixties and the seventies. With over 50 per cent of small and marginal holdings being wholly unirrigated, coefficient of variation of *kharif* production of foodgrains is a better indicator of deprivation for the poor. The coefficient during the three time points is 23.7 per cent, 36.4 per cent and 42.1 per cent, respectively. In the past, compensatory movements were observed in the seasonal (*rabi* and *kharif*) production in most of the areas. This is clearly reflected in the lower aggregate coefficient during the sixties but more prominently during the seventies. This phenomenon is gradually declining over time as is reflected by the aggregate coefficient of variation for the eighties. This may have happened due to excessive concentration of resources in smaller and irrigated areas by using the meagre irrigation facilities more for productive purposes rather than protective ones. With the dwindling groundwater level, the impact of the low rainfall has been the most severe on the small and marginal cultivators.

Production of *rabi* foodgrains, which accounts for two-thirds of the total foodgrain production, shows stability. Variability in total production increased during the eighties due to the 1987-88 drought. The fluctuations in oilseed production have fallen rapidly during this period in spite of a remarkable growth in production (Hanumanta, Rao, 1988) (Fig. 2).

Overall, agricultural production did not show signs of increased fluctuations in spite of a high growth in agricultural production during the past 15 years.[1]

The district level production figures show very large variations in foodgrain production over a period of time. In Barmer, for example, the annual production of foodgrains varied widely: 28,000; 164,000, negligible, negligible and 456,000 tonnes during the five consecutive

Table 1
Agricultural Performance in Rajasthan During Last Four Decades*

Ag. years	Decadal average production			Decadal coefficient of variation		
ending	Foodgrain	Non-foodgrain	All crops	Foodgrain	Non-foodgrain	All crops
1961-70	71	81	72	18.63	26.96	16.87
1971-80	104	102	104	18.12	17.17	16.48
1981-90	123	194	137	20.51	35.89	21.22
1991-00	170	448	222	20.58	11.92	15.18

Note: *Based on index numbers of agricultural production.

Table 2
Agricultural Performance in Recent Years

	Production (mln. tonnes)[1]		Per capita production (kg)	
Year	Foodgrain	Oilseed	Foodgrain	Oilseed
1987-88	4.8	1.16	118	28
1988-89	10.7	1.91	262	47
1989-90	8.5	1.85	204	44
1990-91	10.9	2.35	255	55
1991-92	8.0	2.71	181	62
1992-93	11.5	2.54	254	56
1993-94	7.0	2.31	151	50
1994-95	11.7	2.83	247	60
1995-96	9.6	3.07	197	63
1996-97	12.8	3.49	257	70
1997-98	14.0	3.15	274	62
1998-99	12.9	3.82	246	73
1999-00	10.8	3.41	201	63
2000-01	10.4	2.04	189	37

Source: Government of Rajasthan, *Statistical Abstracts*, various years.

Table 3
Per Capita Average Foodgrain Production by Districts during the Period 1996-97 to 2000-01

Per capita foodgrain production(kg)	Share in foodgrain production	Share in state's population		Districts
		Total	Rural	
300 to 700	40	24	25	Hanumangarh, Bundi, Ganganagar, Sawaimadhopur, Karoli, Dausa, Bharatpur, Alwar
200-300	27	25	26	Chittor, Tonk, Bhilwara, Banswara, Jhalawar, Baran Dholpur, Sikar, Churu
190-200	6	6	5	Kota, Jhunjhunu
100-160	24	38	34	Nagaur, Dungarpur, Udaipur, Bikaner, Jaipur, Rajsamand, Pali, Ajmer, Sirohi, Jalore
60-100	3	10	10	Barmer, Jodhpur, Jaisalmer

Source: Author's calculations.

Fig. 1
Agricultural Instability in Rajasthan: Five Years Moving S.D. of Annual Growth Rates of Production

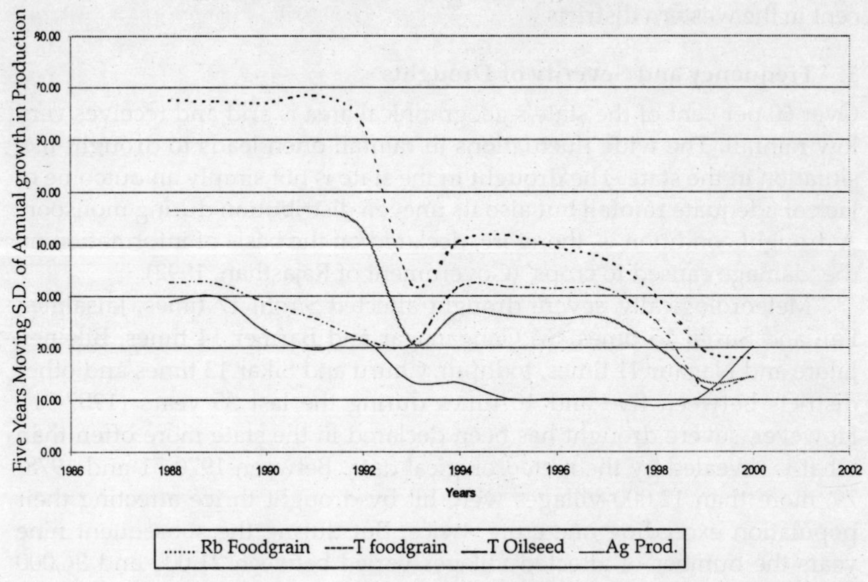

Fig. 2
Average Per Capita Production of Foodgrains

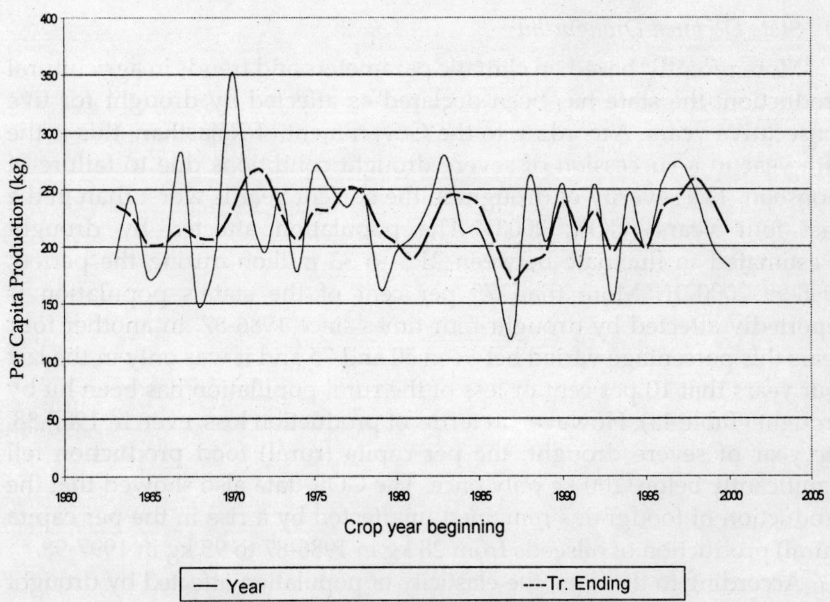

years, 1966-71, and more recently (during 1983-93) as: 290, 157, 21, 37, 1 (one only), 96, 174, 286 and 72,000 tonnes. The coefficient of variation of agricultural production during the period 1962-73, was as high as 71 per cent in the western districts.

3. Frequency and Severity of Droughts

Over 60 per cent of the state's geographical area is arid and receives very low rainfall. The wide fluctuations in rainfall often leads to drought-like situation in the state. The drought in the state is not simply an outcome of lack of adequate rainfall but also its uneven distribution during monsoon. A drought condition is, therefore, declared on the basis of information on the 'damage caused to crops' (Government of Rajasthan, 1992).

Meteorologically, severe drought affected Sirohi 17 times, Jaisalmer, Pali and Sirohi 15 times, Sri Ganganagar and Barmer 14 times, Bikaner, Jalore and Nagaur 11 times, Jodhpur, Churu and Sikar 13 times and other districts between five and 10 times during the last 35 years (1957-91). However, severe drought has been declared in the state more often than what is revealed by the meteorological data. Between 1970-71 and 1978-79, more than 12,000 villages were hit by drought thrice affecting their population exceeding one crore, twice. But during the subsequent nine years the number of affected villages varied between 21,000 and 36,000 (with a population varying from 1.7 to 3.2 crore respectively) over a period of seven years. According to meteorological sources, each district was affected on an average for half the number of years comprising this period (GOR, 1992).

(i) State Declared Drought-hit

More recently, based on climatic parameters and trends in agricultural production, the state has been declared as affected by drought for five consecutive years. According to the Government of Rajasthan, this is the fifth year in a succession of severe drought conditions due to failure of monsoon. The severity of drought in the current year is worst than in the past four years (GOR, 2003). The population affected by drought is estimated to fluctuate between 21.5 to 33 million during the period, 1998-99–2000-01. More than 75 per cent of the state's population is reportedly affected by drought four times since 1986-87. In another four years this percentage varied between 50 and 75 and it was only in the last four years that 10 per cent or less of the rural population has been hit by drought (Table 4a). However, in terms of production loss, even in 1987-88, the year of severe drought, the per capita (rural) food production fell significantly below 200 kg only once. The GOR data also showed that the production of foodgrains remained unaffected by a rise in the per capita (rural) production of oilseeds from 28 kg in 1986-87 to 95 kg in 1997-98.

According to the data, the elasticity of population affected by drought appears to be too high. Table 4b shows such elasticity with respect to variations in foodgrain production and agricultural production. Elasticity of

Table 4a

Frequency and Intensity of Drought in Rajasthan (1986-87 to 2000-01)

Year	Affected number of: Districts	Villages (no.)	Population (in lakh)	Production of: Foodgrain (lakh tonnes)	Oilseed	Rural population: Number (in lakh)	%Affected	Per capita (rural) production (kg) of: Foodgrain	Oilseed
86-87	26	31936	253	68	9	312	81	217	28
87-88	26	36252	317	48	13	319	99	150	39
88-89	17	4497	43	107	19	325	13	327	59
89-90	25	14015	121	85	18	332	36	257	56
90-91	0	0	1	109	24	339	0	323	71
91-92	30	30041	289	80	27	346	84	231	78
92-93	12	4376	35	115	25	354	10	324	71
93-94	25	22586	247	71	24	361	68	195	66
94-95	0	0	1	117	28	369	0	317	76
95-96	29	25475	274	96	31	377	73	254	82
96-97	21	5905	55	128	35	385	14	333	91
97-98	24	4633	15	140	33	393	4	357	84
98-99	20	20069	215	129	38	401	54	322	95
99-00	26	23406	262	108	34	409	64	264	83
2000-01	31	30583	330	100	20	418	79	239	48

Source: Government of Rajasthan (2003a).

Table 4b

Relationship between Agricultural Production and Reported Population Affected by Drought

	Regression coefficient	t- value	Level of significance	R-square
(Constant)	7.55	0.90	0.38	0.45
Ln of the index of agri-production	-6.89	-3.11	0.01	
Time (T)	0.35	2.61	0.02	
Dependent variable: Ln of Population affected by drought				
(Constant)	7.88	0.96	0.36	
Time (T)	0.25	2.31	0.04	0.47
Ln of per capita foodgrain production	-5.92	-3.25	0.01	
Dependent variable: Ln of Population affected by drought				
(Constant)	-298.39	-1.04	0.32	0.84
Per capita foodgrain production (kg)	-2.03	-7.74	0.00	
Time (T)	10.88	3.35	0.01	
Dependent variable: rural population affected by drought (numbers in lakh)				
(Constant)	21.94	0.28	0.78	0.84
Per capita foodgrain production (kg)	-0.57	-8.00	0.00	
Time (T)	1.92	2.18	0.05	
Dependent variable: % affected				

population affected by agricultural production at 6.89 implies that a 15 per cent fall in agricultural production is estimated to affect the entire rural population. The corresponding elasticity *with respect to* per capita foodgrain production is 5.92. While variations in agricultural production do affect the rural population, those in such magnitudes are untenable. This is particularly important during this year, 2002-03, when the likely estimates of foodgrain production are at the all time low of 5.2 million tonnes since 1987-88 and less than 40 per cent of the 2001-02 figure of 14 million tonnes (GOR, 2003a).

III. ACCESS TO FOOD, CONSUMPTION EXPENDITURE AND POVERTY

1. Access to Food

In periods of distress such as drought, the poverty position as revealed by the 1999-2000 poverty estimates appear to be a contradiction of facts. On the basis of these estimates, the centre has asked the state government to identify BPL families so that effective poverty alleviation measures could be initiated with a rather focused perspective. The estimate of rural poverty given by the GOI is 13.4 per cent as against those by various scholars, which vary from 13.4 to 20.6. Has poverty in the state really declined to 13.4 per cent as estimated by GOI? Isn't the estimate of even 20.6 per cent rather low? Do the poverty estimates provide a distorted picture of an otherwise poor state? We shall examine these questions in the following analyses.

Although there is no unanimity amongst poverty specialists on the Expert Group's method of poverty measurement, no serious disagreements were evident until the 1999-2000 results were made public. The estimates of poverty at the sub-region level for the year 1993-94 are given below. According to NIRD (1999), rural poverty declined from 33.21 per cent in 1987-88 to 26.45 per cent in 1993-94. Incidentally, it merits mention here that 1987-88 was the worst drought year in the state since 1968-69— production of foodgrains that year fell to 4.8 mt from a high of 10.1mt during 1983-84.

Clearly, foodgrain production in 1993-94 put at 7.0 mt was not too encouraging either. Therefore, any decline in poverty, if it really happened, may be attributed more to factors other than agricultural performance, some of which are discussed below. While agricultural performance affects poverty levels (Ahluwalia, 1978), the relationship may not be as strong as it was 30 years ago. It contributes directly to employment and income of a household besides contributing to them through the multiplier effect. One may argue that such a multiplier effect has weakened due to a shift in the rural production base of non-food goods to urban centers of mass production. But this does not undermine its effect in terms of enhancing employment and incomes.

The estimates of NIRD also show that in the west and the north-eastern Rajasthan, only 5.8 per cent of the people were very poor, their consumption levels being less than 75 per cent of the poverty line consumption level. Similarly, in south and south-eastern Rajasthan, 16 and 16.2 per cent were very poor (Table 5). Further, if one draws the historical series on poverty (Datt, 1998), while absolute poverty in the state is declining rather slowly, the poverty gap is declining fast and the depth of poverty (square of poverty gap) even faster. Between 1968-69 and 1993-94, the head count ratio of poverty declined from 67.2 to 47.5, the poverty gap from 25.0 to 11.7, while the depth of poverty declined from 12.1 to 4.1. One may argue that the pattern has continued since then and different dimensions of poverty have been observed to decline further. As indicated above, we shall examine below the role of various factors that affect poverty in the state.

Table 5
Poverty Estimates by Region, 1993-94

	Head count			Share of	Poverty estimates in	
Region	Poor	V. poor	Mod. poor	Poor (%)	1987-88	1999-00
West	25.5	5.8	19.6	33	-	-
North-east	17.8	5.8	12.0	29	-	-
South	45.9	16.0	29.9	22	-	-
South-east	34.8	16.2	18.6	16	-	-
Rajasthan	26.46	-	-	100	33.21	13.4

Notes: West : GNR, Nagaur, Jodhpur, Churu, Pali, Barmer, Bikaner, Jalore, Sirohi, Jaisalmer
North-east : Ajmer, Alwar, Bharatpur, Bhilwara, Dholpur, Jaipur, Jhunjhunu, Sawaimadhopur, Sikar, Tonk.
South : Udaipur, Banswara, Dungarpur
South-east : Bundi, Chittor, Jhalawar, Kota

Source: National Institute of Rural Development (1999).

Per capita SDP of the state has grown at the rate of 4.8 per cent per annum during 1992-97 (computed at 1979-81 prices) and 4.32 per cent during 1997-99 (at 1993-94 prices). Agricultural performance in the state during 1994-99 had been excellent—production of foodgrains increased from 7.0 mt during 1993-94 to 12.8 mt in 1995-96 and further to 14 mt during 1997-98. Foodgrain production in 1998-99 was 12.9 mt and the production of oilseeds, another major crop-group, recorded similar growth during the reference period (see Table 2). To the extent that agricultural performance affects poverty levels, the five year period preceding the NSSO survey period should have witnessed a significant decline in poverty levels. In this context the specific factors that determine poverty levels are discussed below:

(i) Share of Foodgrains and Food in Total Expenditure

The share of foodgrains in total consumption expenditure in the state is estimated at less than 30 per cent for the bottom decile of households. It further declined to 25 per cent for the 25th percentile point (Table 6 and fig. 3) as against the all-India figure of 41 per cent for the bottom decile which declined to 33 per cent for the fourth decile. Expenditure on other

Table 6

Value of Consumption (Rs.) for a Period of 30 Days in Rural Rajasthan (1999-2000)

Monthly per capita expenditure (Rs.)	Per HH	Thousand persons	Value of consumption (Rs.) Food-grain	Milk etc.	Other food	Total food	Expenditure Non-food	Total
Up to 340	105	129	86	33	93	180	110	290
340-380	61	74	98	54	130	228	134	362
380-420	83	97	100	66	149	249	151	400
420-470	115	127	105	76	166	271	176	446
470-525	123	131	112	94	191	303	194	497
525-615	156	156	118	117	226	343	224	567
615-775	187	171	123	157	281	404	279	683
775-950	84	62	137	194	342	479	365	844
Over 950	85	54	157	302	516	672	571	1243
All	1000	1000	112	110	214	327	222	549

Source: Government of India, NSSO Report (2001), p. 457.

Fig. 3

Share of Foodgrain to Total Food and Total Consumption Expenditure

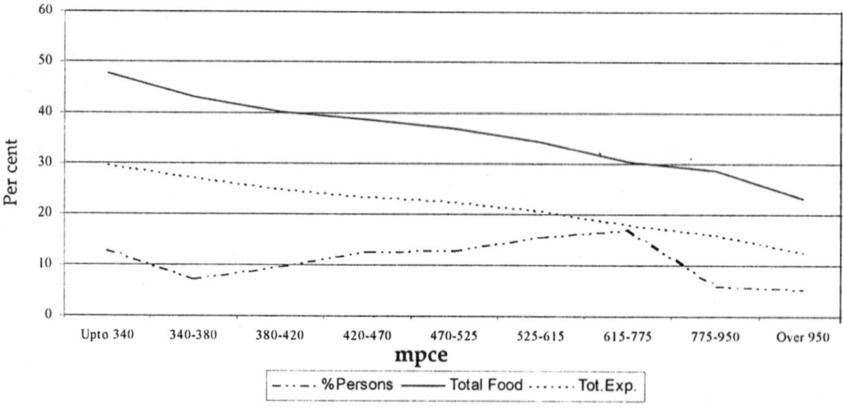

food items (costlier calories) such as milk, meat, edible oil, sugar, spices, fruits and beverages, etc., exceeds that on foodgrains even for the bottom decile of households. At the third decile point, such expenditure exceeds two-thirds of the total food expenditure, while at the all-India level such a ratio is achieved for the median household. Therefore, even without entering the debate on whether the poverty has declined to 13 per cent or to 20 per cent, such indicators do point to an improvement in the consumption behavior of the poor.[2] Accordingly, the state appears to have improved in respect of both the availability of and the access to food during the last decade, in spite of a very high population growth.

(ii) Nutritional Intake

Statistics reveal that a large part of the population in the state has an adequate intake of nutrients even during the priods of low agricultural production. The percentage of persons in the state getting less than 90 per cent of the recommended calorie intake is the lowest among all the Indian states—during 1993-94, when the per capita production of foodgrain was only 150 kg, just 23 per cent of the state's population was provided less than 90 per cent of the recommended calorie intake. During 1999-2000, the estimated population getting less than this amount was 24.3 per cent. Significantly, the figures compare well with those for Punjab (27.6 and 31.0), Haryana (28.2 and 30.2) and all-India (42.0 and 45.2), respectively for 1993-94 and 1900-2000. Protein and fat intake (per consumer unit) of the state's population corresponding to the bottom decile of the expenditure distribution exceeds 70 g and 40 g respectively during 1999-2000.[3] The average consumption of calories and protein is the highest at 3029 kcal and 96.1 g, while that of fat is marginally lower only than in Haryana and Punjab. Even in terms of micro-nutrient intake, the situation in the state is generally better than in other Indian states. Thus, the average intake of calcium (734 mg), iron (31 mg), thiamin (2.58 mg), niacin (21.1 mg) and vitamin C (46 mg) is among the highest in Indian states and exceeds the required daily allowance (RDA) as per the ICMR norms by a comfortable margin (GOI, 1998). The average intake of riboflavin (1.23 mg) and vitamin A (400 units), falls marginally short of the RDA. This does not ensure, however, that people in Rajasthan are secure in terms of their micro-nutrient requirements. The NFHS-2 reports that 16 per cent of the women were suffering from moderate to severe anaemia. The number of children reported to have moderate to severe anaemia is, however, much higher (at 62 per cent). However, such iron-deficiency may not be directly attributed to food insecurity arising out of income deficit, as Punjab and Haryana, amongst the richest states in India, report equal magnitudes of iron deficiency amongst their population (Smith et al., 2000).

2. Estimating Transitory Food Insecurity

Macro estimates of the magnitude of loss in income/employment due to agricultural instability may be approximated in proportion to the production loss. Alternative estimates may be obtained by multiplying the area cultivated under different crops by the laour input per hectare (Gill, 2002). In drought prone areas, however, cultivated areas often differ from the harvested areas. Thus, a better way of estimating employment loss would be to use labour input per ton of crop production during normal years, preferably over a triennium. Based on the CACP data, and estimate of total employment per ton of production varies based on cost of cultivation data between 23 man-days in wheat to 46 man-days in *bajra*. In between we have *barley* (30 man-days), *Soybean* (39 man-days) *Rape* and *Mustard* (33 man-days). For some minor crops such as sesame the estimated manpower requirement per ton of output is 220 man-days, primarily due to their very low productivity. (0.1 to 0.2 ton per hectare.). Applying these values to the agricultural production data it is easy to see that the total employment from crop production fluctuated between 50 to

70 crore man-days during the nineties. This implies a loss of 20 crore man-days of direct employment from agriculture and the corresponding income loss. What is important, however, from the viewpoint of food security is the distribution of such losses and its impact on consumption. It may be possible to provide some estimates by examining changes in consumption, provided there are no external interventions. Providing food security during the periods of drought through direct food assistance programmes forms part of the government mandate in India. Estimates of consumptions, therefore, capture consumption both through domestic resources and income transfers. However, it would be difficult to assess the extent of such insecurity. At best one may get a feel of the vulnerable groups/regions. Let us examine the three (quinquinnial) NSSO surveys on consumption, viz., 1987-88, 1993 and 1999-2000 during the last decade and a half. The 1987-88 survey refers to an extreme stress situation. The per capita foodgrain production at 120 kg during the year can be compared only with the previous low at 148 kg during 1968-69. This also refers to the minimum triennium average of per capita foodgrain production at 170 kg. The reference period of 1993-94 is again a drought year with per capita foodgrain production at 153 kg and triennium average production at 196 kg. The corresponding figures for 1999 and 2000 are 182 kg and 210 kg respectively. Table 7 shows data on calorie consumption (average and for the bottom decile), protein and fat consumption for the three reference periods. The average calorie intake *does not show* any significant fall during 1987-88 (Table 8) when compared to other reference points nor do the estimated calorie intake values corresponding to the bottom two deciles. Both the 1987-88 and the 1993-94 estimates on nutrient intake correspond to the lowest point in agricultural production in the recent past.

What comes out clearly, however, is the problem region of the state with respect to the level of poverty and inadequate nutrition—south Rajasthan. Table 5 shows the highest concentration of rural poverty at 46 per cent in this region, which is predominantly tribal. Table 4 shows that the calorie intake level of the fifth decile matches those of the bottom decile elsewhere. The bottom deciles consumption shows a deficit of 500 to 900 kcal as compared to other regions of the state.

Table 7
Inter-temporal Changes in Nutrient Intake

Reference Year	Average consumption of			Calorie consumption of bottom two decile of MPCE		Below 90% of the RCI*
	Calorie	Protein	Fat	I	II	
1983	2433	75	42			28
1987-88	2493	-	-	1853#	2021#	-
1993-94	2470	79	52			23
1999-2000	2425	77	54	1800	2038	24

Note: 1. * Recommended calorie intake (2400 kcal).
2. # -Author's calculations.

Source: Derived from Central Sample (Ist sub-round) estimates of consumption.

Table 8
Calorie Intake at the Decile Points, 1987-88

Decile points	Regions (state sample estimates) Western	North-east	Southern	South-east	Rajasthan	Central sample
I	1737	1802	1191	1936	1655	1853
II	1814	1988	1309	2188	1878	2021
III	2070	2190	1378	2280	2073	2115
IV	2228	2349	1568	2417	2241	2268
V	2306	2473	1744	2730	2395	2452
VI	2409	2637	1904	2963	2567	2631
VII	2493	2600	2392	3114	2593	–

Source: Authors calculations. Derived from State Sample (Ist sub-round) estimates of consumption.

IV. TOWARDS ACHIEVING FOOD SECURITY IN RAJASTHAN

The state government has initiated various measures towards effecting an improvement in the status of food security in the state. These include strengthening of agricultural infrastructure including irrigation facilities, development of regulated markets, roads, etc., and gearing up the livestock sector, which provides resilience to the rural economy. These are briefly discussed below:

1. Strengthening the Agricultural Base

The overall agricultural performance in the state appears to be impressive considering that large areas in it are under dry land agriculture. Much of the agricultural growth in the past two decades may be attributed to the state's policies and initiatives towards harnessing available water resources for irrigation. Net irrigated area in the state increased from 29.8 lakh hectares in 1981 to 56.1 lakh hectares in 2000, contributing to twice as much in gross cropped area implying a cropping intensity of 200 in these areas. Gross cropped area in the state increased from 173.5 lakh hectares in 1980-81 to 223.3 lakh hectares in 1997-98, resulting in (i) increasing the area under foodgrains with high productivity and stability in the production stream; and (ii) providing farmers with more flexibility to experiment with a more remunerative cropping pattern. Of the total increase of 29.3 lakh hectares in gross irrigated area during the period 1980-81 to 1997-98, 34 per cent was allocated to wheat, 43 per cent to rapeseed and mustard, and the remaining to other cash crops such as cotton, spices, fruits and vegetables, and high value medicinal crops. Such diversification in the cropping pattern was possible as the domestic production of foodgrains kept pace with the growing demand and food security was ensured by an effective public distribution system and other food assistance programmes.

2. Boosting the Livestock Economy

According to the livestock census for 1997-98, the number of she-buffalo and cattle and that of goat and sheep in Rajasthan was estimated at 16.5

million, 16.9 and 14.3 million, respectively approximating to two large and four small ruminants per rural household in the state. In terms of its share of the total production in the country, the state accounts for 10 per cent of milk, 40 per cent of mutton and 42 per cent of wool produced in the country. Besides providing nutritious food, the livestock population also adds to stability to the income stream, thus providing resilience to the rural economy. Notably, fluctuations in the income from the livestock, both seasonal and cyclical, are far lower than from agriculture.

3. Revamping the Public Distribution System and Initiating Food Assistance Programmes

In spite of its limitations, the public distribution system has proved to be the cornerstone of food security in the state. This is evident from the number of studies that have highlighted the limitations and role of the PDS in strengthening food security in the state (Sagar, 1998; Bahuguna, 1999 and Bhargav, 2001). The two components of the PDS are: fair-price shops (FPS) and targeted food assistance programmes. In rural Rajasthan the former accounted for over 76 per cent of the total FPS in the state in 1992-93. Several studies based on 46th round of NSS data on 'Utilisation of the Public Distribution System' for the period, July 1986-June 1987, reveal a high rural bias in its operations—the ratio of rural to urban percentage of consumption from the PDS is the highest at 3.00 in the state. On the other hand, the corresponding figures for Kerala, Andhra Pradesh, Tamil Nadu, Karnataka and all-India are: 1.20, 1.35, 1.06, 0.64 and 0.70, respectively. Yet the average consumption from the PDS in the state is comparatively low at 9.36 kg as against 46.65 kg in Kerala and 29.3 kg in Andhra Pradesh. Moreover, in spite of the fact that 1986-87 was a drought year, 91.2 per cent of the rural population in Rajasthan did not purchase any cereals from the PDS. The purchase of foodgrains from the FPS is a function of the difference between market price and the issue price. Using the monthly data for the period 1984-1994 on off-take and the difference between the issue price and the market price, it is estimated that a one per cent increase in this difference increases the off-take from the PDS by 0.5 per cent (Sagar, 1998). The difference between the issue price and the market price has gradually declined since the liberalisation of the Indian economy in 1991 and indeed has become negative in a number of years since then. As a result, the general component of the PDS has ceased to be of much importance for providing a price advantage. What remains beneficial, however, is the infrastructure provided by the FPS: it is the nearest shop in large parts of rural Rajasthan, particularly in tribal areas, even today (Table 9).

The price advantage component of food security is now focused on the targeted sections of the rural population by revamping the public distribution system. Introduced in August 1991, the revamped public distribution system (RPDS) extends greater benefits in the form of extra quantities of foodgrains at further subsidised rates. The state became a

Table 9
Access to Infrastructure Facilities in Rajasthan

Infrastructure facility	Within village		Below 2 km		2-5 km		Above 5 km	
	Tribal	Non-tribal	Tribal	Non-tribal	Tribal	Non-tribal	Tribal	Non-tribal
Market/haat	34	143	123	114	458	381	385	362
Fair-price shop	137	161	292	187	416	467	155	185
PHC/sub-centre	82	126	123	89	385	417	410	368
Maternity centre	20	9	33	35	199	133	748	823
Hospital	4	8	33	53	217	196	746	743
Dispensary	46	112	141	88	503	412	310	388
Nutrition centre	372	253	155	48	281	153	192	546
Primary school*	651	725	256	174	93	94	0	7

Note : *As nutrition centre for the mid-day meals Scheme.
Source: *Sarvekshana*, July-September, 1994, Table 1 (Rajasthan), p. S-42.

major beneficiary of this scheme with 138 of its blocks covered under the Desert Development Programme (DDP), Desert Prone Area Programme (DPAP) and Integrated Tribal Development Programme (ITDP) targeting a population of 2.50 crore. These areas suffer from food insecurity on account of both a deficit in foodgrain production and a large variability in annual production. In its new reincarnation as the targeted public distribution scheme (TPDS), households identified as below the poverty line (BPL) are given 20 kg of foodgrains at half the issue price. During the drought years the central government extends the eligibility for obtaining wheat at the BPL prices to all the families living in drought-hit areas.

Other food assistance programmes of the state include *Antyodaya Ann Yojana* (AAY), which provides 25 kg of wheat per month to the poorest households at Rs. 2 per kg, and the *Annpurna Programme* which provides 10 kg a month free to old, poor and destitute. The two bags of wheat at every Panchayat Samiti, with the onus of providing food to the depressed distributed on behalf of the *Sarpanch* should go a long way in preventing hunger death; in addition the Mid-day Meal Scheme and Supplementary Nutrition Programme target the school-going children, and pregnant and lactating mothers respectively. Food for Work Programme (FWP) is targeted to the transitory food insecure, and foodgrain released by the central government forms a significant part of the FWP.

4. Diversification of Rural Economy

With the rapid expansion of infrastructure facilities and road networks in rural areas of the state it is not only easier to move between destinations but also seek employment. The length of village roads in the state increased from 11,887 km in 1980 to over 51,000 km in 1998-99. The state highways during the same period increased from 3,666 km to 10,000 km. The number of registered jeeps (a type of multi-utility vehicles plying in rural areas) recorded a six-fold increase—from 16,000 to 96,000—during the same period. The number of registered tractors increased from 43,000 to 377,000 during the same period. Both buses and trucks witnessed similar increases during the last two decades.

In spite of these achievements the state fares poorly in terms of accepted norms of road length—the road length per 100 sq. km in the state is only 47 km as against the national average of 67 km. Further, the distance from the all-weather roads exceeds 5 km for over 25 per cent of the villages in the state.

The improvement in infrastructure facilities is also reflected in the growth of employment in non-agricultural (non-crops and plantation) rural enterprises, which increased at the rate of 3.92 per cent per annum, during 1990-98. This is besides the growth of employment opportunities in urban areas.

5. Alternative Sources of Income/Employment

Both the 55th round NSS data on rural non-farm (RNF) employment as well as the Census data point to significant growth in RNF employment in Rajasthan. The state ranks among the major states where RNF employment has increased by the highest percentage points after Assam and Haryana during the period 1972-73–1999-00. (App. Table A1).

The 50th round (1993-94) of NSS Employment survey shows the diversification in income sources in a drought year. Yet, in over 97 per cent of the sample households, the self-employed in agriculture received income from agriculture, while 45 per cent of such households received other farm incomes, mainly from animal husbandry. Even 49 per cent of agricultural labour and 71 per cent of other labour households received income from cultivation (Table 10). Experience with the recent drought (1999-2000), which coincided with the quinquinnial consumption/employment survey affecting 64 per cent of the rural population, was no different.

In yet another study, with the same reference period, in three different agro-economic areas in Rajasthan (Sagar, 2001), a large number of households were engaged in employment other than in their usual

Table 10

Number of Households Reporting Receipt of Income from Specified Sources (in '000)

Household type	Farm income		Wage income	Non-farm income	Others	Per cent
	Cultivation	Other				
Self-employed in non-agriculture	531	228	224	821	62	11
Agricultural labour	487	261	950	41	18	10
Other labour	717	341	940	63	24	16
Self-employed in agriculture	974	446	222	80	42	54
Others	524	192	557	63	77	9
All	796	364	442	151	42	100
Estimated. no of hh.(00)	45995	21057	25544	8720	2416	57798

Source: Sarvekshana, October-December, 1997, Table-1R (Rajsthan p. S-230).

household activity (Table 11). The study designed to assess the impact of inequalities on human fertility and migration and hence on agricultural sustainability, also examined the alternative sources and magnitude of income in the three areas representing low assets—low inequality (Bhilwara in semiarid south Rajasthan), migration (Nagaur in arid west) and groundwater depletion (Jhunjhunu in arid north) with extensive energisation of the groundwater draft. Fifty-three per cent of the households in the agriculturally rich Jhunjhunu as against 90 per cent households in the resource-poor Bhilwara, earn income from sources other than agriculture. Wages and remittances in Bhilwara, on an average, contributed two-thirds of the total income household and in Jhunjhunu and Nagaur nearly half the total income. In the largely unirrigated arid district, Nagaur, more than one-third of income of the largest land-ownership classes was derived from non-agricultural sources (Table 12). To sum up, alternative income sources define livelihood patterns that reduce vulnerability to food insecurity and enhance income levels.

Table 11

Percentage Distribution of Households Deriving Income from Non-farm Activities Other than Agriculture

Sector of employment	Districts: Nagaur	Bhilwara	Jhunjhunu	Total
Unclassified	4	0	1	2
Primary	11	10	3	9
Secondary	2	8	1	4
Tertiary	50	69	46	56
Civil services	1	5	2	3
All classes	68 (212)	93 (213)	53 (166)	73 (591)

Note: Figures in parentheses indicate sample size.
Source: Sagar (2001).

Table 12

Percentage Share of Alternative Sources of Income in Gross Household Income by Size Class of Holding

	Bhilwara			Jhunjhunu			Nagaur		
	Farm produce	Wages	Remitt-ances	Farm produce	Wages	Remitt-ances	Farm produce	Wages	Remitt-ances
Landless	13	78	9	3	97	0	9	48	23
Up to 0.5 ha	33	62	5	24	65	12	31	53	16
0.5-1 ha	28	63	7	40	43	16	25	43	28
1-2 ha	42	46	12	37	36	17	41	44	11
2-3 ha	78	18	0	40	20	25	41	34	19
3-4 ha	79	21	0	63	30	5	51	40	3
4-6 ha	36	46	19	62	9	20	46	29	20
6-8 ha				88	10	3	60	8	28
Over 8 ha				79	0	8	43	52	5
All classes	36	56	8	45	32	15	39	39	17

Source: Sagar (2001).

V. CHALLENGES TO FOOD SECURITY IN RAJASTHAN

By major indicators food security in the state appears to have improved in spite of its recording the highest population growth in India in recent years. That agricultural and rural development in the state could keep pace with its rapidly growing population may be a matter of satisfaction, the fact remains that, this has been achieved at the cost of resource degradation in large parts of the state. As a result, continuation of such pressure on natural resources may not ensure sustainable food security. What is equally significant in this context is the high rate of population growth in the state—which witnessed the highest decadal increase in population during 1991-2000. A third issue relates to the central government policies to restrict income transfers through food assistance and the TPDS. We shall discuss some of these impediments in the task of achieving food security in Rajasthan below:

1. Growing Pressure of Population

In spite of various initiatives taken by the state government and the civil society during the past several decades there has been little impact on the population growth in the state. The decadal increase in its population during 1991-2001 continues to be high at 28.33 as compared to 28.44 during 1981-91. The all-India decadal variation has declined from 23.56 to 21.34. As such the growth in population may primarily be attributed to the higher birth rate at 31.6 as against the all-India figure of 26.4 per thousand, What is worse is that the fertility level in the state is declining at a slower rate than in India—the birth rate in the state having declined from 34.3 in 1991 to 31.5 in 1998.

Most of the districts that are experiencing high population growth are food-deficit districts, namely, western arid districts of Jaisalmer, Jodhpur, Barmer and Sirohi, which have witnessed decadal population growth at 47.5, 33.8, 36.8 and 30.0 per cent, respectively. Other districts where high population growth has been recorded are the major city districts with 40 to 50 per cent urban population. These include Ajmer, Jaipur, Bikaner and Udaipur, which produce adequate foodgrains for the rural population but where rapid urbanisation reduces the per capita availability. Equally noteworthy is the high population growth in eastern districts bordering Uttar Pradesh, including Dausa, Karauli, Dholpur, Alwar, which have better agro-climatic conditions and thus offer good scope for agricultural development.

2. Depleting Groundwater

As discussed above much of the growth in agriculture has been contributed by expansion in the irrigated area—the net irrigated area in the state having increased from 2.06 million hectares in 1970 to 5.61 million hectares in 2000. Most of such expansion in the irrigation base is contributed by groundwater—the share of groundwater in net irrigated area having increased from 52.8 per cent in 1970 to 68.9 per cent during

2000. In a region of low and erratic rainfall, such development of groundwater has resulted in large parts of the state going 'dark'. Dark zones are the areas where the stage of groundwater development, defined as assessed draft (pumpage) as a percentage of the total replenishable ground-water, approaches 100. The stage of groundwater development was 69 per cent in 1998 and exceeded 100 per cent in the year 2001. The situation is critical in several districts. Nagaur, Jodhpur, Barmer and Jalore in the western arid Rajasthan and Jhunjhunu, Jaipur, Alwar, Ajmer, Bharatpur, Dausa, Dholpur and Sikar districts of the northeast have already developed 94 to 178 per cent of their potential and are facing a serious threat of over-exploitation. It is estimated that groundwater levels had declined between 3 to 10 meters throughout central and eastern Rajasthan between 1984 and 1994. The situation has worsened since then. Today, only the districts with surface water as the major source of irrigation are in the safe zones (App. Table A2, column 3).

3. Shrinking Share of Income Transfers

The BPL households' population based on estimates derived from an unusually good reference year may jeopardise the food security of a large number of transitory poor households. As mentioned above, the reference year for the 55th round of NSSO survey on consumer expenditure is preceded by a series of five good crop years during which the average per capita production of foodgrains and oilseed exceeded 317 kg and 85 kg, respectively. However, since 1999-2000, the state has been experiencing a continuous decline in agricultural production and as a result the 2002-03 drought is likely to be as bad as the one in 1987-88. Poverty figures based on the 1999-2000 data are very low at 13.4 per cent. Although some scholars have questioned the validity of such low figures, these are now being used to restrict the number of BPL families identified for income transfers through programmes such as the TPDS and other food assistance programmes. For a region of low agricultural fluctuations, while this may not be an invalid procedure for identifying BPL households, it may adversely affect food security in a state like Rajasthan.

We had mentioned earlier that the calorie intake of the bottom decile was not affected by the severe drought of the year 1987-88, implying that their food security was ensured. But this was achieved only after pumping in substantial resources. Drought relief expenditure on the 1987-88 drought at Rs. 950 crore was a third of the total Seventh Plan expenditure of Rs. 3,100 crore. Drought of 2002-2003 may need similar expenditures to ensure food security of this vulnerable region. The estimated total expenditure on drought relief is likely to exceed Rs. 30,000 crore till July 2003.[5] This is fine for a year of extreme drought. However, by fixing the percentage share of BPL households to 13.4 per cent and sticking to this number for the next five years, the likelihood of supplying cheaper food to the transitory food insecure households (now outside the BPL net), in years of lower stress, may be seriously affected.

4. Weak Infrastructure

Within the framework of a wider definition of food security, there are other parameters, which are a cause for concern. These include indicators on health, education and gender bias in development and access indicators. Considerable progress has been achieved in respect of the indicators of social development. As discussed above, the average intake of micro-nutrients in Rajasthan is among the highest in Indian states. (GOI, 1998). Yet the state is amongst the laggards in this respect. The status of undernutrition among women and children is far below the desired levels. According to the NFHS (1998-99), over 50 per cent children below five years were found to be mild to moderately undernourished both by the height for age and weight for age criteria. Similarly, 82.3 per cent children were estimated to be anaemic and 62 per cent of them moderately to severely affected. The percentage of women suffering from moderate to severe anaemia was estimated at 16.2 per cent. The percentage of ever-married women with Body Mass Index (BMI) below 18.5 kg/m^2 in the state was 36.1 per cent in spite of the fact that consumption of both major nutrients (calorie and proteins) and micro-nutrients among them is amongst the highest in the country. This clearly indicates the failures and inequities on the food security front in the state. Many of these failures may have nothing to do with the availability of and access to adequate food—in which case, such states as Punjab and Haryana would have performed better than states with lower calorie and protein intakes such as Kerala. What is intriguing, for example, is that the incidence of undernutrition in Punjab was reported at 47 per cent by the 1992 NFHS, according to the weight for age criterion. The corresponding percentage for Rajasthan was 41.6 and for Haryana 37.9. By the 1998-99 NFHS, the nutrition status of the rural population in Punjab improved to 28.6 per cent while in Rajasthan it drifted lower to 50.6 per cent. More significantly, the total correlation between the percentage of population consuming below 2,700 calories (NSSO 1999-2000) and that of child-malnutrition (NFHS, 1998-99) is -0.39. The correlation is statistically significant at 10 per cent probability level (App. Table A3). This implies that the higher the food intake (including its more equitable distribution across households as reflected in the calorie gap and depth of calorie deprivation) in a state the higher is the child malnutrition.

Some of the causes of malnutrition may be morbidity, faulty food habits and biases in the intra-household distribution of food. But equally important is the thin spread of medical facilities (see Table 9). For over 75 per cent villages the nearest hospital/maternity centre is more than 5 km away and for more than 37 per cent villages the distance from the nearest primary health centre, sub-centre or dispensary exceeds 5 km. Thus, much more than the elimination of hunger would be needed to ensure nutrition security in the state. This includes adopting more innovative approaches to the provision of health facility besides improving the efficiency of the existing infrastructure.

5. Adjusting to the Liberalisation Shocks

Much has been written and debated about the likely impact of the WTO and other liberalisation policies. We do not intend to look into these issues afresh. However, some of these policies have affected the farmers in the state adversely while transferring benefits to the consumers elsewhere. The former included farmers who had shifted to mustard cultivation in the eighties following the introduction of the public distribution system, along with appropriate technology and related public policy initiatives. This crop requires low irrigation and hence suits well the agro-climatic environment of the state. Rational diversion of resources towards mustard did help all size classes of farmers to increase incomes significantly. This also helped the expansion of the edible oils industry in the state. Farmers in the state appear to have suffered the first shocks of liberalised import policies when the country's import of edible oils started growing rapidly. Imports of edible oils increased from 200,000 tonnes in 1992-93 to 2.1 million tonnes in 1997-98 and then to 4.4, 4.5 and 4.8 million tonnes in the subsequent three years.

The policy measures which led to the influx of imports were: (i) removal of quantitative restrictions; (ii) progressive reduction in customs duties from 65 per cent in 1994-95 to 15 per cent in 1999-2000; and (iii) a near halving of international prices of oils due to excess supply. Self-sufficiency in edible oils during 1992-2001 reduced from 97 per cent to 55 per cent. Imports of cheap palm oil during 1998-2001 adversely affected the oilseed economy of the state by making mustard cultivation unviable for a large section of the farmers. The state had to procure mustard crop as the prices moved far below the minimum support price. At the support price, industry was not lifting the stocks of mustard seed.[6] As a result, oilseed production in the state declined during this period from 3.8 mt to 2.0 mt. A part of this decline is due to the drought, but a significant part of the production loss is attributed to cropping pattern shifts. The consequent loss in income and employment in the farm sector was compounded by the heavy losses sustained by the edible oil industry in the state. According to a memorandum submitted by Rajasthan Mustard Oil Industries Association, as many as 90 per cent of the small industrial units have suffered because of the liberalised import policy. There is of course no denying that the poor in Rajasthan as elsewhere benefited by the fall in edible oil prices. However, if the total employment and income effect of such a policy is taken into account, gains in welfare substantially get reduced. Taking a long-term perspective, whereby the cost of providing alternative employment and/or reviving a sick industrial sector is considered, such a policy may have resulted in a net welfare loss. It is generally agreed that international prices of food products are more volatile than the domestic markets.[7] Already there are signs that import prices of edible oil have started increasing. Should the country opt to import at higher prices or save the domestic edible oil sector? This may be an issue which involves wider policy considerations but small economies or regions which specialise in a commodity or two must prepare to cope with such policies. During the early nineties, when the price ratio of wheat did not allow a rational allocation of *rabi* area in favor of wheat, the CACP recommended a sharp increase in the support price of wheat in one single year. This would have been done either because wheat is the crop most suited to the agro-climatic conditions of Punjab or because of intense lobbying by farmers' interest groups. It is more likely that the factors were operational. No such effort was visible for saving the growers of mustard in the state.

VI. CONCLUSIONS

To sum up, the state has so far been successful in improving food security. However, in the efforts to achieve this objective it had to face formidable challenges such as depleting resource base and an equally fast growing population. Uncertainties created by the new economic environment, if not handled carefully, can compound the uncertainties created by nature. Climatic fluctuations are a normal feature of the state and therefore cannot be done away with except by making the resource use more sustainable. Resource use policies pursued so far, have not succeeded in arresting resource degradation. The policy of giving liberal electric connections for energisation of wells/tubewells, even in grey areas of the state is a case in point. The severe drought this year will test the efficacy of state polices in tiding over the crisis besides providing lessons for ensuring a sustainable food security.

Appendix

App. Table A1

Share of Rural Non-farm Employment to Total Rural Employment: Male Workers

State	1972-73	1983	1993-94	1999-2000	Change (1972-99)
Andhra Pradesh	19.3	22.6	24.5	25.6	6.3
Assam	15.2	20.7	21.8	35.3	20.1
Bihar	17.2	18.7	18.0	21.1	3.9
Gujarat	16.4	20.3	28.9	28.6	12.2
Haryana	20.0	28.5	38.9	41.2	21.2
Karnataka	15.6	18.3	21.1	21.6	6.0
Kerala	45.0	42.2	47.0	57.3	12.3
Madhya Pradesh	10.6	12.7	14.7	15.8	5.2
Maharastra	19.8	20.3	24.8	26.2	6.4
Orissa	17.6	21.8	21.2	23.2	5.6
Punjab	20.7	22.6	31.9	36.2	15.5
Rajasthan	15.9	19.2	30.3	32.7	16.8
Tamil Nadu	25.4	31.3	36.2	37.7	12.3
Uttar Pradesh	18.7	21.0	23.7	28.2	9.5
West Bengal	22.7	26.8	35.2	33.5	10.8

Source: Bhowmik (2002), p. 723.

App. Table A2
Deficit Districts with High Population Growth

District	Foodgrain production@ ('000 tonnes)	Stage of groundwater development*	Population (2001)		Decadal growth		Per capita production	
			Total	Rural	'81-91	'91-01	Total	Rural
Jaisalmer	32	78	508	430	41.7	47.5	62	73
Jodhpur	230	174	2881	1908	29.1	33.8	80	120
Barmer	166	102	1964	1819	28.3	36.8	84	91
Jalor	154	195	1448	1338	28.5	26.8	106	115
Sirohi	102	93	851	700	20.6	30.0	120	146
Ajmer	261	116	2180	1306	20.0	26.1	120	200
Pali	233	79	1819	1428	16.6	22.4	128	163
Rajsamand	131	93	986	858	18.0	19.9	133	153
Jaipur	794	145	5252	2659	38.7	35.1	151	299
Bikaner	255	73	1674	1079	42.7	38.2	152	236
Udaipur	411	97	2632	2142	24.5	27.4	156	192
Dungarpur	174	67	1107	1027	28.1	26.6	157	169
Nagaur	437	131	2774	2297	31.7	29.3	158	190
Jhunjhunu	370	178	1913	1518	30.6	20.9	194	244
Kota	311	74	1569	730	35.9	28.5	198	426
Churu	396	68	1923	1387	30.8	24.6	206	285
Sikar	476	109	2287	1815	33.8	24.1	208	262
Dholpur	218	107	983	806	28.1	31.1	222	270
Baran	238	67	1022	849	27.3	26.2	232	280
Jhalawar	276	96	1180	1012	21.9	23.3	234	273
Banswara	360	24	150	1393	30.3	29.8	239	258
Bhilwara	483	106	2010	1595	21.6	26.1	240	303
Tonk	326	61	1211	958	24.4	24.2	269	340
Chittaurgarh	526	114	1803	1513	20.4	21.5	292	348
Alwar	894	118	2991	2556	30.8	30.2	299	350
Bharatpur	642	94	2098	1689	27.1	27.1	306	380
Dausa	405	100	1317	1181	30.8	32.4	308	343
Karauli	419	72	1206	1033	28.7	30.0	348	406
S. Madhopur	420	83	1117	903	27.2	27.4	376	465
Ganganagar	772	67	1788	1336	18.3	17.5	432	578
Bundi	451	65	961	782	25.8	24.8	469	576
Hanumangarh	886	86	1517	1214	44.6	24.3	584	730

Notes: @ Average during quinquennium ending 1999-2000.
* Reference year 2001.

Source: Rathore (2002).

App. Table A3
Calorie Deprivation and Child Malnutrition in Indian States

State	% consuming below 2700 cal/cu		Calorie gap (FGT-1) (ref. 2200 cal/p)		Calorie severety (FGT-2) (ref. 2200 cal/p)		Child mal-nutrition (<2 S.D.)*
	1983	1999-00	1983	1999-00	1983	1999-00	
Andhra	54	68	12.9	15	4.5	4.8	27
Bihar	53	60	13.4	12.8	4.6	3.8	54
Gujarat	62	68	15.1	15.9	5.4	4.9	44
Haryana	40	45	9.1	7.8	3.6	2	50
H.Pradesh	30	41	7.4	5.8	3.1	1.2	41
J&K	30	28	6.3	3.8	2.3	0.8	39
Karnataka	53	69	14.7	16.9	5.6	5.7	37
Kerala	72	67	22.6	16.8	9.3	5.6	22
M.Pradesh	48	67	10.9	15.2	3.8	4.8	51
Maharashtra	59	69	13.6	15.3	4.3	4.7	40
Orissa	59	60	15.3	11.9	5.6	3.3	44
Punjab	36	46	8.8	8.5	3.6	2.2	39
Rajasthan	40	40	13.1	6.8	8	1.7	52
T.Nadu	73	78	25.9	21.9	13.2	8	29
U.Pradesh	43	49	10.1	9.6	3.4	2.7	56
W.Bengal	67	64	19.4	13.2	8.1	3.9	42

Note: *By the *Weight for Age* criterion.
Source: Meenakashi and Vishwanathan (2003).

Notes

1. The relative stability in agricultural production in the state would be severely affected by the agricultural performance during the year, 2002-03.
2. Such values of the share of foodgrains in total food expenditure are achieved only at the eighth decile of the distribution of consumption expenditure in 1973-74 (see GOI, 1977, NSSO Report 240, pp. 13 and 32).
3. Derived from Table 1R (Rajasthan) of the NSS. Report No. 47.
4. *Rajasthan Patrika*, February 27, 2003.
5. The state government seeks to create 56 crore man-days of employment at the minimum wages (Rs. 60/day), through the Food for Works programme during the 2002-03 drought. Most of the cost of the FFW programme would be covered by the centre through the food component (10 kg of wheat at Rs. 4.60 per kg and Rs. 14 as the cash component). The state has so far received 2.91 million tons and is allocated another one million ton of wheat at the BPL price. Besides the Calamity relief fund contribution of the state (between Rs. 200 to 300 crore), has also received Rs. 790 crore from the National Calamity Contingency Fund.
6. Advertisements by NAFED were placed in local dailies for this purpose (see *Dainik Bhaskar*, January 18, 2002 and *Rajasthan Patrika*, February 26, 2002).
7. The central government, in the 2003-04 budget has announced a package for the coffee and cashew growers of the southern states, who have suffered from the decline in international prices of the two commodities. Such measures, on an adhoc basis or motivated by considerations of political economy, may significantly impact on the food security of a region.

References

Ahluwalia, M.S. (1978), "Rural Poverty and Agricultural Performance in India", *Journal of Development Studies*, Vol. 14.

Bahuguna, Nalini (1996), *Cost of Reaching the Poor: An Evaluation of PDS in Urban Rajasthan*, Ph.D Thesis. University of Rajasthan, Jaipur.

Bhargav, Pradip (2001), "Food Security and the Public Distribution System in Rajasthan", in Asthana, M.D. and Madrano, Padro (eds.), *Towards Hunger Free India: Agenda and Perspectives*, Manohar, New Delhi.

Bhowmik, S.K. (2002), "Employment Diversification in Rural India: A State Lavel Analysis", *Indian Journal of Labour Economics*, Vol. 45, No. 4.

Datt, Gaurav (1998), "Poverty in India and Indian States: An Update", *Indian Journal of Labour Economics*, Vol. 41, No. 2.

Government of India (2001), Level and Pattern of Consumer Expenditure in India, 1999-2000, NSS 55th Round (July 1999-June 2000), NSSO, Report No. 457, May.

——(2001), *Nutritinal Intake in India 1999-2000*, NSS 55th Round (July 1999-June 2000), NSSO Report No. 471, August.

——(1998), *India Nutrition Profile*, Department of Women and Child Development, Ministry of Human Resource Development, Government of India.

——(1977), *Tabes on Consumes Expenditure, Twenty Eight Round*, (October 1973-June 1974), NSS. Report No. 240.

GOR (1992), *Perspective Plan for Mitigating and Strategic Management of Drought in Rajasthan*. Government of Rajasthan, Department of Relief, Jaipur.

——(2003), *Interim Memorandum on Scarcity*, Government of Rajasthan Samvat 2059, Jaipur.

——(2003a), *Economic Review*, Government of Rajasthan, *2002-03*, Taipur.

Gill, S.S. (2002), "Agricultural Crop Technology and Employment Generation in Punjab", in Johl, S.S. and Ray, S.K. (eds.), Future of Agriculture in Punjab, Centre for Research in Rural and Industrial Development, Chandigarh.

Hanumanta Rao, C.H. et al (1988), *Unstable Agriculture and Drought*, Vikas Publishing House, New Delhi.

IIPS (2001), *National Family Health Survey NFHS-2, 1992-93, India*, International Institute of Population Studies, Mumbai.

Meenakshi, J.V. and Vishwanathan, Brinda (2000), "Calorie Deprivation in Rural India", 1983-1999-2000, *Economic and Political Weekly*, January 25, 2003, pp. 369-375.

NIRD (1999), *India Rural Development Report: Regional Disparities in Development and Poverty*, National Institute of Rural Development, Hyderabad.

Rathore, M.S. (2002), *Droughts and State Failure: Unwilling to Learn and Unwilling to Distribute*, Institute of Development, Jaipur (Mimeo).

Sagar, V. (2001), *Impact of Inequalities on Human Fertility, Migration and on Agricultural Sustainability*, Institute of Development Studies, Jaipur (mimeo).

—— (2000), "Public Distribution System and Food Security in a Region of Large Agricultural Instability", in Krishnaji, N. and Krishnan, T.N. (eds.), *Public Support for Food Security*, Sage Publications, New Delhi.

Smith, L.C. and Haddad, L. (2000), *Explaining Child Malnutrition in Developing Countries: A Cross-Country Analysis*, Research Report 111, International Food Policy Research Institute, Washington, D.C.

World Bank (1986), *Poverty and Hunger: Issue & Options for Food Security in Developing Countries*, A World Bank Policy Study, Washington, D.C.

12

Food and Power in Bihar and Jharkhand: The Political Economy of the Functioning of the Public Distribution System

Jos Mooij

I. INTRODUCTION

Public distribution of foodgrains in India is a national policy, which exists in all states. In some states, however, the public distribution system (PDS) works much better than in other states. The undivided State of Bihar (now the new Bihar and Jharkhand) is one of the states in which the policy works poorly. It is important to understand why this is the case. Generally, policy changes and recommendations do not take the specificities of particular states into account. Yet, for the PDS performance to improve in Bihar and Jharkhand, it is absolutely necessary to understand why it works as it works, what the main bottlenecks are and where there are possibilities for improvement, if any. This paper makes such an attempt: it describes the PDS in Bihar and Jharkhand, not only in terms of how it fails and what it does not accomplish, but also in terms of what it is and what it does. The activities and interests of the various actors involved in the PDS are described, and it is shown that many people do benefit from the present set-up, but that there are also people within almost all categories of stakeholders who are dissatisfied with the large scale misappropriation of foodgrains. The PDS experience is then put in the context of the wider political economy of Bihar. The paper ends with some general observations regarding the process of food policy making and implementation. Furthermore, it discusses constraints and opportunities for reform of the PDS in Bihar and Jharkhand. It is argued that there is scope for change, but change requires strategic political manoeuvring and initially a low-key approach in order not to awaken and antagonise the strong vested interests.

While Bihar and Jharkhand are among the poorest and most backward states in India, these states have hardly benefited from the public distribution system (PDS). It is estimated that 55 per cent of the population of Bihar lives below the poverty line, while the all-India figure is 36.[1] Economic growth rates are much lower than elsewhere in India. The growth rate in the 1990s in the undivided Bihar (i.e., before bifurcation into the new states of Bihar and Jharkhand took place in November 2000) was 1.0-1.2 per cent, as compared to 6 per cent for the whole of India. Education and health facilities are very poor, and malnutrition is endemic. The World Food Programme classified the undivided state of Bihar as the only state in India suffering from extreme food insecurity (Daly and Bhattacharya, 2001). The calorie intake in 1993-94 was just below 2000 kcal per person per day in rural areas, which was below the all-India rural average and less than it was 20 years earlier.[2] About 31 per cent of the children aged 0-4 years are severely malnourished, and this is more than anywhere else in India (the all-India average is just over 20 per cent).[3] Bihar is not self-sufficient in foodgrains. In the 1990s, the average annual production was 12.2 million tonnes of foodgrains (rice and wheat), which is 128 kg per person per year.[4] In this situation, one could argue that if there is a need for a properly functioning public distribution system somewhere in India, it would be in the states of Bihar and Jharkhand.

The people in Bihar and Jharkhand have, however, hardly benefited from the food distribution programme. As compared to other states, the undivided Bihar received less foodgrains through the PDS. In 1998, the per capita PDS foodgrain off-take from the central pool was 9.5 kg, which was about 50 per cent of the all-India average percapita off-take (Swaminathan, 2000). Moreover, a large proportion of what is lifted in Bihar does not reach the card holders. According to a study conducted to the Tata Economic Consultancy Services (quoted by Asthana, 2000), the all-India diversion of PDS foodgrains is 31 per cent for rice and 26 per cent for wheat. In Bihar these figures are 64 and 44, respectively. The impact of the PDS on poverty and inequality is small. On the whole, this impact is less than what one would like it to be, but in states like Andhra Pradesh, Gujarat, Karnataka and Kerala, the impact is considerably more than in poor states like Bihar, Orissa, Rajasthan and Uttar Pradesh (Radhakrishna et al., 1997).

In general, the fact that different states have benefitted to different extents from the PDS, and in particular, the fact that Bihar has hardly benefitted at all has two main reasons.

1. The different treatment from the Government of India: Some states received much more from the central pool of foodgrains than others. Kerala, for instance, has got a favourable treatment since the mid-1960s onwards. The foodgrain allocation to Bihar, on the other hand, has been very low for a long time.

2. The different political economy within the states: Several factors are important—whether there is surplus foodgrain production or not; the extent to which food distribution is taken up as an issue in populist politics (as in Andhra Pradesh and some other south Indian states); the extent to which there is a powerful, articulated demand from the public for the PDS, etc. In short, the economy,

the characteristics of the state and the political processes, and of the civil society are all likely to be important for understanding the experiences of the PDS in particular states.

The fact that the PDS functions differently in different states calls for a differentiated approach. When there are specific state-wise political economic reasons for good or bad performance in particular states, what is needed are policies which address these issues, i.e., policies adjusted to the local or state-wise constraints and opportunities. This, however, is not happening. The Government of India has developed an all-India public distribution system, with all-India guidelines, and it wants these to be implemented in all the states. Individual state governments have made their own adjustments to some extent, and some states have complemented the GOI policies and subsidies with state-wise programmes. On the whole, however, policy thinking about the PDS happens in terms of grand schemes and big overall solutions. The specificities of particular localities are not sufficiently taken into account.

The rest of this paper will analyse the specificities of the PDS in the undivided Bihar (i.e., the new Bihar and Jharkhand) and will try to explain why the PDS works as it works.[5] The next session is a description of the PDS in Bihar, and the third section focuses on the political economy of Bihar, which explains this poor state of affairs. The paper ends with some general conclusions regarding the processes of policy making and implementation, as well as some specific conclusions regarding the opportunities for improving the implementation of the PDS in Bihar.

II. THE PDS IN BIHAR AND JHARKHAND

According to the 1997 policy document of the GOI, Bihar would be entitled to 1,031 thousand tonnes of subsidised foodgrains for the people below the poverty line. Given the fact that there are about 96 million people, of which 55 per cent live below the poverty line, that is, 53 million poor people, one can calculate that on average, according to this policy, there would be almost 20 kg per poor person per year—a substantial increase as compared to the period prior to the introduction of targeting in 1997.

It is, of course, more accurate to look at actual lifting, rather than at allocation. Lifting in Bihar is good, i.e., after 1997. Before the introduction of targeting, lifting was poor. But since Bihar is entitled to a lot of heavily subsidised foodgrains for below poverty line (BPL) families, it lifts almost all wheat (lifting percentage 96 per cent), and 55 per cent of the allocated rice.[6] If one calculates the lifted BPL foodgrains per month, one arrives at an average foodgrain distribution of 1.4 kg per poor person per month, or about almost 8 kg per poor family (based on GOI estimate that there are 8.6 million families living below the poverty line). The GOI policy is 10 kg per poor person per card. So, according to these calculations, distribution in Bihar comes close to the national policy.

In reality, however, only a part of the PDS foodgrains reaches the card holders in this way. In our fieldwork, we found that many poor people have no red card (that is the card meant for BPL households), and that the foodgrains are often not reaching the PDS shops in the villages (see below). The network of PDS dealers is quite reasonable, by the way. Altogether there are more than 59,000 PDS dealers, which means that there is one PDS dealer per 1630 people.[7]

In this section, the PDS in Bihar will be described in more qualitative terms. The discussion begins with the entry point where various actors are involved.

1. The PDS Dealers

As mentioned above, there are over 59,000 PDS dealers in Bihar and Jharkhand. Their number has increased considerably in the past decade, partly because licences are given to political followers of the ruling party.[8]

The commission on the sale of the PDS commodities is not large, and the official income comes to not more than Rs. 400-600 per month.[9] This is comparable to what a landless labourer may earn, and much lower than the salary of the lowest office staff (attendant or sweeper).[10]

Yet, it is obvious that, despite this low income, it is pretty lucrative to be a fair-price shop dealer. People are willing to pay large amounts of money to get a licence to become such dealer. One of the ways in which the PDS dealers survive and make money is by having so-called bogus cards—ration cards that do not belong to any family but which are kept by the dealers themselves. The commodities they get for these bogus cards are sold in the open market. Apart from that, they also divert part of the rice, wheat, sugar and kerosene which is meant for real card holders.

As long as the fair-price shop dealers pay their monthly bribes to the officials of the Food and Civil Supply Department these officials usually do not undertake any action to stop the malpractices. On the contrary, they even help the PDS dealers cover up their activities by informing them when inspection teams come, etc.

Many dealers are also local level politicians, and several state level politicians started as a PDS dealer—in fact, the food minister in one of the governments in the 1990s also had a PDS shop. In south Bihar we found several examples of block level politicians who had a PDS shop. Whether the PDS shop is helpful in their political career, is difficult to say. But it is plausible that the political affiliations help to get protection in case of shop suspensions which are done in case of alleged malpractices. Various sub-divisional officials told us that they receive regular telephone calls from local MLAs, with a request to cancel such suspensions.

Interestingly, the PDS dealers are very well organised. There is a PDS dealers' association which is very active. Its headquarters is in Patna, where it employs three office workers. In each district, and according to some informants even in each block, there are district and block office bearers. For various new policy issues, individual PDS dealers wait for the instructions from the association before they decide what to do. A specifically interesting phenomenon is that the leader of this organisation—officially he is the secretary—is a very articulated man who is committed to the PDS. He was a follower of Jayaprakash Narayan, and, according to the story he told me, established the PDS dealers' organisation on the advice of J.P. Narayan, because at that time the PDS was seen by them as a socialist policy. This leader does not run a PDS shop himself, but has a large charisma, and as far as I can judge, also a considerable command and authority over the PDS dealers. He has initiated many meetings to protest against the harassment of the officials and corruption of the officials, and he has taken up several court cases, for instance, public interest litigation cases to complain about the fact that some rationing inspectors in Patna were posted for 15-20 years in the same posts while they should have been transferred after three years.

But while the association fights corruption and bureaucratic malpractices in Patna, some of the local level office bearers in the districts pursued mainly their own interests.

2. The Would-be Beneficiaries

Card distribution is poor in Bihar, so there are many poor people who should have a card, but who have never received one. In our fieldwork in south Bihar we found many people complain about the fact that they have never received a card, or that the foodgrains never arrived, or that the dealer made false entries in their cards. On the other hand, we also found villages in which many people were satisfied (Chart 1).

The main problem (see also Chart 1) is that PDS commodities arrive late and irregular, if at all. The villagers are poorly informed, and certainly not in advance. This means that the poorest among them may not have sufficient cash readily available when the foodgrains arrive in the shop. The PDS dealer will only transport so much as he expects to sell within one or two days. In short, there is a physical access problem, in the sense that the commodities may come at irregular intervals or not at all. There is also a problem of economic access, in the sense that the poorest people do not have cash ready at the moment the stocks arrive. Yet, on the positive side, all villagers we interviewed knew about the PDS and knew what a 'red card' (a card meant for the BPL population) was. This, I have been told, was very different 15-20 years ago.

Since 1997, as per Government of India guidelines, vigilance committees have been introduced at various levels: district, sub-divisional, panchayat or ward, and shop level. Membership of the first three types of vigilance committees is almost completely politicised, and it is mainly local level politicians who are appointed (see below). At the shop level, the members are usually selected by the PDS dealers themselves and are often not aware of the tasks they have to do.

During the fieldwork, we tried to find out whether there are examples of positive experiences, for instance, villagers who organised themselves

Chart 1

The PDS in South Bihar (Jharkhand): Experiences in 15 Villages

District/Block	Village	Experience
Palamu District		
Chandwa Block	Village 1	Almost everybody satisfied. The PDS shop run by a cooperative.
	Village 2	Reasonable supply, but rice not available for last few months. Sometimes people have no money when shop is open.
	Village 3	Many poor households without red cards. Erratic supply and false entries in the cards.
	Village 4	Many poor households without red cards. Erratic supply and false entries in the cards; Foodgrains finished within 1-2 days.
	Village 5	Erratic supply, except to local Vigilance Committee members; villagers not informed about stock arrival.
Ranchi District		
Silli Block	Village 1	Poor distribution of red cards; those with red cards purchase the commodities, but often do not have money when foodgrains have arrived; influential people close to the PDS dealer have no problem in lifting.
	Village 2	Random distribution of red cards. Those with cards were satisfied, although supply was irregular.
	Village 3	Reasonable distribution; Some complaints about late arrival of stocks, and stocks finished within three days.
	Village 4	No major complaints. Many people do not take sugar.
	Village 5	Many people without red cards. Some people with red cards had problems to arrange the money when stock had arrived.
Ranchi District		
Kanke Block	Village 1	Village with two shops; one doing well, the other much less: irregular supply of foodgrains, late arrival and foodgrains finished within a day.
	Village 2	Many deserving people without cards, false entries in the cards; Irregular supply of foodgrains; sugar and kerosene somewhat better.
	Village 3	Preferential treatment to people close to the PDS dealer; rice and wheat often not available.
	Village 4	Many people without red cards. Small quantities of rice and wheat in the shop, and poor people sometimes not able to purchase on the day the stocks are available.
	Village 5	Irregular supplies. False entries in the cards. If the foodgrains arrive at all, they are sold out within no time.

Source: Fieldwork done by Alok Deo Singh, 1999. The chart summarises the main findings in 15 villages on the basis of 10 interviews in each village with randomly selected villagers and occasional group interviews. The villages are spread over the blocks: some close to the block capital, others more remote.

to fight for a better PDS system. We came across one interesting example in Bhojpur district, not far from Patna, where villagers had started to protest against malpractices. This was then taken up by the local CPI(ML) leaders and together they had forced the officials to suspend the PDS dealer. But, while these kinds of cases abound in a state like Kerala, where on the whole, the PDS works much better, in Bihar they are rare.

Fortunately, however, there are other people who take up the cause of the consumers/card holders, in particular, some reporters of Hindi newspapers. There are regular small reports in these newspapers about the malpractices which are going on. There are also some reporters who have a special interest in the PDS issues and write regularly about them. Doing this is not easy in Bihar, however. I interviewed one such reporter in Ranchi. He is a journalist of the *Ranchi Express*, and he told me he is regularly threatened when he publishes about the PDS and the mafia involved. He receives anonymous telephone calls, in which he is told that his daughter will be kidnapped or that he will be killed. The following quote is the translation of a newspaper article (September 8, 1999) in the *Prabhat Khabar*, a Hindi newspaper, published from Ranchi.[11]

> A reporter of a local newspaper, Mr. Rajendra Prasad, was arrested in Khunti for writing against the ration mafia. A First Information Report (FIR) was lodged against him by three PDS dealers who had complained to the sub-divisional officer. In the FIR the reporter was alleged to extract money from tribal people and harijans and threaten some PDS dealers to get their licence cancelled if they would not pay him.
>
> It should be mentioned that the reporter Rajendra Prasad has been writing about corruption and blackmarketing of the PDS ration and about smuggling of forest woods of Murhu and Khunti block for the last two years. He has also written several articles about the alleged connection between ration mafia, police and government officials. It is believed that such reports about bungling with the PDS ration in open market have annoyed some PDS dealers who then tried to implicate the reporter in false cases. The reporter has said that police in charge of Murhu and some government officials along with the PDS dealers had already threatened him before for writing such articles. He and his family also used to get threatening telephone calls.
>
> The reporter was arrested at midnight. The police abused him and pulled him forcefully out of the house. They also tried to molest his wife. The three PDS dealers who have lodged the FIR are said to be under the control of a bigger ration mafia operating in the region.

Apart from journalists, there are also a few consumer activists and organisations, mainly active in Patna and other towns. Although food distribution is not their main concern (which is water, electricity supply, etc.), they take some interest in the PDS. Occasionally, they have tried to influence the implementation of the PDS, for instance, by lobbying for the inclusion of a consumer activist in the vigilance committees.

3. The Bureaucracy: The Department of Food and Civil Supplies

Like in all other states, the Department of Food and Civil Supplies has its presence all over the state. The Department is headed by the Commissioner who is also the Secretary. The lowest officials are the supply inspectors. They may have 40-60 PDS dealers to check, and are supposed to visit each of them every month. Above them, in urban areas, there are the marketing inspectors, who are supposed to visit 50 per cent of the shops every month. Then there are assistant district supply officers and district supply officers. In four urban zones, there are Special Officers Rationing (SORs). At the block level, there are mainly two people: the block supply officer and the supply inspector.

The department is very corrupt. There are set amounts that the PDS dealers have to pay to the supply inspectors and this money is redistributed with higher-level officers. These higher-level officers themselves may also be involved in money collection and/or blackmarketeering.

I must say, however, that I can understand the low morale and corruption, especially in the case of the lower level supply officers and inspectors. On one of my trips I visited Karra block in Ranchi. The office of the block supply officer was in a rather dilapidated state. It looked like a shed, with a roof with many holes in it. There was no electricity, also not in construction. In the summer it must be terribly hot; in the rainy season, the rain would come inside through the holes in the roof. The office was hardly furnished. There was one table; and one chair in reasonable condition, and two others on which one could only sit after putting a piece of stone or wood on it. There was one pile of old files somewhere in the corner. Otherwise, there was nothing. The Block Development Officer lived in Ranchi (about three hours by bus), and I would admire him if he would decide to come to this office more than once or twice a week.

Apart from monitoring the distribution process, card distribution is also a task of the bureaucracy. As per official guidelines from the Government of India, "Gram Panchayats and Gram Sabhas should be involved in the initial identification of the eligible families" (Government of India, 1997, p. 3) In Bihar, this is a problem because these institutions do not exist.[12] There have been no elections since 1978. What has happened instead is that the red cards have been sent to the district magistrates; they have passed them on to the sub-divisional officers, who have given them to lower ranks officers, and finally, in many places, the cards were given to the PDS dealers themselves to distribute. It is, hence, not surprising that many of them have kept a considerable part of the cards themselves.

But what is also important to mention in a discussion of the bureaucracy is that, although corruption is very widespread and institutionalised, it is not true that each and every officer is involved to the same extent. There are several honest people as well, or people who feel that they are forced to participate in the system of money collection but who do not like it very much.

One of the problems is, however, the transfer system. Transfers are extremely politicised in Bihar. Many transfers need the clearance from the Chief Minister himself/herself or from the concerned Minister. Sometimes money transfers are involved, because some of the departmental staff members will try to influence their transfers through payment. They will have to earn this money back in the course of 1-3 years. At the higher level of the bureaucracy, the transfers obstruct a longer-term commitment to the PDS. A critical attitude is certainly not rewarded positively. Between 1997 and 1999, there have been three secretaries/commisioners. The two that were transferred in this period were both transferred because they refused to cooperate with the Food Minister in his way of money collection and his decisions about transfers of the departmental staff.

4. The Bureaucracy: The Bihar State Food and Civil Supplies Corporation

The Bihar State Food and Civil Supplies Corporation (SFC) is the only wholesale agent for the PDS foodgrains. There are several major problems with the SFC. There is not sufficient infrastructure (warehouses, vans, etc.) to distribute the foodgrains properly (Jharwal, 1999, p. 46). The mobile vans, meant to bring the foodgrains from the godowns to the shops are all in need of repair or there is no driver or no fuel. The SFC is in an extremely poor financial shape. There is no working capital to purchase the PDS commodities from the FCI; it is the PDS dealers who have to advance the money every month. The Corporation is overstaffed.[13] There are districts in which the SFC still needs to pay 12-24 months salaries to the depot managers and other Corporation staff members. Given this fact, it is not surprising that the assistant godown managers are 'a demoralised lot', as one informant described them, and that illegal sales of the commodities and misappropriation of money occur regularly.[14]

5. The Politicians: Food Minister, Members of the State Legislative Assembly (MLAs) and Local Politicians

The two politicians who were the subsequent food ministers were both very corrupt, even to the extent that they visited the districts themselves to ask for money from the concerned officials. Most Members of the State Legislative Assembly (MLAs) are not very interested in the PDS. Some have some involvement in the sense that they approach officials to do *pairavi*[15] on behalf of the PDS dealers in case of suspensions, etc. However, there are exceptions: MLAs who take a serious interest in the PDS, who have raised questions in the Assembly, or who have started public interest litigation in relation to wrong and incomplete card issuing and improper distribution.

Yet, as compared to south India, there seems to be little interest from the state-level politicians in a properly functioning PDS. In south India, these politicians regard the PDS as something that can give them political mileage, but not so in Bihar. In an earlier paper (Mooij, 1999), I formulated four hypotheses which could explain why politicians in Bihar do not regard the PDS in that way:

1. Politicians in Bihar do not require food to increase their popularity. They pursue other strategies to attract votes.
2. Politicians in Bihar are not capable of making the PDS delivery system function in such a way that they could get political mileage out of it. They do not have sufficient control over the (food) bureaucracy in order to force it to deliver the goods to the

people. Or they cannot control the local level vested interests (PDS dealers, local politicians) sufficiently.

3. The present system in which about 85 per cent of the commodities are diverted to the black market offers the Bihari politicians more than a system which would benefit the consumers/card holders.
4. Politicians in Bihar are faced with a different situation than in south India. The poor in Bihar are too poor for the PDS. Households which are permanently indebted cannot buy the PDS commodities. So, the basic problem is one of demand. This problem cannot be solved by special schemes or proper implementation.

The answer that I gave in that paper, and that is confirmed in subsequent research, is that in any case the first and the third hypotheses contain some truth. The fourth may also be true, but I found that most villagers and card holders whom we interviewed were still interested in the PDS, although, indeed, at times some had problems to arrange the required amounts of money at the required time. The phenomenon described in the second hypothesis may also be true, but I doubt whether it is relevant. Lack of capability only matters when there is a will or an interest to do something.

In my earlier paper (Mooij, 1999), I argued that the present set-up with huge diversions to the open market is more profitable for the politicians than a properly functioning PDS. There are at least three reasons. First, the system offers politicians (mainly MLAs and Members of Parliament) a possibility to offer lucrative posts to fellow caste people or political followers (licences to run the PDS shops or membership of vigilance committees). Second, there is a possibility to extort money from the PDS dealers. The Minister and ruling party politicians may benefit from this money.[16] Third, the payments for transfers of people working within the food bureaucracy is a source of money for the concerned Minister and the Chief Minister. These payments require diversion of foodgrains, as ultimately that is how the money is generated.

6. Mafia and *Rangdars*

We came across many accounts of what people call 'mafia'.[17] Unfortunately, so far I have not been able to get a really good impression of the mafia. It seems the transporters of the PDS foodgrains—there is no doorstep delivery, and the foodgrains are transported by private contractors from the FCI godowns to the block-level warehouses—are important in this mafia. They divert a part of the PDS foodgrains, possibly assisted by FCI people and/or SFC assistant general managers. For a long time, transportation of the PDS commodities was not a lucrative job. But since the introduction of targeting, the price difference between BPL foodgrains and open market foodgrains is huge. Diversion of one truck (10 tonnes), can give an illegal earning of about Rs. 60,000.

At the local level, there are many petty criminals, the so-called *rangdars* who benefit from protection from the local MLAs, and, in turn, these *rangdars* may play a role at election time in booth capturing or threatening people when they cast their votes. Several people told us that *rangdars* can easily force the PDS dealers to give them some money or food. For instance, when there are political rallies, they harass the PDS dealers and force them to contribute some money. According to a Block Development Officer, some *rangdars* may also ask for money from local officials.

This description of the main actors in the PDS system in Bihar is rather gloomy. It shows that there are many problems, and also that there are many people who benefit in one way or another from the way the system works at present. But what is also clear is that there is diversity. Not everybody participates to the same extent in all these malpractices. There is an association of the PDS dealers which takes up some important issues; there are committed journalists; there are a few MLAs who have a serious interest in a better PDS; there are some people within the department as well, who would like the system to function differently. Nevertheless, the overall picture is a rather depressing one.

III. THE POLITICAL ECONOMY

The objective of this section is to locate these characteristics of the PDS in Bihar in the wider context of the Bihar political economy. In a sense, there is nothing special about the way the PDS works. Sharma (1995) reviews the implementation of several anti-poverty programmes in Bihar and concludes that

> [t]he measures taken for direct intervention for poverty removal have (...) produced unsatisfactory results, mainly due to deficiencies in the delivery system. The different organs of the delivery system—panchayats, the bureaucracy, cooperatives, etc.,—have really served the interests of the rich who cornered benefits even from those schemes which were specifically meant for the poor (p. 2601).

1. Ineffectiveness of the Government

Several scholars have pointed at the governmental ineffectiveness in Bihar (Kohli, 1991) or the 'withering away of the state' (Sharma, 1995, p. 2587). There are at least three interrelated aspects to this governmental ineffectiveness: (a) the de-professionalisation of the bureaucracy; (b) the criminalisation of politics; and (c) the violence in the state. I will discuss them briefly and relate them to the PDS.

De-professionalisation is an important characteristic of the Bihar government. The more competent civil servants are replaced almost as soon as they do not give in to the wishes of their political superiors. What matters to ministers is political loyalty, rather than competence. Professionalism is not valued, rather the reverse.

The bureaucracy has not always been like this in Bihar. In fact, for some time, even after Independence, Bihar was regarded as one of the best ruled states.[18] From the 1960s onwards, however, the factions within the ruling upper castes, and joined in the Congress party, began to fight more and more openly amongst themselves. Moreover, from the 1970s onwards, Congress politics had changed in the whole of India, and absolute loyalty to the leader Indira Gandhi became more important than professional competence. Criminalisation of politics also became a more normal phenomenon. (About these developments in Bihar, see Kohli, 1991). This criminalisation is still an important and very tragic characteristics of politics in Bihar. In February 2000, State Assembly elections were going on in Bihar, and the newspapers were very critical of the fact that most political parties had allowed criminals to contest. Some of them were even in jail or released on bail, accused of involvement in rape, fraud, bribery, murder or other criminal cases. In one such newspaper article, the leader of the Samata Party defended his party's policy, by saying that he personally regretted the fact that his party (and other political parties) had so many people with criminal records as MLA candidates, but 'we have to take the winnability factor into account'. Although, this may seem strange to outsiders, it is indeed exactly what is the case. In a state where hardly any thing works, it makes sense for people to vote for musclemen. To quote Prasad (1997, p. 3028).

> The majority of the voters are illiterate and unsophisticated but at the same time socially and politically alert. They do not hold the authority of the government in high esteem. In a state where the administrative machinery has been rendered by and large dysfunctional, the voters are inclined to elect someone who can act tough and 'get things done' by the administration. The search, therefore, is not for the one who can conceive of a good legislation or initiate an informed debate in the house, but for the ones who can armtwist the right person at the right place and have things delivered. This partially explains how and why undesirable elements get nominated by all political parties across the board and why elections in Bihar have been increasingly rough, violent and corrupt.

This brings me to the third aspect: the high level of violence in Bihar society. There is not only violence in politics, but in almost every sphere of life. As Das (1998, p. 3103) observes, "the legitimate economy is stagnant and the only 'growth sector' is crime". The state itself is very violent, but apart from that, the Bihar state has also practically abandoned the idea that it should try to maintain a monopoly over the use of the means of coercion (Kohli, 1991, p. 219). Unable to deal with the resistance of agricultural labourers in various parts of the state, it has encouraged, or in any case not taken any effective action against, the establishment of private armies, the so-called *senas*. These *senas* take law and order in their own hand. They are involved in harassing, assaulting and killing the landless and Dalit population, resulting sometimes in extremely barbaric massacres.[19] These *Senas* are organised along caste lines. There are also counter-attacks from the Dalit population against the local upper caste or OBC landlords.

All these three aspects of governmental ineffectiveness are reflected in the implementation of the PDS in Bihar. The description in the previous section shows the lack of a serious interest among the officials to implement the PDS properly. And those IAS officers in senior positions who are committed and refuse to cooperate with the Minister in activities they regard as illegitimate are transferred sooner rather than later. Some of the people who are involved in food distribution, whether to card holders or to others, are petty or not-so-petty criminals. There is a clear nexus between the PDS dealers and local politicians, who give protection to the dealers. And, it is partly with the help of violence that attempts are made to silence people who protest against the malpractices, as happened in the case of the newspaper reporter referred to above.

The next question to raise is, of course, what the reasons are for this governmental ineffectiveness. What are the structural characteristics of the Bihar economy and society which underlie this state failure. There are, in any case, two important structural characteristics: Bihar's under development and economic stagnation on the one hand, and the changing political landscape and breakdown of the traditional political order on the other.

2. Underdevelopment and Stagnation

In the 1990s Bihar growth rate has been between 1.0 and 1.2 per cent per year, while the national average for the whole of India was around 6 per cent. It has the lowest per capita income of all the major states in India. It is one of the most densely populated states of India (coming third after Kerala and West Bengal). Both industrial and agricultural development are poor.

Ever since Independence, the industrial growth rate in Bihar has been lower than the national average.

> Disturbing as this is, what is more disturbing is that while national industrial growth shows some tendency towards acceleration, there is a clear tendency towards deceleration in Bihar. The average national industrial growth rate as a whole increased from about 5 per cent in the '60s to about 8 per cent in the '80s. During the '60s, Bihar's industrial growth rate was roughly the same as the national growth rate. Since then, it has decelerated from about 5 per cent to about 4 per cent in the '80s. During the '90s the position may have worsened (Gupta, 1997, p. 23).

What is interesting is that the relatively large industries develop more or less at par with industries elsewhere in India. The reason is that these industries, mainly basic metals and transport equipment, do not depend on the local economy, but are integrated in national and global markets. It is especially the small industrial units that depend on local supplies and on the local market for their end products that do very poorly and cause the deceleration (Gupta, 1997, pp. 23-4).

Bihar, thus, is not only a rural, but also a very agricultural society. It has the highest proportion of population living in rural areas (87 per cent, as compared to the national average of 74.3 per cent), next to only Assam (Sharma, 1995, p. 2587), and its population depends to a very large extent on agriculture. There is a retrogression in the employment structure.

Sharma (1995, p. 2589) shows that the share of the primary sector in employment has gone up from 80.23 per cent in 1961 to 82.36 per cent in 1991, while the share of the secondary sector declined from 8.28 per cent in 1961 to 4.64 per cent in 1991. Even the absolute number of people employed in the secondary sector declined.

As a result, an increasing number of people depend on agriculture for their livelihood. The agricultural performance is, however, unfortunately, also not very good. During the first decades after Independence, agricultural growth was very poor, and during the Green Revolution period (1964-65 to 1979-80) when cereal production in India as a whole increased at a 1.8 per cent compound rate, in Bihar the rate was only 0.1 per cent (Blair, 1984, p. 55). Since the mid-1980s the growth rates improved, and became even higher than the national average (Sharma, 1995, p. 2591), but the growth rates decelerated again in the 1990s (Sharma and Kumar, 1998, p. 397). In short, especially in view of the large and increasing population that crucially depends on agriculture for its livelihood, the situation is very problematic.

One of the main reasons for the slow agricultural growth is the prevailing agrarian structure, which is often characterised as semi-feudal. The abolition of the *Zamindari* system after Independence meant the transfer of some lands from the upper castes to the larger occupancy tenants, who were often from the backward castes (mainly Yadavs, Koiris and Kurmis). The 'ceiling legislation' was very poorly implemented. It is estimated that about 10 per cent of the total cultivated land changed hands from the *zamindars* to the intermediate size cultivators.[20] The Green Revolution took hardly place in Bihar, but as far as it took place, it was instrumental in the emergence of a new category of *kulak* farmers. Many of them belong to the upper backward castes, the Yadavs, the Koiris and the Kurmis (Sharma and Kumar, 1998, p. 404).

The term 'semi-feudal' is used to describe the agrarian structure because 'precapitalist' economic relationships such as sharecropping, usury and bonded labour still persist. Sharecropping is the most common form of tenancy in Bihar, and in some areas share croppers account for about 40 per cent of the rural households.[21] To quote Sharma and Kumar (1998, pp. 396-7):

> A study conducted in 1980-81, showed that two-fifths of the rural households leased in land in the plains of Bihar [which the northern part of the State] (...) and about 28 per cent of the total cultivated area was being leased in, of which about 70 per cent was on crop-sharing basis (Prasad et al., 1990). Apart from 50 per cent share in crop output, even straw was shared and almost the entire cost was borne by the sharecropper. The survey further revealed that about three-fifths of the rural households were indebted to the traditional sources of loan (money-lenders, employers, etc.), the corresponding percentage for agricultural labourers being more than 80 per cent and for poor middle peasants more than 60. Almost one-third of the agricultural labourers were attached to employers and almost invariably they had to work exclusively for them.

There were some changes in the 1980s, but according to a more recent study, crop sharing remains the principal form of tenancy.[22]

In this situation of an increasing population depending on a stagnating agriculture, conflicts are bound to arise. The total cake is not growing, but those who dominate the social structure continue to try to increase their share by intensifying surplus appropriation. This is not possible without force, debt bondage, reference to a rigid caste hierarchy and other semi-feudal mechanisms (Kohli, 1991, p. 230; Sharma and Kumar, 1998, p. 399). At the same time, people have become increasingly vocal (see below) and do not accept the extreme exploitation. This has led to very violent rural conflicts.

This underdevelopment and economic stagnation also explains in part why the state itself has become the prize over which rival caste groups are fighting (Frankel, 1989, p. 47). In the absence of economic development and growth of the private sector, the state is the main provider of jobs and other resources. This partly explains why there is still a considerable interest in getting a license to run a PDS shop. Even though, strictly speaking, the business is inviable, it is better than nothing since it gives access to food, relations and local influence.

3. Changing Political Landscape and Breakdown of the Traditional Political Order

But while there is underdevelopment and stagnation in the economic sphere, the changes in the political sphere have been quite dramatic. For a long time the political landscape was fully dominated by the upper castes. When the provinces of Bihar and Orissa were established in 1912, the main beneficiaries were the Kayasthas. This caste group got the lion's share of the higher level government jobs. In succeeding years also the other 'twice born' castes entered the political arena: the Bhumihars, the Rajputs and the Brahmins (Blair, 1984, p. 62). There was much struggle and competition amongst these caste groups, and this rivalry continued after Independence. At the same time, however, there was a basic understanding amongst these caste groups that they should rule Bihar, and together they dominated the Congress party.

The introduction of universal suffrage after Independence necessitated for making some concessions and giving patronage to lower castes,[23] but the first real challenge to the upper caste/Congress hegemony came in 1977, when a non-Congress government was elected in Bihar and reservation policies for backward castes were put on the agenda. The real change came only in 1990 with the ascent of Janata Dal and its leader Laloo Prasad Yadav, who has ruled the state more or less continuously since then.[24]

In caste terms, it is the upper *jatis* among the backward castes who have become the new ruling castes: the Yadavs, the Kurmis and the Koiris. Among them, the Yadavs dominate, both in number and in terms of political representation. The lower backward castes are much less represented in the JD/RJD regime of the 1990s (Kumar, 1999). In class terms, it is the *kulaks*, who have played a major role in the changing political arena. This class of farmers had benefited from the agricultural growth as far as it had taken place, and they had been successful in cornering most of the loans and other benefits from the government. It was this self-aware *kulak* class succeeded in challenging the upper caste/ traditional landlord political dominance.

A second struggle which affected the political landscape in several parts of Bihar is that between upper and backward landlowners on the one hand, and the Dalit or landless population on the other hand. In the last decades there have been forceful movements of the small peasants and landless labourers, fighting for homestead land, the enforcement of minimum wage laws, recognition of sharecroppers rights, etc. (Mitra and Vijayendra, 1982). These fights take and took place under the banner of several organisations: the CPI, the CPI(ML), the Indian People's Front, the Bihar State Kisan Sabha, the Maoist Communist Centre, etc. Some of these groups are underground, and by the law and order establishment of the government they are all clustered together and labeled as 'Naxalites' (Hauser, 1993, pp. 88-89).

The violence with which these movements are countered is horrific. The landowning castes have established their own private armies to deal with the *Dalit* uprisings. The government has allowed the violence to increase and become more and more normal.

Also this second factor (the changing political landscape) is crucial for understanding the governmental ineffectiveness, and together with the first factor (economic stagnation) underlies the failure of the PDS in Bihar.[25] The political mobilisation along caste lines in Bihar and the increasing political representation of the OBC castes have resulted in a situation in which also state resources are distributed mainly along caste lines. In the 1990s, the other backward castes are the main beneficiaries. Moreover, the ongoing violent struggles, the fact that this violence has become normal and the ambiguous position of the Bihar government vis-à-vis this violence, means that the rule of law has given way to the rule of muscle and money power. Those who are powerful often also benefit from political protection. The proper implementation of a policy like the PDS is seriously affected by all this.

IV. CONCLUSION AND DISCUSSION

In this paper I have analysed the way in which the public food distribution is implemented system in Bihar (now Bihar and Jharkhand). This analysis showed that there are many problems. There is large scale misappropriation of foodgrains at all levels; the distribution of cards to BPL families is unsatisfactory; the Bihar State Food and Civil Supplies Corporation is financially not able to perform its task. Many people benefit from the way the public distribution system functions at present. Some PDS dealers get a reasonable income, as do many civil servants and others who are involved in monitoring the system. Politicians too have vested interests in the way the system works.

In the next part of the paper I described the political economy of Bihar. The problems with the PDS are not exceptional; in fact, they are part of larger patterns of governmental ineffectiveness. The reasons behind this failure on the part of the government are economic stagnation and underdevelopment, and the changing political landscape. Given this political economic context in which the PDS is implemented, the observed problems are not surprising. There is almost no growth, so whatever scarce resources are available, they are appropriated through legal or illegal means. In the case of the PDS, these are public resources. They include foodgrains, posts (PDS shop licences, vigilance committee memberships, official postings), and also the discretionary powers to decide about these licences and postings. These are different kind of resources, but they are all scarce and highly valued, and people fight for them. These public resources are all misused and the benefits are (mis) appropriated to a large extent. The appropriation happens partly along caste lines, as this is one of the important mechanisms of how access to state resources is organised in Bihar.

So, the first important point to make is that the form the PDS has taken in this state reflects this wider political economy, and cannot be understood without contextualisation within this background. A second point is that, when this is the case, proposals for reform and improved performance should take this context into account, and are likely to fail when they do not, i.e., when they assume a political economic vacuum in which policies are implemented.

These two points may seem fairly obvious, but they are often not sufficiently realised, and there are structural reasons for that. Policy makers who design policies often do this far away from where these policies have to be implemented. There is not only a geographical distance, but also a social one. Food policies are shaped at the central level, by central-state politicians, but mainly by civil servants. These politicians are less concerned with their immediate popularity than their colleagues at the level of the federal states. The central-state politicians may try to protect the interests of their constituency, but when it comes to general policy matters, they are faced with the necessity to bring down budget deficits, to ensure economic growth, to give and take to/from other political parties in a coalition government, to satisfy international agencies and important collective national interest groups (such as national industrialists or the rich farmers' lobby), etc. The involved bureaucrats are also less aware of the practical and political difficulties at the local level resulting from their policies. The implementation arena, at the state and local level, is a very different one. The state politicians are potentially much closer to the people for whom the policy was meant to make a difference, but also much closer to others who have a vested interest. In a state like Bihar, where there is no articulate demand for a proper implementation, these state-level politicians allow various malpractices around the PDS and continue to benefit from these. The same is true for many of the local bureaucrats involved in policy implementation.

This brings us inevitably to the question, what a more local/state specific policy would look like in the case of Bihar. The political economic context is there to stay, in any case for some time. This is a real constraint, and it makes one wonder whether anything can be done at all. Is there an almost insurmountable bottleneck, which makes all attempts of reforms and improvements futile? Such interpretation is too negative and cynical, although these feelings of powerlessness and futility are widespread, also among many government officials in Bihar itself. Many IAS officers and others have become rather cynical and/or feel that they are wasting their time and talents in the office (but no alternatives are available to them).

Yet, I do think that there are options for reform and improvement. As highlighted above, within almost all categories of people involved there are individuals and organisations who are dissatisfied with the way the PDS functions. So, there are seeds of change. It could be tried to bring these dissident voices together and to mobilise them in an attempt to make some improvements on a small scale. There are precedents of such attempts. Sharma (1995, p. 2600) refers to a few "highly localised success stories".

> Such successes are generally caused by ultra-enthusiasm on the part of a small group of administrators who decide to implement a programme on a 'mission basis' in a rather small area. Mobilisation of the rest of the bureaucracy is done by pressure as well as persuasion, and the small size of the project area enables the group to closely monitor the programme. As is expected, even one small positive step of the administration enthuses the expected beneficiaries to take two steps forward and thus it generates a momentum, ensuring the success of the programme.

Also in the case of the PDS, it could be tried to initiate change on a small scale, by bringing the various dissatisfied stakeholders together, in an attempt to develop practical solutions to the various problems. A small pilot project in one or two blocks will not threaten the vested interests in a serious way. Because the PDS continues in the same manner in all the other blocks and districts, there will be no income loss initially for those people who are used to get an illegal income from the PDS. In due course, of course, this has to change. When the project is successful and people in other parts of the state start demanding something similar, there could be a real income loss. The success will then depend on the strength of the people's demand for a clean PDS.

A number of conditions have to be fulfilled for such a project to work. There has to be a dynamic food secretary/commissioner, who is committed to the PDS. There has to be some financial support and political backing from within, but perhaps also from outside the state. There should be a sufficiently large number of people from all normally benefiting stakeholder groups (the PDS dealers, officials, local politicians,

MLAs) who are dissatisfied and who can be brought together. And the last, but most important, there should be some political awareness and willingness to fight amongst the expected beneficiaries.

Some of the conditions for a change in a positive direction are fulfilled. The last condition, for instance, is fulfilled in several areas of Bihar. Although many people who are caught up in extremely exploitative relations depend for their immediate survival on landlords and moneylenders, they are willing to involve themselves in various struggles. So far, their struggles have hardly centered around the PDS (or any anti-poverty programme for that matter), but there is no reason why they could not be, provided there is a possibility to change things for the better. Other conditions are still to be realised: financial support, some political backing. The realisation of these conditions will not be easy.

Overall, what is needed is a rather unconventional approach in the field of policy making: political manoeuvring, lobbying and strategic alliance building, rather than the formulation of new policy directives from the state capital or from Delhi, more squads or guidelines. Improving food distribution policy has to be a political process in which the (few) well-willing stakeholders come together to act strategically and in which a lot will depend on the pressure exercised by the would-be beneficiaries.

(This paper is one of the outcomes of a larger research project "Social Policies and Legislation in India: From Independence to Structural Adjustment", financed by the Indo-Dutch Programme for Alternatives in Development (IDPAD). I would like to thank Mr. Alok Deo Singh for his research assistance. Earlier drafts of this paper were presented at the Indira Gandhi Institute for Development Research, Mumbai; the Institute of Social Studies, the Hague; and at the national seminar on Food Security in India. The Emerging Challenges in the Context of Economic Liberalisation, Hyderabad, March 2000. I would like to thank the contributors to these seminars and a few others for their comments, in particular David Dunham, Bridget O'Laughlin, Niranjan Pant and Alpa Shah).

Notes

1. "Expert Group on Estimation of Proportion and Number of Poor", constituted by the Planning Commission under the Chairmanship of late Prof. Lakdawalla. The percentages calculated by the Expert Group refer to 1993-94. These figures of the Planning Commission are very high. According to the Market Information Survey of Households of the NCAER, 29 per cent of the Bihar population lived below the poverty line in 1997-98. The all-India figure according to this survey is 17 per cent (Lal et al., 2001, tables 2B and 3). For a recent description of poverty in Bihar in more qualitative terms (see Mukul, 1999).
2. The all-India average in 1993-94 was 2153 kcal. In general, the picture in 1993-94 was worse than twenty years earlier (Swaminathan and Ramachandran, 1999).
3. Data from National Sample Surveys and National Family Health Survey. See Swaminathan and Ramachandran (1999).
4. Data from Department of Agriculture, Patna. 128 kilos per person per year, means 10.7 kilos per person per month. The per capita cereal consumption in 1993-94 was 14.31 kilos in rural Bihar and 12.82 kilos in urban Bihar (Hanumantha Rao, 2000, Table 1).
5. The paper is based on fieldwork done between 1997 and 2000, when the state of Bihar was not yet divided into the new Bihar and Jharkhand. Fieldwork took place around Patna and in south Bihar (now Jharkhand). The undivided state of Bihar is treated here as a homogeneous region, which is of course not correct. Even before bifurcation, there was a difference in the political economy of the north and the south. It is likely that

these differences will only increase after the split of the state, something which would be interesting to study in more detail.

6. These percentages refer to December 1998. *Source*: Bihar State Food and Civil Supplies Corporation.

7. In fact, this means that there are too many PDS dealers, and that the economic viability of the shops has come under further threat (see text).

8. Between 1995 and 1999, the number of PDS shops increased by 11 per cent. In some parts of Bihar, where the RJD was strong and Yadavs the dominant caste, we can say that there was something like a 'Yadavisation' (Hauser, 1997) of the PDS. A few years ago, however, the food commissioner issued an order, saying that new PDS shops should be given to SC/ST. This was exactly in order to stop further Yadavisation of the PDS. This policy was not successful. The percentage of shops allotted to SC/ST category increased only by 4.2 per cent between 1995 and 1999, which is considerably less than the overall shop number increase rate.

9. For example, the monthly allotment to Ranchi district (in October 1997) was: 1853 tonnes wheat for below poverty line (BPL) families, 1237 tonnes rice for BPL families, 629 tonnes wheat for above poverty line (APL) families, 419 tonnes rice for APL families, 218 tonnes sugar and 1,836 kiloliters of kerosene. There were 1,624 PDS dealers in Ranchi district. The commission for the PDS dealers was 3.15 per cent for foodgrains, Rs. 0.09 per liter kerosene and Rs. 5.85 per 100 kg sugar. Altogether this means an average monthly income for each PDS dealer of Rs. 479.57. This is based on full off-take of the commodities. When only 50 per cent is available or lifted by the PDS dealers, the income is proportionately less. There are some additional earnings from the sale of the gunnybags, but there are also expenses. The PDS dealers themselves have to pay the transport of the commodities from the warehouses to their premises. This involves a bullock cart and some payment for the coolies who load and unload the cart. In addition to the official expenses, there are many unofficial expenses, like bribes to warehouse managers to people from the Food and Civil Supplies Department, etc.

10. It is important, however, that being a fair-price shop dealer is normally not a full-time job. Sometimes the dealers do not need more than a few days per month to finish the job. However, their urgency to get rid of the commodities as quickly as possible (and therefore not lift more from the warehouse than they can sell in a short time span) adds to access problems of the consumers/card holders.

11. Translation by Alok Deo Singh.

12. Elections have been held since than in Bihar, but not in Jharkhand.

13. Early 2000, the Corporation had about 2200 employees. For a long time the Ministers were the chairmen of the SFC, and they (mis)used their position to give jobs to people they wanted to give jobs to.

14. Statement based on newspaper reports and interviews with officials of the SFC and some other officials.

15. *Pairavi* is the act of requesting authorities for action in favour of a beneficiary by utilising one's own (*pairvikar's*) position, influence or office. The *pairvikar* is often a politician, and the authority approached is often an official (Verma, n.d., footnote 16).

16. The PDS dealers have to pay regular amounts to the rationing inspectors and the market inspectors. In Patna, the capital, there are 1,100 PDS dealers. They have to pay a fixed amount of Rs. 500 each per month. (This was the amount in October 1997. During later visits higher amounts were also mentioned to me).

    This means that each month about half a million rupees are collected and send up in the hierarchy. Apart from this, the PDS dealers have to pay for special purposes. Because the sector is very well organised it is an easy target for occasional demands for money. As one informant told me: 'Occasionally there are solidarity meetings of the Rashtriya Janata Dal. People come from rural areas, and they have to receive a food packet during the rally. What happens is that the District Magistrate and the district rationing officer call for a meeting of all supply officers. They discuss the problems with the PDS. Then, in the last minute, they say: "You might be knowing, there is a demonstration for the RJD. Please help". Informally all supply officers are informed about how much money they should collect from each PDS dealer. The whole city is divided among the supply officers; each of them has 20-70 PDS dealers to check. They collect Rs. 500 or 1000 from all of them. They say: "You can sell whatever you want on the black market, but please contribute to the rally'". (Interview in Patna, July 9, 1998).

17. This word is also used in Hindi. It is used in a rather loose sense, to refer to criminal activities. It does not refer to the networks and societies of criminals as exist, for instance, in southern Italy.

18. Of course, this is a very one-sided picture. The land reform (ceiling legislation), for instance, was hardly implemented in Bihar, and the so-called stable and more professional government was almost completely dominated by members of the Brahmin or Kayasthas castes (Frankel, 1989).

19. See for instance, Bhatia (1997, 1998) or Hauser (1993). See Bose (1991, Table 2) for an overview of various instances of this kind of violence.

20. Frankel (1989, p. 92), who refers in this context to Prasad (1979).

21. See Mitra and Vijayendra (1982) about Purnea district in north Bihar.

22. A study of the L.B.S. National Academy of Administration conducted in 1990-91, referred to in Sharma and Kumar (1998).

23. In the 1930s already, the three great Sudra communities (Yadavs, Kurmis and Koiris – now all OBCs) had tried to organise themselves in opposition to the high caste Congress. At that time they failed, but given the facts that the Sudra castes in Bihar constitute together almost half of the total population of the State and that political mobilisation in Bihar proceeds to a large extent via caste mobilisation, it was almost inevitable that at some point in time the old order would break down.

24. More or less, because there have been short intermittent periods of 'Presidential Rule', and since 1998 it is no longer Laloo Prasad Yadav himself but his wife who heads the government. In 1998, there was a split in Janata Dal, and Laloo Prasad Yadav now heads the Rashtriya Janata Dal (RJD).

25. Of course, there is no underlying argument here that the previous political landscape was more desirable than the present one. See my earlier footnote 19.

References

Ashtana, M.D. (2000), "Rationale for Recent Changes in Foodgrains Distribution under the Targeted Public Distribution System", Paper presented at a *Seminar on Food Security in India: The Emerging Challenges in the Context of Economic Liberalisation*, held at the Centre for Economic and Social Studies, Hyderabad, March 25-27.

Bhatia, Bela (1998), "After the Bathe Massacre", *Economic and Political Weekly*, Vol. 33, No. 14, pp. 751-52.

—— (1997), "Anatomy of a Massacre: The State of Bihar", *Seminar* 450 , pp. 53-59.

Blair, Harry W. (1984), "Structural Change, the Agricultural Sector, and Politics in Bihar", in Wood, John R. (ed.), *State Politics in Contemporary India: Crisis or Continuity?*, Westview Press, Boulder and London, pp. 53-79.

Bose, Pradip K. (1991), "Mobility and Conflict: Social Roots of Caste Violence in Bihar", in Gupta, Dipankar (ed.), *Social Stratification*, Oxford University Press, Delhi, pp. 369-386.

Daly, Gerald and Bhattacharya, Deepayan (2001), "Food Insecurity and Child Work in Rural India: Space Dimensions," Paper presented at the *IHD-WFP Consultative Workshop on Food Insecurity and Child Work*, March 15-17.

Das, Arvind N. (1998), "India in the Image of Bihar", *Economic and Political Weekly*, Vol. 33, No. 49, pp. 3103-4.

Frankel, Francine R. (1989), "Caste, Land and Dominance in Bihar: Breakdown of the Brahminical Order", in Frankel, Francine R. and Rao, M.S.A (eds.), *Dominance and State Power in Modern India: Decline of a Social Order, Vol. 1*, Oxford University Press, Delhi etc., pp. 46-132.

Government of India (1997), *Focus on the Poor (Guidelines for the Implementation of the Targeted Public Distribution System*, Ministry of Civil Supplies, Consumer Affairs and Public Distribution, New Delhi.

Gupta, Shaibal (1997), "The Enigma that is Bihar Economy", *Seminar 450*, pp. 23-27.

Hanumantha Rao, C.H. (2000), "Declining Demand for Foodgrains in Rural India: Causes and Implications", *Economic and Political Weekly*, Vol. 35, No. 4, pp. 201-206.

Hauser, Walter (1993), "Violence, Agrarian Radicalism and Electoral Politics: Reflections on the Indian People's Front", *Journal of Peasant Studies*, Vol. 21, No. 1, pp. 85-126.

Jharwal, S.M. (1999), *Public Distribution System in India Reassessed*, Manak Publications, New Delhi.

Kohli, Atul (1991), *Democracy and Discontent. India's Growing Crisis of Governability*, Cambridge University Press, Cambridge.

Kumar, Sanjay (1999), "New Phase in Backward Caste Politics in Bihar: Janata Dal on the Decline", *Economic and Political Weekly*, Vol. 34, Nos. 34 and 35, pp. 2472-2480.

Lal, Deepak; Mohan, Rakesh and Natarajan, I. (2001), "Economic Reforms and Poverty Alleviation: A Tale of Two Surveys", *Economic and Political Weekly*, Vol. 36, No. 12, pp. 1017-1028.

Mitra, Manoshi and Vijayendra, T. (1982), "Agricultural Labourers and Peasant Politics: Rural Proletarianisation in Purnea, Bihar", *Journal of Peasant Studies*, Vol. 9, No. 3, pp. 88-118.

Mooij, Jos (1999), "Food Policy in India: The Importance of Electoral Politics in Policy Implementation", *Journal of International Development*, Vol. 11, pp. 625-636.

Mukul (1999), "The Untouchable Present: Everyday Life of Musahars in North Bihar", *Economic and Political Weekly*, Vol. 34, No. 49, pp. 3465-70.

Prasad, Binoy S. (1997), "General Elections, 1996: Major Role of Caste and Social Factions in Bihar", *Economic and Political Weekly*, Vol. 32, No. 47, pp. 3021-3028.

Prasad, Pradhan H. (1979), "Caste and Class in Bihar", *Economic and Political Weekly*, Vol. 14, No. 7-8, pp. 481-484.

Prasad, Pradhan H.; Rodgers, Gerry; Sharma, Alakh N. and Gupta, S. (1990), *Dynamics of Poverty and Employment in Bihar*, A.N. Sinha Institute of Social Studies, Patna (mimeo).

Radhakrishna, R. and Subbarao, K. with Indrakant, S. and Ravi, C. (1997), "India's Public Distribution System: A National and International Perspective." *World Bank Discussion Paper No. 380*, The World Bank, Washington, D.C.

Sharma, Alakh N. (1995), "Political Economy of Poverty in Bihar", *Economic and Political Weekly*, Vol. 30, Nos. 41/42, pp. 2587-2602.

—— and Kumar, Ajay (1998), "Peasant Mobilisation in Bihar: Implications for Rural Labour Markets", in Radhakrishna, R. and Sharma, Alakh N. (eds.), *Empowering Rural Labour in India: Market, State and Mobilisation*, Institute for Human Development, New Delhi, pp. 395-414.

Swaminathan, Madhura (2000), *Weakening Welfare: The Public Distribution of Food in India*, Leftword, New Delhi.

Swaminathan, Madhura and Ramachandran, V.K. (1999), "New Data on Calorie Intakes", *Frontline*, March 12, pp. 109-111.

Verma, R.K. (undated), *Dimensions of Mid-term Lok Sabha Elections in Bihar* (mimeo).

13

The Paradox of Food Insecurity in a Food Surplus State: The Case of Uttar Pradesh

Nisha Srivastava

'In the kingdom of hunger the world is only prosaic—
The moon, when full, is like a browned chapatti....'[1]

It is ironic that food security should be an issue more than five decades after independence. It is also paradoxical that it should be discussed in the context of Uttar Pradesh, a state that lies in the Gangetic plains, one of the most fertile tracts of land in the world. The state has plenty of rich alluvial soil and abundant water and is considered a food surplus state. The worst irony, however, is that food security should be an issue at a time when the country has mountains of foodgrains and overflowing godowns. 'Food security', states the Rome Declaration on World Food Security at the World Food Summit held in 1996, "exists when all people, at all times, have physical and economic access to sufficient, safe and nutritious food to meet their dietary needs and food preferences for an active and healthy life." This definition encompasses multiple dimensions, but in this study, we examine two major aspects of the problem—that of food availability and food access in the state of Uttar Pradesh. The first part looks at food availability and examines food access by looking at poverty trends, food consumption and evidence of malnourishment. The second appraises governmental initiatives in providing food security and the last section outlines the conclusions.

I. AVAILABILITY OF AND ACCESS TO FOOD IN UTTAR PRADESH

1. Food Availability

Uttar Pradesh, together with Punjab and Haryana, may be considered the country's agricultural heartland. The state has rich alluvial soils and adequate water. While Uttar Pradesh has 16 per cent of India's population, it contributes 22 per cent to the total foodgrain production, and is the largest producer of wheat, accounting for 35 per cent of the country's output. It is the second largest producer of rice. The state has the highest milk production (12.93 mln.litres) in the country and is the largest producer of fruits contributing 8 per cent of the fruits and 20 per cent of the vegetables produced in the country.

Estimates show that against the population growth of 2.29 per cent between 1980-81 and 1990-91, the compound growth rate in the net value of agricultural production has been higher, i.e., at 2.95 per cent per annum.

Growth in the production of wheat, rice and sugarcane has been achieved mainly through the growth of yield in each case as the rate of growth of their area, though positive, has been much less important. All other cereals witnessed a negative growth in the area cultivated during the period, 1980-81 to 1992-93.

Whatever the absolute level of production, ultimately, food production has to be judged by the extent to which it meets the food requirement, in both quantitative and qualitative terms, i.e., can production meet the requirements of different kinds of foods that make up a balanced diet for all its citizens? If the state is producing enough food to meet basic norms of food intake, it is said to be 'self-sufficient'. In theory, self-sufficiency of a state is not crucial because inter-state movement of food should make it possible to transport it to deficit states. Nonetheless, in practice, adequate production at the state level is important because it facilitates consumption, particularly in rural areas and by the poor. Table 1 shows the daily allowance of different food items recommended by The Indian Council of Medical Research, and the per capita net production in Uttar Pradesh. The figures calculated by the M.S. Swaminathan Research Foundation (MSSRF, 2001) show that the state produces a surplus of cereals, tubers, sugar, and vegetables, but is deficient in pulses, oilseeds and fruits. The per capita net production of cereals, tubers, and sugar is in fact higher than the average for the country as a whole.

Overall, there are two disquieting features in regard to the adequate availability of food. The first is that there has been stagnation in output in recent years and second, there are large regional imbalances within the state.

Table 1

Per Capita Net Production (gm/day)

Food	Cereals	Tubers	Pulses	Sugar	E. oilseeds	Fruits	Vegetables	Total
ICMR norms	420	75	40	30	22	50	125	
Uttar Pradesh	545.68	116.76	33.62	65.67	7.16	38.17	160.95	968.00
India	430.33	65.73	31.94	41	18.10	58.33	179.22	824.66

Source: MSSRF (2001).

The growth in foodgrain production in the state has decelerated sharply during the last decade. Table 2 shows that while the growth rate of agricultural output was not spectacular, it was steady between 1970 to the beginning of the 1990s. Thereafter, it fell sharply. Moreover, while the growth rate in Uttar Pradesh was higher than that at the national level till the triennium ending 1980-83, in the subsequent periods, it fell below the national average. The relative decline in growth rates of agricultural production does not augur well for the poor who are mainly dependent on this sector for their livelihood.

Table 2
Growth of Agricultural Output in Different Periods

	1970-73 over 1962-65	1980-83 over 1970-73	1990-93 over 1980-83	1996-99 over 1990-93
Uttar Pradesh	2.54	2.77	3.06	2.47
All states	2.08	2.38	3.44	2.83

Source: Bhalla (2001).

Table 3 shows that while wheat, rice and fruit and vegetables recorded modest increases between 1994-95 and 1998-99, the index of production of pulses and oilseeds has fallen. As we shall see, the drop in production of pulses, the chief source of protein for the masses, has had a deleterious impact on protein intake, which has been steadily declining.

Table 3
Indices of Volume of Production of Selected Agricultural Commodities, Uttar Pradesh (1970-71=100)

Crops	1994-95	1995-96	1996-97	1997-98	1998-99*
Wheat	295.4	283.7	312.8	296.9	301.3
Rice	288.0	287.4	326.0	340.6	321.9
Pulses	84.5	76.4	91.2	80.4	77.9
Fruits & veg.	354.4	390.1	491.5	307.7	485.2
Oilseeds	69.4	71.7	78.5	48.2	50.5

Source: Statistical Diary, Uttar Pradesh, Various Issues.

The other major problem with food production is the prevalence of wide regional disparities in agricultural output in the state. Productivity of most food crops is highest in the western region and lowest in the agriculturally poor southern (Bundelkhand) region. Compared to the latter, foodgrain productivity is twice as high in the western region (Table 4).

Table 4
Crop Productivity by Region in Uttar Pradesh (quintal/hectare) in 1993-94

Region	Wheat	Rice	All foodgrains	Potato	Oilseeds
Hills	17.6	20.0	16.4	195.7	10.4
Western	26.6	22.2	21.8	222.9	10.3
Central	21.7	18.8	17.5	181.1	7.2
Eastern	21.8	18.0	17.8	153.2	5.7
Southern	17.7	8.6	11.5	193.6	5.4
Uttar Pradesh	23.1	19.0	18.4	193.6	8.4

Source: Computed from figures given by the Department of Agriculture, Government of Uttar Pradesh.

During the 1980's, there were some healthy signs indicating a levelling of agricultural disparities. Agricultural growth picked up in the poorer regions and both the central and eastern regions registered higher growth rates of foodgrains as well as other crops, compared to the traditionally more dynamic western region. During the period, 1977-80—1987-90, foodgrain production in the eastern region grew at an annual compound rate of 5.81 per cent, which was higher than the growth rate of 4.99 per cent in the central region and of 4.57 per cent in the western region. During the decade, 1980-83—1990-93, the eastern region also experienced a growth rate in potato production of 4.2 per cent annually, compared to 3.72 per cent in the western region.

However, these high growth rates could not be sustained, and the growth rate of foodgrain output in the eastern region fell to 2.68 per cent and to a marginally better rate of 2.89 per cent in the western region between 1987-90 and 1993-96.

We may conclude this subsection on food availability with the observation that while there are some disconcerting features, overall, with proper food management, there is adequate foodgrain output to feed the population of this state. In fact, the state government estimates a surplus of 10 mln. tonnes of foodgrains after meeting the household consumption and other requirements of food.[2]

2. Access to Food

Does the abundance of food translate into adequate access to food for all? No, because large-scale poverty in the state constrains the purchasing power of the poor and other vulnerable sections. The poor suffer from limited access to food and to means of livelihood. Here, we highlight the magnitude of poverty in the state (Table 5) and how this is reflected on the consumption and health of the people. Moreover, we also examine how social and gender-related factors prevent access to food as well as to a balanced diet.

Poverty is a complex phenomenon with many dimensions. It poses formidable difficulties in respect of its definition, methodology and measurement. The Planning Commission defines poverty in terms of a minimal daily calorie intake, i.e., the amount of consumption expenditure

Table 5

Percentage of Population below the Poverty Line in Uttar Pradesh and India

Year	India			Uttar Pradesh		
	Rural	Urban	Total	Rural	Urban	Total
1973-74	56.4	49.0	54.9	56.5	60.1	57.1
1977-78	53.1	45.2	51.3	47.6	52.2	49.1
1983	45.6	40.8	44.5	46.5	49.9	47.1
1987-88	39.1	38.2	38.9	41.1	43.0	41.5
1993-94	37.3	32.4	36.0	42.3	35.4	40.9
1999-00	27.1	23.6	26.1	31.2	30.9	31.6

Source: Government of India (2002).

required for an intake of 2400 calories per person per day in the rural areas and 2100 calories per person per day in the urban areas, allowing also for some minimum expenditure on non-food items. In 1999-2000, an estimated 31.15 per cent of the population in the state were living below the poverty line, 31.22 per cent in the rural areas and 30.89 per cent in the urban areas.[3]

In 2001-02, the number of households below the poverty line was 106.79 lakhs, which was the largest in the country (*Economic Survey, 2001-02*). While in the earlier years the proportion of the poor was higher in urban areas, the situation appears to have changed since 1993-94. Uttar Pradesh has performed poorly in poverty reduction. While the number of persons below the poverty line was 57.1 per cent in the state against the national average of 54.9 per cent in 1973-74, this came down to 31.1 per cent in the state against the national average of 26.1 per cent in 1999-2000.

This prevalence of poverty is reflected in the consumption and health of the poor. Table 6 shows a consistent decline in the intake of cereals by the average person in the state between 1972-73 and 1993-94. Consumption of cereals declined from 16.8 kg to 13.9 kg per capita per month in the rural areas, and from 12.2 kg to 11.1 kg per person in the urban areas each month. The decline was sharpest in the case of coarse cereals, leading some to suggest that there was no real decline but only a change in food preferences in favour of wheat and rice and against the inferior cereals. This is only partially true, as the decline in consumption of course cereals has not been offset by equivalent increases in the intake of other cereals.

Table 6
Consumption of Cereals (kg per capita per month)

Year	Average				Poorest quintile			
	Rice	Wheat	Coarse	Total	Rice	Wheat	Coarse	Total
				Rural areas				
72-73	4.0	8.7	4.1	16.8	2.6	6.1	5.0	13.6
87-88	3.7	10.6	1.0	15.3	2.7	7.2	3.1	13.0
93-94	4.0	9.2	0.8	13.9	3.5	8.1	0.8	12.3
				Urban areas				
72-73	2.4	8.9	1.0	12.2	1.6	7.8	1.8	11.1
87-88	2.4	9.2		11.6	1.9	8.8	0.1	10.8
93-94	2.6	8.4	0.1	11.1	2.3	8.3	0.1	10.7

Source: Planning Commission (2001).

Table 6 further shows the trends in the cereal intake of the poorest 20 per cent of the population. The most disturbing aspect of the picture is the very low cereal intake of the poorest quintile compared to the average intake, and, what is more, the downtrend in even this low level of consumption. Here too, there is a switch on from the coarse cereals to wheat and rice, but the declines in the former are not offset by adequate increases in the intake of the latter.

The situation with respect to calorie intake presents a mixed picture. At the macro level, the average intake in the state rates compares favourably with other states. In 1999-2000, the calorie intake in the rural areas of the state was the fourth highest in the country falling below Haryana, Rajasthan and Punjab. In the urban areas, the ranking of the state was relatively lower and in Orissa, Bihar, Assam and West Bengal the calorie intake (in urban areas) was higher (NSSO, 2001) than in Uttar Pradesh. Uttar Pradesh ranks fourth highest (rural) and third highest (urban) among the major states when it comes to levels of protein intake. The down side is that these levels have been consistently declining. Conversely, fat intake levels are relatively lower than in many other states, but have steadily been rising (Table 7).

Table 7
Per Capita Per Diem Intake of Calorie, Protein and Fat over Different NSS Rounds in Uttar Pradesh

	Calorie (kcal)				Protein (gm)				Fat (gm)			
Year	1972-73	1983	1993-94	1999-2000	1972-73	1983	1993-94	1999-2000	1972-73	1983	1993-94	1999-2000
Rural	2575	2399	2307	2327	76.0	73.0	70.4	69.7	28.0	29.0	35.5	37.6
Urban	2161	2043	2114	2131	62.0	62.0	63.2	62.0	35.0	34.0	41.2	45.5

Source: NSSO (2000).

The food insecurity situation in the state can be assessed in terms of the spread and depth of hunger. The spread is given by the percentage of population consuming less than 1890 kcal, which is 70 per cent less than the norm of 2,700 kcal per capita per day (Table 8). The depth is given by the calorie consumption of the lowest 10 per cent of the population per consumer unit per day. The spread and depth of hunger are generally high in areas of deficit production.

Table 8
Percentage of Population/Households in Uttar Pradesh whose Calorie Intake is Less than the Norm

	Percentage of population consuming less than		Percentage of households consuming less than	
Region	70 % of the norm	90 % of the norm	70 % of the norm	90 % of norm
Rural	8.05	32.9	7.54	29.4
Urban	15.17	46.5	12.51	41.4

Source: NSSO (2000).

In Uttar Pradesh, the fact that 8 to 15 per cent of the population consumes less than 1890 kcal per day, and 33 to 47 per cent of the population consumes less than 90 per cent of the required calorie intake per day, reflects poorly on the nutritional intake in a state that boasts of surplus foodgrain production (NSSO, 1999-2000). This indicates the spread of hunger. On the other hand, the depth of hunger is reflected in the average consumption of the lowest monthly per capita expenditure class (i.e., consumption expenditure of less than Rs. 225 and Rs. 300 in rural and urban areas respectively) (Table 9). The average consumption of this class is just 1466 kcal in rural areas and 1,421 kcal in urban areas, showing that they are seriously undernourished and at risk. However, the percentage of population in this expenditure class is small in Uttar Pradesh—3.6 per cent in rural and 7.16 per cent in urban areas.

Table 9

Per Capita Intake of Calorie, Protein and Fat Per Diem of Household with the Lowest Monthly Per Capita Expenditure

	Per capita per diem intake of		
Area	Calorie (kcal)	Protein (gm)	Fat (gm)
Rural	1466	43.8	15.1
Urban	1421	42.6	19.6

Source: NSSO (2000).

3. People Who Do Not Get Two Square Meals a Day

Are there still people who go hungry or who do not get two square meals a day? People who are destitute or disabled may fall in this category. In such cases hunger may be of a chronic nature—or the people may starve because of a loss of livelihood, natural disasters or vulnerability to other kind of shocks. This may be a temporary phenomenon, and how soon it would be over would depend on the efficiency of governmental and other support systems. Then again, in a situation where there is heavy dependence on agriculture, as in Uttar Pradesh, hunger may be more seasonal in nature, surfacing most during the lean agricultural season when there is a shortage of both work and production. This possibility emerged sharply in a survey of living conditions in the poorest regions of Uttar Pradesh and Bihar, where a study by Srivastava (Srivastava, 2001) showed that of the 1225 households covered in the former (in the Eastern and Bundelkhand regions), 6.2 per cent of the sample households reported going without two square meals for sometime during the year. The households also reported the months in which they did not get even two square meals. In the wheat harvesting season, only 2.8 per cent of such households reported going without two square meals. This increased sharply to 37 per cent in the lean months of August-September. Another time when hunger is at its peak is in January when 33 per cent of such households reported going without two square meals.

The results obtained by the NSS (1999-2000), are similar. About 1.79 per cent households reported that they do not get two square meals either during some months or throughout the year. The breakup by social groups shows that the proportion is highest for the scheduled castes and least for the 'other' castes (Table 10). Table 10 also shows that the central region of the state has the largest proportion of hungry households.

Table 10
Percentage of Households Who Report Getting Adequate Food by Social Group and Region, Uttar Pradesh

	Do all members of your household get enough food everyday?								
Social group	Yes	Some months	No	Total	Region	Yes	Some months	No	Total
ST	98.60	0.45	0.95	100	Western	98.31	1.62	0.07	100
SC	96.34	2.36	1.31	100	Central	96.92	1.05	2.02	100
OBC	98.58	1.03	0.39	100	Eastern	98.76	0.98	0.26	100
Others	99.14	0.67	0.19	100	Bundelkhand	98.99	0.90	0.12	100
Total	98.21	1.23	0.56	100	Total	98.21	1.23	0.56	100

Source: NSS 55th Round, Central Sample.

4. Nutritional Status of Vulnerable Groups

Food security provided to people gets reflected in their health and nutritional status. Lack of food and adequate nutrition lead to ill health, lack of resistance to disease, and impaired mental capacities, all of which in turn perpetuate the vicious cycle of poverty. Life expectancy in Uttar Pradesh is among the lowest in the country with only Assam, Madhya Pradesh and Orissa among the major states having a worse record. In respect of female life expectancy, only Madhya Pradesh has a lower ranking. The Infant Mortality and Death Rates in the state are also dismal—only Madhya Pradesh and Orissa beat Uttar Pradesh to the bottom rank on both these parameters (Planning Commission, 2002). Just as education, livelihood, or assets are not equally accessible to everybody, so also access to food is constrained for some. The poor women, and scheduled castes and tribes are especially vulnerable to food insecurity. The nutritional status of vulnerable groups of the populations are discussed below:

(i) Women

It is ironical that women should suffer from poor health, because in most communities it is they who have the responsibility to feed others in the family—they are the food gatherers and food providers. When it comes to the woman herself, culture ordains that she eats last in the family, and poverty constrains that she eats the least. This complex weave of patriarchy and poverty reflects on the nutritional status of women. The National Family Health Survey (1999-2000) (IIPS, 2001) records the nutritional status for women and children. Their estimates show the marked impact of factors such as caste, gender, region and standard of living on their nutritional status (Table 11).

In Uttar Pradesh, 48.7 per cent women suffer from anaemia, which usually results from nutritional deficiency of iron, vitamin 12 or other nutrients. A woman receives no extra food or care during pregnancy, although her nutritional requirements increase dramatically during this period. She gains only half the weight necessary to have a healthy baby and as many as 46 per cent of pregnant women in Uttar Pradesh are anaemic. Anaemia may have detrimental effects on the health of women

Table 11
Nutritional Status of Women in Uttar Pradesh

	Height		Weight for Height	
	Mean height (cm)	Per cent below 145 cm	BMI	Per cent with BMI below 18.5 kg
Region				
Hill	151.60	8.60	20.20	32.30
West	151.00	14.00	20.50	31.10
Centre	149.50	19.80	19.80	40.10
East	149.80	19.00	19.70	37.50
Bundelkhand	151.70	7.10	19.40	43.10
Standard of living				
Low	149.20	20.60	19.00	44.90
Middle	150.30	16.40	19.70	36.80
High	151.90	11.40	22.10	20.90
Total UP	150.30	16.40	20.00	35.80
India	151.2	13.2	20.3	35.8

Source: IIPS (2001).

and children and may become an underlying cause of maternal mortality in the state. In effect, Uttar Pradesh has the highest maternal mortality rate in the country—707 against 407 nationally. Anaemia also results in an increased risk of premature delivery and low birth weight babies. The prevalence of anaemia in Uttar Pradesh is higher among rural women (49 per cent) than among urban women (46 per cent) and those belonging to SC/STs or other backward classes and illiterate women. Regionwise, nutritional deficiency among women is the highest in the poorer eastern (57.9 per cent) and Bundelkhand (41.2 per cent) regions and lowest in the prosperous western region (37.9 per cent). It is also more prevalent among women from poor households.

Anthropometric data tell us a great deal about the adequacy of food and nutritional intake of people, as also their ability to lead healthy and active lives. The height of an adult, for instance, depends, among other factors, on consumption during childhood and adolescence. Mothers who are short are more likely to have low birth weight babies and those whose height is below the range of 140-150 cm are considered nutritionally at risk. The mean height of women in Uttar Pradesh hovers just around 150 cm (see Table 11). There are large numbers of women (16.4 per cent) who are below 145 cm in height and these are more likely to belong to central and eastern regions of the state, to the SC/ST or backward classes and to the economically deprived classes.

Another measure of nutritional adequacy is the Body Mass Index (BMI), which is the ratio of weight (in kg) to height (in mts. squared). Chronic energy deficiency is usually indicated by a BMI of less than 18.5. In Uttar Pradesh, more than one-third women (36 per cent) have a BMI below this ratio. The proportion of women with low BMI is seen to be relatively high in rural women, those living in the Bundelkhand and central regions, those from the socially discriminated classes, and from poorer households. In fact, women from poor households are twice as likely to suffer from chronic energy deficiency compared to those from better-off households (see Table 11).

(ii) Children

Nutritional deficiency in children has particularly detrimental effects on their psychosocial and physical development, which can scar them for life. Undernourishment among children can be judged on the basis of three indices: weight for age, height for age, and weight for height. Children who are more than 2 SD (standard deviation units) below a predetermined reference median on any of the indices are considered 'undernourished' and those who are more than 3 SD below the reference median are considered as 'severely undernourished'. The data on Table 12 relate to children less than three years of age.

Each of these measures tells us something about different dimensions of nutritional status. The measure, weight for age, captures both chronic and acute undernutrition. If it is more than 2 SD below the reference median the child is considered 'underweight'. The height for age index measures the extent of growth retardation and a child who has 2 SD below the reference median is said to be stunted. Stunting is the result of chronic under nutrition. The third index, weight-for-height, measures the child's body mass with reference to the height. A figure 2 SD below the median reference indicates that the child is wasted—that is, is too thin in relation

Table 12

Percentage of Children under 3 Years of Age Classified as Undernourished on 3 Indices of Nutritional Status in UP

Area	Weight for age		Height for age		Weight for height	
	% below –3 SD	% below –2 SD	% below –3 SD	% below –2 SD	% below –3 SD	% below –2 SD
Urban	16.3	42.6	21.8	46.7	2.4	9.5
Rural	23.1	53.6	32.9	57.3	2.0	11.4
Region						
Hill	16.30	40.80	24.50	43.90	1.60	8.30
West	23.10	50.10	31.70	57.80	1.50	8.20
Centre	22.50	58.20	31.80	58.40	2.50	13.20
East	20.20	50.40	30.00	53.20	2.60	12.50
Bundelkhand	28.50	58.30	34.70	54.70	1.60	15.70
Standard of living						
Low	29.30	61.50	39.00	62.40	2.20	13.40
Middle	21.10	51.10	31.40	56.40	1.80	10.20
High	9.70	34.40	13.40	38.60	2.30	9.80
Sex of child						
Male	19.80	49.60	28.40	53.40	2.10	11.40
Female	24.20	53.90	33.70	57.20	2.00	10.80
UP	21.90	51.70	31.00	55.50	2.10	11.10
Male	16.90	45.30	21.80	44.10	2.90	15.70
Female	19.10	48.90	24.40	47.00	2.70	15.20
India	18.00	47.00	23.00	45.50	2.80	15.50

Source: IIPS (2001).

to his/her height. This may be the consequence of some illness or an inadequate diet.

In Uttar Pradesh, 52 per cent of children are underweight compared to 47 per cent nationally and 56 per cent are too short for their age or stunted, compared to 46 per cent nationally. The proportion of children who are severely undernourished is also very high, 22 per cent according to the weight for age criterion and 31 per cent by the height for age criterion. In addition 11 per cent children in Uttar Pradesh are too thin for their height or wasted. This is lower than the national average of 16 per cent.

The data shows that by and large girls are more likely to be underweight and stunted compared to boys, while boys are more prone to be thin in relation to their height or wasted compared to girls. Children from rural areas are worse off on all the parameters. It also reveals that children from SC and backward caste households fare worse on all indicators reflecting their fragile food security status. The sharpest differences in health outcomes arise from economic disparities. Children from poorer households, where the food situation is tenuous, are more than one and a half times as likely to be disadvantaged on the height or weight indicators compared to children from relatively affluent households.

Overall, more than 74 per cent of children in the state, and the same per cent at the national level, suffer from some level of anaemia.

(iii) Social Groups

Despite years of development, society in the state remains deeply fragmented along caste lines. The Scheduled Castes and Tribes carry the burden of years of systematic social and economic discrimination. Each day is a struggle for food, livelihood, shelter and other basics of life. This manifests itself in lower employment, wages, health and educational outcomes. While affirmative action and conscious policy has benefited a small section of the scheduled castes and tribes, the majority still live lives circumscribed by poverty and discrimination.

Since most tribal and nomadic communities in Uttar Pradesh have been included in the list of Scheduled Castes and not in the Scheduled tribes, the latter are underestimated and form only 1.21 per cent of the population in the rural areas and 0.94 per cent in the urban areas (NSS, 1999-2000). As such, the actual condition of the majority of tribal people is represented by the data given for Scheduled Castes. Table 13 compares the per capita monthly expenditures on various items of food by different social groups. It shows clearly that expenditure on food declines as we go down the social ladder from 'other' castes to 'other Backward castes' and to Scheduled castes. This is so for all items of food, except meat, fish and eggs. Predictably, the divergence in food expenses is less in cereals and greater for other foods such as pulses, milk, oil and sugar.

The lower consumption by and lack of a balanced diet of the discriminated castes is reflected in lower health indicators. The data suggests that children belonging to scheduled caste and backward

Table 13

Monthly Per Capita Expenditure on Food Items by Different Social Groups

Social group	Cereals	Pulses and products	Milk & milk products	Edible oil	Meat, eggs and fish	Vegetables	Fruits	Sugar	Total
ST	95.90	20.29	30.40	18.04	14.26	27.44	3.66	12.12	248.45
SC	96.39	18.99	27.23	15.16	8.34	25.20	4.01	10.50	229.64
OBC	98.23	21.24	45.18	17.16	6.69	26.81	4.60	12.25	258.83
Other	99.20	26.30	66.00	20.37	9.08	31.18	8.22	16.46	315.04

Source: NSSO (2001).

caste families are more likely to be underweight and stunted compared to the others. Similarly, they are more prone to be wasted, that is, thin in relation to their height. They are also more likely to suffer from anaemia compared to children from other castes. Such children face physical and mental health problems throughout their lives. The National Family Health Survey for 1998-99 shows that both infant and under-5 mortality is higher among scheduled castes than among other social groups (Table 14).

Table 14

Percentage of Undernourished Children under 3 Years of Age by Social Class

Area	Weight for age		Height for age		Weight for height	
	% below –3 SD	% below –2 SD	% below –3 SD	% below –2 SD	% below –3 SD	% below –2 SD
SC	24.10	60.30	36.30	63.10	2.80	11.50
ST	33.50	59.40	40.40	69.30	3.20	13.70
OBC	25.60	53.30	32.90	55.70	2.70	13.60
Others	17.60	45.90	26.60	50.30	1.40	9.30
Uttar Pradesh	21.90	51.70	31.00	55.50	2.10	11.10
India	18.00	47.00	23.00	45.50	2.80	15.50

Source: IIPS (2001).

The main reason for such a high level of mortality among these social groups is the poor health and nutrition status of the mother. Her malnutrition is passed down to the unborn child in her womb. This is compounded by inadequate antenatal care, lack of sanitation, lack of information and awareness and backbreaking labour. Fifty-two per cent of scheduled caste women suffer from anaemia as opposed to 45 per cent from 'other' castes. The former are also disadvantaged on other anthropometric indices as shown in Table 15. A higher proportion of women from these castes is below 150 cm in height and suffer from chronic energy deficiency, which is a reflection of both poor food and nutritional intake.

II. GOVERNMENT INITIATIVES IN PROVIDING FOOD SECURITY

What has been the state's response to the issue of food security? What has been its policy and what are the programmes it has adopted to address the issue? How well have they fared in practice? Government interventions

Table 15
Nutritional Status of Women by Social Group

Cast group	Height		Weight for height	
	Mean height (cm)	Per cent below 145 cm	BMI	Per cent with BMI below 18.5 Kg
SC	149.60	18.40	19.40	41.30
ST	149.60	18.90	19.70	32.60
OBC	149.80	18.50	19.60	37.30
Others	151.10	13.50	20.60	31.90
Total UP	150.30	16.40	20.00	35.80
India	151.2	13.2	20.3	35.8

Source: IIPS (2001).

may be clubbed into two types. The first are the food-based interventions that directly provide food to beneficiaries, such as the Public Distribution System which provides subsidised foodgrains to the poor, the Mid-day Meal which provides foodgrains to school-going children, and the Integrated Child Development Services (ICDS), which provides nutritional supplements to young children, pregnant women and lactating mothers. In this section we evaluate the impact of these programmes. In recent months, other food-based programmes such as the Antyodaya Anna Yojana have also been introduced. The second type of interventions are those that aim to reduce poverty and enhance the incomes by a multitude of anti-poverty programmes. These do not directly intervene in the food economy but are important for food security because they enhance purchasing power of the poor. We look at these in this section.

1. The Public Distribution System

As a form of governmental intervention aimed at ensuring the availability of foodgrains at affordable prices, the Public Distribution System, in terms of sheer scale of operations is the only one of it's kind in the world. Under this system the central and the state governments share responsibilities towards achieving its stated objective. The Department of Food and Public Distribution at the centre, which has the mandate to implement the PDS, is responsible for the procurement, movement, storage and bulk allocation of foodgrains. While the state governments bear the responsibility for distributing the same to the consumers through the network of fair-price shops.

The burgeoning subsidy bill and criticisms that the poor were not benefiting adequately from the scheme, led to a major revamping exercise in 1997, resulting in its introduction in a new form, namely the Targeted Public Distribution System (TPDS). A massive exercise was launched to identify below poverty line (BPL) households on the basis of poverty estimates arrived at by the Expert Group on Estimation of Proportion and Number of Poor (Lakdawala Committee). In Uttar Pradesh, 41 per cent households were estimated to lie below the poverty line. Allocations to states were calculated on the basis of the norm of 10 kg per month per BPL family together with an additional amount for above poverty line (APL) households. The latter was ultimately to be phased out. The allocation to BPL households was increased from 10 kg to 20 kg in April 2000 at Rs 4.15 for wheat and Rs. 5.65 for rice, but allocations for APL families remained the same (Rs. 6.10 for wheat and Rs. 8.30 for rice). In July 2001, in view of the overabundant supply position, the allocation for BPL families was further increased to 25 kg.

Has the TPDS been successful in its objective of providing food security cover to the poor? If so, to what extent? We first look at the macro evidence from the NSS 55th round survey and then at the micro field level evidence to find the answers.

Prior to the introduction of the TPDS, the off-take of cereals from the central Pool for distribution in the state was very low. As a percentage of allocation only 19 per cent of wheat and 38 per cent of rice was lifted in 1995-96. The off-take improved dramatically with the introduction of the TPDS and separate allocations were made for BPL and APL households. While the off-take for APL families has been consistently low, that for BPL households increased to 96 per cent for wheat and 87 per cent for rice in 1998-99. During 1999-2000 again the off-take remained impressive at 97 per cent for wheat and 71 per cent for rice. Thereafter the percentages of off-take have again been flagging (Table 16).

It would be legitimate to expect the high off-take from the central pool to get mirrored in increased off-take from the 65,557 rural and 11,905 urban fair-price shops set up all over the state. But alas, it did not. In fact, the latest evidence coming from the NSS 55th round survey paints a grim picture of the PDS utilisation. Table 17 shows the percentage distribution of households by their source of purchase of wheat, rice, sugar and kerosene in the course of the 30 days preceding the survey.

Table 17 reveals that only about 6.64 per cent households in rural areas and about 1.76 per cent in urban areas purchase either some or their entire requirement of rice from the PDS. Similarly, only 6.25 per cent households in rural and 1.25 per cent in urban areas buy some or all their requirement of wheat from the PDS. The commodity, in the supply of which the PDS plays a critical role, is in kerosene: for 79 per cent families in rural Uttar Pradesh and 59 per cent families in urban areas of the state, the PDS is the only or chief source of supply for kerosene. With no electricity in many areas, kerosene lamps serve as the only means of illumination. Table 17 also shows that the PDS supplies either the entire or partial requirement of sugar for 42 per cent families in rural areas and 60 per cent in urban areas.

Thus, it is clear from the survey data that the PDS holds significance for the supply of kerosene and sugar, (the supply of which has been taken out of the purview of the PDS), but has an entirely marginal role to play as a source of supply of cereals. A public programme that seeks to enhance food security should be able to cater to the needs of especially vulnerable groups such as scheduled castes and tribes on a priority basis. Here again,

Table 16

Allocation and Off-take of Wheat and Rice Before and After Introduction of the TPDS

(in '000 tonnes)

	BPL			APL+Addl.			Total		
	Allocation	Off-take	%	Allocation	Off-take	%	Allocation	Off-take	%
				Wheat					
1994-95							1186	203	17
1995-96							1186	226	19
1996-97	-	-	-	-	-	-	1038	894	86
1997-98	640	486	76	367	207	56	1007	693	69
1998-99	768	741	96	351	262	75	1319	1003	76
1999-00	768	748	97	761	61	8	1529	808	53
2000-01	1274	476	37	233	1	1	1507	478	32
2001-02	1603	896	56	250	8	3	1853	904	49
				Rice					
1994-95							550	197	36
1995-96							550	210	38
1996-97	-	-	-	-	-	-	532	357	67
1997-98	315	194	61	127	66	52	442	260	59
1998-99	378	330	87	254	133	52	632	463	73
1999-00	378	267	71	362	97	27	740	364	49
2000-01	619	239	39	119	1	1	737	240	33
2001-02	737	254	34	127	1	1	864	255	30

Note: APL: Above Poverty Line; BPL: Below Poverty Line; ADDL: Additional.
Source: Foodgrains Bulletin, Various Issues, Department of Food & Public Distribution, Government of India.

Table 17

Percentage Distribution of Households according to Source of Purchase

Source	Rice	Wheat	Sugar	Kerosene
		Rural		
PDS only	2.63	1.54	14.35	57.65
Other only	50.08	44.85	47.88	18.03
From both	4.01	4.71	27.97	20.82
Not purchased	43.28	48.91	9.80	3.50
Total	100.00	100.00	100.00	100.00
		Urban		
PDS only	0.31	0.09	16.00	46.72
Other only	85.63	85.54	35.93	29.03
From both	1.45	1.48	43.74	12.36
Not purchased	12.61	12.89	4.34	11.89
Total	100.00	100.00	100.00	100.00

Source: Based on analysis of NSS 55th Round unit record data (Schedule 1.0, Central Sample).

the picture as projected in Table 18 is dismal. It tells us that only that only 4.35 per cent scheduled caste households in rural areas and 1.35 households in urban areas bought rice from the PDS. For wheat the figures were even lower—2.8 per cent households in rural and 0.5 per cent in urban areas accessed the PDS for the purchase of wheat.

Although the percentage of households that access the PDS for the purchase of foodgrains is very small, among those that do, the poor ones predominate. In fact, the poorest, relatively speaking, benefit the most.

Table 18
Distribution of Households by Source of Purchase and by Social Group

Social	Rice: source of purchase						Wheat: source of purchase					
	Rural		Urban		Combined		Rural		Urban		Combined	
group	PDS	Other	PDS	Other	PDS	Other	PDS	Other	PDS	Other	PDS	Other
ST	1.5	98.5	0.0	100.0	1.3	98.7	0.5	99.5	6.7	93.3	1.6	98.4
SC	4.3	95.7	1.4	98.6	4.0	96.0	2.8	97.2	0.5	99.5	2.4	97.6
OBC	1.4	98.6	0.4	99.6	1.2	98.8	1.7	98.3	0.2	99.8	1.3	98.7
Others	1.2	98.8	0.5	99.5	0.9	99.1	1.4	98.6	0.4	99.6	1.0	99.0
Total	2.3	97.7	0.6	99.4	1.9	98.1	2.0	98.0	0.4	99.6	1.5	98.5

Source: Based on analysis of NSS 55th round unit record data (Schedule 1.0, Central Sample).

While, 11 per cent of the poorest households buy either all or some of the rice they need from the PDS, only 2 per cent of the rich households do so (Table 19). This is also the case with wheat. For sugar and kerosene too, a larger percentage of the lower income households make use of the PDS compared to the rich. The pattern appears to be the same for both rural and urban areas. Overall, the PDS plays an insignificant role in catering to cereal consumption needs in urban areas with the situation in rural areas being only marginally better.

This is not a very encouraging commentary on the performance of the vast food security network at least in Uttar Pradesh. Interestingly, it is not as though the government has been complacent on the issue. In fact, since the introduction of the TPDS, there have been several government initiatives to improve its functioning. The Standing Committee of Parliament on Food, Civil Supplies and Public Distribution had recommended in 1996-97 that a comprehensive study should be carried out to know the extent of diversion of commodities from the PDS to the open market. According to the Tata Economic Consultancy Services, which was commissioned for the study, the extent of diversion at the state level was 46 per cent for wheat, 49 per cent for rice, and 36 per cent for sugar. This compared unfavourably with the national estimates which were much lower at 36, 31 and 23 per cent respectively. The findings were discussed at a meeting of State Food Secretaries in 1998, who were of the view that although there was some diversion from the PDS, the study overestimated the extent of diversion. With the difference between the BPL and market prices much larger now, there would certainly be a stronger incentive to divert supplies to the open market and make quick profits. What would be the extent of diversion compared to 1997, when the study was undertaken, is a moot point.

The government has also initiated several changes to improve the transparency and accountability of the PDS to the panchayats. A model Citizens Charter was introduced in November 1997 by the centre for adoption by the states. This charter stipulated essential information such as entitlements, procedure for the issue of ration cards, the right of the public for information and so on. It emphasised the need to constitute of model vigilance committees at all levels. In June 1999, the

Table 19

Percentage Distribution of Households by Source of Purchase and Economic Background

	Rural					Urban					Combined (Rural + Urban)				
	Source					Source					Source				
	PDS	Other	Both	None	All	PDS	Other	Both	None	All	PDS	Other	Both	None	All
Rice															
Very poor	4.1	45.5	8.6	38.4	100	1.2	81.2	4.2	9.9	100	3.5	53.2	7.7	32.2	100
Poor	2.8	49.5	5.2	38.9	100	0.5	84.0	2.5	10.7	100	2.3	56.4	4.6	33.2	100
Non-poor	2.7	49.0	3.4	41.4	100	0.1	86.5	0.9	11.0	100	2.2	57.0	2.8	35.0	100
Rich	1.4	48.4	1.5	45.2	100	0.1	81.4	0.3	15.2	100	1.1	56.2	1.2	38.1	100
All	2.5	47.9	3.8	41.4	100	0.3	83.0	1.4	12.2	100	2.0	55.6	3.3	35.0	100
Wheat															
Very poor	2.7	47.0	10.1	37.4	100	0.4	86.8	4.4	5.9	100	2.2	55.6	8.9	30.6	100
Poor	1.5	45.9	5.9	43.3	100	0.1	84.0	2.6	10.4	100	1.2	53.6	5.2	36.6	100
Non-poor	1.5	44.2	4.0	46.4	100	0.0	85.1	1.0	12.3	100	1.2	52.9	3.4	39.2	100
Rich	0.9	38.9	1.8	54.5	100	0.0	80.5	0.1	16.5	100	0.7	48.7	1.4	45.5	100
All	1.5	42.8	4.5	46.7	100	0.1	83.0	1.4	12.5	100	1.2	51.6	3.8	39.2	100
Sugar															
Very poor	20.3	39.0	16.5	21.7	100	29.8	34.5	30.6	3.1	100	22.4	38.1	19.6	17.7	100
Poor	17.5	45.0	24.5	11.3	100	20.5	29.1	48.3	2.0	100	18.1	41.8	29.3	9.4	100
Non-poor	13.5	47.0	29.9	8.2	100	15.5	30.3	50.2	3.5	100	14.0	43.5	34.2	7.2	100
Rich	10.2	52.3	31.6	4.7	100	8.5	44.3	40.4	6.5	100	9.8	50.4	33.7	5.2	100
All	14.0	46.7	27.3	9.6	100	15.8	35.5	43.2	4.3	100	14.4	44.3	30.8	8.4	100
Kerosene															
Very poor	62.0	15.1	18.6	4.0	100	56.2	30.9	10.2	1.9	100	60.7	18.5	16.8	3.5	100
Poor	57.4	17.2	22.6	2.0	100	55.1	22.1	18.4	3.6	100	57.0	18.2	21.7	2.3	100
Non-poor	56.7	18.2	22.2	2.5	100	49.0	25.9	14.7	8.0	100	55.1	19.8	20.6	3.7	100
Rich	55.8	19.4	19.2	5.1	100	31.7	30.8	7.2	22.0	100	50.2	22.1	16.3	9.1	100
All	56.9	17.8	20.5	3.5	100	44.5	27.7	11.8	11.3	100	54.2	20.0	18.6	5.2	100

Notes: Very poor: population below half the poverty line; poor: above half the poverty line and below poverty line; non: poor above poverty line below double the poverty line; rich: above double the poverty line; none refers to not purchased. All groups are exclusive.

Source: Based on analysis of NSS 55th round unit record data (Schedule 1.0, Central Sample).

government also issued guidelines for the involvement of PRIs at all levels in the PDS so as to ensure greater public participation (Planning Commission, 2001).

In a recent move, the Public Distribution System (Control) Order, 2001, was notified in August 2001. The order relates to (i) identification of beneficiaries; (ii) ration cards; (iii) issue price; (iv) distribution of foodgrains; and (v) monitoring the PDS. State governments were asked, *intra alia,* to review each year the names included in the BPL and *Antyodaya* lists; periodically check the authenticity of ration cards; and issue utilisation certificates to confirm the distribution to eligible beneficiaries. Any violation of the Order would invoke criminal liability under the Essential Commodities Act, 1955.

Clearly, the intentions underlying all these measures and directives are good, but unfortunately, there is little evidence of these being translated into action programmes. At the level of government, at least on paper, all orders are issued, screws tightened and loopholes plugged. Downstream, at the level of the village, the story gets muddied as the evidence from the NSS cited earlier tells us. The unpublished report of a recent survey in several villages of Allahabad district tells the same sordid story of eligible poor not getting BPL cards, of 'missing' rations, and of little accountability of shopkeepers to the public.[4]

While large-scale quantitative surveys paint the larger macro picture and present the overall situation, they do not tell us much about why this is so. We know for instance, that only a small proportion of the scheduled castes and the poor make purchases from the PDS, but why this is so remains unclear. Qualitative surveys give us clues to the 'why' questions. During discussions with the poor in qualitative surveys carried out in some of the poorest regions of Uttar Pradesh (Srivastava, 1998; Kozel and Parker, 1998), several problems associated with the functioning of the PDS were stressed.

PDS shops were meant to benefit the poor, but they were located far away from the hamlets of the poor. Worse, they were invariably located in the hamlets of the rich. The shop owners illustrated and humiliated the poor. One harijan youth recounted an incident when he had gone to buy kerosene.

> "I did not go to buy cereals, because one can pay a little more and buy it from the market. But for kerosene we have no option, and despite the unfair treatment we get from the *kotedar* we have to go. But one day, I was so angry with the insulting behaviour of the *kotedar* that I threw the kerosene right in front of him and vowed I would never go to the shop again."

Despite guidelines to the contrary, there are no fixed days when the shop opened, nor were there any fixed timings. Most people complained that they did not get to know when the rations were being distributed. There were days when they would make many trips to the shop, only to return empty handed. In terms of wages lost, this could be crippling for the poor. Further, the quality of the foodgrains was perceived to be variable. Another problem that hinders optimum utilisation of the PDS is that shopkeepers want buyers to lift their entire entitlement in one go. As the poor do not have enough money to do so, they have to forgo their entire month's quota. Srivastava, in a detailed analysis of the demand for cereals in poor rural households, shows how this is satisfied through complex ways such as home production, giving wages in kind and through the market. He focuses on the importance of the seasonal nature of market demand of the poor, that is, market demand is highest in the lean season. He contends that a well-designed PDS, which could take care of this seasonality, would have the highest demand among the rural poor as well as the maximum impact (Srivastava, 2001).

2. Integrated Child Development Services

With the objective of improving the nutritional and health status of young children, the Integrated Child Development Services (ICDS) Programme was started in the year 1975 in three blocks of the state. The programme, launched with a budget of Rs. 202 crore (excluding Uttaranchal) for the Ninth Plan, now covers 498 blocks. It aimed to set up *Anganwadi* centres, which would provide supplementary nutrition to young children and pregnant and lactating mothers and lay the foundation for later schooling by providing early childhood education.

The *Anganwadi* scheme has been a signal failure in the state (Table 20). This is evident from the fact that 99.37 per cent of households in rural areas of the state had not received any food supplement in the 30 days preceding the survey according to data from the NSS 52nd round (1995-96). The situation was similar in the urban areas and across income quintiles. Except for Bundelkhand where 4 per cent and 7.6 per cent households in rural and urban areas respectively, reported receiving some food supplements, the programme had no impact in any region of the state. Results from other independent surveys paint an equally bleak picture.

In the SLC survey covering eastern Uttar Pradesh and Bundelkhand, a mere 3.41 per cent households reported sending children to the *Anganwadi*.[5] Only 1.11 households said they received the food supplement on most days, while another 1.77 per cent reported receiving it on some days. On an

Table 20

Percentage of Eligible Households which Received Food Supplement, Uttar Pradesh

	Whether food supplement received in last 30 days?					
	Rural			Urban		
MPCE quintile	Yes	No	Total	Yes	No	Total
1	0.35	99.65	100	0.17	99.83	100
2	0.60	99.40	100	2.25	97.75	100
3	1.44	98.56	100	0.22	99.78	100
4	0.38	99.62	100	0.95	99.05	100
5	0.11	99.89	100	0.39	99.61	100
Total	0.63	99.37	100	0.81	99.19	100

Source: Based on analysis of NSS 52nd round data (1995-96).

average a child who attended an anganwadi attended it for only 11 days a month. Some positive marks may be given to the programme because results show that among the households, which sent their children to the anganwadi, 52 per cent belonged to the SC/STs and another 32.7 per cent to the backward castes. The remaining households belonged either to the upper castes or to Muslims. Even here it must be remembered that 93.7 per cent of SC/STs and 97.8 per cent of the backward caste households surveyed did not send their children to an *Anganwadi* centre.

Qualitative surveys in eastern Uttar Pradesh and Bundekhand provide clues on why the ICDS could not achieve its stated objectives (Srivastava, 1998; Khare, 1998). Firstly, there was little, or at best, hazy awareness about the scheme. Secondly, the common perception was that there was widespread pilfering—the nutritional supplement meant for children and women was being sold in the open market or fed to livestock. Thirdly, in several cases upper caste *pradhans* had appointed women from their own family as the *Anganwadi* worker, and the *Anganwadi* centre was located in her own house. This effectively put paid to the possibility of the poor ever approaching the centre. Lastly, there were many villages in the district and all over the state, where the *Anganwadi* worker's post was lying vacant.

3. The Mid-day Meal Scheme

The Mid-day Meal scheme was launched on August 15, 1995, for the benefit of students in primary schools. Some states have opted to provide cooked meals to children in school, while others provide 3 kg of foodgrains a month for 10 months to each student. The foodgrains, either wheat or rice, are supplied free of cost to the states. The FCI, which supplies the foodgrains, makes the charge on the Ministry of Human Resource Development, which is the nodal agency for the scheme. Earlier, the price charged by the FCI till November 2000, was the economic cost of the foodgrains. Since then, the government has decided that the price for the foodgrains supplied under the scheme would be the price applicable for all persons living below the poverty line.

The basic objective of the scheme, which was to supply a nutritious meal to children in primary schools and to encourage daily attendance, has not been met because the state government decided to provide foodgrains to each child rather than meals in school. The other expectations of the scheme, that it would break caste barriers by encouraging children to eat together have also been belied. However, on other counts it has fared well. The Operations Research Group did a countrywide study on the coverage and impact of the mid-day meal scheme during 1997-98. It found that in Uttar Pradesh 76 per cent of the children—75 per cent of boys and 78 per cent of girls—in the eligible age group were covered compared to the national average of 59 per cent. The proportion of SC/ST households covered was 35 per cent and that of SC/ST children was 41 per cent. As many as 87 per cent of households reported that the supply of foodgrains was regular. However, only 4 per

Table 21
Percentage of Eligible Households which Reported Receiving Food Supplement by Region

Region	Whether food supplement received in last 30 days?		
	Yes	No	Total
Hill	0.00	100.00	100
West	0.39	99.61	100
Central	0.18	99.82	100
East	0.57	99.43	100
Bundelkhand	7.56	92.44	100
Total	0.80	99.20	100

Source: Based on analysis of NSS 52nd round data (1995-96).

cent of households said they received the stipulated 3 kg and 96 per cent said they got between 2 to 3 kg. Only 12 per cent of the families who got foodgrains said the quality was poor; while the rest appeared satisfied with the quality of food supplied to the child. In terms of perception of parents, 12 per cent said they said they felt the programme had a positive impact on the nutritional status of children.

4. Other Programmes

Among the other programmes targeted at the poor are the *Antyodaya Anna Yojana* announced in December 2000, for the one crore poorest of the poor BPL families. The scheme, now under implementation in all states, provides for giving each of the Antyodaya families 25 kg of foodgrains at Rs. 2 per kg for wheat and Rs. 3 per kg for rice. This is below the CIP of Rs 4.15 per kg for wheat and Rs 5.65 per kg for rice for the BPL families. The *Sampoorna Gramin Rozgar Yojana* was launched in November 2001 to start food-for-work schemes in all states. It envisaged an allocation of 50 lakh tonnes every year. Under the scheme the foodgrains were to be supplied free of cost, through its nodal agency, which is the Ministry of Rural Development.

There are other programmes which do not benefit the poor directly but do so indirectly by increasing the purchasing power of the poor, which in term has a favourable impact on food security. These include employment programmes such as the JGSY and the EAS, the social assistance programmes, such as the pension schemes and the programme to distribute gram sabha land to the SC/ST. A recent study (Srivastava, 2002) evaluates the implementation of the antipoverty schemes in 20 villages spread over all the regions of the state. The study reports that employment generation programmes have had very little impact in terms of providing employment and wage security. Notably, a very small percentage of casual labourers have benefited under the programmes—a minuscule 7.7 per cent of eligible beneficiaries were provided employment. The number of days of employment generated per person was too small to have any impact on poverty. It varied from just two days to 49 days. Almost four-fifths of the beneficiary labourers received employment for less than 15 days in the reference year and a mere 1.4 per cent secured employment for more than 30 days. Further, because of the limited employment created the possibility of any positive impact on the labour market was minimal. The wage employment programmes have been relatively more successful in the creation of infrastructure, particularly construction of village and link roads, although even here rampant corruption has presented its realisation of the full potential benefits of infrastructure development or development of the region.

III. CONCLUSION

Uttar Pradesh faces a peculiar paradox. It is a food surplus state where cereal and calorie intake are higher than the national averages and the spread and depth of hunger is lower than in the country as a whole. Yet, large numbers of people in the state are food insecure. While it scores highly on food availability it is poor in food access. The poor in the state lack adequate food and a balanced diet leading to nutritional and health problems and growth disorders. The health indicators show that the backward regions of the state and women, children and SC/STs are especially disadvantaged. Above all, the state is characterised by a high level of poverty together with poor infrastructure, poor health facilities, high child and infant mortality, high maternal mortality rates, low literacy and low life expectancy.

The analysis of this study showed the lackadaisical performance of the government's direct interventions on the food front. The Public Distribution System, despite attempts to revitalise it, has largely failed to deliver and the ICDS has not drawn young mothers and children to the *Anganwadis* or improved their nutritional status. There are more positive reports on the Mid-day Meal Scheme but even here the achievement lies in its success in enhancing school enrolments rather than in providing food or nutrition to children. It remains to be seen whether the state government can ensure better implementation of the recently introduced *Sampoorna Gramin Rozgar Yojana*, a universal food-for-work programme aimed at utilising the large stocks of foodgrains to provide food and rural employment, while at the same time building rural infrastructure.

A full discussion on the reasons for the poor performance of government's initiatives in ensuing food security would take into account political economy questions and is beyond the scope of this paper. Here we merely wish to stress that after the 73rd Amendment of the Constitution the government appears to have abdicated its role of ensuring that its schemes are properly implemented to the panchayats, without first bringing about an adequate devolution of finances, or creating—to use the currently fashionable jargon—a level playing field. Village societies remain deeply stratified socially and economically. Thus, though the responsibilities for monitoring, if not implementing, all the programmes have fallen on the panchayats, panchayats have not developed as truly participatory institutions. Gram sabha meetings are rarely held, and are thinly attended when they are. Decisions on beneficiaries and schemes are taken by the dominant elite and not by democratic consensus. Reservations have given dalits and women a foothold in panchayats, but not in exercising power, since they continue to be economically dependent on the upper castes for their livelihood. The threat of violence lurks just below the surface and dampens local efforts at empowering the poor. There is clearly a need for much greater monitoring at all levels and strict and swift action against errant officials in order to tilt the scales in favour of the poor.

As longer the poor remain assetless, they will remain voiceless. The Planning Commission study cited earlier (Srivastava, 2002), shows that the impact of social assistance programmes such as the IAY, pensions and land distribution has been fairly positive. In fact, in the case of land distribution, the positive fallout has been that beneficiaries have mobilised all their own latent resources to optimise benefits. Also, the largest number of beneficiaries for any single programme has been for land distribution. One reason why these programmes as well as the Mid-day Meal scheme appear to be more effective than the others is that they directly benefit the poor and suffer less from an 'agency' problem, that is, there is less need for supervision and monitoring once the benefits are given (Srivastava, 2002). These programmes, therefore, need to be strengthened.

In this context it must be mentioned that one of the first moves of Ms. Mayawati, after she was appointed Chief Minister of the state, was to get a Cabinet resolution passed for amending the Uttar Pradesh Zamindari Abolition and Land Reforms Act 1950, to give SC/ST households and other landless labourers, who were working illegally on gram sabha land, the legal right to the gram sabha land in their possession. Although there are limits to this scheme because of the scarcity of gram sabha land, yet if land which has been encroached upon and seized by the rich, is confiscated and distributed among the poor, it will greatly enhance their food security, but what is more important, give them self-respect. Such orders in the past were not properly implemented and it remains to be seen how faithfully this order is carried out. This by itself, however, may not be enough. The government must give grants for land development and take urgent measures to boost non-farm employment.

Finally, the large stocks of foodgrains offer an excellent opportunity to the government to utilise them to reduce poverty, eradicate food insecurity and improve rural infrastructure. The central government has indicated that it was ready to release foodgrains for various programmes including food for work and mid-day meal scheme for school children free of cost. While retreating from its responsibility of initiating any steps in this direction the centre has stated that the godowns are open and it was for the states to lift the stock. "There is no shortage of foodgrains and if hunger persists, the Centre should not be held responsible."[6] The ball is clearly in the court of the government of Uttar Pradesh. Can it take on the challenge?

(Computing support received from N.K. Singh and Anup Karan in the analysis of NSS 52nd and 55th round, unit record data, is gratefully acknowledged).

Notes

1. Sukanta Bhattacharya, referring to the famine of 1943, in 'Chharpatra' (Saraswat Library, Kolkata, 1967).
2. "Uttar Pradesh—Land of Plenty", *Times of India*, Lucknow, February 17, 2001.
3. Differences in the methodology of successive rounds and the 55th round have made comparisons problematic and have led to much controversy on the estimates of poverty. See among others, Sen (1996); Palmer-Jones, and Sen (2001) on this issue.
4. The study conducted in 2002 by a non-governmental organisation 'Sahyog', was part of the Right to Food Campaign.
5. The UP-Bihar Survey of Living Conditions (SLC) study covered 2250 households in 120 villages of Uttar Pradesh and Bihar. The study was sponsored by the World Bank in 1998. The data here refers only to the villages covered in Uttar Pradesh.
6. Food Minister Shanta Kumar answering a series of questions in the Rajya Sabha as reported in the *Northern India Patrika*, May.

References

Bhalla, G.S. (2001), "Demand and Supply of Food and Foodgrains by 2020", in Asthana, M.D. and Medrano, Pedro (eds.), *Towards Hunger Free India: Agenda and Imperatives*, World Food Programme, New Delhi.

Government of India (2002), *Economic Survey 2001-2002*, Economics Division, Ministry of Finance, New Delhi.

Government of Uttar Pradesh (2000), *Statistical Diary, Uttar Pradesh* (Various Issues), Departmnet of Economics and Statistics, Lucknow.

IIPS (2001), *National Family Health Survey 1998-99, Uttar Pradesh*, International Institute for Population Studies, Mumbai.

Khare, Sandeep (1998), "Qualitative Assessment of Poverty in Tarkullah Village of Gorakhpur", Report prepared for the World Bank Study on *The Contribution of Qualitative Research in Poverty Analysis*, World Bank, Washington, D.C.

Kozel, V. and Parker, B. (1998), *Poverty in Rural India: The Contribution of Qualitative Research in Poverty Analysis*, World Bank, Washington, D.C.

MSSRF (2001), *Food Insecurity Atlas of Rural India*, M.S. Swaminathan Research Foundation, Chennai.

NSSO (2000), *Nutritional Intake in India*, NSS 55th Round, 1999-2000, Ministry of Statistics and Programme Implementation, New Delhi.

—— (2001), *Differences in Level of Consumption among Socio-Economic Groups, 1999-2000*, NSS 55th Round 1999-2000, Ministry of Statistics and Programme Implementation, New Delhi.

Palmer-Jones, Richard and Sen, Kunal (2001), "On India's Poverty Puzzles and Statistics of Povety", *Economic and Political Weekly*, Vol. 36, Issue 3, January 20.

Planning Commission (2002), *National Human Development Report 2001*, New Delhi.

—— (2001), *Report of the Working Group on Public Distribution System and Food Security for the Tenth Five Year Plan* (2002-07), New Delhi.

Sen, Abhijit (1996) "Economic Reforms, Employment and Poverty: Trends and Options", *Economic and Political Weekly*, December 16-22.

Srivastava, Nisha (1998), "Only God Can Save Them': Understanding the Multiple Dimensions of Poverty", Report Prepared for the World Bank Study on *The Contribution of Qualitative Research in Poverty Analysis, World Bank*, Washington, D.C.

Srivastava, Ravi S. (2002), *Anti-Poverty Programmes in Uttar Pradesh: An Evaluation*, Report Prepared for the Planning Commission, Institute for Human Development, New Delhi (mimeo).

—— (2001), "Public Distribution System in Rural Uttar Pradesh", in Asthana, M.D. and Medrano Pedro (eds.), *Towards Hunger Free India: Agenda and Imperatives*, World Food Programme, New Delhi.

PART IV

Grass Roots Experiences

14

Food Security in a Drought-prone Area: A Study in Karnataka

V.M. Rao and R.S. Deshpande

I. INTRODUCTION

The task of providing food security poses many hurdles in drought-prone areas mostly characterised by backwardness and chronic poverty. Given the fragile base of agriculture, growth processes remain sluggish. Shifting to commercial crops, and more recently, hi-tech agriculture, are promising sources of growth but their impact on food security could be far from favourable. Commercial crops raise the incomes of farmers but also make them more vulnerable to vagaries of the market and fluctuations in production. More importantly, commercial crops divert land from coarse cereals which are the local staple foodgrains in drought-prone areas. As regards hi-tech agriculture, it usually remains confined to small enclaves. While it would contribute handsomely to the value of agricultural output, it is far from certain that it would have a beneficial impact on the income and employment of the vast majority of the poor. What the drought-prone areas desperately need is a comprehensive watershed development programme to conserve soil and water resources and to improve the yield of dryland crops across the board. It would seem that in the absence of watershed development the new technologies and practices generated by research—of which there is an abundance—merely languish in laboratories. The question of providing food security in the drought-prone areas needs to be looked at, keeping in mind the prospects for dryland agriculture in the coming years. Equally relevant are the implications for food security of the reforms being contemplated to promote liberalisation and globalisation of Indian economy including agriculture.

The purpose of this paper is to suggest an approach to food security which would be consistent with both the development of rainfed farming and the implementation of reforms regime for agriculture. We make the assumption, which can be easily questioned, that the policies aimed at developing rainfed agriculture and facilitating growth and modernisation of agriculture would perform much better in the future than they had performed in the past. We indeed believe this to be true. However, the most important reason for this assumption is that it would be pointless to work for an effective security system for drought-prone areas, if one starts with the premise right at the beginning that rainfed agriculture would continue to stagnate and that the restrictive policy regime for agriculture would persist.

The plan of the paper is as follows: Section II explains the inadequacies of the present food security system. There is a large literature on this theme and a fair measure of consensus on the flaws with the present system. We enumerate the main shortcomings. More importantly, section II presents the findings of our field investigations on the extent to which the PDS reaches the target groups in drought-prone areas. These findings, as we will see later, play a critical role in our arguments for an alternative system of food security in the drought-prone areas. Section III describes an alternative system and also presents field findings on indicators of feasibility of the system. Finally, section IV presents the concluding comments.

II. CHARACTERISTICS OF THE PRESENT FOOD SECURITY SYSTEM

The present Public Distribution System (PDS) has been criticised by researchers and policy analysts for the following reasons. (See Radhakrishna and Subba Rao, 1997; Jharwal, 1998; Mahendra Dev, 1996; Mahendra Dev and Suryanarayana, 1993; Swaminathan, 1998).

1. The system is inherently costly as it is based on surpluses of two superior cereals—rice and wheat—generated in a few green revolution pockets; Punjab, Haryana and western Uttar Pradesh. These surpluses have to be procured, stored and distributed all over the country.
2. The system is too far centralised, hierarchical and bureaucratic to achieve cost-effectiveness, respond quickly to distress in localised areas and distinguish those in real need for assistance from those who do not need it.
3. Judged by the yardsticks of (a) coverage of vulnerable groups, (b) quality of food security provided, and (c) the impact on the conditions of beneficiaries, the performance of the system is rated as poor. The system is practically absent in some of the hard-core poverty areas.

To an observer from outside India, the present food security system must indeed seem paradoxical. Out of a wide range of cereals grown in India, the PDS has chosen rice and wheat—two superior cereals preferred by the well-to-do consumers rather than the numerous local staples consumed by the poor for generations. While the system is ostensibly for the benefit of the poor, it is not targeted on the poor and has shown little concern to extend its reach to areas where food distress is widespread among the poor. Ideally, a food security system should have a dependable provision to ensure that the poor have the capacity to pay for the foodgrains made available to them. This is not the case in India.

Employment programmes and the PDS operate as separate activities. A link between them could have improved the access of the poor to foodgrains. While food subsidy is growing, one cannot be sure that it is really going to the poor.

The observer during the seventies, on the other hand, would have been full of admiration for the food security system which helped India overcome one of the worst crises it faced since independence. However, it originated as an appendage of the green revolution, the chief concern of which was with a quick breakthrough in foodgrain production—which necessitated concentrating on rice and wheat—and not with food security for the poor or to increasing the production of staples consumed by them. The centrepiece of the green revolution was the farmer in the green revolution areas. Subsidised inputs and credit, research and extension, price support through procurement by the government agencies, were all focused on the green revolution farmer to help him raise yields and production. With the increase in production, the dependence on imports and food aid was eliminated. As the upsurge continued, the surpluses became an embarrassment. Simultaneously, the numbers of the poor and the deprivation suffered by them—particularly their foodgrain needs—assumed a prominent role in Indian policies and in policy research and analysis. The outcome was the coming into being of a countrywide network of the Public Distribution System. Over the decades which have followed, the network has expanded considerably, spatially as well as in terms of quantities of foodgrains handled. However, price support to green revolution farmers continues to be the major objective of food policy with the poor providing only an excuse for the huge subsidies and physical losses in foodgrains involved in the operations of Food Corporation of India. The limited purpose here is only to suggest that the present food security system, viewed as a safety-net for the poor needs to be streamlined.

We now present illustrative findings from the field on how the PDS works in drought-prone areas in Karnataka. The findings are derived from a larger field-based study conducted during July-October 1999, in two districts of Karnataka, namely, Chitradurga and Bijapur.[1] The study covered a block and two villages in each of the two districts (see Annexure for a brief profile of the selected districts and villages). Table 1 indicates the percentage of off-take of rice—the mainstay of the PDS in Karnataka—in recent years. The table covers the two selected districts as well as Bangalore (Urban) District—included to permit comparisons between rural and urban areas.

The percentage of off-take to allotment is an ambiguous indicator to interpret. If the percentage is low it could be because the grains do not reach the delivery point due to problems in delivery mechanisation. Alternatively, the percentage could be low if the consumer households do not lift their quota as they may prefer to purchase their requirements directly from the market. However, a fairly plausible guess, which Table 1 suggests, is that the delivery mechanism works better in urban rather than

Table 1
Percentage of Off-take of Rice to Allotment in Selected Districts in Karnataka

Year	Chitradurga	Bijapur	Bangalore (Urban)	Karnataka (State)
1995	50	32	98	55
1996	60	45	98	82
1997	100	55	100	85
1998	100	96	56	93
1999	100	87	100	91

Source: Directorate of Public Distribution, Department of Food & Civil Supplies, Government of Karnataka, Bangalore.

rural areas and that the deficiencies in this respect seem to be more severe in the rural areas of northern Karnataka. It also needs to be noted that taking the state as a whole, the present system of the PDS is marked by off-take falling short of allotment with the gap between the two being quite wide in some of the years. It is easy to see how the food subsidies fail to reach the intended beneficiaries.

A card holder is entitled to receive 8 kg of rice per month. Table 2 shows that the off-take is the lowest—only 60 per cent of the permitted quota—in Bijapur. Taking the state as a whole, the shortfall is almost 20 per cent. The off-take is noticeably higher in Chitradurga and Bangalore (Urban).

Table 2
Rice Off-take per Household (Card)

District	Per month (kg)
Chitradurga	7.5
Bijapur	5.1
Bangalore (Urban)	6.8
Karnataka	6.2

Household data permit a more pointed assessment of the role that the PDS plays in meeting the foodgrain needs of the target groups. Table 3 shows the per household annual consumption of foodgrains and the percentage of the PDS grains to total consumption across the sample villages. While the share of Chitradurga in the PDS is slightly higher than that of Bijapur, the PDS can hardly be regarded as being a major factor in providing food security to the people in drought-prone areas. Even in the case of the landless, which have a larger PDS share in total consumption of foodgrains than the other categories, the share is likely to come down when the consumption of foodgrains of the landless is adjusted to account for the snacks and meals they get from the employer on working days. The implication is that the landless as also other categories of rural poor are already operating in a liberalised market regime as far as food security is concerned! They obtain the foodgrains they need from normal economic channels—market, employers, own production—with the PDS grains and the associated subsidies making no more than a token contribution to their food needs.

Table 3
Annual Consumption of Foodgrains
(In quintals per household)

Category of rural poor	Annual consumption	Percentage obtained from the PDS
	Chikkamanahalli (Chitradurga dist.)	
Landless	6.29	19
Small holders (less than 2.5 ha)	12.85	9
Medium holders (2.5 ha to 5.0 ha)	14.77	8
Large holders (above 5.0 ha)	21.14	6
	Bommankunte (Chitradurga dist.)	
Landless	6.78	18
Small holders	13.17	9
Medium holders	12.15	10
Large holders	14.27	8
	Chikkalgundi (Bijapur dist.)	
Landless	13.89	9
Small holders	13.14	8
Medium holders	18.12	3
Large holders	24.7	3
	Korti (Bijapur dist.)	
Landless	11.13	11
Small holders	11.56	9
Medium holders	11.04	7
Large holders	29.27	2

Source: Survey data.

A word about why it is imperative to look for an alternative system rather than reforming the present system. First, if reforms for liberalisation and globalisation are implemented substantively, the bottom would fall out of the present food security system, as India is supposed to have a comparative advantage in rice and wheat as exports. Further, considerations relating to the conservation of land and water resources weigh heavily against intensive rice and wheat cultivation in the green revolution pockets which now provide the bulk of procurement made by the Food Corporation of India. Second, the present system has a severe limitation in preventing leakages (ghost cards, losses in storage and transit etc.) and in focusing the benefits on the properly identified poor. Third, the system is well-designed to meet major disasters covering the entire population but has failed in tackling the problem of food distress in normal times or in localised periods of scarcity among scattered groups of the poor.

III. AN ALTERNATIVE SYSTEM: FEATURES AND FEASIBILITY

In the light of the preceding discussion, it would be reasonable to expect the alternative system to have the following features:

1. The system should be based on the local staples consumed by the poor. This would make it possible to decentralise the food security system and economise on the logistic arrangements needed to operate the system. A further advantage of a local staple would be that it would ordinarily figure low in preference ranking by the non-poor and, hence, would be less prone to leakages. The policy support given to the local staples as a constituent of the food security system would benefit the poor as producers and also stimulate growth in the areas of local staples which are usually backward and receive little policy attention.
2. Identification of the poor, selection of those eligible to receive food security assistance and delivery of assistance to them should be organised by local representative bodies in which representatives of the poor participate. There should be provision for a watchdog body to ensure that the system covers all the eligible households. Beneficiary groups, local organisations of people and NGOs may be associated with the operation and monitoring of the system.
3. Physical handling of foodgrains involving purchase, storage, distribution—by the local body organising the food security system, may be minimised. For example, in an employment programme linked system, the beneficiary may receive part of wages in the form of food coupons which could be exchanged for foodgrains in a designated local shop. Similarly, the mid-day meal programme for school children could be operated by the organisation running the school.
4. When disaster strikes, all the tiers of the government—from the central government downwards—would get together to handle the crisis. In normal times, the role of the higher tiers would be minimal, confined to laying down norms for assistance, devolution of funds and overall supervision of the working of the system and its results.

Regarding the feasibility of the alternative system outlined above, we first take note of the changing context which has features that are favourable to the alternative system.

1. The years since the early eighties have witnessed the spread of agricultural growth to areas and crops far beyond the limited pockets where the green revolution took place in the seventies. The yields of most crops improved during the later phase. Two recent studies of agricultural growth since the early eighties visualise a continuation of the trend towards broad-based (area-wise and crop-wise) growth (Sawant and Achuthan, 1995; Ray, 1998). The prospective situation would then be favourable for the emergence of local surpluses in a wide range of foodgrains, provided the policy regime remains conducive to broad-based agricultural growth.
2. The coming into being of the third tier of government at the district and lower levels (Panchayati Raj Institutions, i.e., PRIs) would build up an institutional structure which has a constitutional status and the powers and resources associated with that status. It would be the

responsibility of the PRIs to formulate and implement development programmes in their areas including those meant for the poor. The PRIs would have to organise the tasks associated with the food security system, viz., identification of the poor, location of households eligible for receiving subsidised food assistance and provision of food assistance to such households. Thus, irrespective of the food security system, its decentralisation now appears to be certain.

3. The present system is likely to move towards a breakdown in the not-too-distant future. Removal of food subsidy and linking of issue prices to economic cost of grains procured and distributed by FCI would lead to reduction in off-take. As the prices charged to the poor for the PDS grains are a fixed proportion of the issue price (currently 50 per cent), the poor also would have to pay a higher price for the PDS grains and the off-take by them may also decrease. On the other hand, given the political clout of the farmers in green revolution areas, the support prices paid to them would continue to rise in future along with the quantities of grains they offer to the government. It is necessary to remember that FCI has to purchase whatever the farmers offer, which in years of bumper production could be enormous even for the government to handle. It should be fairly obvious that the growing economic and physical burden caused by the system must eventually exceed its capacity to bear the same.

Our field material also has a few indicators suggesting the feasibility of the alternative system. Table 4 brings out the following interesting points:

1. Production in coarse cereals exceeds consumption by a substantial margin in all the four villages and for all the three size groups of farmers. This is also true of superior cereals, though the margins are narrower and in two groups (medium in Chikkammanahalli and large in Korti) consumption is slightly in excess of production. It would be reasonable to make two propositions based on this clue. First, the farmer households as a whole can be taken as being free from food distress, though there may be cases of individual households subject to such distress. What they need is not so much subsidised foodgrains as opportunities to earn additional incomes, i.e., a wide range of income-augmenting programmes. Second, the selected villages have surpluses in coarse cereals as well as superior cereals which could serve as the base for a decentralised food security system.
2. Coarse cereals are still a significant component in the foodgrain consumption pattern of the farm households. However, the pattern does not remain uniform across the villages. In Chikkammanahalli, coarse cereals continue to be dominant while in Bommanakunte—located in the same block—the shift towards superior cereals is quite noticeable. Somewhat similar differences in pattern are also observed in the Bijapur villages, though both of them are ahead of Chikkammanahalli as regards the shift towards superior cereals. This

Table 4
Production and Consumption of Cereals by Farmer Households
(Quintals per farmer household)

Size-group of farmer	Coarse cereals		Superior cereals	
	Production	Consumption	Production	Consumption
	Chikkamanahalli (Chitradurga dist.)			
Small	13.80	11.43	9.50	1.26
Medium	19.80	11.04	2.40	3.53
Large	43.60	17.48	10.16	3.42
	Bommanakunte (Chitradurga dist.)			
Small	9.50	5.16	18.75	7.47
Medium	8.50	4.56	37.50	7.17
Large	13.90	5.19	54.28	8.52
	Chikkalagundi (Bijapur dist.)			
Small	13.75	7.74	5.50	4.92
Medium	27.00	12.48	7.00	4.80
Large	29.80	17.26	9.00	6.60
	Korti (Bijapur dist.)			
Small	9.50	6.90	8.00	4.24
Medium	22.50	5.70	8.00	4.80
Large	48.20	10.79	16.40	17.57

Source: Survey data.

shift can be taken as another pointer to the food distress among farm households not being widespread but confined to some households during some periods in a year. In such a situation a decentralised system would be particularly efficient and cost-effective.

As the category most vulnerable to food distress is that of the landless, it is important to probe our field material for indicators reflecting the situation in regard to the landless in this respect. Foodgrains consumption per adult unit in different categories of households is presented in Table 5. As was noted earlier, the foodgrains consumption in landless households is likely to be an underestimate owing to the omission of data on meals and snacks received by the members of the household at the work site. Taken by themselves, the consumption figures for the landless households do seem to indicate an intake falling below the norm of 500 grams per day which is often used to judge calorie-adequacy of foodgrain consumption. As a second check, we look at the composition of foodgrains consumption in the landless households. In three out of four selected villages—Bommanakunte, Chikkalagundi and Korti—superior cereals account for almost half of the foodgrain consumption in these households. It is also seen that the landless households in these villages augment their PDS quota of rice and wheat with substantial purchases from the market. It does seem rather implausible that households subject to food distress would behave in this manner showing a clear preference for superior cereals. What seems more plausible is that the meals and snacks received by the members of landless households at the worksite has a substantial coarse cereal content, which makes them shift their own purchases towards superior cereals. It is only in Chikkammanahalli, one of the four selected villages, where both the composition of foodgrains, and the quantum of consumption per adult unit is suggestive of the prevalence of food distress (Table 6).

Table 5
Foodgrain Consumption Per Adult Unit*

(In kg per year)

Village	Economic classification			
	Landless	Small	Medium	Large
Chitradurga dist.				
(i) Chikkamanahalli	104**	178**	232	564***
(ii) Bommankunte	103**	137**	226	344
Bijapur dist.				
(i) Chikkalgundi	138**	330	184**	643***
(ii) Korti	194**	550***	650***	557***

Notes: * Consumption refers only to the total inflow/purchases of foodgrains and adult units only indicate the family members of the household.

** Some members of these households are working as casual labourers and usually eat one meal out of the house, specifically in that of landlords/employers. Therefore, the total food purchases are on the lower side.

*** There are some additional members in the households, who are the casual and permanent labourers. Even though they are not the household members they eat in these households and therefore, the total food purchases are on the higher side.

Source: Survey data.

Table 6
Consumption of Cereals in Landless Households

(In quintals per household)

	Consumption	PDS	Market
Chikkammanahalli (Chitradurga dist.)			
Coarse cereals	4.60		4.36
Superior cereals	1.62	1.20	0.40
Bommankunte (Chitradurge, dist.)			
Coarse cereals	3.36		3.36
Superior cereals	3.22	1.20	1.03
Chikkalgundi (Bijapur dist.)			
Coarse cereals	7.56		4.08
Superior cereals	5.87	1.20	3.11
Korti (Bijapur dist.)			
Coarse cereals	6.48		4.56
Superior cereals	4.29	1.20	2.82

Source: Survey data.

A brief description of how the alternative system visualised by us would operate in drought-prone areas is as:

1. As a part of its mandated function, the village/group of village level panchayats would maintain a list of poor households and other households in the area eligible for the development schemes

formulated and implemented by the panchayat. Initially, the schemes would be handed down by the central/state governments, but eventually the panchayat would play an active role in formulating schemes with adequate financial resources at its disposal.

2. Analytically, the schemes formulated by the panchayats could be classified in three categories: (i) Area development programmes guided by the development strategy at the macro level. Issues such as potentialities of the schemes in the area or desirable crop pattern for the area would have to be considered within a macro framework for the development of the economy; (ii) Area development programmes that indicate the scope and opportunities for employment programmes. The latter could be used as the main instrument to deal with the food distress prevailing in the area as well as with the larger objective of providing income support to the poor. Part of the wages paid to the workers in these programmes could be provided in the form of entitlement to receive a specified quantity of local staple consumed by the poor. The choice in this respect could be left to the worker and the implicit price paid by the worker by foregoing part of wages could also be adjusted to introduce an element of subsidy. The panchayat could evolve a procedure whereby the income support would be provided without direct involvement of the panchayat in the acquisition and distribution of foodgrains, so that these would be left to the normal market channels; (iii) The panchayat would also organise welfare programmes to meet the food and nutrition needs of vulnerable groups like children, nursing mothers and senior citizens for whom employment programmes alone would not be appropriate.
3. The panchayat would view the provision of food security as a part of the broader objective of development of area and of rural people. Accordingly, the emphasis would not be so much on providing relief to those subject to food distress as generation of livelihood opportunities which would obviate the need for relief measures except in times of widespread and extreme distress like famine and drought. The provision of food security would be delinked from giving price support to farmers. The price support policy will be formulated on the basis of the criteria appropriate to that policy. The formulation and implementation of development programmes including the programmes to provide food security would involve the participation of NGOs, beneficiary/user groups and representatives of the poor at all stages. Thus, the alternative system outlined in this paper would combine decentralisation with debureaucratisation and depoliticisation.

IV. CONCLUDING OBSERVATIONS

The present food security system reflects two basic flaws in our policy-making for promoting agricultural and rural development. First, the problems of the relatively better-off sections of farmers receive far more attention in policy-making than the deprivations suffered by the poor. Second, while the areas lagging in development like drought-prone areas urgently need investment and an infrastructure to support and sustain the development process, the emphasis in policies remains on temporary and adhoc relief measures. It is important to realise that this is not a congenial setting for maintaining progress towards decentralisation, debureaucratisation and depoliticisation referred to above. In fact, the PRIs as visualised in the recent constitutional amendments, would need a long time to become operational even in the few states like Karnataka which is regarded as being in the forefront in promoting the PRIs. Hence, it would be rather naive to consider the alternative system described in this paper as a pragmatic alternative at the moment. Rather, it would be more realistic to assume that as the present system becomes more and more unwieldy and unsustainable, the policy makers would be under increasing pressure to look for a viable alternative. Simultaneously, political pressures are likely to gather weight at the PRI level for acquiring more substantive resources and decision-making powers than they have now. Thus, the present system is likely to drift towards the system approximating that described in this paper. Discussion on the present food security system often revolves around how it can be improved by (a) focusing the PDS on the poor; (b) excluding the better-off; and (c) reducing leakages and corruption. While improvements in the system are welcome, our plea is that the present food security system needs to be assessed in relation to the broader context of the changing agricultural and poverty scenario in India. This seems to suggest that what is urgently required is a thoroughgoing restructuring of the system rather than piece-meal improvements in it.

Appendix

We selected two districts representing two distinct drought-prone regions of Karnataka. The southern drought-prone region has a different agro-eco-system as compared to the agro-eco-system of northern drought-prone plains of Karnataka. The specific differences arise on account of rainfall pattern, its variability, vegetation, forest cover and type of forest, soils, crop season, and consumption pattern and non-farm economic activities. Chitradurga district falls in southern Karnataka whereas Bijapur district represents the northern drought zone. In the second stage in the process of selection of the study area, we selected Challakere taluka from Chitradurga district and Bilagi taluka from Bijapur district for locating the study villages. These two talukas represent the district characteristics. We give below a few specificities of the selected villages.

1. Bommankunte and Chikkammanhalli

These two villages come under the Challakere taluka of Chitradurga district. Challakere taluka is a typical rain fed area of south Karnataka. Only 11 per cent of its area is under irrigation and coarse cereals dominate the cropping pattern. Jowar, Ragi and Bajra are the major crops along with groundnut cotton and paddy.

Bommankunte is a village situated in the interior area, 12 km away from the main road. Ragi is the staple food in the village. There are an equal number of cultivators and agricultural labourers in the village. The village does not have proper drinking water facility and has to depend on nearby villages for its requirements. The PDS shop is situated in a nearby village. Chikkammanhalli is situated on the main road and hence has easy access to the market, which makes quite a difference to the development and decision-making process of the villagers. The village has a primary school and a PDS shop. Here, the number of cultivators exceeds that of agricultural labourers. Most of the requirements in the households are purchased from the taluka Headquarters.

2. Chikkalgundi and Korti

These villages, located in Bilagi taluka of Bijapur district, were selected to represent the drought zone of northern Karnataka. Jowar and Bajra are the staple foodgrains of the selected region. These two crops along with cotton and sunflower dominate the cropping pattern. Chikkalgundi village is an interior village having no direct road link with the market, whereas, Korti village is situated on the main road with easy access to the town of Bagalkot. Both villages have a school and public health unit each. They also have a PDS shop each, but its functioning has not been to the satisfaction of the consumers.

Note

1. The selected districts represent the southern and northern rainfed region of Karnataka with differential cropping and consumption pattern.

References

Jharwal, S.M. (1998), *Public Distribution System in India Reassessed*, Manak Publications, New Delhi.

Mahendra Dev, S. (1996), "Food Security: PDS *vs.* EGS: A Tale of Two States", *Economic and Political Weekly*, Vol. 31, No. 27.

——and Suryanarayana, M.H. (1991), "Is PDS Urban Biased and Pro Rich? An Evaluation", *Economic and Political Weekly*, Vol. 26, No. 41.

Radhakrishna, R. and Subba Rao (1997), "India's Public Distribution: A National and International Perspective", *World Bank Discussion Paper, No. 380,* Poverty and Social Development Department, World Bank, Washington, D.C.

Ray, S.K. (1998), *Sources of Change in Crop Output*, Institute of Economic Growth, Delhi.

Sawant, S.D. and Achuthan, C.V. (1995), "Agricultural Growth Across Crops and Regions: Emerging Trends and Patterns", *Economic and Political Weekly*, Vol. 30, No.2.

Swaminathan, Madhura (1998), "Understanding the Costs of the Food Corporation of India", *Economic and Political Weekly*, Vol. 34, No. 52, December 25.

15

Perspectives of Women on Food Security : A Case Study of a Tribal Village in West Bengal, 1993 to 1998

Amitava Mukherjee

I. INTRODUCTION

The literature on hunger and food in development economics has been growing over the years. There has been extensive research and discussion on how much poor people eat and how much food they can turn into energy. Some believe that these debates are closely related to the need to establish a poverty line; others maintain that these debates are important for policy formulation. Whatever be the rationale, it is unfortunate that either for establishing the poverty line or for policy formulation, the perspective of those who are concerned most—namely, the poor themselves—has remained largely ignored. This study is an attempt at filling this gap in a partial way.

What kind of food do the poor women and men and children consume to fill their stomach? What type of food relieves them from the pangs of hunger in times of stress, caused by a natural or man-made calamity? In a patriarchal society, where gender discrimination is a matter of public history, who decides on intra-household allocation of food everyday? Do the poor people find out every day the extent of food shortfall they face? And if so, how? What coping mechanisms do they adopt to make good the shortfall or be able to survive with the food shortages? These are some of the questions we will try to address in this paper.

Any discussion on issues relating to food and hunger (read starvation at times!) with poor people who silently suffer the pangs of hunger almost as a matter of routine, is not easy. It requires a lot of tact and effort. In a society where food consumption and self-respect are interwoven, not all people are willing to participate in a session to discuss what they think about such questions. "They often use the interrogative form when replying, showing a mock contempt of the person making the inquiry—a common practice in India. In addition, estimates of food consumption should be taken as such. As one man put it: "we don't measure how much food goes into our stomach" (Beck, 1994).

Generally, it is observed that if both husband and wife work, the woman earned less than the man, but the household still has enough to meet their daily needs. However, employment is available for only half the year at most, and so the poor are forced to reduce their consumption. Most people in a poor economy like ours, spend most of their daily earnings on purchasing food on a regular basis. On an average, people are said to face food shortages of upto 25 per cent, except during certain months. The general nutritional pattern shows that the poorest people spend 80 per cent or more of their income on food and yet are able to meet only 80 per cent of their nutritional needs (Lipton, 1983).

This then forms the background to this study. The Village Krishna Rakshit Chak (KRC) is in Arjum Mouza in Kharagpur Block of Midnapore district of West Bengal. It is one of the backward districts of West Bengal which has been declared as a fully literate district by the government having been covered under the literacy mission. The district is predominantly an agricultural district, with very little industry. There are two agricultural seasons: *Aman* from Ashardh to Kartick, and *Boro* from Magh to Baisakh.

We visited KRC in 1993, in an attempt to study the dynamics of the rural economy in a tribal village based on the perception of the villagers. As a first step a food calendar was prepared by the village women, which provided valuable insights into the different dimensions of food insecurity and hunger, as portrayed by poor tribal women. Women are traditionally responsible for harvesting and gathering food, and its processing and intra-household distribution.

We revisited the village in May 1995 and then again in April 1998 in order to discern and discuss with the villagers the changes in food insecurity and hunger that may have occurred in respect of the poor households of the village between 1993 and 1995, and between 1995 and 1998. A second food calendar was prepared in 1995 and a third one, in 1998. We have attempted here to present our findings and a brief analysis of the same, during the three visits under reference.

II. CONCEPTUAL SPECIFICATIONS

- There is enough food available in the system to match everyone's need;
- People have access to food;
- People have the capacity (purchasing power) to access food;
- Food that is available is culturally acceptable;
- Food accessed and consumed by the people have adequate nutrition; and
- There are no institutional sanctions against consumption of such food (Mukherjee, 1997).

The above position can also be derived from Sen's Entitlement and Deprivation Thesis (ED Thesis) (Sen, 1982; Dreze and Sen, 1988, 1989), according to which food insecurity can be seen to occur when a person does not have enough to eat, which is different from saying that 'there isn't enough to eat'. Whether and how food insecurity is related to food availability is a matter of factual investigation. Food insecurity statements, according to the ED Thesis, relate to the relationship of person to food (Sen, 1982).

In a private market economy, ownership relations and their mapping with others, play an important role in determining food insecurity at the household level amongst others. The extent to which an individual is 'food insecure' depends upon both the individual's ownership of food and on the exchange entitlement mapping that he or she faces. Such entitlement mapping includes time-based entitlements, production-based entitlement and own labour entitlement.

Clearly, the ED Thesis's approach to the food insecurity of an individual concentrates on her/his ability to command food through the legal means available, including the use of production possibilities, trade opportunities, entitlements vis-à-vis the state, and other methods of acquiring food. Individuals are food insecure either because they do not have the ability to command enough food, or because this is not used to avoid food insecurity. But entitlement failures, direct or indirect, would affect the food security situation of individuals. Such failure can be a direct entitlement failure or a trade entitlement failure. The latter can occur either because of an autonomous production decline, resulting from the destruction caused by a pest attack or floods, or due to an induced decline in output, caused by, say, insufficiency of demand. Further, entitlement failure can occur due to economic changes and unfavourable exchange entitlements, such as a sharp fall in the price of non-food items and a steep rise in the price of foodstuff.

It is against this backdrop, that we analyse the perspectives of the villagers of Krishna Rakshit Chak as emanating from the three food calendars.

III. THE METHODOLOGY AND PROCESS

1. The Context

Before describing and analysing the perspectives of the villagers, it is important to have an overview of the methodology and process, to put the discussion in perspective. In Bengal, traditions, practices, customs and usage have all enjoined upon rural women to assume automatic responsibility for a large number of activities. These include collecting fuel (from different sources) and fodder; gathering food from forests and commons; fetching potable water and fodder, often travelling long distances; cooking for the household; child rearing besides carrying out a host of household chores and farm operations. That these activities are laborious, time-consuming and provide critical support to rural life is not always recognised. They are often not visible and tangible in economic terms (and indeed not fully accounted for in economic analysis and national accounting). It is, therefore, important to understand the perspective of rural women on issues such as food (in) security.

We have, thus, described here three food calendars made by rural women in 1993, 1995 and in 1998, referred to earlier and have analysed the same to get an idea of what the women have to say on food security in Krishna Rakshit Chak. This has given us a ringside view of three aspects of village life. The first is the view of the knowledge-base of rural women in gathering food from forests and common property resources and micro-environments (see Chambers, 1990 for a definition of micro-environment), the second, a glimpse of their role in such procurement and the third, the seasonality of food availability, its shortage and the dependence of villagers on food from common property resources, forests and micro-environments.

The processes of preparing the Food Calendars of 1995 and 1998 have been similar to that of the food calendar of 1993 (Mukherjee and Mukherjee, 1994), except that in the case of the later calendars, the women were already in the know of the 'technology'. Also, there was no need for us to build a fresh rapport with the villagers, especially the women, as the earlier visits and communications had already helped establish a good deal of understanding with them.

2. The Community

The inhabitants of Krishna Rakshit Chak are poor and belong to the Lodha tribe, who were given by the colonial rulers the appellation of a 'criminal tribe'. The village has 49 households as per the villagers, which figure may be at slight variance with the 1991 Census figures. Most of the households are landless.

A review of the secondary data and a discussion with the people generally revealed that poor people bought food from the local shops and markets mainly from the wages they get for the labour they sell. Food was purchased generally on a daily basis, as the poor households did not have surplus cash to hold a stock of food. There is a ration shop to which the poor households are attached and rice bought from the ration shop was cheaper than that bought from the local market with cash. Almost all the households access the ration shop at one time or the other depending on whether their cash flow coincides with the day on which the ration shop opens. The supplies from the ration shop were erratic and the quality of rice supplied was not very good—being graded (in government's terminology) as 'fair average quality' or FAQ. Whatever else the poor households consumed had to be bought in the open market, barring wages received in grain in the village.

In the three repeated exercises, we encouraged the women to prepare food calendars, as a part of the process of participatory learning to learn more about their food security situation. At the beginning, in 1993, women were hesitant and shy, but once prodded, they got engrossed in intricate details of food consumption, procurement and intra-household distribution of food. Using various locally available materials like stones, pebbles, leaves, etc., and traditional knowledge of time and space, women drew on the ground months (as per the Bengali calendar) and identified various parameters related to food insecurity.

Across different months and between different commodities, the women of Krishna Rakshit Chak have only indicated relative changes in consumption and not those in the absolute quantity of food consumed during the different months of the year. For instance, each column in the food calendars has to be read as 'stand alone' indicating the relative amount of the particular food item (named as the Column Head) that is available in different months. In column 1, of Table 1, women indicate the pattern of rice consumption through the 12 months of the year. The numbers 15, against Magh and 9 against Phalgun (in column 1 of Table 1) show straight way that consumption of rice in Magh was higher than in Phalgun. Similarly, the number 2 against Poush indicates that the consumption of rice in Poush was even lower than in Phalgun, and so on. These numbers do not indicate the absolute quantities of rice consumed during these months, such as 15 kg in Magh, 9 kg in Phalgun and 2 kg in Poush. Additionally, the numbers across the columns are non-additive and not comparable. Thus, the numbers 15 under rice against Magh and 13 under potatoes against Magh do not indicate that the consumption of rice was higher than that of potatoes in Magh. This is the scheme followed in all the tables showing the food calendars.

IV. THE 1993 FOOD CALENDAR

The 1993 food calendar was prepared in the month of Magh, corresponding to mid-January 1993 and hence starts with Magh. The Bengali calendar year starts in Baisakh, corresponding to mid-April to mid-May. The 1993 food calendar is reproduced in Table I.

1. The Two Food Systems

The different kinds of food consumed by the poor people come from two sources: (i) cultivable land which produced crops such as rice, potato, etc., through the application of technology, and (ii) common property resources (CPRs), micro-environments and forests, which are net resources of food items like fish, fruits, honey, gums, small animals, birds, tubers, small leaves, vegetables, etc. These could be gleaned and collected from land belonging to richer farmers in the neighbouring village. The former type of food may be termed as derived from the primary food system and the latter as that from the secondary food system. Food consumed by people from the primary food system, does not regenerate once harvested unless there are specific interventions from human beings, whereas much of the food from the secondary food system is regenerated without human interventions (Mukherjee, 1993 and 1994).

Table 1
Seasonal Food Calendar, 1993

Month	Rice	Potatoes	Pulses	Vegetables # #	Fruits #	Food from CPRs and water sources	Others from wild
1	2	3	4	5	6	7	8
Magh (mid-Jan. to mid-Feb.)	***	***	****	Cabbage			Wild borums and wild rabbits
Phalgun (mid-Feb. to mid-March)	******* **	******** ***	**	Spinach			Neem leaves
Chaitra (mid-March to mid-April)	****	****	**	Pumpkin		Fish and wild water plants	
Baisakh (mid-April to mid-May)	****	***	*	*Pui* leaves and herbs	Mango Jackfruit	Fish, snails and wild water plants	
Jyaistha (mid-May to mid June)	****	****	**	Lotus leaves and herbs	Mango Jackfruit	Fish, wild water plants	
Ashardh (mid-June to mid-July)	*****	***	***	*Jhinge* (nearer to *sukini*)			
Srabon (mid-July to mid-Aug.)	****	****	****	Green papaya			
Bhadra (mid-Aug. to mid-Sept.)	****	***	***	Green banana		Fish and snails	
Ashwin (mid-Sept. to mid-Oct.)	****	***	**				
Kartick (mid-Oct. to mid-Nov.)	**	***	**	Radish, leaves			
Ahgrahayan (mid-Nov. to mid-Dec.)	****	****	****	Tomatoes			
Poush (mid-Dec. to mid-Jan.)	*****	*********	******	Brinjals		Wild rabits	

Notes:1. The number of 'star' marks under column heads 'Rice', 'Potatoes', 'Pulses' represent the number of stones used by the villagers to show the consumption of the relative item of food.
2. # Fruits from some trees growing near ponds and elsewhere in the village.
3. # # Vegetables are from CPR and forests.
4. Facilitator: Neela Mukherjee.

Source: Prepared by Women's Group, Krishna Rakshit Chak, Midnapore, West Bengal, February 4, 1993.

Thus, the concept of the secondary food system is slightly different in the KRC, because the concept of CPRs in the district is different. There are two ways in which the CPRs can be defined. The traditional definition of CPRs includes common grazing lands, perambokes, sacred groves, village ponds, rivers and rivulets, etc., whose ownership is not recorded in the name of any individual private institution or private individuals but is vested in the state or its agencies. There is a broader definition of CPRs , which includes the elements of the traditional definition of CPRs, and also the rights available to the community to use the usufructs of resources owned and possessed by individuals. Such access could be the outcome of a process of negotiation, bargaining or conflict between poor villagers and the relatively richer farmers. Examples of the latter are drinking water drawn from wells, ripe fruits that fall from fruit trees in orchards owned by individuals, herbs collected from ponds and crops and vegetables gleaned from lands owned by individual farmers. The CPRs in Krishna Rakshit Chak is as delineated by the 'broader definition' of CPRs.

The poor villagers of KRC not only collected, gathered and hunted food from the CPRs, forests and micro-environments, but also gleaned food from the land of richer farmers, The cabbage, pumpkins, *Jhinge*, papaya, green banana, radish, tomato and brinjals, etc. that the poor villagers collected (from other farmers, lands and gardens) as part of the produce of CPRs, were the crops which the well-off farmers did not harvest from their lands. These products had little commercial value and were of inferior quality either because they were damaged by pests or insects, frost-bitten or hit by hailstorm, or diseased, deformed and discoloured for some reason not known to the villagers. Both systems of food play critical roles in providing food to the villagers of Krishna Rakshit Chak. The importance of the two kinds of food lies not only in respect of the nutritional aspects of food consumed but also in the time when such food is available and the variety and palate that they add to the villager's diet.

2. Seasonal Variations from The Primary Food System

Not only does the food calendar reveal that there are two systems of food which sustain the villagers but also that there are seasonal variations in the availability of food from both the systems. Let us categorise the food consumed from the two systems as: (i) principal food items: rice, potatoes, pulses, etc. and (ii) secondary food items: fish, fruits, honey, gums, normal animals, birds, tubers, snails, leaves, leafy vegetables, etc.

If we look at the seasonal consumption trends in the principal food items, we find that rice consumption reaches a peak in Magh, and then declines until Chaitra to remain stationary through to Ashwin (mid-September to mid-October), after which it further declines by almost half of the earlier period in Kartick and picks up in Agrahayan. Thus, consumption of rice, the principal staple food in Bengal, reaches its lowest level during the hot summer months of Chaitra, Baisakh and Jyaistha, and then continues to be low throughout the monsoon season of Ashardh, Srabon and Bhadra when people have to work very hard. Consumption of rice is thus the lowest when the workload is the highest.

In regard to potatoes, the level of consumption follows approximately the same pattern as the level of consumption of rice for the months of Magh and Phalgun. It then declines sharply and stays at the lower level during the entire period from Chaitra to Agrahayan, to pick up again in Poush.

The consumption of pulses, the third element in the basket of principal food items, shows variations. Its intake touches an all time low in Baisakh and rises in the months of Srabon, Agrahayan and Poush. The consumption of pulses is, therefore, also low during the summer period and the beginning of the monsoon months. This is the time when energy requirements are almost the highest, both to stave off the in harsh climate, collect and preserve fuel for the rainy season and meet energy needs of cultivation processes that are vital, during these months.

3. Seasonal Variation from the Secondary Food System

Some vegetables from the CPRs and forests and food of one kind or the other from the secondary system, are consumed almost all through the year except in Aswin. Fruits from CPRs, such as mangoes and Jackfruit, in the summer months are available only in Baisakh and Jyaistha, while fish, snails and wild water-plants are consumed in Chaitra and Bhadra only. Wild rabbits are hunted in the two winter months of Poush and Magh. There are some other foods, not shown in the food calendar but consumed by all households for different reasons, notable amongst which are Drumstick (Sojnae in local language), Mohua and Kundru. While Mohua flowers are collected during the winter months and stored for later use, Kundru and Drumstick are available as vegetables almost round the year.

The availability of fish from CPRs increases significantly during the summer months of Chaitra,Baisakh and Jyaistha and then again during Bhadra, towards the fag end of the rainy season. The increased availability of fish during the summer months, the villagers explained, was due to the heat itself, which causes the water bodies, pond rivulets, etc., to dry up; thus making the catch easier, thereby increasing the availability of fish. And concurrent with this is also the lean period which leaves the villagers with enough time to venture into fishing and collecting snails and water weeds, which provide the poor not only with food but also money from the sale of a part of the 'catch'. This shores up their sagging income, which in any case is low. As Ashardh sets in, the water bodies swell and fishing becomes more arduous and time-consuming while the people get busy in preparing the fields for cultivation. Fishing and collecting snails start in Bhadra, when due to heavy rains in the months of Ashardh and Srabon, the rivulets, ponds and other water bodies start overflowing and flooding nearby fields and meadows. (The rainfall pattern in Midnapore District is such that the month of Bhadra experiences generally sharp showers on certain days, unlike in Ashardh and Srabon, when the district usually receives heavy rainfall for days on end). As a result of such overflowing, fishes and snails flow into the meadows and fields.

The water recedes after the rain stops (or sometime thereafter) leaving fish and snails in the mud and in small puddles scattered all over the place enabling the villagers to catch them. This jacks up the amount of fish and not snails in the secondary food basket of the villagers. Bhadra is also the month when agricultural activity is at a low key, leaving the villagers of Krishna Rakshit Chak with spare time to indulge in gathering activities. Thus, in Bhadra the consumption of fish is higher than in most of the other months.

Unlike the primary food system, the secondary food system cannot be analysed in terms of variations of individual items, because most of the foods from the secondary system are seasonal and vary from month to month. For instance, cabbage is available in Magh, spinach in Phalgun and pumpkin in Chaitra. Similarly, radish leaves are available in Kartick, tomato in Agrahayan and brinjal in Poush.

There are, nevertheless, certain notable features which warrant comments. The secondary food system provides fibre and nutrition (from green vegetables) in the diet of the villagers of Krishna Rakshit Chak. This is an important function as in the absence of the secondary food system, the quality of the food consumed by the villagers would be so much more deficient in nutrients and vitamins. Secondly animal protein, consumed by the inhabitants of Krishna Rakshit Chak also comes from the CPRs and forests. Had the people no access to the kinds of food they gathered and hunted from the CPRs and forests, viz., wild rabbits, fish and snails, the protein content in the villager's diet would have been much less and thirdly, the foods in terms of their number and protein content that the villagers accessed from the CPRs and forests, are higher when the basket of food from the primary food system is the lightest, viz., the months of Chaitra to Bhadra.

4. Nutrition from Wild Foods

Meat from Capybara, the world's largest rodent, and iguana can have similar protein, fat and energy content as pork, beef and chicken. Moreover, meat from Capybara is several times more efficient at converting food meat than in domestic cattle. Rats have a nutritional score equivalent to beef or mutton (Kyle, 1987). Ants, grubs and caterpillars have similar energy protein and fat as goose liver, pork sausage and beef liver. Beetle larve eaten contain 23.3 grams of protein per 100 grams, while termites contain 58.9 grams of protein per 100 grams as compared to 43.4 gram per 100 grams for smoked river fish.

In terms of food security we outlined in section II earlier, there are elements of food insecurity, both from the perspective of food availability and quality of food. There is a fall in food availability from the primary food system during the months of Chaitra, Baisakh, Jyaistha, Aswin and

Kartick, i.e., people suffer from hunger for at least five months in a year. The quality of food consumed also declines during this period, as is indicated by the consumption basket from the secondary food system. The fall in the consumption of rice, potatoes and pulses during these months indicates a lower level of nutrition.

5. The Hunger Periods

The food calendar reveals that people suffer 'differentiated' hunger, i.e., while they are hungry throughout the year, they are more so during some months. Let us look at columns 2, 3 and 4 of the 1993 Food Calendar. As can be seen from Table 1 there are two 'hunger periods' for the villagers of Krishna Rakshit Chak, as indicated by the star marks in the different columns showing the amount of food items consumed in each case. The first hunger period occurs in the proverbial summer months of Bengal, namely, Chaitra, Baisakh and Jyaistha (mid-March to mid-June) taken together, when the availability of rice and potatoes declines to their lowest level; and the availability and consumption of pulses reaches rock bottom. This fall in the availability of food, coupled with acute paucity of employment in the rural areas during this period (Alagh, 1999), which drastically reduces the capacity of the poor to access food leads to entitlement failure. The food intake from the primary food basket, of the poor villagers of the district reaches a very low level during the first hunger period.

'The second hunger period' occurs during the months of Aswin and Kartick (mid-September to mid-November) when again, apart from lowest levels of consumption of rice (reaching two in Kartick), the availability and consumption of potatoes and pulses dips once again (the consumption of pulses being only two in Aswin). And as revealed by Table 4, this is also the period when employment availability is dismal as the harvesting season is yet to get underway and other economic activities are just not enough to provide income to the poor villagers. The power to access food is, therefore, also very low. There is also a sustained entitlement failure during these two months.

During the first hunger period, the bounty of nature, through the common property resources, forests, etc., comes to the rescue of the villagers (see columns 5, 6 and 7 of Table 1). Fish, snails and waterweeds collected from the water-bodies compensate at least partially the loss in protein intake caused by a fall in consumption of pulses. The reduction in calorie intake, due to a fall in the consumption of rice and potatoes, is partially offset by the consumption of fruits like jackfruits and mangoes from the secondary food system. During the second hunger period, unlike during the first hunger period, there is no 'safety net' provided to the poor villagers to tide over their hunger by the secondary food system in terms of the availability of vegetables, fish, snails and water plants or small animals like rabbits to provide protein. This period is also one which coincides with the festival season of West Bengal, during which popular festivals such as Durga Pooja, Bhai Phota (Bhatri Dwitiya) and Kali Puja (Diwali), are observed on a lavish scale entailing huge social expenditures contributing to increasing the distress of the poor villagers. We will return to a discussion on the role of CPRs in food security later in this paper.

V. THE 1995 FOOD CALENDAR

After about two years, in 1995, we returned to Krishna Rakshit Chak, to meet the villagers to find that nothing much had changed be it the terrain, the landscape, the topography, the people, their property, their huts and even the vagaries of nature. The warmth, the forthrightness and the enthusiasm of the villagers remained undiminished. The women were as enthusiastic as they were in 1993 to work out the food calendar a second time over. There was only one difference: the rural women already had the 'technology' to develop the food calendar and there was scant need to facilitate the production of the calendar. The women used local materials like stones, leaves and sticks to produce the 1995 Food Calendar (Table 2), with the same ease with which they cook food for the households, everyday, 365 days in a year.

Once the food calendar was ready, a discussion was held with the villagers with open ended questions to enliven the discussion and facilitate our understanding of their perspectives. The 1995 Food Calendar was prepared towards the end of Chaitra, so that it begins from the month of Chaitra, though the Bengali Calendar Year starts in Baisakh. However, in order to make the 1995 Food Calendar comparable to the 1993 Food Calendar, we rearranged only the months on the form, so that it may be read as starting (as in the case of 1993 Food Calendar) in Magh (Table 3).

The 1995 Food Calendar reveals that the people of Krishna Rakshit Chak continue to depend on both the primary and the secondary food systems for their sustenance and subsistence. The 1995 Food Calendar exhibits very substantial variations in inter-month consumption of food, reaches the lowest level during the months spanned by Chaitra to Kartick, both months included. Thus, villagers of Krishna Rakshit Chak have a very low level of consumption from mid-March to mid-November, which implies that they have enough food for approximately four months in a year. The dominance of rice and potatoes in the consumption basket of the villagers reflects the food preference of the people in West Bengal. At least one commentator has remarked that Bengalis believe that one cannot feel strong without eating rice (Rizvi, 1986). However, potatoes may not be consumed during Bhadra, Aswin and Kartick. Columns 4 to 9 in Table 3 show that a large part of the diet of the poor households is made up of only rice and potatoes. The consumption of fish and snails is significant only during the months following the monsoons. The consumption of potatoes was discontinued, according to the villagers, during certain months of 1995 because the overall price increases did not allow them the luxury of consuming potatoes between Bhadra and Kartick.

Table 2
Seasonal Food Calendar, 1995

Month	Rice	Potatoes	Pulses	Vegetables # #	Fruits #	Fish	Snails	Others from wild
1	2	3	4	5	6	7	8	9
Chaitra-(mid- March to mid-April)	*****	***						
Baisakh (mid-April to mid-May)		****						
Jyaistha (mid-May to mid-June)	****	***						
Ashardh (mid-June to mid-July)	****	**						
Srabon (mid-July to mid-Aug.)	***							
Bhadra (mid-Aug. to mid-Sept.)	**					****** ***		
Ashwin (mid-Sept. to mid-Oct.)	****	***	**	Radish, leaves		****** ****	*****	
Kartick (mid-Oct. to mid-Nov.)	**	***	**	Tomatoes brinjals		******** ********		
Agrahayan (mid-Nov. to mid-Dec.)	****	****	*****	Cabbage				
Poush (mid-Dec. to mid-Jan.)	*****	***** ****	******	Spinach				*Neem* leaves
Magh (mid-Jan. to mid-Feb.)	****** ******	****** *******	***					
Phalgun (mid-Feb. to mid-March)	****** ***	****** *****	**					

Notes: 1. The number of 'star marks' under column heads 'Rice', 'Potatoes', and 'Pulses' represent the number of stones used by the villagers to show the consumption of the relative item of food.
2. # Fruits from some trees growing near ponds and elsewhere in the village.
3. # # These vegetables are from CPRs and Forests.
4. Facilitator: Neela Mukherjee.

Source: Prepared by Women's Group, Krishna Rakshit Chak, Midnapore, West Bengal.

Table 3
Rearranged Seasonal Food Calendar, 1995

Month	Rice	Potatoes	Pulses	Vegetables ##	Fruits #	Fish	Snails	Others from wild
1	2	3	4	5	6	7	8	9
Magh (mid-Jan. to mid-Feb.)	******** *******	******* *****	****					
Phalgun (mid-Feb. to mid-March)	*******							
Chaitra (mid-March to mid-April)	**	******	**					*Neem* leaves
Baisakh (mid-April to mid-May)	*****	*****	**					
Jyaistha (mid-May to mid-June)	****	****						
Ashardh (mid-June to mid-July)	****	***						
Srabon (mid-July to mid-Aug.)	****	**						
Bhadra (mid-Aug. to mid-Sept.)	**	***						
Ashwin (mid-Sept. to mid-Oct.)	****		**					
Kartick (mid-Oct. to mid-Nov.)	**	******	***					
Agrahayan (mid-Nov. to mid- Dec.)	*****	****	*****					
Poush (mid-Dec. to mid-Jan.)	*****	*****	*****	Leaves				

Notes: 1. The number of 'star marks' under column heads 'Rice', 'Potatoes', and 'Pulses' represent the number of stones used by the villagers to show the consumption of the relative item of food.
2. # Fruits from some trees growing near ponds and elsewhere in the village.
3. # # These vegetables are from CPRs and forests.
4. Facilitator: Neela Mukherjee.

Source: Prepared by Women's Group, Krishna Rakshit Chak, Midnapore, West Bengal.

The consumption of food from the secondary food system, to which we will again return later, deserves a few comments here. Firstly, the poor have virtually no access to vegetables, fruits and other wild fruits from the CPRs, forests and micro-environments, etc. Only fish continued to be available in Magh, Phalgun Bhadra, Aswin and Kartick. The poor villagers did manage to have some snails in Aswin and Kartick. There was none of the fibre, nutrients and minerals that the secondary food system provided in 1993. And more importantly the diet of the villagers had become much less varied and was not palatable, regardless of its nutritive value as depicted in the 1993 Food Calendar.

The variations in the levels of food consumed from month to month show a certain pattern. When more food is available (harvest season), the consumption level goes up; when food availability goes down, (cultivation season and the pre-harvesting season), inter-month variations in the level of food consumption increase and the level of food consumption *per se* falls. It is important to recognise that variations in the level of food consumption of the poor, are brought about by both the 'price effect' and the 'quantity effect', "both of which were more important in 1995 than in 1993, because the role of the secondary food system in providing food to the poor had become less important in 1995 than observed earlier".

VI. THE 1998 FOOD CALENDAR

On our return to the district in 1998, after three years we again started work on preparing the food calendar for 1998. The villagers, particularly the women, were enthusiastic about working on the calendar. As in the case of the 1995 Food Calendar, the 1998 Food Calendar was rearranged as in Table 4. The picture emerging from this calendar reveals a food security situation very similar to that portrayed by the 1993 and 1995 food calendars.

In Agrahayan, Poush and Magh, the food intake from the basket of primary food system is the highest, rice and potatoes being the major items consumed. During Phalgun and Chaitra, there is a fall in the consumption of rice and potatoes, but the villagers still have substantial (relatively speaking) food to eat. By the time the Bengal summer is in full rage, in Baisakh, the consumption of food, particularly rice, falls to a very low level, and continues at that level for seven months till Kartick. The situation assumes extreme severity during the three months of Bhadra, Aswin and Kartick (mid-August to mid-November), when the only food that people have from the basket of principal food is rice, the consumption of potatoes having stopped and no pulses being available.

The 1998 Food Calendar shows a long hunger period from Baisakh through Kartick and a less severe hunger period in the months of Phalgun and Chaitra. Four clear phases are noticeable: phase one runs from Agrahayan to Magh, when people eat the most; phase two covers Phalgun and Chaitra, when people eat less and hunger sets in; phase three, runs

Table 4
Seasonal Food Calendar, 1998

Month	Rice	Potatoes	Pulses	Fruits From CPR	Vegetable from CPR	Fish from CPR	Snails	Others from wild
1	2	3	4	5	6	7	8	9
Baisakh (mid-April to mid-May)	*****	***		Brinjals			Snails	Jhinge
Jyiastha (mid-May to mid-June)	***	***	Yes	Kalmi Sak, Gim Sak, Susmi Sak		Fish	Jal Geri	
Ashardh (mid-June to mid-July)	**	*		Wild potatoes Mushroom		Weeds	Yes	
Srabon (mid-July to mid-Aug.)	**	*						
Bhadra (mid-Aug. to mid-Sept.)	**					Laatha Chang	Snails Samuk	
Ashwin (mid-Sept. to mid-Oct.)	***			Jhinge borbotee Snake gourd				
Kartick (mid-Oct. to mid-Nov.)	***			Sak, Seem Pui sak		Fusati, Magur, Punti		
Agrahayan (mid-Nov. to mid-Dec.)	***	*****	***	**		Magur Chang Fish		
Poush (mid-Dec. to mid-Jan.)	**** **	*		Sak, radish				
Magh (mid-Jan. to mid-Feb.)	*****	******						*Neem* leaves
Phalgun (mid-Feb. to mid-March)	****** **	****	Yes			Some fish		
Chaitra (mid-March to mid-April)	*****	****				Fish, Jhinuk	Yes	Rabits

Notes: 1. The number of 'star marks' under column heads 'Rice', 'Potatoes', and 'Pulses' represent the number of stones used by the villagers to show the consumption of the relative item of food.
2. Facilitator: Neela Mukherjee.

Source: Prepared by the Women's Group, Krishna Rakshit Chak, Midnapore, West Bengal.

over the five-month period from Baisakh to Bhadra when the consumption level of the villagers is at a low level; and phase four is of two months duration between Ashwin and Kartick, when the typical diet of the poor households consists of rice alone.

Food from the secondary food system provides some relief to the poor households. The majority of the vegetables from the secondary food system consist of leaves (called Sakin Benhalg). The only redeeming feature of the 1998 Food Calendar is that the quantum of food available from the water-bodies has seen a dramatic upturn from what we saw in the 1995 Food Calendar. The availability of food from the secondary food system has been fairly high during the period from Baisakh to Bhadra and during Ashwin and Kartick, i.e., during the third and fourth phases of hunger identified above. This indicated that during the difficult hunger months, the people of the district would have suffered ever greater hunger, but for the food that they gathered and collected from the CPRs and forests. In other words, when food from the principal food system declined substantially, food from the secondary food system came to the rescue of the hungry. The range of vegetables, green bananas, *saag* (leafy vegetables), fish, snails and small animals that the secondary food system provided, added variety and palatability apart from increasing the food value of the diet of the households.

Thus, the 1998 Food Calendar shows the same pattern as the 1993 and 1995 food calendars and the inter-month variations in food consumed in 1998 also seems to be a function of the availability of food in the system. However, the importance of food from the secondary food basket in eliminating hunger (or in reducing the severity of hunger) which had dwindled in 1995 vis-à-vis 1993, had returned. And this interestingly enough, came about because (as the villagers told us) a huge tank (called Rajbandh), which used to be auctioned by the panchayat, is now under dispute and could not be auctioned. The right to the produce of the tank remains disputed. As a result, the villagers have access to the produce of the tank, which underlines the importance of the secondary food system in 1998.

VII. SIMILARITIES AND DISSIMILARITIES IN THE THREE FOOD CALENDARS

1. Similarities

Having described briefly the three food calendars, it is possible now to compare them. Let us begin by identifying the similarities.

(i) The persistence of long hunger periods depicted by all the three food calendars. Despite all the talk of our national food security, Krishna Rakshit Chak has remained a pocket of hunger for nearly a decade. This is worrisome, though the intensity and duration of the hunger periods may be different. This implies that despite there being no systemic shortage of food, as reflected in the record harvest from the primary food system, and a burgeoning buffer stock with the government, the experience of hunger has persisted as a common feature in 1993 ,1995 and 1998.

(ii) The dominance of starch in the diet of the villagers remained unaffected all these years. This is a cultural phenomenon, which is similar to what Beck (1994) observed in respect of some other villages of Midnapore, studied by him around the same time, through the questionnaire method. He noted that during the discussion with the villagers in Midnapore, there was a common agreement that it is only rice, the staple grain, that would make the stomach happy. "The stomach won't understand unless it gets rice", as one villager put it to him. Beck even notes that when a sufficient quantity of rice was not available, many poor villagers with whom he interacted would take the water left over from boiling rice (called Bhater Phen), which would fill the stomach, but was usually fed to livestock in richer households.[1]

(iii) The major source of protein for the poor households of Krishna Rakshit Chak remains the food collected from the CPRs, particularly water-bodies and forests and micro-environments. More particularly, the relative dependence on food, particularly protein, from the secondary food system in 1998 and 1995 vis-à-vis 1993 has increased in good measure. However, it is not possible to identify whether the absolute amounts of protein intake from this source have actually increased or decreased either in 1995 or in 1998 from their earlier level.

(iv) The consumption of food is the lowest during the summer months and the rainy season (from Baisakh to Kartick, covering the summer months, the cultivation season and the harvesting season). Thus, food is consumed least during the period when the poor have to work the hardest during Ashardh, Srabon and Bhadra, when they work in cultivation and during Aswin, Kartick and Poush, when they work in harvesting operations as also gleaning from the paddy fields. This is also the period when the workload of the women increases because of their involvement in collecting fuel, making 'cakes' and then storing them for future use. The poorest households meet their needs for cooking by collecting fuel from the CPRs (collection of fuel is considered a traditional and unspoken right), which is mainly in the form of fallen leaves, animal dung, notably cow/bullock dung and dry branches. Crop residues and other forms of fuel are also gathered from homesteads, paddy fields, paths, area around ponds, etc. Gathering of fuel is the exclusive responsibility of women and girl children. But collection of animal dung or other forms of fuel during the monsoon is not possible as leaves do not fall during the rainy season and cattle, goats/sheep are kept in the animal-sheds and stall fed. This is done to protect them from the rain and prevent them from trampling crops or grazing the paddy crop standing in the field. Poor households, therefore, store 'cow/bullock dung cakes' made by the women out of dung gathered in the dry season. This increases the workload of the women in KRC.

(v) The consumption of food from the secondary food system increased during the months when the consumption of rice had to be curtailed. This means that much of the foods are gathered in the pre-*aman* harvest period when seasonal factors combined to the disadvantage of the poor and the price of rice hit a new high. Thus, food from the secondary food system substituted food from the primary food system, particularly potatoes and rice, when these became too expensive for the poor villagers to afford. It also means that villagers in KRC are saved from greater hunger during the summer months by being provided food from the secondary food system, though they still remain hungry.

2. The Dissimilarities

The dissimilarities of the three calendars are important and require some serious thought. These are detailed below:

(i) Pulses, which were important components of the food basket of the villagers of the district (as shown by the 1993 Food Calendar) as they provide proteins to the poor households in our rural areas, did not figure in the diet of the poor in the 1995 Food Calendar. The absence of pulses from the diet of the villagers indicates that the quality of food in terms of its nutritive value had deteriorated in 1995 vis-à-vis 1993.

(ii) The intake of vegetables and fruits, which was significant in the 1993 Food Calendar, was non-existent in the 1995 Food Calendar. This also indicates that the quality of the food basket in terms of vitamins and fibre intake had deteriorated in 1995 as compared to 1993. In the 1998 Food Calendar we find a partial recovery of this intake, particularly in terms of food gathered from water-bodies.

(iii) The consumption of other kinds of food—herbs and leaves from common property resources, forests and micro-environments—had almost disappeared in 1995 and was limited to consumption of fish and snails over periods of two and three months, respectively. This means that elements of the consumption basket shown in the 1993 Food Calendar, which combined palate and variety with nutrition in the food basket of the poor households had disappeared in 1995. Because of the dispute over Rajbandh (a huge tank), the poor households of Krishna Rakshit Chak were again able to catch fish, and collect other food from the tank, which has restored some of the loss in palatability and variety in their food, noticed in the 1995 Food Calendar.

(iv) In the 1993 Food Calendar we had seen two hunger periods (from Chaitra to Jyaistha and from Aswin to Kartick) with some respite in between. From the 1995 and 1998 Food Calendars it is apparent that the people of the districts suffer one long hunger period from Chaitra to Kartick (both months inclusive), spanning almost eight months and increasing in intensity during the latter part of the hunger period, viz., from Bhadra to Kartick. The longer hunger period in the 1998 Food Calendar, however, seems to be a little less painful vis-à-vis that depicted by the 1998 Food Calendar, because of the availability of fishes, snails, etc., from Rajbandh, which were virtually missing in 1995.

The implications of the differences in the three food calendars deserve a few comments. It seems that in 1995 and 1998, the total food consumption *per se* of the poor households of the district had gone down, from an already low level. Concurrently, the quality of food in terms of fibre and vitamin content had also deteriorated in 1995. Thus, relative hunger had increased in 1995. However, because of an exogenous factor, namely a dispute over the usufruct of a water tank, there was some improvement in the palate and quality of food in 1998. In sum, if we compare the 1993, 1995 and 1998 food calendars, the picture remains the same: hunger has increased since 1993, but in 1998 due to greater availability of food from the secondary food system, the severity of hunger has been of lower intensity than 1995. The elongated hunger period of 1995, as opposed to two relatively shorter hunger periods of 1993, continues in 1998.

VIII. THE PROBE

In keeping with the accepted practice of reviewing diagrams in order to have a right understanding of the community's perspectives, we had discussions with the villagers on the food calendars. We have restricted our analysis here to the discussions we had on the 1995 and 1998 food calendars.[2] There were two components of the discussion. One component was on what food was available in 1995 and 1998 and the second on what was not available in 1995, though available in 1993 and what was available in 1998 but not in 1995.

Between 1993, 1995 and 1998 there has been no significant change in the dietary habits of the people in Krishna Rakshit Chak in so far as they continue to prefer and consume rice and potatoes as their principal food. The intake of rice, as seen from column 2 of Tables 3 and 4 roughly corresponds to a U-shaped curve with almost a flat bottom. It is relatively high in Magh and falls steadily to the lowest point in Ashwin and then again rises dramatically in the two months of Agrahayan and Poush. (Agrahayan, Poush and Magh constitute the post-harvest season in Bengal). Clearly, consumption of rice is higher immediately after the harvest and then falls steadily through the spring (called Basanta) and summer, to reach the lowest point during the cultivation season immediately preceding the harvesting of the next crop. In other words consumption of rice apparently varies in direct proportion to its availability in the village: its availability is highest after harvesting in a season and lowest before the harvest in the following season.

The availability being discussed here is not merely availability in terms of rice being available for sale in the shops and that provided to the poor as wages, but also its availability in terms of what they can glean immediately after the harvests, from fields of farmers in adjoining villages, where they work as agricultural labourers. Since gleaning of paddy from paddy-fields recently harvested constitutes an important element of the sources of rice, it is highest in the months of Agrahayan and Poush, i.e., immediately after the harvest of a main crop, or kharif crop. A woman can glean as much as 3 kg of rice per day on the days when they glean. This will be discussed further in a separate section on gleaning afterwards.

We noted earlier that most of the villagers of the district are landless labourers belonging to the Lodha tribe. Basically, they are not producers of rice and potatoes, their principal food, they buy these from the market for consumption by selling their labour or glean paddy and dehusk the gleaned paddy into rice by expanding their labour. The villagers explained, that the level of rice and potato consumption was determined both by the availability of (a) these food items, which regulated the price of food in the market and provided the opportunity to glean; and (b) employment (power to access the available food). Nevertheless, the former was the dominant factor which determined food consumption from the primary food system.

During Agrahayan, employment opportunities are available in the fields and farms for harvesting paddy both in the village and in adjoining villages. The average wage hovers around Rs. 30 per day together with a breakfast of puffed rice. Fortunately, both men and women are able to find some work in the villages. During Poush, while men find work in threshing and winnowing paddy, women find some work in dehusking rice. The Lodhas find if more difficult to get work in Poush than in Agrahayan but, since the availability of rice is higher the price of rice is relatively low. The villagers, therefore, not only consume more rice during the months of Agrahayan and Poush but are also able to buy rice for storing to meet future consumption needs during the next two months, Magh and Phalgun. This is part of their coping strategy to which we will refer again later.

During Magh and Phalgun, the on-farm activities virtually dry up and the villagers consequently make a living by selling fish and fuel and firewood they collect from the water-bodies and forests and common property resources, respectively. Poor households of Krishna Rakshit Chak are able to maintain a certain level of consumption, both from these off-farm earnings and from the stocks of food they have built up during Agrahayan and Poush. From Chaitra onwards, not only do employment opportunities and off-farm incomes dwindle, but the availability of their principal food (rice and potato) in the local market also goes down, resulting in a rise in their prices. There are no fields to glean. As a consequence, the poor households cut into their consumption of rice and progressively reduce the intake of potatoes, until it becomes zero in Bhadra, Aswin and Kartick.

IX. FOOD INSECURITY IN TERMS OF THE ED THESIS

Let us now analyse the food insecurity situation in terms of the ED Thesis according to which there could be food insecurity in the households of the village either due to direct entitlement failure or exchange or trade entitlement failure.

Primary and Secondary Food System during 1993, 1995 and 1998

(i) 1993

If we examine the primary food system during 1993, the villagers being landless, there could not have been any direct entitlement failure because they did not produce their own food, and had no production-based entitlement. There was neither any transfer, particularly due to the collapse of the PDS. There is no trade-based entitlement as the Lodha tribe does not have any assets to trade for food except labour.

Exchange entitlement of the Lodhas was determined by five factors: (i) their ability to find employment and the duration thereof, which was highest in the months of Agrahayan, Poush and Magh, and moderate during Ashardh and Srabon. Exchange entitlement failure faced by the poor households in Chaitra, Baisakh and Jyaistha, and during Aswin and Kartick; (ii) the wages paid to them, which were around Rs. 30 per day plus a meal of 'puffed rice'; (iii) their ability to exchange their labour with nature (embodied in the produce of the CPRs, etc.) from which they acquired food; (iv) the cost of whatever food they brought during the months succeeding other harvests; and (v) the indirect and informal taxes that they are required to pay.

Their food security or insecurity was not dependent on security or insecurity arising out of endowment failure but on entitlement mapping that they faced. In 1993, this insecurity (for five months) was due to reduction in employment opportunities and a rise in food prices. During the remaining seven months of the year, food security was ensured through trade entitlement, made possible by higher employment and higher availability of food due to the harvesting of crops.

(ii) 1995

In 1995, like in 1993, the food insecurity of the Krishna Rakshit Chak households in terms of the primary food system was due to exchange entitlement failure, caused by a fall in employment and rise in food prices. The two hunger periods of the 1993 Food Calendar extended into one long hunger period from Chaitra to Kartick, because of the general rise in prices that had forced the villagers to forego consumption of potatoes and reduce the consumption of rice in Bhadra, Aswin and Kartick.

If we look at the secondary food system, depicted by the 1993 Food Calendar, poor households of the districts had a direct entitlement to food from the system. They could reduce hunger because their direct entitlement from CPR and the micro-environment was not jeopardised.

Turning to the 1995 Food Calendar, there appears to be a direct entitlement failure in the secondary food system faced by the poor households. Such entitlement failure is caused, both by a reduction in output of food in the system and by denial of access to such food by others, who owned some of these sources of food—who in effect, partook the nature of alienation of land from the landowner, who engages in food production.

Significantly, direct entitlement of the poor of secondary food was reduced due to the emergence of a market for secondary food and a general decline in the economic conditions of a few of those who owned some of sources of the secondary food system. Thus, one can infer that, as in the case of the secondary food system as depicted in the 1995 Food Calender, direct entitlement failure can occur where there is a change in the market for such goods. But access to the secondary food system improved in 1998, as the efforts at privatisation of CPRs did not succeed.

We can interpret the collection, gathering and hunting of food from the secondary food system as the exchange-based entitlement, as the poor households exchanged their labour for the food they got from the CPRs, forests, etc. In that event one could have said that there was an exchange entitlement failure as the rate of exchange of food from the secondary system vis-à-vis labour moved adversely against the poor households of the district in 1995. But this may not be appropriate because though the poor households were exchanging labour for food, the CPRs, forests and micro-environments did not receive anything in exchange for the food they provided.

(iii) 1998

In the case of the 1998 Food Calendar, the situation of food insecurity from the primary food system, was caused by a failure of exchange entitlement. The pattern was similar to what was seen in 1993 and 1995. However, the direct entitlement failure from the secondary food system, which increased food insecurity in the district in 1995, was eliminated, at least partially, in 1998. This was so because the poor villagers could exchange their labour for the food gathered and collected from Rajbandh (the tank whose usufruct could not be auctioned and hence became available for the villagers' consumption). The dispute regarding ownership of the produce of Rajbandh, thus, turned out to be the saviour of the people of the district.

X. FOOD CONSUMPTION TRENDS IN KRC

Wild food means food consumed by the poor but not cultivated by them. These are generally gathered from the sides of paths, ponds, swamps, the jungle and overgrown areas that are found in patches around the villages and accessible forests. They are, therefore, gathered free of cost and for the most part without restriction.

Villagers generally said that they gathered and collected food from the secondary food system as a way of coping with food shortages in times of stress, and such food was eaten regularly, especially during the rainy season when agricultural employment was limited and the price of food the highest. Gathering of food from this system is done whenever and wherever possible. We did not get any quantitative estimate of food gathered and consumed from the secondary food system, but the 1993, 1995 and the 1998 food calendars reveal that food of one kind or the other from the secondary food system the villagers of KRC consumed were not, however, all the time 'wild-food' as Beck found in the other villages of Midnapore. Many of these foods were vegetables and 'domesticated food'.

Mohua is a part of the lives of the people in KRC, who use Mohua to produce liquor, which is an integral part of the cultural and social life of the Lodhas of KRC, as in every other tribal society in that part of the country. Mohua fruit is boiled and eaten with spice. Mohua flower is dried, broken and mixed with pounded rice (called *chirae* in local language) or fried rice and made into sweet. It is used as a source of fodder and the villagers of KRC also sell Mohua to boost household income. (As a matter of fact, it is one of the major non-timber forest products in tribal India).

Notably, though the villagers of KRC are Lodhas they did not make any mention of lizards (Goshap), minor lizards and rats as being parts of their diet. Whether consumption of such meat, which is not consumed by the general public, formed part of the diet of the villagers or whether these were not abundantly available in KRC are issues which require further investigation. The possibility of the former is somewhat bleak because of two reasons: one, there were repeated rounds of participatory sessions over a long period of time and second, the 1998 Food Calendar was prepared by the villagers, amongst whom there were non-poor participants as well.

We have seen earlier that whereas there were two hunger periods in the 1993 Food Calendar, the hunger period in the 1995 and 1998 food calendars ran almost eight months at a stretch. We also indicated that the peak segment of the hunger period of Bhadra, Aswin and Kartick as also the earlier segment from Chaitra to Srabon were more severe than the two smaller hunger periods shown by the 1993 Food Calendar. A look at columns 2,3 and 4 of Table 1, and columns 2,3 and 4 of Table 3 makes it clear that the length of the hunger period in 1995 had increased by about 60 per cent between 1993 and 1995 and continued to be so in 1998.

A comparison of columns 5 to 8 of Table 1 with corresponding columns of Table 3 reveals interesting features. Whereas in the hunger period of the 1993 Food Calendar, 'hunger food' came from the CPRs, etc., for the poor households of the district which reduced the intensity of hunger, in 1998, the availability of such food was too little during the extended hunger period. Thus, not only has the hunger period been extended but the depth of such hunger also increased over the years. In effect, the poor households suffered from hunger in 1995 and in 1998 over longer periods than in 1993, and as a result, were comparatively more hungry as well.

It was a rather distressing revelation that cabbage, pumpkin, spinach, *Pui Saag*, leaves, herbs, green banana, mango, jackfruit, wildwater plants, etc., had all disappeared in 1995 and 1998. During and around 1993, the poor households had managed access to sizeable amounts of these hunger foods from the fields and tanks of relatively well-off farmers. But from 1995 onwards, due to these well-off farmers' inability to make both ends meet in the face of rising prices, they denied the other poor's access to these foods. This was attributed to two reasons. Firstly, because of the increasing difficulty faced by the farmers they have started selling these hunger foods produced in their fields in the local market to supplement the household income. The average 'ongoing prices' (in 1995) of some of these foods in the nearby Charkabar, Khemasuli, Tangra, Golbazar and Kalai Kunda Gate No. 2 markets were as follows: Bitter gourd: @ Re. 1 for three pieces; *Susmi Saag*: @ Re. 1 for three bundles; *Kalmi Saag*: @ Rs. 2 per kg; *Thankuni Saag*: @ Rs. 3.50 per kg and snails and fish at various prices. Secondly, following from the first, because of their economic difficulty, people started buying these poor quality foods, which no one picked up in the market. Thus, the emergence of a market for poor quality food also contributed towards reducing the food availability from the secondary food system.

In 1998, the market situation remained the same except for one significant change in the secondary food system scenario: the Gram Panchayat, within whose jurisdiction KRC falls, could not auction the usufruct right of Rajbandh (the tank) in KRC due to a dispute and hence villagers had access to its production. Thus, the supply of food from the secondary food system had increased because of the access of the poor to the production of this tank. Some food provided by the CPRs, etc., was again available in 1998 for consumption. Judged from that perspective, the households were less hungry in 1998 than they were in 1995.

XI. FALL IN FOOD OUTPUT

However, villagers pointed out that in 1995 and in 1998 the total output of hunger food *per se* had also fallen on account of two factors. One, because of the use of chemical fertilisers and 'medicines' in the paddy fields to deal with pests and insects, the water in these water bodies gets polluted, leading to a fall in the availability of fish, snails, etc., from these sources. Second, as the area under common lands (on which a portion of hunger food grew) is shrinking these lands are being privatised and diverted to other uses. This is similar to what Beck found in other Midnapore villages. He noted that "wild foods available locally were continually declining as more land was put to agricultural use and the wild foods are either marketed or more villagers tried to collect them".

Despite their increasing scarcity, the knowledge of location and methods of preparation of wild foods still exist among the people. They do not deny that they go and gather these foods, which is unlike the others who out of shame deny that they consume food from the forests, CPRs and micro-environments.

It has also been pointed out that the collection of fuel, particularly twigs and wood, is becoming progressively more difficult which means that poor households are buying fuel. Occasionally, the outlay on buying fuel is not inconsequential in as much as, the cost of three sack-full of dry leaves is Rs. 50, which is enough to meet three days' fuel needs of a household. The amount spent on buying fuel makes inroads into the level of consumption of the poor. This is strikingly similar to what was reported to by Beck (1994): "If we don't collect wood or leaves how will we cook. If there isn't any fuel we have to cut the amount we eat and buy a sack of *guti* that costs 10-12 rupees. We can't get any cow/bullock dungs as the cows aren't allowed out into the fields. There are many mango gardens in the village, we have to cut wet wood and dry it. Wood is getting more and more scarce and things are getting worse".

Scarcity of fuel causes great problems for girl children and women, as this increases the time spent on collection and they have to divert money from food to fuel, earlier collected for free. The social forestry programmes of the government were helpful because they were nearer to the villages providing leaves and fuel-wood as well, though access to these groves are not always guaranteed as there is a negotiated access available.

XII. COPING STRATEGIES IN KRC

Hunger is therefore a certainty which the villagers of KRC endure every year and it is increasing over the years. In such a situation, they have only a few choices: to regulate food consumption, to borrow food from neighbours/relatives, and to take loans to buy food, at the extortionist's high rate of interest. Villagers of KRC exercise the last option cautiously because of the triple burden it imposes: the monetary burden, the psychological burden concerning repayment, and dependence on the moneylender, who is in many cases, the shopkeeper.

In the matter of food curtailment, the poor adopted the tactic of staying at home to save energy and keep a fast while sleeping or lying down. This is similar to what Lipton (1983) and Hertmann and Boyce (1983), found in other areas of Bengal and Bangladesh. The villagers of KRC opted to spread their hunger rather than meet immediate hunger needs and they did so by making one meal stretch into two, or eat every alternate day, a phenomenon widely prevalent in South Asia (Van Schendel, 1989; Dreze, 1988; Caldwell et al., 1986). As we noted earlier (section IX) villagers of KRC would buy, earn or glean food in the months of Agrahayan and Poush, and save the same, in order to stave off hunger in Magh and Phalgun. In other words, the villagers preferred to tolerate some intensity of hunger at the present in order to safeguard against future hunger which would probably be even more severe, a strategy also found in Howrah district of West Bengal (Bharati and Basu, 1988).

Reduction in consumption by the villagers at a point of time, therefore, was effected in an attempt to stave off future hunger and circumvent the possibility of being compelled to take loans from the moneylenders and consequently make them dependent on the latter. Women combined the roles of both mother and cook, who ate last and many a times only the leftovers. The practice prevalent among women was that of eating last and eating the leftovers, internalising the iniquitous norms set out by the custodians of the patriarchal system that operates in the rural areas in India. (World Bank, 1989). Greenough (1982) remarked that "the patriarchal values of Bengali Hindu societies required priority to be given to the feeding of the male members of the household so as to ensure the continuance of the male line". "Even in normal times men are fed first in peasant households. Women eat even after the men, receiving a smaller and poorer share of food" (Arnold, 1985, p. 89). And when food is in short supply, or when disease strikes, the male children get more attention and food resources.

XIII. CONCLUSION

The fact that we produce around 202 million tonnes of food and that the government holds buffer stocks in excess of the warranted level, may give the illusion of food security at the national level, though pockets of the hungry persist. Despite huge strides made by the state in increasing agricultural productivity (Rogaly, Hariss, White and Bose, 1999), the establishment and successful functioning of the Panchayati Raj system and the PDS system, which we are told, 'works', and despite significant land reform measures taken to provide land to the landless and register the tenants (Ghosh, 1999) the hard fact is that a large section of people suffers from hunger. Thus, ensuring (a) a massive food output, (b) the availability of more than adequate food stocks as buffer and (c) a rapid rise in food output at the state and national level is not enough for eliminating hunger. We have to look for food security at a much lower level—that is, at the household level—to secure a hunger-free society.

The nature and intensity of hunger varies from month to month, the situation being worst in the summer and monsoon months. Villagers face long periods of hunger from Chaitra to Kartick and the consumption of food is lowest in the months when it is needed due to workload on account of employment and a harsh climate. The women face an additional workload of maintaining the supply of fuel during the period under reference, when (particularly the latter part of the hunger period), fuel availability from 'conventional sources' gets reduced.

The role of the secondary food system (common property resources, micro-environments and forest, etc.) is critical in reducing hunger of the poor, all through the year but more so during the hunger period. Access to CPRs, micro-environments and forests play a critical role in enabling the hungry villagers to obtain food, diversify income sources and increase the stability of the family livelihood systems. CPRs serve as a source of various kinds of food and the only source of animal protein, fodder, fuel, etc., for household consumption and for sale to supplement income. In effect, the villagers depend heavily on the CPRs for sustaining them. There are two aspects of this dependence that warrant a few comments.

First, the dependence on the CPRs and forests is not constant. It varies from season to season, getting intensified during the slack season. Second, the availability of food and other resources from the CPRs and forests also varies, but the slack season, as it were, for the output from the secondary sources is not co-terminus with that for food availability for the primary food system. This helps the poor villagers to cope with reduction in food supply from the primary food system.

Women are generally known to have a better knowledge of food from the primary and the secondary food systems than men. This is consistent with the findings of Boulding (1976) and Shiva (1988). More generally, the women in the tribal community of Lodhas are the principal gatherers, collectors and gleaners of food from the secondary food system. They, therefore, have special knowledge of the edible produce of the secondary food system.

Collecting food from the secondary food system is time-consuming and entails very hard work. Since there is a disparity in the intra-familial distribution of power, the task of collecting produce from the secondary food system falls on the younger women and girl children, who thus try to ensure that their future food security is preserved in the larger sense. However, since they spend considerable time in collecting and foraging food from the secondary food system, they miss the opportunity of attending schools. This is reflected in the poor literacy rate among women in the village as depicted by the literacy map. The concept of CPR as an element of the secondary food system itself has been distinctly different in the KRC. The women of KRC consider negotiated rights, or their customary right to collect and glean foodgrain and vegetables from the rich farmers' land, even in neighbouring villages, as part of their CPR. This is resulting in a conflict because the kind of foodgrains and vegetables collected and/or gleaned is utilised by the community in KRC and no individual seeks to exerts her/his rights over them, to the exclusion of others, except the person who holds title to the land.

However, there is a positive aspect of this phenomenon. Although the secondary food system robs the young women and girl children of valuable opportunities to study in the village schools (and there is one in the village) as explained above, yet its role in providing women, girl children and even the aged with an independent source of subsistence, cannot be overemphasised. Notably, it eliminates the need for a mediator, which would have resulted in the villagers becoming dependent on able-bodied (younger) males and adults. Thus, the collection of food from the secondary food system needs to be renewed not just as a means of providing sustenance for poor households.but also as a viable method of empowering the women and the vulnerable groups in the society.

XIV. POLICY INITIATIVES

It is imperative to formulate a policy aimed at abating the deterioration and depletion of the CPRs, micro-environment and forests, noting that the

CPRs are the only property to which the poor people like the Lodhas in KRC have access. While the distribution of land to the landless is unexceptionable, a measure to protect the village commons and the micro-environment in the village must be put in place. If the run-off, for instance, from the fields of the better-off farmers pollutes the water-bodies which cut off a vital source of food for the poor, the polluter-pays-principle—must be introduced. And the distribution of land could be from land declared surplus, rather than from CPRs.

There is clearly a need to design interventions to provide money to the poor during the hunger period not as dole, but as a means for generating employment and as credit for opting for self-employment. The record of the state in providing employment is not encouraging and that of the banking system (mass banking system, that is) not exactly flattering. This particularly so, from the gender perspective. Some hope lingers in our mind, that the success in preventing the drought of 1970-73 in Maharashtra from escalating into a full-blown famine, provides those incharge of statecraft with policy options that may help in reducing hunger in other states as well. But on the other hand, the abject failure of the state to prevent millions from migrating out of Bolangir and Kalahandi in Orissa, to prevent starvation in successive years is almost scandalous. The state failed to protect the entitlements to food not only for the most vulnerable households but also for the more vulnerable within the households such as women and children. The EGS did precious little in Tamil Nadu (Guhan, 1981). Thus, in states where the leakages are few and governance is reasonably good, the Maharashtra style EGS may be feasible. Dependence on the instrumentalities of the state may not always be the best course. As has been noted by commentators that even though the state has dealt with the threat of a full-blown famine fairly well (Sen, 1982, Dreze 1988), the report card of the government in dealing with less acute situations, leaves much to be desired. There is a need to look at alternative models, such as the SEWA Model for organising the poor and the Grameen Model for providing credit. The model pursued by several pioneering NGOs in India such as the Working Women's Forum in Tamil Nadu and Karnataka or Banco Sol, in Brazil could also give some pointers for the answer. There is need to move away from the top down systems put in place for delivery of poverty alleviation programmes, which are self-serving and have run out their course. It is not possible to have a long-term solution to the problems of hunger unless we manage several other dependencies. To use Sen's terminology, at the outset, there is a need for laying more emphasis on elementary education and basic health care. It is fashionable to talk of user charges and a reduced role of the state. But given the state of the hunger situation in particular and the poverty scenario in general, the state needs to have a dominant role in these areas. The answer to 'bad governance' is not 'no governance' but better governance. If we cannot refrain from getting into the trap of thinking that the market will do the trick, hunger will prevail amidst us for a long time to come. Markets will not work in the social sectors in the poor rural areas. The example of 'Orissa State Electricity' after the super cyclone that hit the state in 1999, should be enough as a reminder for us.

In the case of KRC, at least the summer vacation could be made to coincide with the time when the women and children are required to work most, in order to collect and gather food from the secondary food system. This will give them time to improve the food security status of their families and create space for them to attend school. This would help in building their future and contribute towards a long-term solution of their hunger problems.

Organising the poor to assert their rights should be accorded high priority and funded by the state, if needed. It is important not only to have entitlements and rights but also to exercise those rights. The lessons learnt about the power of rural organisations in protecting the rights of the poor from the Chipko movement in the Garwal Himalayas is too well known to be laboured upon here. The work of URMUL in Lunkaranar, Bikner, to ensure that water-rights become inviolable; or the role of the poorest families in a village in Nepal in organising themselves to get credit and grain, and in maintaining wage rates and many of the traditional elements of patron-client through severe drought; or the efforts of Vidhayak Sansad in Usgaon, Thane, to secure minimum wages for the tribals, all bring home important lessons in this regard.

Notes

1. Beck (1994) notes that during the Great Bengal Famine of 1943, the hungry people went form house to house asking for Phen and Greenough's comments (1982) has to do with the cultural significance of rice in Bengali culture, as Phen contains little of nutritional value. It may also have been connected to the fact that Phen appears to stave off hunger pains. The tactic of drinking Phen to stave off hunger was used by the poor rural families in Korea, during the Korean War.
2. For a report on our discussions on the 1993 Food Calendar see Mukherjee and Mukherjee (1994).

Reference

Alagh, Y.K. (1999), "Grain of Truth", *The Indian Express*, November.

Arnold, David (1988), "Famines, Social Crisis and Historical Change", Basic Blackwell, Oxford.

Beck, Tony (1994), *The Experience of Poverty*, Intermediate Technology Press, London.

Bharti, P. and A. Basu (1988), "Uncertainties in Food Supply, and Nutritional Deficiencies in Relation to Economic Conditions in a Village Population in Southern West Bengal, India", in De Garine, I and Harrison, G.A. (eds.) *Coping with Uncertainty in Food Supply*, Oxford Science Publication, Clarendon, Oxford.

Caldwell et al. (1986), "Periodic High Risk as a Cause of Fertility Decline in Rural Environment: Survival Strategies in the 1980-83 South Indian Drought", *Economic Development and Cultural Change*, Vol. 3, No. 4.

Dreze, Jean (1988), "Famine, Prevention in India", Paper presented at the World Institute for Development Economics Research, Helsinki (mimeo).

—— and Sen, Amartya (1989), *Hunger and Public Action*, The Clarendon Press, Oxford.

Ghosh, Buddhadeb (1999), "Land Reform: Lessons form West Bengal", in Sinha, B.K. and Pushpendra (eds.), *Land Reforms in India*, Sage, New Delhi.

Greenough, P. (1982), *Prosperity and Misery in Modern Bengal: The Famine of 1943-1944*, Oxford University Press, New York.

Guhan, S. (1981), "Social Security: Lessons and Possibilities from Tamil Nadu Experience", *Bulletin No. 11.*, Madras Institute of Development Studies, Madras.

Hertmann, B. and Boyce, J. (1983), *A Quit Violence: View from a Bangladesh Village*, Zed Books, London.

Kyle, R. (1987), "Rodents under the Carving Knife", *New Scientists*, June, pp. 58-61.

Lipton, Micheal (1983), "Poverty, Undernutrition and Hunger", *World Bank Staff Working Papers No. 597*, The World Bank, Washington, D.C.

Mukherjee, Amitava (1997), "Institutional Sanctions, Choice and the Secondary Food System: Incompleteness of Sen's Entitlement and Deprivation Thesis as an Explanation of Hunger", in George, K.K., et al. (eds.), *Economics, Development and the Quest for Alternatives*, Concept Publishing Company, New Delhi and *Indian Economic Journal*, Vol. 43, No. 4, April-June, 1995-96.

Mukherjee, Neela and Mukherjee, Amitava (1994), "Rural Women and Food Security: What a Food Calender Reveals", *Economic and Political Weekly*, Vol. 29, No. 11, March 12.

Mukherjee, Amitava (1993), *Structural, Putting the First Things, Poverty and Environmental Last*, Segment Books, New Delhi.

Rogaly, B., Hariss, Barbara White and Bose, Sugata (1999), *Sonar Bangla?* Sage, New Delhi.

Rizvi, N. (1986), "Food Categories in Bangladesh and Its Relationship to Food Beliefs and Practices of Valuable Groups", in Khare, R. and Rao, M.S.A. (eds.), *Food, Society and Culture: Aspects of South Asian Food System*, Caroline Academic Press, Durham.

Sen, Amartya (1982), *Poverty and Famines: An Essay on Entitlement and Deprivation*, The Clarendon Press, Oxford.

Shiva, Vandana (1988), *Staying Alive: Women, Ecology and Survival in India*, Kali for Women, Delhi.

Van Schedel, W. (1989), "Self-Rescue and Survival: The Rural Poor and Bangladesh", in Lieten, G. et al. (eds.), *Women, Migrants and Tribals, Survival Strategies in Asia*, Manohar, Delhi.

World Bank (1989), *Gender and Poverty in India*, The World Bank, Washington, D.C.

16

Learning from Micro-level Experiences in Food Security: The Case of Mountain Villages in Uttaranchal

Nira Ramachandran

I. INTRODUCTION

India has, over the past few decades, achieved commendable success in foodgrain production and maintaining stability of supplies, but ensuring access to food, particularly at the level of the household, remains to a large extent, an elusive goal. Added to this is another dimension—that of ensuring adequate nutrition. Recent surveys indicate that 50 per cent of the children in rural India suffer from malnutrition, while 15 per cent are severely malnourished.[1] Low birth weights account for 50 per cent of infant mortality and 20 per cent of all maternal mortality is caused by nutritional anaemia. A study by UNFPA (1999) shows that around one-third of the country's population, i.e., around 320 million (1997), are 'food insecure' or those consuming less than 80 per cent of the minimum calorific requirement. Thus, while the country may have achieved its initial objective of preventing starvation deaths, the undermining of its human resources and productive capacity due to malnutrition remains a serious problem.

Various research studies document the emerging trends in the country's food scenario—the changing preference for fine cereals as against coarse grains, the increasing dominance of oils, sugar, meat, milk and milk products over foodgrains in the family food basket and even the tendency to purchase food supplies from the open market, rather than from the fair-price shop due to parity in prices. The overall macro picture that emerges is one of sufficient/surplus cereal production, the predominance of rice and wheat over other grains and the diminishing consumption of pulses and other sources of vegetable protein. Coupled with this trend is the declining role of the public distribution system, particularly in view of the emphasis on reducing subsidies and refining targeting, which gives rise to the very real apprehension that the food and nutrition security of the most vulnerable groups may be further curtailed.

In this context, the current food policy focus on staples alone begins to appear redundant. The situation calls for a more comprehensive policy providing support to a diverse package of food products and effective programmes for transfer. However, in a country as diverse as India, policy directives originating in macro-level generalisations may impact differently on populations in different regions and produce results, which are widely divergent from those originally intended. Thus, micro-level studies become necessary inputs to food policy formulation.

This paper attempts to assess the food security and nutrition status of the population in remote mountain villages of the district of Garhwal, Uttaranchal. The field study was conducted with the objective of testing a set of participatory tools for RFSNA (Rapid Food Security and Nutrition Analysis) designed by the FAO for the purpose of formulating and implementing National Plans of Action for Nutrition (NPANs) in developing countries. While the objective of the study was to inquire into the state of food security and nutrition, the participatory exercises yielded a wealth of information on related issues including agriculture, employment, income, education, health, gender disparities, child care, availability of basic services, interaction with government functionaries and the functioning of food and health-related government programmes. The techniques used provide a quick and inexpensive method of assessment compared to conventional household surveys, and could prove to be an effective tool when cross-country studies are required on a large scale.

II. THE STUDY AREA: A PROFILE

The district of Garhwal is one of the 13 districts of the newly created Himalayan state of Uttaranchal. The district extends from the fertile valley of the river Ganga and its tributaries into the inhospitable upper reaches of the Himalayas and lies almost entirely within the Himalayan mountain system bounded by other hill districts of the state and traversed by the rivers, Bhagirathi and Alaknanda, which meet at Devprayag to form the river Ganga.

The 2001 Census places the population of the district at 6,96,850. The urban segment accounts for only about 10 per cent of the total population and is concentrated in six towns: Pauri, Srinagar, Bah Bazaar, Kotdwara, Landsdowne and Dogadda. The rural population is distributed over 3,236 villages—small, sparsely populated and widely scattered, with a distinct cultural identity. Its rugged terrain and inaccessibility have resulted in self-contained and internally homogenous settlements with little or no interaction with the plains. Outside influence, if any, is confined to areas bordering the main highways.

The interior of the district, focussed on the administrative headquarters—Pauri, is relatively inaccessible with its steep and rugged terrain and difficult climatic conditions, particularly during the monsoons and in winter. The district is characterised by substantial out-migration of the males in the working age group. Thus, women-headed households dominate, with women bearing the brunt of farming, as well as dealing with household chores, especially the collection of fuel, fodder and drinking water. The flip side of this lopsided sex ratio is that gender discrimination in the form of educational or nutritional disparities, as exist in the rest of the country, are unknown here. However, where work is concerned, be it farm labour or household chores, the onus is entirely on the women folk. Traditionally, men only plough the fields at the start of the sowing season (twice a year), and that too because of the traditional taboo on ploughs for womenfolk. The remaining agricultural or livestock-rearing tasks, including the heavy work of harvesting, fall on women alone. While education has had considerable impact, as can be seen in the almost 100 per cent school enrolment rates and significantly higher adult literacy levels as compared to the neighbouring state of Uttar Pradesh, traditional life styles and technology persist.

1. Lack of Infrastructure

Endowed with vast potential in the form of forest, mineral and water resources, the district remains backward due to lack of infrastructure and planned utilisation of available resources. The only source of livelihood is subsistence farming. The lack of markets, distance from the plains, high transport costs and marginal land holdings make commercial farming inviable. Fragmented landholdings, many as small as 100 square metres scattered among the terraced hillsides, do not allow for mechanisation, even if it were affordable. Irrigation is restricted to the fields at the valley bottom bordering the numerous small streams. Power supply is too erratic to resort to pumping irrigation water. The District Administration discourages the use of chemical fertilisers and pesticides to avoid the danger of polluting the drinking water supplies through run off down the steep slopes.

The staple crops of wheat (September-June) and rice (May-September) are supplemented by small millets (*Mandwa* and *Jhangora*), soy bean and a variety of pulses (*urad, masoor, rajma* and *channa*). Productivity is very low, averaging only about 10 quintals per hectare as compared to about 40 in the plains. In the high altitude fields, productivity falls to as low as 2-3 quintals per hectare. The government is engaged in promoting research for developing more suitable, quick-ripening varieties to increase the number of crops per year, but these high-priced seeds have few buyers. Chemical fertiliser inputs are as low as 3 kg per hectare. Annual crop output is barely sufficient to supply 3-4 months of food for the family. Thus, the region is heavily dependent on the public distribution system (PDS), which supplies subsidised foodgrain, sugar and fuel (kerosene oil) through its network of fair-price shops.

Climatic conditions are conducive to the development of horticulture. A variety of fruits and vegetables flourish in the area, but the lack of cooperatives or local markets has discouraged efforts at commercialisation. A few fruit trees and some vegetable patches can be seen scattered among the homesteads, but even kitchen gardens are restricted to the economically better-off families.

While livestock (mainly cows and bullocks) are found in large numbers, milk production is minimal. Local breeds yield barely 1-2 litres of milk per animal per day. Attempts at improving breeds through importing Jersey cows have failed as the lack of green fodder soon reduces the productivity of the better breeds. Government schemes for transporting bales of dry fodder from the plains are being implemented in an attempt to raise dairy production. Earlier schemes to grow fodder in the hills were abandoned, as input costs were higher than the market value of the fodder produced. The government has also implemented a dairy promotion scheme with milk routes being established to collect even a small output from villages on the route, which is then centrally collected, pasteurised and marketed. This has achieved only limited success. Landless families eke out an existence as agricultural labourers or small artisans, being paid in cash or kind or both.

2. The Sample Villages

Two sample villages were selected with the help of local officials—a medium-sized village located on the road (Gad Kamargaon) with access to electricity, piped water, and primary school, and a large village (Kevars) not connected by road, but with similar infrastructure facilities.

(i) Gad Kamargaon

The village of Gad Kamargaon has 82 households, of which 27 belong to the Scheduled Castes and are located in an isolated hamlet about a kilometre away from the main village. The total population is 435 with women far outnumbering the men (240 females to 195 males). Twenty-three families have been classed below the poverty line. The village has a total area of 37.64 hectares, of which about 18 hectares are available for cultivation, 12 hectares are under pasture and groves and the remaining eight hectares are not cultivable. Of the cultivated area, only 5 per cent is irrigated. The livestock numbers 104 with a predominance of cows.

The village has piped drinking water and electricity. There is a primary school, but the primary health centre is at a distance of 1 km. The nearest market is 2 km distant, while the nearest town 'Pauri' is about 12 km away.

(ii) Kevars

Kevars is a village dating back five to six generations. It is larger than Gad Kamargaon with 182 households, of which 60 households are below the poverty line and 52 belong to the scheduled caste community. However, not all scheduled caste households are below the poverty line (only 29 scheduled caste households fall in the BPL category). The population numbers 1001. Of a total area of 270 hectares, forests cover 20 hectares and the cropped area is 121 hectares, of which only five hectares are irrigated. By far the largest portion, i.e., 224 hectares, is barren and uncultivated. Livestock numbers 613, of which cows and bullocks account for nearly 60 per cent and sheep and goats another 30 per cent. The village has piped drinking water and electricity, a primary school, a junior high school and a fair-price shop. The main road, however, is 2 km away and can be reached only *via* a steep footpath. The nearest market is at a distance of 2 km, the nearest town, Pauri being 6 km from the road head. While the road is metalled and well maintained, adverse weather conditions can lead to the area being cut off for several days, even weeks at a time.

III. METHODOLOGY

1. Creating the Information Base

Secondary data on demographic and socio-economic characteristics at district, block and village level was collected from the census data-base and from officials at the District Headquarters. Official statistics relating to population, age-wise breakups, economic status, prices, land use, cropping patterns, nutrition statistics, government feeding and vitamin supplementation programmes and immunisation campaigns, etc., were collected from the relevant departments. The field and household level information was gathered both through structured questionnaires and RRA techniques.[1]

The basic tools which are used for Rapid Rural Appraisal were utilised to collect information from the villagers, identify and prioritise their problems and trace the root causes of these as perceived by the respondents. The tool set included social and resource maps, seasonal calendars, daily calendars, pie charts, bar charts, Venn diagrams, problem and objective trees, etc. The methodologies used at the village level included Focus Group Discussion (FGD), Rapid Rural Appraisal (RRA) exercises and Household Interviews. The common problems discussed with the groups were verified by the semi-structured household interview schedule, which was mostly kept open-ended.

An intensive discussion with the District Magistrate at Pauri was revealing in terms of the field level problems faced by the district officials in implementing existing government schemes. Enhancing food security or improving the nutritional status of the population was not given much importance as an objective in the proposed or existing development projects, as the area is not severely deficit in food. The officials did not readily perceive the existence of other food-related problems, such as under-nutrition or malnutrition. Following the discussion with the district magistrate, a meeting was organised with district officials from departments, which directly or indirectly impact upon nutrition. The departments represented were: Health, Women and Child Development, Education, Agriculture, Horticulture and Animal Husbandry. Each of the officials presented the schemes being promoted by their respective departments, indicating the rate of success achieved, the problems faced in implementation, etc. The district level meeting was followed by a meeting with block level officials in order to enquire into the background and identify any problems specific to the block. This block level focus was necessitated by the fact that Garhwal is a very large and diverse district comprising of both agriculturally well developed, accessible plains and backward, remote mountain regions.

The semi-structured interview technique was used in both villages. A stratified sample of 20 households in each village was selected on the basis of discussions with village officials, the participatory exercises and the social map drawn by the villagers. Each of the four team members visited five households. Thus, the entire village was transacted physically, as well as socially. This is particularly important as caste-cum-economic stratification in the villages is clear-cut and distinct.

In the preparatory stage before leaving for the field, the team members met and decided on the points for discussion and the information to be elicited at the village and household level. This set of open-ended questionnaires was then used by the team to gather household information.

The team covered about 10 per cent of the households in the larger village (Kevars) and about 25 per cent of the households in the smaller village (Gad Kamargaon). It was also found that certain questions like those relating to seasonal availability of food, work schedules, seasonal food habits, food preservation, food taboos, etc., tend to elicit the same answers within a village, even within a region. Hence, these questions could be asked at the group level, rather than at the individual/household level.

Members of the team who interviewed the poorer households found that the respondents tended to deflate their incomes and present a more dismal picture in the hope of attracting benefits in the form of doles or government subsidies. However, the discussions with block and village level functionaries, both preceding and following the interviews helped to get the real picture into focus. Also, as the interviews were held on a house to house basis, it was possible to cross-check claims through direct observations.

Since the fieldwork was undertaken in winter there was not much agricultural work for the people and the bad weather conditions contributed to keeping them indoors. As the village panchayat was informed in advance about the visit of the team, a cross-section of the village population with adequate women representatives made themselves available throughout the day, despite their tight daily schedule of household work, which included fetching fodder, fuel and water and taking care of children and livestock.[2] The composition of the participants was heterogeneous and included a cross-section by income, caste, age and gender.

2. Social and Resource Maps

Social and resource maps were prepared through people's participation to enable them to understand the settlement pattern, and get a clear idea of the distance of field, forest, source of water, road network, location of community assets, etc. The participants also identified the houses of the rich, poor, scheduled castes, etc. The group members identified their major problems by ranking and prioritising them on the basis of their severity. In the seasonal calendar, intensity and/or availability with reference to rainfall, cultivation, crop production, vegetable production, work, migration, dependence on the PDS, etc., was indicated for each month of a year. This exercise was carried out with the help of women. Similarly, in the fodder chart, availability of various types of fodder was shown against each month. Several other facets, such as maternal mortality and infant mortality rates over the last five years, the amount of each type of food consumed everyday, the relationship of various officials with the villagers and the extent of coordination between them were also covered.[3] In order to capture the severity of various health problems over the months, a seasonal health calendar was prepared. As the workload on women impacts adversely on their own health as well as caring patterns with reference to children and other family members, an attempt was made to carry out a time use study of women's work in winter and in summer (Table 1). The recall method was used to identify activities carried out at hourly intervals.[4] A food chart was also constructed to

Table 1
Time-use Survey of Women's Activities in Village Gad Kamargaon

Winter	Time (hourly intervals)	Summer
	04.00	Wake up
	05.00	Fetch water
	06.00	
Wake up	07.00	Send children to school
Prepare tea	08.00	Take out cattle, feed them, collect dung
Take out cattle, feed them, collect dung	09.00	Cook food
Cook food, send children to school	10.00	Collect firewood/fodder
Clean house, wash dishes, collect fodder and firewood	11.00	Work in fields, cook food
Work in fields	12.00	Eat
	13.00	Rest
	14.00	Fetch water
Fetch water	15.00	Work in fields
Bring in cattle	16.00	Bring in cattle
Cook food, feed family and eat	17.00	Cook food, serve and eat
Wash dishes	18.00	Fetch water
	19.00	Post harvest activities
	20.00	
Go to bed	21.00	
	22.00	
	23.00	Go to bed

Source: PRA Exercise.

assess the production of various foods and the quantities available to each household across the months. Problem trees and objective trees were drawn to list the major problems and the causal factors as perceived by the participants.

IV. FOOD SUPPLIES AND THE PUBLIC DISTRIBUTION SYSTEM

As mentioned above, the district, in general, and particularly, Block Pauri, is largely dependent on subsistence agriculture. The practice of traditional methods of cultivation, the existence of small and scattered landholdings and the total dependence on the already overburdened women farmers results in low productivity levels with agricultural output being barely sufficient to supply the average household with foodgrain for a period of three to four months. The region is thus heavily dependent on the PDS, which ensures a steady supply of rice, wheat and sugar. Both officials and villagers attested to the effective functioning of the PDS. However, as in other regions, the amount available per family is limited and can thus at best augment, but not entirely substitute foodgrains available from other sources. Thus, seasonal food distress is common among the BPL families, who at times, have to reduce food consumption to a single meal a day.

Paddy is harvested in October and rice supplies last till about May, at the most. Provisions for two to three months' supply is more common. Supplies of coarse grains like *mandwa, jhangora* and pulses, which also run out within the same time span, supplement the rice output. In May, wheat is harvested and food is available till July. The months of August and September are critical for the region, as not only do the foodgrain stocks run out, but this period also coincides with the monsoons, consequent landslides and the cutting off of the region from the plains and access to outside food supplies (Table 2). The government deals with this problem by maintaining three months' stock of wheat and rice in the local godowns. This pattern of seasonal malnutrition has been observed in other parts of the country, e.g., in Orissa, where June is the leanest month (Agnihotri, 1999) in Madhya Pradesh where food shortages peak between July and August and in Chattisgarh, where food begins to run short as early as April (Barme and Ramachandran, 2002).

For landless labourers, this period becomes even more critical as their source of income is agricultural or other manual labour such as construction, which also stops during the rains. However, food shortages do not lead to starvation, as foodgrain stocks are available on credit from the privately-run village shop. The strong social support system in the village also ensures that no one actually faces starvation. This was evident from the case of an aged widow living alone on a meagre government pension in village Kevars, who was provided food by a group of neighbours, in turn. The situation serves to underline the fact that even well-intentioned government schemes like the Old Age Pension Scheme are unable to ensure food security to the beneficiaries, as not only is the amount given, meagre, but also, the money transfer is erratic. In the same

Table 2
Seasonal Calendar: Village Kevars

	March	April	May	June	July	August	September	October	November	December	January	February
Rainfall				Yes	Yes	Yes				Yes	Yes	Yes
Crops		Wheat, peas, mustard		Corn				Soybean	Pulses			
Vegetables			Onion, potato, vegetable marrow		Pumpkin, okra, cucumber, snakegourd				Mustard greens			
Fruit					Peaches, apricots, walnuts							
Agricultural tasks	Plough-hing	Harvesting of wheat, threshing, weeding					Mauring			Harvesting		Ploughing
Wage labour							Yes	Yes	Yes	Yes		
Migration		Yes	Yes									
Food scarcity	Yes	Yes			Yes	Yes						

Source: PRA Exercise.

village (Kevars), around 25-30 households out of a total of 182, were identified, by the village women, as having insufficient food.

A government-sponsored mid-day meals scheme operates for school children in all schools.[5] However, the original concept of a hot meal has been replaced by giving each child three kilos of rice per month, which goes to supplement the family rations.

Diet Patterns

An attempt was made to detail daily and seasonal diet patterns in order to observe whether changing food preferences and diets documented at the macro level hold true in these remote rural areas. It was quite evident from the survey that such changes have not yet percolated to the village level. The daily diet is still heavily dependant on foodgrain, particularly cereals. About two-thirds of the total diet is composed of *rotis* made of *mandwa* or wheat. Pulses account for about 20 per cent of the diet, while green vegetables have a share of about 10 per cent. Vegetables are consumed on a daily basis when plentiful, i.e., during the monsoons. In winter, however, the consumption is reduced to negligible amounts, especially among the low-income households. While the tradition of sun drying certain vegetables like pumpkin, bitter gourd and radish and storing them for winter use, continues, most of the poorer families do not have surplus production to preserve. A balanced diet, including dairy products and animal proteins on a regular basis, is quite unknown, even among the higher income families. Consumption of milk and curd is occasional. Although, nearly every family owns a cow, milk production is very low and milk does not form part of the daily diet, except as a whitener for tea. Many of the BPL (below poverty line) families drink only black tea. Infants receive milk only as long as they are breast-fed. In case the family owns a cow, they may receive milk for a longer period for children (up to the age of 2-3 years). Several of the poorer families feed their infants on a gruel of flour and water. As regards other livestock, only a few families keep goats or chickens which are sacrificed on festive occasions, when family and friends feast on meat. Animal proteins do not form part of the daily diet either in the form of milk, milk-products, eggs, meat or fish. This situation prevails despite the fact that the majority of the families are non-vegetarian and relish animal foods.

V. HEALTH STATUS AND PRACTICES

As mentioned above, in the poorest families, infants are fed on a gruel of flour and water, if the mother cannot breast feed. Significantly, the ICDS worker in village Gad Kamargaon stressed the fact that most women in the village do not have sufficient breast milk to feed the newborn. Thus, it is a common practice to feed infants on diluted cow milk. Powdered milk is quite unknown.

However, data recorded at the ICDS centre in each village reveals that cases of severe infant malnutrition do not exist (Table 3).

Table 3
Levels of Infant Malnutrition in the Sample Villages

Village	Number of children aged		No. weighed in February	Ist grade malnutrition	2nd grade malnutrition
	7-36 months	36-72 months			
Kevars	45	37	23	9	1
Gad Kamargaon	20	70	25	5	–

Source: ICDS Registers in the sample villages.

Children between the ages of three and six years attend the ICDS centre daily for a period of 4 hours (9.00 am–1.00 pm in winter and 8.00 am–12.00 noon in summer). Here they are checked for cleanliness, fed a daily supplement of nutritious biscuits or *panjiri* (a cereal/sugar/ghee mix—80 gram) and given pre-primary training. Children falling in the grade II malnutrition category are given double rations, if their weight is near the grade III cut-off point.[6]

However, children below the age of three years who do not have access to the child care centres tend to be rather neglected. This was found to be the case in the scheduled caste hamlet which was at a distance from the *Anganwadi* centre located in the main village. The overload of work on the women considerably impairs their caring capacity—the infant is usually left alone at home, while the mother works in the fields. This is a major problem in nuclear families.

In the afternoons, the child care centre functions as a mother and infant care centre where pregnant and lactating women are given health care and nutrition advice as well as weekly rations of food supplement (160 gram per day). Children below the age of 36 months are also weighed in these centres. These centres are also used to administer polio drops on fixed dates. The most common type of malnutrition among the pregnant/lactating women and pre-school children apparent from the observations is Iron Deficiency Anaemia (IDA).

Large proportions of women were found to be suffering from back pain and general weakness. This problem, according to the Chief Medical Officer of the District, could be attributed to overwork, inadequate diet and worm infestation due to lack of care in observing personal hygiene and unhygienic surroundings. While piped water was available in both villages, water supplies tend to dry up in summer. The cold climate and shortage of fuel for heating tend to restrict the usage of water. Sanitary toilets were found in the houses of some of the middle and higher income houses, but no common toilets exist. The government does have a loan scheme for the construction of sanitary toilets, but this has not been utilised by all the families. Disposal of household waste is done by either dumping it over the hillside or in the stream (where it further contaminates the water supply) or on the open compost heap. This leads to the problem of flies spreading infectious diseases like diahorrea and dysentery, jaundice and typhoid, which flares up in the warmer months.

Certain foods including buttermilk, green leafy vegetables, whole legumes and eggplant are taboo for pregnant women. It is believed that leafy vegetables eaten by the mother would cause worm infestation in the child. Infants are breast fed immediately after birth. There is no ritual of discarding the colostrum, though this practice did exist in the past. The child is introduced to solids between the ages of four to six months, but this is usually in the form of a piece of salty bread being handed to the baby, rather than carefully prepared weaning foods. The mother is not given any special diet after delivery.

Since the Himalayan region is known for iodine deficiency diseases, an attempt was made to enquire into the availability and use of iodised salt in both villages in general, and at the household level, in particular. While all the respondents were aware of the benefits of consuming iodised salt due to government-sponsored awareness campaigns, none of the low-income families used it, as its price was almost double that of ordinary salt. Unlike in urban areas, salt is purchased in fairly large quantities in these villages, as the salt consumed by the household is also given to the cattle.

However, a group of villagers belonging to the lower castes in village Gad Kamargaon did use iodised salt despite its high price, in response to a local awareness campaign by a Youth Group leader (Nehru Yuva Kendra) who belonged to their caste.

1. Sustaining Livelihoods

While out-migration of young able-bodied males is common, there is no significant trend in the migration of families among the people. The average income per family is about Rs. 3,000 per month. Almost all the families have some amount of cultivable land (15-20 *nali*, i.e., ½ to 1 acre) and some cattle, but large landholdings are rare. However, the percentage of men working in the fields or outside is insignificant. Tradition dictates that men may seek occupations outside the region, the army being the first choice, but working their own fields or taking up petty jobs within the village is frowned upon. As a result, gambling and the consumption of liquor among the men has become a way of life. Negative attitudes and the availability of government assistance have resulted in a well-entrenched dependency syndrome with a general unwillingness to help themselves. There is an obvious lack of motivation and little enterprise in the region—even able-bodied men retired from the army tend to live on their pensions and very rarely turn to another occupation or business venture.

In such a situation none of the households produce excess output to sell. All the farm output is consumed at home within a period of three to four months. For the remainder of the year, they have to depend, to a large extent, on purchased food supplemented by the allocation from the public distribution system. Some of the low-income families report that they have to resort to loans, either in cash or in kind (foodgrain), during the hungry period. These loans are, usually, returnable in the form of labour.

2. Issues for Consideration and Action

Based on the discussion with the district and block officials and the RFSNA carried out in the two selected villages, the team identified certain points for action which were presented at the wrap-up meeting with the officials. These are:

(i) In view of the prevailing seasonal food distress, particularly during the monsoons from July to September when the opportunity for earning a living through manual labour is considerably reduced, could additional job opportunities be created during this period?

(ii) Quick-ripening seeds are being specially developed for these high altitude areas, but there are no takers because of their high price. Could these seeds be initially provided at subsidised rates?

(iii) There is no evidence of preference for fine grains among the villagers. They appear to relish local coarse grains and are aware of their nutritive value, but unfortunately these are not available in fair-price shops or in the open market. Could coarse grains procured from neighbouring areas be supplied through the PDS or through a panchayat-anchored local food security scheme (grain bank)?

(iv) Local diets are totally deficient in proteins. Would it be possible to focus dairy promotion efforts on improving the quantity and quality of household supplies, rather than on commercial production?

(v) Government health programmes focus solely on pregnant and lactating mothers and infants. Since women and children in other age groups also need help could the government broaden the scope of the existing programmes?

(vi) In village Gad Kamargaon, a youth group leader had made a tremendous impact on low-income households, who were all consuming iodised salt because of his campaign, while the better-off and more educated families were not. If a local youth group could make such great impact on the villagers, could they not be actively involved in other health and nutrition improvement endeavours?

(vii) The Himalayan Region has been identified as an IDD (iodine deficiency disorder) endemic region. While all the villagers are aware of the need for using iodised salt, very few use it because of its high cost. Could the government provide iodised salt at subsidised rates? (It appears that a scheme to supply iodised salt through Fair Price Shops will soon be implemented).

(viii) Primary school children are being imparted the basics of nutrition and health education including the vitamin content of different foods, ways in which drinking water can be purified, constituents of a balanced diet, etc. Adults, however, have no access to such information. As such it would be worthwhile to consider whether nutrition education can be incorporated into adult literacy classes.

(ix) In remote and inaccessible areas, self-sufficiency in food seems to be imperative. Could food policy focus on improving local productivity, rather than solely on supplying subsidised food?

VI. CONCLUSIONS AND POLICY IMPLICATIONS

The current food policy evolved in response to certain needs: the need for self-sufficiency in foodgrains and the need to eliminate starvation. We have now reached the point where these two objectives have been to a large extent, realised. The time is now ripe for a change in direction. The most pressing needs in terms of food security today are to combat undernutrition for at least one-third of the population and malnutrition for a much larger proportion of the people. This calls for a widening of the scope of the food policy, as well as a broadening of its objectives. It is no longer sufficient to have a food policy which is merely a 'foodgrain policy' or—to narrow the definition even further—a 'cereal policy'. The urgency of reducing food subsidies as well as ensuring that the investment brings greater returns in terms of a better nourished and healthy population calls for new policy initiatives.

The existing food policy with its focus on foodgrain production and subsidised distribution and the nutrition supplementation programmes of other departments with their emphasis on eliminating child malnutrition and micro-nutrient deficiencies need to be synergised. Experience reveals that sustainable food and nutrition security can be achieved only through food-oriented policies. The provision of food supplements can, at best, be a short-term remedial measure. The most successful approach is likely to be a combined strategy that addresses the needs of both increased production and increased consumption and also meets those of special groups such as children and women of child-bearing age (FAO and ILSI 1997). For example, the high incidence of PEM (protein-energy malnutrition) is being dealt with by providing supplementary feeding to malnourished children and pregnant and lactating women. A more comprehensive approach would be to link this issue with the sharp fall in per capita availability of pulses. Protein deficiency, could perhaps, be stemmed by introducing pulses as an item under the PDS. Apart from boosting the availability of protein, it would also serve to address the problems of regional imbalance in agricultural subsidies. As the field study revealed, even in an area where the majority of the population are non-vegetarian, meat forms only a negligible portion of the diet. Thus, the protein deficiency prevalent in the majority of the low-income diets could be remedied on a more sustainable basis and at a more economic cost by the inclusion of vegetable protein in the diet. In this context, it also becomes necessary to review the forecasts of foodgrain demand made on the basis of the existing trends among predominantly meat-eating populations in other developing countries.

A restructured food policy based on a comprehensive approach as discussed above could be built around the following elements:

(i) Linking of the inclusion of local coarse grains in the PDS with decentralised procurement.

(ii) The enlargement of the PDS commodity basket to meet nutritional requirements by the inclusion of vegetable protein in the form of pulses, soy bean flour, soya nuggets or granules, and, perhaps, even soya or groundnut milk.

(iii) The replacement of sugar distributed through the FPS by *gur or khandsari,* which would have the advantage of being cheaper, providing support to the small-scale *gur/khandsari* units, and forming an additional source of iron and the B-complex vitamins.

(iv) The sale of iodised salt through the PDS at subsidised rates to effectively counter iodine deficiency.

(v) The sale of Nutri biscuits/*Panjiri* at the fair-price shops so that these cheap food supplements are available to the general population at a price, as well as for free distribution to the target groups under the ICDS. This would have the additional advantage of boosting the demand for such products and at the same time encourage the local food processing industry.

Notes

1. As one of the team members was based at the District H.Q., rapport-building with government officials began well in advance of the field trips. This contributed significantly towards ensuring participation in the district and block level meetings which preceded the fieldwork, as well as considerably reduced the time required for conducting the village surveys, as village level workers were briefed in advance by their superior officers.
2. The initial meeting with the villagers was held at a community hall (Panchayat Ghar at Kevars and primary school at Gad Kamargaon), where everybody could assemble. This was important in this part of the country, as casteism is deeply rooted in the social system, as is evidenced in the isolated hamlet outside the main village inhabited by the scheduled castes, apart from many other practices.
3. The officials selected for the exercise included the school teacher, village level worker, Block Development Officer, Auxiliary Nurse-Midwife, ICDS Supervisor, Agricultural Officer, Village Headman, Anganwadi Worker, Forest Guard, Watershed Development Officer, and the Veterinary Officer.
4. The schedule is extremely tight in summer, as there is scarcity of and greater need for water, and so, women tend to get a mere four hours sleep at night apart from an hour's rest during the day, in summer. A substantial amount of time (about four hours) is also devoted to fetching fuelwood and fodder as they often have to walk several kilometers for this purpose. Life is more comfortable for them in winter as they can afford to get up at about 7 am and go to bed as early as 9 pm.
5. There are several government programmes in operation for improving the health and nutrition status in the region. These are sponsored by different departments of the central and state governments. The major schemes being implemented by various ministries are: (i) The Ministry of Health and Family Welfare implements the following programmes: Family Planning Programme, Immunisation Programme, Vitamin A Prophylaxis Programme, PHC (Primary Health Centres), which provide medical facilities within easy reach of every village and also send an Auxiliary Nurse-Midwife (ANM) to every village on a bi-weekly visit. This health worker also carries out health check-ups in the village school and maintains records at the PHC. Midwife kits are provided to traditional village midwives after a three-month training course at the PHC. (ii) Ministry of Women and Child Welfare operates Integrated Child Development Services, which maintain health records and provide health care, health and nutrition education and supplementary feeding to pregnant and lactating mothers, infants and children aged 3-6 years through a network of 308 *Anganwadi*

centres. (iii) Ministry of Food and Consumer Affairs through its Public Distribution System provides subsidised foodgrains, sugar and kerosene oil at differential rates to families above and below the poverty line. While this system exists all over the country, it is the only means of survival during the lean period in the mountains. Thus, it seems to function fairly efficiently and with far less corruption than elsewhere. The Ministry is also associated with the mid-day meals scheme through which every school-going child is issued 3 kg of rice provided he records 85 per cent attendance. (iv) The Ministry of Agriculture and the Department of Animal Husbandry has introduced a Dairy Promotion Scheme to collect small surpluses of milk from villages along a milk route, centralise and market it; The Ministry also implements a programme (White Revolution) to upgrade the livestock, especially milch cows in the areas. (v) The Ministry of Rural Development operates a Fodder Promotion Scheme to reinforce the dairy promotion scheme by increasing supplies of green fodder. The Integrated Rural Development Programme (IRDP) of the Ministry provides loans to BPL families to augment sources of income through self-employment. The Nehru Rozgar Yojana (NRY) provides three months employment with wages in cash-cum-foodgrain to at least one member of each household. The Department of Horticulture supplies improved varieties of seeds and promotes research aimed at producing quick-ripening varieties suitable for high altitude farming and also distributes fruit tree saplings on demand for kitchen gardens and (vi) The Ministry of Forests implements the *Van Panchayat* Scheme aimed at providing a community forest, where villagers can collect fuelwood and fodder under the supervision of the panchayat.

6. For Grade II children, the mothers are advised on improving their diet. Grade III are referred to the primary health centre and given double rations.

Note

1. Indian Council of Medical Science, New Delhi, 1998.

References

Agnihotri, S.B. (1999), "Eliminating Severe Malnutrition in Orissa, Profile of a Campaign", *Economic and Political Weekly*, December 18.

Barme, Catherine and Ramachandran, N. (2002), *Report of the PRA on Food Security Conducted in Selected States for the FAO-WFP Grain Banks Project*, January.

FAO and ILSI (1997), *Preventing Micro-nutrient Malnutrition: A Guide to Food-based Approaches*, Food and Agricultural Organisation and International Life Science Institute, Washington.

UNFPA (1999), *Population, Food Production and Nutrition in India*, United Nations Fund for Population Activities, New Delhi.

17

Food Security System and Its Operation: A Study of Some Villages in the District of Kalahandi, Orissa

K. Sarap and M. Mahamallik

I. INTRODUCTION

This paper deals with some aspects of food security system as it operates in some villages situated in the semiarid drought-prone area of Orissa. More specifically it discusses the access of the rural households to foodgrains as supplied by the Revamped Public Distribution System (RPDS) operating in the area.

Food security is defined as the ability of a household to have access to adequate food for all its members either by producing it or earning enough to buy it in the market. Economists talk about two types of food insecurity, namely, chronic food insecurity and transitory food insecurity. The latter is caused by fluctuations in agricultural output, which are mainly due to uncertain weather conditions. Given the fact that a large fraction of arable area lacks adequate and assured irrigation facilities, it has to depend heavily on the monsoon. A backward area is characterised by low and wide fluctuations in output, widespread poverty, unemployment and limited opportunities for income generation. In view of these constraints, provision of food security to the poor is crucial for households located in such an area. In the absence of adequate income to buy basic food items from the market, these households would either have to consume less or borrow on onerous terms and conditions to mobilise funds for buying them. In a broad sense, therefore, food security would be essential not only in terms of providing adequate food at a reasonable or low price but also generating enough income either through self-employment in own activities, and wage employment provided by the private or state-sponsored programmes.

Over the years, the central and state governments have introduced a number of schemes with the objective of alleviating poverty and providing social security to the poor people. Specifically, these schemes aim at enhancing self-employment, generate wage employment or transfer income to the poor to provide them food security. One such scheme is the Public Distribution System (PDS), which has been regarded as an essential feature of India's food security policy. It addresses the problem of chronic food shortage due to poverty by distributing the public stock of foodgrains at subsidised prices, and making it available for other poverty alleviation programmes. Similarly, the buffer stock policy of the government plays an important role in tackling the problem of transitory food insecurity through price stabilisation by transferring resources from regions of plenty to those of scarcity and/or from a food surplus area to a deficit one.

The provision of food security to the poor, in the context of structural adjustment programmes (SAP) being implemented in the country since 1991, has attracted increasing attention among social scientists in recent years. With the introduction of SAP, there has been a renewed interest in the functioning of the PDS, which has been criticised due to a number of reasons. These include the provision of an increasing and unmanageable subsidy for food thereby making it costly to maintain the leakage of the PDS items to the non-beneficiaries and consequently its marginal impact on food security provided to the vulnerable poor households despite large-scale intervention by the state.[1] In view of these flaws in the working of the PDS a number of suggestions have been made for its better functioning. It has been suggested that commodity-based targeting be introduced whereby the public delivery system supplies only commodities that are likely to be consumed by the poor. Accordingly, coarse cereals have been recommended for such targeting (Bhagwati and Srinivasan, 1993). Ahluwalia has advocated the use of the PDS only to cater to the needs of the very poor and the destitute (Ahluwalia, 1993). Parikh (1994) has suggested that on the basis of cost effectiveness, the PDS be substituted by an employment generation scheme that provides an equivalent amount of subsidy. Bhagwati and Srinivasan have emphasised the need to shift to a system of food stamp, whereby these are fixed in nominal terms or indexed to some commodity. However, all these critics of PDS were more concerned with the fiscal problem associated with the food subsidy than with providing food security to the poor (Mooij, 1999).

Recently, the central government introduced the Targeted Public Distribution System (TPDS) with a view to reducing the subsidy on food and to distribute the subsidised food to poor households only. Given the nature and structure of the food delivery system in a state like Orissa, it is unlikely that the benefits of the TPDS will reach the poor on a large scale. The functioning of the RPDS as it operates in a few villages situated in the district of Kalahandi would lend some support to this argument.

The structure of the paper is as follows: the first section discusses the trends in food production and operation of the PDS in Orissa over the years. The socio-economic characteristics of the study area and the access of rural households to the Revamped Public Distribution System (RPDS) are discussed in the second section. The third section analyses the operation of RPDS in the study areas and the last section presents a brief summary of the main findings of the study.

II. TRENDS IN PRODUCTION AND DISTRIBUTION OF FOOD (THROUGH THE PDS) IN ORISSA

Orissa is one of the few backward states in the country where the growth of the economy is very low with a high incidence of income poverty and malnutrition. About 48.56 per cent of people in the state were living below the poverty line as compared to 36 per cent at all-India level during 1993-94.[2] The state is characterised by a high infant mortality rate (IMR) and a high incidence of malnutrition among its children. During the year 1998, the IMR in Orissa was 98 and about 65 per cent of the children faced some form of malnutrition.

A large section of the state's population comprised of scheduled castes (SCs), scheduled tribes (STs) and casual labour with a high incidence of poverty. For instance, 38.41 per cent of population were SCs and STs, according to the 1991 Census, and the percentage (genderwise) of casual labour in the rural work force was 37.6 (male) and 41.3 (female) during the late 1980s. The economy of the state is predominantly rural with 86.62 per cent people living in rural areas against 74.29 per cent at the all-India level.

Out of the total active labour force in the state, 25 per cent are agricultural labourers and 38.7 per cent are cultivators. The agricultural labourers constituted more than one-third of the labour force in semiarid regions including those in the undivided district of Kalahandi and Bolangir. Of the total operational holdings (39.48 lakh during 1990-91), 80 per cent, forming 46.66 per cent of total operational area, belonged to marginal and small farmers (with holdings up to 5.00 acres). Thus, nearly three-fourths of the state's workforce is dependent on agriculture.

The state's agriculture is characterised by low production with wide fluctuations in crop output (Table 1). This is mainly due to uncertain weather conditions combined with lack of assured irrigation facilities in two-thirds of the arable area. In such a situation a less than normal rainfall results in crop failure and wide fluctuations in crop output leading to scarcity conditions, both, in terms of the availability of foodgrain at a reasonable price and jobs for the rural poor thereby reducing their income to buy foodgrain.

Thus, the state's economy is marked by heavy dependence on an uncertain agriculture. Besides, nearly half of its population lives in chronic poverty with very few employment opportunities.

Given this background, the recent changes that have taken place in the structure of the PDS and its working are discussed below.

1. Revamping of Public Distribution System in the State

In June, 1992, the Government of India launched a drive to 'revamp' the existing PDS, aimed at improving the access of poor households to the PDS

Table 1
Total Production and Allocation of Foodgrains through PDS in Orissa during the Period, 1987-88 to 1997-98 (in lakh metric tonnes)

Year	Total foodgrain	Total cereals	Rice as a % of total	Rice	Wheat	Total	Sugar	K. oil
1	2	3	4	5	6	7=5+6	8	9
1987-88	50.6	40.5	85.68	-	-	-	-	-
1988-89	70.0	58.9	89.98	-	-	-	-	-
1989-90	79.7	68.5	91.68	-	-	-	-	-
1990-91	58.0	54.5	96.88	-	-	4.29	-	-
1991-92	72.3	68.3	97.51	3.70 (54.01)	3.15 (45.98)	6.85	1.57	149832
1992-93	59.6	55.6	96.94	4.60 (65.72)	2.40 (34.28)	7.00	1.60	212348
1993-94	72.2	68.4	96.78	4.64 (63.22)	2.70 (36.78)	7.34	1.60	141493
1994-95	69.0	64.9	97.84	-	-	-	-	-
1995-96	67.8	63.7	97.64	7.90 (69.29)	3.50 (30.71)	11.40	1.58	271728
1996-97	48.1	46.1	95.88	10.20 (69.34)	30.66 (30.66)	14.71	1.79	300008
1997-98	66.1	63.5	97.80	5.95 (73.09)	2.19 (26.91)	8.14	1.68	311419

Note: Figures in parentheses indicate percentage of respective column.
Source: *Economic Survey of Orissa, 1998-99.*

and strengthening the delivery system of essential commodities in certain selected backward areas of the country. The RPDS was introduced in 1700 blocks, with the following objectives: (a) to increase the coverage of the population in the target areas (i.e., the population living in drought-prone areas, tribal areas, certain designated hilly and urban slum areas), (b) to improve the access of poor consumers to the PDS; (c) to increase the range of commodities supplied by the fair-price shops and (d) to provide selected commodities at prices lower than in the general PDS. Later, the scheme was extended to cover 1,775 blocks in the country. In Orissa, the RPDS was implemented in 143 Integrated Tribal Development Programme (ITDP) area and Drought-Prone Area Programme (DPAP) blocks till May 31, 1997. In these blocks new fair-price shops were opened and the allocation of food to them was enhanced.

In 1996, the Government of India decided to convert the universal PDS into a targeted PDS (TPDS), whereby the PDS would be targeted to specific groups. Under the TPDS the whole population was subdivided into two sections: one consisting of families below the poverty line (BPL) and the other those above the poverty line (APL). The block officer identified the BPL families with the help of the panchayat secretary, agricultural officers, and school teachers including persons associated with the National Sample Survey (NSS). Finally, the Gram Sabha approved the identification of the target group and the district officials selectively checked the list. Multiple criteria including household occupation, housing condition, number of earners and assets owned by the household etc., are taken into consideration in order to identify the status of the family. Instead of income level, expenditure analysis was undertaken for the purpose of identification. As per the prevailing policy the BPL families receive 10 kg of foodgrains (common variety of rice in Orissa) per month per family at half the level of the central issue price while keeping intact the already ongoing system of distribution at subsidised issue prices for those above the poverty line. Despite the fact that all these criteria had been adopted to identify the people below the poverty line our enquiries show that many of the poor have been omitted from the list of BPL families. The policy implies not only a reallocation of foodgrains between the BPL and APL families but also between different states within the country.

In Orissa, in all, the 143 RPDS and DPAP blocks where the RPDS was implemented the TPDS was introduced from June 1, 1997 with its focus on the needs of the poor. According to the new system adopted by the state government, all the rural families below the poverty line and enlisted in the BPL list in these blocks (143) are supplied with 10 kg of common rice per family per month at Rs. 2 per kg. All rural families above the poverty line, in those blocks, are supplied with the same quantity of rice per family per month at Rs. 4 per kg. In the remaining 171 blocks, all rural families below the poverty line having an annual income not exceeding Rs. 6000 and enlisted in the BPL list, as well as all the families (card holders) below poverty line in urban areas were also supplied with 10 kg of rice per family per month (*Economic Survey of Orissa, 1997-98*).

During the year 1997 (up to 31.12.1997) essential commodities were distributed to 75.6 lakh ration card holders through 24,571 fair-price shops. Of the total card holders, 82.89 per cent belonged to the rural areas. Similarly, 85.27 per cent of fair-price shops were located in these areas. With this background a brief review of the working of the PDS in the state is discussed below in the context of the need for and production of foodgrains therein.[3]

2. Working of Public Distribution System

The allocation and off-take of PDS commodities in the state, both in terms of total amount and as a percentage of allocation given, is low. The allocation of foodgrains as a result of introduction of the TPDS was 427,000 tonnes (Mooij, 1999), which notably, is below the level allocated during the year 1990 (429,000 tonnes). The off-take of grains from the PDS formed 7.70 per cent of the actual estimated consumption of rice and wheat during the year, 1993-94. Further, even though the state has 5 per cent of the total population of the poor in the country, its share of foodgrains supplied through the PDS was 4.2 per cent during the year 1995-96 (Thamarajakshi, 1997), i.e., before the introduction of the RPDS only about 25 per cent of rural households are reported to have purchased any cereal from fair-price shops. Clearly, the coverage of the PDS in terms of families as well as in that of allocation per household in the state has been very low. Furthermore, the percentage of foodgrains allocated to the state is low despite the fact that it accounts for a large share of the poor of the country. The allocation or supply of commodities to different states by the central government is based largely on demand from the states, which in turn is based on past utilisation in each case. The other factor that affects the demand for as well as the management of the PDS items by the states, is the extent of infrastructure development including the food delivery system prevalent in each state. In the case of Orissa, the lower allocation of foodgrains to the state, appears to be due to a lack of commitment by the state government to a strong public distribution system—which is reflected in the management of demand for these items.

It is noteworthy that even in a poor state like Orissa the amount of foodgrain allocated to the PDS is not lifted by the fair-price shops. There is a large gap between the allocation and off-take of these commodities. For instance, during 1995-96, about 53.70 per cent of allotted rice and 43.19 per cent of allotted wheat were not lifted (Thamarajakshi, 1997)[4] Among the factors that may have contributed to such a situation (Thamarajakshi, 1997, Balakrishnan and Ramaswami, 1997) are: (a) a narrowing of the gap between open market price and issue price of foodgrains supplied through the PDS and (b) a difference in the quality of the goods supplied through the PDS and the open market (Table 2). It is clear from Table 2 that the prices of rice, wheat and some other essential items in the open market have been rising in recent years, which is also reflected in the consumer price indices for agricultural labourers for food and general items (Table 3). Clearly, both the open market retail prices for food and the issue prices of cereals supplied through the PDS have increased substantially in recent years. As a result, the gap between the price of foodgrains in the open market and that of those supplied through the PDS has narrowed. This may discourage consumers from purchasing the PDS grains if the quality of grains supplied by it is not as good as that of those available in the open market.

The effective price paid by the consumers may be higher than the nominal price charged by the dealer given the fact that the cost of transactions of the PDS items is not insignificant (Nair and Sivanandan, 1995; Indrakant, 1995). The high transaction costs of the PDS dealers is due to factors such as the location of the fair-price shop in distant places, uncertainty in the supply of commodities, long waiting time in queues and the use of correct weight and measures. It is also true that the dealer, sometimes includes his transaction costs in the price, and thus increases the commodity prices illegally. Besides, lack of information about the time of supply may lead to a situation in which the card holder has to visit the fair-price shop time and again in order to buy the items. The RPDS rice is distributed by the panchayat secretary/officer, and since the panchayat headquarters is located in one of the villages that fall within the jurisdiction of a panchayat, card holders from the other villages covered

Table 2
Average Retail Market Price and Consumer Price Indices in Orissa

Year	Average retail price of rice	Average retail price of wheat	Average retail price of sugar	Year	Consumer price index of food	Year	Change in indexes of food
1993	5.18	4.48	12.63	1991-92	163	1992-93 over 91-92	5.23
1994	6.37	5.02	14.04	1992-93	172	1993-94 over 92-93	4.97
1995	7.14	5.15	13.48	1993-94	181	1994-95 over 93-94	11.27
1996	7.63	5.52	14.26	1994-95	204	1995-96 over 94-95	13.27
1997	8.22	6.18	15.21	1995-96	235	1996-97 over 95-96	4.86
1998	8.65	7.19	16.57-	1996-97	247	1997-98 over 96-97	3.52
-	-	-	-	1997-98	156	-	-
-	-	-	-	-	-	1997-98 over 1991-92	3633

Source: *Economic Survey of Orissa, 1998-99.*

Table 3
Landholding Pattern and Demographic Characteristics of Households in the Study Villages

Size class (in acres of operated area)	Percentage of HH in the group to total HH	Land owned per HH in acre	Average size of family	Percentage of worker to total members
		V-I		
Landless	36.29(49)	-	4.36	50.46
0.01-1.00	5.18(7)	1.00	4.28	60.00
1.01-2.5	25.18(34)	2.01	4.91	55.68
2.51-5.00	14.81(20)	3.88	5.1	62.74
5.01-10.00	14.07(19)	7.18	5.42	61.16
10.01&>	4.47(6)	16.92	7.67	60.86
Overall	100(135)	2.90	4.90	56.49
		V-II		
Landless	32.8(41)	-	4.02	60.00
0.01-1.00	3.93(5)	0.6	3.6	66.67
1.01-2.5	31.49(40)	1.97	4.25	61.17
2.51-5.00	25.19(32)	3.53	4.40	62.41
5.01-10.00	4.72(6)	7.89	4.67	64.28
10.01&>	2.36(3)	15.33	7.00	80.95
Overall	100(127)	2.26	4.27	62.24
		V-III		
Landless	29.13(37)	-	4.60	53.52
0.01-1.00	14.96(19)	0.72	3.94	48.00
1.01-2.5	38.58(49)	1.79	4.63	54.18
2.51-5.00	13.39(17)	3.59	4.64	50.63
5.01-10.00	3.15(4)	7.19	5.00	50.00
10.01&>	0.79(1)	18.25	7.00	71.42
Overall	100.(127)	1.65	4.55	52.76

Note: Figures in brackets represent absolute number.
Source: Field survey.

by this panchayat have to travel to the panchayat office for getting their quota of rice. Given the underdeveloped infrastructure, especially in respect of roads and communication, the small number of fair-price shops and the fact that the shops are open only for three to four days in a month, the transaction cost for obtaining the food items is crucial for many consumers.

The quality of grains supplied through the PDS[5] may also influence the user's willingness to lift it. The perception of intrinsic quality difference as well as the cost of transaction may be individual/group specific. Similarly, the effective cost of buying grain from the PDS differs among different groups of consumers. Thus, consumers who have access to the PDS, would buy goods from it only if the cost of doing so is lower than the open market price and vice versa (Balakrishna and Ramaswami, 1997).

Factors that Affect Purchase of PDS Grains

The off-take of the PDS grains may vary with the change in seasons in that it may be low during certain periods of the year. It has been found that in the case of wheat the off-take is minimum when the difference between the issue price and the open market price is at its lowest and rises as the gap between the two prices widens. But in backward regions and during lean periods of this state, many poor card holders may not buy the PDS items because of lack of income due to inadequate availability of work even when the issue prices are very low compared to market prices. In such a situation one possibility is to borrow funds from the private moneylender to buy the PDS items when the open market prices of these items are high. It is difficult to obtain loans for such purposes in the rural areas because the lender in these areas knows the purpose for which funds are being borrowed. In case he manages to borrow funds and buy the PDS items he has to repay the loan either in kind or cash obtained by selling the items. Clearly, some users of the PDS may not lift the PDS items due to shortage of funds, or, if they do buy them with the help of borrowed funds, then they have to repay the loan obtained to buy these items (see below). This may discourage them from lifting the items.

Given the low income of users, lower availability of foodgrains from the PDS and the rising open market price, some poor consumers may opt to buy low-priced grains (such as *bajra, gurji, kudos*) as well as resort to collection of minor forest products for their survival. In the tribal semiarid belt of the state, our field information shows that during the periods, March-June and August-September, a large number of poor households purchase these items.

Lastly, the inadequate infrastructure, particularly in the inaccessible rural and tribal areas, especially during the rainy seasons, creates obstacles in the transportation of the PDS goods from the district to the storage agents and from there to the villagers.[6] In view of this constraint, the lack of income during the period when the PDS items are being lifted is a crucial factor in influencing their purchase. In such cases many users may not buy the grains if they are not available in the village or they do not know how to reach the PDS items or have no funds to buy them.

Thus, it is clear that a number of factors including the poor accessibility of fair-price shops, poor quality of goods supplied, low level of income at the time of arrival of the PDS items and rising effective prices of the PDS items affect the purchase of allotted foodgrains to the PDS.[7] In the case of poor households lack of purchasing power limits their access to foodgrains, as explained above.

3. Food Production and Consumption in the State

It has been found that the per capita consumption of cereals in Orissa is relatively higher as compared to other underdeveloped states. For instance, the per capita cereal consumption in rural Orissa has increased from 15.22 kg in 1972-73 to 15.93 kg in 1993-94—an increase of 4.66 per cent (Rao, 2000). By contrast, there was a decrease in per capita consumption of cereals in all other major states as well as at all-India level except in West Bengal.[8] The per capita consumption of cereals is higher despite the fact that the allocation and off-take of cereals for the PDS in the state is low (Thamarajakshi, 1997). The estimated requirement of cereals for the state for 1993-94 was 4.90 million tonnes in comparison with the actual consumption of 6.2 million tonnes (Thamarajakshi, 1997). Further, the trend in the production of cereals during the 1990s varies between 5.5 to 6.8 million tonnes with wide fluctuations. Given such erratic behavior in the production of cereals any shortfall in rainfall may decrease production.

From the food security point of view, the food situation both in terms of the amount of production as well as distribution is unsatisfactory. This is because it is not only the physical access to food—but the purchasing power of the people, which can come through the generation of employment that is important. Considering the fact that more than four-fifths of rural households in the state have very small landholdings and a significant proportion of them hire out labour, in the absence of adequate work their incomes are inadequate to meet the required food consumption. As a result, many of them may have to finance the food expenditure through borrowings from private sources. Our micro studies/findings support this trend (see section II). It is significant that even the allotted foodgrains from the fair-price shops have not been lifted by many consumers during the lean seasons due to lack of work and income.

III. WORKING OF THE RPDS IN KALAHANDI DISTRICT

This section discusses the functioning of the RPDS as it operates in the three villages in the district of Kalahandi situated in the arid zone of the state. The analysis is based on primary survey data specially collected for this purpose. Two blocks, namely, Golamunda (Block I) and Sinapali (Block II), have been chosen and two villages from block I and one village from block II have been selected purposefully by taking into account factors such as distance from the block headquarters, composition of population of the village, availability of infrastructure facilities, etc. Of the three villages selected, Village I is least developed followed by Village II (located in Block I) and Village III (located in Block II). The number of households varied from 127 in Village I to 135 in Village III. More than 60 per cent of households belong to SC and ST categories. The infrastructure facilities available in the villages are given in the Appendix.

Agriculture in all the villages is of a subsistence nature. Irrigation facilities are negligible, which clearly indicates the poor state of agriculture in the area. Farmers utilise modern technology such as HYV seeds and chemical fertilisers in small amounts on their land. Despite the occurrence of crop failure at frequent intervals, state intervention to fight drought or provide employment for drought relief and income generation is very limited.

1. Data Base and Study Area

The study is based on the information collected from all the households residing in the villages. A team of two research scholars, who can speak and write the language known to the people of the study area, one of whom belongs to the area, collected the data. The information relating to socio-economic and demographic conditions and on different aspects of the PDS from all the households in all the villages was collected during three periods: September-November, 1996; March-April, 1997, and August-September, 1997. The scholars later visited all the villages in order to fill up the data gaps.

Information relating to the public distribution system was obtained through a number of sources including the ration card of each card holder, which is checked to verify the entry of items in each period, dealers of fair-price shops, panchayat secretary and other knowledgeable persons in the villages. Further, the problems relating to the PDS were discussed with many individual card holders, dealers and others at the panchayat level in order to obtain information on the actual functioning of the system. Even though one ration card is issued per unit of household, it has been found that each household had more than one card, because it was treated as two units. This is despite the fact that they carry out all production and consumption activities together. Though a household unit is identified by its cooking arrangement, i.e., *chulha* in a house, it comprises families who cultivate the land jointly and share all expenditure incurred and income earned among themselves. This explains why a household may have two or three ration cards. Since the household has been taken as a unit of analysis, the average amount in respect of allotment and off-take per family is a fraction of this allotment and off-take of items allotted to per household. A brief description relating to the socio-economic background of dealers is as follows:

2. Socio-economic Background of Dealers and Households

(i) *Dealers*

As per the norm, the civil supply officer at the block level selects a dealer for the PDS out of the candidates recommended by the Sarpanch of the particular panchayat from the applications submitted by different persons. Even though, theoretically, anybody can apply for a dealership, political connections and the influence exerted by relatives do play a role in the selection of dealers. For instance, out of the three dealers in our studied villages, the dealer in Village I is a large farmer having about 10 acres of landholding. In the second village, the dealer owns six acres of land and is a relative of the Sarpanch of the same panchayat. In the third village, the dealer is a panchayat samiti member who was earlier an active worker of a political party. Clearly, all the three dealers are farmers and enjoy political and social clout in the village by virtue of their connections in the power structure. It is important to note that, of the three dealers, two have been dealers for the last five years and the dealer of the third village had been in the business for the last six years (1991-97).

The dealer has to lift the PDS items from the wholesale godown which is generally located at the block headquarters, and transport them to the village, for which he has to bear the transport and other costs involved. He also has to store the materials in his house. The cost incurred by him includes that for submission of draft to the CSO (block office), cost of transporting the items, labor cost for lifting the items, etc. As the location of the villages varies from 7 to 10 kilometers from the respective block headquarters all the dealers have utilised the bullock cart to transport the items. The dealers have to wait in queues for lifting the items because they come from several villages for this purpose by hiring a bullock cart and labour, which entails loss of time in waiting. Besides, they have to spend at least two days to deposit the draft and lift the items. Our enquiry from the dealers revealed that each of them received 5 kg less of sugar in a bag of one quintal of sugar and 10 kg less of rice at the time of lifting of these items. They said that the practice was maintained by the CSO to make up the losses incurred due to transport of items from the wholesale point to the storage point. It is noted that all the dealers have agriculture as their main occupation and distribute the PDS items in the villages only on three days in a week after getting the supply from the storage point.

In order to meet the expenditure incurred for lifting the items, the dealers charge the card holders 0.25 extra for rice and sugar above the normal issue price besides resorting to other means of raising revenue. This practice varies from region to region. For instance, in another village the dealer charged 0.25 paise and 0.75 paise extra for rice and sugar, respectively. Our enquiry from several card holders corroborated this practice. Besides, the dealers recover some money by selling grain bags and kerosene oil containers. It was found that since all the card holders did not lift the items within the stipulated time either because they were not present in the village or had no money to buy them or for some other reason, the dealers resorted to unfair practices like selling the remaining items in the black market (in the village or outside). It was also found that all the three dealers had obliged some influential persons in the villages by giving them some extra amount above the quota at a slightly higher price. In this way, the dealers have developed good relations with the politically important persons in the village. Furthermore, they also offer bribes in the form of some money to the high officials to win their favour.

It was also found that the dealers did not enter the amount purchased by the card holders in the ration card at the time of distribution of items. Instead, in a majority of cases, they would ask the poor or illiterate cardholders to surrender the cards for making the entry and collect it later.

(ii) Households

The socio-economic profile of households in the study villages discussed below provides a backdrop to the subsequent discussion.

The number and percentage of households belonging to landless, near landless, marginal, and small and medium and large farmers have been given in Table 3. The percentage of landless labour and near landless households to the total number of households varied from 37 per cent in Village II to 44 per cent in Village III. The percentage of farmers having land up to 5.00 acres, including the landless, constituted more than four-fifths of the total households in all the villages. They are mostly vulnerable to chronic poverty and unemployment and thereby food insecurity. This is reflected in their low income and employment status as explained below. Further, in the drought years even the medium farmers are affected adversely due to a decline in crop output.

The demographic features of different categories of households are given in Table 3. The average size of a family per household varied between 4.27 and 4.90 increasing with the size of the landholding. It increased with the rise in the landholding status of households in all the three villages. The worker-dependent ratio varied from 52.76 to 62.24 per cent. It was observed that in the case of landless, marginal and small farm households young children and old persons were engaged in part-time and/or full-time work in order to generate some income. Further, collection of property goods was a common feature of the villages covered in the study, especially among the poor households. By contrast, in medium and large farm families it was mostly the male members who worked in the fields and/or supervised the work of the labourers. The average size of land owned per household in the villages varied between 1.65 and 2.90 acres rising with the improvement in the status of farm households.

3. Employment Opportunities and Income Generation in the Study Villages

For ensuring effective food security to the poor it is essential to augment their purchasing power, which is reflected in their income, in order to enable them to have access to basic necessities such as food. The average number of days of employment (both wage and self-) available to each group of households varied from 94 to 153 days per household (Table 4). It was higher for the landless and land-poor households as compared to the medium and large farm households. Wage employment as a percentage of total employment (given in col. 4) varied from 78 to 90 per cent in the case of the land-poor groups across villages. As regards the number of days of employment obtained per household through JRY-EAS schemes in these villages, we found that its contribution to total wage employment varied from 7 per cent to 10 per cent in the villages (col. 9). In terms of income it varied from 8 per cent to 10 per cent of total wage income. Clearly, its contribution in the generation of employment and income in these villages was very low. On the whole, the amount of income derived from wage employment was low in all the villages.

The sources of income for a household include own (gross) activity, wage employment and free collection from common property (Table 4). It is clear from the table that the average income per household per year was very low for landless and land poor households in all the villages—it was less than half of the poverty line income norm adopted in the state. Of the total income generated, the percentage of income contributed by wage employment varied from 33 to 38 per cent across the villages. For landless and land-poor groups it exceeded three-fourths of their income. Thus, the landless and land-poor households not only had low incomes but had to depend primarily on wage employment,[9] which was very low and uncertain in the study area.

4. Expenditure Pattern of Households

The estimated expenditure on different items incurred by households of different size groups shows that expenditure on food formed about four-fifths of the total expenditure (Table 5). There is some variation in expenditure among the different size groups and in different villages. The expenditure per household of landless and marginal farmers was very low—it was about one-third that of larger farmers. Thus, there was a large inequality in the expenditure incurred by different groups.

The income and expenditure pattern of different size groups of households show that there was a large gap between the expenditure incurred (in percentage terms) and income among the poor groups of households (Table 5). In the case of landless, near landless and marginal farmers the gap was very large, as a result of which, these households had to borrow funds for ensuring their survival in different periods of the year.

IV. ACCESS OF HOUSEHOLDS TO PDS

The access of a household to RPDS is dependent on the identification of its members as residents of a village and inclusion in the list of eligible households for getting a ration card. As such a household has to have a ration card in order to be eligible to get its ration from the PDS. In this sense the household has a nominal access to the PDS. The *real* access to the

Table 4

Availability of Employment (self- and wage) and Income According to Different Size Groups of Households in the Study Villages

Size group (in acres)	Of the total days: Average days of employment	Of the total days: Percentage engaged in own land	Of the total days: Percentage engaged in wage employment	Of the total days: Of the total days engaged in wage employment percentage in JRY-EAS	Of the total income: Average income per HH per year (in Rs.)	Of the total income: Percentage coming from own production	Of the total income: Percentage coming from wage employment	Of the total income: Percentage from JRY-EAS	Of the total wage income: Percentage coming from common property resources	Of the total wage income: Percentage coming from migration
1	2	3	4	5	6	7	8	9	10	11
					V-I					
Landless	211	-	100.0	9.2	6589	-	100.0	8.68	4.97	48.31
0.01-1.00	193	23.6	76.4	3.8	6783	34.2	65.8	3.84	8.23	28.80
1.01-2.5	145	13.2	86.8	7.55	7710	54.4	45.6	15.53	08.07	14.89
2.51-5.00	124	17.5	82.5	2.21	11616	82.3	17.7	03.27	19.99	-
5.01-10.00	62	29.7	70.3	18.07	18994	96.3	3.7	33.14	11.99	-
10.01& above	79	24.0	76.00	-	62338	98.9	1.1	-		-
Overall	135	9.0	91.0	7.37	11851	66.7	33.3	10.07	7.15	34.33
					V-II					
Landless	156	-	100.0	19.6	4845	-	100.0	18.98	15.19	21.39
0.01-1.00	209	5.5	94.5	22.23	6536	21.2	78.8	25.60	35.30	-
1.01-2.5	149	12.2	87.8	1.3	6534	49.7	50.3	15.58	07.89	-
2.51-5.00	83	26.7	73.3	21.32	8199	84.4	15.6	30.21	09.96	-
5.01-10.00	121	23.0	77.0	3.61	21035	91.7	8.3	5.71	35.78	-
10.01 & >	21	100.0	-	-	62887	100.0	-	-	-	-
Overall	132	10.2	89.8	13.11	8425	61.9	38.1	19.09	14.11	10.43
					V-III					
Landless	155	-	100.0	7.2	5214	-	100.0	35.92	5.34	51.50
0.01-1.00	112	23.36	76.64	14.51	4086	33.4	66.6	13.57	22.17	24.36
1.01-2.5	52	60.5	39.5	10.67	4307	80.2	19.7	07.73	42.43	24.56
2.51-5.00	82	38.6	61.4	16.49	9617	91.0	9.0	28.52	50.32	-
5.01-10.00	43	78.8	21.4	38.89	23809	96.8	3.2	19.97	69.19	-
10.01 & >	32	100.0	-	-	62940	100.0	-	-	-	-
Overall	94	22.7	77.2	9.85	6325	62.2	37.8	8.27	16.89	40.19

Source: Field survey.

Table 5
Income and Expenditure Pattern of Different Size Group of Households in the Study Villages

Size group (in acres)	Income per HH per months	Estimated expenditure per HH per months	Percentage of expenditure on food items	Percentage of expenditure on non-food items
		V-I		
Landless	549	612	69.65	30.35
0.01-1.00	565	612	72.75	27.25
1.01-2.5	643	709	72.24	27.76
2.51-5.00	968	763	69.59	30.41
5.01-10.00	1583	938	68.14	31.86
10.01&>	5195	1580	64.44	35.56
Overall	988	748	69.26	30.74
		V-II		
Landless	404	438	71.85	28.15
0.01-1.00	545	462	68.39	31.61
1.01-2.5	544	532	75.63	24.37
2.51-5.00	683	671	74.12	25.88
5.01-10.00	1753	803	79.05	20.95
10.01&>	5240	1250	78.13	21.87
Overall	702	567	74.00	26.00
		V-III		
Landless	434	468	71.21	28.79
0.01-1.00	341	425	75.33	24.67
1.01-2.5	359	489	78.90	21.10
2.51-5.00	801	645	67.97	32.03
5.01-10.00	1984	769	70.24	29.76
10.01&>	5245	1400	71.78	28.22
Overall	527	510	74.00	26.00

Source: Field survey.

PDS is dependent on its members having money to buy the food items from the dealer after showing the ration card to him when he sells them. The purchase of the RPDS items by different groups of households is given in Table 6. It shows that there is some difference, as far as the nominal access is concerned, between the groups of landless, marginal and small farmers and that of medium and large farmers. Most of the households belonging to the latter group bought rice in all the three years. This is also largely true in the case of sugar and kerosene oil. By contrast, for the former groups, access to the PDS varied from 88 to 92 per cent in the case of rice, 70 to 80 per cent in respect of sugar and about 82 per cent in the case of kerosene oil in Village V-I and Village V-III. However, in Village V-II about 70 per cent of poor households bought rice, 64 per cent sugar and 61 per cent kerosene oil. Clearly, more than three-fourths of the poor households and more than 90 per cent of rich households have purchased the RPDS items in the study villages during the period of study. There is some variation in the number of items bought by the households in different years. The maximum number of times the RPDS items were distributed[10] was in 1996.

Clearly, the percentage of households having access to RPDS items in all the villages is very high. More than three-fourths of the poor

Table 6
Percentage of Households Buying RPDS Items according to Different Size Groups during the 1995-97 in the Study Villages

Size group	Rice			Sugar			K.oil		
(in acres)	1995	1996	1997	1995	1996	1997	1995	1996	1997
				V-I					
Landless	83.67	83.67	83.67	61.22	77.55	71.42	71.42	81.63	77.55
0.01-1.00	100.0	100.0	100.0	71.42	100.0	100.0	85.71	85.71	100.0
1.01-2.5	94.11	94.11	94.11	85.29	85.29	85.29	88.23	88.23	88.23
2.51-5.00	85.0	85.0	85.0	70.0	75.0	75.0	85.0	80.0	80.0
5.01-10.00	100.0	100.0	100.0	78.94	89.47	100.0	100.0	94.73	100.0
10.01>	100.0	100.0	100.0	83.33	100.0	100.0	100.0	100.0	100.0
Overall	90.37	90.37	90.37	72.59	82.96	82.23	63.71	85.33	85.93
				V-II					
Landless	60.98	60.98	60.98	48.78	56.1	51.22	43.9	56.01	56.01
0.01-1.00	80.0	80.0	77.5	60.0	40.0	40.0	40.0	80.0	80.0
1.01-2.5	72.5	72.5	77.5	55.0	65.0	67.5	52.5	60.0	65.0
2.51-5.00	81.25	81.25	78.12	75.0	78.13	71.88	59.38	71.88	62.5
5.01-10.00	83.33	83.33	66.67	66.67	66.67	83.33	83.33	83.33	83.33
10.01>	100.0	100.0	-	100.0	100.0	-	100.0	100.0	100.0
Overall	72.44	72.44	74.02	59.84	65.35	63.78	53.54	64.57	63.78
				V-III					
Landless	94.74	94.74	94.74	91.89	91.89	83.78	89.18	94.59	86.48
0.01-1.00	100.0	100.0	100.0	94.73	94.73	89.48	94.73	94.73	84.21
1.01-2.5	91.49	91.49	91.49	79.59	77.55	75.51	75.51	77.55	71.42
2.51-5.00	100.0	100.0	100.0	100.0	94.11	94.11	94.11	100.0	100.0
5.01-10.00	100.0	100.0	100.0	100.0	75.0	50.0	100.0	75.0	50.0
10.01>	100.0	100.0	100.0	100.0	100.0	100.0	100.0	100.0	100.0
Overall	94.49	94.49	94.49	88.97	86.69	81.89	85.83	88.19	81.11

Source: Field survey.

households and more than 90 per cent of the rich households have purchased items from the RPDS depots in the study villages during the period of the study. It was relatively higher in the case of rice in comparison with that of sugar and kerosene oil. Further, the percentage of households buying the items in village V-II was relatively less in comparison with villages V-I and V-III There is some inter-group variation in regard to the buying of these items in all the villages. But these percentages do not give the true picture as far as real access to the RPDS is concerned. For this, one has to know the actual amount received by different categories of households in absolute terms, and the actual amount of off-take in relation to their allotment, which is discussed herein:

1. Allotment and Off-take of PDS Items in the Study Villages

The off-take as a percentage of allotment of rice, sugar and kerosene oil for different years and for different size groups of households have been given in Tables 7 a, b and c. The overall off-take of rice in the backward village V-II and one of the other villages varied from 70 to 75 per cent during 1995 and 52 to 82 per cent during 1997. The percentage in 1996 was higher in both these villages. By contrast, in V-I the off-take during 1995 and 1997 was low in comparison with that in other villages while it was similar during 1996. As far as rice is concerned there was not much variation among different groups and in different years in both the relatively developed villages. However, in the backward village V-II it was lower for the poor groups. Clearly, the off-take of rice by the poor households in different villages was comparatively lower due to the fact that, of the total number of times rice is distributed, some households have either not lifted the full amount at the time when they had gone to buy it or they have just not gone to the shops in particular months. In the case of sugar and kerosene oil the total quantity distributed and the number of times they are distributed per year in all the villages during the study period was low. It was much lower in the backward village V-II.

Utilisation Pattern of BPL Rice

The utilisation pattern of rice received by different categories of households in all the villages is given in Table 8. As the quantity of sugar

Table 7a

Amount of Allotment and Off-take of RPDS Rice per HH during Each Year According to Different Size Group in the Study Villages

	V-I			V-II			V-III		
Size group (in acres)	Per HH off-take of rice (in kg)	Off-take as a % of allot-ment	No. of times received per HH per year	Per HH off-take of rice (in kg)	Off-take as a % of allot-ment	No. of times received per HH per year	Per HH off-take of rice (in kg)	Off-take as a % of allot-ment	No. of times received per HH per year
					1995				
Landless	40.54	45.04	3.97	64.17	71.30	5.46	62.68	76.23	6.18
0.01-1.00	40.00	44.44	4.0	57.5	63.89	5.5	59.15	73.55	5.89
1.01-2.5	40.32	43.45	4.03	65.77	73.08	5.42	56.85	71.06	5.57
2.51-5.00	41.17	43.20	4.11	62.80	69.78	6.28	60.23	75.28	5.82
5.01-10.00	44.37	46.83	4.37	84.0	93.33	7.0	66.75	83.43	6.50
10.01&>	45.00	42.85	4.5	70.0	77.78	5.5	60.0	75.0	6.0
Overall	41.32	44.45	3.57	65.23	70.18	5.78	59.83	74.11	5.88
					1996				
Land less	93.00	77.05	7.9	94.00	78.33	9.2	94.68	76.77	8.34
0.01-1.00	102.85	85.70	8.71	100.0	83.33	10.00	94.84	79.03	11.63
1.01-2.5	95.31	77.01	7.53	93.57	77.98	8.86	96.35	80.29	8.52
2.51-5.00	96.47	75.93	8.52	96.92	80.77	9.42	92.35	76.95	8.29
5.01-10.00	93.68	74.16	8.89	102.0	85.00	11.2	87.50	72.91	8.00
10.01&>	85.00	60.71	8.17	90.0	75.00	9.00	90.0	75.0	9.00
Overall	94.38	76.15	8.11	95.27	77.56	9.29	94.66	78.23	8.93
					1997				
Landless	38.25	47.81	3.37	60.33	50.27	4.63	103.34	83.78	7.5
0.01-1.00	37.14	46.42	3.71	62.5	52.08	4.75	98.94	82.45	7.26
1.01-2.5	37.09	44.95	3.54	28.65	23.87	4.29	97.07	80.89	6.82
2.51-5.00	39.41	46.52	3.17	65.5	54.67	4.84	104.7	87.25	6.76
5.01-10.00	39.47	46.87	3.57	90.0	75.0	5.75	97.0	80.83	7.0
10.01&>	46.67	50.00	3.83	66.67	55.56	5.33	30.0	25.0	3.0
Overall	38.67	46.81	3.47	65.23	52.98	4.65	99.82	82.49	7.07

Source: Field survey.

Table 7b

Amount of Allotment and Off-take of RPDS Sugar per HH during Each Year According to Size Group in the Study Villages

Size group (in acres)	V-I			V-II			V-III		
	Per HH off-take of sugar (in lt.)	No. of times received per HH	Amount received per time	Per HH off-take off sugar (in lt.)	No. of times received per HH	Amount received per time	Per HH off-take of sugar (in lt.)	No. of times received per HH	Amount received per time
				1995					
Landless	3.07	2.6	1.17	3.3	2.5	1.47	7.79	6.47	1.2
0.01-1.00	2.2	2.2	1.0	2.33	1.67	1.4	6.13	5.33	1.15
1.01-2.5	2.6	2.37	1.09	4.0	2.86	1.4	8.25	6.66	1.2
2.51-5.00	3.75	3.0	1.25	9.79	3.5	1.61	11.88	8.11	1.46
5.01-10.00	2.93	2.6	1.12	4.63	5.75	0.8	6.62	5.75	1.15
10.01&>	2.6	2.2	1.18	7.33	4.00	1.83	30	10.0	3.0
Overall	2.94	2.55	1.15	4.43	3.14	1.45	8.46	6.61	1.27
				1996					
Landless	3.82	2.86	1.33	3.17	2.87	1.11	8.79	6.85	1.28
0.01-1.00	3.28	1.85	1.76	4.75	5.0	0.95	7.22	5.55	1.3
1.01-2.5	3.05	2.82	1.04	3.62	2.81	1.29	8.64	7.0	1.23
2.51-5.00	4.13	2.6	1.58	5.1	3.72	1.37	12.9	8.56	1.5
5.01-10.00	3.85	2.82	1.36	4.08	7.0	0.58	8.33	7.33	1.13
10.01&>	4.67	2.5	1.86	7.33	4.67	1.57	22	10.0	2.2
Overall	3.68	2.73	1.35	4.13	3.42	1.21	9.19	6.98	1.32
				1997					
Landless	3.31	2.68	1.23	2.83	2.86	0.99	8.82	6.64	1.32
0.01-1.00	2.64	2.0	1.32	5.0	5.0	1.0	6.31	5.82	1.08
1.01-2.5	2.67	2.31	1.15	2.83	2.37	1.2	7.94	6.19	1.28
2.51-5.00	4.93	3.13	1.57	4.7	3.61	1.3	12.34	7.93	1.55
5.01-10.00	3.63	2.68	1.35	4.2	4.6	0.91	7.5	6.5	1.15
10.01&>	4.0	3.17	1.26	7.67	5.33	1.44	15	8.0	1.87
Overall	3.42	2.63	1.29	4.81	3.05	1.52	8.67	6.56	1.33

Source: Field survey.

and kerosene oil received per household was low, most of the households have utilised these items for self-consumption and did not sell or utilise them for other purposes because the price differential between the RPDS items and open market price was not very high. But in the case of rice the situation was different. The information relates to the year, 1996, as during this year we could obtain reliable data in this regard in all the villages. Further, it was during this year that the items were distributed to households the maximum number of times.

Out of all the households who bought rice through the PDS, 78 to 89 per cent utilised it for self-consumption and of the rest some did so partly for payment of wages and partly to repay the loan borrowed specifically to buy the RPDS items, or for some other purpose (allowing for the amount used for self-consumption). The percentage of households who utilised rice largely for self-consumption differed among different size groups. It declined with the increase in the status of household. For instance, the landless, near landless and marginal farmer groups utilised it mostly for self-consumption and sold the rest of it later in order to repay

Table 7c
Amount of Allotment and Off-take of RPDS Kerosine Oil per Household during Each Year According to Size Group in the Study Villages

Size group (in acres)	V-I			V-II			V-III		
	Per HH off-take of PD$ (in lt.)	No. of times received per HH	Amount received per time	Per HH off-take of PDS k. oil (in lt.)	No. of times received per HH	Amount received per time	Per HH off-take of PDS k. oil (in lt.)	No. of times received per HH	Amount received per time
				1995					
Landless	3.94	3.31	1.18	2.17	2.17	1.0	9.6	7.0	1.37
0.01-1.00	2.83	2.5	1.13	3.25	2.5	1.3	12.05	6.67	1.8
1.01-2.5	4.57	3.87	1.18	1.95	1.9	1.03	8.66	6.89	1.25
2.51-5.00	4.91	3.58	1.36	2.63	2.65	1.11	10.53	7.81	1.34
5.01-10.00	4.26	3.7	1.28	3.3	3.2	1.03	8.25	6.25	1.32
10.01&>	5.83	3.67	1.59	1.5	1.33	1.12	11.5	7.0	1.64
Overall	4.35	3.54	1.25	2.32	2.02	1.06	9.79	9.10	1.07
				1996					
Landless	5.85	4.22	1.38	4.22	4.04	1.04	9.71	6.11	1.58
0.01-1.00	5.0	3.67	1.36	3.5	3.0	1.17	8.02	6.5	1.23
1.01-2.5	4.75	3.76	1.26	4.06	3.96	1.03	9.96	6.42	1.55
2.51-5.00	4.43	3.61	1.51	4.43	4.3	1.03	12.14	7.11	1.7
5.01-10.00	5.8	4.17	1.39	6.2	6.2	1.0	9.83	6.33	1.55
10.01&>	7.83	5.5	1.42	5.3	5.33	1.0	12.0	8.0	1.5
Overall	5.42	4.06	1.37	4.36	4.22	1.04	9.92	6.46	1.54
				1997					
Landless	5.1	3.21	1.59	2.96	2.91	1.01	7.78	6.53	1.19
0.01-1.00	4.14	2.71	1.52	3.38	3.25	1.04	9.25	7.37	1.25
1.01-2.5	4.53	3.33	1.36	3.0	2.73	1.10	8.62	5.82	1.48
2.51-5.00	4.0	2.75	1.45	4.45	4.05	1.10	11.35	6.52	1.73
5.01-10.00	4.46	3.0	1.53	4.2	4.2	1.0	12.25	8.5	1.44
10.01&>	6.33	3.5	1.81	2.3	1.66	1.4	13.0	8.0	1.62
Overall	4.73	3.13	1.52	3.42	3.18	1.07	9.03	6.47	1.39

Source: Field survey.

their loan. By contrast, the medium farm groups utilised about 20 to 30 per cent rice for self-consumption, while the large farmers used none of it for this purpose. Thus, the medium and large farm groups utilised the rice partly for payment of wage and/or partly for selling it in the market (Table 8). As the household was taken as the unit of analysis we found cases of double counting (in terms of the number of households) in the utilisation of rice for self-consumption and repayment of loan. It is noteworthy that even some of the poor households had sold their rice, but only to repay their loan, which they had borrowed from private sources to obtain the PDS rice.

It is clear from the table that the percentage of households who bought the RPDS items out of the loan it obtained from the moneylender/shopkeepers varied from 14 per cent in Village I (least developed) to 25 per cent in Village III (relatively developed) In comparison with that of Village II. Further, this trend was more evident among the landless and marginal and small farm households in comparison with other groups.

Table 8

Sources of Funds Utilised and Amount Received from RPDS by Different Size Group of Households during the Year 1996

Size group (in acres)	Percentage of HH getting PDS item	Percentage of HH directly consuming the items	Percentage of HH used it for wage	Percentage of HH the items	Out of (2) percentage of HH linked with credit	Percentage of HH who bought through credit & sold to repay loan	Estimated required amount per HH per month (in kg)	Received amount as percentage of required rice (in kg)	Allotted rice as percentage required amount (in kg)
					V-I				
Landless	81.63 (40)	100.0	-	10.00*	25.00	10.00	43	18.02	23.26
0.01-1.00	100(7)	100.0	-	14.28*	42.86	14.28	43	19.93	23.26
1.01-2.5	91.17(31)	76.4790. 33	-	16.13*	12.91	6.45	58	13.69	17.78
2.51-5.00	85(17)	76.47	11.74	11.77	-	-	59	13.01	17.95
5.01-10.00	100 (19)	-31.57	42.11	26.32	-	-	60	13.63	17.54
10.01&>	100(6)	-	83.34	16.66	-	-	90	7.67	12.96
Overall	88.89 (120)	78.34	12.5	15.00*	14.17	5.84	54	14.56	19.13
					V-II				
Landless	60.97(25)	100.0	-	18.00*	36.00	16.00	33	23.54	30.30
0.01-1.00	80(4)	100.0	-	25.00*	50.00	25.00	36	23.15	27.18
1.01-2.5	72.50 (31)	93.55	-	6.45*	-	-	46	16.95	21.74
2.51-5.00	81.25 (26)	73.07	7.69	19.24	-	-	52	15.53	20.17
5.01-10.00	83.34 (5)	20.00	40.00	40.00	-	-	64	13.28	18.75
10.01&>	100(3)	-	100	–	-	-	97	7.73	10.30
Overall	74.02 (94)	82.98	7.45	14.89*	11.71	5.32	45	17.64	22.95
					V-III				
Landless	97.29(36)	100.0	-	8.33*	36.11	8.33	35	22.54	29.37
0.01-1.00	100(19)	100.0	-	5.26*	50.00	25.00	36	21.95	27.78
1.01-2.5	87.75(43)	90.69	-	16.27*	20.93	6.97	49	16.39	20.41
2.51-5.00	100(17)	70.59	23.53	11.76*	17.65	5.88	52	14.80	19.23
5.01-10.00	100(4)	25.00	50.00	25.00	-	-	49	14.88	20.41
10.01&>	100(1)	-	100	-	-	-	96	7.81	10.42
Overall	94.48 (120)	89.17	5.84	11.67*	25.00	6.67	44	17.93	22.92

Note: Figures in bracket represents absolute number. * indicates percentage of households who borrowed funds to buy the RPDS items and sold to the creditor to repay the loan.

Source: Field survey.

Clearly, as mentioned earlier in the absence of adequate income, these households had to get a loan from the moneylenders to finance their purchases of the PDS items and many of them sold a certain proportion of their items to them to repay the loan. It is noteworthy that nearly half of the households, who bought the PDS rice out of the loans obtained at very high rates of interest, did not sell the items in the market, but consumed it. In such a situation they would repay the loan later.

It merits mention here that for some poor households, the access to the PDS rice was dependent on the mercy of the moneylenders who provided them funds to buy the items. In reality, their access to it was illusory implying that their *effective* access was very low in these villages. The evidence of allotment and off-take of the RPDS items shows that even if three-fifths of the poor households had ration cards, many of them were unable to buy the allotted amount from the dealers due to lack of funds with them at the time of the arrival of the items in the villages. In such a situation they were forced to borrow the required funds from informal sources to enable them to buy these items and—repaid the loan by selling some of the items to the lender. Some of them were consumed, given the urgency to do so. Thus, needless to say, it is not only the availability of the RPDS items in the villages, but also that of income for the poor which is needed to enable them to have these items.

2. Off-take and Requirement of Rice by Different Groups of Households

We had estimated the requirement of rice for each family on the basis of the amount of rice a household had consumed per day in different periods of the year. In the case of landless and poor farmers this was reported to be 500 grams per adult per day as against 400 grams per adult for medium and large farmers. This, relatively higher amount of per capita rice consumption in the area was due to the fact that most of the poor households consumed rice three to four times a day while the consumption of other items was negligible. It is important to note that the poor households have also supplemented their diet with other cereals like *bajra, gurji* and *mandia* in different periods of the year. The estimated requirement of rice per household per month for different categories of households is given in Table 8, which shows the normative allotment as well as actual off-take of rice per household per month as compared with the actual requirement. The off-take of rice as a percentage of requirement varied from 14.56 to 17.93 for overall households in the villages. In the case of landless and near landless households it varied from 18 to 24 per cent and in that of marginal and small farmers from 17 to 23 per cent. Notably, the landless and other land-poor households had to depend on the market to satisfy three-fourths of their requirement.

Given the fact that a number of factors account for a lower off-take of rice by the poor households, even the of allotment of 20 kg of cereals per household per month as per the new policy will not satisfy even half of their requirement. As a result they have to buy foodgrains at the market price. In such a situation, unless there is an increase in their income, through a variety of measures, the new allotment policy may not serve the purpose of providing food security to the poor in these villages.

V. CONCLUSION

Our analysis of the food delivery system in the state clearly shows that its coverage in terms of percentage of households as well as the amount of foodgrains supplied through it is limited. Several factors including inefficient operation, poor infrastructure, poor quality of grains supplied and lack of income especially among the poor households have contributed to the poor performance of the system. Not surprisingly even the limited amount of foodgrains supplied to the state has not been lifted fully by the fair-price shops. Given such a food delivery system even if more and cheap foodgrains had been allotted to the poor it would have been difficult to reach them.

Considering that at the time when the study was undertaken half the population of the state lived below the poverty line, the effort on the part of the state government to ensure that the poor had better access to food was far from adequate. Essentially its success in reaching food to the poor depended critically on the thrust of its rural development policies, including the employment assurance programme. The micro studies on income and expenditure pattern showed that the majority of the landless and land-poor households had very low levels of income and expenditure and spent more than three-fourths of it on food items. Further, there was a large gap between the expenditure incurred by and income of the poor. The income generated through the employment assurance scheme had been negligible and thus did not contribute towards improving their lot.

The analysis of the access of households in the study area to BPL rice and other commodities revealed that a majority of them had ration cards and bought the food items from the dealers, but the amount supplied and bought by them (especially foodgrain) did not satisfy even a quarter of their actual requirement. Moreover, one-fifth of the poor users, who bought rice, had to obtain funds from the private moneylenders in order to buy grain from the fair-price dealers. These households repaid the loan by selling the same later to the lenders. In such a situation their *effective* access to the RPDS was low. As much as four-fifths of their requirement had come from the market and as such the supply of rice from the RPDS as a proportion of the total requirements was minimal. Furthermore, despite the elaborate criteria to identify the poor one-fourth of the landless and about one-fifth of poor farmers had no ration cards.

In the ultimate analysis, rapid rural development through the provision of irrigation and other rural infrastructure and a large scale employment generation programme is an essential prerequisite for providing effective food security to the poor in the study area.

(The authors are thankful to Sri Gagan Bihari Sahu and Mohan Kumbhar for collection and analysis of data and to Madhura Swaminathan and Jos Mooij for their comments and suggestions on an earlier draft of the paper).

Appendix
Infrastructure Facilities in the Study Villages

Villages	Panchayat office/ distance in km	Block/ distance in km	Nearest bus stop	Nearest railway station	Weekly market	Percentage of SC & ST population to the total	Institutions in the village
V-I	Kaigaon/	Golamunda/ 26km	Jorpada (one bus in a day)	Kesinga/ 48 km	Kaigaon /4 km	52.34	Primary school
V-II	Nandol/ 6 km	Golamun- 48 km	Gundri (one bus in a day)	Kesinga/ 42 km	Badcher gaon/8 km	54.08	Primary school, youth club
V-III	Sinapali/	Sinapali/ 7 km	Khalna (one bus in a day)	Kariar/ 25 km	Sinapali /7 km	70.35	Primary school, youth club

Source: Field Survey.

Notes

1. A number of authors have studied the functioning of the Public Distribution System in the country. These include Radhakrishna and Rao (1994); Radhakrishna et al. (1997); Dev and Suryanarayana, (1991); Rao, (1995); Ahluwalia, (1993); Jharmal, (1999); Swaminathan, (1996); Balakrishna and Ramaswami (1997); Parikh, (1994), Mooij (1999), Thamarajakshi, (1997), to mention a few.
2. The percentage of rural poor in the state, according to Lakdawala Committee, was much higher (57.64 per cent) than the official estimate.
3. This section provides a brief summary of the findings in literature as mentioned in the section I.
4. There is another dimension of this gap between allocation of the PDS foodgrains and what is lifted for distribution at the village level. The dealer of a fair-price shop lifts the allotted amount for the village after paying the storing agent through a draft. At the village level some card holders do not buy the grains either, because they do not have the required information or have no funds or are not available in the village, in which case the dealer sells the amount in the open market. As a result, the actual lifting of the PDS grains would be higher.
5. The poor quality of rice supplied by the PDS is not due to the fact that the Food Corporation of India buys such rice. Rather, it is due to inefficiencies in its operation. In Orissa, about 80 per cent of the requirement of rice is purchased by the government at below market price by a levy imposed on rice mills. There may be connivance between the officials of the FCI/government and the private mill owners whereby the mill owners try to sell poor quality stock to the government sector (which comes to the PDS later) and the better quality in the open market. The Orissa State Civil Supplies Corporation (OSCSC) has been entrusted with the responsibility of storing and distributing rice, wheat, sugar and other essential items, which are allotted by the Government of India (through the FCI) for ultimate distribution to the users of the PDS through fair-price shops.
6. This problem has been widely reported in local newspapers of the state.
7. A number of authors have analysed the reasons for the limited access of rural consumers to the PDS. These include lack of adequate food delivery system, corruption in the delivery system, an urban-biased policy, lack of infrastructure etc., (see footnote 1 for reference).
8. Rao (2000) has analysed the reasons for the declining consumption of foodgrains in the country. The relatively higher per capita cereal consumption in Orissa is possibly due to the fact that the majority of the labour force in the state are involved in agricultural work, which is tenuous, and requires manual labour. The extent of mechanisation is very low so that even for collection of common property items the workers have to travel entailing considerable wastage of time and energy. Further, a majority of the households are not in a position to substitute cereals for other high calorie nutritive foods, such as fruits/milk, eggs etc., because these are costly and thus not affordable

by the households given their own income. Lack of proper infrastructure and the small number of sellers in rural areas are other reasons which explain why these food items are costly in rural areas. Given the rising food prices in recent years, in the state (the indices of consumer price for agricultural labourers have been rising at a faster rate in the state as compared to the all-India level in recent years) many poor households have to substitute inferior cereals such as *bajra, mandia,* and *gurji* for their consumption. Our field information on the consumption behaviour of poor households in western Orissa revealed that the households have to spend more than three-fourths of their expenditure on cereals (see Sarap, 2000).

9. Average days of employment generated through JRY/EAS and percentage of it going to different groups who worked under this scheme in the study villages is as follows: Since the wage rate (which varied from Rs. 18 to Rs. 25 per day in the case of male workers and Rs. 16 to Rs. 22 per day in that of the female worker in private work and Rs. 30 for male and female in JRY-EAS work) is low and the number of days of employment (both self-and wage) are few, the average income received by the households is low.

10. The operation of the RPDS was stopped temporarily in the area after May 1997. Our inquiry from the villages revealed that the lower amount distributed during the year 1995 was due to following reasons: (a) In Village II the items were not distributed to the card holders, but were sold to raise funds for the construction of a temple; and (b) In Village III the ration was sold to raise funds for payment to a teacher appointed in the village primary school. The villagers took a collective decision in this regard in both the villages.

Reference

Ahluwalia, Deepak (1993), "Public Distribution of Food in India: Coverage, Targeting and Leakages", *Food Policy*, Vol. 18, No. 1, pp. 33-54.

Balakrishna, Pulapre and Ramaswami, Bharat (1997), "Quality of Public Distribution System, Why It Matters," *Economic and Political Weekly*. Vol. 30, No. 4, January 25-31.

Bhagwati, Jagdish and Srinivasan, T.N. (1993), *India's Economic Reforms*, Ministry of Finance, Government of India, and New Delhi.

Dev S.M. and Suryanarayana, M.H. (1991), "Is PDS Urban Biased and Pro-rich: An Evaluation", *Economic and Political Weekly*, Vol. 26, No. 41, pp. 2357-2366.

Government of Orissa, *Economic Survey* (various years).

Indrakant, S. (1995), "Food security and Public Distribution System in Andhra Pradesh," *Research Project on Strategies and Financing for Human Development in India*, UNDP, Thiruvananthapuram, Kerala.

Mooij, Jos (1999), Dilemmas in Food Policy, About Institutional Contradictions and Vested Interests, *Economic and Political Weekly*. Vol. 30, No. 52, December 25-31.

Nair, K.N. and Sivanandan, P. (1995), *Food Security and Public Distribution System in Kerala*, Research Project on Strategies and Financing for Human Development in India, UNDP, Thiruvananthapuram, Kerala.

Parikh, K.S. (1994), "Who Gets How Much from, PDS, How Effectively Does it Reach the Poor", *Sarvekshana*, January-March.

Radhakrishna, R. and Hanumantha Rao, K. (1994), "Food Security, Public Distribution and Price Policy", UNDP Studies on *Human Development in India*, Discussion Paper, New Delhi.

——Subbarao, K. with Indrakant, S. and Ravi, C. (1997), "India's Public Distribution System: A National and International Perspective", World Bank, Discussion Paper No. 380, The World Bank, Washington, D.C.

Rao, C.H. Hanumantha (2000), "Declining Demand for Foodgrains in Rural India: Causes and Implications", *Economic And Political Weekly*, Vol. 30, No. 4, January 22-28, pp. 201-206.

Sarap, K. (2000), "Agrarian Structure, Land Reform Measures and Livelihood Pattern in KBK Region, Orissa", A report submitted to State Bank of India, Central Office, Mumbai.

Thamarajakshi, R. (1997), "Economic Reforms and State Intervention in Foodgrain Market", *Economic and Political Weekly*, Vol. 30, No. 30, July 26-August 1, pp. 1894-1900.

PART V

Emerging Perspectives

18

On Improving the Effectiveness of the PDS in Achieving Food Security

Shikha Jha and P.V. Srinivasan

I. INTRODUCTION

The Public Distribution System (PDS) in India is the principal means of making subsidised food available to its consumers. In recent years, however, the system has been criticised on two major counts. The costs of operation have been increasing to unsustainable levels and a large percentage of the poor, especially in rural areas, are kept out of reach of the system. The increasing fiscal pressure on the government provided the impetus to streamline the functioning of the PDS and the deregulation of the domestic foodgrains market. The Government of India, therefore, introduced the Targeted PDS (TPDS) in June 1997, specifically aimed at targeting the food subsidy to the poor. Under it the allocation of foodgrains to states was based on the Planning Commission's estimates of state-wise poverty. The state governments were given the responsibility of implementing targeting mechanisms for reaching the poor. Each family below the poverty line (BPL) was entitled to a quota of 10 kg of foodgrains at subsidised prices (about 50 per cent of the economic costs). Families above the poverty line (APL) received a lower subsidy (90 per cent of economic cost). The basic idea behind this system was to phase out the subsidy to APL families gradually rather than in one go. The consistently rising minimum support price (procurement price) tended to decrease the gap between the open market price and the issue price at which grains are sold to APL families, thereby reducing their demand for the PDS grain. However, the large difference between the BPL issue price and the open market price provided incentives for diversion of the TPDS grains into the open market. Such a leakage coupled with exclusion errors in targeting implied that very little subsidy reached the poor.

Since a large proportion of the population continues to be poor, food security concerns have assumed great importance in India. Widespread poverty and lack of purchasing power implies limited market demand for foodgrains. Increases in food supply without adequate increase in demand means lower prices for farmers, which in turn necessitates price support for farmers from the government. At the same time price support operations can result in excessive stocks with the government in the absence of a food distribution program. Food subsidy to consumers and price support to farmers, are, therefore, complementary to each other. But the current food scenario is marked by a high level of foodgrains output coupled with a large grain reserve in public storage.[1] This is largely due to the efforts of the government to protect farmers through regular increases in the procurement price of grains. These two factors together impose a heavy drain on the exchequer, which responds by increasing the issue price of subsidised grain. The ultimate effect of these policies is to reduce the per unit subsidy to consumers leading to a shortfall in the off-take.[2]

Thus, despite the achievement of self-sufficiency in foodgrains and the prevalence of subsidised distribution of grains since World War II, per capita consumption of the poorest sections of the population continues to be lower than the recommended nutritional levels and as a result a large percentage of children remain underweight. At historical growth rates, Bhalla et al. (1999) estimate a gap between the demand for and supply of cereal to be 25 million tonnes by 2020. Even though consumption preferences are shifting towards non-cereal foods, the food gap may, still be substantial. In this paper, we, therefore, examine the costs and benefits associated with the operation of the PDS and discuss the ways of both cutting costs to improve efficiency and better targeting methods to improve the food security of the poor.

This paper is organised as follows: In the next section we discuss various kinds of costs entailed by the operation of the PDS on the economy and various kinds of benefits derived from it such as stabilisation of food consumption and producer revenues and increases in producer and consumer welfare. We illustrate through simulation exercises how targeting subsidies to the poor can raise the benefit-cost ratio of the system. In section III, we focus on the economic costs of the system. In particular, we examine the role of the Food Corporation of India (FCI) and its costs of storage and distribution operations in relation to those of private agents, especially in recent years. We also discuss possible ways in which the rising government costs can be curtailed and the administration made more efficient. Section IV discusses the issues involved in the targeting of the PDS to the poor and examines the potential benefits that can be obtained through geographic targeting. Policy conclusions and a summary of findings are presented in the final section.

II. CHANGING ROLE OF PDS AND ITS COST EFFECTIVENESS

The PDS in India works alongside a free market. It makes available fixed quotas of foodgrains through ration shops at subsidised 'ration' or 'issue' prices. The role and working of the PDS has undergone several changes since its inception. Initially, its objective was to stabilise prices and consumption in the light of fluctuations in foodgrain output. Later, it also assumed importance as one of the government's most significant anti-poverty programs. The changes witnessed in the last decade were a result of the liberalisation process underway and the structural adjustment programme undertaken by the government since 1991, the year of economic crisis. The reforms in the system focused on removing existing inefficiencies, particularly in costs. The costs of operating the PDS consist of two major components: subsidy costs and administration costs. The subsidy costs occur mainly because the cost at which foodgrains are procured is higher than the price at which they are sold in the PDS. In addition there are procurement incidentals, storage, transport and other administrative costs involved in the procurement and distribution of grain. Theft, damages and other kinds of losses in storage and transit add to these costs. In spite of incurring these costs the effectiveness with which the PDS provides food security to the poor has been low. This is mainly due to two reasons. Since the provision of food subsidy through the PDS has until recently been universal and not specifically targeted at the poor a large proportion of the subsidy has gone to the non-poor. There is also the phenomenon of corruption leading to leakage of a large amount of subsidised grain into the open market. In her study on Bihar, Mooij (1999) found that it was difficult for the PDS dealers to make profits without being corrupt. The administrative efficiency and the level of corruption vary with the state. For the nation as a whole, the estimates of diversion of grain from the PDS to the open market is close to one-third (Ahluwalia, 1993; Howes and Jha, 1992 and GOI, 2000).

1. Escalating Food Subsidies

The recent changes in the food distribution system have been motivated mainly by the need to reduce the food subsidy bill. These changes, however, have concentrated mostly on one aspect of the problem, namely, that quite a large fraction of the benefits accrue to the non-poor in the absence of explicit or implicit targeting. The government seems to have ignored the equally or perhaps more important problem of leakage of benefits due to corruption. Riddled with the problems of rising costs, low income-support and ineffective targeting of subsidies to the poor, the Government of India initiated a new scheme in June 1997—the targeted PDS (TPDS)—to directly target the subsidy to the poor. This scheme is meant to serve families below the poverty line (BPL). Under this scheme the states are required to identify these families and provide them 10 kg of foodgrains per family per month (20 kg with effect from April, 2000), at 50 per cent of the Food Corporation of India's (FCI) economic cost. The supply of grains to the states for this purpose is guaranteed by the central government.[3] The states are free to provide higher quotas/price subsidies by adding from their own resources. The population above the poverty line (APL) would continue to receive foodgrains as per the usual untargeted or universal PDS (UPDS) at a price equal to 90 per cent (now 100 per cent) of the FCI's economic cost.

In recent years the ever-increasing and politically influenced procurement: minimum support price (MSP) has been the main cause for the rising food subsidy bill. It was increased this year again in spite of a recommendation by the Expenditure Reforms Commission (2000) for the freezing of MSP at the previous year's level. During the period, 1992-93 to 1999-2000, the annual increase in MSP exceeded the annual average inflation (*Economic Survey*, 2000-2001). For example, against the annual inflation of 7 per cent measured in terms of wholesale price index, the MSP for rice and wheat grew at the rate of about 10 per cent and 11 per cent, respectively. In 2000-01, it constituted 57 per cent of the economic cost of the FCI for rice and 70 per cent for wheat. Such high and rising support prices have resulted in large stocks in government warehouses, adding further to its costs and subsidy bills.

The current level of MSP, for wheat is much higher than the world price (the f.o.b. price of wheat imports) (Table 1). This policy-induced price distortion is preventing the diversification of agriculture and development of comparative advantage in other high-value crops. Lowering of the MSP would lessen this distortion and also help reduce the costs of PDS and carrying buffer stocks. Liberalising of international trade in foodgrains and use of other instruments like variable levies for price stabilisation would

Table 1
Procurement, Issue Prices and FCI's Sales Realisation (Rs. q)

Year	MSP/ Procurement price	Central issue price BPL	Central issue price APL	FCI's average sales realisation
Rice				
1995-96	603	537	537	613
1996-97	655	537	537	611
1997-98	712	350	700	584
1998-99	776	350	905	612
1999-2000	NA	350	905	700
2000-2001 (BE)	NA	565	1130	NA
Wheat				
1995-96	380	402	402	412
1996-97	475	402	402	433
1997-98	510	250	450	370
1998-99	550	250	650	490
1999-2000	580	250	682	520
2000-2001 (BE)	NA	415	830	NA

Notes: 1. FCI's sales realisation for APL families excludes the realisation from special category states of Jammu & Kashmir, Himachal Pradesh, North-east states, Sikkim and hilly areas of Uttar Pradesh.
2. The levy price of rice is an average for the common variety from eight state, viz., Andhra Pradesh, Haryana, Madhya Pradesh, Orissa, Rajasthan, Punjab, Uttar Pradesh and West Bengal.
3. For the years since the introduction of TPDS, sales realisation is derived as a weighted average of the sales realisation under APL and BPL sales, the weights being 0.4 and 0.6 respectively for BPL and APL.
4. BE, Budget estimate.

Sources: Economic Survey, 2000-2001 and World Bank (1999), Annex. Table 2.2a.

also reduce the high costs of buffer stocking. A recently announced National Policy on Handling and Storage of Foodgrains is aimed at tackling such problems. Among other objectives, this policy envisages encouragement of the private sector for building storage capacities for rental use by government agencies and also development of infrastructure for integrated bulk handling, storage and transportation of foodgrains.

2. Need for Price Support

Inadequate purchasing power among the poor leads to low overall demand for foodgrains. This, coupled with a large supply of foodgrains leads to low food prices creating a need for price support. Thus, so long as the incomes of the poor fail to grow adequately and providing income support is fraught with problems, the need for food subsidy will remain and the only way to reduce the food subsidy bill is to improve the efficiency of the system and reduce the incentives for corruption. Past trends in the various components of costs of foodgrain procurement and the public distribution system indicate that the procurement incidentals and distribution costs (the administrative costs) form a very large fraction

Table 2
Ratio of Total Economic Cost to Procurement Price

Year	Rice	Wheat
1989-90	1.49	1.82
1990-91	1.51	1.67
1991-92	1.53	1.83
1992-93	1.51	1.79
1993-94	1.59	1.89
1994-95	1.49	1.94
1995-96	1.51	1.87
1996-97	1.53	1.87
1997-98	1.51	1.84
1998-99	1.59	1.92
Average	1.52	1.84

Source: Authors' calculations.

of the price at which grain is procured (Table 2). In effect, the cost-benefit ratio of the system turns out to be very high (Table 3). It is noteworthy that the benefit-cost ratio is much lower for wheat than for rice. An important reason for this is that the MSP applies to wheat, whereas rice is procured through a levy on rice millers, which is also reflected in the observation that the total carrying cost of wheat has grown far higher than that of rice (Table 4). Part of the reason for the low benefit-cost ratio is the fact that several indirect benefits are not accounted for. The current functioning of the system is such that the PDS serves a dual purpose : it not only provides subsidy to consumers but also helps in the process of providing price support to the farmers. The PDS combined with the foodgrain procurement policy of the government has also brought about stability in the price of foodgrains, which in turn contributes to macro-economic stability. The increased demand for foodgrains resulting from food

Table 3
Benefit-Cost Calculations for Intervention in Grain Markets (Rs. q)

Year	1990-91	1991-92	1992-93	1993-94	1994-95	1995-96	1996-97
Rice							
a. Market price	480	586	672	718	794	893	989
b. CIP	377	377	437	537	537	537	537
c. Procurement price	338	387	454	519	565	603	655
d. Administrative cost	125	128	131	200	182	223	215
e. Storage cost	48	78	99	105	95	85	133
I. Consumer benefit (a-b)	103	209	235	181	257	356	452
II. Government cost (c+d+e-b)	134	216	247	287	305	374	466
Consumer benefit/ (govt. cost)	0.77	0.97	0.95	0.63	0.84	0.95	0.97
Wheat							
a. Market price	293	348	387	431	465	460	566
b. CIP	280	280	330	402	402	402	402
c. Procurement price	225	275	330	350	360	380	475
d. Administrative cost	105	142	155	216	219	224	248
e. Storage cost	45	85	105	94	119	108	166
I. Consumer benefit (a-b)	13	68	57	29	63	58	164
II. Government cost (c+d+e-b)	95	222	260	258	296	310	487
Consumer benefit/ government cost	0.14	0.31	0.22	0.11	0.21	0.19	0.34
Consumer benefit/ (government cost) Rice and wheat combined	0.51	0.63	0.58	0.39	0.53	0.61	0.65

Source: Authors' calculations.

subsidies leads to multiplier effects, raising the overall growth of the economy. Furthermore, increased food intake results in better nutritional and health outcomes leading to greater human resource development.

The indirect benefits of the PDS can be obtained by its influence on the aggregate demand for foodgrains and the supply response to the consequent changes in prices. Results from a simulation model show that even if the government was to purchase grain at market prices for distribution through the PDS, then, even without direct targeting, the cost-benefit ratio for its operation turns out to be close to unity (Table 5). This is much higher than the historically observed figures reported in Table 3, where only the direct benefits are taken into account. The benefit-cost ratio would be even higher with better targeting.[4] Moreover, the PDS not only brings direct benefits in terms of an increase in consumer surplus but also indirect benefits in terms of increase in producer surplus. The increased demand, due to food subsidy, for a given supply of foodgrains results in a rise in prices and hence an increase in producer surplus.[5] There are also other benefits resulting from the PDS, which may not be readily quantifiable. For example, the PDS stabilises aggregate consumption of foodgrains and aggregate producer revenue in the face of year to year fluctuations in production.

Table 4
Public Foodgrain Stocks and Observed Storage Costs

	Central pool stocks on 1st January (Million tonnes)			Total cost (Rs. crore)			Unit cost (Rs./q)		
Year	Rice	Wheat	Total	Rice	Wheat	Total	Rice	Wheat	Total
1989-90	4	4	9	219	241	460	53	54	54
1990-91	6	6	11	269	254	523	48	45	46
1991-92	9	9	18	679	785	1464	78	85	82
1992-93	9	5	14	851	554	1405	99	105	101
1993-94	10	4	13	995	327	1323	105	94	102
1994-95	11	11	22	1058	1291	2349	95	119	107
1995-96	17	13	30	1480	1396	2876	85	108	95
1996-97	15	17	32	2044	2806	4851	133	166	150
1997-98	13	7	20	1994	1326	3321	155	187	166
1998-99	12	7	18	1803	1255	3057	157	185	167
1999-00	12	13	24	1918	2561	4387	164	202	180
2000-01	14	17	31	2492	3739	6061	175	217	193
2001-02	21	25	46	3871	5830	9427	187	233	206

Notes: 1. Total cost is the product of stocks and unit storage costs.
2. The unit cost for the last three years beginning 1999-2000 is based on simple extrapolation of the previous 10 years' trend.

Source: Author's calculations; data from *Economic Survey* and *Union Budget Documents*, Various Issues.

Table 5
Costs and Benefits of PDS With and Without Targeting

		PDS	
Variable	No PDS	Without targeting	With targeting
Average price (Rs. q)			
Rice	897.9	898.8	902.8
Wheat	510.7	511.7	516.0
Average consumption (million tonnes)			
Rice	67.87	68.13	68.32
Wheat	51.97	51.97	51.15
Average government PDS costs (Rs. crore)	0.0	6955.6	7021.0
Average producer surplus	217758	217974	218579
Change in producer surplus	-	216	821
Average consumer surplus	79401	85666	87420
Change in consumer surplus	-	6265	8019
Benefit-cost ratio for the PDS (rice and wheat combined)			
Consumer surplus / govt. cost		0.900	1.14
Consumer + producer surplus / govt. cost-		0.932	1.26

Note: The figures are obtained from simulation effects of a commodity price stabilisation model using 1995-96 as the base year with the PDS purchases at market prices. For more details see Jha and Srinivasan (1999). Benefit-cost ratio is obtained by dividing the change in consumer and producer surplus by government costs.

Source: Authors' calculations.

Thus, the presence of these indirect benefits resulting from the operation of the PDS implies that PDS reform induced by fiscal adjustment aims to explore alternative means of removing cost inefficiencies, rather than just reducing the size of the distribution system. Although food subsidy has been growing over the years in real terms, it has remained stable as a percentage of GNP, ranging between 0.5 and 0.8 per cent. However, due to lack of effective targeting mechanisms and large-scale leakage due to corruption, the cost effectiveness of extending food subsidy to the poor has been very low. Some studies have shown that the government spends more than Rs. 5 for every rupee that goes as food subsidy to the poor (Parikh, 1994). Several studies have pointed to a large scope for reduction in inefficiencies, both in terms of preventing leakage and improving the reach of the poor and future reforms should concentrate on these issues.

III. ROLE OF FCI IN THE PROVISION OF FOOD SECURITY

1. Procurement, Storage and Distribution

The FCI plays an important role in the distribution of foodgrains in India. The FCI and other public procurement agencies purchase their supplies from producers at pre-announced 'procurement prices' fixed by the central government and sell it to the state civil supplies or food corporations at an issue price, which is also fixed by the government. The state agencies in turn distribute the grain to the public through their network of fair price shops. In the case of wheat the procurement price has mostly acted as a support price, whereas for rice it is a levy on the millers. Of late, however, there has been a situation of surplus, even of rice and pressures are building up for its procurement by the FCI at support rather than levy price. Even in the case of wheat, at times the farmers used to be compelled to sell to the FCI at the procurement price when it fell below the market price. This happened in several ways such as traders not being allowed to bid in the procurement season until the FCI achieved its procurement target. Currently, however, the MSP has become a misnomer. It is fixed at such a high level that the FCI is forced to purchase almost the entire market arrival and there is no element of compulsion or coercion to sell to FCI.

On behalf of the central government, the FCI carries out operations and takes care of all aspects of the system including procurement, renting of warehouses and storage and allocations to the states. The net costs that it incurs in this operation over and above sales realisation through the PDS is reimbursed to it by the central government and is referred to as 'food subsidy'. The FCI maintains a buffer stock in order to stabilise grain prices and to provide minimum support prices to protect the farmers. These prices have been rising significantly, partly due to pressure from various interest lobbies. Table 6 provides a breakup of the total economic cost of the FCI and compares it with the average sales realisation from the distribution of rice and wheat. The economic cost consists of the purchase or procurement price, procurement incidentals, storage or carrying cost and the distribution cost. In the last five years of the nineties each cost component for each grain has grown at a slower rate compared to the growth in the previous five years. The growth rate of total cost has declined by 5 percentage points for rice and 4 percentage points for wheat between these periods. This may be due to better management practices and more efficient use of resources in recent years. For example, storage capacity utilisation has increased from 53 per cent in the early 1990s to 85 per cent in 1999-2000 (Gulati et al., 1996, and GOI, 2001). However, due to various erroneous policies that are being followed including that of steadily raising issue prices and exclusion of a large deserving population by the TPDS, the off-take has declined resulting in falling average sales realisation. The net effect of the rising costs and falling revenue has been that growth rate in unit subsidy, which was lower in the early 1990s (17.7 per cent and 9.8 per cent per annum, respectively for rice and wheat), has risen to 23.8 per cent per annum for rice and 19.7 per cent for wheat in the late 1990s.

2. Performance of FCI *vs.* Private Traders

The above observations lead one to ask as to whether private sector operators function with lower or higher margins than the FCI and whether they can be relied upon for fulfilling certain objectives such as market price stabilisation and movement of goods from surplus to deficit regions. This has been a major point of controversy in the debate on the changing role of the FCI. In this subsection, we put together all existing evidence to enable us to make a comparison. Since government agencies usually have a soft budget constraint they do not have the incentive to carry out cost-saving measures. Grain losses are reported to be large during transit as well as under storage.

As seen from Table 6, the carrying cost of grains has by far been the fastest growing component of total FCI cost. The Bureau of Industrial Costs and Prices (BICP) in its report (GOI, 1991) made several suggestions to improve the efficiency of the FCI in order to reduce its costs of operation. These include cutting down FCI costs by 30 percent by economising on staff strength and ways to improve storage capacity utilisation, which was as low as 34.3 per cent in 1988-89, having declined from a high of 77 per cent in 1984-85. The Report suggested 85 per cent as the optimal level. The storage cost of hired godowns in 1988-89 was Rs. 10.6 per quintal while the owned godowns cost Rs. 16.7 per quintal. Of the latter, staff cost alone constituted 72 per cent, whereas depreciation accounted for 15 per cent. In other words, in general, fixed costs substantially raised the average cost of owning as opposed to hiring warehouses. The latest data for the year 2000 shows that 58.9 per cent of storage capacity is owned by the FCI and 41.1 per cent is hired, while the average capacity utilisation is 85 per cent (GOI, 2001).

Table 6
Economic Cost of FCI: A Breakups (Rs. q)

Year	Procure-ment price	Procure-ment incidentals	Distri-bution cost	Carrying cost	Total cost	Sales reali-sation	Net cost (Subsidy)
Rice							
1989-90	319	30	73	53	475	-	-
1990-91	338	43	82	48	511	-	-
1991-92	387	46	82	78	593	366	227
1992-93	454	32	99	99	683	442	241
1993-94	519	77	123	105	823	500	323
Growth rate	12.68	15.89	12.17	20.72	13.89	15.60	17.74
1994-95	565	53	129	95	842	601	241
1995-96	603	76	147	85	911	613	298
1996-97	655	77	138	133	1003	611	392
1997-98	712	50	155	155	1072	584	488
1998-99	776	115	183	157	1231	612	619
Growth rate	8.02	11.23	7.51	16.06	9.22	-0.12	23.79
Wheat							
1989-90	215	47	74	54	391	-	-
1990-91	225	27	78	45	375	-	-
1991-92	275	54	88	85	502	252	250
1992-93	330	50	105	105	590	279	311
1993-94	350	107	109	94	660	356	304
Growth rate	13.58	22.72	10.75	19.28	15.03	17.28	9.83
1994-95	360	99	120	119	699	408	291
1995-96	380	103	121	108	712	412	300
1996-97	475	111	137	166	890	433	457
1997-98	510	107	136	187	940	370	570
1998-99	550	154	167	185	1056	490	566
Growth rate	11.42	9.19	7.73	14.16	11.02	2.59	19.71

Note: The levy price of rice is an average for the common variety from eight states, viz., Andhra Pradesh, Haryana, Madhya Pradesh, Orissa, Rajasthan, Punjab, Uttar Pradesh and West Bengal.

Sources: Economic Survey, 1999-2000; Jha and Srinivasan (2001) and World Bank (1999), Annex Table 2.2a.

Private traders manage to operate at lower costs for several reasons. At the outset they avoid mandi charges by buying directly from farmers; re-use gunny bags several times (unlike the FCI); move grains by trucks which are more easily available (than railway wagons) and have lower transit losses. In contrast to this, the FCI, which receives subsidised rail freight and credit rates and is not restricted by SCC, ECA and zones, incurs much higher operational costs. Interestingly, the FCI also shows diseconomies of scale despite its large scale of operation and moves its stocks multiple times between its warehouses. In addition, in order to cover their losses due to levy sales to the FCI, the rice millers apparently sell low-quality grains to the FCI reserving good-quality grain for the open market.

This brings to the fore the question: if private operators function with lower costs than the FCI can they be relied upon for fulfilling certain objectives such as market price stabilisation and movement of goods from surplus to deficit regions. While this has been a major point of controversy in the debate on the changing role of the FCI, adequate information for making judgements on the storage costs incurred by private storage agents has not been available.

Among a few estimates that are now available, Jha and Srinivasan (2000) inferred private storage costs from the behaviour of public storage costs by noting that public storage cost rises over time and as the rate of storage capacity utilisation falls. They observed a relationship between these variables and then, based on the recommendations of the Government of India (GOI, 1991), assuming 85 per cent storage capacity utilisation by private agents and the fact that their staff costs were lower than the FCI's by 30 per cent, derived the storage costs of private agents which was about 60 per cent of the FCI cost in 1996-97. This estimate was based on the FCI's capacity utilisation rate of 53 per cent as reported by Gulati et al. (1996). For 1999-2000, the Planning Commission (GOI, 2001) reported a much higher all-India average capacity utilisation rate of 85 per cent of all owned and rented warehouse capacity with the FCI. By applying this rate to the relationship as observed above private storage cost comes to 70 per cent of FCI storage cost in 1999-2000. If we compare the trend in the private cost thus estimated with that in the costs actually incurred by the FCI we see that the slope of the cost curve of the FCI is much steeper in the 1990s than in the early 1980s (Fig. 1). In other words, the annual average actual costs of the FCI are rising faster than they were in the past, which favours the promotion of private stockholding.

Fig. 1
Unit Public and Private Storage Cost

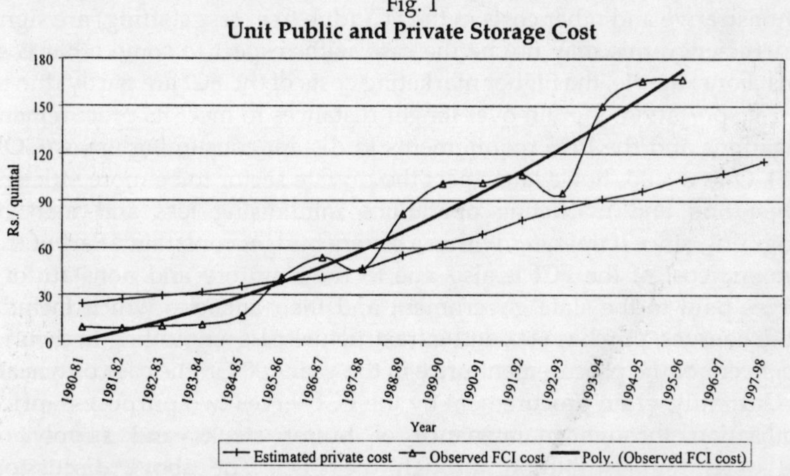

Apart from storage activity, private agents are also involved in the marketing of foodgrains. But, due to a general lack of information on their trade margins, a comparison of FCI costs with those of private operators becomes difficult. However, some early documentation on the relative performance of the FCI versus private operators (Tyagi, 1990) suggests that there is scope for improving the trading efficiency of the FCI. Tyagi's analysis of the data for the period, 1970-71 to 1988-89 clearly revealed that retail margins of private traders were much lower than the post-procurement costs incurred by the FCI. He found that the margin in the distribution of both rice and wheat through private trade was far lower than that through the public channel. A more recent study (World Bank, 1999) also noted that both the procurement/processing and total margins in private trade in rice and wheat are lower than in FCI (Table 7).

Table 7
Wholesale Marketing of Rice and Wheat: Public *vs.* Private Costs (Punjab 1997-98)

Rice marketing				Ratio of private to public costs (%)
Private	Rs. q	Public	Rs. q	
Procurement & processing	157	FCI-procurement agency & processing	179	88
Distribution & wholesaling	20	State distribution agency	13	160
Total	177	Total	191	93
		Wheat marketing		
Wholesale in assembly market	60	FCI-procurement agency & processing	119	51
Wholesale in secondary market	63	State distribution agency	26	247
Total	123	Total	145	85 per cent

Source: World Bank (1999), Annex Table 2.21a.

This clearly suggests that there is scope for improving efficiency in the operations of the FCI. The comparison of FCI margins with those of private traders is, however, not an easy task. While the relatively higher administrative and other costs in the FCI (due to excess staffing) are signs of inefficiency, this may not be the case with respect to some other cost items. For example, the higher marketing costs of the FCI are partly due to the transportation of grain over longer distances to meet its procurement obligations and the PDS requirements in distant consuming areas (GOI, 1985). One would, however, expect the private sector to be more efficient in handling and marketing operations minimising loss and theft of foodgrains, since it operates within a severe budget constraint. Part of the economic cost of the FCI is also due to the statutory and nonstatutory charges paid to the state government and their agencies which include mandi charges, purchase tax and infrastructure cess amounting to around 14 per cent of the procurement price in the year 2000 in the case of wheat.

Currently, grain procurement by the FCI serves two purposes—price stabilisation through maintenance of buffer stocks and supply of foodgrains for distribution through the PDS. The above discussion suggests that the FCI's role can be restricted to maintenance of buffer stocks for the purpose of price stabilisation and PDS grains can be obtained through market purchases. The optimal level of stocks for this purpose would be much less than the current high levels and can be achieved by choosing the floor price of the price band lower than the current minimum support price, which is quite high. The government should set a price band which would insure against the possibility of an excess supply or excess demand situation persisting for a long time and the width of the price band should be such that private agents are left with enough opportunities for inter-temporal arbitrage. Private agents will not be highly speculative in the presence of a credible price stabilisation programme by the government (Balakrishnan and Ramaswami, 1995).

But what should be done to effectively utilise the current stock of almost 60 million tonnes of foodgrains? In the short run, these stocks can be used for schemes such as food-for-work and other anti-poverty programmes. However, the government has to contend with several constraints in doing this. Drèze (2001) pointed out that the poor financial condition of the states made it difficult for them to bear the cash costs or the non-wage component of food-for-work schemes. This partly accounts for the low off-take of the PDS foodgrains by the states from what is allocated to them by the Centre. The governments are not in a position to bear the administrative and other associated costs entailed in operating such schemes. Another problem in disposing of the large stocks is that the total absorption of grains by the various anti-poverty programs currently run in the country is limited. The quantity that can possibly be exported, even at lower than domestic market prices, is in the range of only 3-4 million tonnes. Thus, the scope of anti-poverty programmes would have to be expanded, perhaps involving free distribution of grains, if food stocks have to be reduced substantially. In the long run, of course, such stock build up should be avoided by providing price support to farmers through measures aimed at boosting foodgrain demand (through income generation programmes) rather than raising support prices.

The budgetary savings of the central government realised by limiting the role of the FCI can be used to provide subsidy to the states for the specific purpose of procuring grains through their agencies, private or public, in order to serve the PDS through their network of fair price shops. They can choose the most appropriate way to purchase grain keeping the cost factor in mind. Alternatively, the saved food subsidy could be given to states in the form of food stamps or vouchers, which would be distributed to the households by the local governments/Panchayati Raj institutions (Radhakrishna and Subbarao, 1997).[6] The storage activity can also be decentralised to avoid cross hauling of grain that takes place in a centralised system. While the government has announced its intention to decentralise the system, it should ensure that over time, the states take over the procurement operations and the food subsidy bill of the central government does not rise as in the past. Decentralisation would help to ensure market efficiency and reduce the economic costs of running the PDS. It would also put an end to the trading of blame by the state and central governments for the poor functioning of the system. In the current system "State governments, for instance, complain of inadequate food allotments from the Centre. The Centre, for its part, blames State governments for failing to make full use of their existing allotments." (Drèze, 2001). As seen earlier (Table 5), if the PDS purchases were made at market prices, the benefit cost ratio would, in fact, be higher than the historically observed ratios. The PDS would serve the poor better if, in addition to improving targeting performance, purchases are made from the free market in the nearest and cheapest surplus zone. However, the efficient functioning of private agents would require the removal of restrictions introduced under the Essential Commodities Act such as limits on stock holdings and controls on the movement of grains outside state boundaries. Such controls curtail growth and result in the development of secluded states. For instance, with its continually declining foodgrain production, Orissa depends more on its neighbouring states such as Madhya Pradesh and Andhra Pradesh for its foodgrain supplies, which are not easy to procure through the normal market route. In Tamil Nadu, the zoning policy promotes smuggling out of a particular variety of rice (red boiled—*matta*) that is produced, but not preferred locally for consumption. An immediate solution to such problems lies in removing the interstate restrictions on the movement of foodgrains and in making this policy initiative credible, as there are fears that such restrictions would be imposed again.

Nair (2000) argues that private trade is now emerging as an important source of supply of foodgrains. For instance, despite the formation of the Southern Food Zone in the early sixties, the amount of foodgrain supplied through private trade (17 per cent of total cereal consumption) exceeded the PDS supply and it is now 'likely to be of a higher order'. Due to zonal restrictions, such private trade takes place through illegal channels as the variety of rice preferred in Kerala and produced in Andhra Pradesh and Tamil Nadu has a market only in Kerala and the FCI does not take this factor into account. Interestingly, farmers in these two supplying states require permits from their governments for direct sales outside the state (GOI, 2000). Moreover, with rising production in other states, rice is also smuggled into Kerala from states as distant as Maharashtra, Punjab, Haryana, Madhya Pradesh and Uttar Pradesh. Now the traders are justifiably arguing for freeing of domestic trade in foodgrains so that open market supply could be increased, prices reduced and supply *equalised* among deficit states.

Movement restrictions help the state governments in the levy procurement of foodgrains for the purpose of distributing them through the PDS, especially in the years of shortage when market prices are likely to be at higher levels. However, at the same time these restrictions depress prices during periods of surplus by preventing spatial arbitrage and force the governments to offer price support. Thus, removal of movement restrictions would mean higher costs of procurement during periods of shortage, but lower costs by way of price support during periods of surplus. On balance, there is no reason to believe that the removal of movement restrictions would increase government costs.

IV. TARGETING THE PDS TO THE POOR

1. Problems with the Existing System

As explained above, in order to increase the share of the poor in the benefits from the PDS, the government has in recent years introduced new schemes such as the Revamped PDS (RPDS) and the TPDS. The performance of the TPDS so far does not seem to be satisfactory. Although the ration quota for the poor (the BPL population), has been increased, they are unable to make full use of this quota due to their limited purchasing power. For example, a study by Srivastava (GOI, 2000), shows that the performance of the TPDS in Uttar Pradesh has been highly unsatisfactory. Food subsidy to the poorest groups increased by a meagre amount (1.1 per cent to 1.3 per cent) due to the introduction of the TPDS. The large difference between open market and TPDS prices provided a great incentive for the diversion of grain to the black market with the estimated leakage being 41 per cent. The selection of beneficiaries was not transparent and the basis for selection was "too complicated for the local officials to administer". In the case of Bihar too, the corruption levels are found to be high (Mooij, 1999). The delivery system was weak even before the introduction of the TPDS and not much could be expected in terms of increasing the benefits to the poor.

Several studies have highlighted the different problems associated with the TPDS. One of the major problems with targeting the scheme specifically to the poor is the high cost involved in the correct identification of the target group. Narrow targeting at the level of individual households, for example, requires very detailed data for all households and a complex and expensive process of testing in order to identify the eligible households. The effectiveness of such mechanisms depends on the magnitude of the two possible errors—the errors of exclusion and inclusion. The exclusion error indicates the extent to which the poor are excluded from the list of beneficiaries and the inclusion error, the extent to which the non-poor are included in the list. Direct targeting of the poor through means testing, entails high administrative costs due to the need for repeated periodic identification. The cost of identification of the poor, which is of a recurring nature, can be very high and implementation of such schemes could become cumbersome going by the experiences of other countries.

The costs are further augmented due to widespread leakage to non-poor households by misrepresentation of information. The incentive for leakage has increased due to the larger difference between the open market and ration market prices for BPL families. Thus, although the off-takes are higher for BPL than for APL foodgrains it is not clear how much actually reaches the poor. With persisting distributional problems, it is also not clear as to whether and how the entire allocation would be lifted by the states and then by the consumers. In addition, it was originally envisaged that the APL families will be slowly phased out of the system.

At present, the APL prices are higher than the ruling market prices, which in effect has driven the APL families out of the system. While the central issue price (CIP) was frozen for the BPL families until it was revised upwards last year, there has been a substantial increase in the price for APL families (Table 1). This has led to a lower off-take in the APL category. The net effect seems to be increasing food stocks with the FCI adding further to its storage costs. Due to the poor off-take in the APL category there is not much scope for growth in FCI's average sales realisation. The introduction of the TPDS has also led to the perverse outcome whereby allotment of foodgrains was increased to states with a weak delivery system and reduced to those with greater administrative efficiency since the allotment was based on the prevailing poverty levels in these states (Mooij, 1999).

Replacing a system of universal provision of subsidies with a finely targeted one can lead to serious problems if no provision is made for a safety net to cover those excluded through poor targeting. In particular, such targeting, by leaving out large sections of the so-called APL families, given the controversies surrounding the poverty lines that are being used, is likely to lead to a rising exclusion error. Studies have also shown that since a substantial part of poverty is transient in nature, targeting based on current consumption status is likely to have a lesser impact on chronic poverty as compared to the case of uniform distribution of subsidies to the poor and the non-poor (Jalan and Ravallion, 1998). In short, the whole objective of protecting the poor consumer could get vitiated.

Untargeted programmes, however, are not only a big burden on the government's budget but also spread subsidies thinly across the entire population. Moreover, the benefits sometimes go disproportionately to the non-poor. In order to improve targeting, alternative indirect identification mechanisms based on the observed correlation between different socio-economic characteristics of the population and their poverty status can be used. Typical examples of such characteristics include the household's housing conditions, access to electricity, irrigation facilities, drinking water, etc. In the next sub-section, we analyse the potential gains from the mechanism of geographic targeting.

2. Potential for Geographic Targeting

Geographic targeting that uses the place of residence as the main eligibility criterion can provide an effective way of reaching the poor when there are substantial disparities in living conditions across geographical areas. The administrative cost of geographically targeted programs is expected to be relatively low since their implementation can be facilitated by the existing local administration. Targeting selected regions with a high concentration of poverty can be an effective mechanism for transferring a greater share of benefits to the poor while keeping the total number of beneficiaries unchanged. However, targeting at the level of large administrative areas can entail considerable leakage to the non-poor in these areas, while the poor in other areas remain uncovered. If smaller administrative areas, such as villages or districts are taken as target units the likelihood of identifying regions with a greater concentration of the poor increases. This would help in increasing the coverage of the poor while reducing that of the non-poor.

To illustrate this point, we make some calculations based on the consumption expenditure distribution across rural households in India for the year, 1987-88. The main source of data for estimating the incidence of poverty in India is the National Sample Survey Organisation (NSSO). This survey collects data on households' consumption expenditures at periodic time intervals. The sample size of the NSS is such that statistically significant estimates of poverty indices can be obtained at geographic levels not smaller than what is termed as an NSS region (Dreze and Srinivasan, 2000; Dubey and Gangopadhyay, 1998). The borders of the 'NSS regions' are determined within the states, mostly on the basis of their ago-climatic characteristics, and they are considerably larger than the districts. In the recent NSS survey, pertaining to the year 1987-88 the Indian states were divided into 77 NSS regions and 466 districts. The sample size at the district level is too small to provide statistically significant estimates of the incidence of poverty in the individual districts. However, the use of indirect methods to obtain estimates of poverty for smaller geographic units has become popular in recent years (Bigman et al., 2000 and Hentschel et al., 1998).

These methods involve prediction of poverty on the basis of data on different socio-economic characteristics for each region (say, district) brought together from several sources. These essentially entail two steps (Bigman and Srinivasan, 2001): the first step is an estimation of a relationship between regional incidence of poverty and other characteristics of households in these regions (on which district specific data is also available). The second step is to predict the district-level incidence of poverty in each district based on the above relationship and by using the observed characteristics of households belonging to that district. These estimates can be used to illustrate the gains that can be achieved by selecting smaller administrative units for the purpose of targeting. Since prediction errors could be high we cannot rely much on the individual, and district level poverty estimates. However, we could still place a great deal of reliance on the identification of the poorer groups of districts for the following reason: based on the predicted levels of poverty we can group the districts into different categories, e.g., 'poor', 'moderately poor' and 'least poor' districts, and determine the poverty levels for these groups of districts based on the predictions for individual districts. Since the sample size for these groups of districts is adequate we can directly estimate concentration of poverty in these groups from the survey data. We find that the poverty levels for these groups obtained from our prediction procedure are very close to the estimates derived directly from the survey data. Thus, although the poverty ranking of the individual districts obtained from our prediction procedure may not be reliable, it can be used to identify the group of poorer districts and consider them as target districts.

In estimating the relationship between poverty and other variables, the poverty status of the household (indicated by whether it is above or below the poverty line) is determined from the NSS data. The explanatory variables are obtained from a wide variety of sources that include the population census, the agricultural census, and various other geographical surveys which provide data at the district level. These explanatory variables include among others, population size, fertility rate, literacy rate, infant mortality rate, crop yields, irrigated area, rainfall, etc.

The results show that the choice of the district is preferable to that of the state as the unit for targeting. If available resources permit the coverage of only a limited population, targeting the poorest regions maximises the coverage of the poor. Given this fact, if the target units are chosen to be smaller areas—districts instead of states—we find that more of the poor can be covered by the system. The benefits, however, appear to be small given the distribution of the poor in India (Table 8). Assuming that the total number of people covered by the program is the same we can compare results when we choose alternatively the state or the district as the unit of targeting. In the case of district level targeting we see that more of the poor are covered, reducing the percentage of beneficiaries that are non-poor (the error of inclusion). The improvement in targeting effectiveness as measured by the reduction in the inclusion error is low when district level as opposed to state level targeting is used. This is because the variation in the incidence of poverty across districts is not markedly different from that across states. The head count ratio of poverty

Table 8

Gains from District Level Targeting of PDS

	State level targeting			Equivalent district level targeting			
Target	Total population covered (million)	Poor population covered (million)	Error of inclusion (per cent)	Number of districts covered	Per cent increase in the no. of pocr covered	Number of states which have at least one target district	Error of inclusion (per cent)
Poorest state	68.7	34.8	49.3	37	10.9	7	43.7
Poorest two states	73.1	36.9	49.5	40	10.9	7	44.0
Poorest three states	122.9	60.8	50.5	72	7.7	8	46.4
Poorest four states	149.5	73.3	50.9	88	6.3	8	47.4
Poorest five states	199.2	96.2	51.7	114	5.5	9	48.9
Poorest six states	233.1	111.2	52.3	132	4.9	12	50.0

Notes: 1. In the 'equivalent district targeting' the top ranking districts in terms of poverty are targeted and the number of districts chosen is such that the total population covered is roughly the same as in the case of state level targeting.

2. Error of inclusion refers to the percentage of the PDS beneficiaries who are non-poor.

Source: Authors' calculations.

varies between 15 per cent to 62 per cent at the district level compared to the range of 22.3 per cent to 50.63 per cent at the state level. One could expect the range of variation in poverty to be larger at the village level. Although there is not much reduction in the error, the advantage with district level targeting is that the coverage is spread much wider across the country and not restricted to only a few states.

The distribution of poor districts across different states shows that in the states of Bihar, Himachal Pradesh, Madhya Pradesh, Orissa and Rajasthan most of the districts fall under the 'poor' or 'very poor' category (Table 9). In regions with a greater concentration of poverty the high costs of identification and administration of the TPDS can be avoided since the leakage of benefits to the non-poor will be small for these regions. Universal provision of subsides to these regions is thus likely to be cost effective. For the remaining regions suitable self-targeting mechanisms can be used. For example, the least poor group of regions could be supplied coarse cereals wherever they are available or lower grades of superior cereals, so that there is a self-selection of the poor. Since the number of poor in this group is small, the quantity of coarse cereals required for this purpose would be small and there may not be a supply problem. Or, the supply of foodgrains could be linked to employment generation programs, which also have the self-selection property. In addition, the other targeting criteria that can be used are landlessness,

Table 9

Distribution of Poorer Districts Across States

State	Very poor districts	Poor districts	Moderately poor districts	Least poor districts	Total
Andhra Pradesh	0	5	4	13	22
Bihar	21	12	2	0	35
Gujarat	1	1	1	15	18
Haryana	0	0	3	9	12
Himachal Pradesh	7	3	1	0	11
Karnataka	0	2	11	6	19
Kerala	0	2	3	9	14
Madhya Pradesh	25	13	3	3	44
Maharashtra	0	4	14	7	25
Orissa	5	5	2	0	12
Punjab	0	0	0	12	12
Rajasthan	11	9	6	1	27
Tamil Nadu	0	1	4	13	18
Uttar Pradesh	11	14	24	7	56
West Bengal	6	6	3	0	15
Distribution of total population (per cent)	24.8	25.3	25.5	24.3	100.0
Distribution of poor population (per cent)	33.5	27.26	23.17	16.07	100.0

Notes: Very poor districts are those with HCR $\geq$ 0.47; Poor districts are those with HCR $\geq$ 0.40 and < 0.47; Moderately poor are those with HCR $\geq$0 .32 and <0.40; and Least poor are those with HCR < 0.32.

Source: Authors' calculations.

widowhood, old age, etc. Geographic targeting would also ensure supply of grains to remote and inaccessible rural, hilly and tribal areas where markets are underdeveloped or even nonexistent.

V. CONCLUDING REMARKS

In spite of the enormous tangible and intangible costs entailed in operating the PDS, its effectiveness in providing food security to the poor has been low under the system of universal (or untargeted) provision of food subsidies. Though the system provides low income-support, a large proportion of food subsidy goes to the non-poor and a large amount of grain leaks into the open market due to corruption. The rising costs of operation also make the system increasingly fiscally unsustainable, the net result being a low benefit-cost ratio. In a bid to reduce the food subsidy bill and the diversion of benefits to the non-poor, the Indian government introduced significant changes in the food distribution system in the last few years. The untargeted or universal PDS is being replaced in phases by the targeted PDS in order to restrict the subsidy mainly to the poor. The new system is, however, beset with several problems and does not appear to address the real issues. We argue here that the cost-effectiveness of the system appears to be low partly due to the fact that several indirect benefits of the system go unaccounted. The PDS, for example, not only provides subsidy to consumers but also helps in the process of providing price support to the farmers. The PDS and foodgrain procurement by the government brings about stability in the price of foodgrains, which in turn contributes to macro-economic stability. The increased demand for foodgrains resulting from food subsidies would also lead to multiplier effects, raising the overall growth of the economy. Thus, the presence of such indirect benefits accruing from the operation of the PDS implies that PDS reform induced by fiscal adjustment requires exploring alternative means of removing cost inefficiencies rather than just reducing the size of the distribution system. The effective functioning of the PDS would lead to an adequate increase in demand and reduce the need for providing price support to farmers. It would also avoid the paradoxical situation in which there is widespread hunger alongside mounting stocks of foodgrains.

Each of the components of the economic cost of FCI, consisting of the purchase or procurement price, procurement incidentals, storage and distribution costs, has been growing at a faster rate than revenue (sales realisation) leading to a rising food subsidy bill. The introduction of the TPDS has only magnified the problem. The off-take of foodgrains for distribution to APL families has fallen since the ration prices have risen close to (and at times are even higher than) the open market price. The off-take from the BPL allocation has been impressive, but a large part of the grains is diverted to the black market. The TPDS thus appears to have failed in serving both its objectives. It has succeeded neither in reducing the food subsidy bill nor in providing food subsidies to a greater proportion of the poor. The government should, therefore, now concentrate on tackling the real issues, namely reducing the cost inefficiencies in the procurement and distribution system and controlling the diversion of grain from the PDS to the open market. In the effort towards realising these objectives, while some functions of the FCI can be left to the market, there is a large scope for improving the efficiency of the remaining operations of the FCI. For example, while the FCI's role can be limited to price stabilisation and maintenance of buffer stocks, the central government could provide food subsidy to the states in the form of specific grants linked to their requirements so that the state agencies, private or public, can find the best possible way to procure grains to serve their PDS. This would also lead to decentralisation of storage activities thereby avoiding cross hauling of grain that takes place in a centralised system. The restrictions faced by the private traders under the Essential Commodities Act need to be removed to facilitate this process. Further, liberalising external trade in foodgrains and the use of other instruments of price stabilisation like variable levies would also reduce the high costs of buffer stocking.

Geographical targeting, involving the universal coverage of only those areas that have a high concentration of poverty, can be an effective way of reaching out to more of the poor with a given amount of resources. This would be the case especially when smaller administrative units such as villages are considered for targeting purposes. At this level we can expect substantial disparities in living conditions and, therefore, targeting only the poorer regions is an effective mechanism for transferring a greater share of benefits to the poor while the total number of beneficiaries is kept unchanged. Our analysis in the context of rural India shows that there are positive benefits from choosing smaller geographic units for targeting, although at the level of the district the gains are modest. The exercise also clearly suggests that the universal provision of subsidies is desirable for poorer states such as Bihar, Orissa, Rajasthan and Madhya Pradesh since most of the districts in these states belong to the 'poor' or 'very poor' category. In the other states, on the other hand, universal subsidies could be provided only to the poorer districts. In respect of other districts, self-targeting mechanisms or other direct targeting criteria based on characteristics such as landlessness, old age, widowhood, etc., could be used. Geographical targeting holds promise for bringing the PDS effectively within the reach of a large number of the poor.

Notes

1. In January 2001, the buffer stock of rice and wheat at 46 million tonnes was almost thrice the specified minimum norm. Recent trends indicate that this level is now reaching closer to 60 million tonnes. Many studies have indicated that government stocks are far in excess of optimal levels that can meet the objective of price stabilisation.
2. During 2000-2001, the wheat and rice off-takes were only 2.72 and 5.75 million tonnes against the allocations of 7.51 and 10.96 million tonnes, respectively (*Economic Survey, 2000-2001*, Table 5.7)

3. In addition, workers under Employment Assurance Scheme (EAS)/Jawahar Rojgar Yojana (JRY) would also receive food coupons to be exchanged at fair-price shops for grains at the rate of 1 kg per manday.
4. Targeting of the PDS subsidy entirely to the poorer sections increases aggregate demand for foodgrains since their income elasticity of demand is higher.
5. An important aspect of price determination is the interaction between supply and demand, and hence it is important to model how total demand for grains is related to the PDS quantity and price. The aggregate (free market plus the PDS) demand is obtained by augmenting the income variable in the demand function by the amount of the subsidy, defined as the product of the PDS quantity and the difference between free market and issue prices. Jha and Srinivasan (1999) provide more details on the model.
6. However, operation of food stamps has faced several difficulties in different countries, as described by Jha and Srinivasan (2001).

References

Ahluwalia, D. (1993), "Public Distribution of Food in India: Coverage, Targeting and Leakages", *Food Policy*, Vol. 18, No. 1, pp. 33-54.

Balakrishnan, P. and Ramaswami, B. (1995), "Public Intervention and Private Speculation: The Case of Wheat Procurement in India", *Journal of Quantitative Economics*, Vol. 11, No. 2, pp. 59-83.

Bhalla, G.S.; Hazell, P. and Kerr, J. (1999), "Prospects for India's Cereal Supply and Demand to 2020", *Food, Agriculture and the Environment Discussion Paper 29*, International Food Policy Research Institute (IFPRI), Washington, D.C.

Bigman, D.; Dercon, S.; Guillaume, D. and Lambotte, M. (2000), "Community Targeting for Poverty Reduction in Burkina Faso", *The World Bank Economic Review*, Vol. 14, No. 1, pp. 167-93.

——and Srinivasan, P.V. (2001), *Geographical Targeting of Poverty Alleviation Programs: Methodology and Applications in Rural India*, Indira Gandhi Institute of Development Research (mimeo).

Drèze, J. (2001), "Starving the Poor", *The Hindu*, February 26 and 27.

—— and Srinivasan, P.V. (2000), "Poverty and Inequality in India: Evidence from Regional Data", *Journal of Quantitative Economics*.

Dubey, A. and Gangopadhyay, S. (1998), "Counting the Poor: Where are the Poor in India?", *Sarvekshana Analytical Report No. 1*, Department of Statistics, Government of India.

Expenditure Reforms Commission (2000), *Report on Food Security* (Chairman: K.P. Geethakrishnan, former Finance Secretary), Government of India.

GOI (2001), *Background Note on Public Distribution and Food Security*, Government of India, Development Policy Division, Planning Commission, New Delhi.

——(2000), *Mid-Term Appraisal of Ninth Five Year Plan (1997-2002)*, Planning Commission, New Delhi.

——(1991), *Report on the Operations of the Food Corporation of India*, Bureau of Industrial Costs and Prices, Ministry of Industry, New Delhi.

—— (1985), *Marketing Costs and Margins of Major Agricultural Commodities in India*, Directorate of Marketing and Inspection, Ministry of Rural Development, New Delhi.

Gulati, A.; Sharma, P.K. and Kähkönen, Satu (1996), "The Food Corporation of India: Successes and Failures in Indian Foodgrain Marketing", *IRIS-India Working Paper No. 18*, IRIS Center, University of Maryland, College Park, USA.

Hentschel, J.; Lanjouw, J.; Lanjouw, P. and Poggi, J. (1998), "Combining Census and Survey Data to Study Spatial Dimensions of Poverty", *Policy Research Working Paper*, The World Bank, Washington, D.C.

Howes, S. and Jha, S. (1992), "Urban Bias in the Public Distribution System", *Economic and Political Weekly*, Vol. 27, May 9.

Jalan, J. and Ravallion, M. (1998), "Transient Poverty in Post Reform Rural China", *Journal of Comparative Economics*, Vol. 26, pp. 338-57.

Jha, Shikha, and Srinivasan, P.V. (1999), "Grain Price Stabilisation in India: Evaluation of Policy Alternatives", *Agricultural Economics*, Vol. 21, pp. 93-108.

——(2002), "On Targeting Food Subsidies", in Prabhu, K. Seeta (ed.), *Reforming India's Social Sectors: Strategies and Prospects*, Sage Publications, New Delhi.

Mooij, J. (1999), "Real Targeting: The Case of Food Distribution in India", *Food Policy*, Vol. 24, pp. 49-69

Parikh, K.S. (1994), "Who Gets How Much from PDS: How Effectively Does it Reach the Poor?", *Sarvekshana*, Vol. 17, No. 3, January-March.

Radhakrishna, R., and Subbarao, K., with Indrakant, S. and Ravi, C. (1997), "India's Public Distribution System: A National and International Perspective", *World Bank Discussion Paper No. 380*, The World Bank, Washington, D.C.

Tyagi, D.S. (1990), *Managing India's Food Economy: Problems and Alternatives*, Sage Publications, New Delhi.

World Bank (1999), *India – Foodgrain Marketing Policies: Reforming to Meet Security Needs*, Rural Development Unit, South Asia Region, Working Paper, Report No. 18329, May 27.

19

The Dangers of Narrow Targeting: An Assessment of the Targeted Public Distribution System

Madhura Swaminathan

In 1997, the Government of India introduced the Targeted Public Distribution System (TPDS), which makes a distinction between below-poverty-line (BPL) and above-poverty-line (APL) households with differential entitlements and prices for the two categories. Allocations to APL families, it was announced, would be transitory. That targeting was the first step in a process of excluding large numbers of vulnerable people from the PDS and in changing the character of the PDS was confirmed by the policy announcements in the Budget of March 2000. This paper examines some of the effects of the introduction of the TPDS, including the changes in the Budget of 2000-2001, on food security.[1] The targeting of welfare programmes is a subject of world-wide interest, and the paper begins by reviewing some of the costs of targeting and argues against narrow targeting in India. It then presents a brief assessment of the functioning of the TPDS and concludes with some suggestions for its reform.

I. THE COSTS AND BENEFITS OF TARGETING

Policy makers in India have reached a 'consensus' on the benefits of targeting; they have, however, failed to evaluate the costs of targeting. The costs and benefits of targeting as against universal transfers depend on several factors, factors that are likely to vary across countries and need to be carefully examined before making a choice between targeted and universal schemes. There is a large and growing theoretical literature on the costs of targeting.[2] Some of the major costs of targeting that are relevant to the Indian situation are discussed below:

1. Some Major Costs

(i) Targeting Errors or Errors of Inclusion and Exclusion

In any targeted welfare programme there are two types of errors that occur due to imperfect measurement. Errors of wrong exclusion (Type I errors) refer to the exclusion of genuinely poor or deserving households from a programme, while those wrong inclusion (Type II errors) refer to the inclusion of non-eligible persons or households in a programme.

We can measure these errors on the basis of the number of persons or families that are poor and non-poor and the numbers that are included and excluded by a welfare programme. Following Cornia and Stewart (1993) we can categorise the total number of families, N, as follows:

$$N = P^i + P^e + NP^i + NP^e$$

Where P refers to poor households, NP to non-poor households and the superscripts *i* and *e* to households included and excluded by the programme. With this classification, the error of exclusion can be gauged from the value of P^e, the number of poor households excluded. Alternatively, P^e/P, the proportion of poor households that are excluded or P^e/N, the proportion of all households that are both poor and excluded, can be used to measure the error of exclusion. In a similar way, the error of wrong inclusion can be gauged from NP^i, the number of non-poor families included in the programme, or NP^i/N, or NP^i/NP, that is, the proportion of non-poor wrongly included in the coverage of the targeted programme.

We need to assess the trade-off between the two types of errors. Universal programmes are likely to have low errors of exclusion but high errors of inclusion. On the other hand, a programme targeted to a specific group is likely to have a low error of wrong inclusion but may lead to a high error of exclusion. When one type of error decreases, the other type increases and so we have to attach weights to the two types of errors. Proponents of orthodox reform have implicitly attached a zero weight to errors of inclusion and are thus concerned only with minimising errors of exclusion. This implicit valuation should be recognised openly and be debated, for a strong case can be made for a weighting system that reverses the weights attached to the two types of errors, and places higher weights on errors of exclusion than on errors of inclusion (Cornia and Stewart, 1993). If a high weight is attached to errors of inclusion, then "general subsidies are invariably inferior to targeted schemes" but if a high weight is attached to errors of exclusion, then "general subsidies are invariably superior to targeted schemes" (ibid.).

Any decision on targeting, therefore, calls for some judgement about the relative weights to be assigned to the two types of errors. In making such a judgement, we should note that there is a basic asymmetry in the costs attached to the two types of errors (ibid.). Errors of wrong inclusion result in fiscal or financial cost, that is, higher expenditure due to the inclusion of ineligible beneficiaries. Errors of wrong exclusion, however, lead to welfare costs—that is, costs to individuals and society due to the inadequacy of food, malnutrition, ill health, etc. While fiscal costs are known and easy to measure, it is more difficult to measure the welfare costs of undernutrition although these costs are likely to be high.[3]

(ii) High Cost of Administration

A second major cost in developing countries is that of the administration of targeted programmes. The costs of administration of a welfare programme depend on the nature of institutions and delivery mechanisms in an economy, and on the extent of information available. Targeting raises the costs of delivery and administration, as the target group has to be identified on the basis of specified criteria, say incomes. Given the structure of our economy (which has a large agricultural and self-employed sector) and the ability of administrative organisations to collect accurate information, the costs of administering a targeted programme are likely to be high. These costs, however, vary with the type of targeting—targeting on the basis a criterion such as geographical residence may be easier to implement and is less costly than on that of income or nutritional status.

(iii) Decline in Quality

When programmes that are universal become targeted, their quality tends to deteriorate as the oft-heard phrase 'programmes for the poor are poor programmes suggests van de Walle et al. (1995). For example, the quality of food targeted to the poor tends to deteriorate. Targeted programmes therefore, often end up being inferior to universal programmes. And worsening quality can undermine the objectives of the original programme, as for example, if the quality of food distributed is too bad to be unsafe. To take another example, delivery may become irregular when only the poor are to be provided the benefits.

(iv) Loss of Social Cohesion

Targeting can be invasive and intrusive and result in greater social divisions. Segregating households on the basis of incomes in a country where the poverty line reflects a very low absolute level of income, and where there is a fluidity of households around the poverty line, can lead to social tensions and polarisation. To put it more explicitly very narrow targeting is likely to lead to the exclusion of some genuinely poor households from the programme, and create divisions among the poor. Such divisions can exacerbate existing forms of caste and gender oppression.

(v) Loss of Political Support and Long Run Costs

Lastly, any programme which targets the poor is likely to get less political support than a universal programme resulting in lower allocations for a targeted programme. In other words, the budgetary allocation for a welfare programme depends on the type of the programme, i.e., whether it is a targeted or a universal programme—and typically, allocations fall when a programme becomes targeted. If the budget support for a programme is made endogenous, then targeting may be worse for the poor than a system of universal transfers.[4] There is a good body of evidence from developed and less developed countries to show that political support differs as between universal and targeted transfers. The differences in political support get reflected not only in the size of transfers, both in per capita terms and in terms of total transfers, but also in the very continuation or dismantling of a programme.[5] So the inclusion of the middle classes in a welfare programme may be done on 'purely pragmatic' grounds for they 'play a crucial role in creating, expanding, sustaining, reforming and dismantling the welfare state' (Goodin and Le Grand, 1987).

To sum up, targeting is far from costless, and when all the costs are accounted for, the benefits of targeting may vanish. We thus need to openly recognise and assess the relative costs and benefits of targeting and universal transfers. In a poor country, the most important cost factor, perhaps, is the cost of exclusion. If the errors of exclusion are large, and costs attached to these errors are high, then universal programmes are preferable.

2. The Case against Narrow Targeting

Given the specific features of the Indian situation it is neither desirable nor feasible to implement a policy of narrow targeting based on the income criterion. This argument rests primarily on the costs associated with targeting errors. First, I argue that the target group is very large, thus raising the scope for errors of wrong exclusion; secondly, targeting errors are likely to be large on account of the huge conceptual and practical problems involved in the measurement of incomes and thirdly, wrong exclusion entails large welfare costs. If the costs of exclusion are given a large weightage then a policy of broad targeting or near-universal coverage is preferable. These arguments are set out below:

(i) Minimal Benefits of Targeting

The first part of the argument against narrow targeting is based on the extent of food poverty and insecurity. When food insecurity is widely prevalent, the leakage from a universal programme will be small and the benefits of targeting will be trivial. However, if food insecurity is restricted to a small section of the population, who, therefore need to be provided food subsidies then targeting can be useful. So it is essential to first assess the proportion of the population that requires access to some kind of food security. Let us consider some alternative estimates of the vulnerable population.

If we take the income-poverty line as the criterion of food insecurity, then the target group comprises 35 per cent of the population. In 1993-94, 37 per cent of the rural population and 32 per cent of the urban population (a total of 320 million persons) had expenditures less than the poverty line (Gupta, 1999). The official poverty line in India, however, represents a very low level of absolute expenditure—a fact recognised even in official documents. Further, low and variable incomes imply that a much larger section of the population is vulnerable to income shortfalls than what is observed by means of a static poverty line.[6]

If we use a measure of nutritional outcome, then the target group is much larger. A commonly used indicator of undernutrition among adults is the Body Mass Index (BMI), defined as the ratio of weight (in kilogram) to the square of height (in metre) (Shetty and James, 1994). If the BMI is taken as an indicator of undernutrition, then, according to the surveys of the National Nutrition Monitoring Bureau conducted in seven states in 1993-94, 48 per cent of adult men and women together, were undernourished (NNMB, 1996). In other words, in terms of the BMI criterion, about one-half of the adult population in the country is malnourished. The nutritional status of children is usually measured on the basis of a weight-for-age criterion. The National Family Health Survey (NFHS-1), which was conducted in 24 states in 1992-93, estimated that 53 per cent of boys and girls were undernourished and 21 per cent of the children surveyed were severely undernourished by this criterion (IIPS, 1995). According to the NFHS 1998-99, 47 per cent of children below the age of three were moderately or severely malnourished and 18 per cent were severely malnourished.[7] Since NFHS-1 refers to children up to the age of four, and NFHS-2 to those up to the age of three, the numbers are not strictly comparable, but it is clear that there has been no major improvement in the levels of child nutrition in the 1990s.

In a recent paper on diets in India, Hopper (1999) examined the nutritive value of Indian diets in relation to energy requirements. Based on the NSS consumption data for 1988, he estimated that "56 per cent of the total population fell short of their minimum per capita energy requirement of 1952 kcal/day, and 74 per cent did not meet their minimum protein requirement of 29.8 g/day" (Hopper, 1999). When he adjusted the energy requirement to eliminate wasting and stunting, then 71 per cent of the population failed to meet these energy requirements. Alternatively, if we take the food share (food expenditure as a share of total expenditure) as an indicator of food insecurity then an even larger proportion of the population is categorised as vulnerable.[8] In 1993-94, according to the National Sample Survey on consumption expenditure, the food share was over 70 per cent for the bottom 50 per cent of rural households. Over the next four deciles, it varied between 60 and 70 per cent. It is only among the top 5 per cent of households that the food share was below 50 per cent. If we use a generous cut-off point, namely, a food share of 60 per cent (the yardstick used to identify the poor in China),[9] then the bottom 90 per cent of the population in rural areas and the lower 60 per cent in urban areas would be counted as poor.[10] In other words, about 80 per cent of the total population would have a food share higher than 60 per cent and be eligible for the benefits of the food security programme.

As stated earlier, by using the income poverty line, the target group for a programme of food security was estimated to be just 35 per cent of the population. This criterion, it has been argued, not only indicates a very low absolute level of expenditure but is often an imperfect and inadequate measure of poverty and deprivation (UNDP, 1990). If we thus turn to other indicators of nutritional deprivation and food insecurity then the target group as a proportion of the population ranges from 50 per cent (based on nutritional outcomes) to 70 per cent (based on nutritional requirements) and to 80 per cent (based on food shares). Thus, if we were to identify vulnerable persons on the basis of nutritional intake, nutritional outcomes or expenditure patterns, then it is clear that a large majority of households need to be covered under the programmes of food security.

(ii) Administrative Convenience

With the widening of the target group, based on the use of a realistic criterion, it would be advisable for administrative reasons to have *de facto* universal coverage of food security programmes. Our own experience as well as that of other countries suggest that errors of exclusion are larger for narrowly targeted programmes than for universal schemes. This can be illustrated by the working of the PDS.

Although, up to 1997, the PDS provided universal coverage, in principle, in terms of actual implementation, it is worth noting that in the states, where the coverage of the PDS was extensive and it provided substantive quantities of food per family through an effective distribution network (as in Kerala and to a lesser extent in Andhra Pradesh) the poor had better access to the PDS than the rich.[11] Thus, a more widespread coverage, in practice, was associated with higher inclusion of the poor and lower utilisation by the rich.

A recent study by Dutta and Ramaswami (2001), based on data on household consumption from the National Sample Survey for 1993-94 shows that the utilisation of the PDS in Andhra Pradesh (57 per cent of all households), was much higher than in Maharashtra (33 per cent of all households). The authors also point out that the geographical coverage of the PDS retail outlets in Andhra Pradesh was almost universal whereas it was unlike in Maharashtra. The study further revealed that in terms of utilisation of the PDS by deciles of income groups, "rural Andhra Pradesh does much better than rural Maharashtra in terms of lower errors of (wrong) exclusion while the errors of (wrong) inclusion are comparable between the two states" (ibid.). Finally, it observed that the participation rate (in the PDS) declined with income group, relatively more rapidly in Andhra Pradesh than in Maharashtra. In brief, the important conclusion that emerges from the study is that in states where the functioning of the PDS was better with near universal coverage, the overall utilisation was higher than in others, the errors of exclusion of the poor were relatively lower, and the utilisation fell relatively rapidly with income level. As expected the two targeting errors moved in opposite directions: Andhra Pradesh had higher errors of wrong inclusion but lower errors of wrong exclusion as compared to Maharashtra.[12]

(iii) Welfare Merits Priority

The third and last argument against narrow targeting pertains to the weights to be attached to different types of targeting errors. When there is mass hunger and poverty, priority must be given to welfare in terms of nutritional outcomes, as the errors of wrong exclusion and associated costs of targeting are high in such circumstances. Thus, contrary to the belief of many economists and advisors, a higher weight should be attached to errors of wrong exclusion than to those of wrong inclusion. This underscores the relative importance of broad or near universal targeting in the context of developing economies. For example, a World Bank Study (Kriesel and Zaidi, 1999) on the evaluation of the TPDS in Uttar Pradesh based on the UP-Bihar Survey of Living Conditions conducted in 1997-98, found that 44 per cent of households in the lowest per capita consumption quintile had received BPL cards as compared to 10.8 per cent in the highest quintile. As rightly pointed out, errors of wrong inclusion have been curtailed and the authors conclude that the "allocation of BPL cards in Uttar Pradesh under the TPDS appears to have been fairly well-targeted." They are however, silent on the errors of wrong exclusion, that is, on the problems of 56 per cent of households in the lowest quintile and the 63 per cent of households in the next quintile that did not get BPL cards, and so on. This is despite the fact that poorer households voiced strong support for the PDS and by their own estimates, purchases from the PDS entailed significant net savings. The fact that such large errors of wrong exclusion are neglected can only signify that the authors are more concerned about promoting the targeting at all costs than the welfare of the poor.

To summarise, we have shown that 50 per cent of the total population receives inadequate nourishment and 80 per cent spends a very high share of household incomes on food items. Small fluctuations in incomes, prices and in intakes can thus have serious repercussions on the health and well-being of individuals in a majority of households. This implies that the weight attached to every undernourished person who is wrongly excluded from a targeted programme should be much higher than that attached to a rich person who benefits from the scheme. Broad targeting or near universal coverage, is more inclusive and likely to lower the costs of wrong exclusion, and is therefore should be preferred in such a situation.

II. WORKING OF THE TARGETED PUBLIC DISTRIBUTION SYSTEM

Started in 1942 as a wartime rationing measure the Public Distribution System (PDS) was extended into a universal welfare measure in the sixties designed to ensure that food rations are accessible to all households—rural and urban—with a registered residential address in most parts of the country. Presently, the PDS is a rationing mechanism that entitles households to specified quantities of selected commodities at subsidised prices.

Eligible households are given a ration card that entitles them to buy fixed rations (varying with household size and age composition) of selected commodities. Although the distribution of food rations through the PDS is as per national policy, the exact entitlement (quantity, range of commodities and prices) varies across states, and the responsibility for implementing, monitoring and enforcing legal provisions relating to public delivery rests with state governments. Not surprisingly, there are large inter-state variations in the performance of the PDS.

In 1997, the Government of India introduced the Targeted PDS (TPDS) in an attempt to curtail the food subsidy (GOI, 1997). The new policy aimed at targeting households on the basis of an income criterion, which implied using the income poverty line to demarcate 'poor' and 'non-poor' households. There have been no major evaluations of this policy and its impact has yet to be studied empirically. However, some of the problems of targeting, in principle and in practice, are already visible.

The Targeted PDS differs from earlier variants of the PDS in certain key aspects. First, a distinction between 'below-poverty-line' (BPL) and 'above-poverty-line' (APL) populations is introduced; hereby the two groups are treated differently in terms of quantities and prices.[13] With this, the Government of India initiated a policy of narrow targeting—targeting households with incomes below the official poverty line. Secondly, for 'non-poor' households, a transitory allocation was envisaged—one based on past levels of utilisation (although the period of transition was unspecified). To put it differently, there was no longer a guaranteed entitlement for APL households. The announcements in the Budget for 2000-2001 confirm that the introduction of the TPDS was the first step in moving away from the principle of universal coverage.

The new policy of targeted food distribution has impacted on entitlements, the quantity of foodgrain distributed, prices, and, of course, on coverage. Crucially, it has altered the allocation of foodgrain as between states and as between households within a state. I shall briefly discuss some features of the targeted PDS.

1. Main Features of TDPS

i) The principle of entitlements has been altered from a per capita norm to a family norm. As per the earlier policy, ration scales were typically defined in terms of fixed quantities per person or per unit (with an adult equivalent to two units, and a child equivalent to one unit). Under the Targeted PDS, however, each poor family, irrespective of size and need, is entitled to a uniform quantity of foodgrain.

ii) The entitlements of a household have been reduced sharply so that each poor household is entitled to only 10 kg of grain each month. As against the entitlement the annual level of cereal intake recommended by the Indian Council of Medical Research (ICMR) is 135 kg per person (or 11.25 kg per month). Thus, for a five-member family, the new ration scale of about 2 kg per person per month, provides less than 18 per cent of the recommended intake.

State governments have been advised to revise and lower their ration scales to match the new principle of allocation.[14] For example, with reference to states that offer 15 kg per person, the guidelines note that "it will not be possible to maintain such an *inflated* scale of issue" (ibid., p. 3, emphasis added). Additional allocations demanded by states from the central pool are to be provided at commercially viable prices.[15]

iii) The scheme provides for a dual price policy: while prices of foodgrain for allocation to families identified as BPL are lower than was the case earlier (that is under the universal PDS scheme), central issue prices of grains for allocation to families in the APL category have been raised substantially. As a consequence, in most states, the prices of wheat and rice for APL allocations have risen steeply after the introduction of the Targeted PDS.[16] The Budget of March 2000 increased prices further, and brought them on par with market prices for APL consumers (see below).

iv) Foodgrains were now allocated on the basis of to a new set of principles, according to which 10 kg of foodgrains were to be reserved for allocation to the officially recognised poor population and restrictions were placed on the quantity supplied to the 'non-poor'. States that were providing more than 10 kg of foodgrain per family now have to buy the additional quantity at higher prices even for distribution to the BPL population. As a result, the share of different states in the distribution of foodgrain has altered with the introduction of the TPDS—the states that were earlier ranked at the top in terms of share of all-India distribution lost their positions after 1997. The new policy thus constitutes an "attack on the PDS in those states where it has been functioning well" (Chandrasekhar and Ghosh, 1997).

v) The pattern of allocation as between poor and non-poor categories of households differs significantly across states. This can be illustrated with the help of data on purchases for the period, January to December 1998. In Bihar, a state where the functioning of the PDS is known to be weak, purchases from the PDS have risen sharply consequent to the introduction of the Targeted PDS: purchases of rice and wheat under the BPL category were about five times higher than those under the APL category. Given a weak distribution system and relatively low level of distribution in the past, the state now appears to be only purchasing the cheaper grain allocated for distribution to BPL households. It is difficult to say whether this grain actually reached BPL households or whether it was siphoned off to other consumers at a profit.[17] In Kerala, by contrast, purchases for the APL families were 16 times greater than BPL purchases in the state. This shows that the state was allocated higher quantities of APL grains on the basis of past allocations, and was committed to supplying a certain quantity of foodgrains to the entire population served by the PDS. The state government offered a higher quantity of foodgrains to BPL households than the allocation from the centre, besides providing for the APL population. As there is a large price difference between BPL and APL allocations, (additional allocations being even more expensive), it is clear that state governments that are committed to provide a certain minimum quantity of foodgrains to their population have to now bear the burden of higher costs.

vi) Last but not the least, the method of targeting—based on the income poverty line—has already led to the exclusion of millions of under-nourished people and people who face the risk of undernourishment from the BPL category. Identification of beneficiaries on the basis of a narrow income poverty line is, as I have argued elsewhere, faulty conceptually and difficult to implement, resulting in large errors of exclusion (Swaminathan, 2000). The entire process of selection of households has been slip-shod and arbitrary and has led to the exclusion of many of them.[18] Even the Comptroller and Auditor General of India has been critical of the method of targeting and pointed out that 18 out of 31 states and union territories had not conducted any survey for the identification of BPL families (*Business Line*, February 6, 2001).

Let me illustrate the actual methods and criteria used for the identification of BPL households with the help of a village-level study on the working PDS in a Maharashtra village in (a) 1995, during the universal phase of the PDS, and (b) 2000, after the introduction of the TPDS (Swaminathan and Misra, 2001). The authors reported that the three criteria used by local officials to exclude households from the BPL category were: a household which (a) has a family member employed in a 'service' job, (b) owns a pucca house and (c) owns a television set.

Besides deviating from the official guidelines of the Government of India on the subject, the authors argued that each of the three criteria was arbitrary and provided an unjust basis for the exclusion of a family from the system of subsidised food-provision. Take the criterion of employment in a 'service' job. A service job, as understood by local officials, referred to any non-agricultural employment. It included regular salaried workers such as teachers and government employees as well as persons employed as watchmen or office attendants in private organisations. This argued that in the absence of any information on the actual earnings, size and composition of each household covered, it cannot be known if the salary of one member was adequate to ensure food security to the entire family. The authors then examined household information from their survey of 2000 on households that had been classified as BPL and APL for the purposes of availing the benefits of the PDS and found major mismatches between the Government of India's official criteria for the exclusion of households from the BPL list and the actual procedures adopted at the ground level.

To sum up, the introduction of a targeted PDS has been accompanied by (a) a reduction in entitlements, (b) a lowering in the off-take of foodgrains, and (c) large-scale exclusion of nutritionally vulnerable persons from the BPL category. In effect, the new scheme entails a dual price policy that has raised the cost of foodgrain to the poor. Furthermore, the TPDS is biased against states that attempt to provide higher entitlements or cover a wider section of the population, and transfers the burden of subsidy from the centre to the states.

2. Effect of Changes in the Budget (2000-2001) on Targeted Households

In his budget speech of March 2000, the then Finance Minister announced steep price increases for rice and wheat supplied through fair-price shops and a clear change in policy. Henceforth, central issue prices, that is, prices at which the Food Corporation of India (FCI) sells foodgrains for the PDS to state governments were to be set at half the 'economic cost' incurred by the FCI for BPL households and at the full 'economic cost' for APL households. In effect, wheat would now be available at Rs. 8.40 (against Rs. 6.82) per kg and rice at Rs. 11.70 (against Rs. 9.05) per kg for APL families (Table 1). BPL families would thus be charged Rs. 4.20 (against Rs. 2.50) per kg of wheat and Rs. 5.85 (against Rs. 3.50) per kg of rice. These prices were revised downwards slightly after a few months when the estimates of economic costs were lowered. The new prices were Rs. 8.30 and 11.30 for wheat and rice for APL families and Rs. 4.15 and Rs. 5.65 for wheat and rice respectively for BPL families. These policy changes have had a marked and immediate impact on consumers. This is set out below:

(i) In the first place, the increase in prices of basic foodgrain issued through the PDS have been substantial and will have an adverse impact on the real incomes of millions of consumers (Table 1). For BPL families, the price of rice was hiked by 61 per cent and that of wheat by as much as 65 per cent (after the downward revision). For APL families, the price of wheat has increased by 22 per cent and that of rice, by 25 per cent. Taking a long-term perspective, in real terms, although BPL prices were lower than the prices in the universal PDS in 1996, the rise in prices for BPL families is higher than the rise in 1991 and that of wheat is approximately the same. In other words, the introduction of the TPDS has not resulted in lower prices for the BPL population relative to changes in wholesale prices.

(ii) The new policy has introduced an in-built mechanism for raising prices, so that every rise in procurement prices results in a rise in the issue prices of foodgrains for the poor. It bears an emphasis that procurement prices have risen regularly each year and in recent years (including the most recent announcement) the increases have actually been above those recommended by the Commission on Agricultural Costs and Prices. The inflationary effects of the new policy can hardly be overstated.

Table 1

Central Issue Prices of Rice and Wheat, 1990 to 2001

(Rs. per quintal)

Year	Rice (common)	Wheat
1990-91	289	234
1991-92	377	280
1992-93	377	280
1993-94	437	330
1994-95	537	402
1995-96	537	402
1996-97	537	402
1997-98		
(i) BPL	350	250
(ii) APL	700#	450
1998-1999		
(i) BPL	350*	250
(ii) APL	905#	650
1999-2000		
(i) BPL	350	250
(ii) APL	905#	682
2000-2001 (Mar)		
(i) BPL	585#	420
(ii) APL	1170	840
2000-2001 (Revised)		
(i) BPL	565#	415
(ii) APL	1130	830

Notes: *A hike in BPL prices was announced but then the price change was revoked.
For Grade A (fine and superfine) quality.
From March 2000, the APL price was set at 100 per cent of economic cost and the BPL price was set at 50 per cent of economic cost.

Source: *Economic Survey 2000-2001* (http://indiabudget.nic.in/2000-01/app1.9.pdf).

(iii) The hike in procurement prices, in effect, excludes APL families from the PDS. A comparison of the economic costs of the FCI with wholesale prices and retail prices in different states shows a steady decline in the price advantage enjoyed by the FCI in the 1990s compared to that the 1980s. In situations where the economic cost is higher than the market price, APL consumers will have to pay more for grain in the ration shop than in the open market as is the case in several north Indian states. The exclusion of APL households from the PDS has implications for (a) the consumption and nutrition of a large part of the population, (b) the quality of the programme, (c) the effectiveness of the delivery system, (d) stocks of foodgrains, and, ironically, (e) the central government's food subsidy bill.

(iv) For BPL families, allocations have been doubled (from 10 to 20 kg per family per month) for BPL households. However, despite this increase, which was long overdue, due to the steep rise in the prices, genuinely poor families will have to spend more now on acquiring the same quantity of foodgrains. This will compound the existing hardship for BPL families, who, under the PDS system as it works in many parts of the country, are required to buy the total monthly allocation in one or at best two instalments.

(v) Millions of undernourished persons and the persons vulnerable to undernutrition have already been excluded from the BPL category by means of income targeting.[19] Under the proposed dispensation, the excluded population can no longer have even the limited benefits available to it as a possible part of the APL category.

(vi) Finally, the central government is abdicating its responsibility with respect to the provision of a minimum quantity of cheap food to consumers in all parts of the country. It has decided to transfer the cost of the food subsidy to state governments. Of course, the current policy affects different states differentially, but it targets and penalises states that have performed well—state governments that have shown some commitment to the PDS in the past and wish to continue to provide a sufficient quantity of foodgrains to vulnerable sections of the population at low prices will have now to pay the bill themselves. On the other hand, in states such as Bihar, where the delivery network and administration are already weak and fail notoriously to reach the poor, the new scheme is likely to increase the incentive and scope for diverting foodgrains meant for BPL households to the open market.

The impact of the new changes in policy is visible clearly from the available data on quantities distributed under the PDS. First, let us look at the broad pattern of change during the last 15 years (Table 2). The quantity

Table 2
Availability, Procurement and Public Distribution of Foodgrains, 1985 to 2000

Year	Net availability (NA)	Procurement	Public distribution (PD)	PD/NA (%)
1985	124.8	20.1	15.8	12.7
1986	133.8	19.7	17.3	12.9
1987	134.8	15.7	18.7	13.8
1988	130.8	14.1	18.6	14.2
1989	147.2	18.9	16.4	11.1
1990	144.8	24.0	16.0	11.0
1991	158.6	19.6	20.8	13.1
1992	148.4	17.9	18.8	12.7
1993	149.8	28.0	16.4	10.9
1994	154.8	26.0	14.0	9.1
1995	169.8	22.6	15.3	9.0
1996	165.2	19.8	18.3	11.1
1997	176.2	23.6	17.8	10.1
1998	159.6	26.3	18.4	11.5
1999	169.4	30.8	17.0	10.0
2000	170.5	36.5	12.1	7.1

Note: All quantities are in million tonnes. Figures for 1997 to 2000 are provisional.
Source: Government of India, *Economic Survey (1998-99)* and *Economic Survey (2000-2001)* (*http://indiabudget.nic.in/2000-01/app1.9.pdf*).

of rice and wheat distributed through the PDS network fell from 20.8 million in 1991 to 14 million tonnes in 1994. The quantity of foodgrains supplied through the PDS rose again thereafter but the introduction of targeting has clearly led to a sharp reduction in offtake. The provisional estimate for offtake in 2000 was 12 million tonnes.

More detailed data on quantities allocated and purchased by commodity after the introduction of the Targeted PDS (Table 3) demonstrate that the main factor behind the decline is the total collapse in demand for grain from APL consumers. In the case of wheat, for example, 76.7 per cent of allocations to APL households in 1998-99 were 'lifted' (or distributed); the ratio fell to 38 per cent in 1999-2000 and to a mere 3.8 per cent in 2000-2001. A similar pattern can be observed in the case of APL purchases of rice: the ratio of off-take to allocation fell from 82.8 per cent in 1998-99 to 73.2 per cent in 1999-2000 and further to 21.6 per cent in 2000-2001 (The off-take of rice by APL consumers has not fallen to the same extent as wheat because of the higher demand from the southern states, which have maintained their own subsidy to the PDS). The policy announcement equating issue prices with economic cost thus had the desired effect of excluding APL consumers from the PDS.

Table 3

Allocation and Off-take of Rice and Wheat in the PDS by Poverty Status, 1997-98 to 2000-01

(in '000 tonnes)

	Wheat			Rice		
Year/category	Allocation	Off-take	Off-takes as % of allocation	Allocation	Off-take	Off-takes as % of allocation
1998-99						
BPL	3137.8	2622.0	83.6	3978.6	3348.6	84.2
APL/Addl.	6781.8	5201.4	76.7	8778.4	7272.2	82.8
Total	9919.6	7823.4	78.8	12757.0	10620.8	83.2
1999-2000						
BPL	3173.9	2877.5	90.6	4032.4	3879.3	96.2
APL/Addl.	7001.4	2695.6	38.5	9692.2	7091.2	73.2
Total	10175.3	5573.1	54.8	13724.6	10970.5	79.9
2000-2001*						
BPL	5844.7	3258.9	55.7	7326.6	5356.6	73.1
APL/Addl.	4623.8	174.5	3.8	7474.9	1612.3	21.6
Total	10468.5	3433.4	32.8	14801.5	6968.9	47.1

Notes: The data are for April to March except for 2000-2001, where off-take are up to February 2001. Addl. refers to additional allocations.

Source: Foodgrains Monthly Bulletin, March 2001.

It is noteworthy that the off-take by BPL households in relation to allocation has also fallen, particularly in the case of wheat. This could be due to several reasons including, among others, the lack of access of BPL card-holders to ration shops and foodgrains therein. With the exclusion of the APL from the PDS, it is likely that many fair-price shops became unviable and ceased to operate regularly for a small number of BPL households. Further, even BPL households may not make the effort to buy foodgrains from the ration shops on the few days when it is usually available given the small quantities involved.

As the off-take of cereals from the public distribution system fell, stocks of rice and wheat surpassed minimum requirements by large margins. Whereas actual stocks in July 1992 were below the norm for that period, since 1993, these have been consistently higher than the norm in every quarter. In January 2001, for instance, there were 45.5 million tonnes of foodgrains in the stocks, which is much higher than the norm for the period. Thus, the post-1991 phenomenon of rising food stocks, on the one hand, and falling food off-take from the PDS, on the other hand, has been exacerbated in the last two years with the introduction of the targeted PDS.

III. CONCLUDING REMARKS: DIRECTIONS FOR REFORM

The Targeted PDS was an ill-conceived measure and the introduction of targeting was, as the changes in the Budget for 2000-2001 confirm, the first step in the dismantling of the PDS in India. As expected, the increase in grain prices and restrictions in coverage in the wake of the introduction of the scheme have led to a spiral of lower off-take, higher stocks and higher prices. Further, there is little doubt that the frequent changes in policy in the last few years combined with the exclusion of a large majority of the population from the PDS have undermined the existing delivery network.

Clearly, 'reform' has to take a totally different direction to be successful, namely, to ensure that vulnerable sections of the population have access to a minimum quantity of foodgrain at reasonable prices. Some of the changes required in the present system of grain distribution to make it an effective system for providing food security are outlined below:

First, as I have tried to argue, targeting is very costly in a country with a large population that is undernourished and vulnerable to undernourishment. At the very least, we need to include around 70 to 80 per cent of the population (and a much higher proportion of the rural population) in a scheme of providing minimum nutritional and income support such as the PDS. So, the first step of the reform process must be to redefine the population that is to be *included* in the PDS. Once the size of the population whose nutritional needs are to be covered by the public distribution system, which includes all vulnerable sections of the population, is determined then administrative, fiscal and welfare concerns all indicate that near-universal coverage is a better way to reach the target group than a complicated process which involves the exclusion of those in the highest consumption quintile. A belated recognition of this problem has led to the announcement (in July 2001) that prices for APL consumers in the PDS will be lowered to 70 per cent of the economic cost of grain. This announcement, it is hoped, will bring the consumers back to the fair-price shops resulting in a higher off-take from the PDS.

Secondly, ration quantities should be fixed on a per person norm and the entitlement of each person should be raised so as to provide a measure of minimum nutritional support. Consumption requirements are age and sex-specific and it makes little sense to allocate the same quantity to a one-person adult family as to a 10-person family. It needs to be added here that prior to the introduction of the TPDS, state governments had set such norms. In Kerala, for example, the norm was 13.2 kg per adult per month—an entitlement that went some way in meeting the cereal requirements of a person.

Thirdly, besides being expanded to cover a wider section of the population the PDS must be geared to provide for higher entitlements per person, thus ensuring that all vulnerable groups are able to meet their nutritional requirements. For instance, the provision of about 60 kg per annum per adult (the average off-take in Kerala) to 80 per cent of the population (say 520 million adults and 280 million children) requires that the PDS supplies about 40 million tonnes of foodgrains. At current production levels, this amounts to one-fifth of production. Distribution of foodgrains on this scale is feasible and sustainable if appropriate production and procurement policies are pursued.

Fourthly, there must be greater accountability and transparency in the administration of the PDS at all levels of the delivery network (that is, from the FCI to the fair-price shop owner). The governments, academics, and mass organisations in India have recommended ways of ensuring such transparency.

Lastly, the provision for ensuring effective food security at reasonable costs to the government requires integration of production, procurement and distribution policies. Unless all parts of the food system are strengthened, any talk of isolated issues such as the high costs of the FCI is meaningless. Taking a long-run perspective, if it is only with an expansion of foodgrain production and acceleration in the growth of yields of major foodgrains in relatively backward areas that a system such as the PDS can be sustained. Greater localised procurement and storage as a consequence of higher production in hitherto less developed areas is one way of keeping a check on the costs of distribution. Another suggestions is to set the final procurement price inclusive of taxes (CACP, 1998). These issues deserve to be studies separately. The main point to be noted here is that the costs of the PDS are closely linked to changes in production and production-related policies.

In conclusion, it needs to be stressed that genuine reform of the PDS calls for a reversal of the current policies, and specifically, the policy of narrow targeting to families living below the poverty line.

Notes

1. Many of the arguments in this paper draw on Swaminathan (2000).
2. Useful summary discussions can be found in Burgess and Stern (1991), Cornia and Stewart (1993) and Sen (1992; 1995).
3. Cornia and Stewart (1993) attempted to value the welfare cost of undernutrition in

monetary terms by valuing the effects of undernutrition on (a) short-term labour productivity, (b) long-term productivity *via* phenomena such as growth retardation and (c) inter-generational variables such as reproductive efficiency. They found that the welfare costs of excluding the poor from programmes of food subsidy were very large.

4. For two formal models of this proposition, see Besley (1997) and Gelbach and Pritchett (1996).
5. See Anand and Kanbur (1991) on Sri Lanka and Pinstrup-Andersen (1993) on Colombia.
6. On the implications of income mobility for defining a target group based on a static income poverty line, see Swaminathan (2000).
7. *Business Line*, November 17, 2000.
8. On the food share as an indicator of poverty, see Anand and Harris (1990).
9. See Li Shi (1999).
10. In the United States, for the Food Stamp programme, the poverty line is defined so as to include all those who spend more than one-third of their income on food (Kuhn et al. 1996).
11. See Indrakant (1995), Koshy (1989), Radhakrishna (1996) and Ramachandran (1996).
12. See, also, Swaminathan and Misra (2001) who found, based on a village study in Maharashtra in two time periods, 1995 and 2000, that the errors of wrong inclusion fell sharply with the shift from universal to the Targeted PDS but the errors of wrong exclusion rose steeply at the same time.
13. Although some state governments had systems of dual or multiple ration cards prior to 1997, this is the first time the distinction has been made into national policy by the central government.
14. Ration scales vary by state. Prior to targeting, Kerala provided 13 kg per person per month whereas in Bihar, the entitlement was 8 kg a month.
15. Ration scales vary by state. Prior to targeting, Kerala provided 13 kg per person per month whereas in Bihar, the entitlement was 8 kg a month.
16. In Rajasthan, for example, the price of grade A rice (fine and superfine varieties) rose from Rs. 6.70-7.00 before the TPDS to Rs. 9.70 after the TPDS—an increase of around 40 per cent.
17. Recent fieldwork by Jos Mooij in Bihar suggests that very little grain is reaching genuinely deserving families (seminar presentation, IGIDR, February 2000).
18. On the experience in Maharashtra, see Moghe (1997).
19. The most recent announcement on targeting is a new policy called the *Anna Antyodaya Scheme*, announced on the *Prime Minister's birthday in December 2000*, and launched in March 2001, targeted at the "poorest of the poor" or about 13 per cent of those identified as BPL. Around 50 million people are to be provided rice at Rs. 3 a kg and wheat at Rs. 2 a kg.

References

Anand, S. and Harris, C. (1990), "Food and Standard of Living: An Analysis Based on Sri Lankan Data", in Dreze, J. and Sen, A. (eds.), *The Political Economy of Hunger*, Vol. 1, Clarendon Press, Oxford.

Besley, T. (1997), "Political Economy of Alleviating Poverty: Theory and Institutions", *Annual World Bank Conference on Development Economics, 1996*, International Bank for Reconstruction and Development, pp. 117-134.

Burgess, R. and Stern, N. (1991), "Social Security in Developing Countries: What, Why, Who and How?", in Ahmad, E. et al., *Social Security in Developing Countries*, Clarendon Press, Oxford.

Chandrasekhar, C.P. and Ghosh, J. (1997), "Targeted Public Distribution System: Is It Getting Sore Food to the Poor?", *Business Line*, July 22.

CACP (1998), *Reports of the Commission for Agricultural Costs and Prices for the Crops Sown during 1998-99*, Commission for Agricultural Costs and Prices, Government of India, Ministry of Agriculture, New Delhi.

Cornia, G. A. and Stewart, F. (1993), "Two Errors of Targeting", *Journal of International Development*, Vol. 5, No. 5, pp. 459-490.

Dutta, B. and Ramaswami, B. (2001), "Targeting and Efficiency in the Public Distribution System: Case of Andhra Pradesh and Maharashtra", *Economic and Political Weekly*, Vol. 36, No. 18, May 5, pp. 1524-1532.

Gelbach, J.B. and Pritchett, L.H. (1996), "Does More for the Poor Mean Less for the Poor? The Politics of Tagging", *World Bank Policy Research Working Paper 1523*, Washington.

Goodin, R. E. and Grand, J. le (1987), *Not Only the Poor: The Middle Classes and the Welfare State*, Allen and Unwin, London.

GOI (2001), *Economic Survey*, Government of India, Ministry of Finance, New Delhi.

——(2001), *Foodgrains Monthly Bulletin*, Ministry of Food and Consumer Affairs, Department of Food and Civil Supplies, March 2001, New Delhi.

—— (1997), *Focus on the Poor*, Ministry of Civil Supplies, Consumer Affairs and Public Distribution, New Delhi.

Gupta, S.P. (1999), "Globalisation, Economic Reforms and the Role of Labour", Society for Economic and Social Transition, New Delhi (mimeo).

Hopper, G. R., (1999), "Changing Food Production and Quality of Diet in India", *Population and Development Review*, Vol. 25, No. 3, September.

Indrakant, S. (1995), "Food Security and Public Distribution System in Andhra Pradesh", *Workshop on Food Security and Public Distribution System in India*, Planning Commission, New Delhi, April.

IIPS (1995), *National Family Health Survey 1992-93: India*, International Institute of Population Sciences, Bombay.

Koshy, A.; Gopalakrishnan, A. A.; Vijayachandran, V. and Jayakumar, N. K. (1989), *Report of the Study on Evaluation of the Public Distribution System in Kerala*, Centre for Management Development, Trivandrum.

Kriesel, S. and Zaidi, S. (1999), "The Targeted Public Distribution System in Uttar Pradesh, India—A Evaluation", Draft Paper, The World Bank, Washington, D.C., August.

Kuhn, B. A.; Dunn, P. A.; Smallwood, D.; Hanson, K.; Blaylock, J. and Vogel, S. (1996), "The Food Stamp Programme and Welfare Reform", *Journal of Economic Perspectives*, Vol. 10, No. 2, Spring, pp. 189-198.

Li, Shi (1999), "Urban Poverty Research in China: Some Methodological Issues", Paper prepared for the *International Roundtable on Urban Poverty Research*, Nha Trang, Vietnam, December 13-15.

Moghe, K. (1997), "Redefining the Poor", *Frontline*, Vol. 14, No. 21, October 31.

National Nutrition Monitoring Bureau (1996), *Nutritional Status of Rural Population, Report of NNMB Surveys*, Hyderabad.

Pinstrup-Andersen, P. (1993), "The Role of Food-linked Income Transfers in Efforts to Alleviate Malnutrition", in Lipton, M. and van der Gaag, J. (eds.), *Including the Poor*, World Bank, Washington, D.C.

Radhakrishna, R. (1996), "Food Trends, Public Distribution and Food Security Concerns", *Indian Journal of Agricultural Economics*, Vol. 51, Nos. 1 and 2.

Ramachandran, V. K. (1996), "Kerala's Development Achievements: A Review", in Dreze, J. and Sen, A. (eds.), *Indian Development: Selected Regional Perspectives*, Oxford University Press, Oxford.

Sen, A. (1992), "Poverty Alleviation: Targeting Versus Universalisation", *Convocation Address at Management Development Institute*, Gurgaon, India, July 3.

——(1995), "The Political Economy of Targeting" in van de Walle et al. (eds.), pp. 11-24.

Shetty, P. S. and James, W. P. T. (1994), "Body Mass Index: A Measure of Chronic Energy Deficiency in Adults", *Food and Nutrition Paper* 6, FAO, Rome.

Swaminathan, M. (2000), *Weakening Welfare: The Public Distribution of Food in India*, Left Word Books, New Delhi.

——and Misra, N. (2001), "Errors of Targeting Public Distribution of Food in a Maharashtra Village, 1995-2000", *Economic and Political Weekly*, Vol. 36, No. 26, June 30, pp. 2447-2454.

van de Walle; Nead, D. and Need, K. (eds.) (1995), *Public Spending and the Poor: Theory and Evidence*, A World Bank Book, John Hopkins University Press.

UNDP (1990), *Human Development Report*, United Nations Development Programme, New York.

20

Policies for Nutrition: How Imperative are They?

M. H. Suryanarayana

I. INTRODUCTION

With the majority of studies on poverty confirming a reduction in its incidence during the 1970s and 1980s as a result of agricultural growth and public intervention, there is a general feeling that policy emphasis should be more on growth than on equity and welfare. This apparent realisation has led the government to downplay the role of redistributive policy instruments during the reform era. One such policy question that has not received due attention is that of the nutritional status of the population, the poor in particular. This is so in spite of the fact that the majority of the population is undernourished.[1] Undernourishment is a problem, which has serious long-term implications for daily activities so much so that Pacey and Payne (1985) define undernutrition as "unacceptable penalties in terms of hunger, illness, dysfunction, and risk of dysfunction".[2] The nutritional status has a bearing on efficiency and productivity of labour, the only asset of the poor, and hence, their wages and incomes too.

By and large, the Indian population is not deficient with respect to protein and fat consumption (Minhas, 1991 and Panikar, 1980). Hence, in this paper, we measure the nutritional status in terms of a short-run measure, that is, calorie intake. Policy makers have paid scant attention to the question of nutritional insecurity from this limited perspective, even in this reform era. This could be because of the finding that the per capita calorie intake of the population is declining by choice and not due to any economic constraint—that is, the poor as well as the population in general are diversifying their consumption basket at the cost of calorie intake. As the Expert Group observed: "It has been observed from NSS (National Sample Survey) rounds on household consumption distribution that even for people below the poverty line (both in rural and urban areas) the proportion of expenditure on cereals as also on total foodgrains is falling and at the same time proportion of expenditure on quality food (animal products, fruits, vegetables, etc.) is rising" (Planning Commission, 1993, p. 15).

This finding, even if valid, would only call for an enquiry into the causes of such consumer behavior because this could also be due to inadequate physical access to essential food items.[3] In other words, the finding only calls into question the *design* and *type* of policy instruments used for promoting nutrition security. For instance, consider the principle underlying the formulation of the Targeted Public Distribution System (TPDS). The PDS is essentially an instrument for promoting the intake of food and hence nutrition security by ensuring physical access to foodgrains. But the TPDS is designed as per the poverty criterion and not on the basis of any food security or nutritional status measure (Government of India, 1997).[4] Experts measure the benefits of the PDS in terms of income gain and not the impact on the nutritional status.[5] Similarly, complementary poverty alleviation programmes like the National Rural Employment Programmes lay emphasis on creating durable community assets like roads and irrigation works and not on launching nutritionally relevant projects that would promote health and sanitation like those for setting up health clinics, safe drinking water and toilet facilities.[6] From the human development point of view, the Group's finding emphasises the need for consumer education as is done in Indonesia and Colombia (World Bank, 1993), which would enlighten the poor on making the right choices in order to improve their nutrition levels and health status.

This paper takes up the question of food security and examines how imperative are the policies for nutrition. It is organised as follows: Section II examines the validity of the findings of the Expert Group and what precisely the data on food consumption reveals? Section III describes the contrasting experiences of Kerala and Maharashtra. Section IV examines how far growth and redisrtibutive polices can contribute towards promoting nutrition security across states in India. The final section presents the concluding observations:

II. CHANGES IN CONSUMPTION PATTERN: A MATTER OF CHOICE OR NECESSITY?

Several studies in India as well as countries across the world have shown that with an increases in income, the poor tend to diversify their consumption pattern, that is, express strong preferences for non-basic and non-food items at the margin.[7] A major cost of such consumption diversification is a decline in expenditure elasticities of calories involving increases in the average cost of calories. Recent studies in India have confirmed this pattern for both rural and urban India for the period after 1973-74 (Radhakrishna, 1991). The Expert Group has also come to the same conclusion (Planning Commission, 1993). Given the policy significance of this finding it would be worthwhile to verify how valid these findings are? What are their implications for nutrition security? Do they really justify policy indifference to redistributive issues?[8] Or, do they necessitate constructive policy responses in terms of promoting consumer education backed by efforts to ensure regular availability of necessary items of consumption as is done in Kerala?

1. Analysis of Findings

Radhakrishna (1991) explains his findings in terms of changes in relative prices and consumer tastes. In other words, the observed changes in consumption patterns represent consumer responses to changes in relative prices as part of the effort at welfare maximisation. Even though econometric forecasts and simulations based on demand models may lend some credibility to such conclusions, this empirical question may also be examined from another perspective. This is because these inferences are based on (i) the all-India aggregate estimates and (ii) the data on consumer expenditure proportions at current prices. Hence, they may not be representing consumer responses to changes in relative prices but the average picture of diverse changes across regions resulting from changes in availability conditions. The observed shifts in consumption patterns may not be real but only reflect changes in relative prices. If so, what do the data really imply? This question is examined in this section using the NSS data for all-India rural and urban populations for the period, 1970-71 to 1988-89.

The estimates of expenditure proportion are made both at current and at constant (1970-71) prices. The estimates at constant prices are obtained by using the representative price indices estimated by Jain, Minhas and Tendulkar (Jain and Minhas, 1991; Tendulkar and Jain, 1993). Tables 1 and 2 provide estimates of consumer expenditure proportions across broad commodity groups for the poorest 10 per cent and total populations of rural and urban India at current and constant prices. Consistent with the findings of the Expert Group (Planning Commission, 1993) and Radhakrishna (1991), the estimates at current prices showed a decline in the proportion of expenditure on cereals and an increase in that for all other commodity groups. For instance, the expenditure share of cereals for the poorest of the rural poor (10 per cent) declined from 60.4 per cent in 1970-71 to 42.5 per cent in 1988-89 and that for the remaining items, except clothing, increased.

A similar pattern can be found among the total rural and urban populations. However, when corrected for prices, the estimates show that the reduction in the expenditure share of cereals was much less for all sections. For the rural poorest decile group the reduction was only from 60.4 per cent to 51.2 per cent and not to 42.5 per cent. What is more important is that, contrary to the findings of the Expert Group, there was no uniform increase in the shares of other commodity groups. The shares of meat, fish and eggs, salt and spices in the total consumption (at constant prices) of the rural poorest decile group actually decreased and the relative increases across other food items were very different from those shown by the estimates at current prices. This picture holds good for other decile groups in both rural and urban India. Thus, changes in

Table 1
Consumer Expenditure Proportions (per cent) by Select Decile Groups: All-India Rural

Year	Cereals & c. subst.	Pulses & p. prod-ucts	Milk & m. prod-ucts	Edible oils	Meat, fish & egg	Fruits, veg. & nuts	Sugar	Salt & spices	Bev. & refts	Food total	Pan, tob. & intx.	Fuel & light	Clothing ftwr.	Durb. & misc. goods & services	Non-food total	Total
Decile Group : 0-10																
At current prices																
1970-71	60.42	3.28	1.92	2.92	1.97	4.61	1.87	4.40	1.67	83.05	3.24	8.46	1.89	3.36	16.95	100.00
1988-89	42.50	4.71	3.08	4.78	2.48	7.50	2.46	4.20	2.89	74.61	4.10	10.54	1.71	9.03	25.39	100.00
At 1970-71 prices																
1988/89	51.16	3.05	2.77	4.65	1.59	7.42	2.49	3.69	3.11	79.93	4.11	7.67	1.65	6.65	20.07	100.00
Entire population																
At current prices																
1970-71	40.72	3.77	8.59	3.57	2.83	4.82	3.17	3.43	2.66	73.56	3.23	6.04	7.93	9.24	26.44	100.00
1988-89	26.38	4.08	8.94	4.33	3.50	6.94	2.97	3.00	3.71	63.85	3.40	7.26	8.47	17.02	36.15	100.00
At 1970-71 prices																
1988-89	33.52	2.79	8.47	4.44	2.37	7.24	3.17	2.79	4.21	69.01	3.59	5.57	8.59	13.24	30.99	100.00

Notes: c–cereal; subst.-substitutes; p–pulses; m–milk; bev.–beverages; intx–intoxic, Durb.–Durables, refts–refreshments; tob–tobacco; ftwr–footwear.
Source: Suryanarayana (1995b).

Table 2
Consumer Expenditure Proportions (per cent) by Select Decile Groups: All-India Urban

Year	Cereals & c. subst.	Pulses & p. products	Milk & m. products	Edible oils	Meat, fish & egg	Fruits, veg. & nuts	Sugar, bev & refts	Salt & spices	Food total	Pan, tob. & intx.	Fuel & light	Clothing & ftwr	Durb. & misc. goods & services	Non-food total	Total
							Decile group : 0-10								
At current prices															
1970-71	49.01	4.21	3.91	4.58	2.88	0.97	4.92	7.33	77.79	3.16	8.39	1.19	9.48	22.21	100.00
1988-89	33.98	4.53	6.22	5.51	3.58	7.40	4.06	7.63	72.91	3.18	9.54	1.02	13.34	27.09	100.00
At 19-0-71 prices															
1988-89	39.72	3.01	6.34	5.50	2.63	7.19	3.37	6.96	74.71	2.63	7.09	1.05	14.51	25.29	100.00
							Entire population								
At current prices															
1970-71	23.16	3.10	9.48	4.56	3.60	6.34	2.82	11.35	64.41	2.99	5.96	5.87	20.78	35.59	100.00
1988-89	15.75	3.48	10.02	4.73	3.97	7.58	2.42	9.20	57.15	2.65	6.59	7.17	26.45	42.85	100.00
At 1970-71 prices															
1988-89	18.49	2.32	10.25	4.73	2.92	7.40	2.02	8.43	56.57	2.20	4.92	7.43	28.89	43.43	100.00

Source: Suryanarayana (1995b).

consumption pattern as shown by data at current prices are both distorted and exaggerated by the changes in the relative prices of different items of consumption. This result leads to the following question: If the changes in budgetary allocation across commodity groups were only marginal, how do we explain the increase in average cost of calories?

The increase in the cost of calories cannot be explained entirely in terms of budgetary reallocation as between food and non-food items.[9] This is because even today the rural population (poor) gets about 70 per cent (80 per cent) of their total calorie intake from the cereals (ibid; p. S-68). The corresponding estimates for urban India are about 60 per cent (70 per cent) (NSSO, 1997a, p. S-68). One major reason for the observed increases in the average cost of cereals seems to be the changing composition of the cereal consumption basket. This holds particularly for the rural poor. Of course, as pointed out earlier, Radhakrishna (1991) notes this important change and attributes it to, changes in tastes with increases in income. Academic experts, on the other hand, attribute them to changing relative prices, that is, increases in the prices of coarse cereals relative to those of superior cereals like rice and wheat. They argue that the consumption pattern has shifted in favour of superior cereals as a result of the substitution effect of price changes in their favour. The latter reasoning may not be valid since the consumption pattern has not shifted in favour of cheaper items but costlier cereals. In addition, most importantly, the all-India estimates are only estimates of averages across regions specialising in the production and consumption of different types of cereals. For instance, the poor and subsistence farmers in the dry regions of western and southern India largely consumed the coarse cereals. Till the 1970s, the average cereal consumption basket in different regions of the country largely consisted of a single cereal—rice, wheat or a coarse cereal. Therefore, the question of a substitute grain and its cross price effect were either irrelevant or did not really matter in a consumer's decision making process because of their low budget weight. Of course, it is true that prices of coarse cereals increased faster than those of superior cereals in some years during the late 70s and early 80s. But the average consumer in the poverty belt might not have shifted his cereal consumption away from coarse cereals because of price effects. This is because even today the coarse grains are cheaper than superior cereals. We can therefore conclude that the average consumer has changed his cereal consumption pattern because of changes in availability conditions.

The per capita availability of coarse cereals declined while that of rice and wheat increased during the post-green revolution period. Thus, it is only because of a net decline in the availability of coarse cereals that the poor as well as the general population in rural India have shifted their cereal consumption basket in favour of rice and wheat.

2. Implications of Change in Consumption Pattern of Poor

What do the marginal reallocations of expenditure proportions across different subgroups of food by the poor signify? This may be examined in terms of the observed growth in real expenditure for these different items. Tables 3 and 4 provide estimates of increases in consumer expenditure at constant prices for different commodity groups between 1970-71 and 1988-89 for five poorest decile groups and the total population in rural and urban India. These growth rates are obtained by using base year consumer expenditure share as weights so that they add up to the total increase in real consumer expenditure for the given population group. In rural India, all the poorest decile groups devoted more than 50 per cent of the increase in total expenditure to the food items only.

This is quite pronounced for the poorest three decile groups, for whom, among the food sub-group, cereals & cereal substitutes, milk & milk products, edible oils, fruits, vegetables and nuts accounted for a significant part (more than five per cent) of the increase in total expenditure. This holds good for the fourth and fifth poorest decile groups also except that their expenditure on cereals declined. One possible explanation for this could be changes in institutions. This is the cost (benefit?) of the development process to the poor.

The NSS data, which formed the base for most of the studies on levels of living and consumption pattern, does not provide, in a strict sense, a reliable estimate of distribution parameters. Its emphasis is on obtaining unbiased estimates of the total and mean consumer expenditure and the sample is designed accordingly. For instance, the foodgrain consumption of an employee household obtained by way of perquisites from the employer household is recorded as the food consumption of the latter. This procedure results in underestimation of consumption of the poor and overestimation of those of the rich employer households. During the 1950s and 1960s wage payments in-kind (cooked meals) constituted almost half of the total wage incomes for the labour class. This has given rise to exaggerated estimates of consumption for the richer decile groups. The estimates for 1950s and 1960s report a per capita daily consumption of cereals of almost one kg for the richest decile group. However, increasing casualisation since the 1970s has led to monetisation of the labour market involving reduction in the proportion of wage payment in kind. As a result, underestimation of consumption of the poor has declined and the matching increases in consumption could be representing the increases in monetisation. It is precisely these increases which seem to appear as growth in recorded consumption. From the point of view of the present discussion, what is important are the resultant changes in consumer expenditure allocations. With a decline in wage payment in the form of cooked meals, the poorer wage earners have to resort to the market to buy all the essential cereals and complementary food items. Another possible reason for the apparent, 'diversification of consumption basket' as experts called it, could be increasing landlessness. As a result, the scope for

Table 3

Growth in Monthly Per Capita Consumer Expenditure (At 1970-71 Prices) by Select Decile Groups: All-India Rural

(Percentage increase in 1988-89 over that in 1970-71)

Decile group	Cereals & c. subst.	Pulses & p. prod-ucts	Milk & m. prod-ucts	Edible oils	Meat, fish & egg	Fruits, veg. & nuts	Sugar	Salt & spices	Bev. & refts	Food total	Pan tob. & intx	Fuel & light	Clothing & ftwr.	Durbl. misc. goods & services	Non-food total	Total cons. expe.
0 - 10	5.78	0.67	1.66	3.10	0.09	4.99	1.35	0.38	2.36	20.37	2.07	1.46	0.24	5.25	9.03	29.40
10 - 20	4.65	0.33	1.74	2.58	0.24	5.01	1.35	0.14	2.05	18.00	1.63	1.37	0.41	8.52	11.94	30.02
20 - 30	2.00	0.12	2.17	2.30	0.19	4.78	1.19	-0.13	1.98	14.61	1.28	0.91	0.81	9.04	12.04	26.64
30 - 40	-0.69	-0.04	2.36	1.92	0.04	4.32	0.92	-0.25	1.72	10.30	1.29	0.74	0.04	4.18	6.25	16.55
40 - 50	-1.04	-0.52	1.22	1.57	-0.06	3.96	0.53	-0.34	1.90	7.21	0.85	0.60	0.29	4.11	5.84	13.06
0 - 100	-1.43	-0.50	1.33	1.64	-0.06	3.67	0.55	-0.16	2.27	7.31	0.98	0.49	2.13	6.28	9.89	17.20

Note: Con – Consumer; exp – expenditure.
Source: Suryanarayana (1995b).

Table 4

Growth in Monthly Per Capita Consumer Expenditure (At 1970-71 Prices) by Select Decile Groups: All-India Urban

(Percentage increase in 1988-89 over that in 1970-71)

Decile group	Cereals & c. subst.	Pulses & p. prod-ucts	Milk & m. prod-ucts	Edible oils	Meat fish & egg	Fruits veg. & nuts	Salt & spices	Sugar, Bev. & refts	Food total	Pan tob. & intx.	Fuel & light	Clothing & ftwr.	Durbl. & misc. goods & services	Non-food total	Total cons. expe.
0–10	0.95	-0.42	4.06	2.33	0.42	8.08	-0.68	1.43	16.18	0.16	0.53	0.13	8.77	9.59	25.77
10-20	-1.37	-0.93	3.72	2.03	0.26	8.62	-0.73	1.26	12.86	0.27	0.65	0.72	8.00	9.65	22.51
20–30	-2.53	-0.60	4.12	1.73	0.37	8.72	-0.67	0.84	11.98	0.06	0.45	0.77	8.19	9.47	21.45
30–40	-2.47	-0.54	4.25	1.88	0.02	8.62	-0.71	1.02	12.07	-0.04	0.43	0.99	10.60	11.98	24.05
40–50	-2.06	-0.47	3.89	1.29	0.08	8.78	-0.52	0.75	11.74	0.09	0.19	2.38	11.03	13.69	25.43
0–100	-1.26	-0.35	2.66	1.04	-0.13	2.43	-0.42	-1.37	2.60	-0.39	-0.13	2.93	13.44	15.86	18.46

Source: Suryanarayana (1995b).

obtaining cereals, vegetables and dairy products from the home-grown stock must have declined necessitating market purchases, which are valued at higher market prices in the recorded data set. The poor seem to have resorted to purchases of complementary items like fruits, vegetables, milk etc. from the market, rather than diversified their consumption. Such diversification is essential for nutrition security, if not calorie security, since these items are important sources of protein and other nutrients. In fact, the so-called diversification has not really been at the cost of calorie intake for the poor. The calorie intake of each of the poorest four decile groups of the rural population has consistently increased between 1972-73 and 1993-94 (Table 5). However, the increases in their calorie intake are not enough to ensure the threshold minimum.

Table 5

Estimates of Per Capita Intake of Calories: Rural and Urban All-India

Decile group	Rural			Urban		
	1972-73	1983	1993-94	1972-73	1983	1993-94
0-10	1192.09	1356.31	1460.12	1298.70	1331.76	1443.50
10-20	1591.90	1681.80	1731.32	1575.94	1588.29	1702.40
20-30	1783.40	1847.86	1850.00	1745.94	1724.00	1803.48
30-40	1944.00	1952.00	1971.66	1802.18	1861.19	1896.79
40-50	2115.04	2111.53	2056.48	1980.00	1912.41	1992.81
50-60	2210.00	2229.56	2156.34	2035.48	2046.00	2074.64
60-70	2451.41	2322.00	2275.17	2266.00	2221.13	2186.00
70-80	2581.40	2506.92	2410.00	2382.13	2294.20	2296.74
80-90	2929.00	2779.53	2584.72	2658.75	2500.71	2470.50
90-100	3861.77	3422.49	3034.19	3324.88	3410.30	2843.14
All	2266.00	2221.00	2153.00	2107.00	2089.00	2071.00

Source: Based on NSSO (1983, 1986, 1989 & 1997a).

The same dynamics of change do not hold good for urban India. Urban consumption is largely monetised. With increases in income, the poorest 30 per cent continued to prefer food to non-food items. However, the rest of the urban population seems to have gone in for diversification of the food basket. It is only the richest half who have opted for variety in their consumption basket at the cost of calories in both rural and urban areas (Table 5). The consequent reduction in calorie intake has been more than the increases in that of the poor. As a result, average calorie intake has declined in both rural and urban areas. Inadequate empowerments in the calorie status of the poor coupled with reduction in that of the rich have led to increases in incidence of calorie deficiency in rural and urban India during the era of poverty reduction. At least the poor seem to have utilised the opportunity, thrown up by an improvement in their economic status, to ameliorate their nutritional status. Therefore, the policy emphasis should be on ensuring their physical access to foodgrains and complementary items as done in Kerala. Options to target instruments like the PDS on both poverty and nutrition considerations should be explored. What is noteworthy to note is that the PDS utilisation even by the poor is less than their entitlement not only in a literate state like Kerala but also in other states for reasons like poor quality of the foodgrains. It is no longer true that people are keen to get the benefit of price subsidies. Instead, they prefer quality foodgrains at reasonably stable prices rather than poor quality foodgrains at subsidised prices.[10]

The preceding discussion pertains to the experience of rural and urban areas in the country as a representative of different regions with different consumption patterns and production and availability conditions. Therefore, the question may be examined with reference to individual states with drastically different growth and administrative experience: Kerala and Maharashtra.

III. EXPERIENCE OF KERALA AND MAHARASHTRA

1. Characteristic Features of the States

The choice of Kerala and Maharashtra as case studies is guided by the following considerations. Kerala and Maharashtra differ considerably in terms of their economic structural features and growth experiences. They do not face the same problem of averages, which are encountered at the all-India level. Some of the distinguishing features of these two states and their growth experiences are discussed below:

(i) Level of Development

Kerala has been one of the poorest states of India. Its State Domestic Product (SDP) is very small and below the all-India average. In terms of per capita SDP, Kerala ranked 7th among 15 major states during the period 1959-60 to 1961-62 (Centre for Development Studies, 1977; p. 11); 13 in 1980-81 and 12 in 1990-91 among 21 states of the Indian Union (Government of Kerala, 1993). The growth in per capita SDP during the 1960s was barely one per cent (Kannan, 1995). Per capita SDP increased by 0.06 per cent per annum during the period, 1970-71 to 1980-81, and by 1.40 per cent per annum during the period, 1980-81 to 1990-91, and the growth rates were less than half of that in all-India (Ramachandran, 1995). Agriculture stagnated between the years, 1975-76 and 1985-86 (Kannan and Pushpangadan, 1990) but the SDP in the service sector grew at the rate of 4.37 per cent since the mid-70s (Kannan, 1995). Even though the domestic economy virtually stagnated, Kerala benefited substantially from external remittances, which supplemented the domestic income almost by 50 per cent. Today, it is one of the top three high-wage-rate states (Singh, 1996). Agricultural labourers, particularly women workers, benefited from yield increases. The elasticity of real wages of female workers with respect to per hectare yield is 1.6 per cent, the long-run elasticity being 2.53— the highest across all states (*op.cit*). Next to Punjab and Haryana, women workers wage rates in Kerala are the highest among the Indian states.

Maharashtra, on the other hand, is the third richest state, in terms of per capita SDP and one of the most industrialised and urbanised states in the Indian Union (Government of Maharashtra, 1997). As the state's agriculture is rain-fed, it is characterised by 'medium growth and high instability' in foodgrain production (Mahendra Dev, 1987). The growth and instability in food and non-food production has also varied across regions since the 60s (Mitra, 1990). Further, its agricultural performance with respect to the foodgrain sector has been uneven over time, while the secondary and tertiary sectors, registered increasing growth rates during the three successive decades since 1960. But urbanisation and non-agricultural growth do not seem to have served as a cushion to mitigate the adverse implications of unstable agricultural growth for the rural poor. This is because wages do not adjust with food prices, as is confirmed by the finding that food prices and wages for male and female agricultural labourers are not cointegrated (Ghiara, 1996). As regards female agricultural workers, their wages do not seem to adjust even with productivity improvement. The short-run elasticity of female workers' real wages with respect to yield (being 0.38) is one of the lowest among the Indian states, while the long-run elasticity estimate shows an inelastic response of female agricultural workers' wage rates to changes in agricultural growth. The degree of gender disparity in real wages is also one of the highest in Maharashtra—female workers' wages were only 74 per cent of male workers' wages during 1982-88 (Singh, 1996).

(ii) Agricultural Economy

Kerala's agricultural economy is based largely on commercial crops. In 1991-92, about 58.5 per cent of the operational holdings in rural Kerala was devoted to plantation and orchards and only 25.4 per cent to crop production. At present, it produces only about 25 per cent of its total foodgrain requirement and is a foodgrain deficit state. Thus, its foodgrain consumption basket is virtually monetised. Further, rice, which used to be its staple cereal, even today accounts for about 90 per cent of the total cereal consumption and wheat for the rest. Hence, our statistical analysis of changes in the cost of calories will not be affected by the kind of problems faced at the all-India level.

The bulk of the agricultural operations in Maharashtra, that is about 83.06 per cent of the operational holdings, is field-based. Further, the rural economic structure is not diversified; it consists of agriculture, which has a low yield, and the livestock sector. As much as 82.90 per cent of the operational holdings is devoted to crop production and just 13.00 per cent to livestock in rural Maharashtra in 1991-92 (NSSO, 1997b; p. 37). About 60 per cent of the net sown area is in drought-prone districts. The soil, topography and climate are not conducive to agriculture and the levels of yield of the major crops are very low. As a result, foodgrain production is not sufficient and the state is deficit in this respect. Unlike Kerala, Maharashtra depended largely on coarse cereals, which used to account for about 70 per cent of the total rural cereal consumption and about 40 per cent of that consumed in the urban areas in the 1960s. However, this pattern has changed over time.

Today, rural Maharashtra consumes all the three major types of cereals: rice (28 per cent), wheat (19 per cent) and coarse cereals (53 per cent). The corresponding estimates for urban Maharashtra are: 34, 49; and 17 per cent respectively (Suryanarayana, 1996).

In Kerala, the average size of operational holding has declined over time. In 1991-92, it was 0.35 ha (NSSO, 1997b). The size distribution of landholding has also changed with the bulk of the landholding belonging to the marginal (less than 1.01 ha) category. The marginal landholding, as a proportion of the total number of landholdings, increased from 86.21 per cent in 1970-71 to 91.58 per cent in 1991-92; their share in area increased from 40.05 per cent to 53.27 per cent between the two years. The corresponding estimates for small (1.01-2.00 ha), semi-medium (2.01-4.00 ha) and medium holdings (4.01-10.00 ha) show a decline with respect to both number and area. Large landholdings (0.01 per cent) are virtually non-existent in Kerala, the extent of inequality in the distribution of operational landholding having declined from 64.7 per cent in 1970-71 to 63.6 per cent in 1991-92 (NSSO, 1997b). Thanks to progressive policies pursued by the state government, inter-regional disparities have declined over time.

In Maharashtra, the average size of the operational holding was 4.28 hectares in 1970-71 but declined to 3.11 hectares in 1980-81, 2.64 hectares in 1985-86 and 2.21 hectares in 1990-91 (Government of Maharashtra, 1998). In contrast to Kerala, marginal holding constituted only 43.59 per cent of the total number with a share in area of 6.6 per cent. Other categories declined in number but not with respect to their share in area. As a result, inequality in the distribution of operational landholdings increased, the Gini coefficients being 0.526, 0.571 and 0.598 in 1970-71, 1981-82 and 1991-92 respectively (NSSO, 1997b; p. 26). In sum, resource endowments and levels of development vary across space.

(iii) Rural Employment

Consistent with the picture above, agriculture accounted for 51.2 per cent of the total rural employment in Kerala in 1977-78 (Vaidyanathan, 1986). Wage employment constituted 42.2 per cent of the total employment and 57.1 per cent of wage labour was casual.

In 1977-78, about 80.30 per cent of total rural employment was accounted for by agriculture (*op. cit*) and today the state has the highest percentage number of landless households. Wage employment as a proportion of total employment was only 39.70 per cent, more than half (55.60 per cent) of which was casual in 1977-78 (*op. cit*). This, combined with the fact that it is one of the most urbanised and richest states in the country, would mean marked rural-urban disparities and a high degree of inequality and rural poverty across regions at a point of time.

(iv) Progressive Policies

Kerala is widely known for its progressive policies with respect to the social sector. The 'public policies' enabled Kerala to achieve high levels of human development. As a result, Keralites could exploit employment opportunities in the rest of the country and the world leading to substantial income and foreign remittances into Kerala and hence, growth in the service sector. Further, poverty alleviation policies were designed to promote income and food security of the poor.[11] Hence, in spite of its very poor per capita SDP growth performance, the ranking of Kerala among states in terms of rural per capita consumer expenditure improved substantially during the 1970s and that in terms of urban per capita consumer expenditure during the 1980s.

Kerala has been widely acclaimed for its achievements with respect to literacy, life expectancy and low infant mortality rate. Among the Indian states, it has the distinction of having brought about a reduction in poverty in the shortest possible time. Estimates of inequality and poverty based on the NSS consumption data also show a favourable picture for Kerala. Inequality (Lorenz ratio) in real consumption distribution in rural Kerala increased from 33.04 per cent in 1970-71 to 34.14 per cent in 1977-78, which declined to 30.57 per cent in 1987-88. The corresponding estimates for urban Kerala are: 28.76, 33.09 and 28.01 per cent respectively. Growth in consumption coupled with a decline in inequality had a favourable impact: rural poverty declined from 59.19 per cent in 1973-74 to 51.48 per cent in 1977-78, 29.10 per cent in 1987-88 and finally to 25.76 per cent in 1993-94. The corresponding estimates for urban Kerala are: 62.24, 59.54, 43.36 and 24.55 per cent respectively. The (rural and urban) combined estimate for Kerala declined from 59.71 per cent (13.53 million) in 1973-74 to 52.93 per cent (12.89 million) in 1977-78, 32.08 per cent (9.2 million) in 1987-88 and finally to 25.43 per cent (7.64 million) in 1993-94 (Perspective Planning Division, 1993 and Government of India, 1997).

Maharashtra, on the other hand, has received much acclaim for its public intervention through the Employment Guarantee Scheme (EGS) and its effectiveness in reducing poverty and food insecurity. Since its inception in 1972, the EGS seems to have played an important role in mitigating the adverse implications of the structural features for the poor by (i) reducing the extent of unemployment and underemployment in the state as a result of which the incidence of person day unemployment has decreased much faster in Maharashtra than in India as a whole (Mahendra Dev, 1995); and (ii) stabilising income streams. These factors would form the base for an optimistic assessment of temporal changes in rural poverty suggesting a definite improvement in the economic status of the poor at least since the early 1970s.

The performance of Maharashtra in rural poverty (severity) reduction during the period, 1958-59 to 1990-91, has been found to be the worst (Datt and Ravallion, 1996). While its economic structural features and the development process would only support such findings, public policies pursued would raise questions about them. Datt and Ravallion (1996) find that there was a downtrend in poverty in rural Maharashtra as reflected in the estimates of three different measures of poverty, viz., the headcount index, the poverty-gap index and the squared poverty gap index proposed by Foster, Greer and Thorbecke (1984), for the period 1958-59 to 1990-91. The study finds that Maharashtra stood fourth in terms of progress achieved in raising average household consumption, but the growth process was regressive and hence, the state was the worst performer in terms of reducing poverty. Datt and Ravallion explain the poor performance of Maharashtra relative to Kerala in terms of the adverse initial conditions, because of which poverty (as measured by the headcount index) reduction in Maharashtra was lower by 1.6 percentage points: These included Maharashtra's lower irrigation ratio (5 per cent as against Kerala's 12 per cent), which accounted for a deficit of 0.52 percentage points; lower female literacy rate (93 per thousand against Kerala's 375) resulting in a decline by 0.78 percentage points and high infant mortality rate (107 per thousand against Kerala's 70) leading to a fall by 0.29 percentage points (Datt and Ravallion, 1996, p. 20). Both the incidence and severity of rural poverty is higher in Maharashtra than in all-India. Within Maharashtra, rural poverty is higher than the urban one.

Rural and urban poverty as measured by different measures, in Maharashtra increased till the mid-60s and declined thereafter, which is similar to the findings for the country as a whole. But the frequency and range of fluctuations in poverty was higher for Maharashtra than for all-India. The latter can hardly be attributed to the 'trickle down' mechanism of the growth process, as there was no growth in total consumer expenditure till the mid-70s; but only a decline and a recovery. The limited growth that took place since the 1970s was inequitous in that the growth rates of consumer expenditure for the poorer decile groups were less than the average observed for the rural and urban populations. Inequality (Lorenz ratio) in real consumption distribution actually increased from 25.12 per cent in 1970-71 to 46.68 per cent in 1977-78, which declined to 33.28 per cent in 1987-88 in rural Maharashtra. The corresponding estimates for urban Maharashtra are: 36.24, 38.21 and 36.82 per cent respectively. Rural poverty in Maharashtra increased from 57.71 per cent in 1973-74 to 63.97 per cent in 1977-78, which declined to 40.78 per cent in 1987-88 and finally to 37.93 per cent in 1993-94. The corresponding estimates for urban Maharashtra are: 42.96, 40.61, 38.99 and 35.15 per cent respectively. The estimate for Maharashtra as a whole increased from 52.94 per cent (28.58 million) in 1973-74 to 56.06 per cent (33.10 million) in 1977-78, declined to 40.10 per cent (29.42 million) in 1987-88 and finally to 36.86 per cent (30.52 million) in 1993-94 (Planning Commission, 1993 and Government of India, 1997).

2. Comparative Performance in Nutritional Status

Against the above backdrop, it would be worthwhile to examine the performance of the two states with respect to the nutritional status of their populations:

What is remarkable about Kerala is that there has been an increase in cereal consumption in its rural areas since 1961-62. In fact the state has the distinction of being the only Indian state where average rural cereal consumption increased between 1961-62 and 1990-91 (Suryanarayana, 1996).[12] However, it should be noted that between 1961-62 and 1993-94 the increase in the cereal consumption of the rural population as a whole was only marginal (1.92 per cent), whereas increases for the poorest three decile groups' were 38.57 per cent, 48.74 per cent and 31.71 per cent respectively. In urban Kerala, there was a decline in the cereal consumption of the total population but the poorest three decile groups experienced increases of 58.50 per cent, 42.42 per cent and 26.65 per cent respectively. Consistent with this trend, there was some improvement with respect to three important parameters of nutritional status, viz., calorie, protein and fat intake in Kerala between 1961-62 and 1993-94. The average per capita intake increased from 1631 to 1,965 in rural and from 1,554 to 1,966 in urban Kerala (Panikar, 1980; Tables 6 and 7). Significantly, the bottom 70 per cent of the population enjoyed continuous increases in their calorie, protein and fat consumption between the years, 1972-73, 1983 and 1993-94. As regards urban Kerala, this was true for the bottom 60 per cent of the population. One important reason for this steady improvement in the nutritional status of the rural population in Kerala could be its persistence in adhering to consumption priorities for food items.

In contrast to the situation in Kerala, cereal consumption in rural Maharashtra has declined since 1961-62. Similar to the all-India experience, the decline in the total monthly per capita cereal consumption has occurred largely because of a decline in the consumption of the cheaper coarse cereals from 16.07 kg in 1961-62 to 11.41 kg in 1993-94, which was of the order of 29025 per cent. The decline in the total cereal consumption was more than the average for the poorest decile group (32.63 per cent). Simultaneously,

Table 6

Estimates of Per Capita Intake of Calories, Protein and Fat Per Diem by Decile Groups: Rural Kerala

Decile group	Calorie			Protein			Fat		
	1972-73	1983	1993-94	1972-73	1983	1993-94	1972-73	1983	1993-94
0-10	781.62	1054.07	1168.37	18.90	26.13	28.32	5.95	12.13	13.28
10-20	999.89	1330.18	1493.47	24.38	31.76	36.47	8.69	17.35	18.39
20-30	1138.04	1449.50	1619.76	27.56	34.93	39.66	10.28	19.97	21.84
30-40	1263.98	1585.65	1745.73	30.84	39.19	43.24	12.44	22.19	24.48
40-50	1346.56	1754.00	1896.56	32.92	44.00	48.06	13.92	27.00	29.50
50-60	1569.00	1816.10	1988.80	38.20	45.20	51.04	17.90	28.80	32.62
60-70	1631.18	1961.00	2172.00	39.88	48.00	56.80	19.12	33.00	38.30
70-80	1798.00	2242.01	2231.16	44.40	56.49	58.86	22.40	40.54	40.01
80-90	2158.43	2459.10	2532.88	54.37	62.92	68.64	30.69	47.51	49.71
90-100	2903.29	3188.39	2801.27	74.55	81.38	76.91	51.61	71.52	58.87
All	1559.00	1884.00	1965.00	38.60	47.00	50.80	19.30	32.00	32.70

Source: Based on NSSO (1983, 1986, 1989 and 1997a).

Table 7
Estimates of Per Capita Intake of Calories, Protein and Fat Per Diem by Decile Groups: Urban Kerala

Decile group	Calorie 1972-73	Calorie 1983	Calorie 1993-94	Protein 1972-73	Protein 1983	Protein 1993-94	Fat 1972-73	Fat 1983	Fat 1993-94
0-10	791.05	1085.60	1233.90	19.37	27.19	30.99	6.51	13.16	15.98
10-20	1043.62	1318.84	1482.89	26.06	33.63	38.86	9.96	18.63	21.80
20-30	1181.07	1414.72	1703.96	30.00	37.72	43.31	13.18	21.79	26.60
30-40	1323.15	1672.58	1766.00	33.58	42.60	45.58	15.16	27.37	28.65
40-50	1599.00	1787.84	1880.00	41.10	44.80	49.25	18.20	30.33	32.65
50-60	1665.11	1895.00	1988.48	42.77	47.00	53.15	21.47	34.00	36.56
60-70	1828.86	2201.59	2077.94	47.03	55.54	56.45	26.75	39.12	39.84
70-80	2056.72	2308.02	2188.48	53.41	59.19	59.46	34.41	43.65	43.75
80-90	2495.96	2751.69	2395.97	65.32	70.19	65.73	50.55	61.05	52.24
90-100	3245.46	4054.13	2941.57	82.36	92.14	81.24	74.81	90.90	71.93
All	1723.00	2049.00	1966.00	44.10	51.00	52.40	27.10	38.00	37.00

Source: Based on NSSO (1983, 1986, 1989 and 1997a).

there was also a change in the consumption pattern of superior cereals involving a decline in rice consumption and an increase in wheat consumption; but the increase in wheat consumption was not sufficient to make up for the decline in the consumption of rice and coarse cereals. Urban cereal consumption has virtually been stagnant. A comparison between the terminal years shows that the per capita total cereal consumption of urban Maharashtra declined by 12.95 per cent, mainly due to the decline in coarse cereal consumption. The decline in total cereal consumption was less than the average for the poorest two decile groups of urban Maharashtra. As a consequence, average calorie intake in rural Maharashtra decreased from 2280 in 1960-61 to 2144 in 1983 and further down to 1939 in 1993-94 (Panikar, 1980; Table 8). What should be a cause for worry is the corresponding decline in the calorie intake of all the decile

Table 8
Estimates of Per Capita Intake of Calories, Protein and Fat Per Diem by Decile Groups: Rural Maharashtra

Decile group	Calorie 1972-73	Calorie 1983	Calorie 1993-94	Protein 1972-73	Protein 1983	Protein 1993-94	Fat 1972-73	Fat 1983	Fat 1993-94
0-10	1063.41	1540.19	1333.80	32.12	45.31	40.87	10.28	15.13	16.79
10-20	1420.23	1737.43	1532.24	43.14	50.34	43.95	14.26	18.89	21.82
20-30	1588.21	1851.14	1662.20	47.35	53.58	47.64	15.44	21.19	24.70
30-40	1695.00	1920.00	1765.40	49.70	56.00	50.26	17.70	23.00	27.24
40-50	1818.82	2064.21	1854.20	52.42	59.78	52.34	22.48	25.27	30.85
50-60	1959.00	2155.86	1921.22	55.50	61.75	53.97	27.90	27.89	33.17
60-70	2056.27	2230.00	2028.14	58.47	63.00	56.78	28.56	31.00	35.88
70-80	2152.00	2337.80	2110.50	61.40	66.46	58.85	29.20	34.46	38.23
80-90	2370.71	2544.24	2299.87	67.87	72.82	64.34	31.92	41.50	44.14
90-100	2826.35	3059.13	2882.43	79.03	90.96	79.02	46.27	61.68	62.19
All	1895.00	2144.00	1939.00	54.70	62.00	54.80	24.40	30.00	33.50

Source: Based on NSSO (1983, 1986, 1989 and 1997a).

groups of rural population. As regards the other two nutrients, protein intake declined and fats intake increased between 1983 and 1993-94. In urban Maharashtra, the calorie intake increased from 1916 in 1960-61 to 2028 in 1983, which declined to 1989 in 1993-94 (Panikar, 1980 and Table 9). However, the bottom 40 per cent of the urban population experienced progressive improvement in terms of calories, protein and fat consumption.

Table 9

Estimates of Per Capita Intake of Calories, Protein and Fat per Diem by Decile Groups: Urban Maharashtra

Decile	Calorie			Protein			Fat		
group	1972-73	1983	1993-94	1972-73	1983	1993-94	1972-73	1983	1993-94
0-10	1197.00	1400.22	1471.97	32.43	41.34	42.78	14.24	18.03	21.70
10-20	1513.24	1592.57	1644.80	59.15	47.35	47.03	22.82	24.06	30.04
20-30	1676.00	1719.90	1765.37	51.10	50.01	49.83	28.60	29.02	34.87
30-40	1726.91	1788.68	1850.75	51.42	52.03	52.01	30.91	32.12	38.90
40-50	1778.39	1886.00	1879.85	51.61	54.00	52.63	33.17	39.00	43.00
50-60	1919.00	1999.84	1949.32	52.00	57.48	53.95	39.30	44.21	47.49
60-70	1993.75	2049.21	2089.00	53.95	58.53	58.70	43.41	47.12	53.60
70-80	2181.97	2217.71	2227.16	58.81	61.47	60.99	53.27	58.04	60.38
80-90	2609.00	2695.69	2379.50	69.20	70.22	65.15	66.90	75.03	67.40
90-100	3114.74	2930.16	2632.28	73.34	67.55	71.93	86.39	83.35	81.63
All	1971.00	2028.00	1989.00	55.30	56.00	55.50	41.90	45.00	47.90

Source: Based on NSSO (1983, 1986, 1989 & 1997a).

Can we explain the observed changes in the nutritional status of the people in Kerala in terms of changing consumer preferences and hence absolve the state of any responsibility for effecting such changes. In rural Kerala, the data do show a process of growth in consumption with redistribution. The population as a whole enjoyed an increase in the consumption of 45.29 per cent in 1987-88 over that in 1970-71; but the poorest five decile groups enjoyed even higher growth rates (Table 10). The bottom four decile groups devoted about 40 per cent of the increase in their total expenditure to cereals only. As regards to other food items, the focus was manly on complementary food items like milk, milk-products, edible oil, fruits, vegetables and nuts. Urban Kerala also experienced progressive increases in real consumption across the population, though , it did not opt out of cereals and other basic food items (Table 11).

The process of growth in consumption in Maharashtra, as reflected in the consumer expenditure data, was regressive in the rural and to some extent in the urban sector also (Tables 12 and 13). What is appalling is that, the poor in Maharashtra, in spite of their low levels of living and nutritional status, diversified their consumption pattern at the cost of expenditure on food items leading to a deterioration of their nutritional status. Such a perverse consumer choice could be due to either ignorance or availability constraint. It is in this respect that Kerala has set an example by organising mavveli stores for the provision of basic food items in every nook and corner of the state. In addition, NGOs have also played an important role in

Table 10

Growth in Monthly Per Capita Consumer Expenditure (at 1970-71 Prices) by Select Decile Groups: Kerala (Rural)

(Percentage increase in 1987-88 over that in 1970-71)

Decile group	Cereals & c. subst.	Pulses & p. pro-ducts	Milk & m. pro-ducts	Edible oils	Meat, fish & egg	Fruits, veg. & nuts	Sugar	Salt & spices	Bev. & refts	Food: total	Pan tob. & intx.	Fuel & light	Cloth-ing & ftwr.	Durables & misc. goods & services	Non-food	Total cons. exp.
0 - 10	27.04	-0.40	2.51	2.65	2.07	2.54	2.26	2.76	6.86	48.29	0.16	5.07	1.16	7.96	14.35	62.64
10 - 20	22.91	-0.32	2.45	3.23	2.07	2.59	2.32	3.14.	5.78	44.17	0.54	3.08	2.05	8.12	13.85	58.02
20 - 30	26.01	-0.53	3.93	2.45	1.96	3.02	2.39	3.03	2.55	44.76	0.16	3.73	1.87	8.63	14.45	59.17
30 - 40	22.23	-0.86	3.13	2.11	1.67	2.36	2.43	2.67	3.51	49.592	0.72	3.47	1.99	11.34	17.47	56.66
40 - 50	15.96	-0.71	3.43	1.99	1.78	1.91	2.09	2.31	4.56	33.23	0.57	3.08	2.33	10.32	16.31	49.54
0 - 100	10.30	0.22	4.13	1.69	0.94	1.08	1.30	1.63	4.73	26.02	0.36	1.97	4.35	12.60	19.27	45.29

Source: Suryanarayana (1997b).

Table 11

Growth in Monthly Per Capita Consumer Expenditure (at 1970-71 Prices) by Select Decile Groups: Kerala (Urban)

(Percentage increase in 1987-88 over that in 1970-71)

Decile group	Cereals & c. subst.	Pulses & p. pro-ducts	Milk & m. pro-ducts	Edible oils	Meat, fish & egg	Fruits, veg. & nuts	Salt & spices	Sugar Bev. & refts	Food: total	Pan tob. & intx.	Fuel & light	Cloth-ing & ftwr.	Durbl. & misc. goods & services	Non-food	Total cons. exp.
0-10	7.41	1.60	5.86	0.36	4.30	6.38	0.10	1.11	27.10	1.08	3.05	-0.30	14.46	18.30	45.41
10-20	17.22	1.95	4.77	0.44	4.42	5.95	0.44	3.15	38.33	1.04	3.42	0.55	13.54	18.54	56.86
20-30	12.46	1.52	3.65	0.32	3.63	5.86	0.29	1.02	28.75	-1.05	0.96	2.75	13.09	15.75	44.49
30-40	7.91	1.09	3.86	-0.27	3.14	4.73	0.21	0.12	20.79	-0.78	0.34	2.67	10.92	13.15	33.94
40–50	6.64	0.89	6.10	-0.53	2.55	5.75	-0.08	0.93	22.25	0.51	1.59	0.03	14.00	16.12	38.37
0–100	5.32	0.46	5.09	-0.40	2.67	5.17	0.04	-2.06	16.30	-0.78	0.55	1.96	21.14	22.86	39.17

Source: Suryanarayana (1997b).

Table 12

Growth in Monthly Per Capita Consumer Expenditure (at 1970-71 Prices) by Select Decile Groups: Maharashtra (Rural)

(Percentage increase in 1987-88 over that in 1970-71)

Decile group	Cereals & c. subst.	Pulses & p. pro-ducts	Milk & m. pro-ducts	Edible oils	Meat, fish & egg	Fruits, veg. & nuts	Sugar	Salt & spices	Bev. & refts	Food: total	Pan tob. & intx.	Fuel & light	Cloth-ing & ftwr.	Durbl. & misc. goods & services	Non-food	Total cons. exp.
0 - 10	-0.60	1.03	1.54	1.19	-0.63	2.26	1.78	-0.42	1.37	7.53	1.48	-2.87	0.32	5.29	4.28	11.81
10 - 20	0.35	0.35	0.45	0.76	0.01	1.41	1.17	-0.25	0.76	5.00	0.43	-2.72	0.95	5.01	3.72	8.72
20 - 30	-3.28	-0.23	1.30	0.80	-0.69	1.25	0.92	-0.50	0.41	-0.01	0.85	-1.43	-0.28	3.99	3.12	3.12
30 - 40	-2.84	-0.33	1.64	0.64	-1.36	1.15	0.91	-0.51	0.46	-0.24	0.74	-1.40	-1.19	4.44	2.63	2.39
40 - 50	-0.29	-0.91	1.92	0.32	-2.14	0.62	0.94	0.16	0.81	1.46	0.75	-1.56	-2.57	5.13	1.79	3.25
0 - 100	-0.25	-0.36	0.82	0.91	-0.93	0.77	0.77	0.16	1.79	3.68	0.66	-1.24	-0.80	13.11	11.76	15.42

Source: Suryanarayana (1999).

Table 13

Growth in Monthly Per Capita Consumer Expenditure (at 1970-71 Prices) by Select Decile Groups: Maharashtra (Urban)

(Percentage increase in 1987-88 over that in 1970-71)

Decile group	Cereals & c. subst.	Pulses & p. pro-ducts	Milk & m. pro-ducts	Edible oils	Meat, fish & egg	Fruits, veg. & nuts	Salt & spices	Sugar Bev. & refts	Food: total	Pan tob. & intx.	Fuel & light	Cloth-ing & ftwr.	Durbl. & misc. goods & services	Non-food	Total cons. exp.
0- 0	-8.93	0.15	1.47	1.29	0.07	2.75	-1.41	0.13	-4.49	0.04	-0.71	-0.80	7.56	6.15	1.66
10–20	-6.42	-0.36	2.37	1.77	-0.21	2.92	-1.56	-2.26	-3.73	-0.22	-0.90	-0.74	6.53	4.66	0.94
20-30	-6.46	-0.45	2.97	1.26	-0.09	3.37	-1.37	-1.66	-2.47	-0.31	-0.65	0.24	10.98	10.28	7.81
30-40	-4.01	-0.39	3.39	1.09	-1.35	3.54	-1.03	-2.25	-1.03	-0.03	-0.91	1.71	10.50	11.28	10.24
40-50	-3.75	-0.54	5.41	1.36	-0.47	3.85	-0.96	-2.82	2.07	-0.93	-0.72	0.48	8.18	7.03	9.09
0-100	-1.34	-0.21	1.47	0.66	-0.82	2.34	-0.65	-4.68	-3.21	-0.87	-0.71	3.16	10.57	12.15	8.94

Source: Suryanarayana (1999).

educating the masses on making correct consumption choices. Thus, the contrasting experiences of Kerala and Maharashtra on the growth and redistribution fronts provide a case for designing appropriate policies for redistribution of food items based on nutritional considerations and not on simple statistical estimates of poverty. The following section makes an attempt to quantify the extent of nutritional deprivation, measured in terms of calorie intake, in the two states by rural and urban sectors.

IV. NUTRITIONAL STATUS ACROSS STATES

Statistical estimates of poverty show a decline over time. This, however, is not reflected in the estimates of calorie intake, an important parameter of nutritional status, which, do not show a similar improvement (Suryanarayana, 1998). As with Kerala and Maharashtra, the reasons for this downtrend vary across states. Policy formulation and its effective implementation would call for an appreciation of the causes for the decline in these different parameters. This section seeks to quantify the extent of calorie deficiency across states and examine their distributional properties and their possible policy implications.

Tables 14-17 provide all the relevant estimates of important parameters of calorie distribution in different states by sector. We estimate the incidence of calorie deficiency with reference to the norm of mean level of 2400 calories per capita per day for rural areas and 2100 for the urban areas.[13] In addition to incidence, depth and severity dimensions of calorie shortfall are measured using the Foster-Greer-Thorbecke class of poverty measures.[14] The results for the rural and urban sectors are as follows:

Table 14

Measures of Calorie Intake, Its Distribution and Deficiency Across States: Rural Sector (1993-94)

State	Average calorie intake per capita per diem	Lorenz ratio of calorie intake distribution (%)	Incidence of calorie deficiency (C_0)	Calorie gap index (C_1)	Severity of calorie deficiency (C_2)
Andhra Pradesh	2052	11.25	82.52	16.77	4.62
Assam	1983	8.74	91.68	17.81	4.61
Bihar	2115	11.86	75.01	14.86	4.26
Gujarat	1994	11.78	83.90	18.90	5.51
Haryana	2491	15.65	51.46	9.33	2.44
Karnataka	2073	11.93	76.74	16.22	4.67
Kerala	1965	13.95	81.98	20.44	6.90
Madhya Pradesh	2164	11.84	72.84	13.73	3.64
Maharshtra	1939	11.92	89.12	21.28	6.34
Orissa	2199	10.75	68.42	11.86	3.19
Punjab	2418	12.17	52.77	8.16	1.90
Rajasthan	2470	11.08	45.19	6.72	1.50
Tamil Nadu	1884	13.19	88.11	23.09	7.75
Uttar Pradesh	2307	11.65	62.93	10.23	2.32
West Bengal	2211	10.61	72.14	11.74	2.77
All-India	2153	11.33	74.50	13.75	3.57

Source: Based on NSSO (1996 and 1997a).

Table 15

Elasticities of Different Measures of Calorie Deficiency Shortfall with Reference to (wrt) Mean and Inequality Measures: Rural Sector (1993-94)

	Elasticity wrt average calorie intake			Elasticity wrt inequality (LR) in cereal consumption		
	C_0	C_1	C_2	C_0	C_1	C_2
Andhra Pradesh	-1.69	-3.92	-5.26	-0.25	0.29	0.95
Assam	-1.54	-4.14	-5.73	-0.27	0.11	0.66
Bihar	-2.31	-4.05	-4.98	-0.27	0.40	1.17
Gujarat	-1.30	-3.44	-4.86	-0.22	0.25	0.84
Haryana	-3.08	-4.52	-5.65	0.12	1021	2.29
Karnataka	-1.92	-3.73	-4.94	-0.26	0.36	1.05
Kerala	-1.51	-3.01	-3.93	-0.27	0.27	0.93
Madhya Pradesh	-2.26	-4.30	-5.56	-0.22	0.48	1.26
Maharshtra	-0.80	-3.19	-4.72	-0.15	0.20	0.71
Orissa	-3.10	-4.76	-5.44	-0.26	0.52	1.38
Punjab	-3.90	-5.47	-6.59	0.03	1.05	2.06
Rajasthan	-4.31	-5.71	-6.97	0.13	1.20	2.26
Tamil Nadu	-0.89	-2.82	-3.96	-0.19	0.18	0.72
Uttar Pradesh	-2.95	-5.15	-6.81	-0.11	0.76	1.66
West Bengal	-2.71	-5.14	-6.47	-0.21	0.52	1.33
All-India	-2.31	-4.42	-5.71	-0.24	0.44	1.21

Source: Based on NSSO (1996 and 1997a).

Table 16

Measures of Calorie Intake, its Distribution and Deficiency Across States: Urban Sector (1993-94)

State	Average calorie intake per capita per diem	Lorenz ratio of calorie intake distribution (%)	Incidence of calorie deficiency (C_0)	Calorie gap index (C_1)	Severity of calorie deficiency (C_2)
Andhra Pradesh	1992	10.57	63.31	10.11	2.31
Assam	2108	9.44	54.11	6.27	1.15
Bihar	2188	11.01	44.27	5.94	1.24
Gujarat	2027	10.83	58.67	9.29	2.24
Haryana	2140	9.56	44.90	5.69	1.33
Karnataka	2026	11.55	56.91	9.81	2.57
Kerala	1966	13.15	66.74	12.33	3.42
Madhya Pradesh	2062	9.52	54.32	7.14	1.38
Maharashtra	1989	9.69	68.30	9.68	1.94
Orissa	2261	9.37	30.91	3.87	0.84
Punjab	2089	10.27	52.18	7.61	1.61
Rajasthan	2184	8.73	38.12	4.75	1.06
Tamil Nadu	1922	13.14	69.30	13.50	4.01
Uttar Pradesh	2114	10.68	54.72	6.94	1.39
West Bengal	2131	9.45	47.24	6.04	1.26
All-India	2071	10.51	53.88	8.03	1.76

Source: Based on NSSO (1996 & 1997a).

Table 17
Elasticities of Different Measures of Calorie Deficiency wrt Mean and Inequality Measures: Urban Sector (1993-94)

	Elasticity wrt average calorie intake			Elasticity wrt inequality (LR) in cereal consumption		
	C_0	C_1	C_2	C_0	C_1	C_2
Andhra Pradesh	-3.167	-5.26	-6.75	-0.16	0.68	1.55
Assam	-5.47	-7.63	-8.92	0.02	1.03	2.04
Bihar	-5.02	-6.45	-7.62	0.21	1.31	2.40
Gujarat	-3.52	-5.31	-6.31	-0.12	0.78	1.71
Haryana	-6.54	-6.89	-6.58	0.12	1.15	2.16
Karnataka	-3.33	-4.80	-5.64	-0.12	0.79	1.73
Kerala	-2.74	-4.42	-5.20	-0.17	0.66	1.54
Madhya Pradesh	-4.43	-6.61	-8.31	-0.04	0.94	1.91
Maharashtra	-3.19	-6.06	-7.99	-0.17	0.63	1.047
Orissa	-7.01	-6.99	-7.17	0.54	1.61	2.70
Punjab	-3.78	-5.86	-7.47	-0.01	0.97	1.95
Rajasthan	-5.81	-7.02	-6.98	0.23	1.32	2.36
Tamil Nadu	-2.49	-4.13	-4.73	-0.21	0.56	1.43
Uttar Pradesh	-4.94	-6.89	-7.99	0.03	1.05	2.07
West Bengal	-4.97	-6.82	-7.57	0.07	1.11	2.14
All-India	-3.88	-5.96	-7.15	-0.05	0.90	1.87

Source: Based on NSSO (1996 and 1997a).

1. Rural Sector

The highest incidence of calorie deficiency across states has been recorded in Assam (about 92 per cent), which is twice that of poverty (45.01 per cent) in the state (GOI, 1997; p. 26). On the other hand, Bihar, with an incidence of poverty of 58.21 per cent, tops the 15 states considered here, in this respect, while in terms of calorie deficiency, it ranks eighth with an estimated incidence of 75 per cent. Similarly, while the incidence of rural poverty (15.92 per cent) is one of the least in Andhra Pradesh that of calorie deficiency (82.5 per cent) is the fifth highest. The states of Assam, Bihar, Madhya Pradesh, Maharashtra, Orissa, Uttar Pradesh and West Bengal have witnessed an incidence of rural poverty that is higher than the all-India average, while the corresponding category states for calorie deficiency consisted of Andhra Pradesh, Assam, Bihar, Gujarat, Kerala, Karnataka, Maharashtra and Tamil Nadu. These results clearly suggest that any policy reform which seeks to realise the final objective of human development by promoting the nutritional status of the population should formulate policies (for targeting) with due regard to the nutritional parameters and not any statistical estimate based on monetary measures. This conclusion is further corroborated by estimates of the calorie shortfall gap and the measure of its severity. For instance, while the incidence of poverty in Tamil Nadu is less than the all-India level, the depth and severity of calorie shortfall are the highest in the state.Likewise, Kerala too has a long way to go in improving nutritional standards in spite of its much acclaimed success with respect to poverty alleviation—it ranks third with respect to proportionate calorie shortfall and second with respect to *severity of calorie deficiency* among the 15 states considered here.[15] The estimates of elasticity of calorie deficiency with respect to mean are negative and significant while those with respect to the Lorenz ratio are negative, though negligible, in many cases. This means that an increase in inequality would even reduce the incidence of calorie deficiency, which really shows how poor is the calorie intake status of the population. In other words, the size of the cake itself is so low that any regressive transfer would result in a reduction in the incidence of calorie deficiency.

2. Urban Sector

The inter-state profile with respect to urban calorie deficiency is similar to that obtained for the rural areas. The average calorie intake in urban areas itself is less than the corresponding estimate for the rural areas. For instance, the incidence of urban poverty is the highest in Madhya Pradesh (48.35 per cent) (GOI, 1997; p. 26), but only eighth highest with respect to incidence of calorie deficiency (54.32 per cent). Tamil Nadu ranks first in terms of incidence of calorie deficiency, calorie gap and also severity while it ranks fourth in terms of incidence of urban poverty or expenditure shortfall from the poverty line. The sub-set of states where the incidence of poverty exceeds the all-India average comprises of Andhra Pradesh, Bihar, Karnataka, Madhya Pradesh, Maharashtra, Orissa, Tamil Nadu and Uttar Pradesh, while the corresponding sub-set on the calorie front includes Gujarat and Kerala to the exclusion of Orissa. Urban Kerala, like the rural sector in the state is marked by the high levels of calorie deficiency, gap and severity; it stands third, second and second respectively with respect to these three measures. The elasticity estimates for the urban sector also corroborate the conclusion derived for the rural sector. Our analysis shows that the immediate need seems to be to promote the nutritional status of the population as a whole and not that of any segment of the population.

V. CONCLUSION

The findings on declining poverty during the 1980s have led to a belief that the government should no longer concern itself with any major redistributive exercise. This is all the more so with respect to policies for alleviating nutritional deficiency, because of the apparent finding that the poor, with the improvement in their economic status, have opted for a diversified consumption basket to the neglect of nutritional considerations. This paper examines the empirical basis for such conclusions. It observes that the poor have not diversified their consumption basket to the extent reflected in the estimates at current prices. The data show only marginal inter and intra-reallocation with respect to food and non-food subgroups. At the all-India level, the poorest 40 per cent have only diversified to the extent required by the principle of complementarity among food items. As a result, though their calorie intake has increased consistently, the calorie levels fall short of the normative minimum. This emphasises the need for formulating policies with reference to both poverty and nutritional deficiency considerations. This point is further corroborated with reference to the contrasting growth and redistributive experiences of Kerala and Tamil Nadu. By initiating a set of policies for promoting economic as well as physical access to foodgrains, the government of Kerala could succeed in promoting the wellbeing of its population with respect to both economic and nutritional criteria. Thus, the nutritional status of the state's population has increased consistently over the years unlike in the case of Maharashtra. When it comes to the nation as a whole, the question that needs to be addressed does not seem to be one of how best targeted policies for promoting the nutritional status of a particular section of the population can be pursved. The average level of calorie intake is so low and the incidence of calorie deficiency is so high across states that there is little scope for eradicating the incidence of calorie deficiency by pursuing a targeted policy uniformly across regions. It is therefore imperative that the government initiates policies aimed at improving the nutritional status of the population as a whole by introducing programmes designed to ensure the economic and physical access of all sections of its population to foodgrains and also for guiding consumer choice.

Notes

1. The term 'nutrition' refers to utilising food in such a way as to enable maintenance, day-to-day functioning and growth of mind and body. An individual is 'undernourished' if his intakes of all the essential nutrients fall short of the normative minimum. He is 'malnourished' if his consumption bundle involves inefficient allocation of nutrients due to wrong choice in diet or inefficient processing and use of food due to illness or poor hygiene.
2. Cited in Haddad and Bouis (1991; p. 45).
3. For instance, we do not find such changes in the consumption patterns in Kerala where the state government has taken measures to ensure the availability of food items in almost every nook and corner of the state (see Section 3).
4. Of course, the poverty line as defined and estimated for the base year is anchored in average calorie norm considering both behavioural and normative aspects (Perspective Planning Division, 1981; p. 81). However, estimates of poverty line for subsequent years are made with adjustment accommodating only a weighted average inflation rate and not changes in behavioural and institutional parameters also. Therefore, poverty estimates based on price-adjusted poverty lines would not really tally with estimates of incidence of calorie deficiency (Suryanarayana, 1995b).
5. PDS evaluation in terms of such measures could be misleading when prices are also distorted due to restrictions on inter-regional movement of foodgrains (see Suryanarayana, 1995a).
6. In other words, food by itself is not enough. The efficiency with respect to utilisation of food would be conditional on the health status of the individual, which would depend upon factors like access to safe drinking water and sanitation.
7. See, for instance, Behrman, Deolalikar and Wolfe (1988), Behrman and Deolalikar (1987) and Behrman and Deolalikar (1989).

8. This is not to imply that Radhakrishna (1991) makes a case for policy indifference. On the contrary, he calls for public intervention in the form of programmes like the PDS and supplementary feeding and social intervention for educating the public on the importance of avoiding wasteful consumption, having safe drinking water and better environment (Radhakrishna, 1991; p. 226).
9. Of course, this is an important reason. At current prices, cereals and cereal substitutes accounted for only 25 per cent of the total expenditure of the rural population in 1993-94.
10. There is a misconception among the advocates of reform measures that what matters most for the poor is marginal gain in income and not the quality of food grains. Hence, experts recommend even targeting of the PDS by delivering inferior type of food grains.
11. Kannan (1995) has worked out the money equivalent of benefits of various poverty alleviation programmes (like PDS rice only), school meal programme, supplementary nutrition programme, monthly pension to destitutes, monthly pension to old age agricultural labourers, Integrated Rural Development Programme, National Rural Employment Programme and Rural Landless Employment Guarantee Programme and other subsidiaries) to rural labour households. The benefits per rural labour household in 1983 was Rs 1,395; which was equivalent to 26 per cent of the annual income of the rural labour household or, in per capita terms, 21 per cent of the household consumer expenditure.
12. Average rural and urban per capita cereal consumption declined between 1987-88 and 1993-94 across most of the states including Kerala, though the percentage decline was one of the lowest in Kerala (Suryanarayana, 1997a).
13. The literature is rich in academic debates over the conceptual and measurement issues in this area and it is not the purpose of this section to dwell on these issues.
14. These estimates are made using the POVCAL Programme due to Chen, Shaohua, Gaurav Datt and Martin Ravallion (see Datt, 1994).
15. The estimates on Kerala could be biased due to measurement problems. This is because anthropometric measures and other indicators of health status provide a much better report on Kerala.

References

Behrman, Jere R., Deolalikar, Anil B. (1987), "Will Developing Country Nutrition Improve with Income? A Case Study for Rural South India", *Journal of Political Economy*, Vol. 95, No. 3, pp. 492-507.

——(1989), "Is Variety the Spice of Life? Implications for Calorie Intake", *The Review of Economics and Statistics*, Vol. LXXI, No. 4, pp. 666-672.

——and Wolfe, Barbara L. (1988), "Nutrients: Imacpts and Determinants", *The World Bank Economic Review*, Vol. 2, No. 3, pp. 299-320.

Centre for Development Studies (1977), *Poverty, Unemployment and Development Policy*, Orient Longman, Bombay.

Datt, Gaurav (1994), "Computational Tools for Poverty Measurement and Analysis", *Sarvekshana*, Vol. 18, No. 2, pp. 1-10.

——and Martin Ravallion (1996), "Why Have Some Indian States Done Better than Others at Reducing Rural Poverty?", *Policy Research Working Paper 1594*, Poverty and Human Resources Division, World Bank, Washington, D.C.

Dev, S. Mahendra (1995), "India's (Maharashtra) Employment Guarantee Scheme: Lessons from Long Experience", in von Bruan, Joachim (ed.), *Employment for Poverty Reduction and Food Security*, International Food Policy Research Institute, Washington, D.C., pp. 108-143.

——(1987), "Growth and Instability in Foodgrains Production: An Inter-State Analysis", *Economic and Political Weekly, Review of Agriculture*, Vol. 22, No. 39, pp. A-82 - A-92.

Foster, J.; Greer, J. and Thorbecke, E. (1984), "A Class of Decomposable Poverty Measures", *Econometrica*, Vol.52, pp. 761 - 766.

Ghiara, Ranjeeta (1996), "Determinants of Wages in Rural India: A Cointegration Analysis", *Journal of Quantitative Economics*, Vol. 12, No. 1, pp. 43-56.

Government of India (1997), *Focus on the Poor*, Ministry of Civil Supplies, New Delhi.

Government of Kerala (1993), *Statistics for Planning: 1993*, Department of Economics and Statistics, Thiruvananthapuram.

Government of Maharashtra (1997), *Economic Survey of Maharashtra 1996-97*, Directorate of Economics and Statistics, Planning Department, Mumbai.

——(1998), *Economic Survey of Maharashtra 1997-98*, Directorate of Economics and Statistics, Planning Department, Mumbai.

Haddad, Lawrence and Bouis, Howarth E. (1991), "The Impact of Nutritional Status on Agricultural Productivity: Wage Evidence from The Philippines", *Oxford Bulletin of Economics and Statistics*, Vol. 53, No. 1, pp. 45-68.

Jain, L.R. and Minhas, B.S. (1991), "Rural and Urban Consumer Price Indices by Commodity Groups (States and All India : 1970-71 to 1983)", *Sarvekshana*, Vol. 15, No. 1, pp. 1-21.

Kakwani, N.C. and Subbarao, K. (1990), "Rural Poverty and Its Alleviation in India", *Economic and Political Weekly*, Vol. 15, No. 13.

Kannan, K.P. (1995), "Declining Incidence of Rural Poverty in Kerala", *Economic and Political Weekly*, Vol. 30, Nos 41 & 42, pp. 2651-2662.

——and K. Pushpangadan (1990), "Dissecting Agricultural Stagnation in Kerala: An Analysis across Crops, Seasons and Regions", *Economic and Political Weekly*, Vol. 25, Nos 35 & 36, pp. 1991-2004.

Minhas, B.S. (1991), "On Estimating the Inadequacy of Energy Intake: Revealed Food Consumption Behaviour Versus Nutritional Norm (Nutritional Status of Indian People in 1983)", *The Journal of Development Studies*, Vol. 28, No. 1, pp. 1-38.

Mitra, Ashok K. (1990), "Agricultural Production in Maharashtra: Growth and Instability in the Context of New Technology", *Economic and Political Weekly*, Review of Agriculture, Vol. 25, No. 52, pp. A 146 - A 164.

National Sample Survey Organisation (1997a), "Survey Results on Nutritional Intake in India-NSS 50th Round (July 1993-June 1994)", *Sarvekshana*, Vol. 21, No. 2, pp. S-1 - S-214.

——(1997b), *Operational Land Holdings in India, 1991-92, Salient Features*, Department of Statistics, Ministry of Planning & Programme Implementation, New Delhi.

——(1996), *Level and Pattern of Consumer Expenditure, 5th Quinquennial Survey 1993-94*, Report No. 402, Department of Statistics, Government of India, New Delhi.

——(1989), 'Results on Per Capita Consumption of Cereals for Various Sections of Population: NSS 38th Round (1983)', *Sarvekshana*, Vol. 13, No. 2, pp. S-1-S-176.

——(1986), "Results on the Third Quinquennial Survey on Consumer Expenditure: NSS 38th Round", *Sarvekshana*, Vol. 9, No. 4, pp. S1 – S102.

——(1983), "Survey Results: Per Capita Per Diem Intake of Nutrients, NSS 27th round: October 1972–September 1973", *Sarvekshana*, Vol. 6, Nos. 3-4, Issue No. 18, pp. S1-S88.

Pacey, A. and Payne, P. (eds.) (1985), *Agricultural Development and Nutrtion*, FAO/ UNICEF. Hutchinson/Westview Press. Colorado.

Panikar, P.G.K. (1980), "Inter-regional Variation in Calorie Intake", *Economic and Political Weekly*, Vol. 15, Nos. 41, 42 & 43, pp. 1803-1814.

Planning Commission, (1981), *A Technical Note on the Sixth Plan of India (1980-85)*, Perspective Planning Division, New Delhi.

——(1993), *Report of the Expert Group on Estimation of Proportion and Number of Poor*, New Delhi.

Prabhu, K. Seeta and Sudarshan, R. (2002), *Reforming India's Social Sectors: Poverty Nutrition, Health and Education*, Social Science Press, New Delhi.

Radhakrishna, R. (1991), "Food and Nutrition : Challenge for Policy'" *Journal of the Indian Society of Agricultural Statistics*, Vol. 43, No. 3, pp. 211-227.

Ramachandran, V. K. (1995), *Kerala's Development Achievements: A Review*, Reprint No. 200-1995, Indira Gandhi Institute of Development Research, Mumbai.

Singh, Ram D. (1996), "Female Agricultural Workers' Wages, Male-Female Wage Differentials, and Agricultural Growth in a Developing Country, India", *Economic Development and Cultural Change*, Vol. 45, No. 1, pp.89-123.

Suryanarayana, M.H. (1999), "Poverty, Food Security and Levels of Living: Maharashtra", *Journal of Indian School of Political Economy*, Vol. 11, No. 1, pp. 77-100.

——(1998), "Nutrition Security in India: Problems and Policies", in Prabhu, and Sudarshan, (eds.).

——(1997b), "Poverty Reduction in Kerala: Estimates and Assessment" (forthcoming in a volume in honour of late Prof. T.N. Krishnan).

——(1997a), "Food Policies: Need for an Integrated Perspective", *Productivity*, Vol. 38, No. 2, pp. 207-217.

——(1996), "Food Security and Calorie Adequacy Across States : Implication for Reform", *Journal of Indian School of Political Economy*, Vol. 8, No. 2, pp. 203-265.

——(1995b), "Growth, Poverty and Levels of Living: Hypotheses, Methods and Polices", *Journal of Indian School of Political Economy*, Vol. 7, No. 2, pp. 203-255.

——(1995a), "PDS : Beyond Implicit Subsidy and Urban Bias", *Food Policy*, Vol. 20, No. 4, pp. 259-278.

Tendulkar, S. D. and Jain, L. R. (1993), "In Analysis of Inter-State and Inter-Commodity Group Rural-Urban Consumer Price Indices in India: 1983 to 1988-89", *Journal of Indian School of Political Economy*, Vol. 5, No. 2, pp. 267-299.

Vaidyanathan, A. (1986), "Labour Use in Rural India: A Study of Spatial and Temporal Variations", *Economic and Political Weekly*, Review of Agriculture, Vol. 21, No. 52, pp. A-130 - A-146.

World Bank (1993), *World Development Report 1993: Investing in Health*, Oxford University Press, Oxford.

21

Food Security and the Right to Food

Jean Drèze

This paper consists of three articles initially published in national dailies. Even though they were written in response to specific events, such as the spread of drought across the country in 2000-01 and reports of starvation deaths in Orissa in August 2001, I hope that they have not lost their relevance. If anything, the need to focus on the issues discussed in these essays is even stronger today, as the country gets more and more entangled in the contradictions of 'hunger amidst plenty'. As this book goes to press, the country's food stocks have further increased to 65 million tonnes, and the food subsidy has shot up to more than Rs. 20,000 crore a year; yet hunger and undernutrition continue on a monstrous scale. No less alarming is the deafening silence surrounding this state of affairs. There is a major challenge here for Indian democracy.

I. STARVING THE POOR[1]

There is no greater scam in India at this time than the so-called food subsidy. Under the cover of 'food security', the government is keeping millions of tonnes of food out of reach of poor people.

Even at the best of times, undernutrition levels in India are extraordinarily high. According to the second National Family Health Survey (1998-99), about half of all Indian children are chronically undernourished. The latest Human Development Report places India at the rock bottom of the international scale in this respect, with only Bangladesh doing worse. This year, with drought affecting large parts of the country for the second or third time in a row, undernourishment and starvation could spread even further.

Against this background, unsuspecting observers may welcome the fact that the Indian government is spending about Rs. 10,000 crores this year on the food subsidy. Surely this helps to bring food within reach of poor families? Far from it. The food subsidy is essentially the deficit of the Food Corporation of India (FCI), whose operations are now chiefly geared to keeping food prices *up* rather than down. This has been achieved (temporarily at least) by accumulating massive amounts of food in FCI godowns. Today, foodgrain stocks are approaching 50 million tonnes.

The Indian public is so used to large numbers that it is easy to loose sight of the staggering scale of this hoard. It may help to think of it as the equivalent of one tonne of food for each household below the poverty line. If all the sacks of grain lying in FCI godowns were lined up in a row, the line would stretch for a million kilometres—more than twice the distance from the earth to the moon. When millions of people are undernourished if not starving, hoarding food on this scale—at enormous cost—is nothing short of implicit mass murder.

There are two major reasons why the food subsidy is so large at this time. One pertains to the FCI's high operating costs (including the storage costs). According to one estimate, these accounted for nearly half of the total food subsidy in the mid-1990s. The second reason is that, at this time, the FCI is buying far more food than it is selling. The difference is a net addition to stocks—the latter continue to grow by leaps and bounds.

Ordinary households, for their part, benefit very little from this subsidy. In fact, what they gain on one side from subsidised food obtained from the public distribution system (PDS) pales in comparison to what they loose as a result of having to pay higher food prices in the market. This is all the more so bearing in mind the low quality of the PDS foodgrains. In some areas, it is reported that even BPL (below poverty line) households see little advantage in purchasing food from ration shops rather than from the market, because the price differential is too small to compensate for the quality differential. These households, in other words, effectively gain nothing from subsidised PDS sales; on the other hand, they bear the burden of high food prices in the market as a result of the FCI's hoarding operations.

Meanwhile, unintended constituencies are merrily feeding at the 'food security' trough. Rats and worms are devouring the stocks. Ration-shop dealers, distribution agents and other intermediaries are selling the PDS food on the black market. According to the Planning Commission, 36 per cent of the PDS wheat and 31 per cent of the PDS rice is appropriated by private parties, at the all-India level. All this boosts the 'food subsidy' (i.e., the deficit of the Food Corporation of India), without doing anything for the hungry.

The question arises as to why these mounting stocks are not used to fund a massive expansion of the public distribution system, food-for-work schemes or other anti-poverty programmes. This appears to be largely a matter of political priorities, organisational abilities, and willingness to bear the financial costs associated with such programmes (e.g., the non-wage component of food-for-work schemes). Addressing these 'bottlenecks' is an urgent direction of political action at this time of widespread hardship across the country.

It would be a mistake, however, to assume that income-generation programmes alone would succeed in absorbing the current food stocks.

According to several recent studies, it is only at very low levels of income that foodgrain consumption rises with additional income; beyond that, income increases lead to higher consumption of pulses, vegetables, milk, fat and related items, but foodgrain consumption remains more or less unchanged. This suggests that, after a point, income-generation programmes will not help resolve the fundamental imbalance between foodgrain demand and supply at the prevailing price. Resolving that imbalance ultimately calls for a decline in the relative price of foodgrains. That, in turn, would conflict with a paramount objective of food policy at this time, namely the continuation of relatively high foodgrain prices.

The conviction that food prices have to be 'supported' (i.e., kept up) is so strong and so widespread that it has clouded any reasoned analysis of the social consequences of high food prices. Many people, especially poor people, would gain from a decline in food prices. For agricultural labourers, migrant workers, slum dwellers, in short, all those among the poor who buy most of their food on the market, cheaper food would be a blessing. People living in drought-affected areas that are poorly served by the public distribution sytsem would also get substantial relief from being able to buy cheap food on the market, instead of being at the mercy of the PDS mafia.

What about the farmers? As it is, they have not been doing too well in recent years, with the slowdown of agricultural growth in the nineties followed by widespread drought. Their livelihoods are further threatened, in some cases, by the imminent lifting of quantitative restrictions on agricultural imports in compliance with WTO regulations. Against this background, is it not imperative to sustain high foodgrain prices?

There are two answers to this question. One is that the poorer sections of the farming community benefit very little, if at all, from price support measures. Consider for instance small farmers in, say, Orissa or Jharkhand or Chhattisgarh. These farmers typically sell little grain, if any, on the market; instead, they tend to combine subsistence farming with labour migration and other income-earning activities that allow them to buy non-food commodities. Hence, higher food prices do not help them. What would help them is an improvement in productivity, based for instance on technological innovation and crop diversification. There is an enormous potential for productivity improvement in large parts of the eastern region, which has been grossly neglected. Instead, massive resources have been spent on promoting unsustainable farming patterns in Punjab, Haryana and other privileged areas.

The second answer is that, whatever the pros and cons of lower food prices, it is in any case *not possible* to sustain artificially high prices, short of destroying or exporting the surplus food. Storing surplus food only postpones the problem. Worse, it *aggravates* it, by giving farmers misleading signals to the effect that they should continue growing more foodgrains instead of diversifying their crops. Sooner or later, this is bound to lead to a glut in the foodgrain market and a collapse of market prices, defeating the price-support policy. In fact, declines in market prices have already happened this year in large parts of the country. The glut is likely to intensify after the rabi harvest, especially as private traders are unlikely to take the risk of buying large quantities of food. It is reported that plans are afoot to deal with this impending 'crisis' through official procurement of up to another 20 million tonnes of wheat. But this only amounts to digging the hole deeper and deeper.

Temporarily keeping prices up by storing food at massive public expense is not an effective way of helping needy farmers. In so far as supporting food prices is a sensible objective, the only sustainable and equitable way of doing it is to generate income among the poorer sections of society. This is particularly so at this time of widespread drought, when income-generation programmes can play a crucial role in sustaining people's effective demand for food. The case for using food stocks without delay to fund massive employment programmes (the traditional backbone of drought relief in India) is overwhelming.

Why, then, is so little being done to use food stocks for drought relief purposes? There appear to be three basic constraints, concerned respectively, with political, financial and structural factors.

The political constraint is simply that drought relief is not (at least not yet) a priority in the corridors of power. The poor have never counted for much in India's lopsided democracy, and with the growing orientation of economic policy towards the (so-called) middle class, their concerns have been further marginalised. Drought, for instance, hardly figures in expert discussions of the forthcoming budget.

This political invisibility of drought-related issues struck me after a recent visit to Rajasthan's state secretariat in Jaipur. While some able and public-spirited administrators were hard at work, the dominant mood was one of complacency and abdication. The most common attitude was to downplay the drought, if not blame the victims for their own predicament. One official assured me that the drought was 'media hype', and that people were doing just fine. Another explained to me how he had learnt from Amartya Sen's work that the first sign of a famine is food scarcity and a rise in prices, neither of which could be observed in Rajasthan today. (It is hard to think of a more radical inversion of Sen's analysis.) Asked about the possibility of curbing electricity consumption in Jaipur during the drought period, the Chief Minister proudly told us (P. Sainath and myself) that he had already done it. As he spoke, the lights of Jaipur's lavish wedding parties and glittering avenues were glowing across the evening sky.

A similar feedback emerges from New Delhi's various *bhawans* (Yojana Bhawan, Krishi Bhawan, etc.). A senior official at the Finance Ministry, for instance, assured me that "people do not have the capacity to absorb more food" [sic].

Initially, I took it that all these good people were trying to pull the wool over my eyes. It gradually became clear, however, that they actually believed what they were saying. And to be fair to them, there is little in Jaipur (let alone Delhi) to remind the middle classes that they live in the capital of a drought-affected state. The atmosphere there is one of economic boom and unprecedented opulence, with plenty of internet cafés, smart restaurants and fashionable boutiques. The 'social distance' between government officials and drought-affected people further enhances the political invisibility of the latter's predicament.

The second constraint is financial. The coffers of state governments are empty, making it difficult for them to bear the cash costs of income-generation programmes (e.g., the non-wage component of food-for-work schemes). At the state secretariat in Jaipur, *paise naheen hai* (there is no money) was a constant refrain. Finding money to pay the salaries of government employees is the top priority of the finance wizards, if not the single priority. Rumour has it that all kinds of development schemes have been halted, downsized or postponed for that purpose. Even widow pensions, I was told, had not been paid during the preceding eight months for lack of funds.

The financial constraint is exacerbated by the tendency of different parts of the public sector (e.g., the Food Corporation of India, the state governments, different ministries) to protect their own budgets and 'pass the buck'. State governments, for instance, currently have to buy food from the central government at the 'BPL price'. Thus, the low social cost of food at this time of bloated stocks is not reflected in public accounting practices.

The thought arises, of course, that part of the food stocks could be sold on the market to generate the required cash resources. This brings us to the third issue—the structural constraint. This constraint derives from the primacy of the price-support objective, discussed earlier. If food stocks are released on the market, food prices will fall. This would undermine the central government's commitment to sustain a 'minimum support price' (MSP). In other words, whatever food the government may sell to generate cash resources will, in effect, have to be bought again to sustain the official MSP.

This problem, incidentally, applies not only in relation to the 'overheads' involved in organising (say) employment programmes, but also to wage payments themselves. If wages are paid fully in kind, the market demand for food is bound to decline, compelling the government to procure more food if the MSP is to be sustained. In short, the government cannot have its cake and eat it: either it has to generate independent cash resources for drought-relief programmes, or it has to adopt a lower MSP.

To these three basic constraints, one has to add further impediments of a more routine nature: bureaucratic inertia, infrastructural bottlenecks, lack of communication between ministries, and so on. The 'blame game' between central and state governments is another stumbling block. State governments, for instance, complain of inadequate food allotments from the central government, which for its part, blames state governments for failing to make full use of their existing allotments. Constructive efforts to resolve these differences are few and far between.

In overcoming these constraints, the first step is to ensure that the welfare of drought-affected people becomes a major political priority. That, in turn, is unlikely to happen unless drought-affected people are able to build countervailing power and alter the prevailing biases of public policy. As it happens, a redeeming feature of droughts in contemporary India is that they tend to be periods of intensified political action and popular mobilisation. The 1970-73 drought in Maharashtra led to growing social awareness of the right to work, later enshrined in the state's pioneering 'employment guarantee scheme'. The 1987 drought in Rajasthan gave birth to a powerful movement for the 'people's right to information'. Even the Naxalite movement has important roots in the devastating droughts of the mid-1960s.

This year, similar processes have already begun in some drought-affected states. On February 18, for instance, more than 1,000 farmers and labourers from drought-affected districts of Rajasthan held a public meeting near the state secretariat in Jaipur, in a spirited attempt to make their voices heard. Their startling testimonies exposed the self-satisfied claims of the administration. In one village of Pali district, people have to fetch drinking water from a distance of 20 km. In Rajsamand, the district's largest lake has dried up for the first time in 300 years. In Udaipur district, two starvation deaths have already been reported. In tribal areas of Chittaurgarh, drought-affected families are selling their meagre assets to buy food. In some villages, children are withdrawn from school by impoverished parents. Distress migration and cattle deaths are widespread. As for relief programmes, they are virtually non-existent as things stand: the coverage of relief works is negligible, and even the public distribution system does not function in many areas. Everywhere, people who seek relief are told that 'there is no money' and that 'orders are awaited' for the initiation of relief programmes.

This meeting was a major wake-up call for the state government (and there are early signs of a positive response). Gatherings of this kind also give a sharp sense of the latent political power of the underprivileged. The paradox of mounting food stocks amidst widespread hunger provides a natural rallying point for further popular mobilisation across the country. Therein lies an important hope not only of resolving that paradox but also of achieving more lasting changes in the balance of political power.

II. THE POLITICAL ECONOMY OF HUNGER IN ORISSA[2]

The recent 'starvation deaths' in Kashipur prompted me to re-examine some field notes I had written in April 1999, during a long walk through the 'KBK' (Kalahandi-Bolangir-Koraput) region. As it happens, the walk started in Kashipur. I do not presume to have gained a vast knowledge of the area during this brief journey, but some deep impressions remain.

The breathtaking beauty of western Orissa, and the brighter aspects of tribal life (so beautifully conveyed in Gopinath Mohanty's novel *Paraja*) did not leave any illusion about the harsh conditions of life in the area. I remember how one old man, barely half my height, kindly allowed me to have a go at carrying the load he was taking to the market. I collapsed under the weight. He had another 15 km to go. For this excruciating labour he would earn Rs. 12 or so, at a time when rice was sold for Rs. 10 a kg in the market.

Beyond this anecdote is a sea of hardship and deprivation. In village after village, poor people survived on a spartan diet (e.g., rice and salt), drank unsafe water, and had virtually no access to health care. Diarrhoea was a common cause of death. Real wages were incredibly low. Even on public works programmes, labourers earned as little as Rs. 25 a day.

There were many signs of a crisis of traditional livelihoods, especially in areas that used to practice shifting cultivation. One elderly man sighed: "In the old days, even a single woman's work was enough to feed the family; now, even if the whole family works, we go hungry." Massive environmental degradation clearly contributed to this crisis. In many villages, the surrounding forests had been decimated and forest-based economic activities had virtually disappeared. In some areas, this had been compensated by the expansion of other occupations, such as weaving and the production of cash crops. Elsewhere, labour migration (often described as 'going abroad', e.g., to Nagpur or Hyderabad) was the overwhelming survival strategy. Many villages were almost empty of adult men.

Another prime cause of economic backwardness in KBK is rampant exploitation and corruption. Local *adivasis* and *dalits* are sitting ducks for unscrupulous traders, moneylenders, bootleggers, contractors and bureaucrats. Enormous sums have been poured into 'development' programmes of all hues with no tangible result. In Bhawanipatna, one contractor (who turned out to be a fresh graduate from St. Stephen's College in Delhi) gave me a candid account of the commissions that were 'due' to various officials for any development work at the panchayat level: 3 per cent for the BDO, 5 per cent for the Junior Engineer, 5 per cent for the 'gram panchayat extension officer', 5 per cent for the Block chairman, 2 per cent for the Block clerk, 2 per cent for the Block cashier (sic). When I asked him what happened if, say, the BDO were an honest person, he exclaimed, 'if the BDO is honest, he will stick to his 3 per cent'!

Everywhere we went, the condition of local public services was abysmal. There were plenty of vacant posts in schools, health centres and administrative offices, as government employees strive to avoid being posted in this challenging area. The schooling system was a shambles. I was startled, for instance, to find fairly large villages without a single primary school—something that would be unthinkable in most other states today. The silver lining was the mid-day meal programme: school-going children were getting a cooked lunch, instead of the usual monthly grain rations.

The public distribution system had familiar flaws. Most people had ration cards, and the official entitlements were far from negligible: 10 kg of rice per month for BPL families, at Rs. 2 per kg. But delivery was inadequate and unpredictable. When food happened to reach the local ration shop, people had to rush there at short notice (a whole day's walk in some cases), and rice was distributed on a first-come-first-served basis, with the laggards getting nothing. In two villages where I examined people's ration cards, the average BPL family had received 40 kg of rice over the preceding 12 months, instead of the official 120 kg. In Orissa as elsewhere, government officials blame the people for the low off-take of grain under the public distribution system, but the real problem lies in defective supply arrangements.

Behind all these failures is an 'overarching problem of political marginalisation. As one woman saw it, 'there is no point complaining—nobody is going to listen.'

In many villages, I heard something I have not often heard elsewhere in India: land productivity is declining. Perhaps this trend can be reversed, but it is clear that the long-term answer to rampant poverty in the KBK region is economic diversification. This was already happening in some places, and there was an evident potential for more. Meanwhile, however, the region appears to be going through a phase of extreme vulnerability, when traditional livelihoods have collapsed and alternative economic activities are yet to develop.

These general impressions are corroborated by secondary data. Indeed, recent statistics on Orissa's economy make for depressing reading. To illustrate: during the nineties, the agricultural sector has not grown at all; real agricultural wages have also stagnated; and foodgrain production has declined at about 3 per cent per year. These are all-Orissa figures, and the KBK region probably fares even worse.

Viewed in the light of this development catastrophe, the recent 'starvation deaths' in Kashipur are no surprise. The nineties have witnessed a protracted crisis of traditional livelihoods in western Orissa. Then came a prolonged drought, when the government stabbed the people in the back by hoarding gigantic amounts of food to placate affluent farmers while the hungry millions bore the brunt of high food prices. Finally, in July 2001, relief programmes were prematurely discontinued, just as impoverished farmers and labourers braced themselves for the hardest season of the year. By a cruel irony, the latest tragedy is excessive rain, which, I am told, has destroyed the maize crop in Kashipur.

There are many lessons to learn from Kashipur's starvation deaths, seen in this broader perspective. One of them is that in areas like KBK there is an urgent need for social security arrangements of a permanent nature (involving, for instance, guaranteed slack-season employment combined with direct transfers for those unable to work). The country's massive foodgrain stocks present a unique opportunity to put such arrangements in place. This is how we should think of these stocks, rather than just seeing them as a reserve of food to be rushed to the starving on a temporary and ad hoc basis.

III. RIGHT TO FOOD AND PUBLIC ACCOUNTABILITY[3]

In the month of October, Surguja district in Chhattisgarh looks like a land of milk and honey. Endless waves of green fields, lush forests and clear streams give an impression of natural abundance. These delightful surroundings, however, hide a harsh struggle for survival. Yields are low in Surguja, and most farmers are unable to grow enough food to cover their subsistence needs. When food runs out, they have to migrate in search of work. Those who are unable to migrate try to make ends meet by keeping a few animals, selling wood or collecting *tendu* and other minor forest products. Hunger is widespread, and so are basic diseases like gastroenteritis, which caused hundreds of deaths in Wadrafnagar block last August.

The dismal record of development programmes in the district bears some responsibility for this state of affairs. It would be an exaggeration to say that all these programmes have 'failed'. Examples of useful interventions include the installation of handpumps in many hamlets, state purchases of *tendu* at subsidised rates, and a major expansion of school facilities. However, these are islands of relative success in a sea of inefficiency, corruption and exploitation. Even though large sums have been spent on development schemes, most villages in Surguja are still deprived of basic facilities such as a decent approach road, a health centre or electricity.

The public distribution system (PDS) fits into this broader pattern of dismal basic services, rooted in a breakdown of public accountability. A brief reconnaissance of Wadrafnagar block suggests that the PDS is virtually non-functional in this area. In village after village, ration cards are full of blank entries. The main reason seems to be that the poor are unable to overcome all the hurdles that prevent them from drawing their rations. Consider Jhapar, a tribal village near the border of Uttar Pradesh. It takes about three hours to walk from there to the local ration shop, 12 kilometres away. The shop opens only two or three days each month (in September, it was open for one day only). The opening times are arbitrary and unpredictable. When word reaches Jhapar that grain is being distributed, eligible households have to rustle up enough cash to buy their monthly quota of rice—about Rs. 130, not a small amount in this subsistence economy. Among those who are able to spare the cash, and also to spend a whole day walking to the ration shop and back, some find the shop closed, others are told that the shop has 'run out' of rice. Few households succeed in reaching the end of this obstacle course. Most people are reconciled with the fact that it is futile to expect anything from this rigmarole. They know that they are being short-changed, but feel that little can be done about it. As one resident aptly commented: *Hamaree baat koi naheen manega—ham log lathi chalane wale naheen hai* (nobody is going to listen to us—we are not the sort to wield *lathis*).

Many of these hurdles arise from the fact that the ration-shop dealer has a strong incentive to prevent his customers from buying their ration, and to sell the grain on the open market. In disadvantaged areas like Wadrafnagar, the public simply does not have enough clout to resist this fraud. Many people do not even know their entitlements. In some villages, for instance, they have been told that the monthly quota is only 10 kg, as against the official norm of 20 kg.

In the larger villages on the main road to Ambikapur (the district headquarters), the situation is different. Here people know their entitlements, and they have means of keeping the local dealer on his toes, for instance, through elected representatives or 'vigilance committees'. As a result, off-take from the ration shops is much higher. In fact, the dealers bitterly complain that the public does not 'allow' them to sell on the black market, making the entire business inviable. Indeed, the official 'commissions' are insufficient to cover operational costs (including customary bribes at the FCI godowns). The local dealers envy their counterparts in remote areas, who are able to fleece the public without encountering much resistance.

The whole system looks like it has been designed to fail. Given the inadequacy of official commissions, only those who have enough clout to resist public scrutiny and sell on the black market are likely to bid for ration-shop licences. And once corrupt dealers are in control of the licences, the door is wide open for large-scale diversion of the PDS grain to the black market. According to one dealer, who spoke relatively openly, barely 25 per cent of the food lifted from FCI godowns in Surguja reaches the intended households.

Surguja's experience suggests that the public distribution system is in urgent need of drastic reform, with a special focus on public accountability. Various steps could be taken to improve accountability levels. First, better use can be made of both carrot and stick in handling the ration-shop dealers. Their commissions should be raised, making it possible for them to work honestly, and conditional on that, firm action should be taken against corrupt dealers. Second, gram panchayats and gram sabhas should be empowered to appoint and dismiss ration-shop operators. In Madhya Pradesh and Chhattisgarh, the devolution of supervisory powers to Panchayati Raj institutions has been used with good effect in other contexts, and this approach can perhaps be extended to the public distribution system. Third, in areas such as Surguja, there is a strong case for abolishing the distinction between BPL (below poverty line) and non-BPL households. Aside from creating artificial social divisions in the villages, this distinction has undermined public pressure for an improved PDS (since non-BPL households no longer have a stake in it), without achieving much in terms of cutting costs. Last but not the least, the right to food calls for greater attention from popular organisations and social movements. There is little hope of radical change based on government initiatives alone.

It is perhaps not far-fetched to think that the right to food provides an ideal focus of popular mobilisation at this time of unprecedented 'hunger amidst plenty'. In Wadrafnagar, people were shocked to hear that food mountains are lying idle in FCI godowns across the country (and even in Wadrafnagar block itself). Even otherwise, there is a strong undercurrent of resentment about the rampant exploitation of local communities at the hands of *babus* and *sahukars*, of which the breakdown of the public distribution system is one manifestation. Efforts to translate this resentment into constructive action are likely to be rewarding.

A good example of the galvanising effects of public accountability came up in Raghunathnagar, the site of last August's gastroenteritis epidemic. After this incident, which caused a public uproar, the local health centre was promptly revamped. Now there are qualified doctors, plenty of medicines, and feverish activity—the best health outpost I have seen. It is a pity that this metamorphosis happened only after a wave of deaths.

Perhaps the most effective means of banishing hunger and starvation from Surguja is an 'employment guarantee' programme. Even a limited guarantee (restricted, say, to the lean season) could go a long way in this respect. The country's gigantic food stocks have made such programmes more affordable than ever, and there is no dearth of opportunities for labour-intensive public works in this area. In this connection, it was sobering to find that most villages in Wadrafnagar had not seen any relief works for many years. This year, no relief works had been organised in any of the villages we visited, except Pandari where makeshift work took place for five days shortly before the Chief Minister's visit last August. Even in Pandari, not a single labourer has been paid to date. It is a cruel irony that in the name of 'relief' people are being made to work without payment, like slaves. Here again, lack of public accountability is the key issue.

Notes

1. Originally published in *The Hindu*, February 26 and 27, 2001.
2 Originally published in *Times of India*, September 17, 2001.
3. Originally published in *The Hindu*, December 5, 2001.

Notes on Contributors

Yoginder K. Alagh is currently Chancellor, Nagaland University and Vice-Chairman of Sardar Patel Institute of Economic and Social Research (SPIESR), Ahmedabad. Earlier, he has held several positions such as Union Minister for Power, Planning and Science and Technology; Vice-Chancellor, Jawaharlal Nehru University; Member, Planning Commission; Chairman, Bureau of Industrial Costs and Prices; Chairman, Agricultural Prices Commission; Director, SPIESR; Advisor, Planning Commission, etc. He has been associated with several high level policy/study groups set up by governments and other national/international agencies either as Chairman or as a Member. A Ph.D from the University of Pennsylvania, he has written several books and has published numerous articles on development issues. He is also the Chairman of the Institute for Human Development.

P.C. Bansil head the Techno-Economic Research Institute, New Delhi, founded by him in 1984. He belongs to the first batch of Indian Economic Service and has worked with the FAO for about 15 years in Sri Lanka, Thailand, Rome, Zambia and Libya. He has authored 28 books and reports, besides a large number of documents and papers prepared for various governments. He has published over 400 papers in specialised technical journals. His work experience relates to the formulation, implementation and evaluation of regional plans for agriculture, statistics, marketing, livestock, irrigation, fisheries, forestry, wildlife, national parks, tourism, agro-industries and social sectors like demography, health, education and housing, as well as project identification, formulation and evaluation in these fields.

R.S. Deshpande is a Professor at the Agricultural Economics and Rural Transformation Unit, Institute for Social and Economic Change, Bangalore. He was also earlier a faculty at the Gokhale Institute of Politics and Economics, Pune, for several years. He has written extensively on issues relating to watershed development, poverty, WTO and agriculture, irrigation, food security, etc. He has also served in several committees set up by the government or international agencies.

S. Mahendra Dev is presently the Director of Centre for Economic and Social Studies, Hyderabad. He has written extensively on themes such as agricultural development, poverty and public policy, food security, employment guarantee schemes, social security and farm and non-farm employment. He has been a consultant to many international organisations like the UNDP, World Bank, International Food Policy Research Institute, ESCAP, and has also worked as a member in various committees set up by the Government of India.

Jean Drèze is a Visiting Professor at the Delhi School of Economics and an international authority on development economics. He is also a Member of the Governing Body of the Institute for Human Development.

Amaresh Dubey is Associate Professor in the Department of Economics, North-Eastern Hill University, Shillong. He has co-authored the widely cited monograph on poverty, "Counting the Poor: Where are the Poor in India?" in 1998. He is an accomplished researcher in the area of poverty and other forms of deprivation. He has published more than a dozen papers on these issues in national and international journals.

C.H. Hanumantha Rao is Hon. Fellow and Chairman, Centre for Economic and Social Studies, Hyderabad and Institute of Economic Growth, Delhi. He did his Ph.D from the University of Delhi and worked at the Institute of Economic Growth from 1961 to 1991. His publications include *Technological Change and Distribution of Gains in Indian Agriculture* (1975) and *Agricultural Growth, Rural Poverty and Environmental Degradation in India* (1994). He was a member of the Seventh and Eighth Finance Commissions; and member of the Planning Commission during 1982-86.

S. Harikishan is working as Lecturer in Economics in the Post-graduate Department of Economics, Vivek Varthani College Hyderabad. His areas of interest are agriculture, rural development and food security.

S. Indrakant is a Professor of Economics at Osmania University, Hyderabad, having teaching and research experience of more than 25 years. He has directed eight research projects and is associated with 12 research projects which were sponsored by agencies like UNDP, Ford Foundation, ADB, World Bank, UGC and Governemnt of Andhra Pradesh. He has 22 publications in reputed journals to his credit.

Shikha Jha is a Professor at the Indira Gandhi Institute of Development Research, Mumbai, India. She teaches graduate courses in micro-economics and public economics. Her research interests cover the areas of food security and public economics and her publications cover a range of topics including consumer subsidies, public distribution system, price stabilisation, trade liberalisation, fiscal federalism and fiscal decentralisation.

K.P. Kannan is Fellow and Director of the Centre for Development Studies, Trivandrum. He also holds the Indian Planning Commission Chair in Development Economics at the Centre. He has authored several books and articles on a wide range of development issues including labour, poverty, social security and human development. He has served in various national and international bodies. During 2002-03 he worked as an Expert Member in the Technical Secretariat of the World Commission on Social Dimensions of Globalisation constituted by the International Labour Organisation, Geneva.

Orester Kharpuri is on the faculty of Department of Economics, North-Eastern Hill University, Shillong since 1996. He graduated from North-Eastern Hill University with enviable academic record. He has keen interest in development related issues. Currently he is working on his Ph.D. dissertation in the area of poverty and human development with special emphasis on the socially excluded groups in the north eastern states and has already published a couple of papers on these issues in reputed journals.

Praduman Kumar is Professor of Agricultural Economics at Indian Agricultural Research Institute (IARI), New Delhi. He has written extensively in the areas of total factor productivity, demand and supply projections, small farmers and household food and nutritional security. He has developed a number of econometric models for crops and livestock. He has been honoured with Best Teacher Award of IARI and had been a consultant to FAO, UNDP, United Nations, ESCAP, CGPRT Centre, and several CGIAR institutions including IFPRI and ICRISAT.

M. Mahamallick is Senior Research Scholar, P.G. Department of Economics, Sambalpur University, Sambalpur, Orissa. His research interest includes resource use and livelihood Security.

Surabhi Mittal is Research Associate at National Centre for Agricultural Economics and Policy Research, New Delhi. She is a young scientist and has been working in the areas of total factor productivity, food supply, and rice productivity after her Ph.D. in Agricultural Economics in the year 2001.

Jos Mooij is a Visiting Fellow at the Centre for Economic and Social Studies, Hyderabad. Earlier, she has been a staff member at the Institute of Social Studies, the Hague, the Netherlands. She is working mainly on governance and policy processes with regard to the social sector in India. She is the author of the book, *Food Policy and the Indian State* and *The Public Food Distribution System in South India*, published by Oxford University Press, New Delhi, in 1999 and several articles in international and Indian journals.

Amitava Mukherjee was educated at the Ranchi University, Ranchi; Rice University, Houston; University of South Florida, Tampa, U.S.A.; Stanford University, Stanford; School of Oriental and African Studies, University of London; and London School of Economics and Political Science. He is currently the Chief Technical Advisor, Pro-poor Public Private Sector Partnership, United Nations, at Bangkok and Executive Director (on leave), Development Tracks, a knowledge company in Delhi. He has written and lectured extensively, both in India and abroad (including at the United Nations and World Summits) on food security, hunger and participatory development. He has published a large number of professional reports, articles/papers and about thirty books. His latest publications are *Economic and Social Progress in Jeopardy: HIV/AIDS in the Asian and Pacific Region* (co-authored) (New York: United Nations, 2003) and *Hunger: Theory, Perspectives and Reality* (Aldershot, Sydney etc: Ashgate, forthcoming).

Nira Ramachandran is a development consultant and Senior Visiting Fellow at the Institute for Human Development, New Delhi. Earlier, she was engaged in post-doctoral research on sustainable development as an ICSSR Senior Fellow at the LBSNAA, Mussoorie, where she was also the co-ordinator, Centre for Sustainable Development. She holds a Ph.D in Regional Development from the Jawaharlal Nehru University, New Delhi and has been trained at the Institute for International Studies and Training, Fujinomiya, Japan. She has several publications to her credit including books entitled *Monitoring Sustainability: Indices and Techniques of Analysis* and *Carrying Capacity of Mussorie* (co-author). She has also worked as consultant for international organisations like the WFP, FAO and World Bank.

Vidya Sagar is a Senior Fellow at the Institute of Development Studies, Jaipur and had earlier taught economics at the University of Rajasthan. His research has been mainly on issues related to agricultural and rural development, livestock economy, poverty and food security. He has published several books and a large number of papers in professional journals.

Kailas Sarap is a presently Professor of Economics at Sambalpur University, Sambalpur, Orissa and has been a Visiting Fellow at the University of Namur, Belgium, and Commonwealth Fellow at the University of Oxford. He has previously published a number of articles in leading journals, including the Journal of Peasant Studies, the Cambridge Journal of Economics, Development and Change, Economic and Political Weekly and Indian Economic Review. He has also authored a book entitled *Interlinked Agrarian Markets in Rural India*. His research interests include agrarian relations, land and labour markets, food security and access to credit and health.

Nisha Srivastava teaches economics at the University of Allahabad. She has published several articles in edited books and reputed journals on issues such as social security, gender gaps in employment and organised sector employment. She is co-editing the first Uttar Pradesh Human Development Report. Among the projects she has completed for various national and international organisations are : *Impact of Agricultural Reforms on the Urban Poor; Qualitative Dimensions of Poverty in Uttar Pradesh;* and *Vulnerability and Violence against Women*, carried out for the World Bank. She has also participated in a study on Poverty and the Social Sector in Uttar Pradesh for the Japan Bank for International Cooperation.

P.V. Srinivasan is a Professor at the Indira Gandhi Institute of Development Research, Mumbai, India. His research interests include food security, agricultural price policy and analysis of poverty and inequality. His recent work deals with issues related to managing price risk in foodgrain markets under liberalised external trade and geographic targeting of poverty alleviation programmes.

Madhura Swaminathan, a development economist, is presently a Professor at the Indian Statistical Institute, Kolkata. She is author of *Weakening Welfare: The Public Distribution of Food in India* (LeftWord Books, 2000).

M.H. Suryanarayana is currently a faculty member of the Indira Gandhi Institute of Development Research, Mumbai. He teaches econometrics and his area of research interest is Development Economics.

V.M. Rao is a Honorary Visiting Fellow, Institute for Social and Economic Change, Bangalore. He is also associated with Institute for Human Development, New Delhi and Indian School of Political Economy, Pune. His areas of interest are agricultural and rural development and rural poverty.

Vijay S. Vyas has a Ph.D. degree in Economics from the University of Bombay. He has taught in the University of Bombay, Sardar Patel University and the Indian Institute of Management, Ahmedabad. He was Visiting Scholar at the South Asian Centre of the Boston University, USA. Currently, he is Professor Emeritus in the Institute of Development Studies, Jaipur. He has held senior academic and advisory positions in India and abroad. He was a Member of the Agricultural Prices Commission of the Government of India; Director, Indian Institute of Management, Ahemdabad; Senior Advisor in Agricultural and Rural Development in the World Bank, Washington, D.C.; and Chairman of the Governing Body of Institute for Development Studies, Jaipur. He has been Member and Chairman of several commissions and committees in India and abroad; and is a Member of the Economic Advisory Council to the Prime Minister of India; Central Board of Directors of the Reserve Bank of India; Board of Directors of NABARD, and of the Rajasthan State Planning Board. He has been intimately connected with the NGO and civil rights movement in Rajasthan and India. He has been honoured in India and abroad for his academic, civil and policy related activities.

List of Abbreviations

ACIAR	:	Australian Centre for International Agricultural Research
ADB	:	Asian Development Bank
AIDS	:	Almost Ideal Demand System
AMS	:	Aggregate Measure of Support
ANM	:	Auxiliary Nurse-Midwife
ANP	:	Applied Nutrition Programme
AOA	:	Agreement on Agriculture
APL	:	Above Poverty Line
APSCSC	:	Andhra Pradesh State Civil Supplies Corporation
BDO	:	Block Development Officer
BICP	:	Bureau of Industrial Costs and Prices
BMI	:	Body Mass Index
BOP	:	Balance of Payments
BPL	:	Below Poverty Line
CACP	:	Commission for Agricultural Costs and Prices
CARE	:	Co-operative for American Relief Everywhere
CARG	:	Compound Annual Rate of Growth
CGIAR	:	Consultative Group on International Agricultural Research
CGPRT	:	Coarse Grain, Pulses, Roots and Tuber Crops
CIP	:	Central Issue Price
CPRs	:	Common Property Resources
CPWP	:	Composite Programme for Women and Children
CSO	:	Central Statistical Organisation
CU	:	Consumer Unit
DAP	:	Draught Animal Power
DCP	:	Digestible Crude Protein
DDP	:	Desert Development Programme
DLP	:	District Literacy Programme
EAS	:	Employment Assurance Scheme
EGS	:	Employment Guarantee Scheme
EU	:	European Union
FAO	:	Food and Agriculture Organisation
FAQ	:	Fair Average Quality
FCDS	:	Food Characteristics Demand System
FCI	:	Food Corporation of India
FGD	:	Focus Group Discussion
FIR	:	First Information Report
FOB	:	Freight on Board

FPS : Fair Price Shop
FWP : Food for Work Programme
GATT : General Agreement on Tariffs and Trade
GDP : Gross Domestic Product
GOI : Government of India
HYVs : High-Yielding Varieties
IAS : Indian Administrative Services
IBRD : International Bank for Reconstruction and Development
ICAR : Indian Council of Agricultural Research
ICDS : Integrated Child Development Services
ICMR : Indian Council of Medical Research
ICRISAT : International Crop Research Institute for Semi-Arid Tropics
ICSSR : Indian Council of Social Science Research
IDA : Iron Deficiency Anaemia
IDD : Iodine Deficiency Disorder
IDPAD : Indo-Dutch Programme for Alternatives in Development
IFPRI : International Food Policy Research Institute
ILSI : International Life Science Institute
IMR : Infant Mortality Rate
ITDP : Integrated Tribal Development Programme
JRY : Jawahar Rojgar Yojana
KBK : Kalahandi-Bolangir-Koraput
KRC : Krishna Rakshit Chak
LBSNAA : Lal Bahadur Shastri National Academy of Administration
LRMC : Long Range Marginal Cost
MLA : Member of Legislative Assembly
MPCE : Monthly Per Capita Consumption Expenditure
MSP : Minimum Support Price
NABARD : National Bank for Agriculture and Rural Development
NAFED : National Agricultural Cooperative Marketing Federation
NCAER : National Council of Applied Economic Research
NECC : National Engineering Coordination Committee
NFHS : National Family Health Survey
NGO : Non-Government Organisation
NIRD : National Institute of Rural Development
NNMB : National Nutritional Monitoring Bureau
NPANs : National Plans of Action for Nutrition
NQDS : Normalised Quadratic Demand System
NSS : National Sample Survey
NSSO : National Sample Survey Organisation
OBC : Other Backward Classes
OECD : Organisation for Economic Cooperation and Development
OSCSC : Orissa State Civil Supplies Corporation
PDS : Public Distribution System
PEM : Protein-Energy Malnutrition
PFCE : Private Final Consumption Expenditure
PHC : Primary Health Centre
PRI : Panchayati Raj Institution
QRs : Quantitative Restrictions
RCP : Real Cost of Production

RDA : Required Daily Allowance
RFSNA : Rapid Food Security and Nutrition Analysis
RIDF : Rural Infrastructure Development Fund
RJD : Rashtriya Janata Dal
RNF : Rural Non-Farm
RNFS : Rural Non-Farm Sector
RPDS : Revamped Public Distribution System
RRA : Rapid Rural Appraisal
SAP : Structural Adjustment Programme
SC : Scheduled Caste
SD : Standard Deviation
SDP : State Domestic Product
SDT : Special and Differential Treatment
SFC : State Food Corporation
SLC : Survey of Living Conditions
SNP : Supplementary Nutrition Programme
SORs : Special Officers Rationing
SPS : Sanitary and Phytosanitary Measures
SSG : Special Safeguards
ST : Scheduled Tribe
TDN : Total Digestive Nutrient
TFP : Total Factor Productivity
TLDS : Transcedental Logarithmic Demand System
TPDS : Targeted Public Distribution System
TRIPS : Trade-Related Intellectual Property Rights
UGC : University Grants Commission
UNDP : United Nation Development Programme
UNESCAP : United Nations Economic and Social Commission for Asia and the Pacific
UNFPA : United Nations Fund for Population Activity
UNICEF : United Nations Children Fund
UPDS : Universal Public Distribution System
UR : Uruguay Round
USDA : United States Department of Agriculture
WCED : World Commission on Environment and Development
WFP : World Food Programme
WTO : World Trade Organisation

Glossary

Adivasis	:	Tribals
Anganwadi	:	Centre for pre-school education and serving mother
Anna	:	Grain
Antyodaya	:	A government scheme to provide foodgrains to the poorest
Babus	:	Indian government officials
Bajra	:	A type of inferior cereal
Balwadis	:	A centre initiative to provide supplementary nutrition to children between 0-3 age group
Bazaar	:	Local market
Bhawans	:	Building
Bhumihars	:	A dominant forward caste in Bihar
Bihari	:	Natives of the state of Bihar
Brahmins	:	A forward caste at the top of the caste higher archy
Channa	:	Black gram
Chapati	:	A type of leaf
Choker	:	By-product of grain used to feed livestock
Chulha	:	A fireplace for cooking
Crore	:	One crore equals ten million
Dalit	:	The most oppressed caste, also called schedule caste
Deepam	:	An earthen oil lamp
Ghee	:	Butter
Gram Sabha	:	Village assembly
Gramin	:	Rural
Gur	:	Jaggery
Gurji	:	A type of cereal
Harijan	:	The most oppressed caste, also called schedule caste
Janata Dal	:	A political party
Jatis	:	Caste
Jhangora	:	Coarse cereads
Jowar	:	A type of inferior cereal
Kayasthas	:	A forward caste mostly educated
Khandsari	:	A sweet-dish
Kharif	:	The summer cropping season from April to September
Kisan Sabha	:	Farmers, organisation
Koiris	:	A middle caste in Bihar and Jharkhand, dominant in several pockets

Kotedar : Fair-price shop dealer
Krishi : Agriculture
Kudos : Low quality rice
Kulaks : Rising and powerful middle peasantry
Kurmis : A middle caste in Bihar and Jharkhand, dominant in many areas
Lakh : Ten lakh equals one million
Lathis : Thick wooden sticks
Mahila Samajams : Women co-operative groups
Mandi : Local grains and vegetable market
Mandwa : Coarse cerceale
Soy bean : A kind of pulses, rich in protein
Masoor : Kind of pulse
Matta : Butter milk
Musahars : A very oppressed schedule caste known for its rat-eating habits
Neem : Medicinal tree
Onam : Kerala festival
Pairavi : Act of seeking favour
Pairvikars : Those indulging in the act of seeking favours
Pan : Beetal leaf
Panchayats : Village level government
Panjiri : A type of sweet
Pradhans : Head of village organisation
Pucca : Solid, made of bricks
Rabi : The winter cropping season from October to March
Ragi : A kind of grain
Raithu : A kind of grain
Rajma : A kind of pulse
Rajputs : A dominant forward caste, mostly in north India
Ramzan : An Islamic festival month
Rangdars : Local goons
Rashtriya Janata Dal : A political party dominant in Bihar
Rozgar : Livelihood
Sahukars : Local moneylenders
Samiti : Committee
Sampoorna : Total
Sarpanch : Head of village-level panchayat
Senas : Army
Taluka : An administrative unit below district level
Tendu : A type of leaf used for making bidi
Urad : A kind of pulse
Vanaspati : Edible oil
Yadavs : A dominant middle caste
Yojana : Scheme
Zamindari : The earlier system of land tenure

Index

SUBJECT INDEX

AUTHOR INDEX